Nonlife Actuarial Models

Actuaries must pass exams, but more than that: they must put knowledge into practice. This coherent book supports the Society of Actuaries' short-term actuarial mathematics syllabus while emphasizing the concepts and practical application of nonlife actuarial models. A class-tested textbook for undergraduate courses in actuarial science, it is also ideal for those approaching their professional exams. Key topics covered include loss modeling, risk and ruin theory, credibility theory and applications and empirical implementation of loss models.

Revised and updated to reflect curriculum changes, this second edition includes two brand-new chapters on loss reserving and ratemaking. R replaces Excel as the computation tool used throughout – the featured R code is available on the book's webpage, as are lecture slides. Numerous examples and exercises are provided, with many questions adapted from past Society of Actuaries exams.

YIU-KUEN TSE is an Emeritus Professor with the Singapore Management University. He was a Fellow of the Society of Actuaries. He has published extensively in the areas of financial data analysis and financial risk management, including the book *Financial Mathematics for Actuaries* (third edition, 2021) which he co-authored with Wai-Sum Chan.

INTERNATIONAL SERIES ON ACTUARIAL SCIENCE

The *International Series on Actuarial Science*, published by Cambridge University Press in con-junction with the Institute and Faculty of Actuaries, contains textbooks for students taking courses in or related to actuarial science, as well as more advanced works designed for continuing pro-fessional development or for describing and synthesizing research. The series is a vehicle for publishing books that reflect changes and developments in the curriculum, that encourage the introduction of courses on actuarial science in universities, and that show how actuarial science can be used in all areas where there is long-term financial risk.

A complete list of books in the series can be found at www.cambridge.org/isas. Recent titles include the following:

NONLIFE ACTUARIAL MODELS

Theory, Methods and Evaluation

Second Edition

YIU-KUEN TSE
Singapore Management University

CAMBRIDGE
UNIVERSITY PRESS

CAMBRIDGE
UNIVERSITY PRESS

Shaftesbury Road, Cambridge CB2 8EA, United Kingdom

One Liberty Plaza, 20th Floor, New York, NY 10006, USA

477 Williamstown Road, Port Melbourne, VIC 3207, Australia

314–321, 3rd Floor, Plot 3, Splendor Forum, Jasola District Centre, New Delhi – 110025, India

103 Penang Road, #05–06/07, Visioncrest Commercial, Singapore 238467

Cambridge University Press is part of Cambridge University Press & Assessment, a department of the University of Cambridge.

We share the University's mission to contribute to society through the pursuit of education, learning and research at the highest international levels of excellence.

www.cambridge.org
Information on this title: www.cambridge.org/highereducation/isbn/9781009315074
DOI: 10.1017/9781009315067

First published 2009

Second edition 2023

A catalogue record for this publication is available from the British Library.

A Cataloging-in-Publication data record for this book is available from the Library of Congress.

ISBN 978-1-009-31507-4 Hardback

Additional resources for this publication at www.cambridge.org/tse.

Contents

Preface to the Second Edition

Several changes have been made to the second edition. First, I have added two chapters to cover the topics on loss reserving and ratemaking. Second, the chapter on classical credibility has been rewritten to be less dependent on the Poisson assumption. Also, part of the chapter on Bühlmann credibility has been rewritten for better integration. Third, the sections on "Excel computation notes" have been removed. I use R as the computation tool for this edition and several chapters have a section of "R laboratory." Finally, I have removed some topics from the first edition, including the topics on continuous-time ruin theory and simulation of asset prices. Lecture slides and R codes can be downloaded from the book's webpage: https://sites.google.com/view/nonlifeactuarialmodels.

Yiu-Kuen Tse
Singapore Management University
yktse@smu.edu.sg

Preface to the First Edition

This book is on the theory, methods, and empirical implementation of nonlife actuarial models. It is intended for use as a textbook for senior undergraduates. Users are assumed to have done one or two one-semester courses on probability theory and statistical inference, including estimation and hypothesis testing. The coverage of this book includes all the topics found in Exam C of the Society of Actuaries (Exam 4 of the Casualty Actuarial Society) as per the 2007 Basic Education Catalog. In addition, it covers some topics (such as risk measures and ruin theory) beyond what is required by these exams, and may be used by actuarial students in general.

This book is divided into four parts: loss models, risk and ruin, credibility, and model construction and evaluation. An appendix on the review of statistics is provided for the benefit of students who require a quick summary. Students may read the appendix prior to the main text if they desire, or they may use the appendix as a reference when required. In order to be self contained, the appendix covers some of the topics developed in the main text.

Some features of this book should be mentioned. First, the concepts and theories introduced are illustrated by many practical examples. Some of these examples explain the theory through numerical applications, while others develop new results. Second, several chapters of the book include a section on numerical computation using Excel. Students are encouraged to use Excel to solve some of the numerical exercises. Third, each chapter includes some exercises for practice. Many of these exercises are adapted from past exam questions of the Society of Actuaries.

I would like to thank Tao Yang for painstakingly going through the manuscript and for providing many useful comments and suggestions. Diana Gillooly has professionally guided me through the publication process with admirable patience and efficiency. Clare Dennison has performed a superb job of coordinating the copy editing. I am also grateful to the Society of Actuaries for allowing me to use its past exam questions.

Resources are available at: www.mysmu.edu/faculty/yktse/NAM/NAM base.htm Slides in pdf format can be downloaded from this site, which will facilitate classroom teaching by instructors adopting this book. An errata file will be provided, and the solution manual for instructors is obtainable from the author on request.

Yiu-Kuen Tse
Singapore Management University
yktse@smu.edu.sg

Notation and Convention

1 Abbreviations are used in this book without periods. For example, "probability density function" is referred to as pdf (not p.d.f.) and "moment generating function" is referred to as mgf (not m.g.f.).

2 We do not make distinctions between a random variable and the distribution that describes the random variable. Thus, from time to time we make statements such as: "X denotes the binomial distribution."

3 We use calligraphic fonts to denote commonly used distributions. Discrete distributions are denoted with two alphabets and continuous distributions are denoted with one alphabet. For example, $\mathcal{PN}$ stands for Poisson, $\mathcal{BN}$ stands for binomial, $\mathcal{N}$ stands for normal, and $\mathcal{L}$ stands for lognormal.

4 The following conventions are generally used:

(a) Slanted upper case for random variables, e.g. X.

(b) Slanted lower case for fixed numbers, e.g. x.

(c) Slanted bold-faced upper case for vectors of random variables, e.g. $\boldsymbol{X}$.

(d) Slanted bold-faced lower case for vectors of fixed numbers (observations), e.g. $\boldsymbol{x}$.

(e) Upright bold-faced upper case for matrices of fixed numbers (observations), e.g. $\mathbf{X}$.

5 Natural logarithm is denoted by log, not ln.

Computation Notes

1 All graphs in this book were produced using Matlab. The computation was performed using Gauss and R.
2 Some chapters in the second edition have a section of "R laboratory," where some R codes are included to illustrate the computation.
3 Excel resources in the first edition have been removed. They can be downloaded from the book's web page.

Part I
Loss Models

In this part of the book we discuss actuarial models for claim losses. The two components of claim losses, namely, claim frequency and claim severity, are modeled separately, and are then combined to derive the aggregateloss distribution. In Chapter 1, we discuss the modeling of claim frequency, introducing some techniques for modeling nonnegative integer-valued random variables. Techniques for modeling continuous random variables relevant for claim severity are discussed in Chapter 2, in which we also consider the effects of coverage modifications on claim frequency and claim severity. Chapter 3 discusses the collective risk model and individual risk model for analyzing aggregate losses. The techniques of convolution and recursive methods are used to compute the aggregate-loss distributions.

1

Claim-Frequency Distribution

This book is about modeling the claim losses of insurance policies. Our main interest is nonlife insurance policies covering a fixed period of time, such as vehicle insurance, workers compensation insurance and health insurance. An important measure of claim losses is the claim frequency, which is the number of claims in a block of insurance policies over a period of time. Though claim frequency does not directly show the monetary losses of insurance claims, it is an important variable in modeling the losses.

In this chapter we first briefly review some tools in modeling statistical distributions, in particular, the moment generating function and probability generating function. Some commonly used discrete random variables in modeling claim-frequency distributions, namely, the binomial, geometric, negative binomial and Poisson distributions, are then discussed. We introduce a family of distributions for nonnegative, integer-valued random variables, called the $(a, b, 0)$ class, which includes all the four distributions aforementioned. This class of discrete distributions have found important applications in the actuarial literature. Further methods of creating new nonnegative, integer-valued random variables are introduced. In particular, we discuss the zero-modified distribution, the $(a, b, 1)$ class of distributions, the compound distributions and the mixture distributions.

Learning Objectives

1 Discrete distributions for modeling claim frequency
2 Binomial, geometric, negative binomial and Poisson distributions
3 The $(a, b, 0)$ and $(a, b, 1)$ class of distributions
4 Compound distribution
5 Convolution
6 Mixture distribution

1.1 Claim Frequency, Claim Severity and Aggregate Claim

We consider a block of nonlife insurance policies with coverage over a fixed period of time. The **aggregate claim** for losses of the block of policies is the sum of the monetary losses of all the claims. The number of claims in the block of policies is called the **claim frequency**, and the monetary amount of each claim is called the **claim severity** or **claim size**. A general approach in loss modeling is to consider claim frequency and claim severity separately. The two variables are then combined to model the aggregate claim. Naturally claim frequency is modeled as a nonnegative discrete random variable, while claim severity is continuously distributed.

In this chapter we focus on the claim-frequency distribution. We discuss some nonnegative discrete random variables that are commonly used for modeling claim frequency. Some methods for constructing nonnegative discrete random variables that are suitable for modeling claim frequency are also introduced. As our focus is on short-term nonlife insurance policies, time value of money plays a minor role. We begin with a brief review of some tools for modeling statistical distributions. Further discussions on the topic can be found in the Appendix, as well as the references therein.

1.2 Review of Statistics

Let X be a random variable with **distribution function (df)** $F_X(x)$, which is defined by

$$F_X(x) = \Pr(X \leq x). \tag{1.1}$$

If $F_X(x)$ is a continuous function, X is said to be a **continuous random variable**. Furthermore, if $F_X(x)$ is differentiable, the **probability density function (pdf)** of X, denoted by $f_X(x)$, is defined as

$$f_X(x) = \frac{dF_X(x)}{dx}. \tag{1.2}$$

If X can only take discrete values, it is called a **discrete random variable**. We denote $\Omega_X = \{x_1, x_2, \ldots\}$ as the set of values X can take, called the **support** of X. The **probability function (pf)** of a discrete random variable X, also denoted by $f_X(x)$, is defined as

$$f_X(x) = \begin{cases} \Pr(X = x), & \text{if } x \in \Omega_X, \\ 0, & \text{otherwise.} \end{cases} \tag{1.3}$$

We assume the support of a continuous random variable to be the real line, unless otherwise stated. The rth moment of X about zero (also called the rth raw moment), denoted by $E(X^r)$, is defined as

$$E(X^r) = \int_{-\infty}^{\infty} x^r f_X(x)\, dx, \qquad \text{if } X \text{ is continuous,} \tag{1.4}$$

and

$$E(X^r) = \sum_{x \in \Omega_X} x^r f_X(x), \qquad \text{if } X \text{ is discrete.} \tag{1.5}$$

For convenience, we also write $E(X^r)$ as μ'_r. The **moment generating function (mgf)** of X, denoted by $M_X(t)$, is a function of t defined by

$$M_X(t) = E(e^{tX}), \tag{1.6}$$

if the expectation exists. If the mgf of X exists for t in an open interval around $t = 0$, the moments of X exist and can be obtained by successively differentiating the mgf with respect to t and evaluating the result at $t = 0$. We observe that

$$M_X^r(t) = \frac{d^r M_X(t)}{dt^r} = \frac{d^r}{dt^r} E(e^{tX}) = E\left[\frac{d^r}{dt^r}(e^{tX})\right] = E(X^r e^{tX}), \tag{1.7}$$

so that

$$M_X^r(0) = E(X^r) = \mu'_r. \tag{1.8}$$

If $X_1, X_2, \ldots, X_n$ are **independently and identically distributed (iid)** random variables with mgf $M(t)$, and $X = X_1 + \cdots + X_n$, then the mgf of X is

$$M_X(t) = E(e^{tX}) = E(e^{tX_1 + \cdots + tX_n}) = E\left(\prod_{i=1}^{n} e^{tX_i}\right) = \prod_{i=1}^{n} E(e^{tX_i}) = [M(t)]^n. \tag{1.9}$$

The mgf has the important property that it uniquely defines a distribution. Specifically, if two random variables have the same mgf, their distributions are identical.[1]

If X is a random variable that can only take nonnegative integer values, the **probability generating function (pgf)** of X, denoted by $P_X(t)$, is defined as

$$P_X(t) = E(t^X), \tag{1.10}$$

if the expectation exists. The mgf and pgf are related through the equations

$$M_X(t) = P_X(e^t), \tag{1.11}$$

and

$$P_X(t) = M_X(\log t). \tag{1.12}$$

Given the pgf of X, we can derive its pf. To see how this is done, note that

$$P_X(t) = \sum_{x=0}^{\infty} t^x f_X(x). \tag{1.13}$$

The rth order derivative of $P_X(t)$ is

$$P_X^r(t) = \frac{d^r}{dt^r}\left(\sum_{x=0}^{\infty} t^x f_X(x)\right) = \sum_{x=r}^{\infty} x(x-1)\cdots(x-r+1)t^{x-r} f_X(x). \tag{1.14}$$

---

[1] See Appendix A.8 for more details.

If we evaluate $P_X^r(t)$ at $t = 0$, all terms in the above summation vanish except for $x = r$, which is $r!f_X(r)$. Hence, we have

$$P_X^r(0) = r!f_X(r), \qquad (1.15)$$

so that given the pgf, we can obtain the pf as

$$f_X(r) = \frac{P_X^r(0)}{r!}. \qquad (1.16)$$

In sum, given the mgf of X, the moments of X can be computed through equation (1.8). Likewise, given the pgf of a nonnegative integer-valued random variable, its pf can be computed through equation (1.16). Thus, the mgf and pgf are useful functions for summarizing a statistical distribution.

1.3 Some Discrete Distributions for Claim Frequency

We now review some key results of four discrete random variables, namely, binomial, geometric, negative binomial and Poisson. As these random variables can only take nonnegative integer values, they may be used for modeling the distributions of claim frequency. The choice of a particular distribution in practice is an empirical question to be discussed later.

1.3.1 Binomial Distribution

A random variable X has a binomial distribution with parameters n and θ, denoted by $\mathcal{BN}(n, \theta)$, where n is a positive integer and θ satisfies $0 < \theta < 1$, if the pf of X is

$$f_X(x) = \binom{n}{x} \theta^x (1 - \theta)^{n-x}, \qquad \text{for } x = 0, 1, \ldots, n, \qquad (1.17)$$

where

$$\binom{n}{x} = \frac{n!}{x!(n-x)!}. \qquad (1.18)$$

The mean and variance of X are

$$\mathrm{E}(X) = n\theta \qquad \text{and} \qquad \mathrm{Var}(X) = n\theta(1 - \theta), \qquad (1.19)$$

so that the variance of X is always smaller than its mean.

The mgf of X is

$$M_X(t) = (\theta e^t + 1 - \theta)^n, \qquad (1.20)$$

and its pgf is

$$P_X(t) = (\theta t + 1 - \theta)^n. \qquad (1.21)$$

The expression in equation (1.17) is the probability of obtaining x successes in n independent trials each with probability of success θ. The distribution is symmetric if $\theta = 0.5$. It is positively skewed (skewed to the right) if $\theta < 0.5$, and is negatively skewed (skewed to the left) if $\theta > 0.5$. When n is large, X is approximately normally distributed. The convergence to normality is faster the closer θ is to 0.5.

There is a recursive relationship for $f_X(x)$, which can facilitate the computation of the pf. From equation (1.17), we have $f_X(0) = (1 - \theta)^n$. Now for $x = 1, \ldots, n$, we have

$$\frac{f_X(x)}{f_X(x-1)} = \frac{\binom{n}{x}\theta^x(1-\theta)^{n-x}}{\binom{n}{x-1}\theta^{x-1}(1-\theta)^{n-x+1}} = \frac{(n-x+1)\theta}{x(1-\theta)}, \qquad (1.22)$$

so that

$$f_X(x) = \left[\frac{(n-x+1)\theta}{x(1-\theta)}\right] f_X(x-1). \qquad (1.23)$$

Example 1.1 Plot the pf of the binomial distribution for $n = 10$, and $\theta = 0.2$, 0.4, 0.6 and 0.8.

Solution 1.1 Figure 1.1 plots the pf of $\mathcal{BN}(n, \theta)$ for $\theta = 0.2, 0.4, 0.6$ and 0.8, with $n = 10$.

It can be clearly seen that the binomial distribution is skewed to the right for $\theta = 0.2$ and skewed to the left for $\theta = 0.8$. □

1.3.2 Geometric Distribution

A nonnegative discrete random variable X has a geometric distribution with parameter θ for $0 < \theta < 1$, denoted by $\mathcal{GM}(\theta)$, if its pf is given by

$$f_X(x) = \theta(1 - \theta)^x, \qquad \text{for } x = 0, 1, \ldots . \qquad (1.24)$$

The mean and variance of X are

$$E(X) = \frac{1-\theta}{\theta} \qquad \text{and} \qquad \text{Var}(X) = \frac{1-\theta}{\theta^2}, \qquad (1.25)$$

so that, in contrast to the binomial distribution, the variance of a geometric distribution is always larger than its mean.

The expression in equation (1.24) is the probability of having x failures prior to the first success in a sequence of independent Bernoulli trials with probability of success θ.

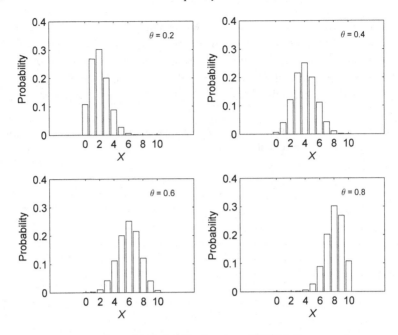

Figure 1.1 Probability function of $\mathcal{BN}(10, \theta)$

The mgf of X is

$$M_X(t) = \frac{\theta}{1 - (1 - \theta)e^t},$$ (1.26)

and its pgf is

$$P_X(t) = \frac{\theta}{1 - (1 - \theta)t}.$$ (1.27)

The pf of X is decreasing in x. It satisfies the following recursive relationship

$$f_X(x) = (1 - \theta)f_X(x - 1),$$ (1.28)

for $x = 1, 2, \ldots$, with starting value $f_X(0) = \theta$.

1.3.3 Negative Binomial Distribution

A nonnegative discrete random variable X has a negative binomial distribution with parameters r and θ, denoted by $\mathcal{NB}(r, \theta)$, if the pf of X is

$$f_X(x) = \binom{x + r - 1}{r - 1} \theta^r (1 - \theta)^x, \qquad \text{for } x = 0, 1, \ldots,$$ (1.29)

where r is a positive integer and θ satisfies $0 < \theta < 1$. The geometric distribution is a special case of the negative binomial distribution with $r = 1$. We may interpret the expression in equation (1.29) as the probability of getting x failures prior to the rth success in a sequence of independent Bernoulli trials with probability of success θ. Thus, $\mathcal{NB}(r, \theta)$ is just the sum of r independently distributed $\mathcal{GM}(\theta)$ variates. Hence, using equation (1.25), we can conclude that if X is distributed as $\mathcal{NB}(r, \theta)$ its mean and variance are

$$E(X) = \frac{r(1 - \theta)}{\theta} \quad \text{and} \quad \text{Var}(X) = \frac{r(1 - \theta)}{\theta^2}, \tag{1.30}$$

so that its variance is always larger than its mean.

Furthermore, using the results in equations (1.9), (1.26) and (1.27), we obtain the mgf of $\mathcal{NB}(r, \theta)$ as

$$M_X(t) = \left[\frac{\theta}{1 - (1 - \theta)e^t} \right]^r, \tag{1.31}$$

and its pgf as

$$P_X(t) = \left[\frac{\theta}{1 - (1 - \theta)t} \right]^r. \tag{1.32}$$

Note that the binomial coefficient in equation (1.29) can be written as

$$\binom{x + r - 1}{r - 1} = \frac{(x + r - 1)!}{(r - 1)! x!}$$
$$= \frac{(x + r - 1)(x + r - 2) \cdots (r + 1) r}{x!}. \tag{1.33}$$

The expression in the last line of the above equation is well defined for any number $r > 0$ (not necessarily an integer) and any nonnegative integer x.[2] Thus, if we define

$$\binom{x + r - 1}{r - 1} = \frac{(x + r - 1)(x + r - 2) \cdots (r + 1) r}{x!}, \tag{1.34}$$

we can use equation (1.29) as a pf even when r is not an integer. Indeed it can be verified that

$$\sum_{x=0}^{\infty} \binom{x + r - 1}{r - 1} \theta^r (1 - \theta)^x = 1, \tag{1.35}$$

for $r > 0$ and $0 < \theta < 1$, so that the extension of the parameter r of the negative binomial distribution to any positive number is meaningful. We shall adopt this extension in any future applications.

The recursive formula of the pf follows from the result

$$\frac{f_X(x)}{f_X(x - 1)} = \frac{\binom{x + r - 1}{r - 1} \theta^r (1 - \theta)^x}{\binom{x + r - 2}{r - 1} \theta^r (1 - \theta)^{x-1}} = \frac{(x + r - 1)(1 - \theta)}{x}, \tag{1.36}$$

---

[2] As factorials are defined only for nonnegative integers, the expression in the first line of equation (1.33) is not defined if r is not an integer.

Table 1.1. *Results of Example 1.2*

x	$r = 0.5$	$r = 1.0$	$r = 1.5$	$r = 2.0$
0	0.6325	0.4000	0.2530	0.1600
1	0.1897	0.2400	0.2277	0.1920
2	0.0854	0.1440	0.1708	0.1728
3	0.0427	0.0864	0.1195	0.1382

so that

$$f_X(x) = \left[\frac{(x + r - 1)(1 - \theta)}{x} \right] f_X(x - 1), \qquad (1.37)$$

with starting value

$$f_X(0) = \theta^r. \qquad (1.38)$$

Example 1.2 Using the recursion formula, calculate the pf of the negative binomial distribution with $r = 0.5, 1, 1.5$ and 2, and $\theta = 0.4$, for $x = 0, 1, 2$ and 3. What is the mode of the negative binomial distribution?

Solution 1.2 From the recursion formula in equation (1.37), we have

$$f_X(x) = \left[\frac{0.6(x + r - 1)}{x} \right] f_X(x - 1), \qquad \text{for } x = 1, 2, \ldots,$$

with starting value $f_X(0) = (0.4)^r$. We summarize the results in Table 1.1.

Note that the modes for $r = 0.5, 1$ and 1.5 are 0, and that for $r = 2$ is 1. To compute the mode in general, we note that, from equation (1.37),

$$f_X(x) > f_X(x - 1) \qquad \text{if and only if} \qquad \frac{(x + r - 1)(1 - \theta)}{x} > 1,$$

and the latter inequality is equivalent to

$$x < \frac{(r - 1)(1 - \theta)}{\theta}.$$

Therefore, the mode of the negative binomial distribution is equal to the non-negative integer part of $(r - 1)(1 - \theta)/\theta$. We can verify this result from Table 1.1. For example, when $r = 2$,

$$\frac{(r - 1)(1 - \theta)}{\theta} = \frac{0.6}{0.4} = 1.5,$$

and its integer part (the mode) is 1.   □

1.3.4 Poisson Distribution

A nonnegative discrete random variable X is said to have a Poisson distribution with parameter λ, denoted by $\mathcal{PN}(\lambda)$, if the pf of X is given by

$$f_X(x) = \frac{\lambda^x e^{-\lambda}}{x!}, \qquad \text{for } x = 0, 1, \ldots, \tag{1.39}$$

where $\lambda > 0$. The mean and variance of X are

$$\mathrm{E}(X) = \mathrm{Var}(X) = \lambda. \tag{1.40}$$

The mgf of X is

$$M_X(t) = \exp\left[\lambda(e^t - 1)\right], \tag{1.41}$$

and its pgf is

$$P_X(t) = \exp\left[\lambda(t - 1)\right]. \tag{1.42}$$

The Poisson distribution is one of the most widely used discrete distributions in empirical applications. It is commonly applied to model the number of arrivals of certain events within a period of time (such as the number of insurance claims in a year), the number of defective items in production and as an approximation of the binomial distribution, among others. We now introduce two properties of the Poisson distribution, which make it convenient to use.

Theorem 1.1 *If $X_1, \ldots, X_n$ are independently distributed with $X_i \sim \mathcal{PN}(\lambda_i)$, for $i = 1, \ldots, n$, then $X = X_1 + \cdots + X_n$ is distributed as a Poisson with parameter $\lambda = \lambda_1 + \cdots + \lambda_n$.*

Proof To prove this result, we make use of the mgf. Note that the mgf of X is

$$\begin{aligned}
M_X(t) &= \mathrm{E}(e^{tX}) \\
&= \mathrm{E}(e^{tX_1 + \ldots + tX_n}) \\
&= \mathrm{E}\left(\prod_{i=1}^{n} e^{tX_i}\right) \\
&= \prod_{i=1}^{n} \mathrm{E}(e^{tX_i}) \\
&= \prod_{i=1}^{n} \exp\left[\lambda_i(e^t - 1)\right] \\
&= \exp\left[(e^t - 1)\sum_{i=1}^{n} \lambda_i\right] \\
&= \exp\left[(e^t - 1)\lambda\right], \tag{1.43}
\end{aligned}$$

which is the mgf of $\mathcal{PN}(\lambda)$. Thus, by the uniqueness of mgf, $X \sim \mathcal{PN}(\lambda)$. $\square$

It turns out that the converse of the above result is also true, as summarized in the following theorem.

Theorem 1.2 *Suppose an event A can be partitioned into m mutually exclusive and exhaustive events A_i, for $i = 1, \ldots, m$. Let X be the number of occurrences of A, and X_i be the number of occurrences of A_i, so that $X = X_1 + \cdots + X_m$. Let the probability of occurrence of A_i given A has occurred be p_i, i.e., $Pr(A_i \mid A) = p_i$, with $\sum_{i=1}^{m} p_i = 1$. If $X \sim \mathcal{PN}(\lambda)$, then $X_i \sim \mathcal{PN}(\lambda_i)$, where $\lambda_i = \lambda p_i$. Furthermore, $X_1, \ldots, X_m$ are independently distributed.*

Proof To prove this result, we first derive the marginal distribution of X_i. Given $X = x$, $X_i \sim \mathcal{BN}(x, p_i)$ for $i = 1, \ldots, m$. Hence, the marginal pf of X_i is (note that $x_i \leq x$)

$$f_{X_i}(x_i) = \sum_{x=x_i}^{\infty} \Pr(X_i = x_i \mid X = x) \Pr(X = x)$$

$$= \sum_{x=x_i}^{\infty} \binom{x}{x_i} p_i^{x_i} (1 - p_i)^{x-x_i} \left[\frac{e^{-\lambda} \lambda^x}{x!} \right]$$

$$= \left[\frac{e^{-\lambda} (\lambda p_i)^{x_i}}{x_i!} \right] \sum_{x=x_i}^{\infty} \frac{[\lambda(1 - p_i)]^{x-x_i}}{(x - x_i)!}$$

$$= \left[\frac{e^{-\lambda} (\lambda p_i)^{x_i}}{x_i!} \right] e^{\lambda(1-p_i)}$$

$$= \frac{e^{-\lambda p_i} (\lambda p_i)^{x_i}}{x_i!}, \tag{1.44}$$

which is the pf of $\mathcal{PN}(\lambda p_i)$.

We now consider the joint pf of $X_1, \ldots, X_m$. Note that given $X = x$, the joint distribution of $X_1, \ldots, X_m$ is multinomial with parameters $x, p_1, \ldots, p_m$.[3] Thus,

$$\Pr(X_1 = x_1, \ldots, X_m = x_m \mid X = x) = \frac{x!}{x_1! \cdots x_m!} p_1^{x_1} \cdots p_m^{x_m}. \tag{1.45}$$

By the multiplication rule of probability, we have

$$f_{X_1 X_2 \cdots X_m}(x_1, \ldots, x_m) = \Pr(X_1 = x_1, \ldots, X_m = x_m \mid X = x) \Pr(X = x)$$

$$= \left(\frac{x!}{x_1! \cdots x_m!} p_1^{x_1} \cdots p_m^{x_m} \right) \frac{e^{-\lambda} \lambda^x}{x!}$$

---

[3] The multinomial distribution is a generalization of the binomial distribution; see DeGroot and Schervish (2002, p. 309).

$$= \prod_{i=1}^{m} \frac{e^{-\lambda p_i}(\lambda p_i)^{x_i}}{x_i!}$$

$$= \prod_{i=1}^{m} f_{X_i}(x_i), \tag{1.46}$$

so that the joint pf of $X_1, \ldots, X_m$ is the product of their marginal pf. This completes the proof that $X_1, \ldots, X_m$ are independent. □

Readers may verify the following recursive relationship of the pf of $\mathcal{PN}(\lambda)$

$$f_X(x) = \left(\frac{\lambda}{x}\right) f_X(x-1), \tag{1.47}$$

with $f_X(0) = e^{-\lambda}$. Finally, we add that when λ is large, $\mathcal{PN}(\lambda)$ is approximately normally distributed.

Example 1.3 The average number of female employees taking sick leave is 1.3 per week, and the average number of male employees taking sick leave is 2.5 per week. What is the probability of finding fewer than 2 sick leaves in a week? You may assume that the numbers of sick leaves in a week for the female and male employees are independent Poisson distributions.

Solution 1.3 From Theorem 1.1, the number of sick leaves in each week is Poisson with mean $1.3 + 2.5 = 3.8$. Thus, the required probability is

$$f_X(0) + f_X(1) = e^{-3.8} + 3.8e^{-3.8} = 0.1074.$$ □

Example 1.4 Bank A has two blocks of loans: housing loans and study loans. The total number of defaults is Poisson distributed with mean 23, and 28% of the defaults are study loans. Bank B has three blocks of loans: housing loans, study loans and car loans. The total number of defaults is Poisson distributed with mean 45, where 21% of the defaults are study loans and 53% are housing loans. The defaults of the two banks are independent. If the loan portfolios of the two banks are merged, find the distribution of the defaults of study loans and car loans.

Solution 1.4 From Theorem 1.2, defaults of study loans of Bank A is Poisson with mean $(23)(0.28) = 6.44$, and that of Bank B is Poisson with mean $(45)(0.21) = 9.45$. Thus, in the merged portfolio, defaults of study loans, by Theorem 1.1, is Poisson with mean $6.44 + 9.45 = 15.89$.

As Bank A has no car loans, defaults of car loans come from Bank B only, which is Poisson distributed with mean $(45)(1 - 0.21 - 0.53) = 11.70$.   □

Table 1.2. *The $(a, b, 0)$ class of distributions*

Distribution	a	b	$f_X(0)$
Binomial: $\mathcal{BN}(n, \theta)$	$-\dfrac{\theta}{1 - \theta}$	$\dfrac{\theta(n + 1)}{1 - \theta}$	$(1 - \theta)^n$
Geometric: $\mathcal{GM}(\theta)$	$1 - \theta$	0	θ
Negative binomial: $\mathcal{NB}(r, \theta)$	$1 - \theta$	$(r - 1)(1 - \theta)$	θ^r
Poisson: $\mathcal{PN}(\lambda)$	0	λ	$e^{-\lambda}$

1.4 The $(a, b, 0)$ Class of Distributions

The binomial, geometric, negative binomial and Poisson distributions belong to a class of nonnegative discrete distributions called the $(a, b, 0)$ class in the actuarial literature. Below is the definition of this class of distributions.

Definition 1.1 A nonnegative discrete random variable X is in the $(a, b, 0)$ class if its pf $f_X(x)$ satisfies the following recursion

$$f_X(x) = \left(a + \frac{b}{x} \right) f_X(x - 1), \qquad \text{for } x = 1, 2, \ldots, \qquad (1.48)$$

where a and b are constants, with given $f_X(0)$.

As an example, we consider the binomial distribution. Equation (1.23) can be written as follows

$$f_X(x) = \left[-\frac{\theta}{1 - \theta} + \frac{\theta(n + 1)}{(1 - \theta)x} \right] f_X(x - 1). \qquad (1.49)$$

Thus, if we let

$$a = -\frac{\theta}{1 - \theta} \qquad \text{and} \qquad b = \frac{\theta(n + 1)}{(1 - \theta)}, \qquad (1.50)$$

the pf of the binomial distribution satisfies equation (1.48) and thus belongs to the $(a, b, 0)$ class. Readers may verify the results in Table 1.2, which show that the four discrete distributions discussed in the last section belong to the $(a, b, 0)$ class.[4]

---

[4] This class of distributions have only four members and no others. See Dickson (2005, Section 4.5.1), for a proof of this result.

The $(a, b, 0)$ class of distributions are defined by recursions starting at $x = 1$, given an initial value $f_X(0)$. By analogy, we can define a class of nonnegative discrete distributions, called the $(a, b, 1)$ class, with recursions starting at $x = 2$ given an initial value $f_X(1)$.

Definition 1.2 A nonnegative discrete random variable X belongs to the $(a, b, 1)$ class if its pf $f_X(x)$ satisfies the following recursion

$$f_X(x) = \left(a + \frac{b}{x} \right) f_X(x - 1), \qquad \text{for } x = 2, 3, \ldots, \qquad (1.51)$$

where a and b are constants, with given initial value $f_X(1)$.

Note that the $(a, b, 0)$ and $(a, b, 1)$ classes have the same recursion formulas, and they differ only at the starting point of the recursion. Also, the probability $f_X(0)$ of a random variable belonging to the $(a, b, 1)$ class need not be zero. Thus, it is possible to create a distribution with a specific probability at point zero and yet a shape similar to one of the $(a, b, 0)$ distributions. This flexibility is of considerable importance because insurance claims of low-risk events are infrequent. It may be desirable to obtain a good fit of the distribution at zero claim based on empirical experience and yet preserve the shape to coincide with some simple parametric distributions. This can be achieved by specifying the zero probability while adopting the $(a, b, 1)$ recursion to mimic a selected $(a, b, 0)$ distribution.

Let $f_X(x)$ be the pf of a $(a, b, 0)$ distribution called the base distribution. We denote $f_X^M(x)$ as the pf that is a modification of $f_X(x)$, where $f_X^M(x)$ belongs to the $(a, b, 1)$ class. The probability at point zero, $f_X^M(0)$, is specified and $f_X^M(x)$ is related to $f_X(x)$ as follows

$$f_X^M(x) = c f_X(x), \qquad \text{for } x = 1, 2, \ldots, \qquad (1.52)$$

where c is an appropriate constant. For $f_X^M(\cdot)$ to be a well-defined pf, we must have

$$1 = f_X^M(0) + \sum_{x=1}^{\infty} f_X^M(x)$$

$$= f_X^M(0) + c \sum_{x=1}^{\infty} f_X(x)$$

$$= f_X^M(0) + c[1 - f_X(0)]. \qquad (1.53)$$

Thus, we conclude that

$$c = \frac{1 - f_X^M(0)}{1 - f_X(0)}. \qquad (1.54)$$

Table 1.3. *Results of Example 1.5*

x	$\mathcal{BN}(4,0.3)$	Zero-modified	Zero-truncated
0	0.2401	0.4000	0
1	0.4116	0.3250	0.5417
2	0.2646	0.2089	0.3482
3	0.0756	0.0597	0.0995
4	0.0081	0.0064	0.0107

Substituting c into equation (1.52) we obtain $f_X^M(x)$, for $x = 1, 2, \ldots$. Together with the given $f_X^M(0)$, we have a $(a, b, 1)$ distribution with the desired zero-claim probability and the same recursion as the base $(a, b, 0)$ distribution. This is called the **zero-modified distribution** of the base $(a, b, 0)$ distribution. In particular, if $f_X^M(0) = 0$, the modified distribution cannot take value zero and is called the **zero-truncated distribution**. The zero-truncated distribution is a particular case of the zero-modified distribution.

Example 1.5 X is distributed as $\mathcal{BN}(4, 0.3)$. Compute the zero-modified pf with the probability of zero equal to 0.4. Also compute the zero-truncated pf.

Solution 1.5 The results are summarized in Table 1.3. The second column of the table gives the pf of $\mathcal{BN}(4, 0.3)$, the third column gives the pf of the zero-modified distribution with $f_X^M(0) = 0.4$, and the fourth column gives the zero-truncated distribution. Note that, using equation (1.54) the constant c of the zero-modified distribution with $f_X^M(0) = 0.4$ is

$$c = \frac{1 - 0.4}{1 - 0.2401} = 0.7896.$$

Thus, $f_X^M(1) = (0.7896)(0.4116) = 0.3250$, and other values of $f_X^M(x)$ are obtained similarly. For the zero-truncated distribution, the value of c is

$$c = \frac{1}{1 - 0.2401} = 1.3160,$$

and the pf is computed by multiplying the second column by 1.3160, for $x = 1$, 2, 3 and 4.

Figure 1.2 plots the pf of $\mathcal{BN}(4, 0.3)$, the zero-modified distribution and zero-truncated distribution.

From the plots, we can see that the zero-modified and zero-truncated distributions maintain similar shapes as that of the binomial distribution for $x \geq 1$. □

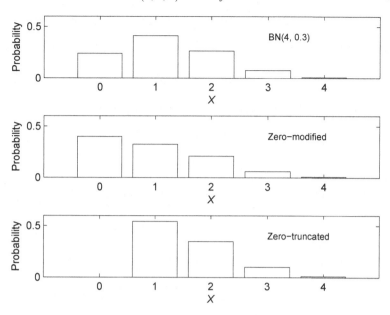

Figure 1.2 Probability functions of $\mathcal{BN}(4, 0.3)$ and its modifications

Example 1.6 X is distributed as $\mathcal{NB}(1.8, 0.3)$. What is the recursion formula for the pf of X? Derive the recursion formula for the zero-modified distribution of X with $f_X^M(0) = 0.6$. Compute the mean and variance of the zero-modified distribution.

Solution 1.6 From Table 1.2, we have

$$a = 1 - \theta = 1 - 0.3 = 0.7,$$

and

$$b = (r - 1)(1 - \theta) = (1.8 - 1)(1 - 0.3) = 0.56.$$

Thus, from equation (1.48), the recursion is

$$f_X(x) = \left(0.7 + \frac{0.56}{x}\right) f_X(x - 1), \quad \text{for } x = 1, 2, \ldots,$$

with the initial value of the recursion equal to

$$f_X(0) = (0.3)^{1.8} = 0.1145.$$

The recursion of the pf of the zero-modified distribution has the same formula as that of X, except that the starting point is $x = 2$ and the initial value is different. To compute the initial value, we first calculate c, which, from equation (1.54), is

$$c = \frac{1 - 0.6}{1 - 0.1145} = 0.4517.$$

Thus, the initial value is

$$f_X^M(1) = cf_X(1) = (0.4517)\left[1.8(0.3)^{1.8}(0.7)\right] = 0.0652,$$

and the recursion of the zero-modified distribution is

$$f_X^M(x) = \left(0.7 + \frac{0.56}{x}\right)f_X^M(x-1), \quad \text{for } x = 2, 3, \dots,$$

with $f_X^M(1) = 0.0652$.

To compute the mean and variance of the zero-modified distribution, we first note that its rth moment is

$$\sum_{x=0}^{\infty} x^r f_X^M(x) = \sum_{x=1}^{\infty} x^r f_X^M(x)$$
$$= c \sum_{x=1}^{\infty} x^r f_X(x)$$
$$= c\,\mathrm{E}(X^r).$$

From equation (1.30), the mean and variance of X are

$$\frac{r(1-\theta)}{\theta} = \frac{(1.8)(0.7)}{0.3} = 4.2,$$

and

$$\frac{r(1-\theta)}{\theta^2} = \frac{(1.8)(0.7)}{(0.3)^2} = 14,$$

respectively. Thus, $\mathrm{E}(X^2) = 14 + (4.2)^2 = 31.64$. Hence, the mean of the zero-modified distribution is $(0.4517)(4.2) = 1.8971$ and its raw second moment is $(0.4517)(31.64) = 14.2918$. Finally, the variance of the zero-modified distribution is $14.2918 - (1.8971)^2 = 10.6928$. $\square$

We have seen that the binomial, geometric, negative binomial and Poisson distributions can be unified under the $(a, b, 0)$ class of distributions. We shall conclude this section with another unifying theme of these four distributions, as presented in the theorem below.

Theorem 1.3 *Let X denote the binomial, geometric, negative binomial or Poisson distributions. The pgf $P_X(t)$ of X can be written as follows*

$$P_X(t \mid \beta) = Q_X[\beta(t - 1)], \tag{1.55}$$

where β is a parameter of X and $Q_X(\cdot)$ is a function of $\beta(t - 1)$ only. In other words, β and t appear in the pgf of X only through $\beta(t-1)$, although the function may depend on other parameters.

Proof First, we show this result for the binomial distribution. From equation (1.21), the pgf of $\mathcal{BN}(n, \theta)$ is

$$P_X(t) = [1 + \theta(t - 1)]^n. \tag{1.56}$$

Thus, equation (1.55) is satisfied with $\theta = \beta$. Next, we prove the result for the negative binomial distribution, as the geometric distribution is a special case of it. From equation (1.32), the pgf of $\mathcal{NB}(r, \theta)$ is

$$P_X(t) = \left[\frac{\theta}{1 - (1 - \theta)t} \right]^r. \tag{1.57}$$

If we define

$$\beta = \frac{1 - \theta}{\theta}, \tag{1.58}$$

then equation (1.57) becomes

$$P_X(t) = \left[\frac{1}{1 - \beta(t - 1)} \right]^r, \tag{1.59}$$

which satisfies equation (1.55). Finally, the pgf of $\mathcal{PN}(\lambda)$ is $P_X(t) = \exp[\lambda(t - 1)]$, which satisfies equation (1.55) with $\lambda = \beta$. $\qquad\square$

This theorem will be used in the next chapter.

1.5 Some Methods for Creating New Distributions

We now introduce two models of statistical distributions through which we can create new distributions. These are the compound distributions and mixture distributions. We may use these methods to create discrete as well as continuous distributions. Our main purpose in this section, however, is to use them to create discrete distributions which may be used to model claim frequency.

1.5.1 Compound Distribution

Let $X_1, \ldots, X_N$ be iid nonnegative integer-valued random variables, each distributed like X. We denote the sum of these random variables by S, so that

$$S = X_1 + \cdots + X_N. \tag{1.60}$$

If N is itself a nonnegative integer-valued random variable distributed independently of $X_1, \ldots, X_N$, then S is said to have a **compound distribution**. The distribution of N is called the **primary distribution**, and the distribution of X is called the **secondary distribution**. We shall use the *primary–secondary* convention to name a compound distribution. Thus, if N is Poisson and X

is geometric, S has a Poisson–geometric distribution. A **compound Poisson** distribution is a compound distribution where the primary distribution is Poisson, for *any* secondary distribution. Terminology such as compound geometric distribution is similarly defined. While N is always integer valued (being the number of summation terms of X_i), X in general may be continuous. In this chapter, we shall only consider the case of nonnegative integer-valued X, in which case S is also nonnegative integer valued.

Let us consider the simple case where N has a degenerate distribution taking value n with probability 1. S is thus the sum of n terms of X_i, where n is fixed. Suppose $n = 2$, so that $S = X_1 + X_2$. Then

$$f_S(s) = \Pr(X_1 + X_2 = s)$$

$$= \sum_{x=0}^{s} \Pr(X_1 = x \text{ and } X_2 = s - x). \tag{1.61}$$

As the pf of X_1 and X_2 are $f_X(\cdot)$, and X_1 and X_2 are independent, we have

$$f_S(s) = \sum_{x=0}^{s} f_X(s) f_X(s - x). \tag{1.62}$$

The above equation expresses the pf of S, $f_S(\cdot)$, as the **convolution** of $f_X(\cdot)$, denoted by $(f_X * f_X)(\cdot)$, i.e.,

$$f_{X_1+X_2}(s) = (f_X * f_X)(s) = \sum_{x=0}^{s} f_X(x) f_X(s - x). \tag{1.63}$$

Convolutions can be evaluated recursively. When $n = 3$, the 3-fold convolution is

$$f_{X_1+X_2+X_3}(s) = (f_{X_1+X_2} * f_{X_3})(s) = (f_{X_1} * f_{X_2} * f_{X_3})(s) = (f_X * f_X * f_X)(s). \tag{1.64}$$

The last equality holds as X_i are identically distributed as X. For $n \geq 2$, the pf of S is the convolution $(f_X * f_X * \cdots * f_X)(\cdot)$ with n terms of f_X, and is denoted by $f_X^{*n}(\cdot)$.

Convolution is in general tedious to evaluate, especially when n is large. The following example illustrates the complexity of the problem.

Example 1.7 Let the pf of X be $f_X(0) = 0.1, f_X(1) = 0, f_X(2) = 0.4$ and $f_X(3) = 0.5$. Find the 2-fold and 3-fold convolutions of X.

Solution 1.7 We first compute the 2-fold convolution. For $s = 0$ and 1, the probabilities are

$$(f_X * f_X)(0) = f_X(0) f_X(0) = (0.1)(0.1) = 0.01,$$

and

$$(f_X * f_X)(1) = f_X(0) f_X(1) + f_X(1) f_X(0) = (0.1)(0) + (0)(0.1) = 0.$$

Table 1.4. *Results of Example 1.7*

x	$f_X(x)$	$f_X^{*2}(x)$	$f_X^{*3}(x)$
0	0.1	0.01	0.001
1	0	0	0
2	0.4	0.08	0.012
3	0.5	0.10	0.015
4		0.16	0.048
5		0.40	0.120
6		0.25	0.139
7			0.240
8			0.300
9			0.125

Other values are similarly computed as follows

$$(f_X * f_X)(2) = (0.1)(0.4) + (0.4)(0.1) = 0.08,$$
$$(f_X * f_X)(3) = (0.1)(0.5) + (0.5)(0.1) = 0.10,$$
$$(f_X * f_X)(4) = (0.4)(0.4) = 0.16,$$
$$(f_X * f_X)(5) = (0.4)(0.5) + (0.5)(0.4) = 0.40,$$

and

$$(f_X * f_X)(6) = (0.5)(0.5) = 0.25.$$

For the 3-fold convolution, we show some sample workings as follows

$$f_X^{*3}(0) = [f_X(0)] \, [f_X^{*2}(0)] = (0.1)(0.01) = 0.001,$$
$$f_X^{*3}(1) = [f_X(0)] \, [f_X^{*2}(1)] + [f_X(1)] \, [f_X^{*2}(0)] = 0,$$

and

$$f_X^{*3}(2) = [f_X(0)] \, [f_X^{*2}(2)] + [f_X(1)] \, [f_X^{*2}(1)] + [f_X(2)] \, [f_X^{*2}(0)]$$
$$= 0.012.$$

Other calculations are similar. Readers may verify the results summarized in Table 1.4.   □

Having illustrated the computation of convolutions, we now get back to the compound distribution in which the primary distribution N has a pf $f_N(\cdot)$. Using the total law of probability, we obtain the pf of the compound distribution S as

$$f_S(s) = \sum_{n=0}^{\infty} \Pr(X_1 + \cdots + X_N = s \mid N = n) f_N(n) = \sum_{n=0}^{\infty} \Pr(X_1 + \cdots + X_n = s) f_N(n),$$

$$(1.65)$$

in which the term $\Pr(X_1 + \cdots + X_n = s)$ can be calculated as the n-fold convolution of $f_X(\cdot)$. However, as the evaluation of convolution is usually quite complex when n is large, the use of equation (1.65) may be quite tedious.

We now discuss some useful properties of S, which will facilitate the computation of its pf.

Theorem 1.4 *Let S be a compound distribution. If the primary distribution N has mgf $M_N(t)$ and the secondary distribution X has mgf $M_X(t)$, then the mgf of S is*

$$M_S(t) = M_N[\log M_X(t)].\tag{1.66}$$

If N has pgf $P_N(t)$ and X is nonnegative integer valued with pgf $P_X(t)$, then the pgf of S is

$$P_S(t) = P_N[P_X(t)].\tag{1.67}$$

Proof The proof makes use of results in conditional expectation, which can be found in Appendix A.11.[5] We note that

$$
\begin{aligned}
M_S(t) &= \mathrm{E}\left(e^{tS}\right)\\
&= \mathrm{E}\left(e^{tX_1 + \ldots + tX_N}\right)\\
&= \mathrm{E}\left[\mathrm{E}\left(e^{tX_1 + \ldots + tX_N} \mid N\right)\right]\\
&= \mathrm{E}\left\{\left[\mathrm{E}\left(e^{tX}\right)\right]^N\right\}\\
&= \mathrm{E}\left\{\left[M_X(t)\right]^N\right\}\\
&= \mathrm{E}\left\{\left[e^{\log M_X(t)}\right]^N\right\}\\
&= M_N[\log M_X(t)].
\end{aligned}\tag{1.68}
$$

For the pgf, we have

$$
\begin{aligned}
P_S(t) &= \mathrm{E}\left(t^S\right)\\
&= \mathrm{E}(t^{X_1 + \ldots + X_N})\\
&= \mathrm{E}\left[\mathrm{E}(t^{X_1 + \ldots + X_N} \mid N)\right]\\
&= \mathrm{E}\left\{\left[\mathrm{E}(t^X)\right]^N\right\}\\
&= \mathrm{E}\left\{\left[P_X(t)\right]^N\right\}\\
&= P_N[P_X(t)].
\end{aligned}\tag{1.69}
$$

$\square$

---

[5] Appendix A.11 discusses other results in conditional expectations, which will be used in later parts of this section.

Equation (1.69) provides a method to compute the pf of S. We note that

$$f_S(0) = P_S(0) = P_N[P_X(0)], \tag{1.70}$$

and, from equation (1.16), we have

$$f_S(1) = P_S'(0). \tag{1.71}$$

The derivative $P_S'(t)$ may be computed by differentiating $P_S(t)$ directly, or by the chain rule using the derivatives of $P_N(t)$ and $P_X(t)$, i.e.,

$$P_S'(t) = \{P_N'[P_X(t)]\}\, P_X'(t). \tag{1.72}$$

Other values of the pf of S may be calculated similarly, although the complexity of the differentiation becomes more involved.

Example 1.8 Let $N \sim \mathcal{PN}(\lambda)$ and $X \sim \mathcal{GM}(\theta)$. Calculate $f_S(0)$ and $f_S(1)$.

Solution 1.8 The pgf of N is

$$P_N(t) = \exp[\lambda(t - 1)],$$

and the pgf of X is

$$P_X(t) = \frac{\theta}{1 - (1 - \theta)t}.$$

From equation (1.67), the pgf of S is

$$P_S(t) = P_N[P_X(t)] = \exp\left[\lambda\left(\frac{\theta}{1 - (1 - \theta)t} - 1\right)\right],$$

from which we obtain

$$f_S(0) = P_S(0) = \exp\left[\lambda\left(\theta - 1\right)\right].$$

Note that as $\theta - 1 < 0$, $f_S(0) < 1$. To calculate $f_S(1)$, we differentiate $P_S(t)$ directly to obtain

$$P_S'(t) = \exp\left[\lambda\left(\frac{\theta}{1 - (1 - \theta)t} - 1\right)\right] \frac{\lambda\theta(1 - \theta)}{[1 - (1 - \theta)t]^2},$$

so that

$$f_S(1) = P_S'(0) = \exp\left[\lambda\left(\theta - 1\right)\right]\lambda\theta(1 - \theta). \qquad \square$$

Suppose the primary distribution of a compound Poisson distribution S has parameter λ, and the secondary distribution has a pgf $P(t)$, then using equation (1.69) the pgf of S is

$$P_S(t) = P_N[P(t)] = \exp\{\lambda[P(t) - 1]\}. \tag{1.73}$$

By the uniqueness of the pgf, equation (1.73) also *defines* a compound Poisson distribution. That is, if a distribution S has a pgf given by equation (1.73), where

λ is a constant and $P(t)$ is a well-defined pgf, then S is a compound Poisson distribution. In particular, the secondary distribution of S has pgf $P(t)$.

We now introduce a recursive method for computing the pf of S, which applies to the case when the primary distribution N belongs to the $(a, b, 0)$ class. This method is called the Panjer (1981) recursion.

Theorem 1.5 *If N belongs to the $(a, b, 0)$ class of distributions and X is a nonnegative integer-valued random variable, then the pf of S is given by the following recursion*

$$f_S(s) = \frac{1}{1 - af_X(0)} \sum_{x=1}^{s} \left(a + \frac{bx}{s}\right) f_X(x) f_S(s - x), \quad for \ s = 1, 2, \ldots, \quad (1.74)$$

with initial value $f_S(0)$ given by equation (1.70).

Proof See Dickson (2005, Section 4.5.2). $\qquad\qquad\qquad\qquad\qquad\qquad\square$

The recursion formula in equation (1.74) applies to the $(a, b, 0)$ class only. Similar formulas, however, can be derived for other classes of primary distributions such as the $(a, b, 1)$ class. Readers will find more details in Dickson (2005).

Example 1.9 Let $N \sim \mathcal{PN}(2)$ and $X \sim \mathcal{GM}(0.2)$. Calculate $f_S(0)$, $f_S(1)$, $f_S(2)$ and $f_S(3)$ using the Panjer recursion.

Solution 1.9 From Example 1.8, we have $f_S(0) = \exp[\lambda(\theta - 1)] = \exp[(2) (0.2 - 1)] = 0.2019$. Evaluating the pf of the geometric distribution, we have $f_X(0) = 0.2, f_X(1) = (0.2)(1 - 0.2) = 0.16, f_X(2) = (0.2)(1 - 0.2)^2 = 0.128$ and $f_X(3) = (0.2)(1 - 0.2)^3 = 0.1024$. From Table 1.2, the parameters a and b of the Poisson distribution are: $a = 0$ and $b = \lambda$. Hence, from equation (1.74) we have

$$f_S(1) = \lambda f_X(1) f_S(0) = (2)(0.16)(0.2019) = 0.0646.$$

This agrees with the answer of $f_S(1) = [f_S(0)] \lambda\theta(1 - \theta) = 0.0646$ from Example 1.8. Similarly, we have

$$f_S(2) = \frac{\lambda}{2} f_X(1) f_S(1) + \lambda f_X(2) f_S(0)$$

$$= (0.16)(0.0646) + (2)(0.128)(0.2019) = 0.0620,$$

and

$$f_S(3) = \frac{\lambda}{3} f_X(1) f_S(2) + \frac{2\lambda}{3} f_X(2) f_S(1) + \lambda f_X(3) f_S(0) = 0.0590. \qquad \square$$

Apart from the pf, it may be of interest to calculate the moments of the compound distribution. It turns out that the mean and variance of a compound distribution can be obtained from the means and variances of the primary and secondary distributions. Thus, the first two moments of the compound distribution can be obtained without computing its pf. The theorem below provides the results.

Theorem 1.6 *Consider the compound distribution defined in equation* (1.60). *We denote* $E(N) = \mu_N$ *and* $Var(N) = \sigma_N^2$, *and likewise* $E(X) = \mu_X$ *and* $Var(X) = \sigma_X^2$. *The mean and variance of S are then given by*

$$E(S) = \mu_N \mu_X, \tag{1.75}$$

and

$$Var(S) = \mu_N \sigma_X^2 + \sigma_N^2 \mu_X^2. \tag{1.76}$$

Proof We use the results in Appendix A.11 on conditional expectations to obtain[6]

$$E(S) = E[E(S \mid N)] = E[E(X_1 + \cdots + X_N \mid N)] = E(N\mu_X) = \mu_N \mu_X. \tag{1.77}$$

From (A.115), we have

$$
\begin{aligned}
Var(S) &= E[Var(S \mid N)] + Var[E(S \mid N)] \\
&= E[N\sigma_X^2] + Var(N\mu_X) \\
&= \mu_N \sigma_X^2 + \sigma_N^2 \mu_X^2,
\end{aligned}
\tag{1.78}
$$

which completes the proof. □

Note that if S is a compound Poisson distribution with $N \sim \mathcal{PN}(\lambda)$, so that $\mu_N = \sigma_N^2 = \lambda$, then

$$Var(S) = \lambda(\sigma_X^2 + \mu_X^2) = \lambda\, E(X^2). \tag{1.79}$$

Theorem 1.6 holds for any compound distribution, whether X is discrete or continuous. This result will be found useful in later chapters when X is the claim severity rather than the claim frequency.

Example 1.10 Let $N \sim \mathcal{PN}(2)$ and $X \sim \mathcal{GM}(0.2)$. Calculate $E(S)$ and $Var(S)$. Repeat the calculation for $N \sim \mathcal{GM}(0.2)$ and $X \sim \mathcal{PN}(2)$.

Solution 1.10 As $X \sim \mathcal{GM}(0.2)$, we have

$$\mu_X = \frac{1 - \theta}{\theta} = \frac{0.8}{0.2} = 4,$$

---

[6] See Appendix A.11 for the interpretation of the expectation operators in equation (1.77).

and

$$\sigma_X^2 = \frac{1 - \theta}{\theta^2} = \frac{0.8}{(0.2)^2} = 20.$$

If $N \sim \mathcal{PN}(2)$, from equation (1.75) we have $E(S) = (4)(2) = 8$. Since N is Poisson, we use equation (1.79) to obtain

$$\text{Var}(S) = 2(20 + 4^2) = 72.$$

For $N \sim \mathcal{GM}(0.2)$ and $X \sim \mathcal{PN}(2)$, $\mu_N = 4$, $\sigma_N^2 = 20$, and $\mu_X = \sigma_X^2 = 2$. Thus, $E(S) = (4)(2) = 8$, and from equation (1.76), we have

$$\text{Var}(S) = (4)(2) + (20)(4) = 88. \qquad \square$$

In Theorem 1.1, we see that the sum of independently distributed Poisson distributions is also Poisson. It turns out that the sum of independently distributed *compound* Poisson distributions has also a *compound* Poisson distribution. Theorem 1.7 states this result.

Theorem 1.7 *Suppose $S_1, \ldots, S_n$ have independently distributed compound Poisson distributions, where the Poisson parameter of S_i is λ_i and the pgf of the secondary distribution of S_i is $P_i(\cdot)$. Then $S = S_1 + \cdots + S_n$ has a compound Poisson distribution with Poisson parameter $\lambda = \lambda_1 + \cdots + \lambda_n$. The pgf of the secondary distribution of S is $P(t) = \sum_{i=1}^{n} w_i P_i(t)$, where $w_i = \lambda_i / \lambda$.*

Proof The pgf of S is

$$P_S(t) = E\left(t^{S_1 + \cdots + S_n}\right)$$

$$= \prod_{i=1}^{n} P_{S_i}(t)$$

$$= \prod_{i=1}^{n} \exp\left\{\lambda_i [P_i(t) - 1]\right\}$$

$$= \exp\left\{\sum_{i=1}^{n} \lambda_i P_i(t) - \sum_{i=1}^{n} \lambda_i\right\}$$

$$= \exp\left\{\sum_{i=1}^{n} \lambda_i P_i(t) - \lambda\right\}$$

$$= \exp\left\{\lambda \left[\sum_{i=1}^{n} \frac{\lambda_i}{\lambda} P_i(t) - 1\right]\right\}$$

$$= \exp\left\{\lambda [P(t) - 1]\right\}. \tag{1.80}$$

Thus, by the uniqueness property of the pgf, S has a compound Poisson distribution with Poisson parameter λ, and the pgf of its secondary distribution is

$P(t)$. Note that $P(t)$ is a well-defined pgf as it is a convex combination (with positive weights that sum to 1) of n well-defined pgf. $\qquad\qquad\square$

Note that if $f_i(\cdot)$ is the pf of the secondary distribution of S_i, then $f(\cdot)$ defined by

$$f(x) = \sum_{i=1}^{n} w_i f_i(x), \qquad \text{for } x = 0, 1, \ldots, \tag{1.81}$$

is the pf of the secondary distribution of S. This can be seen by comparing the coefficients of t^x on both sides of the equation $P(t) = \sum_{i=1}^{n} w_i P_i(t)$. It is easy to see that if all the compound Poisson distributions S_i have the same secondary distribution, then this is also the secondary distribution of S.

Example 1.11 The claim frequency of a block of insurance policies follows a compound Poisson distribution with Poisson parameter 2 and a secondary distribution $\mathcal{BN}(4, 0.4)$. The claim frequency of another block of policies follows a compound Poisson distribution with Poisson parameter 4 and a secondary distribution $\mathcal{GM}(0.1)$. If these two blocks of policies are independent, what is the probability that their aggregate claim frequency is less than 3?

Solution 1.11 Note that the aggregate claim frequency S of the two blocks of policies is the sum of two compound Poisson distributions. Thus, S is itself a compound Poisson distribution with $\lambda = 2 + 4 = 6$. We shall apply the Panjer recursion to compute the distribution of S. To do this, we first consider the pf of the secondary distributions of the blocks of policies. The relevant probabilities of the secondary distribution of the first block of policies are

$$f_1(0) = (0.6)^4 = 0.1296,$$

$$f_1(1) = 4(0.4)(0.6)^3 = 0.3456,$$

$$f_1(2) = 6(0.4)^2(0.6)^2 = 0.3456,$$

and the relevant probabilities of the secondary distribution of the second block of policies are

$$f_2(0) = 0.1, \qquad f_2(1) = (0.1)(0.9) = 0.09, \qquad f_2(2) = (0.1)(0.9)^2 = 0.081.$$

The relevant probabilities of the secondary distribution of S are

$$f(0) = \frac{1}{3}f_1(0) + \frac{2}{3}f_2(0) = 0.1099,$$

$$f(1) = \frac{1}{3}f_1(1) + \frac{2}{3}f_2(1) = 0.1752,$$

and

$$f(2) = \frac{1}{3}f_1(2) + \frac{2}{3}f_2(2) = 0.1692.$$

The pgf of the secondary distribution of S is

$$P(t) = \frac{1}{3}(0.4t + 0.6)^4 + \frac{2}{3}\left(\frac{0.1}{1 - 0.9t}\right),$$

from which we obtain

$$P(0) = \frac{1}{3}(0.6)^4 + \frac{2}{3}(0.1) = 0.1099,$$

This is the probability of zero of the secondary distribution of S, i.e., $f(0)$. Now we have

$$f_S(0) = \exp\{\lambda[P(0) - 1]\} = \exp[6(0.1099 - 1)] = 0.004793,$$

and using the Panjer recursion in equation (1.74), we obtain

$$f_S(1) = 6f(1)f_S(0) = 6(0.1752)(0.004793) = 0.005038,$$

and

$$f_S(2) = \frac{6}{2}f(1)f_S(1) + \frac{(6)(2)}{2}f(2)f_S(0) = 0.007514.$$

Thus, the probability of fewer than 3 aggregate claims is

$$0.004793 + 0.005038 + 0.007514 = 0.017345. \qquad \square$$

1.5.2 Mixture Distribution

New distributions can also be created by mixing distributions. Let $X_1, \ldots, X_n$ be random variables with corresponding pf or pdf $f_{X_1}(\cdot), \ldots, f_{X_n}(\cdot)$ in the common support Ω. A new random variable X may be created with pf or pdf $f_X(\cdot)$ given by

$$f_X(x) = p_1 f_{X_1}(x) + \cdots + p_n f_{X_n}(x), \qquad x \in \Omega, \qquad (1.82)$$

where $p_i \geq 0$ for $i = 1, \ldots, n$ and $\sum_{i=1}^n p_i = 1$. Thus, $\{p_i\}$ form a well-defined probability distribution and we may define a random variable Y by $\Pr(Y = i) = f_Y(i) = p_i$. Hence, X may be regarded as a random variable which is equal to X_i with probability p_i, and Y may be interpreted as a random variable which takes value i if and only if $X = X_i$.

We can check that $f_X(x)$ defined in equation (1.82) is a well-defined pf or pdf. As we are interested in claim-frequency distributions, we shall focus on cases in which $X_1, \ldots, X_n$ are nonnegative integer valued. Let the mean and variance of X_i be μ_i and σ_i^2, respectively. The following theorem gives the mean and variance of X.

Theorem 1.8 *The mean of X is*

$$E(X) = \mu = \sum_{i=1}^{n} p_i \mu_i, \qquad (1.83)$$

and its variance is

$$Var(X) = \sum_{i=1}^{n} p_i \left[(\mu_i - \mu)^2 + \sigma_i^2 \right]. \qquad (1.84)$$

Proof We use the conditional expectation formulas in Appendix A.11. By equation (A.111), we have

$$E(X) = E[E(X \mid Y)]. \qquad (1.85)$$

We denote $E(X \mid Y) = \mu(Y)$, where $\mu(Y) = \mu_i$ if $Y = i$. Thus,

$$E(X) = E[\mu(Y)]$$

$$= \sum_{i=1}^{n} p_i \mu_i. \qquad (1.86)$$

Note that this result can also be derived using equation (1.82) as follows

$$E(X) = \sum_{x=0}^{\infty} x f_X(x)$$

$$= \sum_{x=0}^{\infty} x \left[\sum_{i=1}^{n} p_i f_{X_i}(x) \right]$$

$$= \sum_{i=1}^{n} p_i \left[\sum_{x=0}^{\infty} x f_{X_i}(x) \right]$$

$$= \sum_{i=1}^{n} p_i \mu_i. \qquad (1.87)$$

We now denote $Var(X \mid Y) = \sigma^2(Y)$, where $\sigma^2(Y) = \sigma_i^2$ if $Y = i$. To compute the variance of X we use equation A.115 to obtain

$$Var(X) = E[Var(X \mid Y)] + Var[E(X \mid Y)]$$

$$= E[\sigma^2(Y)] + Var[\mu(Y)]$$

$$= \sum_{i=1}^{n} p_i \sigma_i^2 + \sum_{i=1}^{n} p_i (\mu_i - \mu)^2$$

$$= \sum_{i=1}^{n} p_i \left[(\mu_i - \mu)^2 + \sigma_i^2 \right]. \qquad (1.88)$$

$\square$

A random variable X with pf or pdf given by equation (1.82) has a **mixture distribution**. The random variable Y which determines the probability of occurrence of X_i is called the **mixing distribution**. As Y is discrete, X is called a **discrete mixture**, notwithstanding the fact that it has a continuous distribution if X_i are continuous. Note that X is different from the random variable $X^* = p_1 X_1 + \cdots + p_n X_n$. The exact distribution of X^* is in general difficult to compute. Assuming $\{X_i\}$ are independent,[7] to calculate the distribution of X^* we need to use the convolution method. Also, while the mean of X^* is the same as that of X, its variance is $\sum_{i=1}^{n} p_i^2 \sigma_i^2$, which is smaller than that of X.

Example 1.12 The claim frequency of a bad driver is distributed as $\mathcal{PN}(4)$, and the claim frequency of a good driver is distributed as $\mathcal{PN}(1)$. A town consists of 20% bad drivers and 80% good drivers. What are the mean and variance of the claim frequency of a randomly selected driver from the town?

Solution 1.12 The mean of the claim frequency is

$$(0.2)(4) + (0.8)(1) = 1.6,$$

and its variance is

$$(0.2)\left[(4 - 1.6)^2 + 4\right] + (0.8)\left[(1 - 1.6)^2 + 1\right] = 3.04. \qquad \square$$

We have so far considered discrete mixing distributions. Continuous distributions, however, can also be used as the mixing distribution. For example, consider a Poisson distribution $\mathcal{PN}(\lambda)$. Let $h(\cdot)$ be a function such that $h(\lambda) > 0$ for $\lambda > 0$, and

$$\int_0^\infty h(\lambda)\, d\lambda = 1. \tag{1.89}$$

In other words, $h(\lambda)$ is a properly defined pdf with the Poisson parameter λ treated as the realization of a *random variable*. A new mixture distribution can be created by defining a random variable X with pf given by

$$f_X(x) = \int_0^\infty \frac{e^{-\lambda}\lambda^x}{x!} h(\lambda)\, d\lambda. \tag{1.90}$$

It can be checked that $f_X(\cdot)$ is a well-defined pf. Specifically, $f_X(x) > 0$ for $x = 0, 1, \ldots$, and

$$\sum_{x=0}^\infty f_X(x) = \sum_{x=0}^\infty \int_0^\infty \frac{e^{-\lambda}\lambda^x}{x!} h(\lambda)\, d\lambda = \int_0^\infty \left(\sum_{x=0}^\infty \frac{e^{-\lambda}\lambda^x}{x!} \right) h(\lambda)\, d\lambda = \int_0^\infty h(\lambda)\, d\lambda = 1. \tag{1.91}$$

We now replace the Poisson pf in equation (1.90) by an arbitrary pf $f(x \mid \theta)$, where θ is the parameter of the distribution. With $h(\theta)$ satisfying the conditions

---

[7] Note that this assumption is not relevant for the definition of X with pf or pdf defined in equation (1.82), for which only the *marginal* distributions of X_i are relevant.

Table 1.5. *R functions for some discrete distributions*

Distribution	R function	Arguments
Binomial: $\mathcal{BN}(m,\theta)$	binom(,size,prob)	size $= m$, prob $= \theta$
Geometric: $\mathcal{GM}(\theta)$	geom(,prob)	prob $= \theta$
Negative binomial: $\mathcal{NB}(r,\theta)$	nbinom(,size,prob)	size $= r$, prob $= \theta$
Poisson: $\mathcal{PN}(\lambda)$	pois(,lambda)	lambda $= \lambda$

of a pdf (now treating θ as a random variable), a general formula for a mixture distribution for which the mixing distribution is *continuous* can be obtained. The pf of the mixture distribution is

$$f_X(x) = \int_0^\infty f(x \mid \theta) h(\theta) \, d\theta. \tag{1.92}$$

Note that as $f(x \mid \theta)$ is a pf, $f_X(x)$ is also a pf and X is discrete. On the other hand, equation (1.92) can also be applied to a pdf $f(x \mid \theta)$, in which case $f_X(x)$ is a pdf and X is continuous. With this extension, equation (1.92) defines a **continuous mixture**, notwithstanding the fact that X is discrete if $f(x \mid \theta)$ is a pf. We will see some examples of continuous mixing in later chapters.

1.6 R Laboratory

Table 1.5 provides a selection of R functions for the discrete distributions discussed in this chapter. We provide the names of the R functions describing the distributions, which should be preceded by r (for generating random numbers), p (for computing the distribution function), q (for computing the quantile function, i.e., inverse of the distribution function) or d (for computing the probability function of a discrete random variable or the probability density function of a continuous random variable). Each function must be called with an input argument, which is x (for functions beginning with p or d, representing the arguments (quantiles) of these functions), n (for functions beginning with r, representing the number of observations to generate) or p (for functions beginning with q, representing the probability). Some examples are given in **R Codes 1.1**.

```
#########################################################
# R Codes 1.1
#
# Some examples of usage of functions for discrete
# distributions
#########################################################
```

```
x=c(0,1,2,3)
dbinom(x,4,0.3)      # Table 1.3
pbinom(x,4,0.3)
dnbinom(x,1.5,0.4)   # Example 1.2, Table 1.1
dnbinom(x,1,0.8)
dgeom(x,0.8)         # Same as dnbinom(x,1,0.8)
rpois(10,4.5)        # Generate 10 PN(4.5) observations
```

1.7 Summary and Conclusions

We have discussed some standard nonnegative integer-valued random variables that may be applied to model the claim-frequency distributions. Properties of the binomial, geometric, negative binomial and Poisson distributions are discussed in detail. These distributions belong to the class of $(a, b, 0)$ distributions, which play an important role in the actuarial science literature. Further methods of creating new distributions with the flexibility of being able to fit various shapes of empirical data are introduced, including the compound-distribution and mixture-distribution methods. The computation of the compound distribution requires the convolution technique in general, which may be very tedious. When the primary distribution of the compound distribution belongs to the $(a, b, 0)$ class, the Panjer recursion may be used to facilitate the computation.

Claim events are dependent on the policy terms. Policy modifications such as deductibles may impact the claim events and thus their distributions. The techniques discussed in this chapter may be applied to any policies without reference to whether there are policy modifications. In later chapters we shall examine the relationship between claim-frequency distributions with and without claim modifications.

Exercises

Exercise 1.1 Let $X \sim \mathcal{BN}(n, \theta)$, prove that $E(X) = n\theta$ and $E[X(X - 1)] = n(n - 1)\theta^2$. Hence, show that $\text{Var}(X) = n\theta(1 - \theta)$. Derive the mgf of X, $M_X(t)$.

Exercise 1.2 Let $X \sim \mathcal{GM}(\theta)$, prove that $E(X) = (1 - \theta)/\theta$ and $E[X(X - 1)] = 2(1 - \theta)^2/\theta^2$. Hence, show that $\text{Var}(X) = (1 - \theta)/\theta^2$. Derive the mgf of X, $M_X(t)$.

Exercise 1.3 Let $X \sim \mathcal{PN}(\lambda)$, prove that $E(X) = \lambda$ and $E[X(X - 1)] = \lambda^2$. Hence, show that $\text{Var}(X) = \lambda$. Derive the mgf of X, $M_X(t)$.

Exercise 1.4 Let X^* be the zero-truncated distribution of X, which has pgf $P_X(t)$ and pf $f_X(x)$. Derive an expression for the pgf of X^* in terms of $P_X(\cdot)$ and $f_X(\cdot)$.

Exercise 1.5 Let $S = X_1 + X_2 + X_3$, where X_i are iid $\mathcal{BN}(2, 0.4)$ for $i = 1, 2$ and 3. Compute the pf of S.

Exercise 1.6 What are the supports of the following compound distributions?
(a) Primary distribution: $N \sim \mathcal{NB}(r, \theta)$, secondary distribution: $X \sim \mathcal{PN}(\lambda)$.
(b) Primary distribution: $N \sim \mathcal{NB}(r, \theta)$, secondary distribution: $X \sim \mathcal{BN}(n, \theta)$.
(c) Primary distribution: $N \sim \mathcal{BN}(n, \theta)$, secondary distribution: $X \sim \mathcal{GM}(\theta)$.
(d) Primary distribution: $N \sim \mathcal{BN}(n, \theta)$, secondary distribution: $X \sim \mathcal{BN}(m, \theta)$.

Exercise 1.7 S_1 and S_2 are independent compound Poisson distributions. The Poisson parameter of S_1 is 3 and its secondary distribution is $\mathcal{GM}(0.6)$. The Poisson parameter of S_2 is 4 and its secondary distribution is Bernoulli with probability of success 0.2. If $S = S_1 + S_2$, what is $\Pr(S < 4)$?

Exercise 1.8 Suppose $X \sim \mathcal{GM}(0.1)$, calculate the probability that the zero-modified distribution of X with $f_X^M(0) = 0.3$ is less than 4.

Exercise 1.9 Let $X_1, \dots, X_n$ be nonnegative integer-valued random variables with identical pf $f_X(\cdot)$. A discrete mixture distribution W is created with pf $f_W(x) = p_1 f_{X_1}(x) + \cdots + p_n f_{X_n}(x)$, where $p_i \geq 0$ for $i = 1, \dots, n$ and $\sum_{i=1}^{n} p_i = 1$. Another random variable Y is defined by $Y = p_1 X_1 + \cdots + p_n X_n$.

(a) Compare the mean of W and Y.
(b) If $X_1, \dots, X_n$ are independent, compare the variance of W and Y.

Exercise 1.10 S has a compound Poisson distribution, for which the Poisson parameter of the primary distribution is λ_1. Suppose the secondary distribution of S is also Poisson, with parameter λ_2.

(a) Find the mgf of S.
(b) Find the mean and the variance of S.
(c) Find the probabilities of $S = 0$ and $S = 1$.

Exercise 1.11 S has a compound Poisson distribution with Poisson parameter λ. The secondary distribution X of S follows a logarithmic distribution with parameter β, with pf given by

$$ f_X(x) = \frac{\beta^x}{x(1 + \beta)^x \log(1 + \beta)}, \qquad \beta > 0, \ x = 1, 2, \dots. $$

(a) Derive the pgf of X.
(b) Derive the pgf of S and show that S has a negative binomial distribution. What are the parameters of the negative binomial distribution?

Exercise 1.12 Construct the zero-modified distribution X from the Poisson distribution with $\lambda = 2.5$ so that the probability of zero is 0.55. What is the probability of $X \geq 4$? Find the mean and the variance of X.

Exercise 1.13 Let $X_1 \sim \mathcal{PN}(2)$, $X_2 \sim \mathcal{PN}(3)$ and $S = X_1 + 2X_2$, where X_1 and X_2 are independent. Calculate $\Pr(S = s)$, for $s = 0, 1$ and 2.

Exercise 1.14 S_1 has a compound distribution with primary distribution $\mathcal{PN}(1)$ and secondary distribution $\mathcal{GM}(\theta_1)$. Likewise, S_2 has a compound distribution with primary distribution $\mathcal{PN}(2)$ and secondary distribution $\mathcal{GM}(\theta_2)$, and S_1 and S_2 are independent. Let $S = S_1 + S_2$. Calculate $\Pr(S = s)$, for $s = 0, 1$ and 2, if

(a) $\theta_1 = \theta_2 = 0.2$,
(b) $\theta_1 = 0.2$ and $\theta_2 = 0.4$.

Exercise 1.15 Let $N_i \sim \mathcal{PN}(\lambda_i)$, $i = 1, 2, \ldots, n$, be independently distributed. Define a random variable S by

$$S = x_1 N_1 + x_2 N_2 + \cdots + x_n N_n,$$

where x_i are n different positive numbers.

(a) Derive the pgf of S.
(b) Calculate $\Pr(S = 0)$.

Exercise 1.16 S_1 has a compound distribution with primary distribution $\mathcal{PN}(2)$ and secondary distribution $\mathcal{NB}(4, 0.5)$. S_2 has a compound distribution with primary distribution $\mathcal{NB}(4, 0.5)$ and secondary distribution $\mathcal{PN}(2)$. Calculate the mean and the variance of S_1 and S_2.

Exercise 1.17 X is a mixture of $\mathcal{PN}(\lambda)$ distributions, where $\lambda - 1$ has a $\mathcal{BN}(2, 0.2)$ distribution. Calculate the pgf, the mean and the variance of X.

Exercise 1.18 The number of trips a courier needs to make into the business district each day is distributed as $\mathcal{BN}(2, 0.7)$. The number of stops they have to make in front of traffic lights in each trip follows a $\mathcal{PN}(4)$ distribution. What is the probability that the courier will not make any stop in front of traffic lights on a working day?

Exercise 1.19 The number of sick leaves for male workers are on average three times that of female workers. The number of sick leaves of all workers in a day is Poisson distributed with mean 4.5.

(a) Find the probability of the event of having no sick leave in a day.
(b) Find the probability of the event of having one male sick leave and one female sick leave in a day.

Exercise 1.20 Let $X_1 \sim \mathcal{PN}(1)$ and $X_2 \sim \mathcal{PN}(2)$, where X_1 and X_2 are independent. Calculate $\Pr(X_1 = x)$ and $\Pr(X_2 = x)$ for $x = 0, 1$ and 2. Hence find $\Pr(X_1 + X_2 \leq 2)$. Can you suggest an alternative method to compute $\Pr(X_1 + X_2 \leq 2)$ without calculating the probabilities of X_1 and X_2?

Exercise 1.21 Suppose the nonnegative integer-valued random variable X has pf $f_X(x)$ for $x = 0, 1, \ldots$, and pgf $P_X(t)$. A zero-modified distribution X^* of X has probability at zero of $f_X^M(0)$, where $f_X^M(0) > f_X(0)$. Prove that the pgf of X^*, denoted by $P_{X^*}(t)$ is given by

$$P_{X^*}(t) = 1 - c + cP_X(t),$$

where

$$c = \frac{1 - f_X^M(0)}{1 - f_X(0)}.$$

By recognizing that the pgf of a Bernoulli distribution with probability of success θ is $P(t) = 1 - \theta + \theta t$, show that the above results can be interpreted as saying that any zero-modified distribution is a compound distribution. What are the primary and secondary distributions of this compound distribution? Also, how would you interpret X^* as a mixture distribution?

Exercise 1.22 Show that any geometric–geometric compound distribution can be interpreted as a Bernoulli–geometric compound distribution, and vice versa.

Exercise 1.23 Show that any binomial–geometric compound distribution can be interpreted as a negative binomial–geometric compound distribution, and vice versa.

Exercise 1.24 A diversified portfolio of bonds consist of investment-grade and noninvestment-grade bonds. The number of defaults of investment-grade bonds in each month is Poisson distributed with parameter 0.2, and the number of defaults of noninvestment-grade bonds in each month is independently Poisson distributed with parameter 1. When there is a default, whether it is an investment-grade or noninvestment-grade bond, the loss is $1 million or $2 million with equal probability. Derive the recursive formula for calculating the distribution of the losses of the portfolio in a month.

Exercise 1.25 Let S be a compound distribution, where the primary distribution is $\mathcal{NB}(r, \theta)$ and the secondary distribution is $\mathcal{PN}(\lambda)$. Suppose S^* is a mixture of distributions, with pf

$$f_{S^*}(x) = \sum_{i=0}^{n} f_{Y_i}(x) p_i,$$

where $p_i \geq 0$, $\sum_{i=0}^{n} p_i = 1$ (n may be infinite) and $Y_i \sim \mathcal{PN}(\lambda i)$ (note that $Y_0 = 0$ with probability 1). Let X be a random variable such that $\Pr(X = i) = p_i$, with mgf $M_X(\cdot)$.

(a) What is the pgf of S, $P_S(t)$?

(b) Show that the pgf of S^*, $P_{S^*}(t)$, is given by

$$P_{S^*}(t) = \sum_{i=0}^{n} e^{(t-1)\lambda i} p_i = E[e^{(t-1)\lambda X}] = M_X[\lambda(t-1)].$$

(c) If p_i are such that $X \sim \mathcal{NB}(r, \theta)$, show that $P_{S^*}(t) = P_S(t)$. How would you interpret this result?

Exercise 1.26 X is distributed as $\mathcal{GM}(0.8)$. What is the recursion formula for the pf of X? Derive the recursion formula for the zero-modified distribution of X with $f_X^M(0) = 0.4$. Calculate the mean and the variance of the zero-modified distribution.

Exercise 1.27 S has a binomial-Poisson compound distribution. What is the pgf of the zero-truncated distribution of S?

Exercise 1.28 S has a compound distribution with primary distribution N and secondary distribution X. If $N \sim \mathcal{GM}(0.5)$ and $X \sim \mathcal{PN}(3)$, calculate $f_S(s)$ for $s = 0, 1$ and 2 using Panjer recursion.

Exercise 1.29 Business failures are due to three mutually exclusive risks: market risk, credit risk and operation risk, which account for 20%, 30% and 50%, respectively, of all business failures. Suppose the number of business failures each year is Poisson distributed with mean 4.6.

(a) What is the chance that there are two business failures due to operation risk in a year?

(b) What is the chance that the business failures due to market risk and credit risk are both fewer than two in a year?

(c) Given that there are four business failures in a year, what is the probability that two of these are due to market risk?

Exercise 1.30 What are the mgf and pgf of the following distributions?

(a) Geometric–binomial compound distribution, $\mathcal{GM}(\theta_N)$–$\mathcal{BN}(n, \theta_X)$.

(b) Binomial–Poisson compound distribution, $\mathcal{BN}(n, \theta)$–$\mathcal{PN}(\lambda)$.

(c) Negative binomial–Poisson compound distribution, $\mathcal{NB}(r, \theta)$–$\mathcal{PN}(\lambda)$.

2

Claim-Severity Distribution

Claim severity refers to the monetary loss of an insurance claim. Unlike claim frequency, which is a nonnegative integer-valued random variable, claim severity is usually modeled as a nonnegative continuous random variable. Depending on the definition of loss, however, it may also be modeled as a mixed distribution, i.e., a random variable consisting of probability masses at some points and continuous otherwise.

We begin this chapter with a brief review of some statistical tools for analyzing continuous distributions and mixed distributions. The use of the survival function and techniques of computing the distribution of a transformed random variable are reviewed. Some standard continuous distributions for modeling claim severity are summarized. These include the exponential, gamma, Weibull and Pareto distributions. We discuss methods for creating new claim-severity distributions such as the mixture-distribution method. As losses that are in the extreme right-hand tail of the distribution represent big losses, we examine the right-hand tail properties of the claim-severity distributions. In particular, measures of tail weight such as limiting ratio and conditional tail expectation are discussed. When insurance loss payments are subject to coverage modifications such as deductibles, policy limits and coinsurance, we examine their effects on the distribution of the claim severity.

Learning Objectives

1 Continuous distributions for modeling claim severity
2 Mixed distributions
3 Exponential, gamma, Weibull and Pareto distributions
4 Mixture distributions
5 Tail weight, limiting ratio and conditional tail expectation
6 Coverage modification and claim-severity distribution

2.1 Review of Statistics

In this section we review some results in statistical distributions relevant for analyzing claim severity. These include the survival function, the hazard function and methods for deriving the distribution of a transformed random variable.

2.1.1 Survival Function and Hazard Function

Let X be a continuous random variable with df $F_X(x)$ and pdf $f_X(x)$. The **survival function (sf)** of X, denoted by $S_X(x)$, is the complement of the df,[1] i.e.,

$$S_X(x) = 1 - F_X(x) = \Pr(X > x). \tag{2.1}$$

The pdf can be obtained from the sf through the equation

$$f_X(x) = \frac{dF_X(x)}{dx} = -\frac{dS_X(x)}{dx}. \tag{2.2}$$

While the df $F_X(x)$ is monotonic nondecreasing, the sf $S_X(x)$ is monotonic nonincreasing. Also, we have $F_X(-\infty) = S_X(\infty) = 0$ and $F_X(\infty) = S_X(-\infty) = 1$. If X is nonnegative, then $F_X(0) = 0$ and $S_X(0) = 1$.

The **hazard function (hf)** of a nonnegative random variable X, denoted by $h_X(x)$, is defined as[2]

$$h_X(x) = \frac{f_X(x)}{S_X(x)}. \tag{2.3}$$

If we multiply both sides of the above equation by dx, we obtain

$$
\begin{aligned}
h_X(x)\, dx &= \frac{f_X(x)\, dx}{S_X(x)} \\
&= \frac{\Pr(x \le X < x + dx)}{\Pr(X > x)} \\
&= \frac{\Pr(x \le X < x + dx \text{ and } X > x)}{\Pr(X > x)} \\
&= \Pr(x < X < x + dx \mid X > x), \tag{2.4}
\end{aligned}
$$

where we have made use of the results in Appendix A.2 to obtain the second line of the equation. Thus, $h_X(x)\, dx$ can be interpreted as the conditional probability of X taking value in the infinitesimal interval $(x, x + dx)$ given $X > x$. In the life

---

[1] The survival function is also called the **decumulative distribution function**. In this book, we use the term survival function.

[2] The hazard function is also called the *hazard rate* or the *failure rate*. In the survival analysis literature, it is called the *force of mortality*.

contingency and survival analysis literature, the hf of the age-at-death random variable is a very important tool for analyzing mortality and life expectancy. We shall see that it is an important determinant of the tail behavior of claim-severity distributions.

Given the pdf or sf, we can compute the hf using equation (2.3). The reverse can be obtained by noting that equation (2.3) can be written as

$$h_X(x) = -\frac{1}{S_X(x)} \left(\frac{dS_X(x)}{dx} \right) = -\frac{d \log S_X(x)}{dx}, \qquad (2.5)$$

so that

$$h_X(x) \, dx = -d \log S_X(x). \qquad (2.6)$$

Integrating both sides of the equation, we obtain

$$\int_0^x h_X(s) \, ds = -\int_0^x d \log S_X(s) = -\left. \log S_X(s) \right]_0^x = -\log S_X(x), \qquad (2.7)$$

as $\log S_X(0) = \log(1) = 0$. Thus, we have

$$S_X(x) = \exp \left(-\int_0^x h_X(s) \, ds \right), \qquad (2.8)$$

from which the sf can be calculated given the hf. The integral in the above equation is called the **cumulative hazard function**.

The sf is defined for both continuous and discrete random variables. If X is a discrete random variable, the last expression on the right-hand side of equation (2.2) is replaced by the difference of the sf, i.e., $f_X(x_i) = S_X(x_{i-1}) - S_X(x_i)$, where x_i are values in increasing order in the support of X. We will, however, use the hf only for continuous random variables.

Example 2.1 Let X be a uniformly distributed random variable in the interval $[0, 100]$, denoted by $\mathcal{U}(0, 100)$.[3] Compute the pdf, df, sf and hf of X.

Solution 2.1 The pdf, df and sf of X are, for $x \in [0, 100]$,

$$f_X(x) = 0.01,$$
$$F_X(x) = 0.01x,$$

and

$$S_X(x) = 1 - 0.01x.$$

From equation (2.3) we obtain the hf as

$$h_X(x) = \frac{f_X(x)}{S_X(x)} = \frac{0.01}{1 - 0.01x},$$

which increases with x. In particular, $h_X(x) \to \infty$ as $x \to 100$. $\qquad \square$

---

[3] See Appendix A.10.3 for a brief discussion of uniform distribution.

2.1.2 Mixed Distribution

Some random variables may have a mixture of discrete and continuous parts. A random variable X is said to be of the **mixed type** if its df $F_X(x)$ is continuous and differentiable except for some values of x belonging to a countable set Ω_X.[4] Thus, if X has a mixed distribution, there exists a function $f_X(x)$ such that[5]

$$F_X(x) = \Pr(X \le x) = \int_{-\infty}^{x} f_X(x)\, dx + \sum_{x_i \in \Omega_X,\, x_i \le x} \Pr(X = x_i). \tag{2.9}$$

The functions $f_X(x)$ and $\Pr(X = x_i)$ together describe the density and mass function of the mixed random variable X. Whether a random variable X is of the continuous, discrete or mixed type, we may use the convenient **Stieltjes integral** to state that, for any constants a and b,[6]

$$\Pr(a \le X \le b) = \int_{a}^{b} dF_X(x), \tag{2.10}$$

which is equal to

$$\int_{a}^{b} f_X(x)\, dx, \qquad \text{if } X \text{ is continuous,} \tag{2.11}$$

$$\sum_{x_i \in \Omega_X,\, a \le x_i \le b} \Pr(X = x_i), \qquad \text{if } X \text{ is discrete with support } \Omega_X, \tag{2.12}$$

and

$$\int_{a}^{b} f_X(x)\, dx + \sum_{x_i \in \Omega_X,\, a \le x_i \le b} \Pr(X = x_i), \qquad \text{if } X \text{ is mixed.} \tag{2.13}$$

2.1.3 Expected Value of Function of Random Variable

Consider a function $g(\cdot)$. The expected value of $g(X)$, denoted by $\mathrm{E}[g(X)]$, is defined as

$$\mathrm{E}[g(X)] = \int_{-\infty}^{\infty} g(x)\, dF_X(x)$$

$$= \int_{-\infty}^{\infty} g(x) f_X(x)\, dx + \sum_{x_i \in \Omega_X} g(x_i)\, \Pr(X = x_i), \tag{2.14}$$

for a general mixed distribution X. If X is continuous, we have

$$\mathrm{E}[g(X)] = \int_{-\infty}^{\infty} g(x) f_X(x)\, dx, \tag{2.15}$$

---

[4] We use the term *mixed* random variable to denote one consisting of discrete and continuous parts. This should be distinguished from the *mixture* distributions described in Sections 1.5.2 and 2.3.2.

[5] Note that $f_X(x)$ is the derivative of $F_X(x)$ at the points where $F_X(x)$ is continuous and differentiable, but it is not the pdf of X. In particular, $\int_{-\infty}^{\infty} f_X(x)\, dx \ne 1$.

[6] For the definition of Stieltjes integral, see Ross (2006, p. 404).

and when it is discrete we have

$$E[g(X)] = \sum_{x_i \in \Omega_X} g(x_i) f_X(x_i). \tag{2.16}$$

If X is continuous and nonnegative, and $g(\cdot)$ is a nonnegative, monotonic and differentiable function, the following result holds[7]

$$E[g(X)] = \int_0^\infty g(x) \, dF_X(x) = g(0) + \int_0^\infty g'(x)[1 - F_X(x)] \, dx, \tag{2.17}$$

where $g'(x)$ is the derivative of $g(x)$ with respect to x. Defining $g(x) = x$, so that $g(0) = 0$ and $g'(x) = 1$, the mean of X can be evaluated by

$$E(X) = \int_0^\infty [1 - F_X(x)] \, dx = \int_0^\infty S_X(x) \, dx. \tag{2.18}$$

Example 2.2 Let $X \sim \mathcal{U}(0, 100)$. Calculate the mean of X using equation (2.15) and verify equation (2.18). Define a random variable Y as follows

$$Y = \begin{cases} 0, & \text{for } X \le 20, \\ X - 20, & \text{for } X > 20. \end{cases}$$

Determine the df of Y and its density and mass function.

Solution 2.2 From equation (2.15) and the results in Example 2.1, the mean of X is given by

$$E(X) = \int_0^{100} x f_X(x) \, dx = \int_0^{100} 0.01x \, dx = 0.01 \left(\frac{x^2}{2} \right]_0^{100} \right) = 0.01 \left(\frac{100^2}{2} \right) = 50.$$

Applying equation (2.18), we have

$$E(X) = \int_0^{100} S_X(x) \, dx = \int_0^{100} (1 - 0.01x) \, dx = 100 - \int_0^{100} 0.01x \, dx = 50.$$

Thus, the result is verified.

To determine the distribution of Y, we note that

$$\Pr(Y = 0) = \Pr(X \le 20) = F_X(20) = 0.2.$$

For $0 < y \le 80$, we have

$$\begin{aligned} \Pr(Y \le y) &= \Pr(Y = 0) + \Pr(0 < Y \le y) \\ &= 0.2 + \Pr(20 < X \le y + 20) \\ &= 0.2 + 0.01y. \end{aligned}$$

---

[7] See Appendix A.3 for a proof.

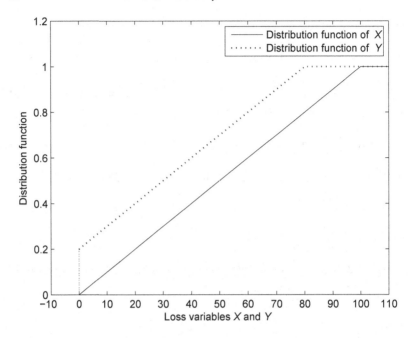

Figure 2.1 Distribution functions of X and Y in Example 2.2

Thus, the df of Y is

$$F_Y(y) = \begin{cases} 0, & \text{for } y < 0, \\ 0.2, & \text{for } y = 0, \\ 0.2 + 0.01y, & \text{for } 0 < y \leq 80, \\ 1, & \text{for } y > 80. \end{cases}$$

Hence, Y has a probability mass of 0.2 at point 0, and has a density function of 0.01 in the interval $(0, 80]$ and zero otherwise. See Figure 2.1 for the graphical illustration of the distribution functions of X and Y. □

2.1.4 Distribution of Function of Random Variable

Let $g(\cdot)$ be a continuous and differentiable function, and X be a continuous random variable with pdf $f_X(x)$. We define $Y = g(X)$, which is also a random variable. Suppose $y = g(x)$ is a one-to-one transformation, i.e., for any value of y, there is a unique value x such that $y = g(x)$. We denote the value of x corresponding to y by $g^{-1}(y)$, where $g^{-1}(\cdot)$ is called the inverse transformation. The theorem below gives the pdf of Y.

Theorem 2.1 *Let X be a continuous random variable taking values in $[a, b]$ with pdf $f_X(x)$, and let $g(\cdot)$ be a continuous and differentiable one-to-one transformation. Denote $a' = g(a)$ and $b' = g(b)$. The pdf of $Y = g(X)$ is*

$$f_Y(y) = \begin{cases} f_X(g^{-1}(y)) \left| \dfrac{dg^{-1}(y)}{dy} \right|, & \text{for } y \in [a', b'], \\ 0, & \text{otherwise.} \end{cases} \tag{2.19}$$

Proof See DeGroot and Schervish (2002, pp. 160–161). $\quad\square$

The restriction of one-to-one transformation may be relaxed by partitioning the domain of the transformation. Thus, suppose the domain of the transformation $g(\cdot)$ can be partitioned as the union of k mutually disjoint sets. Corresponding to each set there exists a function $g_i(\cdot)$ so that for a given value of $y \in [a', b']$, there is a unique x in the ith set with the property $y = g_i(x)$, for $i = 1, \ldots, k$. Then the pdf of Y is given by

$$f_Y(y) = \begin{cases} \sum_{i=1}^{k} f_X(g_i^{-1}(y)) \left| \dfrac{dg_i^{-1}(y)}{dy} \right|, & \text{for } y \in [a', b'], \\ 0, & \text{otherwise.} \end{cases} \tag{2.20}$$

The example below illustrates this result.

Example 2.3 Suppose $X \sim \mathcal{U}(-1, 1)$. Determine the pdf and the df of $Y = X^2$.

Solution 2.3 The pdf of X is

$$f_X(x) = \frac{1}{2}, \qquad \text{for } -1 \leq x \leq 1 \text{ and } 0 \text{ otherwise.}$$

Note that $Y = X^2 = g(X)$ is not a one-to-one transformation. We partition the domain of X into $A_1 = [-1, 0)$ and $A_2 = [0, 1]$, and define the functions $g_i(x) = x^2$, for $x \in A_i$, $i = 1, 2$. Then $g_i(x)$ are one-to-one transformations with respect to their domains, and we have

$$g_1^{-1}(y) = -\sqrt{y}, \qquad \text{for } y \in (0, 1],$$

and

$$g_2^{-1}(y) = \sqrt{y}, \qquad \text{for } y \in [0, 1].$$

Now,

$$f_X(g_i^{-1}(y)) = \frac{1}{2}, \qquad \text{for } i = 1, 2,$$

and

$$\frac{dg_1^{-1}(y)}{dy} = -\frac{1}{2\sqrt{y}} \quad \text{and} \quad \frac{dg_2^{-1}(y)}{dy} = \frac{1}{2\sqrt{y}}, \qquad \text{for } y \in (0, 1].$$

Thus, using equation (2.20), we have

$$f_Y(y) = \frac{1}{2} \left| -\frac{1}{2\sqrt{y}} \right| + \frac{1}{2} \left| \frac{1}{2\sqrt{y}} \right| = \frac{1}{2\sqrt{y}}, \qquad \text{for } y \in (0, 1].$$

The df of Y is

$$F_Y(y) = \int_0^y f_Y(s)\,ds = \frac{1}{2}\int_0^y \frac{1}{\sqrt{s}}\,ds = \sqrt{s}\Big]_0^y = \sqrt{y}.$$

Note that the df can also be derived directly as follows

$$F_Y(y) = \Pr(Y \le y) = \Pr(X^2 \le y) = \Pr(-\sqrt{y} \le X \le \sqrt{y}) = \int_{-\sqrt{y}}^{\sqrt{y}} f_X(x)\,dx = \sqrt{y}.$$

□

2.2 Some Continuous Distributions for Claim Severity

In this section, we review some key results of four continuous random variables, namely, exponential, gamma, Weibull and Pareto. These random variables can only take nonnegative values and may be used for distributions of claim severity. The choice of a particular distribution in practice is an empirical question to be discussed later.

2.2.1 Exponential Distribution

A random variable X has an exponential distribution with parameter λ, denoted by $\mathcal{E}(\lambda)$, if its pdf is

$$f_X(x) = \lambda e^{-\lambda x}, \qquad \text{for } x \ge 0, \tag{2.21}$$

where $\lambda > 0$. The df and sf of X are

$$F_X(x) = 1 - e^{-\lambda x}, \tag{2.22}$$

and

$$S_X(x) = e^{-\lambda x}. \tag{2.23}$$

Thus, the hf of X is

$$h_X(x) = \frac{f_X(x)}{S_X(x)} = \lambda, \tag{2.24}$$

which is a constant, irrespective of the value of x. The mean and variance of X are

$$\text{E}(X) = \frac{1}{\lambda} \qquad \text{and} \qquad \text{Var}(X) = \frac{1}{\lambda^2}. \tag{2.25}$$

The mgf of X is

$$M_X(t) = \frac{\lambda}{\lambda - t}. \tag{2.26}$$

The exponential distribution is often used to describe the interarrival time of an event, such as the breakdown of a machine. It is related to the Poisson distribution. If the interarrival time of an event is distributed as an exponential random variable with parameter λ, which is the reciprocal of the expected waiting time for the event (see equation (2.25)), then the number of occurrences of the event in a unit time interval is distributed as a Poisson with parameter λ.

2.2.2 Gamma Distribution

X is said to have a gamma distribution with shape parameter α and scale parameter β ($\alpha > 0$ and $\beta > 0$), denoted by $\mathcal{G}(\alpha, \beta)$, if its pdf is

$$f_X(x) = \frac{1}{\Gamma(\alpha)\beta^\alpha} x^{\alpha-1} e^{-\frac{x}{\beta}}, \qquad \text{for } x \geq 0. \tag{2.27}$$

The function $\Gamma(\alpha)$ is called the gamma function, defined by

$$\Gamma(\alpha) = \int_0^\infty y^{\alpha-1} e^{-y} \, dy, \tag{2.28}$$

which exists (i.e., the integral converges) for $\alpha > 0$. For $\alpha > 1$, $\Gamma(\alpha)$ satisfies the following recursion

$$\Gamma(\alpha) = (\alpha - 1)\Gamma(\alpha - 1). \tag{2.29}$$

In addition, if α is a positive integer, we have

$$\Gamma(\alpha) = (\alpha - 1)!. \tag{2.30}$$

Both the df and the hf of the gamma distribution are not in analytic form. However, it can be shown that the hf decreases with x if $\alpha < 1$, and increases with x if $\alpha > 1$.[8] The mean and variance of X are

$$\mathrm{E}(X) = \alpha\beta \qquad \text{and} \qquad \mathrm{Var}(X) = \alpha\beta^2, \tag{2.31}$$

and its mgf is

$$M_X(t) = \frac{1}{(1 - \beta t)^\alpha}, \qquad \text{for } t < \frac{1}{\beta}. \tag{2.32}$$

From equation (2.30), $\Gamma(1) = 1$. Thus, from equation (2.27) we can see that the pdf of $\mathcal{G}(1, \beta)$ is the same as that of $\mathcal{E}(1/\beta)$, and the exponential distribution is a special case of the gamma distribution. Suppose $X_1, \ldots, X_n$ are independently and identically distributed as $X \sim \mathcal{E}(1/\beta)$, and we define $Y = X_1 + \cdots + X_n$, then the mgf of Y is

$$M_Y(t) = [M_X(t)]^n = \left[\frac{\frac{1}{\beta}}{\frac{1}{\beta} - t} \right]^n = \frac{1}{(1 - \beta t)^n}, \tag{2.33}$$

which is the mgf of $\mathcal{G}(n, \beta)$. Thus, the sum of iid exponential distributions follows a gamma distribution with a positive integer-valued α. A gamma distribution with α being a positive integer is referred to in the literature as an **Erlang distribution**.

---

[8] See Klugman *et al.* (2004, p. 51), for a proof of this result.

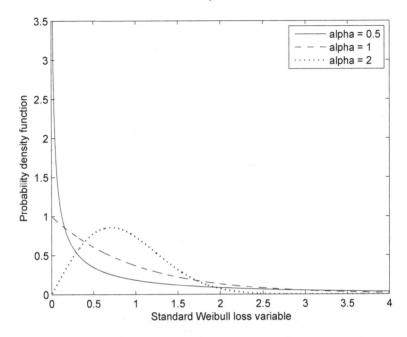

Figure 2.2 Probability density functions of standard Weibull distribution

2.2.3 Weibull Distribution

A random variable X has a 2-parameter Weibull distribution if its pdf is

$$f_X(x) = \left(\frac{\alpha}{\lambda}\right) \left(\frac{x}{\lambda}\right)^{\alpha-1} \exp\left[-\left(\frac{x}{\lambda}\right)^{\alpha}\right], \qquad \text{for } x \geq 0, \qquad (2.34)$$

where α is the shape parameter and λ is the scale parameter. We denote the distribution by $\mathcal{W}(\alpha, \lambda)$, where both α and λ are positive. The mean and variance of X are

$$\mathrm{E}(X) = \mu = \lambda\, \Gamma\left(1 + \frac{1}{\alpha}\right) \qquad \text{and} \qquad \mathrm{Var}(X) = \lambda^2\, \Gamma\left(1 + \frac{2}{\alpha}\right) - \mu^2. \ (2.35)$$

The df of X is

$$F_X(x) = 1 - \exp\left[-\left(\frac{x}{\lambda}\right)^{\alpha}\right], \qquad \text{for } x \geq 0. \qquad (2.36)$$

Due to its complexity, the mgf of the Weibull distribution is not presented here. A Weibull distribution with $\lambda = 1$ is called the standard Weibull, with pdf equal to $\alpha x^{\alpha-1} \exp(-x^{\alpha})$.

We shall see later that there is a close relationship between the exponential distribution and the Weibull distribution. Figure 2.2 shows the pdf of the standard Weibull distribution with different shape parameter α.

2.2.4 Pareto Distribution

A random variable X has a Pareto distribution with parameters $\alpha > 0$ and $\gamma > 0$, denoted by $\mathcal{P}(\alpha, \gamma)$, if its pdf is

$$f_X(x) = \frac{\alpha \gamma^\alpha}{(x + \gamma)^{\alpha+1}}, \qquad \text{for } x \geq 0. \tag{2.37}$$

The df of X is

$$F_X(x) = 1 - \left(\frac{\gamma}{x + \gamma}\right)^\alpha, \qquad \text{for } x \geq 0. \tag{2.38}$$

The hf of X is

$$h_X(x) = \frac{f_X(x)}{S_X(x)} = \frac{\alpha}{x + \gamma}, \tag{2.39}$$

which decreases with x. The kth moment of X exists for $k < \alpha$. For $\alpha > 2$, the mean and variance of X are

$$E(X) = \frac{\gamma}{\alpha - 1} \qquad \text{and} \qquad \text{Var}(X) = \frac{\alpha \gamma^2}{(\alpha - 1)^2(\alpha - 2)}. \tag{2.40}$$

The Pareto distribution was first applied in economics to study income distribution. It does not have a mgf. We shall see in the next section that the Pareto distribution can be derived as a mixture of exponential distributions. In Section 2.4, we discuss some tail properties of the Pareto distribution.

2.3 Some Methods for Creating New Distributions

In this section we discuss some methods for creating new distributions. In particular, we consider the methods of transformation, mixture distribution and splicing.

2.3.1 Transformation of Random Variable

New distributions may be created by transforming a random variable with a known distribution. The easiest transformation is perhaps the multiplication or division by a constant. For example, let $X \sim \mathcal{W}(\alpha, \lambda)$. Consider the **scaling** of X by the scale parameter λ and define

$$Y = g(X) = \frac{X}{\lambda}. \tag{2.41}$$

Using Theorem 2.1, we have $x = g^{-1}(y) = \lambda y$, so that

$$\frac{dg^{-1}(y)}{dy} = \lambda. \tag{2.42}$$

Hence, from equations (2.19) and (2.34), we have

$$f_Y(y) = \frac{\alpha y^{\alpha-1}}{\lambda}[\exp(-y^\alpha)]\lambda = \alpha y^{\alpha-1} \exp(-y^\alpha), \tag{2.43}$$

which is the pdf of a standard Weibull distribution.

Another common transformation is the **power transformation**. To illustrate this application, assume $X \sim \mathcal{E}(\lambda)$ and define $Y = X^{\frac{1}{a}}$ for an arbitrary constant $a > 0$. Thus, $x = g^{-1}(y) = y^a$, and we have

$$\frac{dg^{-1}(y)}{dy} = ay^{a-1}. \tag{2.44}$$

Applying Theorem 2.1 we obtain

$$f_Y(y) = \lambda ay^{a-1} \exp(-\lambda y^a). \tag{2.45}$$

If we let

$$\lambda = \frac{1}{\beta^a}, \tag{2.46}$$

equation (2.45) can be written as

$$f_Y(y) = \frac{a}{\beta^a} y^{a-1} \exp\left[-\left(\frac{y}{\beta}\right)^a\right], \tag{2.47}$$

from which we can conclude $Y \sim \mathcal{W}(a, \beta) \equiv \mathcal{W}(a, 1/\lambda^{\frac{1}{a}})$. Thus, the Weibull distribution can be obtained as a power transformation of an exponential distribution.

We now consider the **exponential transformation**. Let X be normally distributed with mean μ and variance σ^2, denoted by $X \sim \mathcal{N}(\mu, \sigma^2)$. As X can take negative values it is not suitable for analyzing claim severity. However, a new random variable may be created by taking the exponential of X. Thus, we define $Y = e^X$, so that $x = \log y$. The pdf of X is

$$f_X(x) = \frac{1}{\sqrt{2\pi}\sigma} \exp\left[-\frac{(x-\mu)^2}{2\sigma^2}\right]. \tag{2.48}$$

As

$$\frac{d\log y}{dy} = \frac{1}{y}, \tag{2.49}$$

applying Theorem 2.1, we obtain the pdf of Y as

$$f_Y(y) = \frac{1}{\sqrt{2\pi}\sigma y} \exp\left[-\frac{(\log y - \mu)^2}{2\sigma^2}\right]. \tag{2.50}$$

A random variable Y with pdf given by equation (2.50) is said to have a **lognormal distribution** with parameters μ and σ^2, denoted by $\mathcal{L}(\mu, \sigma^2)$. In other words, if $\log Y \sim \mathcal{N}(\mu, \sigma^2)$, then $Y \sim \mathcal{L}(\mu, \sigma^2)$. The mean and variance of $Y \sim \mathcal{L}(\mu, \sigma^2)$ are given by

$$E(Y) = \exp\left(\mu + \frac{\sigma^2}{2}\right), \tag{2.51}$$

and

$$\text{Var}(Y) = \left[\exp\left(2\mu + \sigma^2\right)\right]\left[\exp(\sigma^2) - 1\right]. \tag{2.52}$$

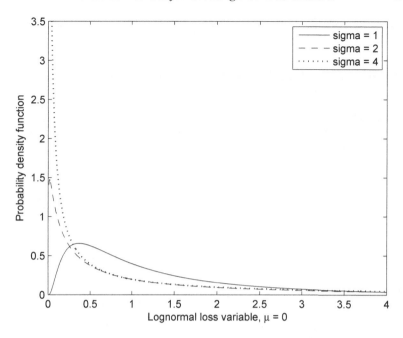

Figure 2.3 Probability density functions of $\mathcal{L}(0, \sigma^2)$

A lognormal distribution is skewed to the right. Figure 2.3 presents the pdf of some lognormal distributions with $\mu = 0$ and $\sigma = 1, 2$ and 4.

2.3.2 *Mixture Distribution*

In Section 1.5.2 we discuss the creation of a new distribution as a finite mixture of pdf or pf. For continuous distributions, a finite mixture can be created from n pdf. Thus, if $X_1, \ldots, X_n$ are random variables with corresponding pdf $f_{X_1}(\cdot), \ldots, f_{X_n}(\cdot)$, a new random variable X may be created with pdf $f_X(\cdot)$ given by

$$f_X(x) = p_1 f_{X_1}(x) + \cdots + p_n f_{X_n}(x), \tag{2.53}$$

where $p_i \geq 0$ for $i = 1, \ldots, n$ and $\sum_{i=1}^{n} p_i = 1$. We now formally extend this to continuous mixing (a brief discussion of this is in Section 1.5.2).

Let X be a continuous random variable with pdf $f_X(x \mid \lambda)$, which depends on the parameter λ. We allow λ to be the realization of a random variable Λ with support Ω_Λ and pdf $f_\Lambda(\lambda \mid \theta)$, where θ is the parameter determining the distribution of Λ, sometimes called the **hyperparameter**. A new random variable Y may then be created by *mixing* the pdf $f_X(x \mid \lambda)$ to form the pdf

$$f_Y(y \mid \theta) = \int_{\lambda \in \Omega_\Lambda} f_X(y \mid \lambda) f_\Lambda(\lambda \mid \theta) \, d\lambda. \tag{2.54}$$

Thus, Y is a mixture distribution and its pdf depends on θ. Unlike equation (2.53), in which the mixing distribution is discrete, the distribution of Y given in equation (2.54) is a continuous mixture as its mixing distribution is represented by the pdf $f_\Lambda(\lambda \mid \theta)$. The example below illustrates an application of continuous mixing.

Example 2.4 Assume $X \sim \mathcal{E}(\lambda)$, and let the parameter λ be distributed as $\mathcal{G}(\alpha, \beta)$. Determine the mixture distribution.

Solution 2.4 We have

$$f_X(x \mid \lambda) = \lambda e^{-\lambda x},$$

and

$$f_\Lambda(\lambda \mid \alpha, \beta) = \frac{1}{\Gamma(\alpha)\beta^\alpha} \lambda^{\alpha-1} e^{-\frac{\lambda}{\beta}}.$$

Thus,

$$\begin{aligned}
\int_0^\infty f_X(x \mid \lambda) f_\Lambda(\lambda \mid \alpha, \beta) \, d\lambda &= \int_0^\infty \lambda e^{-\lambda x} \left[\frac{1}{\Gamma(\alpha)\beta^\alpha} \lambda^{\alpha-1} e^{-\frac{\lambda}{\beta}} \right] d\lambda \\
&= \int_0^\infty \frac{\lambda^\alpha \exp\left[-\lambda \left(x + \frac{1}{\beta} \right) \right]}{\Gamma(\alpha)\beta^\alpha} \, d\lambda \\
&= \frac{\Gamma(\alpha+1)}{\Gamma(\alpha)\beta^\alpha} \left[\frac{\beta}{\beta x + 1} \right]^{\alpha+1} \\
&= \frac{\alpha}{\beta^\alpha} \left[\frac{\beta}{\beta x + 1} \right]^{\alpha+1}.
\end{aligned}$$

If we let $\gamma = 1/\beta$, the above expression can be written as

$$\frac{\alpha}{\beta^\alpha} \left[\frac{\beta}{\beta x + 1} \right]^{\alpha+1} = \frac{\alpha \gamma^\alpha}{(x + \gamma)^{\alpha+1}},$$

which is the pdf of $\mathcal{P}(\alpha, \gamma)$. Thus, the gamma–exponential mixture has a Pareto distribution. We also see that the distribution of the mixture distribution depends on α and β (or α and γ). □

In the above example, we may consider the exponential distribution as a *conditional distribution* given the parameter Λ and denote this by $X \mid \Lambda \sim \mathcal{E}(\Lambda)$. The distribution of Λ is the *mixing distribution*, with the mixture distribution regarded as the *unconditional distribution* of X.

As the mixture distribution is Pareto, from equation (2.40) we may conclude that the unconditional mean and variance of X are (when $\alpha > 2$)

$$E(X) = \frac{1}{(\alpha - 1)\beta} \qquad \text{and} \qquad \text{Var}(X) = \frac{\alpha}{(\alpha - 1)^2(\alpha - 2)\beta^2}. \qquad (2.55)$$

However, as the mixing technique does not always give rise to a straightforward pdf, its mean and variance may not be directly obtainable from a standard distribution. The example below illustrates the computation of the mean and variance of a continuous mixture using rules of **conditional expectation.** For the mean, we use the following result

$$E(X) = E\left[E\left(X \mid \Lambda\right)\right]. \tag{2.56}$$

For the variance, we use the result in equation (A.115), which can be rewritten in the current context as[9]

$$\text{Var}(X) = E\left[\text{Var}(X \mid \Lambda)\right] + \text{Var}\left[E(X \mid \Lambda)\right]. \tag{2.57}$$

Example 2.5 Assume $X \mid \Lambda \sim \mathcal{E}(\Lambda)$, and let the parameter Λ be distributed as $\mathcal{G}(\alpha, \beta)$. Calculate the unconditional mean and variance of X using rules of conditional expectation.

Solution 2.5 As the conditional distribution of X is $\mathcal{E}(\Lambda)$, from equation (2.25) we have

$$E(X \mid \Lambda) = \frac{1}{\Lambda}.$$

Thus, from equation (2.56), we have

$$E(X) = E\left(\frac{1}{\Lambda}\right)$$
$$= \int_0^\infty \frac{1}{\lambda}\left[\frac{1}{\Gamma(\alpha)\beta^\alpha} \lambda^{\alpha-1} e^{-\frac{\lambda}{\beta}}\right] d\lambda$$
$$= \frac{\Gamma(\alpha-1)\beta^{\alpha-1}}{\Gamma(\alpha)\beta^\alpha}$$
$$= \frac{1}{(\alpha-1)\beta}.$$

From equation (2.25), we have

$$\text{Var}(X \mid \Lambda) = \frac{1}{\Lambda^2},$$

so that using equation (2.57), we have

$$\text{Var}(X) = E\left(\frac{1}{\Lambda^2}\right) + \text{Var}\left(\frac{1}{\Lambda}\right) = 2E\left(\frac{1}{\Lambda^2}\right) - \left[E\left(\frac{1}{\Lambda}\right)\right]^2.$$

---

[9] See Appendix A.11 for a proof of the result, which has been used in the proof of Theorem 1.6.

As

$$\begin{aligned}
E\left(\frac{1}{\Lambda^2}\right) &= \int_0^\infty \frac{1}{\lambda^2}\left[\frac{1}{\Gamma(\alpha)\beta^\alpha}\lambda^{\alpha-1}e^{-\frac{\lambda}{\beta}}\right]d\lambda \\
&= \frac{\Gamma(\alpha-2)\beta^{\alpha-2}}{\Gamma(\alpha)\beta^\alpha} \\
&= \frac{1}{(\alpha-1)(\alpha-2)\beta^2},
\end{aligned}$$

we conclude

$$\text{Var}(X) = \frac{2}{(\alpha-1)(\alpha-2)\beta^2} - \left[\frac{1}{(\alpha-1)\beta}\right]^2 = \frac{\alpha}{(\alpha-1)^2(\alpha-2)\beta^2}.$$

These results agree with those in equation (2.55) obtained directly from the Pareto distribution. □

2.3.3 Splicing

Splicing is a technique to create a new distribution from standard distributions using different pdf in different parts of the support. Suppose there are k pdf, denoted by $f_1(x), \ldots, f_k(x)$, defined on the support $\Omega_X = [0, \infty)$, a new pdf $f_X(x)$ can be defined as follows

$$f_X(x) = \begin{cases}
p_1 f_1^*(x), & x \in [0, c_1), \\
p_2 f_2^*(x), & x \in [c_1, c_2), \\
\vdots & \vdots \\
p_k f_k^*(x), & x \in [c_{k-1}, \infty),
\end{cases} \tag{2.58}$$

where $p_i \geq 0$ for $i = 1, \ldots, k$ with $\sum_{i=1}^k p_i = 1$, $c_0 = 0 < c_1 < c_2 \cdots < c_{k-1} < \infty = c_k$, and $f_i^*(x)$ is a legitimate pdf based on $f_i(x)$ in the interval $[c_{i-1}, c_i)$ for $i = 1, \ldots, k$. For the last condition to hold, we define

$$f_i^*(x) = \frac{f_i(x)}{\int_{c_{i-1}}^{c_i} f_i(x)\,dx}, \qquad \text{for } x \in [c_{i-1}, c_i). \tag{2.59}$$

It is then easy to check that $f_X(x) \geq 0$ for $x \geq 0$, and

$$\int_0^\infty f_X(x)\,dx = 1. \tag{2.60}$$

Note that while $f_X(x)$ is a legitimate pdf, it is in general not continuous, as the splicing causes jumps at the points $c_1, \ldots, c_{k-1}$. The example below illustrates the method.

Example 2.6 Let $X_1 \sim \mathcal{E}(0.5)$, $X_2 \sim \mathcal{E}(2)$ and $X_3 \sim \mathcal{P}(2, 3)$, with corresponding pdf $f_i(x)$ for $i = 1, 2$ and 3. Construct a spliced distribution using

$f_1(x)$ in the interval $[0, 1)$, $f_2(x)$ in the interval $[1, 3)$ and $f_3(x)$ in the interval $[3, \infty)$, so that each interval has a probability content of one third. Also, determine the spliced distribution so that its pdf is continuous, without imposing equal probabilities for the three segments.

Solution 2.6 We first compute the probability of each pdf $f_i(x)$ in their respective interval. For $x \in [0, 1)$, we have

$$\int_0^1 f_1(x)\, dx = \int_0^1 0.5e^{-0.5x}\, dx = 1 - e^{-0.5} = 0.3935.$$

For $x \in [1, 3)$, we have

$$\int_1^3 f_2(x)\, dx = e^{-2} - e^{-6} = 0.1329,$$

and for $x \in [3, \infty)$, we have, from equation (2.38)

$$\int_3^\infty f_3(x)\, dx = \left(\frac{3}{3+3}\right)^2 = 0.25.$$

Now $p_1 = p_2 = p_3 = 1/3$. Thus, from equations (2.58) and (2.59), $f_X(x)$ is equal to

$$\frac{1}{3}\left(\frac{0.5e^{-0.5x}}{0.3935}\right) = 0.4236e^{-0.5x}, \qquad \text{for } x \in [0, 1),$$

$$\frac{1}{3}\left(\frac{2e^{-2x}}{0.1329}\right) = 5.0179e^{-2x}, \qquad \text{for } x \in [1, 3),$$

and

$$\frac{1}{3}\left[\frac{(2)(3)^2}{(0.25)(x+3)^3}\right] = \frac{24}{(x+3)^3}, \qquad \text{for } x \in [3, \infty).$$

If the spliced pdf is to be continuous, we require $p_1 f_1^*(1) = p_2 f_2^*(1)$, i.e.,

$$p_1\left(\frac{f_1(1)}{0.3935}\right) = p_2\left(\frac{f_2(1)}{0.1329}\right),$$

and similarly

$$p_2\left(\frac{f_2(3)}{0.1329}\right) = (1 - p_1 - p_2)\left(\frac{f_3(3)}{0.25}\right).$$

Solving for the above simultaneous equations we obtain $p_1 = 0.3728$, $p_2 = 0.1410$ and $p_3 = 0.4862$. □

2.4 Tail Properties of Claim Severity

Claims with large losses undermine the viability of insurance contracts. Thus, in modeling losses special efforts must be made in analyzing the behavior of extreme values. For claim severity the extreme values occur in the upper (right-hand) tail of the distribution. A distribution with high probability of heavy loss is said to have a **fat tail**, **heavy tail** or **thick tail**, which may be interpreted in the relative or absolute sense. While it is difficult to define *thickness*, some measures may be used as indicators. First, the existence of moments is an indication of whether the distribution has a thick tail. For example, the gamma distribution has moments of all order, which indicates that the probability of extreme values dies down quite fast. In contrast, the Pareto distribution has moments only up to order α. Hence if $\alpha < 2$, the Pareto distribution has *no variance*. This is an indication of a thick-tail distribution.

To compare the tail behavior of two distributions, we may take the **limiting ratio** of their sf. The faster the sf approaches zero, the thinner is the tail. However, as the sf of a distribution always tends to zero, the ratio of two sf at the tail end has to be computed using the l'Hôpital rule. Thus, if $S_1(x)$ and $S_2(x)$ are the sf of the random variables X_1 and X_2, respectively, with corresponding pdf $f_1(x)$ and $f_2(x)$, we have

$$\lim_{x \to \infty} \frac{S_1(x)}{S_2(x)} = \lim_{x \to \infty} \frac{S_1'(x)}{S_2'(x)} = \lim_{x \to \infty} \frac{f_1(x)}{f_2(x)}. \tag{2.61}$$

The example below compares the limiting ratio of the Pareto and gamma distributions.

Example 2.7 Let $f_1(x)$ be the pdf of the $\mathcal{P}(\alpha,\gamma)$ distribution, and $f_2(x)$ be the pdf of the $\mathcal{G}(\theta,\beta)$ distribution. Determine the limiting ratio of these distributions, and suggest which distribution has a thicker tail.

Solution 2.7 The limiting ratio of the Pareto versus the gamma distribution is

$$\lim_{x \to \infty} \frac{f_1(x)}{f_2(x)} = \lim_{x \to \infty} \frac{\dfrac{\alpha\gamma^\alpha}{(x+\gamma)^{\alpha+1}}}{\dfrac{1}{\Gamma(\theta)\beta^\theta} x^{\theta-1} e^{-\frac{x}{\beta}}}$$

$$= \alpha\gamma^\alpha \Gamma(\theta)\beta^\theta \lim_{x \to \infty} \frac{e^{\frac{x}{\beta}}}{(x+\gamma)^{\alpha+1} x^{\theta-1}}.$$

As the exponential function tends to infinity faster than the power function, the ratio of the right-hand side of the above equation tends to infinity as x tends to infinity. Thus, we conclude that the Pareto distribution has a thicker tail than the gamma distribution. This conclusion is congruent with the conclusion drawn based on the comparison of the moments. □

Another important determinant of tail thickness is the hf. Consider a random variable X with sf $S_X(x)$. For any $d > 0$, the ratio

$$\frac{S_X(x+d)}{S_X(x)} < 1. \tag{2.62}$$

This ratio measures the rate of decrease of the upper tail, and, using equation (2.8), it can be expressed in terms of the hf as follows

$$\frac{S_X(x+d)}{S_X(x)} = \frac{\exp\left(-\int_0^{x+d} h_X(s)\,ds\right)}{\exp\left(-\int_0^x h_X(s)\,ds\right)}$$

$$= \exp\left(-\int_x^{x+d} h_X(s)\,ds\right)$$

$$= \exp\left(-\int_0^d h_X(x+s)\,ds\right). \tag{2.63}$$

Thus, if the hf is a decreasing function in x, $\exp\left(-\int_0^d h_X(x+s)\,ds\right)$ is increasing in x, which implies the ratio $S_X(x+d)/S_X(x)$ increases in x. This is an indication of a thick-tail distribution. On the other hand, if the hf is an increasing function in x, the ratio $S_X(x+d)/S_X(x)$ decreases in x, suggesting low probability of extreme values. As mentioned in Section 2.2.2, the gamma distribution with $\alpha > 1$ has an increasing hf, the exponential distribution has a constant hf and both the gamma distribution with $\alpha < 1$ and the Pareto distribution have decreasing hf. Thus, in terms of increasing tail thickness based on the hf, we have the ordering of: (a) gamma with $\alpha > 1$, (b) exponential and (c) gamma with $\alpha < 1$ and Pareto.

We may also quantify extreme losses using quantiles in the upper end of the loss distribution. The **quantile function (qf)** is the inverse of the df. Thus, if

$$F_X(x_\delta) = \delta, \tag{2.64}$$

then

$$x_\delta = F_X^{-1}(\delta). \tag{2.65}$$

$F_X^{-1}(\cdot)$ is called the quantile function and x_δ is the δ-quantile (or the 100δth percentile) of X. Equation (2.65) assumes that for any $0 < \delta < 1$ a unique value x_δ exists.[10]

---

[10] If $F_X(\cdot)$ is not continuous, the inverse function may not exist. On the other hand, if $F_X(\cdot)$ is flat in some neighborhoods, there may be multiple solutions of the inverse. To get around these difficulties, we may define the quantile function of X by $F_X^{-1}(\delta) = \inf\{x : F_X(x) \geq \delta\}$.

Example 2.8 Let $X \sim \mathcal{E}(\lambda)$ and $Y \sim \mathcal{L}(\mu, \sigma^2)$. Derive the quantile functions of X and Y. If $\lambda = 1$, $\mu = -0.5$ and $\sigma^2 = 1$, compare the quantiles of X and Y for $\delta = 0.95$ and 0.99.

Solution 2.8 From equation (2.22), we have

$$F_X(x_\delta) = 1 - e^{-\lambda x_\delta} = \delta,$$

so that $e^{-\lambda x_\delta} = 1 - \delta$, implying

$$x_\delta = -\frac{\log(1 - \delta)}{\lambda}.$$

For Y we have

$$\begin{aligned}
\delta &= \Pr(Y \le y_\delta) \\
&= \Pr(\log Y \le \log y_\delta) \\
&= \Pr(\mathcal{N}(\mu, \sigma^2) \le \log y_\delta) \\
&= \Pr\left(Z \le \frac{\log y_\delta - \mu}{\sigma}\right),
\end{aligned}$$

where Z follows the standard normal distribution.

Thus,

$$\frac{\log y_\delta - \mu}{\sigma} = \Phi^{-1}(\delta),$$

where $\Phi^{-1}(\cdot)$ is the quantile function of the standard normal. Hence, $y_\delta = \exp\left[\mu + \sigma\Phi^{-1}(\delta)\right]$.

For X, given the parameter value $\lambda = 1$, $E(X) = \text{Var}(X) = 1$ and $x_{0.95} = -\log(0.05) = 2.9957$. For Y with $\mu = -0.5$ and $\sigma^2 = 1$, from equations (2.51) and (2.52) we have $E(Y) = 1$ and $\text{Var}(Y) = \exp(1) - 1 = 1.7183$. Hence, X and Y have the same mean, while Y has a larger variance. For the quantile of Y we have $\Phi^{-1}(0.95) = 1.6449$, so that

$$y_{0.95} = \exp\left[\mu + \sigma\Phi^{-1}(0.95)\right] = \exp(1.6449 - 0.5) = 3.1420.$$

Similarly, we obtain $x_{0.99} = 4.6052$ and $y_{0.99} = 6.2112$. Thus, Y has larger quantiles for $\delta = 0.95$ and 0.99, indicating it has a thicker upper tail. Figure 2.4 presents a comparison of the pdf of the two loss random variables in the upper tail.   □

Given the tolerance probability $1 - \delta$, the quantile x_δ indicates the loss which will be exceeded with probability $1 - \delta$. However, it does not provide information about how bad the loss might be if loss exceeds this threshold. To address this issue, we may compute the expected loss conditional on the threshold being exceeded. We call this the **conditional tail expectation (CTE)** with tolerance probability $1 - \delta$, denoted by CTE_δ, which is defined as

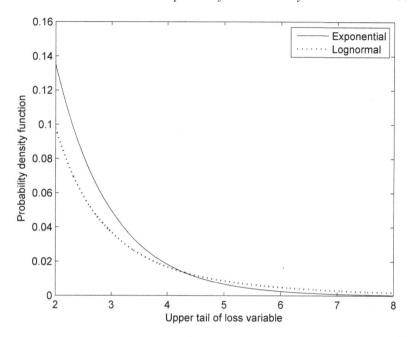

Figure 2.4 Upper tails of pdf of $\mathcal{E}(1)$ and $\mathcal{L}(-0.5, 1)$

$$\text{CTE}_\delta = E(X \mid X > x_\delta). \qquad (2.66)$$

To compute CTE_δ we first define the conditional pdf of X given $X > x_\delta$, denoted by $f_{X \mid X > x_\delta}(x)$. Using conditional law of probability, this quantity is given by

$$f_{X \mid X > x_\delta}(x) = \frac{f_X(x)}{\Pr(X > x_\delta)} = \frac{f_X(x)}{S_X(x_\delta)}, \qquad \text{for } x \in (x_\delta, \infty). \qquad (2.67)$$

Thus,

$$\begin{aligned}
\text{CTE}_\delta &= \int_{x_\delta}^{\infty} x f_{X \mid X > x_\delta}(x) \, dx \\
&= \int_{x_\delta}^{\infty} x \left[\frac{f_X(x)}{S_X(x_\delta)} \right] dx \\
&= \frac{\int_{x_\delta}^{\infty} x f_X(x) \, dx}{1 - \delta}. \qquad (2.68)
\end{aligned}$$

Example 2.9 For the loss distributions X and Y given in Example 2.8, calculate $\text{CTE}_{0.95}$.

Solution 2.9 We first consider X. As $f_X(x) = \lambda e^{-\lambda x}$, the numerator of the last line of equation (2.68) is

$$\int_{x_\delta}^{\infty} \lambda x e^{-\lambda x} \, dx = -\int_{x_\delta}^{\infty} x \, de^{-\lambda x}$$

$$= -\left(xe^{-\lambda x} \Big]_{x_\delta}^{\infty} - \int_{x_\delta}^{\infty} e^{-\lambda x}\, dx \right)$$

$$= x_\delta e^{-\lambda x_\delta} + \frac{e^{-\lambda x_\delta}}{\lambda},$$

which, for $\delta = 0.95$ and $\lambda = 1$, is equal to

$$3.9957 e^{-2.9957} = 0.1998.$$

Thus, $\text{CTE}_{0.95}$ of X is

$$\frac{0.1998}{0.05} = 3.9957.$$

The pdf of the lognormal distribution is given in equation (2.50). Thus, the numerator of (2.68) is

$$\int_{y_\delta}^{\infty} \frac{1}{\sqrt{2\pi}\sigma} \exp\left[-\frac{(\log x - \mu)^2}{2\sigma^2} \right] dx.$$

To compute this integral, we define the transformation

$$z = \frac{\log x - \mu}{\sigma} - \sigma.$$

As

$$\exp\left[-\frac{(\log x - \mu)^2}{2\sigma^2} \right] = \exp\left[-\frac{(z+\sigma)^2}{2} \right]$$

$$= \exp\left(-\frac{z^2}{2} \right) \exp\left(-\sigma z - \frac{\sigma^2}{2} \right),$$

and

$$dx = \sigma x\, dz = \sigma \exp(\mu + \sigma^2 + \sigma z)\, dz,$$

we have

$$\int_{y_\delta}^{\infty} \frac{1}{\sqrt{2\pi}\sigma} \exp\left[-\frac{(\log x - \mu)^2}{2\sigma^2} \right] dx = \exp\left(\mu + \frac{\sigma^2}{2} \right) \int_{z^*}^{\infty} \frac{1}{\sqrt{2\pi}} \exp\left(-\frac{z^2}{2} \right) dz$$

$$= \exp\left(\mu + \frac{\sigma^2}{2} \right) [1 - \Phi(z^*)],$$

where $\Phi(\cdot)$ is the df of the standard normal and

$$z^* = \frac{\log y_\delta - \mu}{\sigma} - \sigma.$$

Now we substitute $\mu = -0.5$ and $\sigma^2 = 1$ to obtain

$$z^* = \log y_{0.95} - 0.5 = \log(3.1421) - 0.5 = 0.6449,$$

so that $\text{CTE}_{0.95}$ of Y is

$$\text{CTE}_{0.95} = \frac{e^0 \left[1 - \Phi(0.6449)\right]}{0.05} = 5.1900,$$

which is larger than that of X. Thus, Y gives rise to more extreme losses compared to X, whether we measure the extreme events by the upper quantile or CTE. $\qquad\qquad\square$

2.5 Effects of Coverage Modifications

To reduce risks and/or control problems of **moral hazard**,[11] insurance companies often modify the policy coverage. Examples of such modifications are **deductibles**, **policy limits** and **coinsurance**. These modifications change the amount paid by the insurance companies in case of a loss event. For example, with deductibles the insurer does not incur any payment in a loss event if the loss does not exceed the deductible. Thus, we need to distinguish between a **loss event** and a **payment event**. A loss event occurs whenever there is a loss, while a payment event occurs only when the insurer is liable to pay for (some or all of) the loss.

In this section, we study the distribution of the *loss to the insurer* when there is coverage modification. To begin with, we define the following notations:

1 $X =$ amount paid in a loss event when there is no coverage modification, also called the **ground-up loss**

2 $X_L =$ amount paid in a loss event when there is coverage modification, also called the **cost per loss**

3 $X_P =$ amount paid in a payment event when there is coverage modification, also called the **cost per payment**

Thus, X and X_P are positive and X_L is nonnegative. Now we consider some coverage modifications and their effects on the loss-amount variable X_L and the payment-amount variable X_P.

2.5.1 Deductible

An insurance policy with a per-loss deductible of d will not pay the insured if the loss X is less than or equal to d, and will pay the insured $X - d$ if the loss X

---

[11] Moral hazard refers to the situation in which the insured behaves differently from the way they would behave if they were fully exposed to the risk, such that the risk of burden is transferred to the insurer. For example, in vehicle insurance, an insured may drive less carefully, knowing that the insurer will pay for the damages in accidents.

exceeds d. Thus, the amount paid in a loss event, X_L, is given by[12]

$$X_L = \begin{cases} 0, & \text{for } X \leq d, \\ X - d, & \text{for } X > d. \end{cases} \quad (2.69)$$

If we adopt the notation

$$x_+ = \begin{cases} 0, & \text{for } x \leq 0, \\ x, & \text{for } x > 0, \end{cases} \quad (2.70)$$

then X_L may also be defined as

$$X_L = (X - d)_+. \quad (2.71)$$

Note that $\Pr(X_L = 0) = F_X(d)$. Thus, X_L is a mixed-type random variable. It has a probability mass at point 0 of $F_X(d)$ and a density function of

$$f_{X_L}(x) = f_X(x + d), \qquad \text{for } x > 0. \quad (2.72)$$

Furthermore,

$$F_{X_L}(x) = F_X(x + d) \qquad \text{and} \qquad S_{X_L}(x) = S_X(x + d), \qquad \text{for } x > 0. \quad (2.73)$$

The random variable X_P, called the **excess-loss variable**, is defined only when there is a payment, i.e., when $X > d$. It is a conditional random variable, defined as $X_P = X - d \,|\, X > d$.

X_P follows a continuous distribution if X is continuous, and its pdf is given by[13]

$$f_{X_P}(x) = \frac{f_X(x + d)}{S_X(d)}, \qquad \text{for } x > 0. \quad (2.74)$$

Its sf is computed as

$$S_{X_P}(x) = \frac{S_X(x + d)}{S_X(d)}, \qquad \text{for } x > 0. \quad (2.75)$$

Figure 2.5 plots the df of X, X_L and X_P.

Note that in empirical applications only data on payments are available. When the loss X is less than or equal to d, a claim is not made and the loss information is not captured. Thus, for a policy with deductible only X_P is observed, and some information about X and X_L is lost.[14]

---

[12] The deductible defined in equation (2.69) is called an **ordinary deductible**. A deductible policy may also pay 0 when $X \leq d$ and X when $X > d$, in which case it is called a **franchise deductible**.

[13] In the life-contingency literature with X being the **age-at-death** variable, X_P is the future lifetime variable *conditional* on an entity reaching age d, and its expectation given in equation (2.77) is called the **expected future lifetime** or **mean residual lifetime**.

[14] Using the terminology in the statistics literature, X_L has a **censored distribution**, while X_P has a **truncated distribution**. Empirically, loss data are truncated.

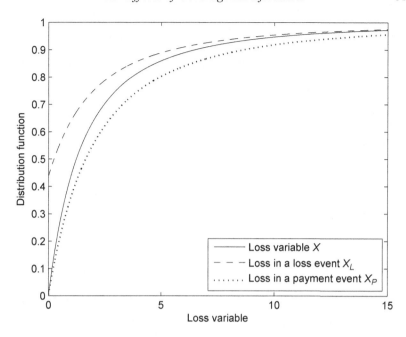

Figure 2.5 Distribution functions of X, X_L and X_P

The mean of X_L can be computed as follows

$$
\begin{aligned}
E(X_L) &= \int_0^\infty x f_{X_L}(x)\,dx \\
&= \int_d^\infty (x - d) f_X(x)\,dx \\
&= -\int_d^\infty (x - d)\,dS_X(x) \\
&= -\left[(x - d)S_X(x)]_d^\infty - \int_d^\infty S_X(x)\,dx \right] \\
&= \int_d^\infty S_X(x)\,dx.
\end{aligned} \tag{2.76}
$$

On the other hand, the mean of X_P, called the **mean excess loss**, is given by the following formula

$$
\begin{aligned}
E(X_P) &= \int_0^\infty x f_{X_P}(x)\,dx \\
&= \int_0^\infty x \left[\frac{f_X(x + d)}{S_X(d)} \right] dx \\
&= \frac{\int_0^\infty x f_X(x + d)\,dx}{S_X(d)}
\end{aligned}
$$

$$= \frac{\int_d^\infty (x - d) f_X(x)\, dx}{S_X(d)}$$

$$= \frac{E(X_L)}{S_X(d)}. \tag{2.77}$$

Note that we can also express X_P as $X_P = X_L \,|\, X_L > 0$. Now using conditional expectation, we have

$$E(X_L) = E(X_L \,|\, X_L > 0) \Pr(X_L > 0) + E(X_L \,|\, X_L = 0) \Pr(X_L = 0)$$
$$= E(X_L \,|\, X_L > 0) \Pr(X_L > 0)$$
$$= E(X_P) \Pr(X_L > 0), \tag{2.78}$$

which implies

$$E(X_P) = \frac{E(X_L)}{\Pr(X_L > 0)} = \frac{E(X_L)}{S_{X_L}(0)} = \frac{E(X_L)}{S_X(d)}, \tag{2.79}$$

as proved in equation (2.77).

There is also a relationship between $E(X_P)$ and CTE_δ. From equation (2.68) and the fourth line of equation (2.77), we have

$$E(X_P) = \frac{\int_d^\infty x f_X(x)\, dx - d \int_d^\infty f_X(x)\, dx}{S_X(d)} = \frac{\int_d^\infty x f_X(x)\, dx - d[S_X(d)]}{S_X(d)} = \text{CTE}_\delta - d, \tag{2.80}$$

where $\delta = 1 - S_X(d)$. This equation can also be derived by observing

$$E(X_P) = E(X - d \,|\, X > d) = E(X \,|\, X > d) - E(d \,|\, X > d) = \text{CTE}_\delta - d. \tag{2.81}$$

Thus, CTE_δ and $E(X_P)$ are mathematically equivalent. An important difference is that δ in CTE_δ is typically large (say, 0.95 or 0.99) as it measures the upper-tail behavior of the loss distribution. In contrast, the deductible d is typically in the lower tail of the loss distribution.

Example 2.10 For the loss distributions X and Y given in Examples 2.8 and 2.9, assume there is a deductible of $d = 0.25$. Calculate $E(X_L)$, $E(X_P)$, $E(Y_L)$ and $E(Y_P)$.

Solution 2.10 For X, we compute $E(X_L)$ from equation (2.76) as follows

$$E(X_L) = \int_{0.25}^\infty e^{-x}\, dx = e^{-0.25} = 0.7788.$$

Now $S_X(0.25) = e^{-0.25} = 0.7788$. Thus, from equation (2.77), $E(X_P) = 1$. For Y, we use the results in Example 2.9. First, we have

$$E(Y_L) = \int_d^\infty (y - d) f_Y(y)\, dy = \int_d^\infty y f_Y(y)\, dy - d[S_Y(d)].$$

Replacing y_δ in Example 2.9 by d, the first term of the above expression becomes

$$\int_d^\infty y f_Y(y)\, dy = \int_d^\infty \frac{1}{\sqrt{2\pi}\sigma} \exp\left[-\frac{(\log y - \mu)^2}{2\sigma^2}\right] dy = \exp\left(\mu + \frac{\sigma^2}{2}\right)[1 - \Phi(z^*)],$$

where

$$z^* = \frac{\log d - \mu}{\sigma} - \sigma = \log(0.25) - 0.5 = -1.8863.$$

As $\Phi(-1.8863) = 0.0296$, we have

$$\int_d^\infty \frac{1}{\sqrt{2\pi}\sigma} \exp\left[-\frac{(\log y - \mu)^2}{2\sigma^2}\right] dy = 1 - 0.0296 = 0.9704.$$

Now,

$$S_Y(d) = \Pr\left(Z > \frac{\log d - \mu}{\sigma}\right) = \Pr(Z > -0.8863) = 0.8123.$$

Hence,

$$E(Y_L) = 0.9704 - (0.25)(0.8123) = 0.7673,$$

and

$$E(Y_P) = \frac{0.7673}{0.8123} = 0.9446. \qquad \square$$

It turns out that the mean loss in a loss event for the lognormal distribution has important applications in the finance literature.[15] We summarize this result in the following theorem.

Theorem 2.2 *Let* $Y \sim \mathcal{L}(\mu, \sigma^2)$, *then for a positive constant* d,

$$E[(Y - d)_+] = \exp\left(\mu + \frac{\sigma^2}{2}\right)[1 - \Phi(z^*)] - d[1 - \Phi(z^* + \sigma)], \qquad (2.82)$$

where

$$z^* = \frac{\log d - \mu}{\sigma} - \sigma. \qquad (2.83)$$

Proof The derivation in Example 2.10 shows that

$$E[(Y - d)_+] = \int_d^\infty (y - d) f_Y(y)\, dy = \int_d^\infty y f_Y(y)\, dy - d[S_Y(d)], \qquad (2.84)$$

and

$$\int_d^\infty y f_Y(y)\, dy = \exp\left(\mu + \frac{\sigma^2}{2}\right)[1 - \Phi(z^*)]. \qquad (2.85)$$

---

[15] This result is closely related to the celebrated Black–Scholes option pricing formula (see Exercise 2.28).

Now

$$S_Y(d) = \Pr\left(Z > \frac{\log d - \mu}{\sigma}\right) = 1 - \Phi(z^* + \sigma). \tag{2.86}$$

Combining equations (2.84) through (2.86), we obtain equation (2.82). □

Comparing the results in Examples 2.8 through 2.10, we can see that although the lognormal loss distribution has thicker tail than the exponential loss distribution (note that they are selected to have the same mean), its mean loss in a loss event and mean amount paid in a payment event are smaller than those of the exponential loss distribution. This echoes the point that the deductible is set at the lower tail of the loss distribution, which influences the overall mean of the modified loss.

If we subtract the loss amount with deductible from the loss amount without deductible, the result is the reduction in loss due to the deductible, which is equal to $X - (X - d)_+$. Thus, the expected reduction in loss due to the deductible is

$$\mathrm{E}(X) - \mathrm{E}\left[(X - d)_+\right] = \mathrm{E}(X) - \mathrm{E}(X_L). \tag{2.87}$$

Now we define the **loss elimination ratio** with deductible d, denoted by LER(d), as the ratio of the expected reduction in loss due to the deductible to the expected loss without the deductible, which is given by

$$\mathrm{LER}(d) = \frac{\mathrm{E}(X) - \mathrm{E}(X_L)}{\mathrm{E}(X)}. \tag{2.88}$$

Example 2.11 Calculate LER(0.25) for the loss distributions X and Y given in Examples 2.8 through 2.10.

Solution 2.11 For X, we have

$$\mathrm{LER}(0.25) = \frac{1 - 0.7788}{1} = 0.2212.$$

Similarly, LER(0.25) for Y is $1 - 0.7673 = 0.2327$. Thus, the deductible of amount 0.25 has caused a bigger percentage reduction in the loss for the lognormal loss distribution than for the exponential loss distribution. □

Finally, we note that for any loss distribution X, higher raw moments of X_L and X_P can be computed as follows

$$\mathrm{E}(X_L^k) = \int_d^\infty (x - d)^k f_X(x)\, dx, \tag{2.89}$$

and

$$\mathrm{E}(X_P^k) = \frac{\int_d^\infty (x - d)^k f_X(x)\, dx}{S_X(d)} = \frac{\mathrm{E}(X_L^k)}{S_X(d)}. \tag{2.90}$$

Table 2.1. *Proof of equation* (2.94)

	$X < q$	$X \geq q$
$X \wedge q$	X	q
$(X - q)_+$	0	$X - q$
$(X \wedge q) + (X - q)_+$	X	X

2.5.2 Policy Limit

For an insurance policy with a **policy limit**, the insurer compensates the insured up to a preset amount, say, u. If a policy has a policy limit but no deductible, then the amount paid in a loss event is the same as the amount paid in a payment event. We denote the amount paid for a policy with a policy limit by X_U. If we define the binary operation $\wedge$ as the minimum of two quantities, so that

$$a \wedge b = \min\{a, b\}, \tag{2.91}$$

then

$$X_U = X \wedge u, \tag{2.92}$$

i.e.,

$$X_U = \begin{cases} X, & \text{for } X < u, \\ u, & \text{for } X \geq u. \end{cases} \tag{2.93}$$

X_U defined above is called the **limited-loss variable**. It is interesting to note that the loss amount with a policy limit and the loss amount with a deductible are closely related. Specifically, for any arbitrary positive constant q, the following identity holds

$$X = (X \wedge q) + (X - q)_+. \tag{2.94}$$

This relationship is verified in Table 2.1, from which we can see that the two sides of equation (2.94) are equal, whether $X < q$ or $X \geq q$.

Thus, $(X \wedge u) = X - (X - u)_+$, which can be interpreted as the saving to the insurer if the policy has a *deductible* of amount u. With the identity in equation (2.94), LER can be written as

$$\text{LER}(d) = \frac{E(X) - E\left[(X - d)_+\right]}{E(X)} = \frac{E(X) - [E(X) - E(X \wedge d)]}{E(X)} = \frac{E(X \wedge d)}{E(X)}. \tag{2.95}$$

2.5.3 Coinsurance

An insurance policy may specify that the insurer and insured share the loss in a loss event, which is called **coinsurance**. We consider a simple coinsurance policy in which the insurer pays the insured a fixed portion c of the loss in a loss event, where $0 < c < 1$. Under pure coinsurance the insurer pays damages whenever there is a loss. We denote X_C as the payment made by the insurer with coinsurance. Thus,

$$X_C = cX, \tag{2.96}$$

where X is the loss without policy modification. Using Theorem 2.1, the pdf of X_C is

$$f_{X_C}(x) = \frac{1}{c} f_X \left(\frac{x}{c} \right), \tag{2.97}$$

and it is also true that

$$E(X_C) = c\, E(X). \tag{2.98}$$

Now we consider a policy with a deductible of amount d and a **maximum covered loss** of amount u ($u > d$). Thus, the policy limit is of amount $u - d$. In addition, assume the policy has a coinsurance factor c ($0 < c < 1$). We denote the loss random variable in a loss event of this insurance policy by X_T, which is given by

$$X_T = c\left[(X \wedge u) - (X \wedge d) \right] = c\left[(X - d)_+ - (X - u)_+ \right]. \tag{2.99}$$

It can be checked that X_T defined above satisfies

$$X_T = \begin{cases} 0, & \text{for } X < d, \\ c(X - d), & \text{for } d \le X < u, \\ c(u - d), & \text{for } X \ge u. \end{cases} \tag{2.100}$$

From equation (2.99) we have

$$E(X_T) = c\left\{ E\left[(X - d)_+ \right] - E\left[(X - u)_+ \right] \right\}, \tag{2.101}$$

which can be computed using equation (2.76).

Example 2.12 For the exponential loss distribution X and lognormal loss distribution Y in Examples 2.8 through 2.11, assume there is a deductible of $d = 0.25$, maximum covered loss of $u = 4$ and coinsurance factor of $c = 0.8$. Calculate the mean loss in a loss event of these two distributions.

Solution 2.12 We use equation (2.101) to calculate $E(X_T)$ and $E(Y_T)$. $E[(X - d)_+]$ and $E[(Y - d)_+]$ are computed in Example 2.10 as 0.7788 and 0.7673, respectively. We now compute $E[(X - u)_+]$ and $E[(Y - u)_+]$ using the method in Example 2.10, with u replacing d. For X, we have

$$E\left[(X - u)_+ \right] = \int_u^\infty e^{-x}\, dx = e^{-4} = 0.0183.$$

For Y, we have $z^* = \log(4) - 0.5 = 0.8863$ so that $\Phi(z^*) = 0.8123$, and

$$S_Y(u) = \Pr\left(Z > \frac{\log(u) - \mu}{\sigma}\right) = \Pr(Z > 1.8863) = 0.0296.$$

Thus,

$$E\left[(Y - u)_+\right] = (1 - 0.8123) - (4)(0.0296) = 0.0693.$$

Therefore, from equation (2.101), we have

$$E(X_T) = (0.8)\,(0.7788 - 0.0183) = 0.6084,$$

and

$$E(Y_T) = (0.8)(0.7673 - 0.0693) = 0.5584.$$

We concluded from Example 2.10 that the mean loss with a deductible of 0.25 is lower for the lognormal distribution than the exponential. Now the maximum covered loss brings about a bigger reduction in loss for the lognormal distribution as it has a thicker tail than the exponential. Thus, the resulting mean loss for the lognormal distribution is further reduced compared to that of the exponential. □

To compute the variance of X_T, we may use the result $\mathrm{Var}(X_T) = E(X_T^2) - [E(X_T)]^2$. When $c = 1$, $E(X_T^2)$ can be evaluated from the following result

$$E(X_T^2) = E\left[(X \wedge u)^2\right] - E\left[(X \wedge d)^2\right] - 2d\{E\left[(X \wedge u)\right] - E\left[(X \wedge d)\right]\}. \quad (2.102)$$

To prove the above equation, note that

$$E(X_T^2) = E\left\{[(X \wedge u) - (X \wedge d)]^2\right\}$$
$$= E\left[(X \wedge u)^2\right] + E\left[(X \wedge d)^2\right] - 2E\left[(X \wedge u)(X \wedge d)\right]. \quad (2.103)$$

Now we have

$$E\left[(X \wedge u)(X \wedge d)\right] = \int_0^d x^2 f_X(x)\,dx + d\int_d^u x f_X(x)\,dx + du[1 - F_X(u)]$$

$$= \int_0^d x^2 f_X(x)\,dx + d\left[\int_0^u x f_X(x)\,dx - \int_0^d x f_X(x)\,dx\right]$$
$$\quad + du[1 - F_X(u)]$$

$$= \int_0^d x^2 f_X(x)\,dx + d^2[1 - F_X(d)]$$
$$\quad + d\left[\int_0^u x f_X(x)\,dx + u[1 - F_X(u)]\right]$$
$$\quad - d\left[\int_0^d x f_X(x)\,dx + d[1 - F_X(d)]\right]$$

$$= E\left[(X \wedge d)^2\right] + d\{E\left[(X \wedge u)\right] - E\left[(X \wedge d)\right]\}. \quad (2.104)$$

Substituting equation (2.104) into (2.103), we obtain the result in equation (2.102). Finally, if the policy has a deductible d but no policy limit (i.e., $u = \infty$), we have

$$
\begin{aligned}
\mathrm{E}(X_L^2) &= \mathrm{E}\left[(X - d)_+^2\right] \\
&= \mathrm{E}\left\{[X - (X \wedge d)]^2\right\} \\
&= \mathrm{E}(X^2) - \mathrm{E}\left[(X \wedge d)^2\right] - 2d\{\mathrm{E}(X) - \mathrm{E}\left[(X \wedge d)\right]\}.
\end{aligned}
\tag{2.105}
$$

2.5.4 Effects of Inflation

While loss distributions are specified based on current experience and data, inflation may cause increases in the costs. On the other hand, policy specifications (such as deductible) remain unchanged for the policy period. To model the effects of inflation, we consider a one-period insurance policy and assume the rate of price increase in the period to be r. We use a tilde to denote inflation-adjusted losses. Thus, the inflation-adjusted loss distribution is denoted by $\tilde{X}$, which is equal to $(1+r)X$. For an insurance policy with deductible d, the loss in a loss event and the loss in a payment event with inflation adjustment are denoted by $\tilde{X}_L$ and $\tilde{X}_P$, respectively. As the deductible is not inflation adjusted, we have

$$
\tilde{X}_L = (\tilde{X} - d)_+ = \tilde{X} - (\tilde{X} \wedge d),
\tag{2.106}
$$

and

$$
\tilde{X}_P = \tilde{X} - d \mid \tilde{X} - d > 0 = \tilde{X}_L \mid \tilde{X}_L > 0.
\tag{2.107}
$$

For any positive constants k, a and b, we have

$$
k(a - b)_+ = (ka - kb)_+ \qquad \text{and} \qquad k(a \wedge b) = (ka) \wedge (kb).
\tag{2.108}
$$

Thus, the mean inflation-adjusted loss is given by

$$
\begin{aligned}
\mathrm{E}(\tilde{X}_L) &= \mathrm{E}\left[(\tilde{X} - d)_+\right] \\
&= \mathrm{E}\left[(1 + r)\left(X - \frac{d}{1+r}\right)_+\right] \\
&= (1 + r)\,\mathrm{E}\left[\left(X - \frac{d}{1+r}\right)_+\right].
\end{aligned}
\tag{2.109}
$$

Similarly, we can also show that

$$
\mathrm{E}(\tilde{X}_L) = (1 + r)\left\{\mathrm{E}(X) - \mathrm{E}\left[X \wedge \left(\frac{d}{1+r}\right)\right]\right\}.
\tag{2.110}
$$

From equation (2.107), we have

$$
\mathrm{E}(\tilde{X}_P) = \mathrm{E}(\tilde{X}_L \mid \tilde{X}_L > 0) = \frac{\mathrm{E}(\tilde{X}_L)}{\Pr(\tilde{X}_L > 0)}.
\tag{2.111}
$$

As

$$\Pr(\tilde{X}_L > 0) = \Pr(\tilde{X} > d) = \Pr\left(X > \frac{d}{1+r}\right) = S_X\left(\frac{d}{1+r}\right), \qquad (2.112)$$

we conclude

$$\mathrm{E}(\tilde{X}_P) = \frac{\mathrm{E}(\tilde{X}_L)}{S_X\left(\dfrac{d}{1+r}\right)}. \qquad (2.113)$$

For a policy with a policy limit u, we denote the loss in a loss event by $\tilde{X}_U$. Thus,

$$\tilde{X}_U = \tilde{X} \wedge u = (1+r)\left[X \wedge \left(\frac{u}{1+r}\right)\right], \qquad (2.114)$$

and

$$\mathrm{E}(\tilde{X}_U) = (1+r)\,\mathrm{E}\left[X \wedge \left(\frac{u}{1+r}\right)\right]. \qquad (2.115)$$

If we consider a policy with deductible d, maximum covered loss u and coinsurance factor c, and denote the loss in a loss event with inflation by $\tilde{X}_T$, then, similar to equation (2.99), we have

$$\tilde{X}_T = c\left[(\tilde{X} \wedge u) - (\tilde{X} \wedge d)\right] = c\left[(\tilde{X} - d)_+ - (\tilde{X} - u)_+\right]. \qquad (2.116)$$

The mean loss in a loss event is then given by

$$\begin{aligned}
\mathrm{E}(\tilde{X}_T) &= c(1+r)\left\{\mathrm{E}\left[X \wedge \left(\frac{u}{1+r}\right)\right] - \mathrm{E}\left[X \wedge \left(\frac{d}{1+r}\right)\right]\right\} \\
&= c(1+r)\left[\mathrm{E}\left(X - \frac{d}{1+r}\right)_+ - \mathrm{E}\left(X - \frac{u}{1+r}\right)_+\right].
\end{aligned} \qquad (2.117)$$

2.5.5 Effects of Deductible on Claim Frequency

If the loss incurred in a loss event is less than the deductible, no claim will be made. Thus, the deductible affects the distribution of the claim frequency. Suppose N denotes the claim frequency when the insurance policy has no deductible, and N_D denotes the claim frequency when there is a deductible of amount d. Let $P_N(t)$ and $P_{N_D}(t)$ be the pgf of N and N_D, respectively. We define I_i as the random variable taking value 1 when the ith loss is larger than d (i.e., the loss gives rise to a claim event) and 0 otherwise, and assume I_i to be iid as I. Furthermore, let $\Pr(I = 1) = v$, so that the pgf of I is

$$P_I(t) = 1 - v + vt. \qquad (2.118)$$

We note that

$$N_D = I_1 + \cdots + I_N, \qquad (2.119)$$

so that N_D is a compound distribution, with N being the primary distribution and I the secondary distribution. Hence, from equation (1.69), we have

$$P_{N_D}(t) = P_N[P_I(t)] = P_N[1 + v(t-1)]. \tag{2.120}$$

The above equation can be further simplified if N belongs to the $(a,b,0)$ class. From Theorem 1.3, if N belongs to the $(a,b,0)$ class of distributions, the pgf of N can be written as

$$P_N(t \mid \beta) = Q_N[\beta(t-1)], \tag{2.121}$$

where β is a parameter of the distribution of N and $Q_N(\cdot)$ is a function of $\beta(t-1)$ only. Thus,

$$\begin{aligned} P_{N_D}(t) &= P_N[P_I(t)] \\ &= Q_N\{\beta[P_I(t)-1]\} \\ &= Q_N[\beta v(t-1)] \\ &= P_N(t \mid \beta v), \end{aligned} \tag{2.122}$$

so that N_D has the same distribution as N, with the parameter β replaced by βv (while the values of other parameters, if any, remain unchanged).

Example 2.13 Consider the exponential loss distribution $\mathcal{E}(1)$ and lognormal loss distribution $\mathcal{L}(-0.5, 1)$ discussed in Examples 2.8 through 2.12. Assume there is a deductible of $d = 0.25$, and the claim frequencies for both loss distributions without deductibles are (a) $\mathcal{PN}(\lambda)$, and (b) $\mathcal{NB}(r,\theta)$. Find the distributions of the claim frequencies with the deductibles.

Solution 2.13 We first consider the probability v of the deductible being exceeded. From Example 2.10, $v = 0.7788$ for the $\mathcal{E}(1)$ loss, and $v = 0.8123$ for the $\mathcal{L}(-0.5, 1)$ loss. For (a), when $N \sim \mathcal{PN}(\lambda)$, $N_D \sim \mathcal{PN}(0.7788\lambda)$ if the loss is $\mathcal{E}(1)$, and $N_D \sim \mathcal{PN}(0.8123\lambda)$ if the loss is $\mathcal{L}(-0.5, 1)$. This results from the fact that λ equals β defined in equation (2.121) (see the proof of Theorem 1.3).
 For (b), when $N \sim \mathcal{NB}(r,\theta)$, from equation (1.59), we have

$$P_N(t) = \left[\frac{1}{1-\beta(t-1)}\right]^r,$$

where

$$\beta = \frac{1-\theta}{\theta}$$

so that

$$\theta = \frac{1}{1+\beta}.$$

Thus, when the loss is distributed as $\mathcal{E}(1)$, $N_D \sim \mathcal{NB}(r, \theta^*)$ with θ^* given by

$$\theta^* = \frac{1}{1 + 0.7788\beta} = \frac{\theta}{\theta + 0.7788(1 - \theta)}.$$

Likewise, when the loss is distributed as $\mathcal{L}(-0.5, 1)$, $N_D \sim \mathcal{NB}(r, \theta^*)$ with θ^* given by

$$\theta^* = \frac{\theta}{\theta + 0.8123(1 - \theta)}. \qquad \square$$

2.6 R Laboratory

Table 2.2 provides a selection of R functions for the continuous distributions discussed in this chapter. A set of four R functions, beginning with r, p, q or d, is available for each distribution.[16] For $X \sim \mathcal{P}(\alpha, \gamma)$, pareto computes the related functions for $Y = X + \gamma$. The function pareto is in the package EnvStats. Some examples for the use of these functions are given in **R Codes 2.1**.

```
############################################################
# R Codes 2.1
#
# Some examples of usage of functions for continuous
# distributions
############################################################

library(EnvStats)

p=c(0.95,0.99)              # Example 2.8
qexp(p,1)                   # Quantiles of exponential
qlnorm(p,-0.5,1)            # Quantiles of lognormal
qpareto(0.9,6,4)-6          # Exercise 2.16, quantile
                            # of P(4,6) at 0.9
ppareto(8,6,4)             # Pr(X<2), X is P(4,6)
```

2.7 Summary and Conclusions

We have discussed the use of some standard continuous distributions for modeling claim-severity distributions. Some methods for creating new distributions

---

[16] See Section 1.6 for the details.

Table 2.2. *R functions for some continuous distributions*

Distribution	R function	Arguments
Exponential: $\mathcal{E}(\lambda)$	exp(,rate)	rate $= \lambda$
Gamma: $\mathcal{G}(\alpha, \beta)$	gamma(,shape,scale)	shape $= \alpha$, scale $= \beta$
Weibull: $\mathcal{W}(\alpha, \lambda)$	weibull(,shape,scale)	shape $= \alpha$, scale $= \lambda$
Pareto: $\mathcal{P}(\alpha, \gamma)$	pareto(,location,shape)	location $= \gamma$, shape $= \alpha$
Lognormal: $\mathcal{L}(\mu, \sigma^2)$	lnorm(,meanlog,sdlog)	meanlog $= \mu$, sdlog $= \sigma$

are introduced, and these include the methods of transformation, mixing and splicing. The right-hand tail properties of these distributions are important for modeling extreme losses, and measures such as quantiles, limiting ratios and conditional tail expectations are often used. We derive formulas for calculating the expected amount paid in a loss event and in a payment event. Policies may be modified to give rise to different payment functions, and we consider policy modifications such as deductible, policy limit and coinsurance. Methods of calculating the mean loss subject to policy modifications are presented. For the $(a, b, 0)$ class of claim-frequency distributions, we derive the effects of deductibles on the distribution of the claim frequency.

We have assumed that the ground-up loss distribution is independent of the policy modification. For example, we assume the same claim-severity distribution whether there is a deductible or not. This assumption may not be valid as the deductible may affect the behavior of the insured and thus the claim-severity distribution. Such limitations of the model, however, are not addressed in this chapter.

Exercises

Exercise 2.1 Prove that raw moments of all orders exist for the gamma distribution $\mathcal{G}(\alpha, \beta)$, and that only raw moments of order less than α exist for the Pareto distribution $\mathcal{P}(\alpha, \gamma)$.

Exercise 2.2 The inverse exponential distribution X has the following pdf:

$$f_X(x) = \frac{\theta e^{-\frac{\theta}{x}}}{x^2}, \qquad \text{for } \theta > 0.$$

(a) Find the df, sf and hf of X.
(b) Derive the median and the mode of X.

Exercise 2.3 The inverse Weibull distribution X has the following df:

$$F_X(x) = e^{-\left(\frac{\theta}{x}\right)^{\tau}}, \qquad \text{for } \theta, \tau > 0.$$

(a) Find the sf, pdf and hf of X.
(b) Derive the median and the mode of X.

Exercise 2.4 Suppose X has the following hf:

$$h_X(x) = \frac{1}{100 - x}, \qquad \text{for } 0 \leq x < 100.$$

(a) Find the sf, df and pdf X.
(b) Calculate the mean and the variance of X.
(c) Calculate the median and the mode of X.
(d) Calculate the mean excess loss for $x = 10$.

Exercise 2.5 Suppose X has the following pdf:

$$f_X(x) = \frac{3x(20 - x)}{4,000}, \qquad \text{for } 0 < x < 20 \text{ and } 0 \text{ otherwise.}$$

(a) Find the sf, df and hf of X.
(b) Calculate the mean and the variance of X.
(c) Calculate the median and the mode of X.
(d) Calculate the mean excess loss for $x = 8$.

Exercise 2.6 A Pareto distribution has mean 4 and variance 32. What is its median?

Exercise 2.7 Let $X \sim \mathcal{E}(2)$ and $Y \sim \mathcal{P}(3, 4)$. Suppose Z is a mixture of X and Y with equal weights. Find the mean and the median of Z. [**Hint:** Use the function `uniroot` in R to compute the median.]

Exercise 2.8 If the pdf of X is $f_X(x) = 2xe^{-x^2}$, for $0 < x < \infty$ and 0 otherwise, what is the pdf of $Y = X^2$?

Exercise 2.9 If $X \sim \mathcal{U}(-\pi/2, \pi/2)$ (see Appendix A.10.3), what is the pdf of $Y = \tan X$? [**Hint:** $d \tan^{-1} y / dy = 1/(1 + y^2)$.]

Exercise 2.10 There is a probability of 0.2 that the loss X is zero. Loss occurs with density proportional to $1 - x/20$ for $0 < x \leq 20$.

(a) What is the df of X?
(b) Find the mean and the variance of X.
(c) What is $x_{0.8}$?

Exercise 2.11 Suppose X has a probability mass of 0.4 at $x = 0$ and has a density proportional to x^3 for $0 < x \leq 1$, and 0 elsewhere.

(a) What is the df of X?
(b) Find the mean and the variance of X.
(c) What is $x_{0.8}$?

Exercise 2.12 Use the mgf to calculate the skewness (see equation A.28) of $\mathcal{G}(\alpha, \beta)$.

Exercise 2.13 Construct a two-component spliced distribution, where the density of its first component, for $0 \leq x < 0.8$, is proportional to an exponential density with parameter $\lambda = 2$ and the density of its second component, for $0.8 \leq x < \infty$, is proportional to a gamma density with $\alpha = 2$ and $\beta = 0.5$. Apply continuity restriction to the spliced distribution.

Exercise 2.14 Suppose $X | \Lambda \sim \mathcal{E}(\Lambda)$ and Λ is uniformly distributed in the interval $[1,5]$.

(a) Calculate the unconditional mean and variance of X using equations (2.56) and (2.57).
(b) Determine the unconditional pdf of X, and hence calculate $E(X)$ and $Var(X)$.
   [**Hint:** You may use the result $\int_0^\infty \frac{e^{-ax} - e^{-bx}}{x} \, dx = \log\left(\frac{b}{a}\right)$.]

Exercise 2.15 Suppose $X \sim \mathcal{G}(\alpha, \beta)$. If $\beta = 2$ and $\alpha - 1$ is distributed as $\mathcal{PN}(2.5)$, calculate the unconditional mean and variance of X.

Exercise 2.16 Let $X \sim \mathcal{P}(4, 6)$, calculate $x_{0.9}$ and $CTE_{0.9}$.

Exercise 2.17 Let $X \sim \mathcal{E}(\lambda)$, and d be the amount of the deductible.

(a) What is the df of $X_L = (X - d)_+$?
(b) What is the df of $X_P = X - d | X > d$?
(c) Find the pdf of X_P and $E(X_P)$.

Exercise 2.18 Let $X \sim \mathcal{P}(2, 5)$, and $d = 1$ be the amount of the deductible.

(a) Calculate $E(X_P)$.
(b) Calculate $E(X \wedge d)$.
(c) Calculate $LER(d)$.

Exercise 2.19 X_i are iid $\mathcal{G}(\alpha, \beta)$, for $i = 1, 2, \ldots, n$. Using the mgf, show that $S = X_1 + X_2 + \cdots + X_n$ is distributed as $\mathcal{G}(n\alpha, \beta)$.

Exercise 2.20 X is a mixture of exponential distributions $\mathcal{E}(\lambda_1)$ and $\mathcal{E}(\lambda_2)$ with the following pdf:

$$f_X(x) = p\lambda_1 e^{-\lambda_1 x} + (1 - p)\lambda_2 e^{-\lambda_2 x}, \qquad 0 < x, \, 0 < p < 1.$$

(a) Derive the df of X.
(b) Calculate $E[(X - d)_+]$.

Exercise 2.21 The pdf of the claim severity X is $f_X(x) = 0.02x$, for $0 \leq x \leq 10$. An insurance policy has a deductible of $d = 4$, calculate the expected loss payment in a payment event.

Exercise 2.22 Policy loss X is distributed as $\mathcal{U}(0, 100)$, with a deductible of $d = 20$ and a maximum covered loss of $u = 80$. Calculate $E(X_P)$ and $Var(X_P)$.

Exercise 2.23 Policy loss X is distributed as $\mathcal{P}(5, 100)$, with a deductible of $d = 10$ and a maximum covered loss of $u = 50$. Calculate the expected loss in a loss event.

Exercise 2.24 Policy loss X is distributed as $\mathcal{E}(0.01)$. If there is a deductible of $d = 8$, calculate the mean and the variance of X_L.

Exercise 2.25 Suppose claim severity X is distributed as $\mathcal{E}(0.01)$. The policy has a deductible of $d = 20$, maximum covered loss of $u = 200$ and coinsurance factor of $c = 0.8$. Calculate the expected loss in a loss event. Subject to inflation adjustment of 5%, with no adjustments in policy factors, what is the expected payment per loss?

Exercise 2.26 Policy loss X_T has a deductible of d and maximum covered loss of u. If the coinsurance factor is c, the rate of inflation is r and the loss in a loss event with inflation is $\tilde{X}_T$, prove that

$$
E(\tilde{X}_T^2) = c^2(1 + r)^2 \left\{ E[(X \wedge \tilde{u})^2] - E[(X \wedge \tilde{d})^2] \right.
$$
$$
\left. - 2\tilde{d} \left(E[X \wedge \tilde{u}] - E[(X \wedge \tilde{d})] \right) \right\},
$$

where $\tilde{u} = u/(1 + r)$ and $\tilde{d} = d/(1 + r)$.

Exercise 2.27 Assume $X \mid \Lambda \sim \mathcal{PN}(\Lambda)$, and let the parameter Λ be distributed as $\mathcal{G}(\alpha, \beta)$. Show that $X \sim \mathcal{NB}(\alpha, 1/(1 + \beta))$.

Exercise 2.28 The Black–Scholes model of pricing a European call option on a nondividend-paying stock states that the price C of the European call option with exercise price x and time to maturity t is equal to the discounted expected payoff at maturity. That is, we have

$$
C = e^{-rt} E\left[(\tilde{S} - x)_+ \right],
$$

where $\tilde{S}$ is the stock price at maturity and r is the riskfree rate of interest. Here $\tilde{S}$ is assumed to be lognormally distributed. Specifically, we assume

$$
\log \tilde{S} \sim \mathcal{N} \left(\log S + \left(r - \frac{\sigma_{\tilde{S}}^2}{2} \right) t, \sigma_{\tilde{S}}^2 t \right),
$$

where S is the current stock price and σ_S is the volatility parameter of the stock. Using Theorem 2.2 and the above assumption, prove that

$$
C = S\Phi(d_1) - xe^{-rt}\Phi(d_2),
$$

where

$$d_1 = \frac{\log\left(\dfrac{S}{x}\right) + \left(r + \dfrac{\sigma_S^2}{2}\right) t}{\sigma_S \sqrt{t}},$$

and

$$d_2 = \frac{\log\left(\dfrac{S}{x}\right) + \left(r - \dfrac{\sigma_S^2}{2}\right) t}{\sigma_S \sqrt{t}}.$$

This is the celebrated Black–Scholes formula.

Questions Adapted from SOA Exams

Exercise 2.29 Let $X \sim \mathcal{P}(\alpha, \gamma)$. Derive the pdf of $Y = \log(1 + X/\gamma)$.

Exercise 2.30 The claim frequency of a policy with no deductible is distributed as $\mathcal{NB}(3, 0.2)$. The claim severity is distributed as $\mathcal{W}(0.3, 100)$. Determine the expected number of claim payments when the policy has a deductible of 20.

Exercise 2.31 Suppose $X \sim \mathcal{E}(0.001)$. Calculate the coefficient of variation, i.e., the ratio of the standard deviation to the mean, of $(X - 2{,}000)_+$.

3

Aggregate-Loss Models

Having discussed models for claim frequency and claim severity separately, we now turn our attention to modeling the aggregate loss of a block of insurance policies. Much of the time we shall use the terms aggregate loss and aggregate claim interchangeably, although we recognize the difference between them as discussed in the last chapter. There are two major approaches in modeling aggregate loss: the individual risk model and the collective risk model. We shall begin with the individual risk model, in which we assume there are n independent loss prospects in the block. As a policy may or may not have a loss, the distribution of the *loss* variable in this model is of the mixed type. It consists of a probability mass at point zero and a continuous component of positive losses. Generally, exact distribution of the aggregate loss can only be obtained through the convolution method. The De Pril recursion, however, is a powerful technique to compute the exact distribution recursively when the block of policies follows a certain setup.

On the other hand, the collective risk model treats the aggregate loss as a compound process, with the primary process being the claim frequency and the secondary process being the claim severity. The Panjer recursion can be used to compute the distribution of the aggregate loss if the claim-frequency distribution belongs to the $(a, b, 0)$ class and the claim-severity distribution is *discretized* or approximated by a discrete distribution. In particular, the compound Poisson process has some useful properties in applications, and it can also be used as an approximation for the individual risk model. Finally, we consider the effects of a stop-loss reinsurance on the distribution of the aggregate loss.

Learning Objectives

1 Individual risk model
2 Collective risk model

3.1 Individual Risk and Collective Risk Models

The aggregate loss of a block of insurance policies is the sum of all losses incurred in the block. It may be modeled by two approaches: the **individual risk model** and the **collective risk model**. In the individual risk model, we denote the number of policies in the block by n. We assume the loss of each policy, denoted by X_i, for $i = 1, \ldots, n$, to be *independently and identically distributed* as X. The aggregate loss of the block of policies, denoted by S, is then given by

$$S = X_1 + \cdots + X_n. \tag{3.1}$$

Thus, S is the sum of n iid random variables each distributed as X, where n is a fixed number. Note that typically most of the policies have zero loss, so that X_i is zero for these policies. In other words, X follows a mixed distribution with a probability mass at point zero. Although X_i in equation (3.1) are stated as being iid, the assumption of identical distribution is not necessary. The individual risk model will be discussed in Section 3.2.

The aggregate loss may also be computed using the collective risk model, in which the aggregate loss is assumed to follow a compound distribution. Let N be the number of losses in the block of policies, and X_i be the amount of the ith loss, for $i = 1, \ldots, N$. Then the aggregate loss S is given by

$$S = X_1 + \cdots + X_N. \tag{3.2}$$

The compound process as stated above was introduced in equation (1.60), in which $X_1, \ldots, X_N$ are assumed to be iid nonnegative integer-valued random variables representing claim frequencies. The purpose was then to create a new nonnegative integer-valued compound distribution to be used to model the claim-frequency distribution. In equation (3.2), however, $X_1, \ldots, X_N$ are assumed to be iid as the claim-severity random variable X, which is the secondary distribution of the compound distribution; while N is the claim-frequency random variable representing the primary distribution. Furthermore, N and X are assumed to be independent. The distributions of the claim frequency and claim severity have been discussed extensively in the last two chapters. Note that X_i are defined differently in equations (3.1) versus (3.2). In equation (3.1) X_i is the loss (which may be zero) of the ith policy, whereas in equation (3.2)

X_i is the loss amount in the ith loss event and is positive with probability 1. The collective risk model will be discussed in Section 3.3.[1]

There are some advantages in modeling the claim frequency and claim severity separately, and then combine them to determine the aggregate-loss distribution. For example, expansion of insurance business may have impacts on the claim frequency but not the claim severity. On the other hand, cost control (or general cost increase) and innovation in technology may affect the claim severity with no effects on the claim frequency. Furthermore, the effects of coverage modifications may impact the claim-frequency distribution and claim-severity distribution differently. Modeling the two components separately would enable us to identify the effects of these modifications on the aggregate loss.

3.2 Individual Risk Model

The basic equation of the individual risk model stated in equation (3.1) specifies the aggregate loss S as the sum of n iid random variables each distributed as X. Thus, the mean and variance of S are given by

$$\mathrm{E}(S) = n \,\mathrm{E}(X) \qquad \text{and} \qquad \mathrm{Var}(S) = n \,\mathrm{Var}(X). \tag{3.3}$$

To compute the mean and variance of S, we need the mean and variance of X. Let the probability of a loss be θ and the probability of no loss be $1 - \theta$. Furthermore, we assume that when there is a loss, the loss amount is Y, which is a positive continuous random variable with mean μ_Y and variance σ_Y^2. Thus, $X = Y$ with probability θ, and $X = 0$ with probability $1 - \theta$. We can now write X as

$$X = IY, \tag{3.4}$$

where I is a Bernoulli random variable distributed independently of Y, so that

$$I = \begin{cases} 0, & \text{with probability } 1 - \theta, \\ 1, & \text{with probability } \theta. \end{cases} \tag{3.5}$$

Thus, the mean of X is

$$\mathrm{E}(X) = \mathrm{E}(I)\mathrm{E}(Y) = \theta \mu_Y, \tag{3.6}$$

and its variance, using equation (A.118) in Appendix A.11, is

$$\begin{aligned} \mathrm{Var}(X) &= \mathrm{Var}(IY) \\ &= [\mathrm{E}(Y)]^2 \,\mathrm{Var}(I) + \mathrm{E}(I^2)\mathrm{Var}(Y) \\ &= \mu_Y^2 \,\theta(1 - \theta) + \theta \,\sigma_Y^2. \end{aligned} \tag{3.7}$$

---

[1] In Chapter 1 we use X to denote the claim frequency. From now onward, however, we shall use N to denote the claim frequency.

Equations (3.6) and (3.7) can be plugged into equation (3.3) to obtain the mean and variance of S.

Example 3.1 Assume there is a chance of 0.2 that there is a claim. When a claim occurs the loss is exponentially distributed with parameter $\lambda = 0.5$. Find the mean and variance of the claim distribution. Suppose there are 500 independent policies with this loss distribution, compute the mean and variance of their aggregate loss.

Solution 3.1 The mean and variance of the loss in a loss event is

$$\mu_Y = \frac{1}{\lambda} = \frac{1}{0.5} = 2,$$

and

$$\sigma_Y^2 = \frac{1}{\lambda^2} = \frac{1}{(0.5)^2} = 4.$$

Thus, the mean and variance of the loss incurred by a random policy are

$$E(X) = (0.2)(2) = 0.4,$$

and

$$\text{Var}(X) = (2)^2(0.2)(1 - 0.2) + (0.2)(4) = 1.44.$$

The mean and variance of the aggregate loss are

$$E(S) = (500)(0.4) = 200,$$

and

$$\text{Var}(S) = (500)(1.44) = 720. \qquad \square$$

3.2.1 Exact Distribution Using Convolution

The general technique to compute the exact distribution of the sum of independent random variables is by convolution. We discussed the convolution for sums of discrete nonnegative random variables in Section 1.5.1. We now consider the case of convolution of the continuous and mixed type random variables.

Let $X_1, \ldots, X_n$ be n independently distributed nonnegative continuous random variables with pdf $f_1(\cdot), \ldots, f_n(\cdot)$, respectively. Here we have relaxed the assumption of identically distributed losses, as this is not required for the computation of the convolution. We first consider the distribution of $X_1 + X_2$, the pdf of which is given by the 2-fold convolution

$$f^{*2}(x) = f_{X_1+X_2}(x) = \int_0^x f_1(x-y)f_2(y)\, dy = \int_0^x f_2(x-y)f_1(y)\, dy. \qquad (3.8)$$

The pdf of $X_1 + \cdots + X_n$ can be calculated recursively. Suppose the pdf of $X_1 + \cdots + X_{n-1}$ is given by the $(n-1)$-fold convolution $f^{*(n-1)}(x)$, then the pdf of $X_1 + \cdots + X_n$ is the n-fold convolution given by

$$f^{*n}(x) = f_{X_1 + \ldots + X_n}(x) = \int_0^x f^{*(n-1)}(x-y) f_n(y)\, dy = \int_0^x f_n(x-y) f^{*(n-1)}(y)\, dy.$$
(3.9)

It is clear that the above formulas do not assume identically distributed components X_i.

Now we consider the case where X_i are mixed-type random variables, which is typical of an individual risk model. We assume that the pf–pdf of X_i is given by

$$f_{X_i}(x) = \begin{cases} 1 - \theta_i, & \text{for } x = 0, \\ \theta_i f_{Y_i}(x), & \text{for } x > 0, \end{cases}$$
(3.10)

in which $f_{Y_i}(\cdot)$ are well-defined pdf of positive continuous random variables. The df of $X_1 + X_2$ is given by the 2-fold convolution in the Stieltjes-integral form, i.e.,[2]

$$F^{*2}(x) = F_{X_1 + X_2}(x) = \int_0^x F_{X_1}(x-y)\, dF_{X_2}(y) = \int_0^x F_{X_2}(x-y)\, dF_{X_1}(y). \quad (3.11)$$

The df of $X_1 + \cdots + X_n$ can be calculated recursively. Suppose the df of $X_1 + \cdots + X_{n-1}$ is given by the $(n-1)$-fold convolution $F^{*(n-1)}(x)$, then the df of $X_1 + \cdots + X_n$ is the n-fold convolution

$$F^{*n}(x) = F_{X_1 + \ldots + X_n}(x) = \int_0^x F^{*(n-1)}(x-y)\, dF_{X_n}(y) = \int_0^x F_{X_n}(x-y)\, dF^{*(n-1)}(y).$$
(3.12)

For the pf–pdf given in equation (3.10), we have[3]

$$F^{*n}(x) = \int_0^x F^{*(n-1)}(x-y) f_{X_n}(y)\, dy + (1 - \theta_n) F^{*(n-1)}(x).$$
(3.13)

In particular, if $X_1, \ldots, X_n$ are iid, with $\theta_i = \theta$ and $f_{Y_i}(x) = f_Y(x)$, for $i = 1, \ldots, n$, then

$$F^{*n}(x) = \theta \int_0^x F^{*(n-1)}(x-y) f_Y(y)\, dy + (1 - \theta) F^{*(n-1)}(x).$$
(3.14)

While the expressions of the pf–pdf of the sums of X_i can be written in convolution form, the computations of the integrals are usually quite complex. To implement the convolution method in practice we may first *discretize* the continuous distribution, and then apply convolution to the discrete distribution on

---

[2] See A.2 and A.3 in the Appendix for the use of Stieltjes integral.
[3] Compare this equation with equation (A.15) in Appendix A.3.

the computer. Assume the discretized approximate distribution of X_i has the pf $f_i(x)$ for $x = 0, \ldots, m$ and $i = 1, \ldots, n$.[4] Then the 2-fold convolution $X_1 + X_2$ is

$$f^{*2}(x) = \sum_{y=0}^{x} f_1(x-y) f_2(y) = \sum_{y=0}^{x} f_2(x-y) f_1(y), \qquad \text{for } x = 0, \ldots, 2m,$$

(3.15)

and the n-fold convolution is given by

$$f^{*n}(x) = \sum_{y=0}^{x} f^{*(n-1)}(x-y) f_n(y) = \sum_{y=0}^{x} f_n(x-y) f^{*(n-1)}(y), \qquad \text{for } x = 0, \ldots, nm.$$

(3.16)

In the equations above, some of the probabilities in the summation are zero. For example, in equation (3.15) $f_1(\cdot)$ and $f_2(\cdot)$ are zero for $y > m$ or $x - y > m$.

Example 3.2 For the block of insurance policies defined in Example 3.1, approximate the loss distribution by a suitable discrete distribution. Compute the df $F_S(s)$ of the aggregate loss of the portfolio for s from 110 through 300 in steps of 10, based on the discretized distribution.

Solution 3.2 We approximate the exponential loss distribution by a discrete distribution taking values $0, 1, \ldots, 10$. As the df of $\mathcal{E}(\lambda)$ is $F_X(x) = 1 - \exp(-\lambda x)$, we approximate the pf by

$$f_X(x) = (0.2) \left\{ \exp\left[-\lambda(x - 0.5)\right] - \exp\left[-\lambda(x + 0.5)\right] \right\}, \qquad \text{for } x = 1, \ldots, 9,$$

with

$$f_X(0) = 0.8 + (0.2)[1 - \exp(-0.5\lambda)],$$

and

$$f_X(10) = (0.2) \exp(-9.5\lambda).$$

The discretized approximate pf of the loss is
    Note that the mean and variance of the loss random variable, as computed in Example 3.1, are 0.4 and 1.44, respectively. In comparison, the mean and variance of the discretized approximate loss distribution given in Table 3.1 are 0.3933 and 1.3972, respectively.
    Using the convolution method, the df of the aggregate loss S for selected values of s is given in Table 3.2. □

---

[4] We assume that the maximum loss of a policy is m, which is a realistic assumption in practice, as insurance policies may set maximum loss limits. We shall not distinguish between the continuous claim-severity distribution and its discretized version by different notations. The discrete distribution may also be an empirical distribution obtained from claim data.

Table 3.1. *Discretized probabilities*

x	$f_X(x)$	x	$f_X(x)$
0	0.8442	6	0.0050
1	0.0613	7	0.0031
2	0.0372	8	0.0019
3	0.0225	9	0.0011
4	0.0137	10	0.0017
5	0.0083		

Table 3.2. *The df of S by convolution*

s	$F_S(s)$	s	$F_S(s)$
110	0.0001	210	0.7074
120	0.0008	220	0.8181
130	0.0035	230	0.8968
140	0.0121	240	0.9465
150	0.0345	250	0.9746
160	0.0810	260	0.9890
170	0.1613	270	0.9956
180	0.2772	280	0.9984
190	0.4194	290	0.9994
200	0.5697	300	0.9998

The computation of the convolution is very intensive if n is large. In the next section we present an efficient exact solution due to De Pril (1985, 1986) using a recursive method when the block of insurance policies follow a specific setup.

3.2.2 Exact Distribution Using the De Pril Recursion

The De Pril recursion provides a method to compute the aggregate-loss distribution of the individual risk model. This method applies to blocks of insurance policies which can be stratified by the sum assured and the claim probability. Specifically, we assume that the portfolio of insurance policies consist of J different claim probabilities θ_j, for $j = 1, \ldots, J$, and each policy has an insured amount of $i = 1, \ldots, I$ benefit units, which is a suitably standardized monetary amount. We assume there are n_{ij} independent policies with insured amount of i benefit units and claim probability of θ_j, for $i = 1, \ldots, I$ and $j = 1, \ldots, J$. If we denote the aggregate loss of the block by S and the pf of S by $f_S(s)$, $s = 0, \ldots, n$, where $n = \sum_{i=1}^{I} \sum_{j=1}^{J} i n_{ij}$. then $f_S(s)$ can be computed using the following theorem.[5]

---

[5] Note that n is the maximum loss of the block of policies.

Theorem 3.1 *The pf of S, $f_S(s)$, satisfies the following equation, known as the De Pril (1985, 1986) recursion formula*

$$f_S(s) = \frac{1}{s} \sum_{i=1}^{\min\{s,I\}} \sum_{k=1}^{\left[\frac{s}{i}\right]} f_S(s - ik)h(i, k), \qquad \text{for } s = 1, \ldots, n, \qquad (3.17)$$

where $[x]$ denotes the integer part x,

$$h(i, k) = \begin{cases} i(-1)^{k-1} \sum_{j=1}^{J} n_{ij} \left(\dfrac{\theta_j}{1 - \theta_j}\right)^k, & \text{for } i = 1, \ldots, I, \\ 0, & \text{otherwise,} \end{cases} \qquad (3.18)$$

and the recursion has the following starting value

$$f_S(0) = \prod_{i=1}^{I} \prod_{j=1}^{J} (1 - \theta_j)^{n_{ij}}. \qquad (3.19)$$

Proof See Dickson (2005, Section 5.3), for the proof. □

The De Pril recursion formula is computationally intensive for large values of s and I. However, as θ_j are usually small, $h(i, k)$ is usually close to zero for large k. An approximation can thus be obtained by choosing a truncation parameter K in the summation over k in equation (3.17).[6] We denote the resulting pf by $f_S^K(s)$, which can be computed as

$$f_S^K(s) = \frac{1}{s} \sum_{i=1}^{\min\{x,I\}} \sum_{k=1}^{\min\{K,\left[\frac{s}{i}\right]\}} f_S^K(s - ik)h(i, k), \qquad (3.20)$$

with $f_S^K(0) = f_S(0)$.

3.2.3 Approximations of the Individual Risk Model

As the aggregate loss S in equation (3.1) is the sum of n iid random variables, its distribution is approximately normal when n is large, by virtue of the Central Limit Theorem. The (exact) mean and variance of S are given in equations (3.3), (3.6) and (3.7), which can be used to compute the approximate distribution of S. Thus,

$$\Pr(S \le s) = \Pr\left(\frac{S - E(S)}{\sqrt{\text{Var}(S)}} \le \frac{s - E(S)}{\sqrt{\text{Var}(S)}}\right)$$

$$\simeq \Pr\left(Z \le \frac{s - E(S)}{\sqrt{\text{Var}(S)}}\right)$$

$$= \Phi\left(\frac{s - E(S)}{\sqrt{\text{Var}(S)}}\right). \qquad (3.21)$$

---

[6] Dickson (2005) suggested that $K = 4$ is usually sufficient for a good approximation.

Table 3.3. *Number of policies for Example 3.3*

Benefit units i ($,000)	Claim probability group			
	$j = 1$	$j = 2$	$j = 3$	$j = 4$
1	30	40	50	60
2	40	50	70	80
3	70	60	80	90
Claim probability θ_j	0.0015	0.0024	0.0031	0.0088

The normal approximation holds even when the individual risks are not identically distributed. As in the case of the De Pril setup, the claim probability varies. The mean and variance of S, however, can be computed as follows under the assumption of independent risks

$$E(S) = \sum_{i=1}^{I} \sum_{j=1}^{J} i \, n_{ij} \, \theta_j, \qquad (3.22)$$

and

$$\text{Var}(S) = \sum_{i=1}^{I} \sum_{j=1}^{J} i^2 \, n_{ij} \, \theta_j (1 - \theta_j). \qquad (3.23)$$

Equation (3.21) can then be used to compute the approximate df of the aggregate loss.

Example 3.3 A portfolio of insurance policies have benefits of 1, 2 or 3 thousand dollars. The claim probability may be 0.0015, 0.0024, 0.0031 or 0.0088. The number of policies with claim amount i thousands and claim probability θ_j are summarized in Table 3.3. Calculate the distribution of the aggregate claim using (a) the De Pril recursion with the exact formula, (b) the De Pril recursion with truncation at $K = 2$, and (c) the normal approximation.

Solution 3.3 Using equations (3.22) and (3.23), the mean and variance of the aggregate loss S are computed as 6.8930 and 16.7204, respectively. These values are plugged into equation (3.21) to obtain the normal approximation (with the usual continuity correction). Table 3.4 gives the results of the exact De Pril method, the truncated De Pril method and the normal approximation. The numbers in the table are the df at selected values of aggregate loss s.

It can be seen that the truncated De Pril approximation works very well, even for a small truncation value of $K = 2$. On the other hand, the normal approximation is clearly inferior to the truncated De Pril approximation.

Table 3.4. *Aggregate-loss df at selected values*

	Method		
Aggregate loss s	De Pril (exact)	De Pril (truncated, $K = 2$)	Normal approximation
0	0.03978	0.03978	0.05897
5	0.40431	0.40431	0.36668
10	0.81672	0.81670	0.81114
15	0.96899	0.96895	0.98235
20	0.99674	0.99668	0.99956
25	0.99977	0.99971	1.00000

Although the computation of the exact De Pril recursion is very efficient, its application depends on the assumption that the portfolio of insurance policies can be stratified according to the particular setup. □

Example 3.4 For the portfolio of policies in Example 3.1, calculate the df of the aggregate loss at s = 180 and 230 using normal approximation. Compare the answers against the answers computed by convolution in Example 3.2.

Solution 3.4 From Example 3.1, the mean and standard deviation of the aggregate loss S are, respectively, 200 and $\sqrt{720}$ = 26.8328. Using normal approximation, we have

$$\Pr(S \leq 180) \simeq \Pr\left(Z \leq \frac{180.5 - 200}{26.8328}\right) = \Phi(-0.7267) = 0.2337,$$

and

$$\Pr(S \leq 230) \simeq \Pr\left(Z \leq \frac{230.5 - 200}{26.8328}\right) = \Phi(1.1367) = 0.8722.$$

The corresponding results obtained from the convolution method in Example 3.2 are 0.2772 and 0.8968. The differences in the answers are due to (a) discretization of the exponential loss in the convolution method, and (b) the use of normal approximation assuming sufficiently large block of policies. □

3.3 Collective Risk Model

As stated in equation (3.2), the collective risk model specifies the aggregate loss S as the sum of N losses, which are independently and identically distributed as the claim-severity variable X. Thus, S follows a compound distribution, with N being the primary distribution and X the secondary distribution. We have discussed compound distributions in Section 1.5, in which both the primary and secondary distributions are nonnegative discrete random variables. Some properties of the compound distributions derived in Section 1.5 are applicable to the collective risk model in which the secondary distribution is continuous. We shall review some of these properties, and apply the results in Chapter 1 to study the aggregate-loss distribution. Both recursive and approximate methods will be considered for the computation of the aggregate-loss distribution.

3.3.1 Properties of Compound Distributions

First, as proved in Theorem 1.4, the mgf $M_S(t)$ of the aggregate loss S is given by

$$M_S(t) = M_N [\log M_X(t)], \tag{3.24}$$

where $M_N(t)$ and $M_X(t)$ are, respectively, the mgf of N and X. Furthermore, if the claim-severity takes nonnegative discrete values, S is also nonnegative and discrete, and its pgf is

$$P_S(t) = P_N [P_X(t)], \tag{3.25}$$

where $P_N(t)$ and $P_X(t)$ are, respectively, the pgf of N and X. Second, Theorem 1.6 also applies to the aggregate-loss distribution. Thus, the mean and variance of S are

$$E(S) = E(N)E(X), \tag{3.26}$$

and

$$\text{Var}(S) = E(N)\text{Var}(X) + \text{Var}(N) [E(X)]^2. \tag{3.27}$$

These results hold whether X is continuous or discrete. Third, if S_i has a compound Poisson distribution with claim-severity distribution X_i, which may be continuous or discrete, for $i = 1, \ldots, n$, then $S = S_1 + \cdots + S_n$ has also a compound Poisson distribution. As shown in Theorem 1.7, the Poisson parameter λ of S is the sum of the Poisson parameters $\lambda_1, \ldots, \lambda_n$ of $S_1, \ldots, S_n$, respectively. In addition, the secondary distribution X of S is the mixture distribution of $X_1, \ldots, X_n$, where the weight of X_i is λ_i/λ.

When X is continuous, we extend the result in equation (1.65) to obtain the pdf of S as

$$f_S(s) = \sum_{n=1}^{\infty} f_{X_1 + \cdots + X_n \mid n}(s) f_N(n)$$

$$= \sum_{n=1}^{\infty} f^{*n}(s) f_N(n), \tag{3.28}$$

where $f^{*n}(\cdot)$ is the n-fold convolution given in equation (3.9). Thus, the exact pdf of S is a weighted sum of convolutions, and the computation is highly complex.

There are some special cases for which the compound distribution can be analytically derived. Theorem 3.2 provides an example.

Theorem 3.2 *For the compound distribution specified in equation* (3.2), *assume* $X_1, \ldots, X_N$ *are iid* $\mathcal{E}(\lambda)$, *and* $N \sim \mathcal{GM}(\theta)$. *Then the compound distribution* S *is a mixed distribution with a probability mass of* θ *at* 0 *and a continuous component of* $\mathcal{E}(\lambda\theta)$ *weighted by* $1 - \theta$.

Proof From Section 2.2, the mgf of $X \sim \mathcal{E}(\lambda)$ is

$$M_X(t) = \frac{\lambda}{\lambda - t},$$

and from Section 1.3 the mgf of $N \sim \mathcal{GM}(\theta)$ is

$$M_N(t) = \frac{\theta}{1 - (1 - \theta)e^t}.$$

Thus, using equation (3.24), we conclude that the mgf of S is

$$
\begin{aligned}
M_S(t) &= M_N\left[\log M_X(t)\right] \\
&= \frac{\theta}{1 - (1 - \theta)\left(\dfrac{\lambda}{\lambda - t}\right)} \\
&= \frac{\theta(\lambda - t)}{\lambda\theta - t} \\
&= \frac{\theta(\lambda\theta - t) + (1 - \theta)\lambda\theta}{\lambda\theta - t} \\
&= \theta + (1 - \theta)\left(\frac{\lambda\theta}{\lambda\theta - t}\right).
\end{aligned}
$$

Thus, $M_S(t)$ is the weighted average of 1 and $\lambda\theta/(\lambda\theta - t)$, which are the mgf of a degenerate distribution at 0 and the mgf of $\mathcal{E}(\lambda\theta)$, respectively, with the weights being θ for the degenerate distribution and $1 - \theta$ for $\mathcal{E}(\lambda\theta)$. Hence, the aggregate loss is a mixed distribution, with a probability mass of θ at 0 and a continuous component of $\mathcal{E}(\lambda\theta)$ weighted by $1 - \theta$.   □

Analytic solutions of compound distributions are not common. In what follows we discuss some approximations making use of recursions, as well as normal approximations assuming sufficiently large samples.

3.3.2 Panjer Recursion

Theorem 1.5 provides the efficient Panjer recursion method to compute the exact distribution of a compound process which satisfies the conditions that (a) the primary distribution belongs to the $(a, b, 0)$ class, and (b) the secondary

Table 3.5. *Discretized probabilities*

x	$f_X(x)$	x	$f_X(x)$
0	0.2212	6	0.0252
1	0.3064	7	0.0153
2	0.1859	8	0.0093
3	0.1127	9	0.0056
4	0.0684	10	0.0085
5	0.0415		

distribution is discrete and nonnegative integer valued. Thus, if a continuous claim-severity distribution can be suitably discretized, and the primary distribution belongs to the $(a, b, 0)$ class, we can use the Panjer approximation to compute the distribution of the aggregate loss.

Example 3.5 Consider the block of insurance policies in Examples 3.1 and 3.2. Approximate the distribution of the aggregate loss using the collective risk model. You may assume a suitable discretization of the exponential loss, and that the primary distribution is Poisson.

Solution 3.5 Unlike the case of Example 3.2, the loss variable X in the collective risk model is the loss in a loss event (not the loss of a random policy). The discretized distribution would take positive values, and we use the following formulas to compute the pf of the discretized distribution[7]

$$f_X(x) = \exp\left[-\lambda(x - 0.5)\right] - \exp\left[-\lambda(x + 0.5)\right], \qquad \text{for } x = 1, \dots, 9,$$

with

$$f_X(0) = 1 - \exp\left(-0.5\lambda\right),$$

and

$$f_X(10) = \exp\left(-9.5\lambda\right).$$

The pf is summarized in Table 3.5.

As the probability of a claim is 0.2, and there are 500 policies in the portfolio, the expected number of claims is $(0.2)(500) = 100$. Thus, we assume the primary distribution to be Poisson with mean 100. From Table 1.2, the parameters of the $(a, b, 0)$ class are: $a = 0$, $b = 100$, and $f_X(0) = 0.2212$. Thus, from equation (1.70), we have

$$f_S(0) = \exp\left[(100)(0.2212 - 1)\right] = \exp(-77.88).$$

---

[7] It may seem contradictory to have a nonzero probability of zero loss when X is defined as the loss in a loss event. We should treat this as an approximation of the continuous loss distribution rather than an assumption of the model.

Table 3.6. *The df of S by the Panjer recursion*

s	$F_S(s)$	s	$F_S(s)$
110	0.0003	210	0.6997
120	0.0013	220	0.8070
130	0.0052	230	0.8856
140	0.0164	240	0.9375
150	0.0426	250	0.9684
160	0.0932	260	0.9852
170	0.1753	270	0.9936
180	0.2893	280	0.9975
190	0.4257	290	0.9991
200	0.5684	300	0.9997

The Panjer recursion in equation (1.74) becomes

$$f_S(s) = \sum_{x=1}^{s} \frac{100x}{s} f_X(x) f_S(s - x).$$

As $f_X(x) = 0$ for $x > 10$, the above equation can be written as

$$f_S(s) = \sum_{x=1}^{\min\{s,10\}} \frac{100x}{s} f_X(x) f_S(s - x).$$

The df $F_S(s)$ of the aggregate loss of the portfolio for s from 110 through 300 in steps of 10 is presented in Table 3.6.   □

Note that the results in Tables 3.2 and 3.6 are quite similar. The results in Table 3.2 are exact (computed from the convolution) for the individual risk model given the discretized loss distribution. On the other hand, the results in Table 3.6 are also exact (computed from the Panjer recursion) for the collective risk model, given the assumptions of Poisson primary distribution and the discretized loss distribution. These examples illustrate that the individual risk model and the collective risk model may give rise to similar results when their assumptions concerning the claim frequency and claim severity are compatible.

3.3.3 Approximations of the Collective Risk Model

Under the individual risk model, if the number of policies n is large, by virtue of the Central Limit Theorem the aggregate loss is approximately normally distributed. In the case of the collective risk model, the situation is more complex, as the number of summation terms N in the aggregate loss S is random. However, if the mean number of claims is large, we may expect the normal approximation to work. Thus, using the mean and variance formulas of S in equations (3.26) and (3.27), we may approximate the df of S by

$$\Pr(S \le s) = \Pr \left(\frac{S - E(S)}{\sqrt{\text{Var}(S)}} \le \frac{s - E(S)}{\sqrt{\text{Var}(S)}} \right) \simeq \Phi \left(\frac{s - E(S)}{\sqrt{\text{Var}(S)}} \right). \qquad (3.29)$$

Example 3.6 Assume the aggregate loss S in a collective risk model has a primary distribution of $\mathcal{PN}(100)$ and a secondary distribution of $\mathcal{E}(0.5)$. Approximate the distribution of S using the normal distribution. Compute the df of the aggregate loss for $s = 180$ and 230.

Solution 3.6 From equation (3.26) we have

$$E(S) = E(N)E(X) = (100) \left(\frac{1}{0.5} \right) = 200,$$

and

$$\begin{aligned} \text{Var}(S) &= E(N)\text{Var}(X) + \text{Var}(N) \, [E(X)]^2 \\ &= (100) \left[\frac{1}{(0.5)^2} \right] + (100) \left(\frac{1}{0.5} \right)^2 \\ &= 800. \end{aligned}$$

Thus, we approximate the distribution of S by $\mathcal{N}(200, 800)$. Note that this model has the same mean as that of the portfolio of policies in the individual risk model in Example 3.4, while its variance is larger than that of the individual risk model, which is 720. Also, this model has the same expected number of claims and the same claim-severity distribution in a loss event as the individual risk model. Using the normal approximation the required probabilities are

$$\Pr(S \le 180) \simeq \Pr \left(Z \le \frac{180.5 - 200}{\sqrt{800}} \right) = \Phi(-0.6894) = 0.2453,$$

and

$$\Pr(S \le 230) \simeq \Pr \left(Z \le \frac{230.5 - 200}{\sqrt{800}} \right) = \Phi(1.0783) = 0.8596. \qquad \square$$

The normal approximation makes use of only the first two moments of S. Higher-order moments can be derived for S and may help improve the approximation. Dickson (2005, Section 4.3), shows that the compound Poisson process is skewed to the right (i.e., positively skewed) regardless of the shape of the secondary distribution. Improvements in the approximation may be achieved using more versatile approximations, such as the translated gamma distribution, which can capture the skewness of the distribution. An example can be found in Dickson (2005, Section 4.8.2).

3.3.4 Compound Poisson Distribution and Individual Risk Model

In Example 3.5 we compute the distribution of the aggregate loss using the collective risk model by way of the Panjer recursion, whereas the parameter of the primary distribution is selected based on the individual risk model and the secondary distribution is a discretized version of the random loss in a loss event. We now provide a more formal justification of this approximation, as well as some extensions.

We consider the individual risk model

$$S = X_1 + \cdots + X_n, \tag{3.30}$$

with n policies. The policy losses are independently distributed with pf–pdf $f_{X_i}(\cdot)$, which are not necessarily identical. Note that X_i can be regarded as having a compound Bernoulli distribution. The primary distribution N_i of X_i takes value 0 with probability $1 - \theta_i$ and 1 with probability θ_i, and the secondary distribution has a pdf $f_{Y_i}(\cdot)$, so that

$$f_{X_i}(x) = \begin{cases} 1 - \theta_i, & \text{for } x = 0, \\ \theta_i f_{Y_i}(x), & \text{for } x > 0. \end{cases} \tag{3.31}$$

Thus, S is the sum of n compound Bernoulli distributions. This distribution is in general intractable and convolution has to be applied to compute the exact distribution. From Theorem 1.7, however, we know that the sum of n compound Poisson distributions has also a compound Poisson distribution. As the Panjer recursion provides an efficient method to compute the compound Poisson distribution, an approximate method to compute the distribution of S is available by approximating the compound Bernouli distributions X_i by compound Poisson distributions $\tilde{X}_i$. Thus, we define $\tilde{X}_i$ as a compound Poisson distribution, where the Poisson parameter is $\lambda_i = \theta_i$ and the secondary distribution has a pdf $f_{Y_i}(\cdot)$. Thus, the means of the primary distributions of X_i and $\tilde{X}_i$ are the same, and they have the same secondary distributions. We now define

$$\tilde{S} = \tilde{X}_1 + \cdots + \tilde{X}_n, \tag{3.32}$$

which, by virtue of Theorem 1.7, has a compound Poisson distribution with Poisson parameter

$$\lambda = \lambda_1 + \cdots + \lambda_n = \theta_1 + \cdots + \theta_n. \tag{3.33}$$

The pdf of the secondary distribution of $\tilde{S}$ is

$$f_{\tilde{X}}(x) = \frac{1}{\lambda} \sum_{i=1}^{n} \lambda_i f_{Y_i}(x). \tag{3.34}$$

With a suitable discretization of $f_{\tilde{X}}(\cdot)$, the distribution of $\tilde{S}$ can be computed using Panjer's recursion, which provides an approximation of the distribution of S.

Finally, if X_i are identically distributed with $\theta_i = \theta$ and $f_{Y_i}(\cdot) = f_Y(\cdot)$, for $i = 1, \ldots, n$, then we have

$$\lambda = n\theta \qquad \text{and} \qquad f_{\tilde{X}}(\cdot) = f_Y(\cdot). \tag{3.35}$$

This approximation was illustrated in Example 3.5.

3.4 Coverage Modifications and Stop-Loss Reinsurance

In Section 2.5 we discuss the effects of coverage modifications on the distributions of the claim frequency and claim severity. Depending on the model used for the aggregate-loss distribution, we may derive the effects of coverage modifications on aggregate loss through their effects on the claim frequency and severity.

We first consider the effects of a deductible of amount d. For the individual risk model, the number of policies n remains unchanged, while the policy loss X_i becomes the loss amount of the claim after the deductible, which we shall denote by $\tilde{X}_i$. Thus, the pf–pdf of $\tilde{X}_i$ is[8]

$$f_{\tilde{X}_i}(x) = \begin{cases} 1 - \theta_i + \theta_i F_{Y_i}(d), & \text{for } x = 0, \\ \theta_i f_{Y_i}(x + d), & \text{for } x > 0. \end{cases} \tag{3.36}$$

For the collective risk model the primary distribution of the compound distribution, i.e., the distribution of the claim frequency, is now modified, as discussed in Section 2.5.5. Also, the secondary distribution is that of the claim after the deductible, i.e., $\tilde{X}$ with pdf given by

$$f_{\tilde{X}}(x) = \frac{f_X(x + d)}{1 - F_X(d)}, \qquad \text{for } x > 0. \tag{3.37}$$

Second, we consider the effects of a policy limit u. For the individual risk model, the number of policies again remains unchanged, while the claim-severity distribution is now capped at u. If we denote the modified claim-severity distribution by $\tilde{X}_i$, then the pf–pdf of $\tilde{X}_i$ is given by

$$f_{\tilde{X}_i}(x) = \begin{cases} 1 - \theta_i, & \text{for } x = 0, \\ \theta_i f_{Y_i}(x), & \text{for } 0 < x < u, \\ \theta_i \left[1 - F_{Y_i}(u) \right], & \text{for } x = u, \\ 0, & \text{otherwise.} \end{cases} \tag{3.38}$$

For the collective risk model, the primary distribution is not affected, while the secondary distribution $\tilde{X}$ has a pf–pdf given by

$$f_{\tilde{X}}(x) = \begin{cases} f_X(x), & \text{for } 0 < x < u, \\ 1 - F_X(u), & \text{for } x = u, \\ 0, & \text{otherwise.} \end{cases} \tag{3.39}$$

---

[8] The definition of Y_i is in equation (3.31).

Insurance companies may purchase reinsurance coverage for a portfolio of policies they own. The coverage may protect the insurer from aggregate loss S exceeding an amount d, called **stop-loss reinsurance**. From the reinsurer's point of view this is a policy with a deductible of amount d. Thus, the loss to the reinsurer is $(S - d)_+$. As shown in equation (2.76), we have

$$E\left[(S - d)_+\right] = \int_d^\infty \left[1 - F_S(s)\right] ds, \qquad (3.40)$$

which can be computed as

$$E\left[(S - d)_+\right] = \int_d^\infty (s - d) f_S(s)\, ds \qquad (3.41)$$

when S is continuous, or

$$E\left[(S - d)_+\right] = \sum_{s > d} (s - d) f_S(s) \qquad (3.42)$$

when S is discrete.

If S takes on integer values only, but d is not an integer, then interpolation is required to compute the expected loss. Given a stop-loss amount d, let $\underline{d}$ be the largest integer and $\overline{d}$ be the smallest integer such that $\underline{d} \le d < \overline{d}$, and $\underline{d} + 1 = \overline{d}$. Then[9]

$$
\begin{aligned}
E\left[(S - d)_+\right] &= \int_d^\infty \left[1 - F_S(s)\right] ds \\
&= \int_d^{\overline{d}} \left[1 - F_S(s)\right] ds + \int_{\overline{d}}^\infty \left[1 - F_S(s)\right] ds \\
&= (\overline{d} - d)\left[1 - F_S(\underline{d})\right] + E\left[(S - \overline{d})_+\right].
\end{aligned}
\qquad (3.43)
$$

Note that if we consider $d = \underline{d}$ in equation (3.43), we have, after rearranging terms,

$$E\left[(S - (d+1))_+\right] = E\left[(S - d)_+\right] - \left[1 - F_S(d)\right], \qquad (3.44)$$

for any integer $d > 0$. This is a convenient recursive formula to use for computing the expected loss at integer-valued deductibles.

From equation (3.44) we have

$$1 - F_S(\underline{d}) = E\left[(S - \underline{d})_+\right] - E\left[(S - \overline{d})_+\right], \qquad (3.45)$$

so that equation (3.43) can be written as

$$
\begin{aligned}
E\left[(S - d)_+\right] &= (\overline{d} - d)\left\{E\left[(S - \underline{d})_+\right] - E\left[(S - \overline{d})_+\right]\right\} + E\left[(S - \overline{d})_+\right] \\
&= (\overline{d} - d)\,E\left[(S - \underline{d})_+\right] + (d - \underline{d})\,E\left[(S - \overline{d})_+\right].
\end{aligned}
\qquad (3.46)
$$

Thus, $E\left[(S - d)_+\right]$ is obtained by interpolating $E\left[(S - \underline{d})_+\right]$ and $E\left[(S - \overline{d})_+\right]$.

---

[9] Note that $F_S(s) = F_S(\underline{d})$ for $\underline{d} \le s < \overline{d}$.

Example 3.7 Assume the aggregate loss S follows a compound Poisson distribution with Poisson parameter λ, and the claim-severity distribution follows a Pareto distribution with parameters α and γ, namely, $\mathcal{P}(\alpha, \gamma)$, where $\alpha > 2$. Compute the mean and the variance of S. If policies are modified with a deductible of d, compute the mean and the variance of the aggregate loss $\tilde{S}$.

Solution 3.7 Without the deductible, the claim-frequency distribution N has mean and variance λ, and the mean and variance of the claim severity X are, from equation (2.40),

$$E(X) = \frac{\gamma}{\alpha - 1} \quad \text{and} \quad \text{Var}(X) = \frac{\alpha\gamma^2}{(\alpha - 1)^2(\alpha - 2)}.$$

Hence, from equations (3.26) and (3.27), we have

$$E(S) = E(N)E(X) = \frac{\lambda\gamma}{\alpha - 1},$$

and

$$\text{Var}(S) = \lambda \left\{ \text{Var}(X) + [E(X)]^2 \right\}$$

$$= \lambda \left[\frac{\alpha\gamma^2}{(\alpha - 1)^2(\alpha - 2)} + \left(\frac{\gamma}{\alpha - 1} \right)^2 \right]$$

$$= \frac{\lambda\gamma^2}{(\alpha - 1)^2} \left[\frac{\alpha}{\alpha - 2} + 1 \right]$$

$$= \frac{2\lambda\gamma^2}{(\alpha - 1)(\alpha - 2)}.$$

With a deductible of amount d, from equation (2.118) the claim-frequency distribution $\tilde{N}$ is Poisson with parameter λv, where $v = \Pr(X > d)$. Using the distribution function of $\mathcal{P}(\alpha, \gamma)$ given in equation (2.38), we have

$$v = \left(\frac{\gamma}{d + \gamma} \right)^\alpha.$$

From equations (2.37) and (3.37), the pdf of the modified claim severity $\tilde{X}$ is

$$f_{\tilde{X}}(x) = \frac{\dfrac{\alpha\gamma^\alpha}{(x + d + \gamma)^{\alpha+1}}}{\left(\dfrac{\gamma}{d + \gamma} \right)^\alpha}$$

$$= \frac{\alpha(d + \gamma)^\alpha}{[x + (d + \gamma)]^{\alpha+1}}, \quad \text{for } x > 0.$$

Thus, the modified claim severity $\tilde{X}$ is distributed as $\mathcal{P}(\alpha, d + \gamma)$. Now we can conclude

$$E(\tilde{S}) = E(\tilde{N})E(\tilde{X})$$
$$= \lambda \left(\frac{\gamma}{d+\gamma}\right)^\alpha \left(\frac{d+\gamma}{\alpha-1}\right)$$
$$= \frac{\lambda\gamma^\alpha}{(\alpha-1)(d+\gamma)^{\alpha-1}}$$
$$= E(S) \left(\frac{\gamma}{d+\gamma}\right)^{\alpha-1},$$

which is less than $E(S)$. Furthermore,

$$\mathrm{Var}(\tilde{S}) = \lambda v \left\{ \mathrm{Var}(\tilde{X}) + [E(\tilde{X})]^2 \right\}$$
$$= \lambda \left(\frac{\gamma}{d+\gamma}\right)^\alpha \left[\frac{\alpha(d+\gamma)^2}{(\alpha-1)^2(\alpha-2)} + \left(\frac{d+\gamma}{\alpha-1}\right)^2\right]$$
$$= \lambda \left(\frac{\gamma}{d+\gamma}\right)^\alpha \left(\frac{d+\gamma}{\alpha-1}\right)^2 \left(\frac{\alpha}{\alpha-2}+1\right)$$
$$= \lambda \left(\frac{\gamma}{d+\gamma}\right)^\alpha \left[\frac{2(d+\gamma)^2}{(\alpha-1)(\alpha-2)}\right]$$
$$= \mathrm{Var}(S) \left(\frac{\gamma}{d+\gamma}\right)^{\alpha-2},$$

which is less than $\mathrm{Var}(S)$.   □

Example 3.8 An insurer pays 80% of the aggregate loss in excess of the deductible of amount 5 up to a maximum payment of 25. Aggregate claim amounts S are integers and the following expected losses are known: $E[(S-5)_+] = 8.52$, $E[(S-36)_+] = 3.25$ and $E[(S-37)_+] = 2.98$. Calculate the expected amount paid by the insurer.

Solution 3.8 If d is the stop-loss amount, then

$$0.8(d-5) = 25,$$

which implies $d = 36.25$.

Thus, the amount paid by the insurer is $0.8[(S-5)_+ - (S-36.25)_+]$, so that the expected loss is $0.8(E[(S-5)_+] - E[(S-36.25)_+])$. From equation (3.46), we have

$$E[(S-36.25)_+] = 0.75\,E[(S-36)_+] + 0.25\,E[(S-37)_+]$$
$$= (0.75)(3.25) + (0.25)(2.98)$$
$$= 3.1825.$$

Thus, the insurer's expected loss is

$$0.8(8.52 - 3.1825) = 4.27. \qquad \square$$

Example 3.9 Aggregate loss S takes values in multiples of 10. If $E[(S-20)_+] = 12.58$ and $F_S(20) = 0.48$, calculate $E[(S-24)_+]$ and $E[(S-30)_+]$.

Solution 3.9 Using equation (3.44) by modifying the increments of claim amounts as 10, we obtain

$$E[(S-30)_+] = E[(S-20)_+] - 10[1 - F_S(20)] = 12.58 - (10)(0.48) = 7.78.$$

Thus, from equation (3.46), we have

$$E[(S-24)_+] = (0.6)(12.58) + (0.4)(7.78) = 10.66. \qquad \square$$

3.5 R Laboratory

R Codes 3.1 provides the codes to compute the distribution of the aggregate loss for the collective risk model. Example 3.5 is used for illustration, where the primary distribution is $\mathcal{PN}(100)$ and the secondary distribution is $\mathcal{E}(0.5)$. The continuous secondary distribution is discretized, with the approximate probability function given in Table 3.5. Our codes use the formula given in equation (3.28). The convolution is computed using the function gconv in the package SensitivityCaseControl. We truncate the Poisson primary distribution with infinite support to a maximum value of 400. The computed distribution function for the aggregate loss can be compared against the results in Table 3.6 based on the Panjer recursion.

```
##########################################################
# R Codes 3.1
#
# Computation of the aggregate loss distribution in
# Example 3.5
##########################################################

library(SensitivityCaseControl) # To use function
                                 # gconv( )

cm=matrix(0,400,500)             # For s: 0 to 399 and
                                 #        n: 1 to 500
```

```
fx=c(0.2212,0.3064,0.1859,0.1127,0.0684,0.0415,0.0252,
     0.0153,0.0093,0.0056,0.0085)
                         # Prob funct of discretized
                         # secondary distribution
nv=seq(1,500,1)
prp=dpois(nv,100)        # Prob funct of primary
                         # distribution PN(100)
h=fx
cm[1:length(fx),1]=fx
for (j in 2:500)
{
h=gconv(fx,h)            # Prob funct of sum of j losses
                         # by convolution
cm[1:min(length(h),400),j]=h[1:min(length(h),400)]
}
pm=cm%*%prp              # Prob funct of aggregate loss S,
                         # s from 0 to 399
fpm=cumsum(pm)           # Dist funct of aggregate loss S,
                         # s from 0 to 399
s=seq(110,300,10)        # Select s
cbind(s,fpm[s])          # Output df at values of s
```

3.6 Summary and Conclusions

We have discussed the individual risk and collective risk models for analyzing
the distribution of aggregate loss. Both models build upon assumptions of the
claim-frequency and claim-severity distributions. While exact distributions are
available for both models their computation may be very intensive. Table 3.7
summarizes the exact as well as approximate methods for the computation of
the aggregate-loss distribution.

The Panjer recursion can be extended to other classes of primary distributions, and some results are provided in Dickson (2005). When the portfolio
sizes of insurance policies are large, computation of the exact distribution often
encounters underflow or overflow problems. Klugman *et al.* (2008) discuss
some of the computational stability issues.

Exercises

Exercise 3.1 The primary distribution of a compound distribution S is
$\mathcal{NB}(2, 0.25)$, and its secondary distribution is $\mathcal{PN}(\lambda)$. If $f_S(0) = 0.067$,
calculate λ.

Table 3.7. *Methods for computing the aggregate-loss distribution*

Model	Exact methods	Approximate methods
Individual risk	1 Convolution: with discretized claim-severity distribution 2 De Pril recursion: with specific setup of policy stratification	1 Normal approximation 2 Compound Poisson distribution and Panjer recursion
Collective risk	1 Convolution: with discretized claim-severity distribution and assumed primary distribution 2 Panjer recursion: Primary distribution follows $(a, b, 0)$ class, secondary distribution discretized 3 Some limited analytic results	1 Normal approximation

Exercise 3.2 The primary distribution of a compound distribution S is $\mathcal{BN}(4, \theta)$, and its secondary distribution is $\mathcal{GM}(\beta)$. If $f_S(0) = 0.4$ and $f_S(1) = 0.04$, find θ and β.

Exercise 3.3 The primary distribution of a compound distribution S is $\mathcal{PN}(\lambda_1)$, and its secondary distribution is $\mathcal{PN}(\lambda_2)$. If the mean and the variance of S are 2 and 5, respectively, determine λ_1 and λ_2.

Exercise 3.4 A portfolio has 100 independent insurance policies. Each policy has a probability of 0.8 making no claim, and a probability of 0.2 making a claim. When a claim is made, the loss amount is 10, 50 and 80 with probabilities of 0.4, 0.4 and 0.2, respectively. Calculate the mean and the variance of the aggregate claim of the portfolio.

Exercise 3.5 A portfolio has n independent insurance policies. Each policy has a probability of $1 - \theta$ making no claim, and a probability of θ making a claim. When a claim is made, the loss amount is distributed as $\mathcal{G}(\alpha, \beta)$. Determine the mgf of the aggregate claim of the portfolio.

Exercise 3.6 There are two independent insurance policies. The claim frequency of each policy follows a $\mathcal{BN}(4, 0.1)$ distribution. When there is a claim the claim amount follows the zero-truncated $\mathcal{BN}(5, 0.4)$ distribution. What is the probability that the aggregate claim of these two policies is (a) zero and (b) one?

Exercise 3.7 There are two independent insurance policies. The claim frequency of each policy follows a $\mathcal{NB}(2, 0.2)$ distribution. When there is a claim the claim amount follows the $\mathcal{BN}(4, 0.5)$ distribution. What is the probability that the aggregate claim of these two policies is (a) zero and (b) one?

Exercise 3.8 A portfolio has 5 independent policies. Each policy has equal probability of making 0, 1 and 2 claims. Each claim is distributed as $\mathcal{E}(0.05)$. Determine the mgf of the aggregate loss of the portfolio.

Exercise 3.9 An insurance policy has probabilities of 0.6, 0.2, 0.1 and 0.1 of making 0, 1, 2 and 3 claims, respectively. The claim severity is 1 or 2 with equal probability. Calculate the mean and the variance of the aggregate loss of the policy.

Exercise 3.10 An insurance policy has claims of amount 0, 10 and 20 with probabilities of 0.7, 0.2 and 0.1, respectively. Calculate the probability that the aggregate claim of 4 independent policies is not more than 50.

Exercise 3.11 In a collective risk model S has a binomial compound distribution with primary distribution $\mathcal{BN}(2, 0.6)$. The individual claims are 1, 2 and 3, with probabilities of 0.5, 0.3 and 0.2, respectively. Determine the pgf of S.

Exercise 3.12 An insurer has 5 independent policies. Each policy has a probability of 0.2 making a claim, which takes a value of 1 or 2 with a probability of 0.3 and 0.7, respectively.

(a) Using Panjer's recursion, determine the probability that the aggregate claim is less than 5.
(b) Using convolution, determine the probability that the aggregate claim is less than 5.

Exercise 3.13 X_1 and X_2 are iid mixed-type random variables, with $f_{X_1}(0) = f_{X_2}(0) = 0.5$ and a constant density in the interval $(0, 2]$. Determine the df of $X_1 + X_2$.

Exercise 3.14 A portfolio has 500 independent policies. Each policy has a probability of 0.6 making no claim, and a probability of 0.4 making a claim. Claim amount is distributed as $\mathcal{P}(3, 20)$. Determine an approximate chance that the aggregate claim is larger than 2,500.

Exercise 3.15 The number of claims N of an insurance portfolio has the following distribution: $f_N(0) = 0.1, f_N(1) = 0.4, f_N(2) = 0.3$ and $f_N(3) = 0.2$. The claim amounts are distributed as $\mathcal{E}(0.4)$ and are independent of each other as well as the claim frequency. Determine the variance of the aggregate claim.

Exercise 3.16 The number of claims per year of an insurance portfolio is distributed as $\mathcal{PN}(10)$. The loss amounts are distributed as $\mathcal{U}(0, 10)$. Claim frequency and claim amount are independent, and there is a deductible of 4 per loss. Calculate the mean of the aggregate claim per year.

Exercise 3.17 Claim severity X is distributed as $\mathcal{U}(0, 10)$. An insurance policy has a policy limit of $u = 8$. Calculate the mean and the variance of the aggregate loss of 20 independent policies, if each policy has a probability of 0.2 of a claim and 0.8 of no claim.

Exercise 3.18 Aggregate loss S follows a compound distribution with primary distribution $\mathcal{NB}(3, 0.3)$. The claim severity is distributed as $\mathcal{P}(3, 20)$. Compute the mean and the variance of S. If the policies are modified with a deductible of $d = 5$, compute the mean and the variance of the aggregate loss $\tilde{S}$.

Exercise 3.19 Let N_1 and N_2 be independent Poisson distributions with $\lambda = 1$ and 2, respectively. How would you express $S = -2N_1 + N_2$ as a compound Poisson distribution?

Exercise 3.20 Aggregate loss S follows a compound distribution. The primary distribution is $\mathcal{PN}(20)$ and the secondary distribution is $\mathcal{U}(0, 5)$. If the policies are modified with a deductible of $d = 1$ and a maximum covered loss of $u = 4$, compute the mean and the variance of the modified aggregate loss $\tilde{S}$.

Exercise 3.21 In a portfolio of 100 independent policies the probabilities of one claim and no claim are 0.1 and 0.9, respectively. Suppose claim severity is distributed as $\mathcal{E}(0.2)$ and there is a maximum covered loss of 8, approximate the probability that the aggregate loss is less than 50.

Exercise 3.22 Portfolio A consists of 50 insurance policies, each with a proba-bility 0.8 of no claim and a probability 0.2 of making one claim. Claim severity is distributed as $\mathcal{E}(0.1)$. Portfolio B consists of 70 insurance policies, each with a probability 0.7 of no claim and a probability 0.3 of making one claim. Claim severity is distributed as $\mathcal{P}(3, 30)$.

(a) Calculate the mean and the variance of the aggregate loss of the combined portfolio based on the individual risk model.
(b) How would you approximate the aggregate loss of the combined portfolio using a collective risk model? Determine the mean and the variance of the aggregate loss of the combined portfolio based on the collective risk model.

Questions Adapted from SOA Exams

Exercise 3.23 The aggregate loss S is distributed as a compound binomial dis-tribution, where the primary distribution is $\mathcal{BN}(9, 0.2)$. Claim severity X has pf: $f_X(1) = 0.4, f_X(2) = 0.4$ and $f_X(3) = 0.2$. Calculate $\Pr(S \leq 4)$.

Exercise 3.24 Aggregate claim S can only take positive integer values. If $\mathrm{E}\left[(S-2)_+\right] = 1/6$, $\mathrm{E}\left[(S-3)_+\right] = 0$ and $f_S(1) = 1/2$, calculate the mean of S.

Exercise 3.25 You are given that $E[(S-30)_+] = 8$, $E[(S-20)_+] = 12$ and the only possible aggregate claim in $(20, 30]$ is 22, with $f_S(22) = 0.1$. Calculate $F_S(20)$.

Exercise 3.26 Aggregate losses follow a compound Poisson distribution with parameter $\lambda = 3$. Individual losses take values 1, 2, 3 and 4 with probabilities 0.4, 0.3, 0.2 and 0.1, respectively. Calculate the probability that the aggregate loss does not exceed 3.

Exercise 3.27 Aggregate losses follow a compound distribution. The claim frequency has mean 100 and standard deviation 25. The claim severity has mean 20,000 and standard deviation 5,000. Determine the normal approximation of the probability that the aggregate loss exceeds 150% of the expected loss.

Part II
Risk and Ruin

This part of the book is about two important and related topics in modeling insurance business: measuring risk and computing the likelihood of ruin. In Chapter 4 we introduce various measures of risk, which are constructed with the purpose of setting premium or capital. We discuss the axiomatic approach of identifying risk measures that are coherent. Specific measures such as Value-at-Risk, conditional tail expectation, and the distortion-function approach are discussed. Chapter 5 analyzes the probability of ruin of an insurance business in a discrete-time framework. Probabilities of ultimate ruin and ruin before a finite time are discussed. We show the interaction of the initial surplus, premium loading, and loss distribution on the probability of ruin.

4

Risk Measures

As insurance companies hold portfolios of insurance policies that may result in claims, it is a good management practice to assess the exposure of the company to such risks. A risk measure, which summarizes the overall risk exposures of the company, helps the company evaluate if there is sufficient capital to overcome adverse events. Risk measures for blocks of policies can also be used to assess the adequacy of the premium charged. Since the Basel Accords, financial institutions such as banks and insurance companies have elevated their efforts to assess their internal risks as well as communicating the assessments to the public.

In this chapter we discuss various measures of risks. We introduce the axioms proposed by Artzner *et al.* (1999), which define the concept of a *coherent* risk measure. Risk measures based on the premium principle, such as the expected-value principle, variance principle and standard-deviation principle, are discussed. This is followed by the capital-based risk measures such as the Value-at-Risk and the conditional tail expectation. Many of the risk measures used in the actuarial literature can be viewed as the integral of a distortion function of the survival distribution of the loss variable, or the mean of the risk-adjusted loss. Further risk measures that come under this category are risk measures defined by the hazard transform and the Wang (2000) transform.

Learning Objectives

1 Axioms of coherent risk measures
2 Risk measures based on premium principles
3 Risk measures based on capital requirements
4 Value-at-Risk and conditional tail expectation
5 Distortion function
6 Proportional hazard transform and Wang transform

4.1 Uses of Risk Measures

Risk management is of paramount importance for the management of a firm. The risks facing a firm can be generally classified under **market risk** (exposure to potential loss due to changes in market prices and market conditions), **credit risk** (risk of customers defaulting) and **operational risk** (any business risk that is not a market or credit risk). The risk management process should be a holistic process covering the analysis of risk incidents, assessment of management control, reporting procedures and prediction of risk trends. While a risk management process is multidimensional, measuring risk is the core component of the process.

In this chapter we focus on measuring the risks of an insurance company. A major risk an insurance company encounters is the loss arising from the insurance policies. In other words, our focus is on the operational risk of the firm. We shall discuss various measures that attempt to summarize the potential risks arising from the possible claims of the insurance policies. Thus, the measures will be based on the loss random variables. Such measures may be used by an insurance company in the following ways.

Determination of Economic Capital
Economic capital is the capital a firm is required to hold in order to avoid insolvency. It is a buffer against unexpected losses, and may differ from the available capital of the firm. The size of the economic capital is dependent on the level of credit standing the firm expects to achieve or the probability of insolvency the firm is prepared to tolerate. The first step in the calculation of economic capital often involves the quantification of the possible risks of the firm.

Determination of Insurance Premium
Insurance premium is the price demanded by the insurance company for transferring the risk of loss from the insured to the insurer. The premium charged should vary directly with the potential loss. Thus, appropriately measuring the risk is important for the determination of the insurance premium.

It should be noted that in practice the determination of premium often depends on other factors such as competition in the industry and strategic marketing concerns. In this book, however, we consider premium determination principles purely from the point of view of compensation for potential losses.

Internal Risk Management
Risk measures are important inputs to internal risk management and control. A firm may set targets on different segments of the business based on certain risk measures. Internal evaluation will be much easier if clear and well-defined targets for risk measures are available.

External Regulatory Reporting

Concerned about the solvency of insurance companies, various regulatory bodies have attempted to institutionalize the regulatory framework of reporting, as well as step up the supervision of such reports. Risk measures form a main part of the reporting system.

Since the Basel Accord I in 1988 and the Basel Accord II in 2004, risk assessment and reporting have assumed important profiles in many financial institutions. A survey of the best practice in the industry in enterprise risk management can be found in Lam (2003). McNeil *et al.* (2005) provide an introductory description of the Basel Accords as well as some regulatory developments in the insurance industry.

In what follows we first describe some simple risk measures based on the premium principle. We then introduce the axiomatic approach of Artzner *et al.* (1999) for identifying desirable properties of a risk measure. Some risk measures based on capital requirements are then discussed, and a unifying theme on risk measures using distortion functions concludes this chapter.

Prior to introducing some premium-based risk measures, we first provide a formal definition of a risk measure based on a random loss X, which is the aggregate claim of a block of insurance policies.[1]

Definition 4.1 A risk measure of the random loss X, denoted by $\varrho(X)$, is a real-valued function $\varrho : X \to \mathbb{R}$, where $\mathbb{R}$ is the set of real numbers.

As a loss random variable, X is nonnegative. Thus, the risk measure $\varrho(X)$ may be imposed to be nonnegative for the purpose of measuring insurance risks. However, if the purpose is to measure the risks of a portfolio of assets, X may stand for the *change* in portfolio value, which may be positive or negative. In such cases, the risk measure $\varrho(X)$ may be positive or negative.

4.2 Some Premium-Based Risk Measures

We denote the mean and the variance of the random loss X by μ_X and σ_X^2, respectively. The **expected-value principle premium** risk measure is defined as

$$\varrho(X) = (1 + \theta)\mu_X, \tag{4.1}$$

where $\theta \geq 0$ is the **premium loading factor**. Thus, the loading in excess of the mean loss μ_X is $\theta\mu_X$. In the special case of $\theta = 0$, $\varrho(X) = \mu_X$ and the risk measure is called the **pure premium**.

---

[1] In this chapter we use X to denote the aggregate loss random variable rather than S, which has other notational use.

Note that in the expected-value premium risk measure, the risk depends only on the mean μ_X and the loading factor θ. Thus, two loss variables with the same mean and same loading will have the same risk, regardless of the higher-order moments such as the variance. To differentiate such loss distributions, we may consider the **variance principle premium** risk measure defined by

$$\varrho(X) = \mu_X + \alpha\sigma_X^2, \tag{4.2}$$

or the **standard-deviation principle premium** risk measure defined by

$$\varrho(X) = \mu_X + \alpha\sigma_X, \tag{4.3}$$

where $\alpha \geq 0$ in equations (4.2) and (4.3) is the loading factor. Under the variance premium and standard-deviation premium risk measures, the loss distribution with a larger dispersion will have a higher risk. This appears to be a reasonable property. However, these two risk measures yet have quite different properties, as we shall see later. Thus, the choice of a risk measure is not a trivial task. In the next section we introduce some properties of risk measures that are deemed to be desirable. The selection of risk measures may then be focused on the set of risk measures that satisfy these properties.

4.3 Axioms of Coherent Risk Measures

Artzner *et al.* (1999) suggest four axioms of measures of risk. They argue that these axioms "should hold for any risk measure that is to be used to effectively regulate or manage risks." A risk measure that satisfies these four axioms is said to be **coherent**. We summarize these axioms as follows.[2]

Axiom 4.1 (Translational invariance (T)) For any loss variable X and any nonnegative constant a, $\varrho(X + a) = \varrho(X) + a$.

Axiom T states that if the loss X is increased by a fixed amount a, then the risk increases by the same amount.

Axiom 4.2 (Subadditivity (S)) For any loss variables X and Y, $\varrho(X + Y) \leq \varrho(X) + \varrho(Y)$.

Axiom S implies that an insurance company cannot reduce its risk by splitting its business into smaller blocks. It also says that consolidating blocks of policies does not make the company more risky.

---

[2] Artzner *et al.* (1999) consider X that can be positive or negative. As we have restricted our interest to nonnegative X for insurance losses, we have modified their axioms accordingly.

Axiom 4.3 (Positive homogeneity (PH)) For any loss variable X and any nonnegative constant a, $\varrho(aX) = a\varrho(X)$.

This axiom is at all reasonable as it ensures that changing the monetary units of the risks does not alter the risk measure.

Axiom 4.4 (Monotonicity (M)) For any loss variables X and Y such that $X \leq Y$ under all states of nature, $\varrho(X) \leq \varrho(Y)$.

Axiom M states that if the loss of one risk is no more than that of another risk under all states of nature, the risk measure of the former risk cannot be more than that of the latter.

Example 4.1 Show that, under Axiom PH, $\varrho(0) = 0$. Hence, prove that if Axioms M and PH hold, $\varrho(X) \geq 0$ for $X \geq 0$.

Solution 4.1 First we note that $\varrho(0) = \varrho(a0)$ for all a. Now with Axiom PH, we have $\varrho(a0) = a\varrho(0)$ for all $a \geq 0$. Thus, we conclude $\varrho(0) = a\varrho(0)$ for all $a \geq 0$, which implies $\varrho(0) = 0$.

Now for $X \geq 0$, we have, from Axiom M, $\varrho(X) \geq \varrho(0)$, and we conclude $\varrho(X) \geq 0$. $\qquad\square$

If we apply Axiom T to a coherent risk measure and assume $X = 0$, then for any nonnegative constant a we have $\varrho(a) = \varrho(X+a) = \varrho(X)+a = \varrho(0)+a = a$. This result says that if a risk takes a constant value, a coherent risk measure of the risk must be equal to this constant. Thus, for a coherent risk measure based on the premium principle, the loading for a constant risk must be equal to zero. Consequently, we say that a coherent risk measure has **no unjustified loading**.

If the loss X has a finite support with maximum value x_U, then a risk defined by $Y = x_U$ satisfies $X \leq Y$. From Axiom M, a coherent risk measure must satisfy $\varrho(X) \leq \varrho(Y) = \varrho(x_U) = x_U$. Thus, a coherent risk is bounded above by the maximum loss. A premium that satisfies this condition is said to have the property of **no ripoff**.[3]

Example 4.2 Show that the expected-value premium risk measure satisfies Axioms S, PH and M, but not T.

Solution 4.2 For any risks X and Y, we have

$$\varrho(X+Y) = (1 + \theta)\mathrm{E}(X+Y)$$

---

[3] It can also be shown that a coherent risk measure satisfies the condition $\varrho(X) \geq \mu_X$. A proof of this result is given in Artzner (1999).

$$= (1 + \theta)\mathrm{E}(X) + (1 + \theta)\mathrm{E}(Y)$$
$$= \varrho(X) + \varrho(Y).$$

Thus, Axiom S holds. Now for $Y = aX$ with $a \geq 0$, we have

$$\varrho(Y) = (1 + \theta)\mathrm{E}(Y) = (1 + \theta)\mathrm{E}(aX) = a(1 + \theta)\mathrm{E}(X) = a\varrho(X),$$

which proves Axiom PH. For two risks X and Y, $X \geq Y$ implies $\mu_X \geq \mu_Y$. Thus,

$$\varrho(X) = (1 + \theta)\mu_X \geq (1 + \theta)\mu_Y = \varrho(Y),$$

and Axiom M holds. To examine Axiom T, we consider an arbitrary constant $a > 0$. Note that, if $\theta > 0$,

$$\varrho(X + a) = (1 + \theta)\mathrm{E}(X + a) > (1 + \theta)\mathrm{E}(X) + a = \varrho(X) + a.$$

Thus, Axiom T is not satisfied if $\theta > 0$, which implies the expected-value premium is in general not a coherent risk measure. However, when $\theta = 0$, Axiom T holds. Thus, the pure premium risk measure is coherent. $\square$

It can be shown that the variance premium risk measure satisfies Axiom T, but not Axioms S, M and PH. On the other hand, the standard-deviation premium risk measure satisfies Axioms S, T and PH, but not Axiom M. Readers are invited to prove these results (see Exercises 4.2 and 4.3).

The axioms of coherent risk narrow down the set of risk measures to be considered for management and regulation. However, they do not specify a unique risk measure to be used in practice. Some risk measures (such as the pure premium risk measure) that are coherent may not be a suitable risk measure for some reasons. Thus, the choice of which measure to use depends on additional considerations.

4.4 Some Capital-Based Risk Measures

We now introduce some risk measures constructed for the purpose of evaluating economic capital.

4.4.1 Value-at-Risk (VaR)

Value-at-Risk (VaR) is probably one of the most widely used measures of risk. Simply speaking, the VaR of a loss variable is the minimum value of the distribution such that the probability of the loss larger than this value is not more than a given probability. In statistical terms, VaR is a quantile as defined in Section 2.4. We now define VaR formally as follows.

Definition 4.2 Let X be a random variable of loss with continuous df $F_X(\cdot)$, and δ be a probability level such that $0 < \delta < 1$, the Value-at-Risk at probability level δ, denoted by $\mathrm{VaR}_\delta(X)$, is the δ-quantile of X. That is,

$$\mathrm{VaR}_\delta(X) = F_X^{-1}(\delta) = x_\delta. \tag{4.4}$$

The probability level δ is usually taken to be close to 1 (say, 0.95 or 0.99), so that the probability of loss X exceeding $\mathrm{VaR}_\delta(X)$ is not more than $1 - \delta$, and is thus small. We shall write VaR at probability level δ as VaR_δ when the loss variable is understood.

If $F_X(\cdot)$ is a step function (as when X is not continuous), there may be some ambiguity in the definition of $F_X^{-1}(\delta)$. Thus, a more general definition of $\mathrm{VaR}_\delta(X)$ is

$$\mathrm{VaR}_\delta(X) = \inf \{x \in [0, \infty) : F_X(x) \geq \delta\}. \tag{4.5}$$

Example 4.3 Find VaR_δ of the following loss distributions X: (a) $\mathcal{E}(\lambda)$, (b) $\mathcal{L}(\mu, \sigma^2)$, and (c) $\mathcal{P}(\alpha, \gamma)$.

Solution 4.3 For (a), from Example 2.8, we have

$$\mathrm{VaR}_\delta = -\frac{\log(1 - \delta)}{\lambda}.$$

For (b), from Example 2.8, the VaR is

$$\mathrm{VaR}_\delta = \exp\left[\mu + \sigma \Phi^{-1}(\delta)\right].$$

For (c), from equation (2.38), the df of $\mathcal{P}(\alpha, \gamma)$ is

$$F_X(x) = 1 - \left(\frac{\gamma}{x + \gamma}\right)^\alpha,$$

so that its quantile function is

$$F_X^{-1}(\delta) = \gamma(1 - \delta)^{-\frac{1}{\alpha}} - \gamma,$$

and

$$\mathrm{VaR}_\delta = F_X^{-1}(\delta) = \gamma\left[(1 - \delta)^{-\frac{1}{\alpha}} - 1\right]. \qquad \square$$

Example 4.4 Find VaR_δ, for $\delta = 0.95, 0.96, 0.98$ and 0.99, of the following discrete loss distribution

$$X = \begin{cases} 100, & \text{with prob } 0.02, \\ 90, & \text{with prob } 0.02, \\ 80, & \text{with prob } 0.04, \\ 50, & \text{with prob } 0.12, \\ 0, & \text{with prob } 0.80. \end{cases}$$

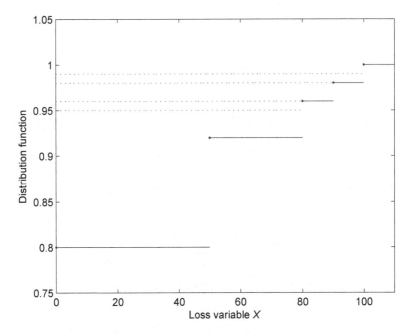

Figure 4.1 Distribution function of loss and VaR of Example 4.4

Solution 4.4 As X is discrete, we use the definition of VaR in equation (4.5). The df of X is plotted in Figure 4.1. The dotted horizontal lines correspond to the probability levels 0.95, 0.96, 0.98 and 0.99. Note that the df of X is a step function. For VaR_δ we require the value of X corresponding to the probability level equal to or next-step higher than δ. Thus, VaR_δ for $\delta = 0.95, 0.96, 0.98$ and 0.99, are, respectively, 80, 80, 90 and 100.   □

As the distribution function is monotonic, it is easy to see that VaR satisfies Axiom M for coherency. Thus, if $X \leq Y$ under all states of nature,

$$\Pr(X \leq \text{Var}_\delta(Y)) \geq \Pr(Y \leq \text{Var}_\delta(Y)) \geq \delta, \qquad (4.6)$$

which implies $\text{Var}_\delta(X) \leq \text{Var}_\delta(Y)$ and Axiom M holds. Now for any risk X and any positive constant a, let $Y = X + a$. We have

$$\begin{aligned}
\text{VaR}_\delta(X + a) &= \text{VaR}_\delta(Y) \\
&= \inf\{y : \Pr(Y \leq y) \geq \delta\} \\
&= \inf\{x + a : \Pr(X + a \leq x + a) \geq \delta\} \\
&= a + \inf\{x : \Pr(X + a \leq x + a) \geq \delta\} \\
&= a + \inf\{x : \Pr(X \leq x) \geq \delta\} \\
&= a + \text{VaR}_\delta(X), \qquad (4.7)
\end{aligned}$$

so that Axiom T holds. Furthermore, if we let $Y = aX$ for $a \geq 0$, we have

$$
\begin{aligned}
\text{VaR}_\delta(aX) &= \text{VaR}_\delta(Y) \\
&= \inf\{y : \text{Pr}(Y \leq y) \geq \delta\} \\
&= \inf\{ax : \text{Pr}(aX \leq ax) \geq \delta\} \\
&= \inf\{ax : \text{Pr}(X \leq x) \geq \delta\} \\
&= a\,[\inf\{x : \text{Pr}(X \leq x) \geq \delta\}] \\
&= a\,\text{VaR}_\delta(X), \quad\quad\quad\quad\quad\quad\quad\quad (4.8)
\end{aligned}
$$

and Axiom PH holds.

While VaR satisfies Axioms M, T and PH, it does not satisfy Axiom S and is thus not coherent. A counter-example which illustrates that VaR is not subadditive can be found in Artzner *et al.* (1999).

4.4.2 Conditional Tail Expectation and Related Measures

A drawback of VaR is that it only makes use of the cut-off point corresponding to the probability level δ and does not use any information about the tail distribution beyond this point. The conditional tail expectation (CTE) corrects for this. As stated in equation (2.66), the CTE at probability level δ, denoted by $\text{CTE}_\delta(X)$ (or CTE_δ when the loss variable is understood) is defined as

$$
\text{CTE}_\delta(X) = \text{E}(X \mid X > x_\delta). \quad\quad\quad\quad (4.9)
$$

When X is continuous, the above can be written as

$$
\text{CTE}_\delta(X) = \text{E}\,[X \mid X > \text{VaR}_\delta(X)], \quad\quad\quad\quad (4.10)
$$

which will be used as the definition of CTE as a risk measure, and this definition also applies to discrete losses. Analogous to the excess-loss variable defined in Section 2.5.1, we consider the loss in excess of the VaR conditional on it being exceeded, i.e.,

$$
X - \text{VaR}_\delta(X) \mid X > \text{VaR}_\delta(X). \quad\quad\quad\quad (4.11)
$$

The mean of this conditional excess, called the **conditional VaR**, is denoted by $\text{CVaR}_\delta(X)$ (or CVaR_δ when the loss variable is understood) and defined as[4]

$$
\text{CVaR}_\delta(X) = \text{E}\,[X - \text{VaR}_\delta(X) \mid X > \text{VaR}_\delta(X)]. \quad\quad\quad\quad (4.12)
$$

The above equation can be written as

$$
\begin{aligned}
\text{CVaR}_\delta(X) &= \text{E}\,[X \mid X > \text{VaR}_\delta(X)] - \text{E}\,[\text{VaR}_\delta(X) \mid X > \text{VaR}_\delta(X)] \\
&= \text{CTE}_\delta(X) - \text{VaR}_\delta(X), \quad\quad\quad\quad\quad\quad (4.13)
\end{aligned}
$$

---

[4] This definition follows Denuit *et al.* (2005). CVaR is also alternatively taken as synonymous with CTE.

which is analogous to equation (2.81), with the deductible replaced by VaR.
    If we use VaR_δ as the economic capital, the **shortfall** of the capital is

$$(X - \text{VaR}_\delta)_+. \tag{4.14}$$

When X is continuous, $\text{VaR}_\delta = x_\delta$ and the **mean shortfall** is

$$\begin{aligned} \text{E}\left[(X - x_\delta)_+\right] &= \text{E}\left[X - x_\delta \,|\, X > x_\delta\right]\text{Pr}(X > x_\delta) \\ &= (1 - \delta)\,\text{CVaR}_\delta, \end{aligned} \tag{4.15}$$

and we have, from equations (4.13) and (4.15),

$$\begin{aligned} \text{CTE}_\delta &= x_\delta + \text{CVaR}_\delta \\ &= x_\delta + \frac{1}{1 - \delta}\text{E}\left[(X - x_\delta)_+\right], \end{aligned} \tag{4.16}$$

which relates CTE_δ to the mean shortfall.[5] To evaluate CTE_δ, we consider

$$\text{CTE}_\delta = \text{E}(X \,|\, X > x_\delta) = \frac{1}{1 - \delta}\int_{x_\delta}^\infty x f_X(x)\, dx. \tag{4.17}$$

Using change of variable $\xi = F_X(x)$, the integral above can be written as

$$\begin{aligned} \int_{x_\delta}^\infty x f_X(x)\, dx &= \int_{x_\delta}^\infty x\, dF_X(x) \\ &= \int_\delta^1 x_\xi\, d\xi, \end{aligned} \tag{4.18}$$

which implies

$$\text{CTE}_\delta = \frac{1}{1 - \delta}\int_\delta^1 x_\xi\, d\xi. \tag{4.19}$$

Thus, CTE_δ can be interpreted as the *average* of the quantiles exceeding x_δ.
    On the other hand, when X is not necessarily continuous, equation (4.17) is
replaced by the Stieltjes integral

$$\text{CTE}_\delta = \text{E}(X \,|\, X > \text{VaR}_\delta) = \frac{1}{1 - \bar{\delta}}\int_{x \in (\text{VaR}_\delta, \,\infty)} x\, dF_X(x), \tag{4.20}$$

where

$$\bar{\delta} = \text{Pr}(X \leq \text{VaR}_\delta). \tag{4.21}$$

---

[5] Note that mathematically CVaR is equivalent to $\text{E}(X_P)$ (see equation (2.80)), and the mean
shortfall is equivalent to $\text{E}(X_L)$ (see equation (2.78)).

However, as $\bar{\delta} \geq \delta$, equation (4.20) implies that we may be using less than the worst $1 - \delta$ portion of the loss distribution in computing CTE_δ. To circumvent this problem, we use the following formula (see Hardy, 2003, p. 164)

$$\text{CTE}_\delta = \frac{(\bar{\delta} - \delta)\text{VaR}_\delta + (1 - \bar{\delta})\text{E}(X|X > \text{VaR}_\delta)}{1 - \delta}, \qquad (4.22)$$

which is a weighted average of VaR_δ and $\text{E}(X|X > \text{VaR}_\delta)$. We shall adopt this formula for CTE_δ in subsequent discussions. When $\bar{\delta} = \delta$ (as when X is continuous), equation (4.22) reduces to $\text{CTE}_\delta = \text{E}(X|X > \text{VaR}_\delta)$.

An expression analogous to the right-hand side of equation (4.19) is

$$\frac{1}{1 - \delta} \int_\delta^1 \text{VaR}_\xi \, d\xi, \qquad (4.23)$$

which is sometimes called the **tail Value-at-Risk**, denoted by $\text{TVaR}_\delta(X)$ (or TVaR_δ when the loss variable is understood). Expression (4.23) is an alternative way of writing equation (4.22), whether or not X is continuous. Hence, TVaR_δ and CTE_δ (as defined by equation (4.22)) are equivalent.

Example 4.5 Find CTE_δ and CVaR_δ of the following loss distributions X: (a) $\mathcal{E}(\lambda)$, (b) $\mathcal{L}(\mu, \sigma^2)$, and (c) $\mathcal{P}(\alpha, \gamma)$ with $\alpha > 1$.

Solution 4.5 For $\mathcal{E}(\lambda)$, CTE_δ was computed in Examples 2.8 and 2.9, i.e.,

$$\text{CTE}_\delta = \frac{e^{-\lambda x_\delta}}{1 - \delta} \left[x_\delta + \frac{1}{\lambda} \right] = x_\delta + \frac{1}{\lambda}.$$

Thus, CVaR_δ is given by

$$\text{CVaR}_\delta = \text{CTE}_\delta - x_\delta = \frac{1}{\lambda}.$$

For $\mathcal{L}(\mu, \sigma^2)$, we have, from Example 2.9,

$$\text{CTE}_\delta = \frac{1}{1 - \delta} \left\{ \exp\left(\mu + \frac{\sigma^2}{2} \right) [1 - \Phi(z^*)] \right\},$$

where

$$z^* = \frac{\log x_\delta - \mu}{\sigma} - \sigma,$$

and x_δ is obtained from Example 2.8 as

$$x_\delta = \exp\left[\mu + \sigma\Phi^{-1}(\delta) \right].$$

Thus,

$$\begin{aligned} z^* &= \frac{\mu + \sigma\Phi^{-1}(\delta) - \mu}{\sigma} - \sigma \\ &= \Phi^{-1}(\delta) - \sigma. \end{aligned}$$

CVaR$_\delta$ of $\mathcal{L}(\mu, \sigma^2)$ is

$$\text{CVaR}_\delta = \frac{1}{1-\delta}\left\{\exp\left(\mu + \frac{\sigma^2}{2}\right)[1 - \Phi(z^*)]\right\} - \exp\left[\mu + \sigma\Phi^{-1}(\delta)\right].$$

For $\mathcal{P}(\alpha, \gamma)$ we compute the integral in equation (4.17) as

$$\int_{x_\delta}^\infty x f_X(x)\, dx = \alpha\gamma^\alpha \int_{x_\delta}^\infty \frac{x}{(x+\gamma)^{\alpha+1}}\, dx$$

$$= -\gamma^\alpha\left\{\left.\frac{x}{(x+\gamma)^\alpha}\right]_{x_\delta}^\infty - \int_{x_\delta}^\infty \frac{dx}{(x+\gamma)^\alpha}\right\}$$

$$= -\gamma^\alpha\left\{-\frac{x_\delta}{(x_\delta+\gamma)^\alpha} + \left.\left[\frac{1}{(\alpha-1)(x+\gamma)^{\alpha-1}}\right]\right]_{x_\delta}^\infty\right\}$$

$$= x_\delta\left(\frac{\gamma}{x_\delta+\gamma}\right)^\alpha + \frac{\gamma^\alpha}{(\alpha-1)(x_\delta+\gamma)^{\alpha-1}}.$$

Substituting the result

$$\delta = 1 - \left(\frac{\gamma}{x_\delta+\gamma}\right)^\alpha$$

in Example 4.3 into the above equation, we obtain

$$\int_{x_\delta}^\infty x f_X(x)\, dx = (1-\delta)\left[x_\delta + \frac{x_\delta+\gamma}{\alpha-1}\right].$$

Thus, from equation (4.17) we conclude

$$\text{CTE}_\delta = x_\delta + \frac{x_\delta+\gamma}{\alpha-1}$$

$$= \frac{\gamma}{\alpha-1} + \frac{\alpha x_\delta}{\alpha-1},$$

and CVaR$_\delta$ is given by

$$\text{CVaR}_\delta = \text{CTE}_\delta - x_\delta = \frac{x_\delta+\gamma}{\alpha-1}. \qquad \square$$

Example 4.6 Calculate CTE$_\delta$ for the loss distribution given in Example 4.4 for $\delta = 0.95, 0.96, 0.98$ and 0.99. Also, calculate TVaR corresponding to these values of δ.

Solution 4.6 As X is not continuous we use equation (4.22) to calculate CTE$_\delta$. Note that VaR$_{0.95}$ = VaR$_{0.96}$ = 80. For $\delta = 0.95$, we have $\bar{\delta} = 0.96$. Now,

$$E(X \mid X > \text{VaR}_{0.95} = 80) = \frac{90(0.02) + 100(0.02)}{0.04} = 95,$$

so that from equation (4.22) we obtain

$$\text{CTE}_{0.95} = \frac{(0.96 - 0.95)80 + (1 - 0.96)95}{1 - 0.95} = 92.$$

For $\delta = 0.96$, we have $\bar{\delta} = 0.96$, so that

$$\text{CTE}_{0.96} = \text{E}(X \,|\, X > \text{VaR}_{0.96} = 80) = 95.$$

For TVaR_δ, we use equation (4.23) to obtain

$$\text{TVaR}_{0.95} = \frac{1}{1 - 0.95} \int_{0.95}^1 \text{VaR}_\xi \, d\xi = \frac{1}{0.05} \left[(80)(0.01) + (90)(0.02) + (100)(0.02) \right] = 92,$$

and

$$\text{TVaR}_{0.96} = \frac{1}{1 - 0.96} \int_{0.96}^1 \text{VaR}_\xi \, d\xi = \frac{1}{0.04} \left[(90)(0.02) + (100)(0.02) \right] = 95.$$

For $\delta = 0.98$, we have $\bar{\delta} = 0.98$, so that

$$\text{CTE}_{0.98} = \text{E}(X \,|\, X > \text{VaR}_{0.98} = 90) = 100,$$

which is also the value of $\text{TVaR}_{0.98}$. Finally, for $\delta = 0.99$, we have $\bar{\delta} = 1$ and $\text{VaR}_{0.99} = 100$, so that $\text{CTE}_{0.99} = \text{VaR}_{0.99} = 100$. On the other hand, we have

$$\text{TVaR}_{0.99} = \frac{1}{1 - 0.99} \int_{0.99}^1 \text{VaR}_\xi \, d\xi = \frac{(100)(0.01)}{0.01} = 100.$$

$\square$

When X is continuous, CTE satisfies Axioms M, T, PH and S, and is thus coherent. Let a be any positive constant. We have

$$\begin{aligned}
\text{CTE}_\delta(X + a) &= \text{E}\left[X + a \,|\, X + a > \text{VaR}_\delta(X + a) \right] \\
&= \text{E}\left[X + a \,|\, X > \text{VaR}_\delta(X) \right] \\
&= a + \text{E}\left[X \,|\, X > \text{VaR}_\delta(X) \right] \\
&= a + \text{CTE}_\delta(X), \quad\quad\quad\quad\quad\quad\quad (4.24)
\end{aligned}$$

so that CTE is translational invariant. Likewise,

$$\begin{aligned}
\text{CTE}_\delta(aX) &= \text{E}\left[aX \,|\, aX > \text{VaR}_\delta(aX) \right] \\
&= \text{E}\left[aX \,|\, X > \text{VaR}_\delta(X) \right] \\
&= a\,\text{E}\left[X \,|\, X > \text{VaR}_\delta(X) \right] \\
&= a\,\text{CTE}_\delta(X), \quad\quad\quad\quad\quad\quad\quad (4.25)
\end{aligned}$$

so that CTE is positively homogeneous. If two continuous loss distributions X and Y satisfy the condition $X \le Y$, we have $x_\delta \le y_\delta$ for $\delta \in (0, 1)$. Thus, from equation (4.21),

$$\begin{aligned}
\text{CTE}_\delta(X) &= \frac{1}{1 - \delta} \int_\delta^1 x_\xi \, d\xi \\
&\le \frac{1}{1 - \delta} \int_\delta^1 y_\xi \, d\xi \\
&= \text{CTE}_\delta(Y), \quad\quad\quad\quad\quad\quad\quad (4.26)
\end{aligned}$$

and CTE is monotonic. Finally, a proof of the subadditivity of CTE can be found in Denuit *et al.* (2005).

4.5 More Premium-Based Risk Measures

In this section, we discuss further risk measures based on the premium principle. Various features of these measures will be explored.

4.5.1 Proportional Hazard Transform and Risk-Adjusted Premium

The premium-based risk measures introduced in Section 4.2 define risk based on a loading of the expected loss. As shown in equation (2.18), the expected loss μ_X of a nonnegative continuous random loss X can be written as

$$\mu_X = \int_0^\infty S_X(x) \, dx. \tag{4.27}$$

Thus, instead of adding a *loading* to μ_X to obtain a premium we may *redefine* the distribution of the losses by shifting more probability weighting to the high losses. Suppose $\tilde{X}$ is distributed with sf $S_{\tilde{X}}(x) = [S_X(x)]^{\frac{1}{\rho}}$, where $\rho \geq 1$, then the mean of $\tilde{X}$ is[6]

$$E(\tilde{X}) = \mu_{\tilde{X}} = \int_0^\infty S_{\tilde{X}}(x) \, dx = \int_0^\infty [S_X(x)]^{\frac{1}{\rho}} \, dx. \tag{4.28}$$

The parameter ρ is called the **risk-aversion index**. Note that

$$\frac{dE(\tilde{X})}{d\rho} = -\frac{1}{\rho^2} \int_0^\infty [S_X(x)]^{\frac{1}{\rho}} \log [S_X(x)] \, dx > 0, \tag{4.29}$$

(as $\log [S_X(x)] < 0$), so that the premium increases with ρ, justifying the risk-aversion index interpretation of ρ.

The distribution of $\tilde{X}$ is called the **proportional hazard (PH) transform** of the distribution of X with parameter ρ.[7] If we denote $h_X(x)$ and $h_{\tilde{X}}(x)$ as the hf of X and $\tilde{X}$, respectively, then from equations (2.2) and (2.3), we have

$$\begin{aligned}
h_{\tilde{X}}(x) &= -\frac{1}{S_{\tilde{X}}(x)} \left(\frac{dS_{\tilde{X}}(x)}{dx} \right) \\
&= -\frac{1}{\rho} \left(\frac{[S_X(x)]^{\frac{1}{\rho}-1} S_X'(x)}{[S_X(x)]^{\frac{1}{\rho}}} \right) \\
&= -\frac{1}{\rho} \left(\frac{S_X'(x)}{S_X(x)} \right) \\
&= \frac{1}{\rho} h_X(x), \tag{4.30}
\end{aligned}$$

---

[6] Given $S_X(x)$ is a well-defined sf, $S_{\tilde{X}}(x)$ is also a well-defined sf.

[7] In general, the PH transform only requires the parameter ρ to be positive. In the context of risk loading, however, we consider PH transforms with $\rho \geq 1$. It can be shown that $E(\tilde{X}) \geq E(X)$ if and only if $\rho \geq 1$.

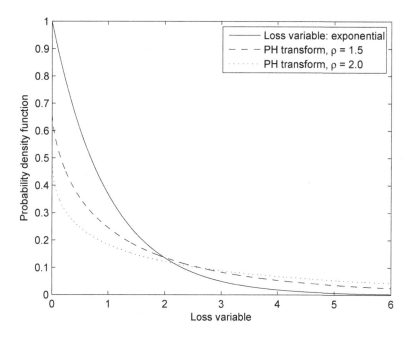

Figure 4.2 Probability density functions of $\mathcal{E}(1)$ and its PH transforms

so that the hf of $\tilde{X}$ is *proportional to* the hf of X. As $\rho \geq 1$, the hf of $\tilde{X}$ is less than that of X, implying that $\tilde{X}$ has a thicker tail than that of X. Also, $S_{\tilde{X}}(x) = [S_X(x)]^{\frac{1}{\rho}}$ declines slower than $S_X(x)$ so that $\mu_{\tilde{X}} > \mu_X$, the difference of which represents the loading.

Example 4.7 If $X \sim \mathcal{E}(\lambda)$, find the PH transform of X with parameter ρ and the risk-adjusted premium.

Solution 4.7 The sf of X is $S_X(x) = e^{-\lambda x}$. Thus, the sf of the PH transform is $S_{\tilde{X}}(x) = \left(e^{-\lambda x}\right)^{\frac{1}{\rho}} = e^{-\frac{\lambda}{\rho}x}$, which implies $\tilde{X} \sim \mathcal{E}(\lambda/\rho)$. Hence, the risk-adjusted premium is $E(\tilde{X}) = \rho/\lambda \geq 1/\lambda = E(X)$.

Figure 4.2 plots the pdf of $X \sim \mathcal{E}(1)$ and its PH transforms for $\rho = 1.5$ and 2.0. It can be seen that the PH transforms have thicker tails than the original loss distribution. □

Example 4.8 If $X \sim \mathcal{P}(\alpha, \gamma)$ with $\alpha > 1$, find the PH transform of X with parameter $\rho \in [1, \alpha)$ and the risk-adjusted premium.

Solution 4.8 The sf of X is

$$S_X(x) = \left(\frac{\gamma}{\gamma + x}\right)^{\alpha},$$

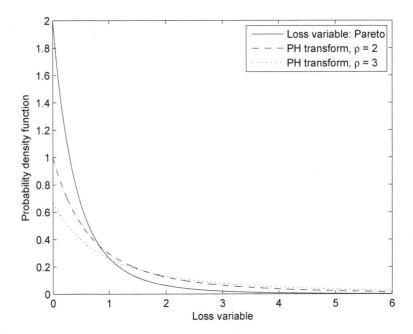

Figure 4.3 Probability density functions of $\mathcal{P}(4, 2)$ and its PH transforms

with mean

$$\mu_X = \frac{\gamma}{\alpha - 1}.$$

The sf of $\tilde{X}$ is

$$S_{\tilde{X}}(x) = [S_X(x)]^{\frac{1}{\rho}} = \left(\frac{\gamma}{\gamma + x}\right)^{\frac{\alpha}{\rho}},$$

so that $\tilde{X} \sim \mathcal{P}(\alpha/\rho, \gamma)$. Hence, the mean of $\tilde{X}$ (the risk-adjusted premium) is

$$\mu_{\tilde{X}} = \frac{\gamma}{\frac{\alpha}{\rho} - 1} = \frac{\rho\gamma}{\alpha - \rho} > \frac{\gamma}{\alpha - 1} = \mu_X.$$

Figure 4.3 plots the pdf of $X \sim \mathcal{P}(4, 2)$ and its PH transform for $\rho = 2$ and 3. It can be seen that the PH transforms have thicker tails than the original loss distribution. □

It can be shown that $\mu_{\tilde{X}}$ as a risk measure satisfies the properties of positive homogeneity, monotonicity and translational invariance. It also has the property of no ripoff. Readers are invited to prove these results (see Exercise 4.4). By virtue of Theorem 4.1 presented later, it is also subadditive. Hence, the PH risk measure is coherent.

4.5.2 Esscher Transform and Risk-Adjusted Premium

The PH transform puts more weights on the right-hand tail of the loss distribution through the transformed sf. An alternative method to shift the weights to the right is to transform the pdf directly. Thus, if X has pdf $f_X(x)$, we may define a loss distribution $\tilde{X}$ with pdf $f_{\tilde{X}}(x)$ by

$$f_{\tilde{X}}(x) = w(x)f_X(x). \tag{4.31}$$

To put more weights on the right-hand tail of the loss distribution, we require $w'(x)$ to be positive and, in addition, $f_{\tilde{X}}(x)$ must be a well-defined pdf. Thus, we consider the following weighting function

$$w(x) = \frac{e^{\rho x}}{M_X(\rho)} = \frac{e^{\rho x}}{\int_0^\infty e^{\rho x}f_X(x)\,dx}, \qquad \rho > 0, \tag{4.32}$$

where

$$M_X(\rho) = \int_0^\infty e^{\rho x}f_X(x)\,dx = \mathrm{E}(e^{\rho X}) \tag{4.33}$$

is the mgf of X. It is easy to see that

$$w'(x) = \frac{\rho e^{\rho x}}{M_X(\rho)} > 0, \qquad \rho > 0, \tag{4.34}$$

and that

$$\int_0^\infty f_{\tilde{X}}(x)\,dx = \int_0^\infty w(x)f_X(x)\,dx = \int_0^\infty \left[\frac{e^{\rho x}}{\int_0^\infty e^{\rho x}f_X(x)\,dx}\right]f_X(x)\,dx = 1. \tag{4.35}$$

Thus,

$$f_{\tilde{X}}(x) = \frac{e^{\rho x}f_X(x)}{\int_0^\infty e^{\rho x}f_X(x)\,dx} = \frac{e^{\rho x}f_X(x)}{M_X(\rho)}, \qquad \rho > 0, \tag{4.36}$$

is a well-defined pdf. The distribution of $\tilde{X}$ defined by the pdf in equation (4.36) is called the **Esscher transform** of X with parameter ρ. A risk measure based on the premium principle can be constructed as the expected value of the Esscher transform of X, i.e., the risk-adjusted premium. Specifically, we define the Esscher premium as

$$\varrho(X) = \mathrm{E}(\tilde{X}) = \mu_{\tilde{X}} = \int_0^\infty xf_{\tilde{X}}(x)\,dx = \frac{\int_0^\infty xe^{\rho x}f_X(x)\,dx}{M_X(\rho)} = \frac{\mathrm{E}(Xe^{\rho X})}{\mathrm{E}(e^{\rho X})}. \tag{4.37}$$

It can be shown that $d\varrho(X)/d\rho \geq 0$ (see Denuit *et al.*, 2005, Section 2.5.5) so that ρ can be interpreted as the risk-aversion index. To identify the distribution of $\tilde{X}$, we may use its mgf, which is given by

$$M_{\tilde{X}}(t) = \mathrm{E}(e^{t\tilde{X}}) = \int_0^\infty e^{tx}f_{\tilde{X}}(x)\,dx = \frac{\int_0^\infty e^{tx}e^{\rho x}f_X(x)\,dx}{M_X(\rho)} = \frac{M_X(\rho + t)}{M_X(\rho)}. \tag{4.38}$$

Example 4.9 If $X \sim \mathcal{E}(\lambda)$, calculate the Esscher transform of X with parameter $\rho \in (0, \lambda)$ and the risk-adjusted premium.

Solution 4.9 From equation (2.26) the mgf $M_X(\rho)$ of X is

$$M_X(\rho) = \frac{\lambda}{\lambda - \rho},$$

so that the mgf $M_{\tilde{X}}(t)$ of the Esscher transform $\tilde{X}$ with parameter ρ is

$$M_{\tilde{X}}(t) = \frac{M_X(\rho + t)}{M_X(\rho)} = \frac{\lambda - \rho}{\lambda - \rho - t}.$$

Thus, $\tilde{X} \sim \mathcal{E}(\lambda - \rho)$. The risk-adjusted premium is

$$\varrho(X) = \mu_{\tilde{X}} = \frac{1}{\lambda - \rho} > \frac{1}{\lambda} = \mu_X. \qquad \square$$

We conclude this section by stating that the Esscher premium is subadditive, translational invariant and does not allow ripoff. However, this risk measure is not positively homogeneous and violates monotonicity. Thus, it is not coherent. Readers are invited to prove these results (see Exercise 4.5).

4.6 Distortion-Function Approach

The **distortion function** is a mathematical device to construct risk measures. We define below a distortion function and its associated risk measure, and then show that some of the risk measures we have discussed belong to this class of risk measures.

Definition 4.3 A distortion function is a nondecreasing function $g(\cdot)$ satisfying $g(1) = 1$ and $g(0) = 0$.

Suppose X is a loss random variable with sf $S_X(x)$. As the distortion function $g(\cdot)$ is nondecreasing and $S_X(\cdot)$ is nonincreasing, $g(S_X(x))$ is a nonincreasing function of x. This can be seen by noting that the derivative of $g(S_X(x))$ is (assuming $g(\cdot)$ is differentiable)

$$\frac{dg(S_X(x))}{dx} = g'(S_X(x))S_X'(x) \leq 0. \qquad (4.39)$$

Together with the property that $g(S_X(0)) = g(1) = 1$ and $g(S_X(\infty)) = g(0) = 0$, $g(S_X(x))$ is a well-defined sf over the support $[0, \infty)$. We denote the random variable with this sf as $\tilde{X}$, which may be interpreted as a risk-adjusted loss random variable, and $g(S_X(x))$ is the risk-adjusted sf.

We further assume that $g(\cdot)$ is concave down (i.e., $g''(x) \leq 0$ if the derivative exists), then the pdf of $\tilde{X}$ is

$$f_{\tilde{X}}(x) = -\frac{dg(S_X(x))}{dx} = g'(S_X(x))f_X(x), \tag{4.40}$$

and we note that

$$\frac{dg'(S_X(x))}{dx} = g''(S_X(x))S_X'(x) \geq 0. \tag{4.41}$$

Thus, $g'(S_X(x))$ is nondecreasing. Comparing equation (4.40) with equation (4.31), we can interpret $g'(S_X(x))$ as the weighting function to *scale up* the pdf of the loss at the right-hand tail.

Definition 4.4 Let X be a nonnegative loss random variable. The distortion risk measure based on the distortion function $g(\cdot)$, denoted by $\varrho(X)$, is defined as

$$\varrho(X) = \int_0^\infty g(S_X(x)) \, dx. \tag{4.42}$$

Thus, the distortion risk measure $\varrho(X)$ is the mean of the risk-adjusted loss $\tilde{X}$. The class of distortion risk measures include the following measures we have discussed.[8]

Pure Premium Risk Measure
This can be seen easily by defining

$$g(u) = u, \tag{4.43}$$

which satisfies the conditions $g(0) = 0$ and $g(1) = 1$, and $g(\cdot)$ is nondecreasing. Now

$$\varrho(X) = \int_0^\infty g(S_X(x)) \, dx = \int_0^\infty S_X(x) \, dx = \mu_X, \tag{4.44}$$

which is the pure premium risk measure.

Proportional Hazard Risk-Adjusted Premium Risk Measure
This can be seen by defining

$$g(u) = u^{\frac{1}{\rho}}, \qquad \rho \geq 1. \tag{4.45}$$

VaR Risk Measure
For VaR_δ we define the distortion function as

$$g(S_X(x)) = \begin{cases} 0, & \text{for } 0 \leq S_X(x) < 1 - \delta, \\ 1, & \text{for } 1 - \delta \leq S_X(x) \leq 1, \end{cases} \tag{4.46}$$

---

[8] More examples of distortion risk measures can be found in Wirch and Hardy (1999).

which is equivalent to

$$g(S_X(x)) = \begin{cases} 0, & \text{for } x > \text{VaR}_\delta, \\ 1, & \text{for } 0 \leq x \leq \text{VaR}_\delta. \end{cases} \tag{4.47}$$

Hence,

$$\varrho(X) = \int_0^\infty g(S_X(x))\, dx = \int_0^{\text{VaR}_\delta} dx = \text{VaR}_\delta. \tag{4.48}$$

CTE Risk Measure

For CTE$_\delta$, we define the distortion function as (subject to the condition X is continuous)

$$g(S_X(x)) = \begin{cases} \dfrac{S_X(x)}{1-\delta}, & \text{for } 0 \leq S_X(x) < 1-\delta, \\[2mm] 1, & \text{for } 1-\delta \leq S_X(x) \leq 1, \end{cases} \tag{4.49}$$

which is equivalent to

$$g(S_X(x)) = \begin{cases} \dfrac{S_X(x)}{1-\delta}, & \text{for } x > x_\delta, \\[2mm] 1, & \text{for } 0 \leq x \leq x_\delta. \end{cases} \tag{4.50}$$

Hence,

$$\varrho(X) = \int_0^\infty g(S_X(x))\, dx = \int_0^{x_\delta} dx + \int_{x_\delta}^\infty \frac{S_X(x)}{1-\delta}\, dx = x_\delta + \int_{x_\delta}^\infty \frac{S_X(x)}{1-\delta}\, dx. \tag{4.51}$$

Now using integration by parts, we have

$$\int_{x_\delta}^\infty S_X(x)\, dx = xS_X(x)]_{x_\delta}^\infty + \int_{x_\delta}^\infty xf_X(x)\, dx$$

$$= -x_\delta(1-\delta) + \int_{x_\delta}^\infty xf_X(x)\, dx. \tag{4.52}$$

Substituting equation (4.52) into equation (4.51), we obtain

$$\varrho(X) = \frac{1}{1-\delta}\int_{x_\delta}^\infty xf_X(x)\, dx, \tag{4.53}$$

which is equal to CTE$_\delta$ by equation (4.17).

Risk measures based on distortion functions form a very important class. This approach is very easy to use to create new risk measures. More importantly, this class of risk measures have very desirable properties, as summarized in the following theorem.

Theorem 4.1 *Let $g(\cdot)$ be a concave-down distortion function. The risk measure of the loss X defined in equation* (4.42) *is translational invariant, monotonic, positively homogeneous and subadditive, and is thus coherent.*[9]

Proof See Denuit *et al.* (2005, Section 2.6.2.2). □

4.7 Wang Transform

Wang (2000) proposed the following distortion function

$$g(u) = \Phi \left[\Phi^{-1}(u) + \rho \right], \qquad (4.54)$$

where $\Phi(\cdot)$ is the df of the standard normal and ρ is the risk parameter taking positive values. Note that $\Phi(\cdot)$ is only used to define the transform and no normality assumption is made for the loss distribution. Equation (4.54) is known as the Wang transform.

We can easily verify that $g(0) = 0$ and $g(1) = 1$. In addition, denoting $\varphi(\cdot)$ as the pdf of the standard normal and $x = \Phi^{-1}(u)$, we have

$$\frac{dg(u)}{du} = \frac{\varphi(x+\rho)}{\varphi(x)} = \exp\left(-\rho x - \frac{\rho^2}{2}\right) > 0, \qquad (4.55)$$

and

$$\frac{d^2 g(u)}{du^2} = -\frac{\rho \varphi(x+\rho)}{[\varphi(x)]^2} < 0. \qquad (4.56)$$

Thus, the Wang transform is increasing and concave down. Denoting $\tilde{X}$ as the Wang-transformed variable of the loss distribution X, the risk measure of X based on the Wang transform is defined as the risk-adjusted premium

$$\varrho(X) = E(\tilde{X}) = \int_0^\infty \Phi \left[\Phi^{-1}(S_X(x)) + \rho \right] dx. \qquad (4.57)$$

It can be seen that

$$\frac{d\varrho(X)}{d\rho} = \int_0^\infty \varphi \left[\Phi^{-1}(S_X(x)) + \rho \right] dx > 0. \qquad (4.58)$$

This implies the risk measure $\varrho(X)$ increases with ρ, which represents the risk aversion.

Example 4.10 If $X \sim \mathcal{N}(\mu, \sigma^2)$, find the distribution of the loss under the Wang transform, and the risk-adjusted premium.

---

[9] Note that VaR$_\delta$ is a step function and is thus not concave-down. In contrast, CTE$_\delta$ is concave-down. See Wirch and Hardy (1999).

Solution 4.10 The sf of X is

$$S_X(x) = 1 - \Phi\left(\frac{x - \mu}{\sigma}\right) = \Phi\left(-\frac{x - \mu}{\sigma}\right).$$

The sf of the Wang-transformed variable $\tilde{X}$ is

$$
\begin{aligned}
S_{\tilde{X}}(x) &= g(S_X(x)) \\
&= \Phi\left[\Phi^{-1}(S_X(x)) + \rho\right] \\
&= \Phi\left[\Phi^{-1}\left(\Phi\left(-\frac{x - \mu}{\sigma}\right)\right) + \rho\right] \\
&= \Phi\left[\left(-\frac{x - \mu}{\sigma}\right) + \rho\right] \\
&= \Phi\left[-\frac{x - (\mu + \rho\sigma)}{\sigma}\right] \\
&= 1 - \Phi\left[\frac{x - (\mu + \rho\sigma)}{\sigma}\right].
\end{aligned}
$$

Thus, $\tilde{X} \sim \mathcal{N}(\mu + \rho\sigma, \sigma^2)$ and the risk-adjusted premium is $\varrho(X) = \mathrm{E}(\tilde{X}) = \mu + \rho\sigma$. $\qquad\square$

Example 4.11 If $X \sim \mathcal{L}(\mu, \sigma^2)$, find the distribution of the loss under the Wang transform, and the risk-adjusted premium.

Solution 4.11 The sf of X is

$$S_X(x) = 1 - \Phi\left[\frac{\log x - \mu}{\sigma}\right] = \Phi\left[-\frac{\log x - \mu}{\sigma}\right].$$

The sf of the Wang-transformed variable $\tilde{X}$ is

$$
\begin{aligned}
S_{\tilde{X}}(x) &= g(S_X(x)) \\
&= \Phi\left[\Phi^{-1}\left(\Phi\left[-\frac{\log x - \mu}{\sigma}\right]\right) + \rho\right] \\
&= \Phi\left[-\frac{\log x - \mu}{\sigma} + \rho\right] \\
&= 1 - \Phi\left[\frac{\log x - (\mu + \rho\sigma)}{\sigma}\right].
\end{aligned}
$$

Thus, $\tilde{X} \sim \mathcal{L}(\mu + \rho\sigma, \sigma^2)$ and the risk-adjusted premium is

$$\varrho(X) = \mathrm{E}(\tilde{X}) = \exp\left(\mu + \rho\sigma + \frac{\sigma^2}{2}\right). \qquad\square$$

Examples 4.10 and 4.11 show that the Wang-transformed loss remains in the same family of the original loss distribution for the case of normal and lognormal losses. Another advantage of the Wang transform is that it can be applied to measure risks of assets as well, in which case ρ will take negative values. More details of this can be found in Wang (2000).

4.8 Summary and Conclusions

We have discussed the uses of risk measures for insurance business. The risk measures may be constructed for the determination of economic capital or for setting insurance premium. The four axioms of desirable properties proposed by Artzner *et al.* (1999) help to narrow down the choice of risk measures, although they do not specifically identify a unique choice. Risk measures satisfying these axioms are said to be coherent. A class of risk measures that are coherent are those constructed based on concave-down distortion functions. This class of risk measures include the conditional tail expectation, the PH transform risk-adjusted premium and the Wang transform risk-adjusted premium. On the other hand, the commonly used risk measure Value-at-Risk is not coherent.

Many distortion functions depend on a risk-aversion parameter, which in turn determines the risk-adjusted premium. Theory is often unable to identify the risk-aversion parameter. Some recent works (Jones *et al.*, 2006, and Jones and Zitikis, 2007) consider the estimation of the risk-aversion parameter, and test the equality of the risk measures.

Quantile-based risk measures have received much attention since the emergence of VaR. In the actuarial science and risk management literature, however, the terminologies for quantile-based risk measures such as VaR, CVaR and CTE have not been standardized. Further details and extensions can be found in Denuit *et al.* (2005) and Dowd and Blake (2006).

Exercises

Exercise 4.1 When the loss random variable X is not continuous, show that $\text{CTE}_\delta(X)$ computed according to equation (4.20) is larger than or equal to $\text{TVaR}_\delta(X)$ given in equation (4.23).

Exercise 4.2 Prove that the risk measure based on the variance premium satisfies Axiom T, but not Axioms S, M and PH.

Exercise 4.3 Prove that the risk measure based on the standard-deviation premium satisfies Axioms S, T and PH, but not Axiom M.

Exercise 4.4 Prove that the risk measure based on the expected value of the PH transform satisfies Axioms PH, M and T. It also has the property of no ripoff.

Exercise 4.5 Prove that the risk measure based on the Esscher premium satisfies Axioms S and T, but not M and PH.

Exercise 4.6 Let X be a nonnegative loss random variable distributed as $\mathcal{G}(\alpha, \beta)$. Find the Esscher premium risk measure with risk parameter ρ, where $\rho \in [0, 1/\beta)$.

Exercise 4.7 Let $X \sim \mathcal{W}(\alpha, \lambda)$. Determine $\text{VaR}_\delta(X)$ and the PH premium with parameter ρ.

Exercise 4.8 Suppose $c \in (0, 1)$ and the df of the loss random variable X is $F_X(x) = cx$ for $x \in [0, 1)$ and 1 when $x \geq 1$.

(a) Plot the df of X.
(b) Compute $E(X)$.
(c) Determine $\text{Var}_\delta(X)$ for $\delta \in (0, 1)$.
(d) Determine $\text{CTE}_\delta(X)$ for $\delta \in (0, c)$.

Exercise 4.9 The loss random variable X has the following pf:

x	$f_X(x)$
60	0.04
50	0.04
40	0.22
30	0.30
20	0.30
10	0.10

Calculate $\text{VaR}_\delta(X)$ for $\delta = 0.90, 0.95$ and 0.99, and $\text{CTE}_\delta(X)$ for $\delta = 0.90$ and 0.95.

Exercise 4.10 Calculate the risk-adjusted premium risk measure of the PH transform with risk-aversion index ρ for the following loss distributions:

(a) $\mathcal{U}(0, 2b)$,
(b) $\mathcal{E}(1/b)$,
(c) $\mathcal{P}(2, b)$,

where $b > 0$ and $1 < \rho < 2$. Note that all the above distributions have expected loss b. Now consider $\rho = 1.2, 1.5$ and 1.8, and compute the PH premium for the above loss distributions as a function of b. Comment on your results.

Exercise 4.11 Let $X \sim \mathcal{U}(0, b)$.

(a) Determine the pure premium and the expected-value premium with loading θ.

(b) Determine the variance premium and standard-deviation premium with loading α.

(c) Determine $\text{VaR}_\delta(X)$, and calculate $\text{CTE}_\delta(X)$ using equation (4.19).

(d) Calculate $\text{CTE}_\delta(X)$ using equation (4.17) and verify that the answer is the same as in (c).

(e) Calculate $\text{CVaR}_\delta(X)$ using equation (4.12) and $\text{TVaR}_\delta(X)$ using equation (4.23).

Exercise 4.12 Let $X \sim \mathcal{E}(\lambda)$.

(a) Determine the pure premium and the expected-value premium with loading θ.

(b) Determine the variance premium and standard-deviation premium with loading α.

(c) Determine $\text{VaR}_\delta(X)$, and calculate $\text{CTE}_\delta(X)$ using equation (4.19).

(d) Calculate $\text{CTE}_\delta(X)$ using equation (4.17) and verify that the answer is the same as in (c).

(e) Calculate $\text{CVaR}_\delta(X)$ using equation (4.12) and $\text{TVaR}_\delta(X)$ using equation (4.23).

Exercise 4.13 If loss follows a compound Poisson distribution with parameter λ and $\mathcal{G}(\alpha, \beta)$ as the secondary distribution, determine the expected-value premium with a loading of 20%. If the same premium is charged under the variance principle, what is the loading used?

Exercise 4.14 If loss follows a compound Poisson distribution with parameter λ and $\mathcal{G}(\alpha, \beta)$ as the secondary distribution, determine the Esscher premium with parameter ρ.

Exercise 4.15 Losses X and Y have the following distribution:

$$\Pr(X = 0, Y = 0) = \Pr(X = 0, Y = 3) = \Pr(X = 6, Y = 6) = \frac{1}{3}.$$

Show that $\Pr(X \leq Y) = 1$, but that the Esscher premium of X with parameter 0.5 is larger than that of Y.

Exercise 4.16 The losses in two portfolios, denoted by P_1 and P_2, have identical distributions of 100 with probability 4% and zero with probability 96%. Suppose P_1 and P_2 are independent.

(a) Determine $\text{VaR}_{0.95}(P_1)$ and $\text{VaR}_{0.95}(P_2)$.

(b) Determine the distribution of $P_1 + P_2$.

(c) Calculate $\text{VaR}_{0.95}(P_1 + P_2)$ and $\text{VaR}_{0.95}(P_1) + \text{VaR}_{0.95}(P_2)$. Comment on your results.

Exercise 4.17 The loss random variable X has the following pf:

x	$f_X(x)$
500	0.08
400	0.12
300	0.35
200	0.45

Calculate $\text{VaR}_{0.9}(X)$, $\text{CTE}_{0.9}(X)$, $\text{CVaR}_{0.9}(X)$ and $\text{TVaR}_{0.9}(X)$.

Exercise 4.18 Let $X \sim \mathcal{N}(\mu, \sigma^2)$. Show that

$$E\left[(X - x_\delta)_+\right] = \sigma\varphi\left(\Phi^{-1}(\delta)\right) - \sigma\Phi^{-1}(\delta)(1 - \delta),$$

for $0 < \delta < 1$. Note that the expression on the right-hand side depends on σ and δ only.

Exercise 4.19 Let $X \sim \mathcal{L}(\mu, \sigma^2)$. Show that

$$E\left[(X - x_\delta)_+\right] = \exp\left(\mu + \frac{\sigma^2}{2}\right) \Phi\left(\sigma - \Phi^{-1}(\delta)\right) - \exp\left(\mu + \sigma\Phi^{-1}(\delta)\right)(1 - \delta),$$

for $0 < \delta < 1$.

Exercise 4.20 U and V are two loss distributions. The sf of U is $S_U(x) = 0.25$ for $0 \le x < 4$ and zero for $4 \le x$. The sf of V is $S_V(x) = (2/(2+x))^3$.

(a) Show that $E(U) = E(V) = 1$, and $\text{Var}(U) = \text{Var}(V) = 3$.
(b) Determine the PH risk-adjusted premium of U and V with parameter $\rho < 3$.

5

Ruin Theory

We consider models for analyzing the surplus of an insurance portfolio. Suppose an insurance business begins with a start-up capital, called the initial surplus. The insurance company receives premium payments and pays claim losses. The premium payments are assumed to be coming in at a constant rate. When there are claims, losses are paid out to policyholders. Unlike the constant premium payments, losses are random and uncertain, in both timing and amount. The net surplus through time is the excess of the initial capital and aggregate premiums received over the losses paid out. The insurance business is in ruin if the surplus falls to or below zero. The main purpose of this chapter is to consider the probability of ruin as a function of time, the initial surplus and the claim distribution. Ultimate ruin refers to the situation where in ruin occurs at finite time, irrespective of the time of occurrence.

We consider the situation in which premium payments and claim losses occur at discrete time. We derive recursive formulas for the probability of ultimate ruin given the initial surplus. These recursive formulas require the value of the probability of ultimate ruin when the start-up capital is zero. Formulas for the probability of ruin before fixed finite times are also derived. To obtain bounds for the probability of ultimate ruin, we introduce Lundberg's inequality.

Ruin probabilities are measures of risk. They express risk as a dynamic process and relate ruin to the counteracting factors of premium rates and claim-loss distributions. Our discussions, however, will be restricted only to discrete-time models.

Learning Objectives

1 Surplus function, premium rate and loss process
2 Probability of ultimate ruin
3 Probability of ruin before a finite time
4 Adjustment coefficient and Lundberg's inequality

5.1 Discrete-Time Surplus and Events of Ruin

We assume that an insurance company establishes its business with a start-up capital of u at time 0, called the **initial surplus**. It receives premiums of one unit per period at the end of each period. Loss claim of amount X_i is paid out at the end of period i for $i = 1, 2, \ldots$. We assume X_i are independently and identically distributed as the loss random variable X. Thus, we have a discrete-time model in which the **surplus** at time n with initial capital u, denoted by $U(n; u)$, is given by[1]

$$U(n; u) = u + n - \sum_{i=1}^{n} X_i, \qquad \text{for } n = 1, 2, \ldots. \tag{5.1}$$

Note that the *numeraire* of the above equation is the amount of premium per period, or the premium rate. All other variables are measured as multiples of the premium rate. Thus, the initial surplus u may take values of $0, 1, \ldots$, times the premium rate. Likewise, X_i may take values of j times the premium rate with pf $f_X(j)$ for $j = 0, 1, \ldots$. We denote the mean of X by μ_X and its variance by σ_X^2. Furthermore, we assume X is of finite support, although in notation we allow j to run to infinity.

If we denote the premium loading by θ, then we have

$$1 = (1 + \theta)\mu_X, \tag{5.2}$$

which implies

$$\mu_X = \frac{1}{1 + \theta}. \tag{5.3}$$

We shall assume positive loading so that $\mu_X < 1$. Also, we have a model in which expenses and time value of money are not considered. The business is said to be in **ruin** if the surplus function $U(n; u)$ falls to or below zero sometime after the business started, i.e., at a point $n \geq 1$. Specifically, we have the following definition of ruin.

Definition 5.1 Ruin occurs at time n if $U(n; u) \leq 0$ for the first time at n, for $n \geq 1$.

Note that an insurance business may begin with zero start-up capital. According to the above definition, the insurance business is not in ruin at time 0 even if the initial surplus is zero. A main purpose of the model is to analyze the surplus

---

[1] We may regard the premium and the loss as the total amount received and paid, respectively, over each period. Surplus is only computed at the end of each period, and equation (5.1) is appropriate as there is no interest in our model.

and the probability of ruin. Given the initial surplus u, we define $T(u)$ as the **time of ruin** as follows.

Definition 5.2 The time-of-ruin random variable $T(u)$ is defined as

$$T(u) = \min \{n \geq 1 : U(n; u) \leq 0\}. \tag{5.4}$$

As long as there exists a finite n such that $U(n; u) \leq 0$, the event of ruin has occurred. However, for some realizations, such a finite value of n may not exist, in which case ruin does not occur. Thus, $T(u)$ may not have a finite value and is, in this sense, an *improper* random variable. A key interest in analyzing the surplus function is to find the probability that $T(u)$ has a finite value, i.e., the **probability of ultimate ruin**.

Definition 5.3 Given an initial surplus u, the probability of ultimate ruin, denoted by $\psi(u)$, is

$$\psi(u) = \Pr(T(u) < \infty). \tag{5.5}$$

Apart from the probability of ultimate ruin, it may also be of interest to find the probability of ruin at or before a finite time. We define the probability of ruin at or before a finite time as follows.

Definition 5.4 Given an initial surplus u, the probability of ruin by time t, denoted by $\psi(t; u)$, is

$$\psi(t; u) = \Pr(T(u) \leq t), \qquad \text{for } t = 1, 2, \ldots. \tag{5.6}$$

Both $\psi(u)$ and $\psi(t; u)$ are important measures of the risks of ruin. In the following section, we present some recursive methods for the computation of these functions and some bounds for their values in discrete time.

5.2 Discrete-Time Ruin Theory

In this section we first derive recursive formulas for the computation of the probability of ultimate ruin. We then consider the calculation of the probability of ruin by a finite time, and finally we derive the Lundberg inequality in discrete time.

5.2.1 Ultimate Ruin in Discrete Time

We first consider the probability of ultimate ruin when the initial surplus is 0, i.e., $\psi(0)$. At time 1, if there is no claim, which occurs with probability $f_X(0)$, then the surplus accumulates to 1 and the probability of ultimate ruin is $\psi(1)$. On the other hand, if $X_1 \geq 1$, which occurs with probability $S_X(0) = 1 - F_X(0) = \Pr(X \geq 1)$, then the business ends in ruin. Thus, we have

$$\psi(0) = f_X(0)\psi(1) + S_X(0), \tag{5.7}$$

from which $\psi(1)$ can be computed given $\psi(0)$. Similarly, for $u = 1$, we have

$$\psi(1) = f_X(0)\psi(2) + f_X(1)\psi(1) + S_X(1). \tag{5.8}$$

The above equation can be generalized to larger values of u as follows

$$\psi(u) = f_X(0)\psi(u+1) + \sum_{j=1}^{u} f_X(j)\psi(u+1-j) + S_X(u), \qquad \text{for } u \geq 1. \tag{5.9}$$

Rearranging equation (5.9), we obtain the following recursive formula for the probability of ultimate ruin

$$\psi(u+1) = \frac{1}{f_X(0)} \left[\psi(u) - \sum_{j=1}^{u} f_X(j)\psi(u+1-j) - S_X(u) \right], \qquad \text{for } u \geq 1. \tag{5.10}$$

To apply the above equation we need the starting value $\psi(0)$, which is given by the following theorem.

Theorem 5.1 *For the discrete-time surplus model,* $\psi(0) = \mu_X$.

Proof We first rearrange equation (5.7) to obtain

$$f_X(0) \left[\psi(1) - \psi(0) \right] = \left[1 - f_X(0) \right] \psi(0) - S_X(0), \tag{5.11}$$

and equation (5.9) to obtain

$$f_X(0) \left[\psi(u+1) - \psi(u) \right] = \left[1 - f_X(0) \right] \psi(u)$$
$$- \sum_{j=1}^{u} f_X(j)\psi(u+1-j) - S_X(u), \quad \text{for } u \geq 1. \tag{5.12}$$

Now adding equations (5.11) and (5.12) for $u = 0, \ldots, z$, we obtain

$$f_X(0) \sum_{u=0}^{z} \left[\psi(u+1) - \psi(u) \right] = \left[1 - f_X(0) \right] \sum_{u=0}^{z} \psi(u)$$
$$- \sum_{u=1}^{z} \sum_{j=1}^{u} f_X(j)\psi(u+1-j) - \sum_{u=0}^{z} S_X(u), \tag{5.13}$$

the left-hand side of which can be written as

$$f_X(0) \left[\psi(z+1) - \psi(0) \right]. \tag{5.14}$$

We now simplify the second term on the right-hand side of equation (5.13) as

$$\sum_{u=1}^{z}\sum_{j=1}^{u} f_X(j)\psi(u+1-j) = \sum_{u=1}^{z}\sum_{r=1}^{u} f_X(u+1-r)\psi(r)$$

$$= \sum_{r=1}^{z}\psi(r)\sum_{u=r}^{z} f_X(u+1-r)$$

$$= \sum_{r=1}^{z}\psi(r)\sum_{u=1}^{z+1-r} f_X(u), \tag{5.15}$$

where in the first line above we have applied the change of index $r = u + 1 - j$, and in the second line we have reversed the order of the summation indexes u and r. Now substituting equation (5.15) into (5.13), we have

$$f_X(0)[\psi(z+1) - \psi(0)] = [1 - f_X(0)]\sum_{u=0}^{z}\psi(u) - \sum_{r=1}^{z}\psi(r)\sum_{u=1}^{z+1-r} f_X(u) - \sum_{u=0}^{z} S_X(u)$$

$$= [1 - f_X(0)]\,\psi(0) + \sum_{r=1}^{z}\psi(r)\left[1 - \sum_{u=0}^{z+1-r} f_X(u)\right] - \sum_{u=0}^{z} S_X(u)$$

$$= [1 - f_X(0)]\,\psi(0) + \sum_{r=1}^{z}\psi(r)S_X(z+1-r) - \sum_{u=0}^{z} S_X(u). \tag{5.16}$$

Now $\psi(z+1) \to 0$ as $z \to \infty$, and as X is of finite support, we have

$$\sum_{r=1}^{z}\psi(r)S_X(z+1-r) \to 0 \tag{5.17}$$

when $z \to \infty$. Thus, when $z \to \infty$, we conclude from equation (5.16) that

$$-f_X(0)\psi(0) = [1 - f_X(0)]\,\psi(0) - \sum_{u=0}^{\infty} S_X(u), \tag{5.18}$$

so that

$$\psi(0) = \sum_{u=0}^{\infty} S_X(u) = \mu_X, \tag{5.19}$$

where the last equality of the above equation is due to the discrete analog of equation (2.18). □

Example 5.1 The claim variable X has the following distribution: $f_X(0) = 0.5$, $f_X(1) = f_X(2) = 0.2$ and $f_X(3) = 0.1$. Calculate the probability of ultimate ruin $\psi(u)$ for $u \geq 0$.

Solution 5.1 The survival function of X is $S_X(0) = 0.2 + 0.2 + 0.1 = 0.5$, $S_X(1) = 0.2 + 0.1 = 0.3$, $S_X(2) = 0.1$ and $S_X(u) = 0$ for $u \geq 3$. The mean of X is

$$\mu_X = (0)(0.5) + (1)(0.2) + (2)(0.2) + (3)(0.1) = 0.9,$$

which can also be calculated as

$$\mu_X = \sum_{u=0}^{\infty} S_X(u) = 0.5 + 0.3 + 0.1 = 0.9.$$

Thus, from Theorem 5.1 $\psi(0) = 0.9$, and from equation (5.7), $\psi(1)$ is given by

$$\psi(1) = \frac{\psi(0) - S_X(0)}{f_X(0)} = \frac{0.9 - 0.5}{0.5} = 0.8.$$

From equation (5.8), we have

$$\psi(2) = \frac{\psi(1) - f_X(1)\psi(1) - S_X(1)}{f_X(0)} = \frac{0.8 - (0.2)(0.8) - 0.3}{0.5} = 0.68,$$

and applying equation (5.10) for $u = 2$, we have

$$\psi(3) = \frac{\psi(2) - f_X(1)\psi(2) - f_X(2)\psi(1) - S_X(2)}{f_X(0)} = 0.568.$$

As $S_X(u) = 0$ for $u \geq 3$, using equation (5.10) we have, for $u \geq 3$,

$$\psi(u + 1) = \frac{\psi(u) - f_X(1)\psi(u) - f_X(2)\psi(u - 1) - f_X(3)\psi(u - 2)}{f_X(0)}.$$

Using the above recursive equation we compute $\psi(u)$ for u up to 30. The results are plotted in Figure 5.1, from which it is clear that $\psi(u)$ is a monotonic decreasing function of u. To obtain a probability of ultimate ruin of less than 1%, the initial surplus must be at least 26.   □

Example 5.2 The claim variable X can take values 0 or 2 with the following probabilities: $f_X(0) = p$ and $f_X(2) = q = 1 - p$, where $p > 0.5$. Calculate the probability of ultimate ruin $\psi(u)$ for $u \geq 0$.

Solution 5.2 The survival function of X is $S_X(0) = S_X(1) = q$ and $S_X(u) = 0$ for $u \geq 2$. Thus, $\psi(0) = \mu_X = S_X(0) + S_X(1) = 2q < 1$. For $u = 1$, we have, from equation (5.7),

$$\psi(1) = \frac{\psi(0) - S_X(0)}{f_X(0)} = \frac{2q - q}{p} = \frac{q}{p}.$$

When $u = 2$, we apply equation (5.10) to obtain

$$\psi(2) = \frac{\psi(1) - S_X(1)}{f_X(0)}$$

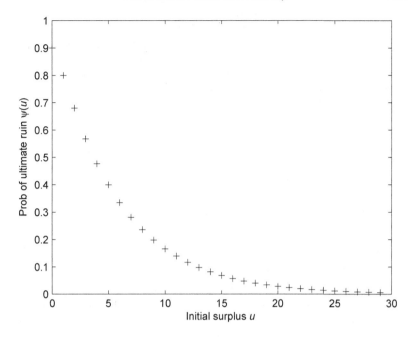

Figure 5.1 Probability of ultimate ruin in Example 5.1

$$= \frac{1}{p} \left(\frac{q}{p} - q \right)$$

$$= \left(\frac{q}{p} \right)^2 .$$

To derive a general formula for $\psi(u)$, we observe that

$$\psi(u) = \left(\frac{q}{p} \right)^u$$

holds for $u = 1$ and 2. Assuming the formula holds for $u - 1$ and u with $u \geq 2$, we can show that it also holds for $u + 1$. To do this we apply equation (5.10) to obtain

$$\psi(u + 1) = \frac{1}{f_X(0)} \left[\psi(u) - f_X(2)\psi(u - 1) \right]$$

$$= \frac{1}{p} \left[\left(\frac{q}{p} \right)^u - q \left(\frac{q}{p} \right)^{u-1} \right]$$

$$= \frac{1}{p} \left(\frac{q}{p} \right)^{u-1} \left(\frac{q}{p} - q \right)$$

$$= \left(\frac{q}{p} \right)^{u+1} .$$

Thus, the general formula is established by induction. $\qquad\square$

5.2.2 Finite-Time Ruin in Discrete Time

We now consider the probability of ruin at or before a finite time point t given an initial surplus u. First we consider $t = 1$ given initial surplus u. As defined in equation (5.6), $\psi(t; u) = \Pr(T(u) \leq t)$. If $u = 0$, the ruin event occurs at time $t = 1$ when $X_1 \geq 1$. Thus,

$$\psi(1; 0) = 1 - f_X(0) = S_X(0). \tag{5.20}$$

Likewise, for $u > 0$, we have

$$\psi(1; u) = \Pr(X_1 > u) = S_X(u). \tag{5.21}$$

Thus, $\psi(1; u)$ are easily obtained from equations (5.20) and (5.21) for $u \geq 0$. We now consider $\psi(t; u)$ for $t \geq 2$ and $u \geq 0$. Note that the event of ruin occurring at or before time $t \geq 2$ may be due to (a) ruin at time 1, or (b) loss of j at time 1 for $j = 0, 1, \ldots, u$, followed by ruin occurring within the next $t - 1$ periods. When there is a loss of j at time 1, the surplus becomes $u + 1 - j$ at time 1, so that the probability of ruin within the next $t - 1$ periods is $\psi(t - 1; u + 1 - j)$. Thus, we conclude that

$$\psi(t; u) = \psi(1; u) + \sum_{j=0}^{u} f_X(j)\psi(t - 1; u + 1 - j). \tag{5.22}$$

Hence, $\psi(t; u)$ can be computed as follows

1 Construct a table with time t running down the rows for $t = 1, 2, \ldots$, and u running across the columns for $u = 0, 1, \ldots$.
2 Initialize the first row of the table for $t = 1$ with $\psi(1; u) = S_X(u)$. Note that if M is the maximum loss in each period, then $\psi(1; u) = 0$ for $u \geq M$.
3 Increase the value of t by 1 and calculate $\psi(t; u)$ for $u = 0, 1, \ldots$, using equation (5.22). Note that the computation requires the corresponding entry in the first row of the table, i.e., $\psi(1; u)$, as well as some entries in the $(t-1)$th row. In particular, the $u+1$ entries $\psi(t-1; 1), \ldots, \psi(t-1; u+1)$ in the $(t-1)$th row are required.[2]
4 Re-do Step 3 until the desired time point.

The example below illustrates the computation of the probabilities.

Example 5.3 As in Example 5.1, the claim variable X has the following distribution: $f_X(0) = 0.5, f_X(1) = f_X(2) = 0.2$ and $f_X(3) = 0.1$. Calculate the probability of ruin at or before a finite time t given initial surplus u, $\psi(t; u)$, for $u \geq 0$.

---

[2] Note that if $f_X(j) = 0$ for $j > M$, we only require the entries $\psi(t-1; \max\{1, u+1-M\}), \ldots, \psi(t-1; u+1)$ in the $(t-1)$th row.

Table 5.1. *Results of Example 5.3*

Time t	0	1	2	3	4	5	6
				Initial surplus u			
1	0.500	0.300	0.100	0.000	0.000	0.000	0.000
2	0.650	0.410	0.180	0.050	0.010	0.000	0.000
3	0.705	0.472	0.243	0.092	0.030	0.007	0.001

Solution 5.3 The results are summarized in Table 5.1 for $t = 1, 2$ and 3, and $u = 0, 1, \ldots, 6$.

The first row of the table is $S_X(u)$. Note that $\psi(1; u) = 0$ for $u \geq 3$, as the maximum loss in each period is 3. For the second row, the details of the computation are as follows. First, $\psi(2; 0)$ is computed as

$$\psi(2; 0) = \psi(1; 0) + f_X(0)\psi(1; 1) = 0.5 + (0.5)(0.3) = 0.65.$$

Similarly,

$$\psi(2; 1) = \psi(1; 1) + f_X(0)\psi(1; 2) + f_X(1)\psi(1; 1) = 0.3 + (0.5)(0.1) + (0.2)(0.3) = 0.41,$$

and

$$\psi(2; 2) = \psi(1; 2) + f_X(0)\psi(1; 3) + f_X(1)\psi(1; 2) + f_X(2)\psi(1; 1) = 0.18.$$

We use $\psi(3; 3)$ to illustrate the computation of the third row as follows

$$\begin{aligned}
\psi(3; 3) &= \psi(1; 3) + f_X(0)\psi(2; 4) + f_X(1)\psi(2; 3) + f_X(2)\psi(2; 2) + f_X(3)\psi(2; 1) \\
&= 0 + (0.5)(0.01) + (0.2)(0.05) + (0.2)(0.18) + (0.1)(0.41) \\
&= 0.092.
\end{aligned}$$

Figure 5.2 plots the probabilities of ruin given three values of initial surplus, $u = 0, 5$ and 10. $\qquad\square$

5.2.3 Lundberg's Inequality in Discrete Time

The recursive formulas presented in the last two sections compute the exact probability of ruin given the initial surplus. We now introduce the Lundberg inequality, which provides an upper bound for the probability of ultimate ruin as long as the mgf of the loss distribution exists. Prior to stating the Lundberg inequality, however, we first define an important quantity called the **adjustment coefficient** as follows.

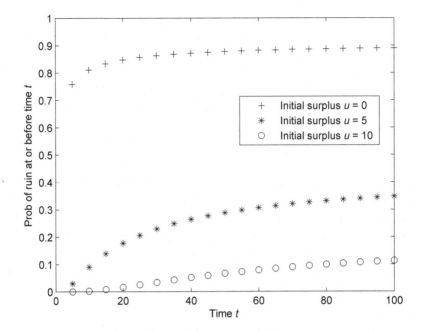

Figure 5.2 Probability of ruin by a finite time in Example 5.3

Definition 5.5 Suppose X is the loss random variable. The adjustment coefficient, denoted by r^*, is the positive value of r that satisfies the following equation

$$\mathrm{E}\left[\exp\left\{r(X-1)\right\}\right] = 1. \tag{5.23}$$

Note that $\mathrm{E}\left[\exp\left\{r(X-1)\right\}\right]$ is the mgf of $X-1$ (i.e., the deficit per period) evaluated at r, or $M_{X-1}(r)$. To show that a positive root r^* exists, we first define the function $\varphi(r)$ as follows

$$\varphi(r) = \mathrm{E}\left[\exp\left\{r(X-1)\right\}\right]. \tag{5.24}$$

Now we note the following properties of $\varphi(r)$

1 $\varphi(0) = 1$ and $\varphi(r)$ is decreasing at $r = 0$. The latter result arises from the fact that

$$\varphi'(r) = \mathrm{E}\left[(X-1)\exp\left\{r(X-1)\right\}\right], \tag{5.25}$$

so that

$$\varphi'(0) = \mathrm{E}\left[X-1\right] = \mu_X - 1 < 0. \tag{5.26}$$

2 $\varphi(r)$ is concave upward for $r > 0$, as

$$\varphi''(r) = \mathrm{E}\left[(X-1)^2 \exp\left\{r(X-1)\right\}\right] > 0, \qquad \text{for } r > 0. \tag{5.27}$$

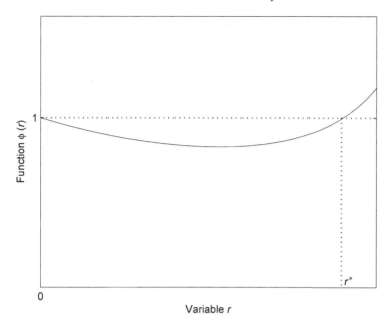

Figure 5.3 A plot of $\varphi(r)$

Furthermore, suppose there exits $x^* > 1$, such that $\Pr(X \geq x^*) > 0$. Then $\varphi(r) \geq e^{r(x^*-1)} \Pr(X \geq x^*)$, which tends to ∞ as r tends to ∞. These results show that the typical shape of $\varphi(r)$ is as in Figure 5.3, for which there is a unique value $r^* > 0$ satisfying equation $\varphi(r^*) = 1$ for the existence of the adjustment coefficient.

Example 5.4 Assume the loss random variable X follows the distribution given in Examples 5.1 and 5.3. Calculate the adjustment coefficient r^*.

Solution 5.4 Equation (5.23) is set up as follows

$$0.5e^{-r} + 0.2 + 0.2e^r + 0.1e^{2r} = 1,$$

which is equivalent to

$$0.1w^3 + 0.2w^2 - 0.8w + 0.5 = 0,$$

for $w = e^r$. We solve the above equation numerically to obtain $w = 1.1901$, so that $r^* = \log(1.1901) = 0.1740$.   □

We now state Lundberg's inequality in the following theorem.

Theorem 5.2 *For the discrete-time surplus function, the probability of ultimate ruin satisfies the following inequality*

$$\psi(u) \le \exp(-r^* u), \tag{5.28}$$

where r^* is the adjustment coefficient.

Proof We shall show that all finite-time ruin probabilities satisfy inequality (5.28), i.e.,

$$\psi(t; u) \le \exp(-r^* u), \qquad \text{for } t \ge 1, \tag{5.29}$$

so that the inequality holds for the probability of ultimate ruin. We first note that $\exp\left[-r^*(u + 1 - j)\right] \ge 1$ for $j \ge u + 1$. Thus, for $t = 1$, the probability of ruin is, from equation (5.21),

$$\begin{aligned}
\psi(1; u) &= \sum_{j=u+1}^{\infty} f_X(j) \\
&\le \sum_{j=u+1}^{\infty} e^{-r^*(u+1-j)} f_X(j) \\
&\le \sum_{j=0}^{\infty} e^{-r^*(u+1-j)} f_X(j) \\
&= e^{-r^* u} \sum_{j=0}^{\infty} e^{r^*(j-1)} f_X(j) \\
&= e^{-r^* u} \, \mathrm{E}\left[r^*(X-1)\right] \\
&= e^{-r^* u}.
\end{aligned} \tag{5.30}$$

To prove the result by induction, we assume inequality (5.29) holds for a $t \ge 1$. Then, for $t + 1$ the probability of ruin is, from equation (5.22),

$$\begin{aligned}
\psi(t+1; u) &= \psi(1; u) + \sum_{j=0}^{u} \psi(t; u + 1 - j) f_X(j) \\
&\le \sum_{j=u+1}^{\infty} f_X(j) + \sum_{j=0}^{u} e^{-r^*(u+1-j)} f_X(j) \\
&\le \sum_{j=u+1}^{\infty} e^{-r^*(u+1-j)} f_X(j) + \sum_{j=0}^{u} e^{-r^*(u+1-j)} f_X(j) \\
&= \sum_{j=0}^{\infty} e^{-r^*(u+1-j)} f_X(j)
\end{aligned}$$

$$= e^{-r^* u} \sum_{j=0}^{\infty} e^{r^* (j-1)} f_X(j)$$

$$= e^{-r^* u} \, \mathrm{E}\left[r^* (X - 1) \right]$$

$$= e^{-r^* u}. \tag{5.31}$$

Hence, inequality (5.28) holds for all finite time. $\qquad\square$

The upper bound of the probability of ultimate ruin $e^{-r^* u}$ decreases with the initial surplus u, which is intuitive. The example below compares the upper bound with the exact values for the problem in Example 5.1.

Example 5.5 Assume the loss random variable X follows the distribution given in Examples 5.1 and 5.4. Calculate the Lundberg upper bound for the probability of ultimate ruin for $u = 0, 1, 2$ and 3.

Solution 5.5 From Example 5.4, the adjustment coefficient is $r^* = 0.1740$. The Lundberg upper bound for $u = 0$ is 1, and for $u = 1, 2$ and 3, we have $e^{-0.174} = 0.8403$, $e^{-(2)(0.174)} = 0.7061$ and $e^{-(3)(0.174)} = 0.5933$, respectively. These figures may be compared against the exact values computed in Example 5.1, namely, 0.8, 0.68 and 0.568, respectively. $\qquad\square$

Note that equation (5.23) can be written as

$$e^{-r} M_X(r) = 1, \tag{5.32}$$

or

$$\log M_X(r) = r. \tag{5.33}$$

We can establish that (see Exercise 5.1)

$$\left. \frac{d \log M_X(r)}{dr} \right|_{r=0} = \mu_X, \tag{5.34}$$

and

$$\left. \frac{d^2 \log M_X(r)}{dr^2} \right|_{r=0} = \sigma_X^2, \tag{5.35}$$

so that the Taylor series approximation of $\log M_X(r)$ is

$$\log M_X(r) \simeq r \mu_X + \frac{r^2 \sigma_X^2}{2}. \tag{5.36}$$

Thus, equation (5.33) can be written as

$$r \simeq r \mu_X + \frac{r^2 \sigma_X^2}{2}, \tag{5.37}$$

the solutions of which are $r = 0$ and

$$r^* \simeq \frac{2(1 - \mu_X)}{\sigma_X^2}. \tag{5.38}$$

For the loss distribution X in Example 5.4, its variance is 1.09. Based on the approximation in equation (5.38), the approximate adjustment coefficient is 0.1835, which is larger than the exact value of 0.1740.

5.3 Summary and Conclusions

The surplus of a block of insurance policies traces the excess of the initial surplus and premiums received over claim losses paid out. The business is said to be in ruin if the surplus falls to or below zero. We discuss the probabilities of ultimate ruin as well as ruin before a finite time. We also present recursive formulas to compute these probabilities, which depend on the initial surplus, the premium loading factor and the distribution of the claim losses. An upper bound of the probability of ultimate ruin can be calculated using Lundberg's inequality.

Exercises

Exercise 5.1 Suppose the mgf of the claim-severity random variable X is $M_X(r)$ for $r \in [0, \gamma)$. Let the mean and variance of X be μ_X and σ_X^2, respectively. Show that

$$\left. \frac{d \log M_X(r)}{dr} \right|_{r=0} = \mu_X,$$

and

$$\left. \frac{d^2 \log M_X(r)}{dr^2} \right|_{r=0} = \sigma_X^2.$$

Exercise 5.2 You are given the following information about a block of insurance policies.

(a) There is an initial surplus of 2 at time zero. Premium per period is 1 and is paid at the beginning of each period. Surplus earns 5% interest in each period.
(b) The claims at the end of period 1, 2 and 3 are, 0.2, 1.5 and 0.6, respectively.

Find the surplus at the beginning of period 4 (prior to premium payment).

Exercise 5.3 Claim severity in each period has the following distribution: $f_X(0) = 0.5, f_X(1) = 0.3, f_X(2) = 0$ and $f_X(3) = 0.2$. Find the probability of ultimate ruin if the initial surplus is 4.

Exercise 5.4 Claim severity per period is distributed as $\mathcal{BN}(4, 0.2)$. Calculate the probability of ruin at or before time 3 if the initial surplus is 3.

Exercise 5.5 In a discrete-time surplus model, the claim severity in each period is distributed as $\mathcal{GM}(0.6)$. Determine the adjustment coefficient and the maximum probability of ultimate ruin if the initial surplus is 3.

Exercise 5.6 In a discrete-time surplus model, the claim severity in each period is distributed as $\mathcal{PN}(0.7)$. Determine the adjustment coefficient and the maximum probability of ultimate ruin if the initial surplus is 2.

Exercise 5.7 In a discrete-time surplus model, the claim severity in each period is distributed as $\mathcal{BN}(2, 0.4)$. Determine the adjustment coefficient and the maximum probability of ultimate ruin if the initial surplus is 2.

Exercise 5.8 A discrete-time surplus function has initial surplus of 6 (exclusive of the first-year premium). Annual premiums of 3 are paid at the beginning of each year. Losses each year are 0 with probability 0.6 and 10 with probability 0.4, and are paid at the end of the year. Surplus earns interest of 6% annually. Determine the probability of ruin by the end of the second year.

Exercise 5.9 A discrete-time surplus function has initial surplus of 8 (exclusive of the first-year premium). Annual losses X have the following distribution

x	$\Pr(X = x)$
0	0.50
10	0.30
20	0.10
30	0.10

Premiums equaling the annual expected loss are paid at the beginning of each year. If the surplus increases in a year, dividend equaling half of the increase is paid out at the end of the year. Determine the probability of ruin by the end of the second year.

Question Adapted from SOA Exams

Exercise 5.10 You are given the following information about a block of insurance policies:

(a) The initial surplus is 1. The annual premium collected at the beginning of each year is 2.

(b) The distribution of loss X each year is $f_X(0) = 0.6$, $f_X(2) = 0.3$ and $f_X(6) = 0.1$.

(c) Capital at the beginning of the year earns 10% income for the year. Losses are paid and income is collected at the end of each year.

Calculate the finite-time probability of ruin $\psi(3; 1)$.

Part III

Credibility

Credibility theory provides the basic analytical framework for pricing insurance products. The importance of combining information about the recent experience of the individuals versus the aggregate past experience has been recognized in the literature through the classical approach. Rigorous analytical treatment of the subject started with Hans Bühlmann, and much work has been accomplished by him and his students. Bühlmann's approach provides a simple solution to the Bayesian method and achieves optimality within the subset of linear predictors. In this part of the book, we introduce the classical approach, the Bühlmann approach, the Bayesian method, as well as the empirical implementation of these techniques.

6

Classical Credibility

Credibility models were first proposed in the beginning of the twentieth century to update predictions of insurance losses in light of recently available data of insurance claims. The oldest approach is the limited-fluctuation credibility method, also called the classical approach, which proposes to update the loss prediction as a weighted average of the prediction based purely on the recent data and the rate in the insurance manual. Full credibility is achieved if the amount of recent data is sufficient, in which case the updated prediction will be based on the recent data only. If, however, the amount of recent data is insufficient, only partial credibility is attributed to the data, and the updated prediction depends on the manual rate as well.

We consider the calculation of the minimum size of the data above which full credibility is attributed to the data. For cases where the data are insufficient we derive the partial-credibility factor and the updating formula for the prediction of the loss. The classical credibility approach is applied to update the prediction of loss measures such as the frequency of claims, the severity of claims, the aggregate loss and the pure premium of a block of insurance policies.

Learning Objectives

1 Basic framework of credibility
2 The limited-fluctuation (classical) credibility approach
3 Full credibility
4 Partial credibility
5 Prediction of claim frequency, claim severity, aggregate loss and pure premium

6.1 Framework and Notations

We consider a block of insurance policies, referred to as a **risk group**. Examples of risk groups of interest are workers of a company covered under a workers accident compensation scheme, employees of a firm covered under employees health insurance and a block of vehicle insurance policies. The risk group is covered over a period of time (say, one year) upon the payment of a premium. The premium is partially based on a rate specified in the manual, called the **manual rate**, and partially on the specific risk characteristics of the group. Based upon the recent **claim experience** of the risk group, the premium for the next period will be revised. Credibility theory concerns the updating of the prediction of the claim for the next period using the recent claim experience and the manual rate. The revised prediction determines the insurance premium of the next period for the risk group.

Credibility theory may be applied to different measures of claim experience. We summarize below the key factors of interest and define our notations to be used subsequently:

Claim frequency: The number of claims in the period is denoted by N.

Aggregate loss: We denote the amount of the ith claim by X_i and the aggregate loss by S, so that
$S = X_1 + X_2 + \cdots + X_N$.

Claim severity: The average claim severity is the sample mean of $X_1, \ldots, X_N$, i.e., $\bar{X} = S/N$.

Pure premium: Let E be the number of exposure units of the risk group, the pure premium P is defined as $P = S/E$.

The loss measures N, X_i, S, $\bar{X}$ and P are random variables determined by uncertain events, while the exposure E is a known constant measuring the size of the risk group. For workers compensation and employees health insurance, E may be measured as the number of workers or employees covered under the policies. X_i are assumed to be independently and identically distributed as X.

We denote generically the predicted loss based on the manual by M, and the observed value of the loss based on recent data of the experience of the risk group by D. Thus, M and D may refer to the predicted value and observed value, respectively, of N, S, $\bar{X}$ and P. The **classical credibility** approach (also called the **limited-fluctuation credibility** approach) proposes to formulate the updated prediction of the loss measure as a weighted average of D and M. The weight attached to D is called the **credibility factor**, and is denoted by Z, with $0 \leq Z \leq 1$. Thus, the updated prediction, generically denoted by U, is given by

$$U = ZD + (1 - Z)M. \qquad (6.1)$$

Example 6.1 The loss per worker insured in a ship-building company was $230 last year. If the pure premium per worker in a similar industry is $292 and the credibility factor of the company (the risk group) is 0.46, calculate the updated predicted pure premium for the company's insurance.

Solution 6.1 We have $D = 230$, $M = 292$ and $Z = 0.46$, so that from equation (6.1) we obtain

$$U = (0.46)(230) + (1 - 0.46)(292) = \$263.48,$$

which will be the pure premium charged per worker of the company next year. □

From equation (6.1) we observe that U is always between the experience measure D and the manual rate M. The closer Z is to 1, the closer the updated predicted value U will be to the observed measure D. The credibility factor Z determines the relative importance of the data in calculating the updated prediction. **Full credibility** is said to be achieved if $Z = 1$, in which case the prediction depends upon the data only but not the manual. When $Z < 1$, the data are said to have **partial credibility**. Intuitively, a larger data set would justify a larger Z.

For the classical frequentist approach in statistics with no extraneous (or prior) information, estimation and prediction are entirely based on the data available. Thus, in the frequentist statistical framework one might say that all data have full credibility. The credibility theory literature, however, attempts to use the extraneous (or prior) information (as provided by insurance manuals) to obtain an improved update of the prediction.

6.2 Full Credibility

The classical credibility approach determines the minimum data size required for the experience data to be given full credibility (namely, for setting $Z = 1$). The minimum data size for setting $Z = 1$ is called the **standard for full credibility**. We denote W generically as the loss variable of interest, which may be claim frequency N, claim severity X or aggregate loss S. In this section, we derive the formulas for the computation of the full-credibility standards for these loss measures.

6.2.1 Full Credibility for a Generic Loss Variable

Assume that the generic loss variable W has mean μ_W and variance σ_W^2. Suppose a sample of n loss measures is available. For the cases of claim counts N and aggregate losses S, n is the number of periods of loss data. For the case of claim severity X, n is the number of claim amounts observed. We need to determine the minimum sample size n for full credibility to be achieved. This value depends on a **precision parameter** k and a **confidence parameter** α. In the classical (limited fluctuation) credibility approach, full credibility is achieved if the probability of the mean loss $\bar{W}$ being within $100k\%$ of the expected loss μ_W is not less than $1 - \alpha$, called the **coverage probability**. This condition can be written as

$$\Pr(\mu_W - k\mu_W \leq \bar{W} \leq \mu_W + k\mu_W) \geq 1 - \alpha. \tag{6.2}$$

Assuming $\bar{W}$ to be approximately normally distributed, the probability on the left-hand side of (6.2) can be evaluated as

$$\Pr\left(\mu_W - k\mu_W \leq \bar{W} \leq \mu_W + k\mu_W\right)$$

$$= \Pr\left(-\frac{k\mu_W}{\frac{\sigma_W}{\sqrt{n}}} \leq \frac{\bar{W} - \mu_W}{\frac{\sigma_W}{\sqrt{n}}} \leq \frac{k\mu_W}{\frac{\sigma_W}{\sqrt{n}}}\right)$$

$$= \Pr\left(\frac{\bar{W} - \mu_W}{\frac{\sigma_W}{\sqrt{n}}} \leq \frac{k\mu_W}{\frac{\sigma_W}{\sqrt{n}}}\right) - \Pr\left(\frac{\bar{W} - \mu_W}{\frac{\sigma_W}{\sqrt{n}}} \leq -\frac{k\mu_W}{\frac{\sigma_W}{\sqrt{n}}}\right)$$

$$\simeq \Phi\left(\frac{k\mu_W}{\frac{\sigma_W}{\sqrt{n}}}\right) - \Phi\left(-\frac{k\mu_W}{\frac{\sigma_W}{\sqrt{n}}}\right)$$

$$= 2\Phi\left(\frac{k\mu_W}{\frac{\sigma_W}{\sqrt{n}}}\right) - 1, \tag{6.3}$$

where $\Phi(\cdot)$ is the distribution function of the standard normal variate.

Example 6.2 Suppose a loss measure has a mean of 30 and a standard deviation of 65. A sample of 620 such losses are observed. (a) What is the probability that the sample mean of the losses is within 10% of the true mean? (b) Within what percentage of the true mean will the sample mean be observed with a probability of 96%? You may assume the sample mean to be normally distributed.

Solution 6.2 For (a) we are given the precision parameter of $k = 0.1$. As $\mu_W = 30$, $\sigma_W = 65$ and $n = 620$, we have

$$\frac{k\mu_W}{\frac{\sigma_W}{\sqrt{n}}} = \frac{0.1(30)}{\frac{65}{\sqrt{620}}} = 1.1492.$$

As $\Phi(1.1492) = 0.8748$, the probability that the sample mean of the losses is within 10% of the true mean is $2(0.8748) - 1 = 0.7495$.

For (b), we need to find k such that

$$2\Phi\left(\frac{k(30)}{\frac{65}{\sqrt{620}}}\right) - 1 = 0.96 \Rightarrow \Phi(11.4922k) = \frac{1.96}{2} = 0.98.$$

As $\Phi^{-1}(0.98) = 2.0537$, we have $k = 2.0537/11.4922 = 17.87\%$. ☐

We denote z_δ as the 100δth percentile of the standard normal distribution, i.e., $\Phi(z_\delta) = \delta$. Standard for full credibility requires the probability in expression (6.3) to be at least $1 - \alpha$, i.e.,

$$2\Phi\left(\frac{k\mu_W}{\frac{\sigma_W}{\sqrt{n}}}\right) - 1 \geq 1 - \alpha$$

$$\Rightarrow \Phi\left(\frac{k\mu_W}{\frac{\sigma_W}{\sqrt{n}}}\right) \geq 1 - \frac{\alpha}{2}$$

$$\Rightarrow \frac{k\mu_W}{\frac{\sigma_W}{\sqrt{n}}} \geq z_{1-\frac{\alpha}{2}}$$

$$\Rightarrow \sqrt{n}\left(\frac{\mu_W}{\sigma_W}\right) \geq \frac{z_{1-\frac{\alpha}{2}}}{k}$$

$$\Rightarrow n \geq \left(\frac{\sigma_W^2}{\mu_W^2}\right)\left(\frac{z_{1-\frac{\alpha}{2}}}{k}\right)^2 = \left(\frac{\sigma_W^2}{\mu_W^2}\right)\lambda_F, \quad (6.4)$$

where

$$\lambda_F = \left(\frac{z_{1-\frac{\alpha}{2}}}{k}\right)^2. \quad (6.5)$$

We let

$$\lambda_W = \left(\frac{\sigma_W^2}{\mu_W^2}\right)\lambda_F, \quad (6.6)$$

which is the **standard for full credibility** for the loss variable W.

Example 6.3 Consider the loss variable in Example 6.2. (a) If $k = 0.05$, compute the standard for full credibility for coverage probability of 90% and 95%. (b) If the required coverage probability is 92%, compute the standard for full credibility for coverage within 5% and 10% of the expected mean loss.

Table 6.1. λ_F *for selected values of α and k*

α	Coverage probability	k		
		10%	5%	1%
0.20	80%	164	657	16,424
0.10	90%	271	1,082	27,055
0.05	95%	384	1,537	38,415
0.01	99%	664	2,654	66,349

Solution 6.3 We first compute

$$\frac{\sigma_W^2}{\mu_W^2} = \left(\frac{65}{30}\right)^2 = 4.6944.$$

For (a), if the coverage probability is 90%, we have

$$1 - \alpha = 0.9 \Rightarrow 1 - \frac{\alpha}{2} = 1 - \frac{0.1}{2} = 0.95.$$

Thus, the full-credibility standard for coverage probability of 90% is

$$4.6944 \left(\frac{z_{0.95}}{0.05}\right)^2 = 5,080.36.$$

Similarly, the full-credibility standard for coverage probability of 95% is

$$4.6944 \left(\frac{z_{0.975}}{0.05}\right)^2 = 7,213.34.$$

For (b), $\alpha = 0.08$ so that when $k = 5\%$ the standard for full credibility is

$$4.6944 \left(\frac{z_{1-\frac{0.08}{2}}}{0.05}\right)^2 = 4.6944 \left(\frac{z_{0.96}}{0.05}\right)^2 = 5,755.20.$$

Similarly, when $k = 10\%$ the standard for full credibility is

$$4.6944 \left(\frac{z_{0.96}}{0.1}\right)^2 = 1,438.80. \qquad \square$$

The standard for full credibility λ_W depends on the mean and variance of the loss variable W, as well as λ_F. Given the precision parameter k, λ_F increases with the required coverage probability $1 - \alpha$. Likewise, given the required coverage probability $1 - \alpha$, λ_F increases with the required accuracy (i.e., λ_F increases when k drops). Table 6.1 presents the values of λ_F for selected values of α and k.

Recall that the sample size n stands for the number or periods (for N and S) or the number of claim payments (for X). The full-credibility standard is

$$n \geq \left(\frac{\sigma_W^2}{\mu_W^2}\right) \lambda_F, \qquad (6.7)$$

which can be rewritten as

$$n\mu_W \geq \left(\frac{\sigma_W^2}{\mu_W}\right) \lambda_F. \tag{6.8}$$

If we substitute $\bar{W}$ for μ_W in the left-hand side of the above equation, the full-credibility standard can also be stated as

Total losses (total claim counts for $W = N$ or

$$\text{total claim payments for } W = X, S) \geq \left(\frac{\sigma_W^2}{\mu_W}\right) \lambda_F. \tag{6.9}$$

Equations (6.7) and (6.9) state generically the full-credibility standard in two forms. We shall call these criteria for full credibility C1 and C2, respectively. In what follows we shall elaborate on these criteria specifically for claim frequency N, claim severity X and aggregate loss S.

6.2.2 Full Credibility for Claim Frequency

We assume claim frequency N has mean μ_N and variance σ_N^2. Using criterion C2 in equation (6.9), we consider the minimum number of loss counts in one period to justify full credibility for the next period. We further assume N to be distributed as a Poisson variate with parameter λ, so that $\mu_N = \sigma_N^2 = \lambda$. The standard for full credibility is then given by

$$\text{Total claim counts last period} \geq \left(\frac{\sigma_N^2}{\mu_N}\right) \lambda_F = \lambda_F. \tag{6.10}$$

Example 6.4 If an insurance company requires a coverage probability of 99% for the number of claims to be within 5% of the true expected claim frequency, how many claims in the recent period are required for full credibility? If the insurance company receives 2,890 claims this year from the risk group and the manual list of expected claims is 3,000, what is the updated expected number of claims next year? Assume the claim-frequency distribution is Poisson and the normal approximation applies.

Solution 6.4 We compute λ_F using equation (6.5) to obtain

$$\lambda_F = \left(\frac{z_{0.995}}{0.05}\right)^2 = \left(\frac{2.576}{0.05}\right)^2 = 2,653.96.$$

Hence, 2,654 claims are required for full credibility. As the observed claim frequency of 2,890 is larger than 2,654, full credibility is attributed to the data, i.e., $Z = 1$. Thus, $1 - Z = 0$, and from equation (6.1) the updated estimate of the expected number of claims in the next period is 2,890. Note that as full credibility is attained; the updated prediction does not depend on the manual value of $M = 3,000$. ☐

Example 6.5 If an insurance company decides to assign full credibility for 800 claims or more, what is the required coverage probability for the number of claims to be within 8% of the expected value? Assume the claim-frequency distribution is Poisson and the normal approximation applies.

Solution 6.5 The standard for full credibility for claim counts of one period based on the Poisson assumption is λ_F. To find the coverage probability when 800 claims are sufficient to acquire full credibility to within 8% of the true mean, we apply equation (6.5) to find α. Thus,

$$800 = \lambda_F = \left(\frac{z_{1-\frac{\alpha}{2}}}{k}\right)^2 \Rightarrow z_{1-\frac{\alpha}{2}} = 0.08\sqrt{800} = 2.2627,$$

from which we obtain $\alpha = 0.0237$. Hence, the coverage probability is $1 - \alpha = 97.63\%$. ☐

Standard for full credibility is sometimes expressed in terms of the number of exposure units. If the number of exposure units is E and the probability of a claim for each unit is θ, the expected number of claims is $E\theta$. The example below illustrates an application of the minimum standard based on exposure units.

Example 6.6 Recent experience of a workers compensation insurance has established the mean accident rate to be 0.045 and the standard for full credibility of claims to be 1,200. For a group with a similar risk profile, what is the minimum number of exposure units (i.e., number of workers in the group) required for full credibility?

Solution 6.6 As the standard for full credibility has been established to be 1,200 for claim frequency, we have

$$1,200 = E\theta = (0.045)E \Rightarrow E = \frac{1,200}{0.045} = 26,667 \text{ workers.} \quad ☐$$

So far we have adopted the assumption that the number of claims follows a Poisson distribution. We now consider alternatives where credibility for claim frequency is considered under other assumptions.

As an illustration, we assume that the claim frequency N is distributed as a binomial random variable with parameters E and θ, i.e., $N \sim \mathcal{BN}(E, \theta)$. Thus, θ is the probability of a claim and E is the number of exposure units. The mean and variance of N are $\lambda_N = E\theta$ and $\sigma_N^2 = E\theta(1 - \theta)$. The standard for full credibility based on the expected number of claims, as given by equation (6.9), is

$$E\theta \geq \left(\frac{E\theta(1 - \theta)}{E\theta} \right) \lambda_F = (1 - \theta)\lambda_F. \tag{6.11}$$

This can also be expressed in terms of the minimum amount of exposure units as

$$E \geq \frac{(1 - \theta)\lambda_F}{\theta}. \tag{6.12}$$

As $(1 - \theta)\lambda_F < \lambda_F$, the standard for full credibility under the binomial assumption is less than that under the Poisson assumption. However, as θ is typically small, $1 - \theta$ is close to 1 and the difference between the two models is usually small.

Example 6.7 Assume full credibility is based on 99% coverage of observed claim frequency within 1% of the true mean. Compare the standard for full credibility for claim frequency based on assumptions of Poisson claim frequency versus binomial claim frequency with the probability of claim per policy being 0.05.

Solution 6.7 From Table 6.1, full-credibility standard for claim frequency requires an expected claim frequency of 66,349, or exposure of 66,349/0.05 = 1.327 million units, if Poisson assumption is adopted. Under the binomial assumption, the expected claim number is $66,349(1 - 0.05) = 63,031.55$. In terms of exposure, we require $63,031.55/0.05 = 1.261$ million units. □

6.2.3 Full Credibility for Claim Severity

We now consider the standard for full credibility when the loss measure of interest is claim severity X. Let the mean and variance of X be μ_X and σ_X^2, respectively, and denote the full-credibility standard for X by λ_X. Using C1 of equation (6.7), we have

$$\lambda_X = \left(\frac{\sigma_X^2}{\mu_X^2} \right) \lambda_F = C_X^2 \lambda_F, \tag{6.13}$$

where $C_X = \sigma_X/\mu_X$ is the **coefficient of variation** of X. Using C2 of equation (6.9), we may also state the full credibility standard as

$$\text{Total amount of loss payments} \geq \left(\frac{\sigma_X^2}{\mu_X} \right) \lambda_F. \tag{6.14}$$

Thus, if the experienced claim frequency exceeds $C_X^2 \lambda_F$, the sample mean of the loss claims $\bar{X}$ will be the estimator for the expected severity of the next period (i.e., the manual rate will not be relevant). Note that to implement the methodology in practice, the coefficient of variation has to be estimated from the sample.

Example 6.8 What is the standard for full credibility for claim severity with $\alpha = 0.01$ and $k = 0.05$, given that the mean and variance estimates of claim severity are 1,000 and 2,000,000, respectively?

Solution 6.8 From Table 6.1, we have $\lambda_F = 2,654$. Thus, using equation (6.13), the standard for full credibility for severity is

$$\left[\frac{2,000,000}{(1,000)(1,000)} \right] 2,654 = 5,308 \text{ claims.} \qquad \square$$

In this example, the standard for full credibility is higher for claim severity than for claim frequency. As shown in equation (6.13), the standard for full credibility for severity is higher (lower) than that for claim frequency if the coefficient of variation of X is larger (smaller) than 1.

Example 6.9 Data for the claim experience of a risk group in the current period show the following: (a) there are 542 claims, and (b) the sample mean and variance of the claim severity are, respectively, 48 and 821. For $\alpha = 0.01$ and $k = 0.1$, do the data justify full credibility for claim frequency and claim severity for the next period?

Solution 6.9 From Table 6.1, the standard for full credibility for claim frequency at $\alpha = 0.01$ and $k = 0.1$ is 664, which is larger than the claim frequency of 542. Thus, full credibility is not attained for claim frequency. To calculate the standard for full credibility for severity, we use equation (6.13) to obtain

$$C_X^2 \lambda_F = \left[\frac{821}{(48)^2} \right] 664 = 236.61.$$

As $542 > 236.61$, full credibility is attained for claim severity. $\qquad \square$

In deriving the standard for full credibility for severity, we do not make use of the assumption of Poisson distribution for claim frequency. The number of claims, however, must be large enough to justify the normal approximation for the distribution of the average loss per claim $\bar{X}$.

6.2.4 *Full Credibility for Aggregate Loss*

We adopt the results in equations (6.7) and (6.8) for aggregate loss S. Let μ_S and σ_S^2 be the mean and variance of S, respectively. We assume the collective risk model for which S has a compound distribution, with N being the primary distribution and X being the secondary distribution. Thus, $\mu_S = \mu_N \mu_X$ and $\sigma_S^2 = \mu_N \sigma_X^2 + \mu_X^2 \sigma_N^2$. We let n be the total number of periods with aggregate losses calculated for each period. From C1 of equation (6.7) the full-credibility standard for S is

$$n \geq \left(\frac{\sigma_S^2}{\mu_S^2}\right) \lambda_F = \left[\frac{\mu_N \sigma_X^2 + \mu_X^2 \sigma_N^2}{\mu_N^2 \mu_X^2}\right] \lambda_F. \tag{6.15}$$

Alternatively, using C2 of equation (6.8), the full-credibility standard can be stated as

$$\text{Total amount of aggregate losses in } n \text{ periods} \geq \left[\frac{\mu_N \sigma_X^2 + \mu_X^2 \sigma_N^2}{\mu_N \mu_X}\right] \lambda_F, \tag{6.16}$$

or

$$\text{Total number of claims in } n \text{ periods} \geq \left[\frac{\mu_N \sigma_X^2 + \mu_X^2 \sigma_N^2}{\mu_N \mu_X^2}\right] \lambda_F. \tag{6.17}$$

The above results do not presume any specific distributions for N and X. If we further assume that N is Poisson distributed with parameter λ, then the above conditions can be simplified. First, the condition based on C1 in equation (6.15) is

$$n \geq \left[1 + \frac{\sigma_X^2}{\mu_X^2}\right] \frac{\lambda_F}{\lambda} = (1 + C_X^2) \frac{\lambda_F}{\lambda}. \tag{6.18}$$

Similarly, based on C2 in equations (6.16) and (6.17) we have

$$\text{Total amount of aggregate losses in } n \text{ periods} \geq \left[\mu_X + \frac{\sigma_X^2}{\mu_X}\right] \lambda_F, \tag{6.19}$$

and

$$\text{Total number of claims in } n \text{ periods} \geq \left[1 + \frac{\sigma_X^2}{\mu_X^2}\right] \lambda_F = (1 + C_X^2) \lambda_F. \tag{6.20}$$

From equations (6.10) and (6.20) it can be seen that the standard for full credibility for aggregate loss is always higher than that for claim frequency under the Poisson assumption for N. This result is due to the randomness of both the claim frequency and the claim severity in impacting the aggregate loss. Indeed, as

$$\left(1 + C_X^2\right) \lambda_F = \lambda_F + C_X^2 \lambda_F, \tag{6.21}$$

we conclude that

> Standard for full credibility for aggregate loss
> = Standard for full credibility for claim frequency
> + Standard for full credibility for claim severity.

Example 6.10 A block of health insurance policies has estimated mean severity of 25 and variance of severity of 800. For $\alpha = 0.15$ and $k = 0.08$, calculate the standard for full credibility for claim frequency and aggregate loss. Assume the claim frequency follows a Poisson distribution and normal approximation can be used for the claim-frequency and aggregate-loss distributions. If the block has 400 claims, is full credibility attained?

Solution 6.10 As $z_{0.925} = \Phi^{-1}(0.925) = 1.4395$, we have

$$\lambda_F = \left(\frac{1.4395}{0.08}\right)^2 = 323.78,$$

which is the standard for full credibility for claim frequency. The coefficient of variation of claim severity is

$$\frac{\sqrt{800}}{25} = 1.1314.$$

Thus, using equation (6.18) the standard for full credibility for aggregate loss is

$$[1 + (1.1314)^2]\ 323.78 = 738.24,$$

which is 2.28 times that of the standard for full credibility for claim frequency. As the claim count of 400 is larger than 323.78 but smaller than 738.24, full credibility is attained for the risk group for claim frequency but not for aggregate loss.   □

Example 6.11 Aggregate loss follows a compound distribution, with the secondary (severity) distribution being exponential with mean θ. Full credibility for aggregate loss is to be within 5% of expected aggregate loss 95% of the time. It is known that the variance of the primary distribution is 1.2 times its mean. Determine the minimum total number of claims needed for full credibility for aggregate loss.

Solution 6.11 Using equation (6.17), the minimum total number of claims for full credibility for aggregate loss is

$$\left[\frac{\mu_N \sigma_X^2 + \mu_X^2 \sigma_N^2}{\mu_N \mu_X^2}\right] \lambda_F.$$

With $k = 0.05$ and $1 - \alpha = 95\%$, $\lambda_F = 1,537$ from Table 6.1. As X is exponential with mean θ, $\mu_X = \theta$ and $\sigma_X^2 = \theta^2$. Thus, the minimum total number of claims required is

$$\left[\frac{\mu_N \theta^2 + \theta^2 \sigma_N^2}{\mu_N \theta^2}\right] 1,537 = \left[\frac{\mu_N + 1.2\mu_N}{\mu_N}\right] 1,537 = (2.2)1,537 = 3,381.40. \quad \square$$

6.2.5 Full Credibility for Pure Premium

Pure premium, denoted by P, is the premium per unit exposure charged to cover losses before taking account of expenses and profits. Let the mean and variance of P be μ_P and σ_P^2, respectively. As $P = S/E$, where the number of exposure units E is a constant, we have $\sigma_P/\mu_P = \sigma_S/\mu_S$. Thus, full-credibility standard for aggregate loss can also be used to calculate full-credibility standard for pure premium.

Example 6.12 A block of accident insurance policies has mean claim frequency of 0.03 per policy. Claim-frequency distribution is assumed to be Poisson. If claim severity is distributed lognormally as $\mathcal{L}(5, 1)$, calculate the number of policies required to attain full credibility for pure premium, with $\alpha = 0.02$ and $k = 0.05$. You may assume compound distribution for aggregate loss.

Solution 6.12 The mean and variance of the claim severity distribution $\mathcal{L}(\mu, \sigma^2)$ are, respectively,

$$\mu_X = \exp\left(\mu + \frac{\sigma^2}{2}\right) = \exp(5.5) = 244.6919$$

and

$$\sigma_X^2 = \left[\exp\left(2\mu + \sigma^2\right)\right]\left[\exp(\sigma^2) - 1\right] = 102{,}880.6497.$$

Thus, the coefficient of variation of claim severity is

$$C_X = \frac{\sqrt{102{,}880.6497}}{244.6919} = 1.3108.$$

Now $z_{0.99} = \Phi^{-1}(0.99) = 2.3263$, so that the standard for full credibility for pure premium requires a minimum claim count of (see equation (6.20))

$$(1 + C_X^2)\lambda_F = \left[1 + (1.3108)^2\right]\left(\frac{2.3263}{0.05}\right)^2 = 5{,}884.18.$$

Hence, the minimum number of policies for full credibility for pure premium is

$$\frac{5{,}884.18}{0.03} = 196{,}139. \qquad \square$$

Example 6.13 Aggregate loss follows a compound Poisson distribution. The coefficient of variation of the severity distribution is 3. Determine the full-credibility standard for pure premium to be within 5% of the expected pure premium 95% of the time.

Solution 6.13 We use the criteria for aggregate loss to determine the full standard for pure premium. Note that, however, the mean of the Poisson distribution, as well as the mean and variance of the severity distribution, are unknown. Hence, we can only use equation (6.20) (Equations (6.18) and (6.19) cannot be used) to determine the full-credibility standard. With $k = 0.05$ and $\alpha = 5\%$, we have, from Table 6.1, $\lambda_F = 1,537$. Thus, the minimum number of claims for full credibility for pure premium is

$$(1 + (3)^2)1,537 = 15,370. \qquad \square$$

6.3 Partial Credibility

When the risk group is not sufficiently large, full credibility cannot be attained. In this case, a value of $Z < 1$ has to be determined. For a generic loss variable W, the basic assumption in deriving Z is that the probability of $Z\bar{W}$ lying within the interval $[Z\mu_W - k\mu_W, Z\mu_W + k\mu_W]$ is at least $1 - \alpha$ for given values of k and α. In other words, the coverage probability is achieved after shrinking the sample mean of the losses by a factor of Z, called the **partial-credibility factor**.

Z is determined as follows

$$\Pr\left(Z\mu_W - k\mu_W \leq Z\bar{W} \leq Z\mu_W + k\mu_W\right) \geq 1 - \alpha$$

$$\Rightarrow \Pr\left(-\frac{k\mu_W}{\frac{\sigma_W}{\sqrt{n}}} \leq \frac{Z\bar{W} - Z\mu_W}{\frac{\sigma_W}{\sqrt{n}}} \leq \frac{k\mu_W}{\frac{\sigma_W}{\sqrt{n}}}\right) \geq 1 - \alpha$$

$$\Rightarrow \Pr\left(-\sqrt{n}\frac{k}{Z}\frac{\mu_W}{\sigma_W} \leq \frac{\bar{W} - \mu_W}{\frac{\sigma_W}{\sqrt{n}}} \leq \sqrt{n}\frac{k}{Z}\frac{\mu_W}{\sigma_W}\right) \geq 1 - \alpha$$

$$\Rightarrow \Phi\left(\sqrt{n}\frac{k}{Z}\frac{\mu_W}{\sigma_W}\right) - \Phi\left(-\sqrt{n}\frac{k}{Z}\frac{\mu_W}{\sigma_W}\right) \geq 1 - \alpha$$

$$\Rightarrow \Phi\left(\sqrt{n}\frac{k}{Z}\frac{\mu_W}{\sigma_W}\right) \geq 1 - \frac{\alpha}{2}, \qquad (6.22)$$

so that

$$\sqrt{n}\frac{k}{Z}\frac{\mu_W}{\sigma_W} \geq z_{1-\frac{\alpha}{2}} \qquad (6.23)$$

and

$$Z \leq \left[\frac{k}{z_{1-\frac{\alpha}{2}}}\frac{\mu_W}{\sigma_W}\right]\sqrt{n}. \qquad (6.24)$$

Thus, we take the partial-credibility factor as

$$Z = \sqrt{\frac{n}{\lambda_F}}\left[\frac{\mu_W}{\sigma_W}\right]. \qquad (6.25)$$

Table 6.2. *Summary of partial-credibility factor Z*

Loss measure	Partial-credibility factor Z
Claim frequency	$\sqrt{\dfrac{\text{Total claim counts}}{\lambda_F}}$
Claim severity	$\sqrt{\dfrac{\text{Total claim counts}}{C_X^2 \lambda_F}}$
Aggregate loss/Pure premium	$\sqrt{\dfrac{\text{Total claim counts}}{(1 + C_X^2)\lambda_F}}$

To derive specific results, we further assume that the claim counts are Poisson distributed with mean λ and the aggregate losses follow a compound distribution. The partial-credibility factor for claim frequency is then given by

$$Z = \sqrt{\frac{n\lambda}{\lambda_F}}. \tag{6.26}$$

For a single period of data, we have

$$Z = \sqrt{\frac{\text{Total claim counts}}{\lambda_F}}, \tag{6.27}$$

As λ_F is the full-credibility standard for claim frequency, equation (6.27) is called the **square root rule for partial credibility**. Similar rules can be deduced for other loss variables. Table 6.2 summarizes the square root rules for claim frequency, claim severity and aggregate loss.

Example 6.14 A block of insurance policies had 896 claims this period with mean loss of 45 and variance of loss of 5,067. Full credibility is based on a coverage probability of 98% for a range of within 10% deviation from the true mean. Calculate Z for the claim frequency, claim severity and aggregate loss of the next period.

Solution 6.14 We have $z_{0.99} = \Phi^{-1}(0.99) = 2.3263$, so that the full-credibility standard for claim frequency is

$$\lambda_F = \left(\frac{2.3263}{0.1}\right)^2 = 541.19 < 896.$$

Thus, for claim frequency there is full credibility and $Z = 1$. The estimated coefficient of variation of claim severity is

$$C_X = \frac{\sqrt{5,067}}{45} = 1.5818,$$

so that the standard for full credibility for claim severity is

$$C_X^2 \lambda_F = (1.5818)^2 (541.19) = 1,354.18,$$

which is larger than the sample size 896. Hence, full credibility is not attained for claim severity. The partial-credibility factor is

$$Z = \sqrt{\frac{896}{1,354.18}} = 0.8134.$$

For aggregate loss, the standard for full credibility based on total claim counts is

$$(1 + C_X^2)\lambda_F = 1,895.30 > 896.$$

Thus, full credibility is not attained for aggregate loss, and the partial credibility factor is

$$Z = \sqrt{\frac{896}{1,895.30}} = 0.6876. \qquad \square$$

Example 6.15 Claim severity is distributed as $\mathcal{L}(3,2)$. Classical credibility approach is adopted to predict the mean severity, with a minimum coverage probability of 92% to within 5% of the mean severity. An average loss of 62 per claim is calculated for 6,810 claims. What is the predicted loss for each claim?

Solution 6.15 Based on the lognormal assumption for X, we obtain

$$\mu_X = e^{3+\frac{2}{2}} = 54.5982$$

and

$$\sigma_X^2 = \exp(2(3) + 2)(e^2 - 1) = 19,045.51,$$

so that the coefficient of variation is

$$C_X^2 = \frac{19,045.51}{(54.5982)^2} = 6.3891.$$

Also,

$$\lambda_F = \left(\frac{z_{0.96}}{0.05}\right)^2 = 1,225.96.$$

Hence, the full-credibility standard for claim severity is

$$6.3891(1,225.96) = 7,832.73,$$

and the partial-credibility factor is

$$Z = \sqrt{\frac{6,810}{7,832.73}} = 0.9324.$$

The predicted mean loss per claim is

$$0.9324(62) + (1 - 0.9324)54.5982 = 61.4996. \qquad \square$$

6.4 Summary and Discussions

The computation of the full-credibility standards depends on the given level of probability coverage $1 - \alpha$ and the accuracy parameter k. As Table 6.1 shows, the full-credibility standard has large variations over different values of α and k, and it may be difficult to determine the suitable values to adopt.

Although the classical credibility approach is easy to apply, it is not based on well-adopted statistical principles of prediction. In particular, there are several shortcomings of the approach, such as:

1 This approach emphasizes the role of D. It does not attach any importance to the accuracy of the prior information M.
2 The full-credibility standards depend on some unknown parameter values. The approach does not address the issue of how the calibration of these parameters may affect the credibility.
3 There are some limitations in the assumptions, which are made for the purpose of obtaining tractable analytical results.

Exercises

Exercise 6.1 Claim severity has a mean of 256 and a standard deviation of 532. A sample of 456 claims are observed. Answer the following questions.

(a) What is the probability that the sample mean is within 10% of the true mean?
(b) What is the coefficient of variation of the claim-severity distribution?
(c) What is the coefficient of variation of the sample mean of the claim severity?
(d) Within what percentage of the true mean will the sample mean be observed with a probability of 92%?
(e) What assumptions have you made in answering the above questions?

Exercise 6.2 Assume the aggregate-loss distribution follows a compound distribution with the claim frequency distributed as a Poisson with mean 569, and the claim severity distributed with mean 120 and standard deviation 78.

(a) Calculate the mean and the variance of the aggregate loss.
(b) Calculate the probability that the observed aggregate loss is within 6% of the mean aggregate loss. You may assume aggregate loss to be normally distributed.
(c) If the mean of the claim frequency increases to 620, how might the claim-severity distribution be changed so that the probability in (b) remains unchanged (give one possible answer)?
(d) If the standard deviation of the claim-severity distribution reduces to 60, how might the claim-frequency distribution be changed so that the probability in (b) remains unchanged?

Exercise 6.3 A risk group has 569 claims this period, giving a claim average of 1,290 and standard deviation of 878. Calculate the standard for full credibility for claim frequency and claim severity, where full credibility is based on deviation of up to 6% of the true mean with a coverage probability of 94%. You may assume the claim frequency to be Poisson. Is full credibility attained in each case?

Exercise 6.4 Assume the variance of the claim-frequency distribution is twice its mean (the distribution is not Poisson). Find the standard for full credibility for claim frequency and aggregate loss.

Exercise 6.5 Assume Poisson distribution for claim frequency. Show that the partial-credibility factor for claim severity is $\sqrt{n/(C_X^2 \lambda_F)}$, where n ($< C_X^2 \lambda_F$) is the number of claims.

Exercise 6.6 Assume Poisson distribution for claim frequency. Show that the partial-credibility factor for aggregate loss is $\sqrt{n/[(1 + C_X^2)\lambda_F]}$, where n ($< (1 + C_X^2)\lambda_F$) is the total number of claims over all periods.

Exercise 6.7 The standard for full credibility for claim frequency of a risk group is 2,156. If the full-credibility standard is based on coverage probability of 94%, what is the accuracy parameter k?

(a) If the required accuracy parameter is halved, will the standard for full credibility increase or decrease? What is its new value?
(b) For the standard defined in (a), if the standard for full credibility for claim severity is 4,278 claims, what is the standard for full credibility for aggregate loss based on the total number of claims? You may assume compound Poisson distribution for aggregate loss.

Exercise 6.8 Claim severity is uniformly distributed in the interval $[2000, 3000]$. If claim frequency is distributed as a Poisson, determine the standard for full credibility for aggregate loss based on the total number of claims.

Exercise 6.9 Assume claim frequency to be Poisson. If claim severity is distributed exponentially with mean 356, find the standard for full credibility for aggregate loss in terms of total claim counts. If the maximum amount of a claim is capped at 500, calculate the revised standard for full credibility for aggregate loss.

Exercise 6.10 A block of health insurance policies has 2,309 claims this year, with mean claim of $239 and standard deviation of $457. If full credibility is based on 95% coverage to within 5% of the true mean claim severity, and the prior mean severity is $250, what is the updated prediction for the mean severity next year based on the limited-fluctuation approach?

Exercise 6.11 Claim severity is distributed lognormally with $\mu = 5$ and $\sigma^2 = 2$. Classical credibility approach is adopted to predict mean severity, with a minimum coverage probability of 92% to within 5% of the mean severity. An average loss of 354 per claim was calculated for 6,950 claims for the current year. What is the predicted loss for each claim? If the average loss of 354 was actually calculated for 9,650 claims, what is the predicted loss for each claim? State any assumptions you have made in the calculation.

Exercise 6.12 Claim severity has mean 358 and standard deviation 421. An insurance company has 85,000 insurance policies. Using classical credibility approach with coverage probability of 96% to within 6% of the mean aggregate loss, determine the credibility factor Z if the average claim per policy is (a) 3%, and (b) 5%.

Exercise 6.13 Claim frequency has a binomial distribution with the probability of claim per policy being 0.068. Assume full credibility is based on 98% coverage of observed claim frequency within 4% of the true mean. Determine the credibility factor if there are 68,000 policies.

Questions Adapted from SOA Exams

Exercise 6.14 Claim severity has mean 26. In Year 1, 1,200 claims were filed with mean severity of 32. Based on the limited-fluctuation approach, severity per policy for Year 2 was then revised to 29.82. In Year 2, 1,500 claims were filed with mean severity of 24.46. What is the revised mean severity prediction for Year 3, if the same actuarial assumptions are used as for the prediction for Year 2?

Exercise 6.15 Claim frequency N has a Poisson distribution, and claim size X is distributed as $\mathcal{P}(6, 0.5)$, where N and X are independent. For full credibility of pure premium the observed pure premium is required to be within 2% of the expected pure premium 90% of the time. Determine the expected number of claims required for full credibility.

Exercise 6.16 Aggregate loss follows a compound Poisson distribution, with claim severity distributed as $\mathcal{G}(2, 100)$. Full-credibility standard is based on aggregate loss being within 10% of the expected aggregate loss 95% of the time. Determine the expected number of claims required for full credibility using limited fluctuation credibility.

Exercise 6.17 An insurance company has determined that the limited-fluctuation full-credibility standard is 2,000 if (a) the total number of claims is to be within 3% of the expected value with probability $1 - \alpha$, and (b) the number of claims follows a Poisson distribution. The standard is then changed so that the total cost of claims is to be within 5% of the expected value with probability $1 - \alpha$, where claim severity is distributed as $\mathcal{U}(0, 10000)$. Determine the number of claims for the limited-fluctuation full-credibility standard.

Exercise 6.18 The number of claims is distributed as $\mathcal{NB}(r, 0.25)$, and the claim severity takes values 1, 10 and 100 with probabilities 0.4, 0.4 and 0.2, respectively. If claim frequency and claim severity are independent, determine the expected number of claims needed for an observed aggregate loss to be within 10% of the expected aggregate loss with 95% probability. You may assume aggregate loss to be approximately normally distributed.

7

Bühlmann Credibility

While the classical credibility theory addresses the important problem of combining claim experience and prior information to update the prediction for loss, it does not provide a very satisfactory solution. The method is based on arbitrary selection of the coverage probability and the accuracy parameter. Furthermore, for tractability some restrictive assumptions about the loss distribution have to be imposed.

Bühlmann credibility theory sets the problem in a rigorous statistical framework of optimal prediction, using the least mean squared error criterion. It is flexible enough to incorporate various distributional assumptions of loss variables. The approach is further extended to enable the claim experience of different blocks of policies with different exposures to be combined for improved forecast through the Bühlmann–Straub model.

The Bühlmann and Bühlmann–Straub models recognize the interaction of two sources of variability in the data, namely, the variation due to between-group differences and variation due to within-group fluctuations. We begin this chapter with the setup of the Bühlmann credibility model, and a review of how the variance of the loss variable is decomposed into between-group and within-group variations. We derive the Bühlmann credibility factor and updating formula as the minimum mean squared error predictor. The approach is then extended to the Bühlmann–Straub model, in which the loss random variables have different exposures.

Learning Objectives

1 Basic framework of Bühlmann credibility
2 Variance decomposition
3 Expected value of the process variance
4 Variance of the hypothetical mean

7.1 Framework and Notations

Consider a risk group or block of insurance policies with loss measure denoted by X, which may be claim frequency, claim severity, aggregate loss or pure premium. We assume that the risk profiles of the group are characterized by a parameter θ, which determines the distribution of the loss measure X. We denote the conditional mean and variance of X given θ by

$$E(X \mid \theta) = \mu_X(\theta), \tag{7.1}$$

and

$$\text{Var}(X \mid \theta) = \sigma_X^2(\theta). \tag{7.2}$$

We assume that the insurance company has similar blocks of policies with different risk profiles. Thus, the parameter θ varies with different risk groups. We treat θ as the realization of a random variable Θ, the distribution of which is called the **prior distribution**. When θ varies over the support of Θ, the conditional mean and variance of X become random variables in Θ, and are denoted by $\mu_X(\Theta) = E(X \mid \Theta)$ and $\sigma_X^2(\Theta) = \text{Var}(X \mid \Theta)$, respectively.

Example 7.1 An insurance company has blocks of workers compensation policies. The claim frequency is known to be Poisson with parameter λ, where λ is 20 for low-risk group and 50 for high-risk group. Suppose 30% of the risk groups are low risk and 70% are high risk. What are the conditional mean and variance of the claim frequency?

Solution 7.1 The parameter determining the claim frequency X is λ, which is a realization of the random variable Λ. As X is Poisson, the conditional mean and conditional variance of X are equal to λ. Thus, we have the results in Table 7.1, so that

$$\mu_X(\Lambda) = E(X \mid \Lambda) = \begin{cases} 20, & \text{with probability } 0.30, \\ \\ 50, & \text{with probability } 0.70. \end{cases}$$

Table 7.1. *Results for Example 7.1*

λ	$\Pr(\Lambda = \lambda)$	$E(X \mid \lambda)$	$\text{Var}(X \mid \lambda)$
20	0.3	20	20
50	0.7	50	50

Likewise, we have

$$\sigma_X^2(\Lambda) = \text{Var}(X \mid \Lambda) = \begin{cases} 20, & \text{with probability } 0.30, \\ \\ 50, & \text{with probability } 0.70. \end{cases} \qquad \square$$

Example 7.2 The claim severity X of a block of health insurance policies is normally distributed with mean θ and variance 10. If θ takes values within the interval $[100, 200]$ and follows a uniform distribution, what are the conditional mean and conditional variance of X?

Solution 7.2 The conditional variance of X is 10, irrespective of θ. Hence, we have $\sigma_X^2(\Theta) = \text{Var}(X \mid \Theta) = 10$ with probability 1. The conditional mean of X is Θ, i.e., $\mu_X(\Theta) = \text{E}(X \mid \Theta) = \Theta$, which is uniformly distributed in $[100, 200]$ with pdf

$$f_\Theta(\theta) = \begin{cases} 0.01, & \text{for } \theta \in [100, 200], \\ \\ 0, & \text{otherwise.} \end{cases} \qquad \square$$

The Bühlmann model assumes that there are n observations of losses, denoted by $X = \{X_1, \ldots, X_n\}$. The observations may be losses recorded in n periods and they are assumed to be independently and identically distributed as X, which depends on the parameter θ. The task is to update the prediction of X for the next period, i.e., X_{n+1}, based on X. In the Bühlmann approach, the solution depends on the variation between the conditional means as well as the average of the conditional variances of the risk groups. In the next section, we discuss the calculation of these components, after which we will derive the updating formula proposed by Bühlmann.

7.2 Variance Components

The variation of the loss measure X consists of two components: the variation between risk groups and the variation within risk groups. The first component, variation between risk groups, is due to the randomness of the risk profiles of each group and is captured by the parameter Θ. The second component, variation within risk group, is measured by the conditional variance of the risk group.[1]

We first consider the calculation of the overall mean of the loss measure X. The **unconditional mean** (or **overall mean**) of X measures the overall central

---

[1] Readers may refer to Appendix A.11 for a review of the calculation of conditional expectation and total variance. To economize on notations, we will use X to denote a general loss measure as well as claim severity.

tendency of X, averaged over all the underlying differences in the risk groups. Applying equation (A.111) of iterative expectation, the unconditional mean of X is

$$E(X) = E[E(X \mid \Theta)] = E[\mu_X(\Theta)]. \tag{7.3}$$

Thus, the unconditional mean is the average of the conditional means taken over the distribution of Θ.[2]

For the **unconditional variance** (or **total variance**), the calculation is more involved. The total variance of X is due to the variation in Θ as well as the variance of X conditional on Θ. We use the results derived in Appendix A.11. Applying equation (A.115), we have

$$\text{Var}(X) = E[\text{Var}(X \mid \Theta)] + \text{Var}[E(X \mid \Theta)]. \tag{7.4}$$

Note that $\text{Var}(X \mid \Theta)$ measures the variance of a given risk group. It is a function of the random variable Θ and we call this the **process variance**. Thus, $E[\text{Var}(X \mid \Theta)]$ is the **expected value of the process variance (EPV)**. On the other hand, $E(X \mid \Theta)$ is the mean of a given risk group. We call this conditional mean the **hypothetical mean**. Thus, $\text{Var}[E(X \mid \Theta)]$ is the **variance of the hypothetical means (VHM)**, as it measures the variations in the *means* of the risk groups. Verbally, equation (7.4) can be written as

Total variance = expected value of process variance

+ variance of hypothetical means,   (7.5)

or

Total variance = EPV + VHM.   (7.6)

It can also be stated alternatively as

Total variance = mean of conditional variance

+ variance of conditional mean.   (7.7)

Symbolically, we use the following notations

$$E[\text{Var}(X \mid \Theta)] = E[\sigma_X^2(\Theta)] = \mu_{\text{PV}}, \tag{7.8}$$

and

$$\text{Var}[E(X \mid \Theta)] = \text{Var}[\mu_X(\Theta)] = \sigma_{\text{HM}}^2, \tag{7.9}$$

---

[2] Note that the expectation operations in equation (7.3) have different meanings. The operation in $E(X)$ is taken unconditionally on X. The first (outer) operation in $E[E(X \mid \Theta)]$ is taken over Θ, while the second (inner) operation is taken over X *conditional* on Θ. Lastly, the operation in $E[\mu_X(\Theta)]$ is taken over Θ unconditionally.

so that equation (7.4) can be written as

$$\text{Var}(X) = \mu_{\text{PV}} + \sigma^2_{\text{HM}}. \tag{7.10}$$

Example 7.3 For Examples 7.1 and 7.2, calculate the unconditional mean, the expected value of the process variance, the variance of the hypothetical means and the total variance.

Solution 7.3 For Example 7.1, the unconditional mean is

$$\begin{aligned}
\text{E}(X) &= \text{Pr}(\Lambda = 20)\text{E}(X \mid \Lambda = 20) + \text{Pr}(\Lambda = 50)\text{E}(X \mid \Lambda = 50) \\
&= (0.3)(20) + (0.7)(50) \\
&= 41.
\end{aligned}$$

The expected value of the process variance, EPV, is

$$\begin{aligned}
\text{E}[\text{Var}(X \mid \Lambda)] &= \text{Pr}(\Lambda = 20)\text{Var}(X \mid \Lambda = 20) + \text{Pr}(\Lambda = 50)\text{Var}(X \mid \Lambda = 50) \\
&= (0.3)(20) + (0.7)(50) \\
&= 41.
\end{aligned}$$

As the mean of the hypothetical means (i.e., the unconditional mean) is 41, the variance of the hypothetical means, VHM, is

$$\text{Var}[\text{E}(X \mid \Lambda)] = (0.3)(20 - 41)^2 + (0.7)(50 - 41)^2 = 189.$$

Thus, the total variance of X is

$$\text{Var}(X) = \text{E}[\text{Var}(X \mid \Lambda)] + \text{Var}[\text{E}(X \mid \Lambda)] = 41 + 189 = 230.$$

For Example 7.2, as Θ is uniformly distributed in $[100, 200]$, the unconditional mean of X is

$$\text{E}(X) = \text{E}[\text{E}(X \mid \Theta)] = \text{E}(\Theta) = 150.$$

As X has a constant variance of 10, the expected value of the process variance is

$$\text{E}[\text{Var}(X \mid \Theta)] = \text{E}(10) = 10.$$

The variance of the hypothetical means is[3]

$$\text{Var}[\text{E}(X \mid \Theta)] = \text{Var}(\Theta) = \frac{(200 - 100)^2}{12} = 833.33,$$

and the total variance of X is

$$\text{Var}(X) = 10 + 833.33 = 843.33. \qquad \square$$

---

[3] See Appendix A.10.3 for the variance of the uniform distribution.

If we divide the variance of the hypothetical means by the total variance, we obtain the proportion of the variation in X that is due to the differences in the means of the risk groups. Thus, for Example 7.1, we have

$$\frac{\sigma_{\text{HM}}^2}{\text{Var}(X)} = \frac{189}{230} = 82.17\%,$$

so that 82.17% of the variation in a randomly observed X is due to the differences in the averages of the risk groups. For Example 7.2, this figure is $833.33/843.33 = 98.81\%$.

Example 7.4 The claim severity X of a block of health insurance policies is normally distributed with mean 100 and variance σ^2. If σ^2 takes values within the interval [50, 100] and follows a uniform distribution, find the conditional mean of claim severity, the expected value of the process variance, the variance of the hypothetical means and the total variance.

Solution 7.4 We denote the random variable of the variance of X by Ω. Note that the conditional mean of X does not vary with Ω, and we have $E(X \mid \Omega) = 100$, so that the unconditional mean of X is

$$E(X) = E[E(X \mid \Omega)] = E(100) = 100.$$

As Ω is uniformly distributed in [50, 100], the expected value of the process variance is

$$\text{EPV} = \mu_{\text{PV}} = E[\text{Var}(X \mid \Omega)] = E(\Omega) = 75.$$

For the variance of the hypothetical means, we have

$$\text{VHM} = \sigma_{\text{HM}}^2 = \text{Var}[E(X \mid \Omega)] = \text{Var}(100) = 0.$$

Thus, the total variance of X is 75, which is *entirely* due to the process variance, as there is no variation in the conditional mean. □

Example 7.5 An insurance company sells workers compensation policies, each of which belongs to one of three possible risk groups. The risk groups have claim frequencies N that are Poisson distributed with parameter λ and claim severity X that are gamma distributed with parameters α and β. Claim frequency and claim severity are independently distributed given a risk group, and the aggregate loss is S. The data of the risk groups are given in Table 7.2.

For each of the following loss measures: (a) claim frequency N, (b) claim severity X, and (c) aggregate loss S, calculate EPV, VHM and the total variance.

Table 7.2. *Data for Example 7.5*

Risk group	Relative frequency	Distribution of N: $\mathcal{P}\mathcal{N}(\lambda)$	Distribution of X: $\mathcal{G}(\alpha, \beta)$
1	0.2	$\lambda = 20$	$\alpha = 5, \beta = 2$
2	0.4	$\lambda = 30$	$\alpha = 4, \beta = 3$
3	0.4	$\lambda = 40$	$\alpha = 3, \beta = 2$

Table 7.3. *Results for Example 7.5 (a)*

Risk group	Probability	$\mathrm{E}(N \mid \Lambda) = \mu_N(\Lambda)$	$\mathrm{Var}(N \mid \Lambda) = \sigma_N^2(\Lambda)$
1	0.2	20	20
2	0.4	30	30
3	0.4	40	40

Solution 7.5 (a) Claim frequency We first calculate the conditional mean and conditional variance of N given the risk group, which is characterized by the parameter Λ. As N is Poisson, the mean and variance are equal to Λ, so that we have the results in Table 7.3.

Thus, the EPV is

$$\mu_{\mathrm{PV}} = \mathrm{E}[\mathrm{Var}(N \mid \Lambda)] = (0.2)(20) + (0.4)(30) + (0.4)(40) = 32,$$

which is also equal to the unconditional mean $\mathrm{E}[\mu_N(\Lambda)]$. For VHM, we first calculate

$$\mathrm{E}\{[\mu_N(\Lambda)]^2\} = (0.2)(20)^2 + (0.4)(30)^2 + (0.4)(40)^2 = 1{,}080,$$

so that

$$\sigma_{\mathrm{HM}}^2 = \mathrm{Var}[\mu_N(\Lambda)] = \mathrm{E}\{[\mu_N(\Lambda)]^2\} - \{\mathrm{E}[\mu_N(\Lambda)]\}^2 = 1{,}080 - (32)^2 = 56.$$

Therefore, the total variance of N is

$$\mathrm{Var}(N) = \mu_{\mathrm{PV}} + \sigma_{\mathrm{HM}}^2 = 32 + 56 = 88.$$

(b) Claim severity There are three claim-severity distributions, which are specific to each risk group. We assume that the researcher obtains loss observations from the same risk group, so that they have identical distributions. However, the researcher has no information about the risk parameter Θ. The probabilities of occurrence of the severity distributions, as well as their conditional means and variances are given in Table 7.4, in which $\Gamma = (\alpha, \beta)$ denotes the vector representing the parameters of the claim-severity distribution for the risk group.

Table 7.4. *Results for*
Example 7.5 (b)

Group	Group probability	$E(X\mid\Gamma)$ $=\mu_X(\Gamma)$	$Var(X\mid\Gamma)$ $=\sigma_X^2(\Gamma)$
1	0.2	10	20
2	0.4	12	36
3	0.4	6	12

The right two columns give the conditional mean $\alpha\beta$ and conditional variance $\alpha\beta^2$ corresponding to the three different distributions of claim severity. Similar to the calculation in (a), we have

$$E(X) = E[E(X\mid\Gamma)] = 0.2(10) + 0.4(12) + 0.4(6) = 9.20,$$

and

$$\mu_{PV} = 0.2(20) + 0.4(36) + 0.4(12) = 23.2.$$

To calculate VHM, we first compute the raw second moment of the conditional mean of X, which is

$$E\{[\mu_X(\Gamma)]^2\} = 0.2(10)^2 + 0.4(12)^2 + 0.4(6)^2 = 92.$$

Hence,

$$\sigma_{HM}^2 = Var[\mu_X(\Gamma)] = E\{[\mu_X(\Gamma)]^2\} - \{E[\mu_X(\Gamma)]\}^2 = 92 - (9.20)^2 = 7.36.$$

Therefore, the total variance of X is

$$Var(X) = \mu_{PV} + \sigma_{HM}^2 = 23.2 + 7.36 = 30.56.$$

(c) Aggregate loss   The distribution of the aggregate loss S is determined jointly by Λ and Γ, which we shall denote as Θ. For the conditional mean of S, we have

$$E(S\mid\Theta) = E(N\mid\Theta)E(X\mid\Theta) = \lambda\alpha\beta.$$

For the conditional variance of S, we use the result on compound distribution with Poisson claim frequency stated in equation (A.123), and make use of the assumption of gamma severity to obtain

$$Var(S\mid\Theta) = \lambda[\sigma_X^2(\Gamma) + \mu_X^2(\Gamma)] = \lambda(\alpha\beta^2 + \alpha^2\beta^2).$$

The conditional means and conditional variances of S are summarized in Table 7.5.

The unconditional mean of S is

$$E(S) = E[E(S\mid\Theta)] = (0.2)(200) + (0.4)(360) + (0.4)(240) = 280,$$

Table 7.5. *Results for Example 7.5 (c)*

Group	Group probability	Parameters λ, α, β	$E(S \mid \Theta)$ $= \mu_S(\Theta)$	$\text{Var}(S \mid \Theta)$ $= \sigma_S^2(\Theta)$
1	0.2	20, 5, 2	200	2,400
2	0.4	30, 4, 3	360	5,400
3	0.4	40, 3, 2	240	1,920

and the EPV is

$$\mu_{\text{PV}} = (0.2)(2{,}400) + (0.4)(5{,}400) + (0.4)(1{,}920) = 3{,}408.$$

Also, the VHM is given by

$$\begin{aligned}
\sigma_{\text{HM}}^2 &= \text{Var}[\mu_S(\Theta)] \\
&= E\{[\mu_S(\Theta)]^2\} - \{E[\mu_S(\Theta)]\}^2 \\
&= [(0.2)(200)^2 + (0.4)(360)^2 + (0.4)(240)^2] - (280)^2 \\
&= 4{,}480.
\end{aligned}$$

Therefore, the total variance of S is

$$\text{Var}(S) = 3{,}408 + 4{,}480 = 7{,}888. \qquad \square$$

EPV and VHM measure two different aspects of the total variance. When a risk group is homogeneous so that the loss claims are similar within the group, the conditional variance is small. If all risk groups have similar loss claims within the group, the expected value of the process variance EPV is small. On the other hand, if the risk groups have very different risk profiles across groups, their hypothetical means will differ more and thus the variance of the hypothetical means VHM will be large. In other words, it will be easier to distinguish between risk groups if the variance of the hypothetical means is large and the average of the process variance is small.

We define k as the ratio of EPV to VHM, i.e.,

$$k = \frac{\mu_{\text{PV}}}{\sigma_{\text{HM}}^2} = \frac{\text{EPV}}{\text{VHM}}. \tag{7.11}$$

A small EPV or large VHM will give rise to a small k. The risk groups will be more *distinguishable* in the mean when k is smaller, in which case we may put more weight on the data in updating our revised prediction for future losses. For the cases in Example 7.5, the values of k for claim frequency, claim severity and aggregate loss are, respectively, 0.5714, 3.1522 and 0.7607. For Example 7.4, as $\sigma_{HM}^2 = 0$, k is infinite.[4]

Example 7.6 Frequency of claim per year, N, is distributed as a binomial random variable $\mathcal{BN}(10, \theta)$, and claim severity, X, is distributed as an exponential random variable with mean $c\theta$, where c is a known constant. Given θ, claim frequency and claim severity are independently distributed. Derive an expression of k for the aggregate loss per year, S, in terms of c and the moments of Θ, and show that it does not depend on c. If Θ is 0.3 or 0.7 with equal probabilities, calculate k.

Solution 7.6 We first calculate the conditional mean of S as a function of θ. Due to the independence assumption of N and X, the hypothetical mean of S is

$$E(S\,|\,\Theta) = E(N\,|\,\Theta)E(X\,|\,\Theta) = (10\Theta)(c\Theta) = 10c\Theta^2.$$

Using equation (A.122), the process variance is

$$\begin{aligned}
\text{Var}(S\,|\,\Theta) &= \mu_N(\Theta)\sigma_X^2(\Theta) + \sigma_N^2(\Theta)\mu_X^2(\Theta) \\
&= (10\Theta)(c\Theta)^2 + [10\Theta(1 - \Theta)](c\Theta)^2 \\
&= 10c^2\Theta^3 + 10c^2\Theta^3(1 - \Theta) \\
&= 10c^2\Theta^3(2 - \Theta).
\end{aligned}$$

Hence, the unconditional mean of S is

$$E(S) = E[E(S\,|\,\Theta)] = E(10c\Theta^2) = 10cE(\Theta^2)$$

and the variance of the hypothetical means is

$$\begin{aligned}
\sigma_{HM}^2 &= \text{Var}[E(S\,|\,\Theta)] \\
&= \text{Var}(10c\Theta^2) \\
&= 100c^2\,\text{Var}(\Theta^2) \\
&= 100c^2\{E(\Theta^4) - [E(\Theta^2)]^2\}.
\end{aligned}$$

The expected value of the process variance is

$$\begin{aligned}
\mu_{PV} &= E[\text{Var}(S\,|\,\Theta)] \\
&= E[10c^2\Theta^3(2 - \Theta)] \\
&= 10c^2[2E(\Theta^3) - E(\Theta^4)].
\end{aligned}$$

---

[4] In this case, the data contain no useful information for updating the *mean* of the risk group separately from the overall mean, although they might be used to update the specific group *variance* if required.

Table 7.6. Calculations of Example 7.6

θ	$\Pr(\Theta = \theta)$	θ^2	θ^3	θ^4
0.3	0.5	0.09	0.027	0.0081
0.7	0.5	0.49	0.343	0.2401

Combining the above results we conclude that

$$k = \frac{\mu_{PV}}{\sigma_{HM}^2} = \frac{10c^2[2E(\Theta^3) - E(\Theta^4)]}{100c^2\{E(\Theta^4) - [E(\Theta^2)]^2\}} = \frac{2E(\Theta^3) - E(\Theta^4)}{10\{E(\Theta^4) - [E(\Theta^2)]^2\}}.$$

Thus, k does not depend on c. To compute its value for the given distribution of Θ, we present the calculations in Table 7.6.

Thus, the required moments of Θ are

$$E(\Theta) = (0.5)(0.3) + (0.5)(0.7) = 0.5,$$
$$E(\Theta^2) = (0.5)(0.09) + (0.5)(0.49) = 0.29,$$
$$E(\Theta^3) = (0.5)(0.027) + (0.5)(0.343) = 0.185$$

and

$$E(\Theta^4) = (0.5)(0.0081) + (0.5)(0.2401) = 0.1241,$$

so that

$$k = \frac{2(0.185) - 0.1241}{10\,[0.1241 - (0.29)^2]} = 0.6148.$$

In this example, note that both EPV and VHM depend on c. However, as the effects of c on these components are the same, the ratio of EPV to VHM is invariant to c. Also, though X and N are independent *given* θ, they are correlated *unconditionally* due to their common dependence on Θ. □

7.3 Bühlmann Credibility

Bühlmann's approach of updating the predicted loss measure is based on a linear predictor using past observations. It is also called the **greatest accuracy approach** or the **least squares approach**. Recall that for the classical credibility approach, the updated prediction U is given by (see equation (6.1))

$$U = ZD + (1 - Z)M. \tag{7.12}$$

The Bühlmann credibility method has a similar basic equation, in which D is the sample mean of the data and M is the overall prior mean $E(X)$. The Bühlmann credibility factor Z depends on the sample size n and the EPV to VHM ratio k. In particular, Z varies with n and k as follows:

1 Z increases with the sample size n of the data.

2 Z increases with the *distinctiveness* of the risk groups. As argued above, the risk groups are more distinguishable when k is small. Thus, Z increases as k decreases.

We now state formally the assumptions of the Bühlmann model and derive the updating formula as the **least mean squared error (MSE) linear predictor**.

1 $\boldsymbol{X} = \{X_1, \ldots, X_n\}$ are loss measures that are independently and identically distributed as the random variable X. The distribution of X depends on the parameter θ.

2 The parameter θ is a realization of a random variable Θ. Given θ, the conditional mean and variance of X are

$$\mathrm{E}(X \mid \theta) = \mu_X(\theta), \tag{7.13}$$

and

$$\mathrm{Var}(X \mid \theta) = \sigma_X^2(\theta). \tag{7.14}$$

3 The unconditional mean of X is $\mathrm{E}(X) = \mathrm{E}[\mathrm{E}(X \mid \Theta)] = \mu_X$. The mean of the conditional variance of X is

$$
\begin{aligned}
\mathrm{E}[\mathrm{Var}(X \mid \Theta)] &= \mathrm{E}[\sigma_X^2(\Theta)] \\
&= \mu_{\mathrm{PV}} \\
&= \text{Expected value of process variance} \\
&= \mathrm{EPV},
\end{aligned}
\tag{7.15}
$$

and the variance of the conditional mean is

$$
\begin{aligned}
\mathrm{Var}[\mathrm{E}(X \mid \Theta)] &= \mathrm{Var}[\mu_X(\Theta)] \\
&= \sigma_{\mathrm{HM}}^2 \\
&= \text{Variance of hypothetical means} \\
&= \mathrm{VHM}.
\end{aligned}
\tag{7.16}
$$

The unconditional variance (or total variance) of X is

$$
\begin{aligned}
\mathrm{Var}(X) &= \mathrm{E}[\mathrm{Var}(X \mid \Theta)] + \mathrm{Var}[\mathrm{E}(X \mid \Theta)] \\
&= \mu_{\mathrm{PV}} + \sigma_{\mathrm{HM}}^2 \\
&= \mathrm{EPV} + \mathrm{VHM}.
\end{aligned}
\tag{7.17}
$$

4 The Bühlmann approach formulates a predictor of X_{n+1} based on a linear function of $\boldsymbol{X}$, where X_{n+1} is assumed to have the same distribution as X. The predictor minimizes the mean squared error in predicting X_{n+1} over the joint distribution of Θ, X_{n+1} and $\boldsymbol{X}$. Specifically, the predictor is given by

$$\hat{X}_{n+1} = \beta_0 + \beta_1 X_1 + \cdots + \beta_n X_n, \tag{7.18}$$

where $\beta_0, \beta_1, \ldots, \beta_n$ are chosen to minimize the mean squared error, MSE, defined as

$$\text{MSE} = \text{E}[(X_{n+1} - \hat{X}_{n+1})^2]. \tag{7.19}$$

To solve the above problem we make use of the least squares regression results in Appendix A.17. We define W as the $(n+1) \times 1$ vector $(1, X')'$, and β as the $(n+1) \times 1$ vector $(\beta_0, \beta_1, \ldots, \beta_n)'$. We also write β_S as $(\beta_1, \ldots, \beta_n)'$. Thus, the predictor $\hat{X}_{n+1}$ can be written as

$$\hat{X}_{n+1} = \beta' W = \beta_0 + \beta_S' X. \tag{7.20}$$

The MSE is then given by

$$\begin{aligned}
\text{MSE} &= \text{E}[(X_{n+1} - \hat{X}_{n+1})^2] \\
&= \text{E}[(X_{n+1} - \beta' W)^2] \\
&= \text{E}(X_{n+1}^2 + \beta' WW' \beta - 2\beta' W X_{n+1}) \\
&= \text{E}(X_{n+1}^2) + \beta' \text{E}(WW') \beta - 2\beta' \text{E}(W X_{n+1}).
\end{aligned} \tag{7.21}$$

Thus, the MSE has the same form as RSS in equation (A.167), with the sample moments replaced by the population moments. Hence, the solution of β that minimizes MSE is, by virtue of equation (A.168),

$$\hat{\beta} = [\text{E}(WW')]^{-1} \text{E}(W X_{n+1}). \tag{7.22}$$

Following the results in equations (A.174) and (A.175), we have

$$\begin{aligned}
\hat{\beta}_S &= \begin{pmatrix} \hat{\beta}_1 \\ \hat{\beta}_2 \\ \vdots \\ \hat{\beta}_n \end{pmatrix} \\
&= \begin{bmatrix} \text{Var}(X_1) & \text{Cov}(X_1, X_2) & \cdots & \text{Cov}(X_1, X_n) \\ \text{Cov}(X_1, X_2) & \text{Var}(X_2) & \cdots & \text{Cov}(X_2, X_n) \\ \vdots & \vdots & \cdot & \cdot \\ & & \vdots & \cdot \\ \text{Cov}(X_1, X_n) & \text{Cov}(X_2, X_n) & \cdots & \text{Var}(X_n) \end{bmatrix}^{-1} \begin{bmatrix} \text{Cov}(X_1, X_{n+1}) \\ \text{Cov}(X_2, X_{n+1}) \\ \vdots \\ \text{Cov}(X_n, X_{n+1}) \end{bmatrix}
\end{aligned} \tag{7.23}$$

and

$$\hat{\beta}_0 = E(X_{n+1}) - \sum_{i=1}^{n} \hat{\beta}_i E(X_i) = \mu_X - \mu_X \sum_{i=1}^{n} \hat{\beta}_i. \qquad (7.24)$$

From equation (7.17), we have

$$\text{Var}(X_i) = \mu_{\text{PV}} + \sigma^2_{\text{HM}}, \qquad \text{for } i = 1, \ldots, n. \qquad (7.25)$$

Also, $\text{Cov}(X_i, X_j)$ is given by (for $i \neq j$)

$$\begin{aligned}
\text{Cov}(X_i, X_j) &= E(X_i X_j) - E(X_i)E(X_j) \\
&= E\left[E(X_i X_j \mid \Theta)\right] - \mu_X^2 \\
&= E\left[E(X_i \mid \Theta)E(X_j \mid \Theta)\right] - \mu_X^2 \\
&= E\left\{[\mu_X(\Theta)]^2\right\} - \left\{E\left[\mu_X(\Theta)\right]\right\}^2 \\
&= \text{Var}[\mu_X(\Theta)] \\
&= \sigma^2_{\text{HM}}.
\end{aligned} \qquad (7.26)$$

Thus, equation (7.23) can be written as

$$\hat{\beta}_S = \begin{pmatrix} \hat{\beta}_1 \\ \hat{\beta}_2 \\ \vdots \\ \hat{\beta}_n \end{pmatrix} = \left(\mu_{\text{PV}}\mathbf{I} + \sigma^2_{\text{HM}}\mathbf{1}\mathbf{1}'\right)^{-1} \left(\sigma^2_{\text{HM}}\mathbf{1}\right), \qquad (7.27)$$

where $\mathbf{I}$ is the $n \times n$ identity matrix and $\mathbf{1}$ is the $n \times 1$ vector of ones. We now write

$$k = \frac{\mu_{\text{PV}}}{\sigma^2_{\text{HM}}}, \qquad (7.28)$$

and evaluate the inverse matrix on the right-hand side of equation (7.27) as follows

$$\begin{aligned}
\left(\mu_{\text{PV}}\mathbf{I} + \sigma^2_{\text{HM}}\mathbf{1}\mathbf{1}'\right)^{-1} &= \frac{1}{\mu_{\text{PV}}}\left(\mathbf{I} + \frac{\sigma^2_{\text{HM}}}{\mu_{\text{PV}}}\mathbf{1}\mathbf{1}'\right)^{-1} \\
&= \frac{1}{\mu_{\text{PV}}}\left(\mathbf{I} + \frac{1}{k}\mathbf{1}\mathbf{1}'\right)^{-1}.
\end{aligned} \qquad (7.29)$$

With $\mathbf{1}'\mathbf{1} = n$, it is easy to verify that

$$\left(\mathbf{I} + \frac{1}{k}\mathbf{1}\mathbf{1}'\right)^{-1} = \mathbf{I} - \frac{1}{n+k}\mathbf{1}\mathbf{1}'. \qquad (7.30)$$

Substituting equation (7.30) into equations (7.27) and (7.29), we obtain

$$\hat{\beta}_S = \frac{1}{\mu_{PV}} \left(\mathbf{I} - \frac{1}{n+k} \mathbf{1}\mathbf{1}' \right) (\sigma_{HM}^2 \mathbf{1})$$

$$= \frac{1}{k} \left(\mathbf{I} - \frac{1}{n+k} \mathbf{1}\mathbf{1}' \right) \mathbf{1}$$

$$= \frac{1}{k} \left(\mathbf{1} - \frac{n}{n+k} \mathbf{1} \right)$$

$$= \frac{1}{n+k} \mathbf{1}. \tag{7.31}$$

Note that equation (7.24) can be written as

$$\hat{\beta}_0 = \mu_X - \mu_X \hat{\beta}_S' \mathbf{1}. \tag{7.32}$$

Thus, the least MSE linear predictor of X_{n+1} is

$$\hat{\beta}_0 + \hat{\beta}_S' X = (\mu_X - \mu_X \hat{\beta}_S' \mathbf{1}) + \hat{\beta}_S' X$$

$$= \left(\mu_X - \frac{\mu_X}{n+k} \mathbf{1}'\mathbf{1} \right) + \frac{1}{n+k} \mathbf{1}'X$$

$$= \frac{1}{n+k} \mathbf{1}'X + \frac{k\mu_X}{n+k}. \tag{7.33}$$

Noting that $\mathbf{1}'X = n\bar{X}$, we conclude that

$$\hat{X}_{n+1} = \hat{\beta}_0 + \hat{\beta}_S' X = \frac{n\bar{X}}{n+k} + \frac{k\mu_X}{n+k} = Z\bar{X} + (1 - Z)\mu_X, \tag{7.34}$$

where

$$Z = \frac{n}{n+k}. \tag{7.35}$$

Z defined in equation (7.35) is called the **Bühlmann credibility factor** or simply the **Bühlmann credibility**. It depends on the EPV to VHM ratio k, which is called the **Bühlmann credibility parameter**. The optimal linear forecast $\hat{X}_{n+1}$ given in equation (7.34) is also called the **Bühlmann premium**. Note that k depends only on the parameters of the model,[5] while Z is a function of k and the size n of the *data*. For predicting claim frequency N, the sample size n is the number of periods over which the number of claims is aggregated.[6] For predicting claim severity X, the sample size n is the number of claims. As aggregate loss S refers to the total loss payout per period, the sample size is the number of periods of claim experience.

---

[5] Hence, k is fixed, but needs to be estimated in practice. We shall come back to this issue in Chapter 9.

[6] Note that N is the number of claims per period, say year, and n is the number of periods of claim-frequency experience.

Example 7.7 Refer to Example 7.5. Suppose the claim experience last year was 26 claims with an average claim size of 12. Calculate the updated prediction of (a) the claim frequency, (b) the average claim size and (c) the aggregate loss for next year.

Solution 7.7 (a) Claim frequency From Example 7.5, we have $k = 0.5714$ and $M = E(N) = 32$. Now we are given $n = 1$ and $D = 26$. Hence,

$$Z = \frac{1}{1 + 0.5714} = 0.6364,$$

so that the updated prediction of the claim frequency of this group is

$$U = (0.6364)(26) + (1 - 0.6364)(32) = 28.1816.$$

(b) Claim severity We have $k = 3.1522$ and $M = E(X) = 9.20$, with $n = 26$ and $D = 12$. Thus,

$$Z = \frac{26}{26 + 3.1522} = 0.8919,$$

so that the updated prediction of the claim severity of this group is

$$U = (0.8919)(12) + (1 - 0.8919)(9.20) = 11.6973.$$

(c) Aggregate loss With $k = 0.7607$, $M = E(S) = 280$, $n = 1$ and $D = (26)(12) = 312$, we have

$$Z = \frac{1}{1 + 0.7607} = 0.5680,$$

so that the updated prediction of the aggregate loss of this group is

$$U = (0.5680)(312) + (1 - 0.5680)(280) = 298.1760. \qquad \square$$

Example 7.8 Refer to Example 7.6. Suppose the numbers of claims in the past three years were: 8, 4 and 7, with the corresponding average amount of claim in each of the three years being 12, 19 and 9. Calculate the updated prediction of the aggregate loss for next year for $c = 20$ and 30.

Solution 7.8 We first calculate the average aggregate loss per year in the past three years, which is

$$\frac{1}{3}[(8)(12) + (4)(19) + (7)(9)] = 78.3333.$$

As shown in Example 7.6, $k = 0.6148$, which does not vary with c. As there are three observations of S, the Bühlmann credibility factor is

$$Z = \frac{3}{3 + 0.6148} = 0.8299.$$

The unconditional mean of S is

$$\mathrm{E}[\mathrm{E}(S \mid \Theta)] = 10c\mathrm{E}(\Theta^2) = (10)(0.29)c = 2.9c.$$

Hence, using equation (7.34), the updated prediction of S is

$$(0.8299)(78.3333) + (1 - 0.8299)(2.9c),$$

which gives a predicted value of 74.8746 when $c = 20$, and 79.8075 when $c = 30$. $\qquad\square$

We have derived the Bühlmann credibility predictor for future loss as the linear predictor (in X) that minimizes the mean squared prediction error in equation (7.19). However, we can also consider the problem of a linear *estimator* (in X) that minimizes the squared error in estimating the *expected* future loss, i.e., $\mathrm{E}\big[(\mu_{n+1} - \hat{\mu}_{n+1})^2\big]$, where $\mu_{n+1} = \mathrm{E}(X_{n+1}) = \mu_X$ and $\hat{\mu}_{n+1}$ is a linear estimator of μ_{n+1}. Readers are invited to show that the result is the same as the Bühlmann credibility predictor for future loss (see Exercise 7.5). Thus, we shall use the terminologies Bühlmann credibility predictor for future loss and Bühlmann credibility estimator of the expected loss interchangeably.

7.4 Bühlmann–Straub Credibility

An important limitation of the Bühlmann credibility theory is that the predictors X_i are assumed to be *identically* distributed. This assumption is violated if the predictors are based on different numbers of observed losses. The **Bühlmann–Straub credibility model** extends the Bühlmann theory to cases where the loss data X_i are not identically distributed.

We now state formally the assumptions of the Bühlmann–Straub model and present the updating formula as the least MSE linear predictor. Let $\{X_{ij}\}$ be a set of loss observations that are independently and identically distributed as the random variable X, for $i = 1, \ldots, n$ and $j = 1, \ldots, m_i$. The distribution of X depends on the risk parameter θ. Given θ, the mean of X_{ij} is $\mu_X(\theta)$ and its variance is $\sigma_X^2(\theta)$, i.e., $\mathrm{E}(X|\theta) = \mu_X(\theta)$ and $\mathrm{Var}(X|\theta) = \sigma_X^2(\theta)$. Across different risk groups, the mean of the process variance is $\mu_{\mathrm{PV}} = \mathrm{E}[\sigma_X^2(\Theta)]$ and the variance of the hypothetical mean is $\sigma_{\mathrm{HM}}^2 = \mathrm{Var}[\mu_X(\Theta)]$.

We define[7]

$$X_i = \frac{1}{m_i} \sum_{j=1}^{m_i} X_{ij}. \tag{7.36}$$

To clarify the notations, we consider the following examples:

---

[7] For simplicity, we use the notation X_i instead of the usual notation $\bar{X}_i$ for a sample mean. This also enables us to use the same prediction equation as in (7.18).

1 **Claim frequency:** Let X_{ij} be the number of claims of the jth insured in year i, for $i = 1, \ldots, n$ and $j = 1, \ldots, m_i$. Thus, there are n years of data with m_i insured in year i. X_i is the average number of claims per insured in year i.

2 **Claim severity:** Let X_{ij} be the amount of the jth claim in the ith block of policies, for $i = 1, \ldots, n$ and $j = 1, \ldots, m_i$. Thus, there are n blocks of policies with m_i claims for the ith block. The policies are assumed to belong to the same risk group. X_i is the average claim amount over all claims from the ith block.

3 **Aggregate loss:** Let X_{ij} be the aggregate loss in the jth period for the ith block of policies, for $i = 1, \ldots, n$ and $j = 1, \ldots, m_i$. Thus, there are n blocks of policies with m_i periods of aggregate loss data for the ith block of policies. X_i is the average aggregate loss per period for the ith block.

The Bühlmann–Straub approach formulates a predictor for a single future loss, denoted by X_{n+1}, based on a linear function of $X = \{X_1, \ldots, X_n\}$. The predictor minimizes the mean squared error in predicting X_{n+1} over the joint distribution of Θ, X_{n+1} and X. Specifically, the predictor is given by[8]

$$\hat{X}_{n+1} = \beta_0 + \beta_1 X_1 + \cdots + \beta_n X_n, \tag{7.37}$$

where $\beta_0, \beta_1, \ldots, \beta_n$ are chosen to minimize the MSE as defined in equation (7.19). The solution of this problem depends on the mean and variance of the components of X. First, the conditional mean of X_i is

$$
\begin{aligned}
\mathrm{E}(X_i \mid \theta) &= \mathrm{E}\left[\frac{1}{m_i}\sum_{j=1}^{m_i} X_{ij} \mid \theta\right] \\
&= \frac{1}{m_i}\sum_{j=1}^{m_i}\mathrm{E}[X_{ij}\mid\theta] \\
&= \frac{1}{m_i}[m_i \mu_X(\theta)] \\
&= \mu_X(\theta). \tag{7.38}
\end{aligned}
$$

Thus, the unconditional mean of X_i is $\mathrm{E}(X_i) = \mathrm{E}[\mu_X(\Theta)] = \mu_X$. Next, the conditional variance of X_i is

$$
\begin{aligned}
\mathrm{Var}(X_i \mid \theta) &= \frac{1}{m_i^2}\mathrm{Var}\left(\sum_{j=1}^{m_i} X_{ij} \mid \theta\right) \\
&= \frac{1}{m_i^2}\sum_{j=1}^{m_i}\mathrm{Var}\left(X_{ij} \mid \theta\right)
\end{aligned}
$$

---

[8] Note that the prediction is for a single future loss (not a mean as the single suffix defined in equation (7.36) might have suggested). Also, X_i in the right-hand sides of equations (7.37) and (7.18) are differently defined. The former are sample means, while the latter are single observations.

$$= \frac{1}{m_i^2} \sum_{j=1}^{m_i} \sigma_X^2(\theta)$$

$$= \frac{\sigma_X^2(\theta)}{m_i}, \tag{7.39}$$

so that the mean of the conditional variance of X_i is

$$E[\text{Var}(X_i \mid \Theta)] = E\left[\frac{\sigma_X^2(\Theta)}{m_i}\right]$$

$$= \frac{\mu_{\text{PV}}}{m_i}, \tag{7.40}$$

where $\mu_{\text{PV}} = E[\sigma_X^2(\Theta)]$. Furthermore, the variance of the conditional mean is

$$\text{Var}[E(X_i \mid \Theta)] = \text{Var}[\mu_X(\Theta)]$$

$$= \sigma_{\text{HM}}^2, \tag{7.41}$$

so that the total variance of X_i is

$$\text{Var}(X_i) = \frac{\mu_{\text{PV}}}{m_i} + \sigma_{\text{HM}}^2. \tag{7.42}$$

In addition, following the derivation as in equation (7.26), we have $\text{Cov}(X_i, X_j) = \sigma_{\text{HM}}^2$ for $i \neq j$. Equation (7.27) can be written as

$$\hat{\boldsymbol{\beta}}_S = \begin{pmatrix} \hat{\beta}_1 \\ \hat{\beta}_2 \\ \vdots \\ \hat{\beta}_n \end{pmatrix} = \left(\mathbf{V} + \sigma_{\text{HM}}^2 \mathbf{1}\mathbf{1}'\right)^{-1} \left(\sigma_{\text{HM}}^2 \mathbf{1}\right), \tag{7.43}$$

where $\mathbf{V}$ is the $n \times n$ diagonal matrix

$$\mathbf{V} = \mu_{\text{PV}} \begin{bmatrix} m_1^{-1} & 0 & 0 & \cdot & 0 \\ 0 & m_2^{-1} & 0 & \cdot & 0 \\ 0 & 0 & \cdot & \cdot & \cdot \\ \cdot & \cdot & \cdot & \cdot & \cdot \\ 0 & 0 & \cdot & \cdot & m_n^{-1} \end{bmatrix}. \tag{7.44}$$

It can be verified that

$$\left(\mathbf{V} + \sigma_{\text{HM}}^2 \mathbf{1}\mathbf{1}'\right)^{-1} = \mathbf{V}^{-1} - \frac{\sigma_{\text{HM}}^2 (\mathbf{V}^{-1}\mathbf{1})(\mathbf{1}'\mathbf{V}^{-1})}{1 + \sigma_{\text{HM}}^2 \mathbf{1}'\mathbf{V}^{-1}\mathbf{1}}. \tag{7.45}$$

Thus, denoting

$$m = \sum_{i=1}^{n} m_i \tag{7.46}$$

and $m = (m_1, \ldots, m_n)'$, we have

$$\mathbf{V}^{-1} - \frac{\sigma_{\text{HM}}^2 (\mathbf{V}^{-1}\mathbf{1})(\mathbf{1}'\mathbf{V}^{-1})}{1 + \sigma_{\text{HM}}^2 \mathbf{1}'\mathbf{V}^{-1}\mathbf{1}} = \mathbf{V}^{-1} - \frac{1}{\mu_{\text{PV}}} \left(\frac{\sigma_{\text{HM}}^2 mm'}{\mu_{\text{PV}} + m\sigma_{\text{HM}}^2} \right), \tag{7.47}$$

so that from equation (7.43) we have

$$\begin{aligned}
\hat{\boldsymbol{\beta}}_S &= \left[\mathbf{V}^{-1} - \frac{1}{\mu_{\text{PV}}} \left(\frac{\sigma_{\text{HM}}^2 mm'}{\mu_{\text{PV}} + m\sigma_{\text{HM}}^2} \right) \right] (\sigma_{\text{HM}}^2 \mathbf{1}) \\
&= \left(\frac{\sigma_{\text{HM}}^2}{\mu_{\text{PV}}} \right) m - \left(\frac{\sigma_{\text{HM}}^2}{\mu_{\text{PV}}} \right) \left(\frac{\sigma_{\text{HM}}^2 mm}{\mu_{\text{PV}} + m\sigma_{\text{HM}}^2} \right) \\
&= \left(\frac{\sigma_{\text{HM}}^2}{\mu_{\text{PV}}} \right) \left(1 - \frac{\sigma_{\text{HM}}^2 m}{\mu_{\text{PV}} + m\sigma_{\text{HM}}^2} \right) m \\
&= \frac{\sigma_{\text{HM}}^2 m}{\mu_{\text{PV}} + m\sigma_{\text{HM}}^2}.
\end{aligned} \tag{7.48}$$

We now define

$$\bar{X} = \frac{1}{m} \sum_{i=1}^{n} m_i X_i = \frac{1}{m} m' X \tag{7.49}$$

and

$$k = \frac{\mu_{\text{PV}}}{\sigma_{\text{HM}}^2} \tag{7.50}$$

to obtain

$$\hat{\boldsymbol{\beta}}_S' X = \frac{\sigma_{\text{HM}}^2 m' X}{\mu_{\text{PV}} + m\sigma_{\text{HM}}^2} = \frac{m}{m+k} \bar{X} = Z\bar{X}, \tag{7.51}$$

where

$$Z = \frac{m}{m+k}. \tag{7.52}$$

If we replace X in equation (7.51) by $\mathbf{1}$, we have

$$\hat{\boldsymbol{\beta}}_S' \mathbf{1} = Z, \tag{7.53}$$

so that from equation (7.32) we obtain

$$\hat{\beta}_0 = \mu_X - \mu_X \hat{\boldsymbol{\beta}}_S' \mathbf{1} = (1 - Z)\mu_X. \tag{7.54}$$

Combining the results in equations (7.51) and (7.54), we conclude that

$$\hat{X} = \hat{\beta}_0 + \hat{\boldsymbol{\beta}}_S' X = Z\bar{X} + (1 - Z)\mu_X, \tag{7.55}$$

where Z is defined in equation (7.52).

Table 7.7. *Data for Example 7.9*

Year	Number of insureds	Number of claims
1	100	7
2	200	13
3	250	18
4	280	–

Example 7.9 The number of accident claims or each insured within a risk group is distributed as a binomial random variable $\mathcal{BN}(2, \theta)$, and the claim incidences are independent across insureds. The probability θ of the binomial has a beta distribution across different risk groups with parameters $\alpha = 1$ and $\beta = 10$. The data in Table 7.7 are given for a block of policies in a risk group. Calculate the Bühlmann–Straub credibility prediction of the number of claims in the fourth year.

Solution 7.9 Let m_i be the number of insureds in Year i, and X_i be the number of claims per insured in Year i. Define X_{ij} as the number of claims for the jth insured in Year i, which is distributed as $\mathcal{BN}(2, \theta)$. Thus, we have

$$E(X_i \mid \Theta) = \frac{1}{m_i} \sum_{j=1}^{m_i} E(X_{ij} \mid \Theta) = 2\Theta,$$

and

$$\sigma_{\text{HM}}^2 = \text{Var}[E(X_i \mid \Theta)] = \text{Var}(2\Theta) = 4\text{Var}(\Theta).$$

As Θ has a beta distribution with parameters $\alpha = 1$ and $\beta = 10$, we have[9]

$$\text{Var}(\Theta) = \frac{\alpha\beta}{(\alpha + \beta)^2(\alpha + \beta + 1)} = \frac{10}{(11)^2(12)} = 0.006887.$$

For the conditional variance of X_i, we have

$$\text{Var}(X_i \mid \Theta) = \frac{2\Theta(1 - \Theta)}{m_i}.$$

Thus,

$$\mu_{\text{PV}} = 2E[\Theta(1 - \Theta)].$$

As

$$E(\Theta) = \frac{\alpha}{\alpha + \beta} = 0.0909,$$

[9] See Appendix A.10.6 for the moments of the beta distribution.

we have

$$\mu_{PV} = 2[E(\Theta) - E(\Theta^2)]$$
$$= 2\left\{E(\Theta) - \left(\text{Var}(\Theta) + [E(\Theta)]^2\right)\right\}$$
$$= 2\{0.0909 - [0.006887 + (0.0909)^2]\} = 0.1515.$$

Thus,

$$k = \frac{\mu_{PV}}{\sigma_{HM}^2} = \frac{0.1515}{(4)(0.006887)} = 5.5.$$

As $m = 100 + 200 + 250 = 550$, we have

$$Z = \frac{550}{550 + 5.5} = 0.9901.$$

Now

$$\mu_X = E[E(X_i \mid \Theta)] = (2)(0.0909) = 0.1818$$

and

$$\bar{X} = \frac{7 + 13 + 18}{550} = 0.0691.$$

Thus, the predicted number of claims per insured in the risk group is

$$(0.9901)(0.0691) + (1 - 0.9901)(0.1818) = 0.0702,$$

and the predicted number of claims in the risk group in Year 4 is

$$(280)(0.0702) = 19.66. \qquad \square$$

Example 7.10 The number of accident claims incurred per year for each insured in a risk group is a Bernoulli random variable with probability θ. Across different risk groups the value of θ is 0.1 with probability 0.8 and 0.2 with probability 0.2. For all risk groups each claim may be of amount 20, 30 or 40, with equal probabilities. Claim frequency and claim severity are assumed to be independent for each insured. The data for the total claim amount of a risk group are given in Table 7.8.

Table 7.8. *Data for Example 7.10*

Year	Number of insureds	Total claim amount
1	100	240
2	200	380
3	250	592
4	280	–

Calculate the Bühlmann–Straub credibility prediction of the pure premium and total loss in the fourth year for this risk group.

Solution 7.10 Let X_{ij} be the claim amount for the jth insured in Year i, each of which is distributed as $X = NW$, where

$$N = \begin{cases} 0, & \text{with probability } 1 - \Theta, \\ \\ 1, & \text{with probability } \Theta, \end{cases}$$

and $W = 20, 30$ and 40, with equal probabilities. We have

$$E(N \mid \Theta) = \Theta,$$

and

$$\text{Var}(N \mid \Theta) = \Theta(1 - \Theta).$$

We evaluate the moments of Θ to obtain

$$E(\Theta) = (0.1)(0.8) + (0.2)(0.2) = 0.12,$$

and

$$E(\Theta^2) = (0.1)^2(0.8) + (0.2)^2(0.2) = 0.016.$$

Also,

$$E(W) = \frac{20 + 30 + 40}{3} = 30,$$

and

$$E(W^2) = \frac{(20)^2 + (30)^2 + (40)^2}{3} = 966.6667,$$

so that

$$E(X \mid \Theta) = E(N \mid \Theta)E(W) = 30\Theta.$$

Using equations (A.118), we have

$$\begin{aligned} \text{Var}(X \mid \Theta) &= E(W^2)\text{Var}(N \mid \Theta) + [E(N \mid \Theta)]^2 \text{Var}(W) \\ &= 966.6667\Theta(1 - \Theta) + \Theta^2[966.6667 - (30)^2] \\ &= 966.6667\Theta - 900\Theta^2. \end{aligned}$$

Thus, EPV is

$$\mu_{\text{PV}} = E[\text{Var}(X \mid \Theta)] = (966.6667)(0.12) - (900)(0.016) = 101.60,$$

and VHM is

$$
\begin{aligned}
\sigma_{\mathrm{HM}}^2 &= \mathrm{Var}[\mathrm{E}(X \,|\, \Theta)] \\
&= \mathrm{Var}(30\Theta) \\
&= 900 \left\{ \mathrm{E}(\Theta^2) - [\mathrm{E}(\Theta)]^2 \right\} \\
&= 900[0.016 - (0.12)^2] \\
&= 1.44.
\end{aligned}
$$

Thus,

$$
k = \frac{\mu_{\mathrm{PV}}}{\sigma_{\mathrm{HM}}^2} = \frac{101.60}{1.44} = 70.5556.
$$

As $m = 100 + 200 + 250 = 550$,

$$
Z = \frac{550}{550 + 70.5556} = 0.8863.
$$

Now

$$
\bar{X} = \frac{240 + 380 + 592}{550} = 2.2036,
$$

and

$$
\mu_X = \mathrm{E}(X) = 30\mathrm{E}(\Theta) = (30)(0.12) = 3.60,
$$

so that the Bühlmann–Straub prediction for the pure premium is

$$
(0.8863)(2.2036) + (1 - 0.8863)(3.60) = 2.3624,
$$

and the Bühlmann–Straub prediction for the total claim amount in Year 4 is

$$
(280)(2.3624) = 661.4638. \qquad \square
$$

7.5 Summary and Discussions

The Bühlmann–Straub credibility model is a generalization of the Bühlmann credibility model, and we summarize its main results again here. Let X_{ij}, $i = 1, \ldots, n$, and $j = 1, \ldots, m_i$ be independently and identically distributed as the loss variable X. Let X_i be the mean for the ith period or ith block of policies over m_i losses.

Let

$$
\mu_{\mathrm{PV}} = m_i \, \mathrm{E}[\mathrm{Var}(X_i \,|\, \Theta)], \tag{7.56}
$$

and

$$
\sigma_{\mathrm{HM}}^2 = \mathrm{Var}[\mathrm{E}(X_i \,|\, \Theta)], \tag{7.57}
$$

then the Bühlmann–Straub prediction of X is

$$
\hat{X} = Z\bar{X} + (1 - Z)\mu_X, \tag{7.58}
$$

where $\mu_X = E(X)$ and

$$\bar{X} = \frac{1}{m} \sum_{i=1}^{n} m_i X_i, \qquad (7.59)$$

and

$$Z = \frac{m}{m+k}, \qquad (7.60)$$

with

$$k = \frac{\mu_{PV}}{\sigma_{HM}^2}. \qquad (7.61)$$

In the special case where the exposures of all periods are the same, say $m_i = \bar{m}$ for $i = 1, \ldots, n$, then

$$\bar{X} = \frac{1}{n} \sum_{i=1}^{n} X_i, \qquad (7.62)$$

and

$$Z = \frac{n\bar{m}}{n\bar{m} + \dfrac{\mu_{PV}}{\sigma_{HM}^2}} = \frac{n}{n + \dfrac{\mu_{PV}}{\bar{m}\sigma_{HM}^2}}. \qquad (7.63)$$

If $\bar{m} = 1$, Z in equation (7.63) is the same as Z in equation (7.35). Thus, the Bühlmann–Straub credibility predictor can be specialized to the Bühlmann credibility predictor.

For the examples given in this chapter we assume that the variance components are known. In practice, they have to be estimated from the data. In Chapter 9 we shall consider the empirical implementation of the Bühlmann and Bühlmann–Straub credibility models when EPV and VHM are unknown. While we have proved the optimality of the Bühlmann predictor in the class of *linear* predictors, it turns out that its optimality may be more general. We shall see the details of this in the next chapter.

Exercises

Exercise 7.1 Refer to Example 7.6. Calculate the unconditional covariance between X and N, $\mathrm{Cov}(X, N)$.

Exercise 7.2 Refer to Example 7.6. Find the Bühlmann credibility parameters for claim frequency N and claim severity X.

Exercise 7.3 Refer to Example 7.6. If the claim-severity distribution X is gamma with parameters $\alpha = c\theta$ and $\beta = 1/c$, derive an expression of the Bühlmann credibility parameter k for the aggregate loss per year S in terms of c.

Exercise 7.4 Refer to Example 7.8. Calculate the updated prediction for claim frequency and claim severity for next year, for $c = 20$ and 30.

Exercise 7.5 Following the setup in Section 7.3, let $X = \{X_1, \ldots, X_n\}$ be a random sample of losses that are independently and identically distributed as the random variable X, the distribution of which depends on a risk parameter θ. Denote $\mu_{n+1} = E(X_{n+1})$, and consider the problem of estimating μ_{n+1} by a linear function of X, denoted by $\hat{\mu}_{n+1}$, that minimizes the mean squared error $E\left[(\mu_{n+1} - \hat{\mu}_{n+1})^2\right]$. Show that $\hat{\mu}_{n+1}$ is the same as the Bühlmann credibility predictor for future loss given in equations (7.34) and (7.35).

Questions Adapted from SOA Exams

Exercise 7.6 The Bühlmann credibility assigned for estimating X_5 based on $X_1, \ldots, X_4$ is $Z = 0.4$. If the expected value of the process variance is 8, calculate $\text{Cov}(X_i, X_j)$ for $i \neq j$.

Exercise 7.7 The annual number of claims of a policy is distributed as $\mathcal{GM}(1/(1 + \theta))$. If Θ follows the $\mathcal{P}(\alpha, 1)$ distribution, where $\alpha > 2$, and a randomly selected policy has x claims in Year 1, derive the Bühlmann credibility estimate of the expected number of claims of the policy in Year 2.

Exercise 7.8 For a portfolio of insurance policies the annual claim amount X of a policy has the following pdf:

$$f_X(x \mid \theta) = \frac{2x}{\theta^2}, \qquad 0 < x < \theta.$$

The prior distribution of Θ has the following pdf:

$$f_\Theta(\theta) = 4\theta^3, \qquad 0 < \theta < 1.$$

A randomly selected policy has claim amount 0.1 in Year 1. Determine the Bühlmann credibility estimate of the expected claim amount of the selected policy in Year 2.

Exercise 7.9 The number of claims in a year of a selected risk group follows the $\mathcal{PN}(\lambda)$ distribution. Claim severity follows the $\mathcal{E}(1/\theta)$ distribution and is independent of the claim frequency. If $\Lambda \sim \mathcal{E}(1)$ and $\Theta \sim \mathcal{PN}(1)$, and Λ and Θ are independent, determine the Bühlmann credibility parameter k for the estimation of the expected annual aggregate loss.

Exercise 7.10 An insurance company sells two types of policies with the following characteristics:

Type of policy	Proportion of policies	Annual claim frequency, Poisson
1	θ	$\lambda = 0.5$
2	$1 - \theta$	$\lambda = 1.5$

A randomly selected policyholder has one claim in Year 1. Determine the Bühlmann credibility factor Z of this policyholder.

Exercise 7.11 Claim frequency follows a Poisson distribution with mean λ. Claim size follows an exponential distribution with mean 10λ and is independent of claim frequency. If the distribution of Λ has pdf

$$f_\Lambda(\lambda) = \frac{5}{\lambda^6}, \qquad \lambda > 1,$$

calculate the Bühlmann credibility parameter k.

Exercise 7.12 Two risks have the following severity distributions:

Claim amount	Probability of claim amount for Risk 1	Probability of claim amount for Risk 2
250	0.5	0.7
2,500	0.3	0.2
60,000	0.2	0.1

If Risk 1 is twice as likely to be observed as Risk 2 and a claim of 250 is observed, determine the Bühlmann credibility estimate of the expected second claim amount from the same risk.

Exercise 7.13 Claim frequency in a month is distributed as $\mathcal{PN}(\lambda)$, and the distribution of Λ is $\mathcal{G}(6, 0.01)$. The following data are available:

Month	Number of insureds	Number of claims
1	100	6
2	150	8
3	200	11
4	300	–

Calculate the Bühlmann–Straub credibility estimate of the expected number of claims in Month 4.

Exercise 7.14 The number of claims made by an individual insured in a year is distributed as $\mathcal{PN}(\lambda)$, where Λ is distributed as $\mathcal{G}(1, 1.2)$. If 3 claims are observed in Year 1 and no claim is observed in Year 2, calculate the Bühlmann credibility estimate of the expected number of claims in Year 3.

Exercise 7.15 Annual claim frequency of an individual policyholder has mean λ, which is distributed as $\mathcal{U}(0.5, 1.5)$, and variance σ^2, which is distributed as exponential with mean 1.25. A policyholder is selected randomly and found to have no claim in Year 1. Using Bühlmann credibility, estimate the expected number of claims in Year 2 for the selected policyholder.

Exercise 7.16 You are given the following joint distribution of X and Θ:

	Θ	
X	0	1
0	0.4	0.1
1	0.1	0.2
2	0.1	0.1

For a given (but unknown) value of Θ and a sample of 10 observations of X with a total of 10, determine the Bühlmann credibility premium.

Exercise 7.17 There are four classes of insureds, each of whom may have zero or one claim, with the following probabilities:

	Number of claims	
Class	0	1
A	0.9	0.1
B	0.8	0.2
C	0.5	0.5
D	0.1	0.9

A class is selected randomly, with probability of one fourth, and four insureds are selected at random from the class. The total number of claims is two. If five insureds are selected at random from the same class, determine the Bühlmann credibility estimate of the expected total number of claims.

Exercise 7.18 An insurance company has a large portfolio of insurance policies. Each insured may file a maximum of one claim per year, and the probability of a claim for each insured is constant over time. A randomly selected insured has a probability 0.1 filing a claim in a year, and the variance of the claim probability of individual insured is 0.01. A randomly selected individual is found to have filed no claim over the past 10 years. Determine the Bühlmann credibility estimate for the expected number of claims the selected insured will file over the next 5 years.

Exercise 7.19 A portfolio of insurance policies comprises 100 insureds. The aggregate loss of each insured in a year follows a compound distribution, where the primary distribution is $\mathcal{NB}(r, 1/1.2)$ and the secondary distribution is $\mathcal{P}(3, 1000)$. If the distribution of r is exponential with mean 2, determine the Bühlmann credibility factor Z of the portfolio.

Exercise 7.20 An insurance company has a large portfolio of employee compensation policies. The losses of each employee are independently and identically distributed. The overall average loss of each employee is 20, the variance of the hypothetical means is 40 and the expected value of the process variance is 8,000. The following data are available in the past three years for a randomly selected policyholder:

Year	Average loss per employee	Number of employees
1	15	800
2	10	600
3	5	400

Determine the Bühlmann–Straub credibility premium per employee for this policyholder.

Exercise 7.21 Claim severity has mean μ and variance 500, where the distribution of μ has a mean of 1,000 and a variance of 50. The following three claims were observed: 750, 1,075 and 2,000. Calculate the Bühlmann estimate of the expected claim severity of the next claim.

Exercise 7.22 Annual losses are distributed as $\mathcal{G}(\alpha, \beta)$, where β does not vary with policyholders. The distribution of α has a mean of 50, and the Bühlmann credibility factor based on two years of experience is 0.25. Calculate the variance of the distribution of α.

Exercise 7.23 The aggregate losses per year per exposure of a portfolio of insurance risks follow a normal distribution with mean μ and standard deviation 1,000. You are given that μ varies by class of risk as follows:

Class	μ	Probability of class
A	2,000	0.6
B	3,000	0.3
C	4,000	0.1

A randomly selected risk has the following experience over three years:

Year	Number of exposures	Aggregate losses
1	24	24,000
2	30	36,000
3	26	28,000

Calculate the Bühlmann–Straub estimate of the expected aggregate loss per exposure in Year 4 for this risk.

Exercise 7.24 The annual loss of an individual policy is distributed as $\mathcal{G}(4, \beta)$, where the mean of the distribution of β is 600. A randomly selected policy had losses of 1,400 in Year 1 and 1,900 in Year 2. Loss data for Year 3 were misfiled and the Bühlmann credibility estimate of the expected loss for the selected policy in Year 4 based on the data for Years 1 and 2 was 1,800. The loss for the selected policy in Year 3, however, was found later to be 2,763. Determine the Bühlmann credibility estimate of the expected loss for the selected policy in Year 4 based on the data of Years 1, 2 and 3.

Exercise 7.25 Claim frequency in a month is distributed as $\mathcal{PN}(\lambda)$, where λ is distributed as $\mathcal{W}(2, 0.1)$. You are given the following data:

Month	Number of insureds	Number of claims
1	100	10
2	150	11
3	250	14

Calculate the Bühlmann–Straub credibility estimate of the expected number of claims in the next 12 months for 300 insureds. [**Hint:** You need to compute the natural logarithm of the gamma function.]

8

Bayesian Approach

In this chapter we consider the Bayesian approach in updating the prediction for future losses. We consider the derivation of the posterior distribution of the risk parameters based on the prior distribution of the risk parameters and the likelihood function of the data. The Bayesian estimate of the risk parameter under the squared-error loss function is the mean of the posterior distribution. Likewise, the Bayesian estimate of the mean of the random loss is the posterior mean of the loss conditional on the data.

In general, the Bayesian estimates are difficult to compute, as the posterior distribution may be quite complicated and intractable. There are, however, situations where the computation may be straightforward, as in the case of conjugate distributions. We define conjugate distributions and provide some examples for cases that are of relevance in analyzing loss measures. Under specific classes of conjugate distributions, the Bayesian predictor is the same as the Bühlmann predictor. Specifically, when the likelihood belongs to the linear exponential family and the prior distribution is the natural conjugate, the Bühlmann credibility estimate is equal to the Bayesian estimate. This result provides additional justification for the use of the Bühlmann approach.

Learning Objectives

1 Bayesian inference and estimation
2 Prior and posterior pdf
3 Bayesian credibility
4 Conjugate prior distribution
5 Linear exponential distribution
6 Bühlmann credibility versus Bayesian credibility

8.1 Bayesian Inference and Estimation

The classical and Bühlmann credibility models update the prediction for future losses based on recent claim experience and existing prior information. In these models, the random loss variable X has a distribution that varies with different risk groups. Based on a sample of n observations of random losses, the predicted value of the loss for the next period is updated. The predictor is a weighted average of the sample mean of X and the prior mean, where the weights depend on the distribution of X across different risk groups.

We formulate the aforementioned as a statistical problem suitable for the Bayesian approach of statistical inference and estimation. The setup is summarized as follows:[1]

1 Let X denote the random loss variable (such as claim frequency, claim severity and aggregate loss) of a risk group. The distribution of X is dependent on a parameter θ, which varies with different risk groups and is hence treated as the realization of a random variable Θ.

2 Θ has a statistical distribution called the **prior distribution**. The **prior pdf** of Θ is denoted by $f_{\Theta}(\theta \mid \gamma)$ (or simply $f_{\Theta}(\theta)$), which depends on the parameter γ, called the **hyperparameter**.

3 The conditional pdf of X given the parameter θ is denoted by $f_{X \mid \Theta}(x \mid \theta)$. Suppose $X = \{X_1, \ldots, X_n\}$ is a random sample of X, and $x = (x_1, \ldots, x_n)$ is a realization of X. The conditional pdf of X is

$$f_{X \mid \Theta}(x \mid \theta) = \prod_{i=1}^{n} f_{X \mid \Theta}(x_i \mid \theta). \tag{8.1}$$

We call $f_{X \mid \Theta}(x \mid \theta)$ the **likelihood function**.

4 Based on the sample data x, the distribution of Θ is updated. The conditional pdf of Θ given x is called the **posterior pdf**, and is denoted by $f_{\Theta \mid X}(\theta \mid x)$.

5 An estimate of the mean of the random loss, which is a function of Θ, is computed using the posterior pdf of Θ. This estimate, called the **Bayes estimate**, is also the predictor of future losses.

Bayesian inference differs from classical statistical inference in its treatment of the prior distribution of the parameter θ. Under classical statistical inference, θ is assumed to be *fixed* and *unknown*, and the relevant entity for inference is the likelihood function. For Bayesian inference, the prior distribution has an important role. The likelihood function and the prior pdf jointly determine the posterior pdf, which is then used for statistical inference.

---

[1] For convenience of exposition, we assume all distributions (both the prior and the likelihood) are continuous. Thus, we use the terminology "pdf" and compute the marginal pdf using integration. If the distribution is discrete, we need to replace "pdf" by "pf," and use summation instead of integration. A brief introduction to Bayesian inference can be found in Appendix A.15.

We now discuss the derivation of the posterior pdf and the Bayesian approach of estimating Θ.

8.1.1 Posterior Distribution of Parameter

Given the prior pdf of Θ and the likelihood function of X, the joint pdf of Θ and X can be obtained as follows

$$f_{\Theta X}(\theta, x) = f_{X|\Theta}(x \mid \theta) f_\Theta(\theta). \tag{8.2}$$

Integrating out θ from the joint pdf of Θ and X, we obtain the marginal pdf of X as

$$f_X(x) = \int_{\theta \in \Omega_\Theta} f_{X|\Theta}(x \mid \theta) f_\Theta(\theta) \, d\theta, \tag{8.3}$$

where Ω_Θ is the support of Θ.

Now we can turn the question around and consider the conditional pdf of Θ given the data x, i.e., $f_{\Theta|X}(\theta \mid x)$. Combining equations (8.2) and (8.3), we have

$$
\begin{aligned}
f_{\Theta|X}(\theta \mid x) &= \frac{f_{\Theta X}(\theta, x)}{f_X(x)} \\
&= \frac{f_{X|\Theta}(x \mid \theta) f_\Theta(\theta)}{\int_{\theta \in \Omega_\Theta} f_{X|\Theta}(x \mid \theta) f_\Theta(\theta) \, d\theta}.
\end{aligned} \tag{8.4}
$$

The posterior pdf describes the distribution of Θ based on prior information about Θ and the sample data x. Bayesian inference about the population as described by the risk parameter Θ is then based on the posterior pdf.

Example 8.1 Let X be the Bernoulli random variable which takes value 1 with probability θ and 0 with probability $1 - \theta$. If Θ follows the beta distribution with parameters α and β, i.e., $\Theta \sim \mathcal{B}(\alpha, \beta)$, calculate the posterior pdf of Θ given X.[2]

Solution 8.1 As X is Bernoulli, the likelihood function of X is

$$f_{X|\Theta}(x \mid \theta) = \theta^x (1 - \theta)^{1-x}, \qquad \text{for } x = 0, 1.$$

Since Θ is assumed to follow the beta distribution with hyperparameters α and β, the prior pdf of Θ is

$$f_\Theta(\theta) = \frac{\theta^{\alpha-1}(1 - \theta)^{\beta-1}}{B(\alpha, \beta)}, \qquad \text{for } \theta \in (0, 1),$$

---

[2] See Appendix A.10.6 for some properties of the $\mathcal{B}(\alpha, \beta)$ distribution. The support of $\mathcal{B}(\alpha, \beta)$ is the interval $(0, 1)$, so that the distribution is suitable for modeling probability as a random variable.

where $B(\alpha, \beta)$ is the beta function defined in equation (A.102). Thus, the joint pf–pdf of Θ and X is

$$f_{\Theta X}(\theta, x) = f_{X|\Theta}(x \mid \theta) f_\Theta(\theta) = \frac{\theta^{\alpha+x-1}(1-\theta)^{(\beta-x+1)-1}}{B(\alpha, \beta)},$$

from which we compute the marginal pf of X by integration to obtain

$$f_X(x) = \int_0^1 \frac{\theta^{\alpha+x-1}(1-\theta)^{(\beta-x+1)-1}}{B(\alpha, \beta)}\, d\theta$$
$$= \frac{B(\alpha+x, \beta-x+1)}{B(\alpha, \beta)}.$$

Thus, we conclude

$$f_{\Theta|X}(\theta \mid x) = \frac{f_{\Theta X}(\theta, x)}{f_X(x)}$$
$$= \frac{\theta^{\alpha+x-1}(1-\theta)^{(\beta-x+1)-1}}{B(\alpha+x, \beta-x+1)},$$

which is the pdf of a beta distribution with parameters $\alpha+x$ and $\beta-x+1$. □

Example 8.2 In Example 8.1, if there is a sample of n observations of X denoted by $X = \{X_1, \dots, X_n\}$, compute the posterior pdf of Θ.

Solution 8.2 We first compute the likelihood of X as follows

$$f_{X|\Theta}(x \mid \theta) = \prod_{i=1}^n \theta^{x_i}(1-\theta)^{1-x_i}$$
$$= \theta^{\sum_{i=1}^n x_i}(1-\theta)^{\sum_{i=1}^n (1-x_i)},$$

and the joint pf–pdf is

$$f_{\Theta X}(\theta, x) = f_{X|\Theta}(x \mid \theta) f_\Theta(\theta)$$
$$= \left[\theta^{\sum_{i=1}^n x_i}(1-\theta)^{\sum_{i=1}^n (1-x_i)}\right]\left[\frac{\theta^{\alpha-1}(1-\theta)^{\beta-1}}{B(\alpha, \beta)}\right]$$
$$= \frac{\theta^{(\alpha+n\bar{x})-1}(1-\theta)^{(\beta+n-n\bar{x})-1}}{B(\alpha, \beta)}.$$

As

$$f_X(x) = \int_0^1 f_{\Theta X}(\theta, x)\, d\theta$$
$$= \int_0^1 \frac{\theta^{(\alpha+n\bar{x})-1}(1-\theta)^{(\beta+n-n\bar{x})-1}}{B(\alpha, \beta)}\, d\theta$$
$$= \frac{B(\alpha+n\bar{x}, \beta+n-n\bar{x})}{B(\alpha, \beta)},$$

we conclude that

$$f_{\Theta|X}(\theta|x) = \frac{f_{\Theta X}(\theta,x)}{f_X(x)}$$
$$= \frac{\theta^{(\alpha+n\bar{x})-1}(1-\theta)^{(\beta+n-n\bar{x})-1}}{B(\alpha+n\bar{x}, \beta+n-n\bar{x})},$$

and the posterior pdf of Θ follows a beta distribution with parameters $\alpha + n\bar{x}$ and $\beta + n - n\bar{x}$. $\qquad\square$

Note that the denominator in equation (8.4) is a function of x but not θ. Denoting

$$K(x) = \frac{1}{\int_{\theta \in \Omega_\Theta} f_{X|\Theta}(x|\theta)f_\Theta(\theta)\,d\theta}, \qquad (8.5)$$

we can rewrite the posterior pdf of Θ as

$$f_{\Theta|X}(\theta|x) = K(x)f_{X|\Theta}(x|\theta)f_\Theta(\theta)$$
$$\propto f_{X|\Theta}(x|\theta)f_\Theta(\theta). \qquad (8.6)$$

$K(x)$ is free of θ and is a **constant of proportionality**. It scales the posterior pdf so that it integrates to 1. The expression $f_{X|\Theta}(x|\theta)f_\Theta(\theta)$ enables us to identify the functional form of the posterior pdf in terms of θ without computing the marginal pdf of X.

Example 8.3 Let $X \sim \mathcal{BN}(m, \theta)$, and $X = \{X_1, \ldots, X_n\}$ be a random sample of X. If $\Theta \sim \mathcal{B}(\alpha, \beta)$, what is the posterior distribution of Θ?

Solution 8.3 From equation (8.6), we have

$$f_{\Theta|X}(\theta|x) \propto f_{X|\Theta}(x|\theta)f_\Theta(\theta)$$
$$\propto \left[\theta^{n\bar{x}}(1-\theta)^{\sum_{i=1}^n (m-x_i)}\right]\left[\theta^{\alpha-1}(1-\theta)^{\beta-1}\right]$$
$$\propto \theta^{(\alpha+n\bar{x})-1}(1-\theta)^{(\beta+mn-n\bar{x})-1}.$$

Comparing the above equation with equation (A.101), we conclude that the posterior pdf belongs to the class of beta distributions. We can further conclude that the hyperparameters of the beta posterior pdf are $\alpha + n\bar{x}$ and $\beta + mn - n\bar{x}$. Note that this is done without computing the expression for the constant of proportionality $K(x)$ nor the marginal pdf of X. $\qquad\square$

8.1.2 Loss Function and Bayesian Estimation

We now consider the problem of estimating $\mu_X(\Theta) = E(X|\Theta)$ given the observed data x. The Bayesian approach of estimation views the estimator as a decision rule, which assigns a value to $\mu_X(\Theta)$ based on the data. Thus, let $w(x)$ be an estimator of $\mu_X(\Theta)$. A nonnegative function $L[\mu_X(\Theta), w(x)]$, called the **loss function**, is then defined to reflect the penalty in making a wrong decision about $\mu_X(\Theta)$. Typically, the larger the difference between $\mu_X(\Theta)$ and $w(x)$, the larger the loss $L[\mu_X(\Theta), w(x)]$. A commonly used loss function is the **squared-error loss function** (or **quadratic loss function**) defined by

$$L[\mu_X(\Theta), w(x)] = [\mu_X(\Theta) - w(x)]^2. \tag{8.7}$$

Other popularly used loss functions include the **absolute-error loss function** and the **zero-one loss function**.[3] We assume, however, that the squared-error loss function is adopted in Bayesian inference.

Given the decision rule and the data, the expected loss in the estimation of $\mu_X(\Theta)$ is

$$E\{L[\mu_X(\Theta), w(x)] \mid x\} = \int_{\theta \in \Omega_\Theta} L[\mu_X(\Theta), w(x)] f_{\Theta \mid X}(\theta \mid x) \, d\theta. \tag{8.8}$$

It is naturally desirable to have a decision rule that gives as small an expected loss as possible. Thus, for any given x, if the decision rule $w(x)$ assigns a value to $\mu_X(\Theta)$ that minimizes the expected loss, then the decision rule $w(x)$ is called the **Bayes estimator** of $\mu_X(\Theta)$ with respect to the chosen loss function. In other words, the Bayes estimator, denoted by $w^*(x)$, satisfies

$$E\{L[\mu_X(\Theta), w^*(x)] \mid x\} = \min_{w(\cdot)} E\{L[\mu_X(\Theta), w(x)] \mid x\}, \tag{8.9}$$

for any given x. For the squared-error loss function, the decision rule (estimator) that minimizes the expected loss $E\{[\mu_X(\Theta) - w(x)]^2 \mid x\}$ is[4]

$$w^*(x) = E[\mu_X(\Theta) \mid x]. \tag{8.10}$$

Thus, for the squared-error loss function, the Bayes estimator of $\mu_X(\Theta)$ is the posterior mean, denoted by $\hat{\mu}_X(x)$, so that[5]

$$\hat{\mu}_X(x) = E[\mu_X(\Theta) \mid x] = \int_{\theta \in \Omega_\Theta} \mu_X(\theta) f_{\Theta \mid X}(\theta \mid x) \, d\theta. \tag{8.11}$$

In the credibility literature (where X is a loss random variable), $\hat{\mu}_X(x)$ is called the **Bayesian premium**.

---

[3] For estimating θ with the estimator $\hat{\theta}$, the absolute-error loss function is defined by $L[\theta, \hat{\theta}] = |\theta - \hat{\theta}|$ and the zero-one loss function is defined by $L[\theta, \hat{\theta}] = 0$ if $\hat{\theta} = \theta$ and 1 otherwise.

[4] See DeGroot and Schervish (2002, p. 348), for a proof of this result.

[5] The Bayes estimator based on the absolute-error loss function is the posterior median, and the Bayes estimator based on the zero-one loss function is the posterior mode. See DeGroot and Schervish (2002, p. 349), for more discussions.

An alternative way to interpret the Bayesian premium is to consider the prediction of the loss in the next period, namely, X_{n+1}, given the data x. To this effect, we first calculate the conditional pdf of X_{n+1} given x, which is

$$f_{X_{n+1} \mid X}(x_{n+1} \mid x) = \frac{f_{X_{n+1}X}(x_{n+1}, x)}{f_X(x)}$$

$$= \frac{\int_{\theta \in \Omega_\Theta} f_{X_{n+1}X \mid \Theta}(x_{n+1}, x \mid \theta) f_\Theta(\theta) \, d\theta}{f_X(x)}$$

$$= \frac{\int_{\theta \in \Omega_\Theta} \left[\prod_{i=1}^{n+1} f_{X_i \mid \Theta}(x_i \mid \theta)\right] f_\Theta(\theta) \, d\theta}{f_X(x)}. \tag{8.12}$$

As the posterior pdf of Θ given X is

$$f_{\Theta \mid X}(\theta \mid x) = \frac{f_{\Theta X}(\theta, x)}{f_X(x)} = \frac{\left[\prod_{i=1}^{n} f_{X_i \mid \Theta}(x_i \mid \theta)\right] f_\Theta(\theta)}{f_X(x)}, \tag{8.13}$$

we conclude

$$\left[\prod_{i=1}^{n} f_{X_i \mid \Theta}(x_i \mid \theta)\right] f_\Theta(\theta) = f_{\Theta \mid X}(\theta \mid x) f_X(x). \tag{8.14}$$

Substituting (8.14) into (8.12), we obtain

$$f_{X_{n+1} \mid X}(x_{n+1} \mid x) = \int_{\theta \in \Omega_\Theta} f_{X_{n+1} \mid \Theta}(x_{n+1} \mid \theta) f_{\Theta \mid X}(\theta \mid x) \, d\theta. \tag{8.15}$$

Equation (8.15) shows that the conditional pdf of X_{n+1} given X can be interpreted as a mixture of the conditional pdf of X_{n+1}, where the mixing density is the posterior pdf of Θ.

We now consider the prediction of X_{n+1} given X. A natural predictor is the conditional expected value of X_{n+1} given X, i.e., $E(X_{n+1} \mid x)$, which is given by

$$E(X_{n+1} \mid x) = \int_0^\infty x_{n+1} f_{X_{n+1} \mid X}(x_{n+1} \mid x) \, dx_{n+1}. \tag{8.16}$$

Using equation (8.15), we have

$$E(X_{n+1} \mid x) = \int_0^\infty x_{n+1} \left[\int_{\theta \in \Omega_\Theta} f_{X_{n+1} \mid \Theta}(x_{n+1} \mid \theta) f_{\Theta \mid X}(\theta \mid x) \, d\theta\right] dx_{n+1}$$

$$= \int_{\theta \in \Omega_\Theta} \left[\int_0^\infty x_{n+1} f_{X_{n+1} \mid \Theta}(x_{n+1} \mid \theta) \, dx_{n+1}\right] f_{\Theta \mid X}(\theta \mid x) \, d\theta$$

$$= \int_{\theta \in \Omega_\Theta} E(X_{n+1} \mid \theta) f_{\Theta \mid X}(\theta \mid x) \, d\theta$$

$$= \int_{\theta \in \Omega_\Theta} \mu_X(\theta) f_{\Theta \mid X}(\theta \mid x) \, d\theta$$

$$= E[\mu_X(\Theta) \mid x]. \tag{8.17}$$

Thus, the Bayesian premium can also be interpreted as the conditional expectation of X_{n+1} given X.

In summary, the Bayes estimate of the mean of the random loss X, called the Bayesian premium, is the posterior mean of X conditional on the data x, as given in equation (8.11). It is also equal to the conditional expectation of future loss given the data x, as shown in equation (8.17). Thus, we shall use the terminologies Bayesian estimate of expected loss and Bayesian predictor of future loss interchangeably.

8.1.3 Some Examples of Bayesian Credibility

We now revisit Examples 8.2 and 8.3 to illustrate the calculation of the Bayesian estimate of the expected loss.

Example 8.4 Let X be the Bernoulli random variable which takes value 1 with probability θ and 0 with probability $1 - \theta$, and $X = \{X_1, \ldots, X_n\}$ be a random sample of X. If $\Theta \sim \mathcal{B}(\alpha, \beta)$, calculate the posterior mean of $\mu_X(\Theta)$ and the expected value of a future observation X_{n+1} given the sample data.

Solution 8.4 From Example 8.2, we know that the posterior distribution of Θ given x is beta with parameters $\alpha^* = \alpha + n\bar{x}$ and $\beta^* = \beta + n - n\bar{x}$. As X is a Bernoulli random variable, $\mu_X(\Theta) = \mathrm{E}(X \mid \Theta) = \Theta$. Hence, the posterior mean of $\mu_X(\Theta)$ is $\mathrm{E}(\Theta \mid x) = \alpha^*/(\alpha^* + \beta^*)$. Now the conditional pdf of X_{n+1} given Θ is

$$
f_{X_{n+1} \mid \Theta}(x_{n+1} \mid \theta) = \begin{cases} \theta, & \text{for } x_{n+1} = 1, \\ 1 - \theta, & \text{for } x_{n+1} = 0. \end{cases}
$$

From equation (8.15), the conditional pdf of X_{n+1} given x is

$$
f_{X_{n+1} \mid X}(x_{n+1} \mid x) = \begin{cases} \mathrm{E}(\Theta \mid x) = \dfrac{\alpha^*}{\alpha^* + \beta^*}, & \text{for } x_{n+1} = 1, \\[2mm] 1 - \mathrm{E}(\Theta \mid x) = 1 - \dfrac{\alpha^*}{\alpha^* + \beta^*}, & \text{for } x_{n+1} = 0. \end{cases}
$$

Now we apply the above results to equation (8.16) to obtain the conditional mean of X_{n+1} given x as[6]

$$
\mathrm{E}(X_{n+1} \mid x) = (1) \left[f_{X_{n+1} \mid X}(1 \mid x) \right] + (0) \left[f_{X_{n+1} \mid X}(0 \mid x) \right]
$$
$$
= \frac{\alpha^*}{\alpha^* + \beta^*},
$$

which is equal to the posterior mean of Θ, $\mathrm{E}(\Theta \mid x)$. □

---

[6] Note That X_{n+1} is a discrete random variable and we have to replace the integration in equation (8.16) by summation.

Example 8.5 Let $X \sim \mathcal{BN}(2, \theta)$, and $X = \{X_1, \ldots, X_n\}$ be a random sample of X. If $\Theta \sim \mathcal{B}(\alpha, \beta)$, calculate the posterior mean of $\mu_X(\Theta)$ and the expected value of a future observation X_{n+1} given the sample data.

Solution 8.5 From Example 8.3, we know that the posterior distribution of Θ is beta with parameters $\alpha^* = \alpha + n\bar{x}$ and $\beta^* = \beta + 2n - n\bar{x}$. As X is a binomial random variable, $\mu_X(\Theta) = E(X \mid \Theta) = 2\Theta$. Hence, the posterior mean of $\mu_X(\Theta)$ is $E(2\Theta \mid x) = 2\alpha^*/(\alpha^* + \beta^*)$. Now the conditional pdf of X_{n+1} given Θ is

$$f_{X_{n+1} \mid \Theta}(x_{n+1} \mid \theta) = \binom{2}{x_{n+1}} \theta^{x_{n+1}} (1 - \theta)^{2 - x_{n+1}}, \qquad x_{n+1} \in \{0, 1, 2\}.$$

From equation (8.15), the conditional pdf of X_{n+1} given x is

$$f_{X_{n+1} \mid X}(x_{n+1} \mid x) = \begin{cases} E[(1 - \Theta)^2 \mid x], & \text{for } x_{n+1} = 0, \\[2mm] 2E[\Theta(1 - \Theta) \mid x], & \text{for } x_{n+1} = 1, \\[2mm] E[\Theta^2 \mid x], & \text{for } x_{n+1} = 2. \end{cases}$$

Now we apply the above results to equation (8.16) to obtain the conditional mean of X_{n+1} given x as

$$\begin{aligned} E(X_{n+1} \mid x) &= (1) \left[f_{X_{n+1} \mid X}(1 \mid x) \right] + (2) \left[f_{X_{n+1} \mid X}(2 \mid x) \right] \\ &= 2E[\Theta(1 - \Theta) \mid x] + 2E[\Theta^2 \mid x] \\ &= 2E[\Theta \mid x] \\ &= \frac{2\alpha^*}{\alpha^* + \beta^*}, \end{aligned}$$

which is equal to the posterior mean of $\mu_X(\Theta)$. □

Examples 8.4 and 8.5 illustrate the equivalence of equations (8.11) and (8.16). The results can be generalized to the case when X is a binomial random variable with parameters m and θ, where m is any positive integer. Readers may wish to prove this result as an exercise (see Exercise 8.1).

Example 8.6 X is the claim-severity random variable that can take values 10, 20 or 30. The distribution of X depends on the risk group defined by parameter Θ, which are labeled 1, 2 and 3. The relative frequencies of risk groups with Θ equal to 1, 2 and 3 are, respectively, 0.4, 0.4 and 0.2. The conditional distribution of X given the risk parameter Θ is given in Table 8.1.

A sample of 3 claims with $x = (20, 20, 30)$ is observed. Calculate the posterior mean of X. Compute the conditional pf of X_4 given x, and calculate the expected value of X_4 given x.

Table 8.1. *Data for Example 8.6*

θ	$\Pr(\Theta = \theta)$	$\Pr(X = x \mid \theta)$		
		$x = 10$	$x = 20$	$x = 30$
1	0.4	0.2	0.3	0.5
2	0.4	0.4	0.4	0.2
3	0.2	0.5	0.5	0.0

Solution 8.6 We first calculate the conditional probability of x given Θ as follows

$$f_{X \mid \Theta}(x \mid 1) = (0.3)(0.3)(0.5) = 0.045,$$

$$f_{X \mid \Theta}(x \mid 2) = (0.4)(0.4)(0.2) = 0.032,$$

and

$$f_{X \mid \Theta}(x \mid 3) = (0.5)(0.5)(0) = 0.$$

Thus, the joint pf of x and Θ is

$$f_{\Theta X}(1, x) = f_{X \mid \Theta}(x \mid 1) f_\Theta(1) = (0.045)(0.4) = 0.018,$$

$$f_{\Theta X}(2, x) = f_{X \mid \Theta}(x \mid 2) f_\Theta(2) = (0.032)(0.4) = 0.0128,$$

and

$$f_{\Theta X}(3, x) = f_{X \mid \Theta}(x \mid 3) f_\Theta(3) = 0(0.2) = 0.$$

Thus, we obtain

$$f_X(x) = 0.018 + 0.0128 + 0 = 0.0308,$$

so that the posterior distribution of Θ is

$$f_{\Theta \mid X}(1 \mid x) = \frac{f_{\Theta X}(1, x)}{f_X(x)} = \frac{0.018}{0.0308} = 0.5844,$$

$$f_{\Theta \mid X}(2 \mid x) = \frac{f_{\Theta X}(2, x)}{f_X(x)} = \frac{0.0128}{0.0308} = 0.4156,$$

and $f_{\Theta \mid X}(3 \mid x) = 0$. The conditional means of X are

$$E(X \mid \Theta = 1) = (10)(0.2) + (20)(0.3) + (30)(0.5) = 23,$$

$$E(X \mid \Theta = 2) = (10)(0.4) + (20)(0.4) + (30)(0.2) = 18,$$

and

$$E(X \mid \Theta = 3) = (10)(0.5) + (20)(0.5) + (30)(0) = 15.$$

Thus, the posterior mean of X is

$$E[E(X \mid \Theta) \mid x] = \sum_{\theta=1}^{3} [E(X \mid \theta)] f_{\Theta \mid X}(\theta \mid x)$$

$$= (23)(0.5844) + (18)(0.4156) + (15)(0) = 20.92.$$

Now we compute the conditional distribution of X_4 given x. We note that

$$f_{X_4 \mid X}(x_4 \mid x) = \sum_{\theta=1}^{3} f_{X_4 \mid \Theta}(x_4 \mid \theta) f_{\Theta \mid X}(\theta \mid x).$$

As $f_{\Theta \mid X}(3 \mid x) = 0$, we have

$$f_{X_4 \mid X}(10 \mid x) = (0.2)(0.5844) + (0.4)(0.4156) = 0.2831,$$

$$f_{X_4 \mid X}(20 \mid x) = (0.3)(0.5844) + (0.4)(0.4156) = 0.3416,$$

and

$$f_{X_4 \mid X}(30 \mid x) = (0.5)(0.5844) + (0.2)(0.4156) = 0.3753.$$

Thus, the conditional mean of X_4 given x is

$$E(X_4 \mid x) = (10)(0.2831) + (20)(0.3416) + (30)(0.3753) = 20.92,$$

and the result

$$E[\mu_X(\Theta) \mid x] = E(X_4 \mid x)$$

is verified. $\qquad\square$

8.2 Conjugate Distributions

A difficulty in applying the Bayes approach of statistical inference is the computation of the posterior pdf, which requires the computation of the marginal pdf of the data. However, as the Bayes estimate under squared-error loss is the mean of the posterior distribution, the estimate cannot be calculated unless the posterior pdf is known.

It turns out that there are classes of prior pdfs, which, together with specific likelihood functions, give rise to posterior pdfs that belong to the same class as the prior pdf. Such prior pdf and likelihood are said to be a **conjugate** pair. In Example 8.1, we see that if the prior pdf is beta and the likelihood is Bernoulli, the posterior pdf also follows a beta distribution, albeit with hyperparameters different from those of the prior pdf. In Example 8.3, we see that if the prior pdf is beta and the likelihood is binomial, then the posterior pdf is also beta, though with hyperparameters different from those of the prior. Thus, in these cases, the observed data x do not change the class of the prior, they only change the parameters of the prior.

A formal definition of **conjugate prior distribution** is as follows. Let the prior pdf of Θ be $f_\Theta(\theta \mid \gamma)$ where γ is the hyperparameter. The prior pdf $f_\Theta(\theta \mid \gamma)$ is conjugate to the likelihood function $f_{X \mid \Theta}(x \mid \theta)$ if the posterior pdf is equal to $f_\Theta(\theta \mid \gamma^*)$, which has the same functional form as the prior pdf but, generally, a different hyperparameter γ^*. In other words, the prior and posterior belong to the same family of distributions.

We adopt the convention of "prior-likelihood" to describe the conjugate distribution. Thus, as shown in Examples 8.1 and 8.3, beta–Bernoulli and beta–binomial are conjugate distributions. We now present further examples of conjugate distributions which may be relevant for analyzing random losses. More conjugate distributions can be found in Table A.3 in the Appendix.

8.2.1 The Gamma–Poisson Conjugate Distribution

Let $X = \{X_1, X_2, \ldots, X_n\}$ be iid $\mathcal{PN}(\lambda)$. We assume $\Lambda \sim \mathcal{G}(\alpha, \beta)$. As shown in Appendix A.16.3, the posterior distribution of Λ is $\mathcal{G}(\alpha^*, \beta^*)$, where

$$\alpha^* = \alpha + n\bar{x} \tag{8.18}$$

and

$$\beta^* = \left[n + \frac{1}{\beta}\right]^{-1} = \frac{\beta}{n\beta + 1}. \tag{8.19}$$

Hence, the gamma prior pdf is conjugate to the Poisson likelihood.

8.2.2 The Beta–Geometric Conjugate Distribution

Let $X = \{X_1, X_2, \ldots, X_n\}$ be iid $\mathcal{GM}(\theta)$. If the prior pdf of Θ is $\mathcal{B}(\alpha, \beta)$, then, as shown in Appendix A.16.4, the posterior distribution of Θ is $\mathcal{B}(\alpha^*, \beta^*)$, with

$$\alpha^* = \alpha + n \tag{8.20}$$

and

$$\beta^* = \beta + n\bar{x}, \tag{8.21}$$

so that the beta prior is conjugate to the geometric likelihood.

8.2.3 The Gamma–Exponential Conjugate Distribution

Let $X = \{X_1, X_2, \ldots, X_n\}$ be iid $\mathcal{E}(\lambda)$. If the prior distribution of Λ is $\mathcal{G}(\alpha, \beta)$, then, as shown in Appendix A.16.5, the posterior distribution of Λ is $\mathcal{G}(\alpha^*, \beta^*)$, with

$$\alpha^* = \alpha + n \qquad (8.22)$$

and

$$\beta^* = \left[\frac{1}{\beta} + n\bar{x}\right]^{-1} = \frac{\beta}{1 + \beta n\bar{x}}. \qquad (8.23)$$

Thus, the gamma prior is conjugate to the exponential likelihood.

8.3 Bayesian versus Bühlmann Credibility

If the prior distribution is conjugate to the likelihood, the Bayes estimate is easy to obtain. It turns out that for the conjugate distributions discussed in the last section, the Bühlmann credibility estimate is equal to the Bayes estimate. The examples below give the details of these results.

Example 8.7 (gamma–Poisson case) The claim-frequency random variable X is assumed to be distributed as $\mathcal{PN}(\lambda)$, and the prior distribution of Λ is $\mathcal{G}(\alpha, \beta)$. If a random sample of n observations of $X = \{X_1, X_2, \ldots, X_n\}$ is available, derive the Bühlmann credibility estimate of the future claim frequency, and show that this is the same as the Bayes estimate.

Solution 8.7 As $X_i \sim$ iid $\mathcal{P}(\lambda)$, we have

$$\mu_{\text{PV}} = \mathrm{E}[\sigma_X^2(\Lambda)] = \mathrm{E}(\Lambda).$$

Since $\Lambda \sim \mathcal{G}(\alpha, \beta)$, we conclude that $\mu_{\text{PV}} = \alpha\beta$. Also, $\mu_X(\Lambda) = \mathrm{E}(X \mid \Lambda) = \Lambda$, so that

$$\sigma_{\text{HM}}^2 = \mathrm{Var}[\mu_X(\Lambda)] = \mathrm{Var}(\Lambda) = \alpha\beta^2.$$

Thus,

$$k = \frac{\mu_{\text{PV}}}{\sigma_{\text{HM}}^2} = \frac{1}{\beta},$$

and the Bühlmann credibility factor is

$$Z = \frac{n}{n+k} = \frac{n\beta}{n\beta + 1}.$$

The prior mean of the claim frequency is

$$M = \mathrm{E}[\mathrm{E}(X \mid \Lambda)] = \mathrm{E}(\Lambda) = \alpha\beta.$$

Hence, we obtain the Bühlmann credibility estimate of future claim frequency as

$$U = Z\bar{X} + (1 - Z)M$$
$$= \frac{n\beta\bar{X}}{n\beta + 1} + \frac{\alpha\beta}{n\beta + 1}$$
$$= \frac{\beta(n\bar{X} + \alpha)}{n\beta + 1}.$$

The Bayes estimate of the expected claim frequency is the posterior mean of Λ. From Section 8.2.1, the posterior distribution of Λ is $\mathcal{G}(\alpha^*, \beta^*)$, where α^* and β^* are given in equations (8.18) and (8.19), respectively. Thus, the Bayes estimate of the expected claim frequency is

$$E(X_{n+1} \mid \boldsymbol{x}) = E[E(X_{n+1} \mid \Lambda) \mid \boldsymbol{x}]$$
$$= E(\Lambda \mid \boldsymbol{x})$$
$$= \alpha^* \beta^*$$
$$= (\alpha + n\bar{X}) \left[\frac{\beta}{n\beta + 1} \right]$$
$$= U,$$

which is the Bühlmann credibility estimate. $\square$

Example 8.8 (beta–geometric case) The claim-frequency random variable X is assumed to be distributed as $\mathcal{GM}(\theta)$, and the prior distribution of Θ is $\mathcal{B}(\alpha, \beta)$, where $\alpha > 2$. If a random sample of n observations of $X = \{X_1, X_2, \ldots, X_n\}$ is available, derive the Bühlmann credibility estimate of the future claim frequency, and show that this is the same as the Bayes estimate.

Solution 8.8 As $X_i \sim$ iid $\mathcal{G}(\theta)$, we have

$$\mu_X(\Theta) = E(X \mid \Theta) = \frac{1 - \Theta}{\Theta},$$

and

$$\sigma_X^2(\Theta) = \text{Var}(X \mid \Theta) = \frac{1 - \Theta}{\Theta^2}.$$

Assuming $\Theta \sim \mathcal{B}(\alpha, \beta)$, we first compute the following moments

$$E\left(\frac{1}{\Theta}\right) = \int_0^1 \frac{1}{\theta} \left[\frac{\theta^{\alpha-1}(1 - \theta)^{\beta-1}}{B(\alpha, \beta)} \right] d\theta$$
$$= \frac{B(\alpha - 1, \beta)}{B(\alpha, \beta)}$$
$$= \frac{\alpha + \beta - 1}{\alpha - 1},$$

and

$$E\left(\frac{1}{\Theta^2}\right) = \int_0^1 \frac{1}{\theta^2}\left[\frac{\theta^{\alpha-1}(1-\theta)^{\beta-1}}{B(\alpha,\beta)}\right]d\theta$$

$$= \frac{B(\alpha-2,\beta)}{B(\alpha,\beta)}$$

$$= \frac{(\alpha+\beta-1)(\alpha+\beta-2)}{(\alpha-1)(\alpha-2)}.$$

Hence, the expected value of the process variance is

$$\mu_{\text{PV}} = E[\sigma_X^2(\Theta)]$$

$$= E\left(\frac{1-\Theta}{\Theta^2}\right)$$

$$= E\left(\frac{1}{\Theta^2}\right) - E\left(\frac{1}{\Theta}\right)$$

$$= \frac{(\alpha+\beta-1)(\alpha+\beta-2)}{(\alpha-1)(\alpha-2)} - \frac{\alpha+\beta-1}{\alpha-1}$$

$$= \frac{(\alpha+\beta-1)\beta}{(\alpha-1)(\alpha-2)},$$

and the variance of the hypothetical means is

$$\sigma_{\text{HM}}^2 = \text{Var}[\mu_X(\Theta)]$$

$$= \text{Var}\left(\frac{1-\Theta}{\Theta}\right)$$

$$= \text{Var}\left(\frac{1}{\Theta}\right)$$

$$= E\left(\frac{1}{\Theta^2}\right) - \left[E\left(\frac{1}{\Theta}\right)\right]^2$$

$$= \frac{(\alpha+\beta-1)(\alpha+\beta-2)}{(\alpha-1)(\alpha-2)} - \left(\frac{\alpha+\beta-1}{\alpha-1}\right)^2$$

$$= \frac{(\alpha+\beta-1)\beta}{(\alpha-1)^2(\alpha-2)}.$$

Thus, the ratio of μ_{PV} to σ_{HM}^2 is

$$k = \frac{\mu_{\text{PV}}}{\sigma_{\text{HM}}^2} = \alpha - 1,$$

and the Bühlmann credibility factor is

$$Z = \frac{n}{n+k} = \frac{n}{n+\alpha-1}.$$

As the prior mean of X is

$$M = E(X) = E[E(X \mid \Theta)] = E\left(\frac{1 - \Theta}{\Theta}\right) = \frac{\alpha + \beta - 1}{\alpha - 1} - 1 = \frac{\beta}{\alpha - 1},$$

the Bühlmann credibility prediction of future claim frequency is

$$\begin{aligned}
U &= Z\bar{X} + (1 - Z)M \\
&= \frac{n\bar{X}}{n + \alpha - 1} + \frac{\alpha - 1}{n + \alpha - 1}\left(\frac{\beta}{\alpha - 1}\right) \\
&= \frac{n\bar{X} + \beta}{n + \alpha - 1}.
\end{aligned}$$

To compute the Bayes estimate of future claim frequency we note, from Section 8.2.2, that the posterior distribution of Θ is $\mathcal{B}(\alpha^*, \beta^*)$, where α^* and β^* are given in equations (8.20) and (8.21), respectively. Thus, we have

$$\begin{aligned}
E(X_{n+1} \mid x) &= E[E(X_{n+1} \mid \Theta) \mid x] \\
&= E\left(\frac{1 - \Theta}{\Theta} \mid x\right) \\
&= \frac{\alpha^* + \beta^* - 1}{\alpha^* - 1} - 1 \\
&= \frac{\beta^*}{\alpha^* - 1} \\
&= \frac{n\bar{X} + \beta}{n + \alpha - 1},
\end{aligned}$$

which is the same as the Bühlmann credibility estimate.   □

Example 8.9 (gamma–exponential case) The claim-severity random variable X is assumed to be distributed as $\mathcal{E}(\lambda)$, and the prior distribution of Λ is $\mathcal{G}(\alpha, \beta)$, where $\alpha > 2$. If a random sample of n observations of $X = \{X_1, X_2, \ldots, X_n\}$ is available, derive the Bühlmann credibility estimate of the future claim severity, and show that this is the same as the Bayes estimate.

Solution 8.9 As $X_i \sim$ iid $\mathcal{E}(\lambda)$, we have

$$\mu_X(\Lambda) = E(X \mid \Lambda) = \frac{1}{\Lambda},$$

and

$$\sigma_X^2(\Lambda) = \text{Var}(X \mid \Lambda) = \frac{1}{\Lambda^2}.$$

Since $\Lambda \sim \mathcal{G}(\alpha, \beta)$, the expected value of the process variance is

$$\mu_{\text{PV}} = E[\sigma_X^2(\Lambda)]$$

$$= E\left(\frac{1}{\Lambda^2}\right)$$

$$= \int_0^\infty \frac{1}{\lambda^2}\left[\frac{\lambda^{\alpha-1}e^{-\frac{\lambda}{\beta}}}{\Gamma(\alpha)\beta^\alpha}\right]d\lambda$$

$$= \frac{1}{\Gamma(\alpha)\beta^\alpha}\int_0^\infty \lambda^{\alpha-3}e^{-\frac{\lambda}{\beta}}\,d\lambda$$

$$= \frac{\Gamma(\alpha-2)\beta^{\alpha-2}}{\Gamma(\alpha)\beta^\alpha}$$

$$= \frac{1}{(\alpha-1)(\alpha-2)\beta^2}.$$

The variance of the hypothetical means is

$$\sigma^2_{\text{HM}} = \text{Var}[\mu_X(\Lambda)] = \text{Var}\left(\frac{1}{\Lambda}\right) = E\left(\frac{1}{\Lambda^2}\right) - \left[E\left(\frac{1}{\Lambda}\right)\right]^2.$$

Now

$$E\left(\frac{1}{\Lambda}\right) = \int_0^\infty \frac{1}{\lambda}\left[\frac{\lambda^{\alpha-1}e^{-\frac{\lambda}{\beta}}}{\Gamma(\alpha)\beta^\alpha}\right]d\lambda$$

$$= \frac{\Gamma(\alpha-1)\beta^{\alpha-1}}{\Gamma(\alpha)\beta^\alpha}$$

$$= \frac{1}{(\alpha-1)\beta},$$

so that

$$\sigma^2_{\text{HM}} = \frac{1}{(\alpha-1)(\alpha-2)\beta^2} - \left[\frac{1}{(\alpha-1)\beta}\right]^2$$

$$= \frac{1}{(\alpha-1)^2(\alpha-2)\beta^2}.$$

Thus, we have

$$k = \frac{\mu_{\text{PV}}}{\sigma^2_{\text{HM}}} = \alpha - 1,$$

and the Bühlmann credibility factor is

$$Z = \frac{n}{n+k} = \frac{n}{n+\alpha-1}.$$

The prior mean of X is

$$M = E\left[E(X\,|\,\Lambda)\right] = E\left(\frac{1}{\Lambda}\right) = \frac{1}{(\alpha-1)\beta}.$$

Hence we obtain the Bühlmann credibility estimate as

$$U = Z\bar{X} + (1 - Z)M$$

$$= \frac{n\bar{X}}{n+\alpha-1} + \frac{\alpha-1}{n+\alpha-1}\left[\frac{1}{(\alpha-1)\beta}\right]$$

$$= \frac{\beta n\bar{X}+1}{(n+\alpha-1)\beta}.$$

To calculate the Bayes estimate, we note, from Section 8.2.3, that the posterior pdf of Λ is $\mathcal{G}(\alpha^*, \beta^*)$, where α^* and β^* are given in equations (8.22) and (8.23), respectively. Thus, the Bayes estimate of the expected claim severity is

$$E(X_{n+1} \mid x) = E\left(\frac{1}{\Lambda} \mid x\right)$$

$$= \frac{1}{(\alpha^* - 1)\beta^*}$$

$$= \frac{1 + \beta n\bar{X}}{(\alpha + n - 1)\beta}$$

$$= U,$$

and the equality of the Bühlmann estimate and the Bayes estimate is proven.   □

We have shown that if the conjugate distributions discussed in the last section are used to model loss variables, where the distribution of the loss variable follows the likelihood function and the distribution of the risk parameters follows the conjugate prior, then the Bühlmann credibility estimate of the expected loss is equal to the Bayesian estimate. In such cases, the Bühlmann credibility estimate is said to have **exact credibility**. Indeed, there are other conjugate distributions for which the Bühlmann credibility is *exact*. For example, the Bühlmann estimate for the case of normal-normal conjugate has exact credibility. In the next section, we discuss a general result for which the Bühlmann credibility estimate is exact.

8.4 Linear Exponential Family and Exact Credibility

Consider a random variable X with pdf or pf $f_{X|\Theta}(x \mid \theta)$, where θ is the parameter of the distribution. X is said to have a **linear exponential distribution** if $f_{X|\Theta}(x \mid \theta)$ can be written as

$$f_{X|\Theta}(x \mid \theta) = \exp\left[A(\theta)x + B(\theta) + C(x)\right], \tag{8.24}$$

for some functions $A(\theta)$, $B(\theta)$ and $C(x)$. By identifying these respective functions it is easy to show that some of the commonly used distributions in the

Table 8.2. *Some linear exponential distributions*

Distribution	$\log f_{X\mid\Theta}(x\mid\theta)$	$A(\theta)$	$B(\theta)$	$C(x)$
Binomial, $\mathcal{BN}(m,\theta)$	$\log(_mC_x)+x\log\theta$ $+(m-x)\log(1-\theta)$	$\log\theta-\log(1-\theta)$	$m\log(1-\theta)$	$\log(_mC_x)$
Geometric, $\mathcal{GM}(\theta)$	$\log\theta+x\log(1-\theta)$	$\log(1-\theta)$	$\log\theta$	0
Poisson, $\mathcal{PN}(\theta)$	$x\log\theta-\theta-\log(x!)$	$\log\theta$	$-\theta$	$-\log(x!)$
Exponential, $\mathcal{E}(\theta)$	$-\theta x+\log\theta$	$-\theta$	$\log\theta$	0

actuarial science literature belong to the linear exponential family. Table 8.2 summarizes some of these distributions.[7]

If the likelihood function belongs to the linear exponential family, we can identify the prior distribution that is conjugate to the likelihood. Suppose the distribution of Θ has two hyperparameters, denoted by α and β. The **natural conjugate** of the likelihood given in equation (8.24) is

$$f_\Theta(\theta\mid\alpha,\beta)=\exp\left[A(\theta)a(\alpha,\beta)+B(\theta)b(\alpha,\beta)+D(\alpha,\beta)\right],\qquad(8.25)$$

for some functions $a(\alpha,\beta)$, $b(\alpha,\beta)$ and $D(\alpha,\beta)$. To see this, we combine equations (8.24) and (8.25) to obtain the posterior pdf of Θ conditional on the sample $X=\{X_1,X_2,\ldots,X_n\}$ as

$$f_{\Theta\mid X}(\theta\mid x)\propto\exp\left\{A(\theta)\left[a(\alpha,\beta)+\sum_{i=1}^n x_i\right]+B(\theta)\left[b(\alpha,\beta)+n\right]\right\}.\qquad(8.26)$$

Hence, the posterior pdf belongs to the same family as the prior pdf with parameters α^* and β^*, assuming they can be solved uniquely from the following equations

$$a(\alpha^*,\beta^*)=a(\alpha,\beta)+n\bar{x},\qquad(8.27)$$

and

$$b(\alpha^*,\beta^*)=b(\alpha,\beta)+n.\qquad(8.28)$$

---

[7] For convenience we use θ to denote generically the parameters of the distributions instead of the usual notations (e.g., θ replaces λ for the parameter of the Poisson and exponential distributions). $_mC_x$ in Table 8.2 denotes the combinatorial function.

Table 8.3. *Examples of natural conjugate priors*

Conjugate distribution	$\log f_{\Theta}(\theta \mid \alpha, \beta)$	$a(\alpha, \beta)$	$b(\alpha, \beta)$
gamma–Poisson	$(\alpha - 1)\log\theta - \dfrac{\theta}{\beta} - \log\Gamma(\alpha, \beta)$	$\alpha - 1$	$\dfrac{1}{\beta}$
beta–geometric	$(\alpha - 1)\log\theta + (\beta - 1)\log(1 - \theta)$ $- \log B(\alpha, \beta)$	$\beta - 1$	$\alpha - 1$
gamma–exponential	$(\alpha - 1)\log\theta - \dfrac{\theta}{\beta} - \log\Gamma(\alpha, \beta)$	$\dfrac{1}{\beta}$	$\alpha - 1$

For the Poisson, geometric and exponential likelihoods, we identify the functions $a(\alpha, \beta)$ and $b(\alpha, \beta)$, and summarize them in Table 8.3. The natural conjugate priors are then obtainable using equation (8.25).[8]

The results above enable us to compute the prior pdf (up to a scaling factor) using equation (8.25). To illustrate the calculation of the posterior pdf, we consider the gamma–Poisson conjugate distribution. As $a(\alpha, \beta) = \alpha - 1$, we have, from equation (8.27),

$$\alpha^{*} - 1 = \alpha - 1 + n\bar{x}, \tag{8.29}$$

which implies

$$\alpha^{*} = \alpha + n\bar{x}. \tag{8.30}$$

Also, from equation (8.28), we have

$$\frac{1}{\beta^{*}} = \frac{1}{\beta} + n, \tag{8.31}$$

which implies

$$\beta^{*} = \left[\frac{1}{\beta} + n\right]^{-1}. \tag{8.32}$$

Thus, the results are the same as in equations (8.18) and (8.19).

Having seen some examples of linear exponential likelihoods and their natural conjugates, we now state a theorem which relates the Bühlmann credibility estimate to the Bayes estimate.

Theorem 8.1 *Let X be a random loss variable. If the likelihood of X belongs to the linear exponential family with parameter θ, and the prior distribution of*

---

[8] In Table 8.3, the function $D(\alpha, \beta)$, which defines the scaling factor, is ignored. The case of the binomial likelihood and its natural conjugate is left as an exercise (see Exercise 8.2).

Θ *is the natural conjugate of the likelihood of X, then the Bühlmann credibility estimate of the mean of X is the same as the Bayes estimate.*

Proof See Klugman *et al.* (2008, Section 20.3.7) or Jewell (1974) for a proof of this theorem.[9] □

When the conditions of Theorem 8.1 hold, the Bühlmann credibility estimate is the same as the Bayes estimate and is said to have **exact credibility**. When the conditions of the theorem do not hold, the Bühlmann credibility estimator generally has a larger mean squared error than the Bayes estimator. The Bühlmann credibility estimator, however, still has the minimum mean squared error in the class of linear estimators based on the sample. The example below illustrates a comparison between the two methods, as well as the sample mean.

Example 8.10 Assume the claim frequency X over different periods are iid as $\mathcal{PN}(\lambda)$, and the prior pf of Λ is

$$
\Lambda =
\begin{cases}
1, & \text{with probability } 0.5, \\
2, & \text{with probability } 0.5.
\end{cases}
$$

A random sample of $n = 6$ observations of X is available. Calculate the Bühlmann credibility estimate and the Bayes estimate of the expected claim frequency. Compare the mean squared errors of these estimate as well as that of the sample mean.

Solution 8.10 The expected claim frequency is $E(X) = \Lambda$. Thus, the mean squared error of the sample mean as an estimate of the expected claim frequency is

$$
\begin{aligned}
E\left[(\bar{X} - \Lambda)^2\right] &= E\left\{E\left[(\bar{X} - \Lambda)^2 \mid \Lambda\right]\right\} \\
&= E\left\{[\text{Var}(\bar{X} \mid \Lambda)]\right\} \\
&= E\left[\frac{\text{Var}(X \mid \Lambda)}{n}\right] \\
&= \frac{E(\Lambda)}{n} \\
&= \frac{1.5}{6} \\
&= 0.25.
\end{aligned}
$$

[9] Note that the proofs in these references require a transformation of the parameters of the prior pdf, so that the prior pdf is expressed in a form different from equation (8.24).

We now derive the Bühlmann credibility estimator. As $\mu_X(\Lambda) = E(X \mid \Lambda) = \Lambda$ and $\sigma_X^2(\Lambda) = \text{Var}(X \mid \Lambda) = \Lambda$, we have

$$\mu_{PV} = E[\sigma_X^2(\Lambda)] = E(\Lambda) = 1.5,$$

and

$$\sigma_{HM}^2 = \text{Var}[\mu_X(\Lambda)] = \text{Var}(\Lambda) = (0.5)(1 - 1.5)^2 + (0.5)(2 - 1.5)^2 = 0.25.$$

Thus, we have

$$k = \frac{\mu_{PV}}{\sigma_{HM}^2} = \frac{1.5}{0.25} = 6,$$

and the Bühlmann credibility factor is

$$Z = \frac{n}{n+6} = \frac{6}{6+6} = 0.5.$$

As the prior mean of X is

$$M = E[E(X \mid \Lambda)] = E(\Lambda) = 1.5,$$

the Bühlmann credibility estimator is

$$U = Z\bar{X} + (1 - Z)M = 0.5\bar{X} + (0.5)(1.5) = 0.5\bar{X} + 0.75.$$

Given $\Lambda = \lambda$, the expected values of the sample mean and the Bühlmann credibility estimator are, respectively, λ and $0.5\lambda + 0.75$. Thus, the sample mean is an unbiased estimator of λ, while the Bühlmann credibility estimator is generally not. However, when λ varies as a random variable the expected value of the Bühlmann credibility estimator is equal to 1.5, which is the prior mean of X, and so is the expected value of the sample mean.

The mean squared error of the Bühlmann credibility estimate of the expected value of X is computed as follows

$$
\begin{aligned}
E\left\{[U - E(X)]^2\right\} &= E\left[(0.5\bar{X} + 0.75 - \Lambda)^2\right] \\
&= E\left\{E\left[(0.5\bar{X} + 0.75 - \Lambda)^2 \mid \Lambda\right]\right\} \\
&= E\left\{E\left[0.25\bar{X}^2 + (0.75)^2 + \Lambda^2 + 0.75\bar{X} - 1.5\Lambda - \Lambda\bar{X} \mid \Lambda\right]\right\} \\
&= E[0.25(\text{Var}(\bar{X} \mid \Lambda) + [E(\bar{X} \mid \Lambda)]^2) \\
&\quad + E\left\{(0.75)^2 + \Lambda^2 + 0.75\bar{X} - 1.5\Lambda - \Lambda\bar{X} \mid \Lambda\right\}] \\
&= E\left[0.25\left(\frac{\Lambda}{6} + \Lambda^2\right) + (0.75)^2 + \Lambda^2 + 0.75\Lambda - 1.5\Lambda - \Lambda^2\right] \\
&= E\left[0.25\left(\frac{\Lambda}{6} + \Lambda^2\right) + (0.75)^2 - 0.75\Lambda\right] \\
&= E\left(0.25\Lambda^2 - 0.7083\Lambda + 0.5625\right) \\
&= 0.25\left[(1)(0.5) + (2)^2(0.5)\right] - (0.7083)(1.5) + 0.5625 \\
&= 0.1251.
\end{aligned}
$$

Hence, the mean squared error of the Bühlmann credibility estimator is about half of that of the sample mean.

As the Bayes estimate is the posterior mean, we first derive the posterior pf of Λ. The marginal pf of X is

$$f_X(x) = \sum_{\lambda \in \{1,2\}} f_{X \mid \Lambda}(x \mid \lambda) \Pr(\Lambda = \lambda)$$

$$= 0.5 \left[\sum_{\lambda \in \{1,2\}} \left(\prod_{i=1}^{6} \frac{\lambda^{x_i} e^{-\lambda}}{x_i!} \right) \right]$$

$$= 0.5 \left[\left(\frac{1}{e^6} \prod_{i=1}^{6} \frac{1}{x_i!} \right) + \left(\frac{1}{e^{12}} \prod_{i=1}^{6} \frac{2^{x_i}}{x_i!} \right) \right]$$

$$= K, \qquad \text{say.}$$

Thus, the posterior pdf of Λ is

$$f_{\Lambda \mid X}(\lambda \mid x) = \begin{cases} \dfrac{0.5}{e^6 K} \left(\displaystyle\prod_{i=1}^{6} \frac{1}{x_i!} \right), & \text{for } \lambda = 1, \\[4mm] \dfrac{0.5}{e^{12} K} \left(\displaystyle\prod_{i=1}^{6} \frac{2^{x_i}}{x_i!} \right), & \text{for } \lambda = 2. \end{cases}$$

The posterior mean of Λ is

$$\mathrm{E}(\Lambda \mid x) = \frac{0.5}{e^6 K} \left(\prod_{i=1}^{6} \frac{1}{x_i!} \right) + \left(\frac{1}{e^{12} K} \prod_{i=1}^{6} \frac{2^{x_i}}{x_i!} \right).$$

Thus, the Bayes estimate is a highly nonlinear function of the data, and the computation of its mean squared error is intractable. We estimate the mean squared error using simulation as follows:[10]

1 Generate λ with value of 1 or 2 with probability of 0.5 each.

2 Using the value of λ generated in Step 1, generate 6 observations of X, $x_1, \ldots, x_6$, from the distribution $\mathcal{PN}(\lambda)$.

3 Compute the posterior mean of Λ of this sample using the expression

$$\frac{0.5}{e^6 K} \left(\prod_{i=1}^{6} \frac{1}{x_i!} \right) + \left(\frac{1}{e^{12} K} \prod_{i=1}^{6} \frac{2^{x_i}}{x_i!} \right).$$

4 Repeat Steps 1 through 3 m times. Denote the values of λ generated in Step 1 by $\lambda_1, \ldots, \lambda_m$, and the corresponding Bayes estimates computed in Step 3 by $\hat{\lambda}_1, \ldots, \hat{\lambda}_m$. The estimated mean squared error of the Bayes estimate is

---

[10] The methodology of simulation is covered in detail in Chapters 14 and 15.

$$\frac{1}{m} \sum_{i=1}^{m} (\hat{\lambda}_i - \lambda_i)^2.$$

We perform a simulation with $m = 100{,}000$ runs. The estimated mean squared error is 0.1105. Thus, the mean squared error of the Bayes estimate is lower than that of the Bühlmann credibility estimate (0.1251), which is in turn lower than that of the sample mean (0.25).   □

8.5 R Laboratory

R Codes 8.1 provides the codes to estimate the mean squared error of the Bayes estimate in Example 8.10. We also estimate the mean squared errors of the sample mean and the Bühlmann premium, which are found to be 0.24851 and 0.12509, respectively.

```
######################################################################
# R Codes 8.1
#
# Estimation of MSE of the Bayes estimate in Example 8.10
######################################################################

set.seed(1)              # Set seed
LT=NULL                  # Initialize sample of true lambdas
LE=NULL                  # Initialize sample of Bayes estimates of
                         #   lambda
LM=NULL                  # Initialize sample of sample means
LBM=NULL                 # Initialize sample Buhlmann premiums
m=100000                 # Set simulation runs
for (i in 1:m)
{
lambda=sample(2,1)       # Sample true lambda, 1 or 2
x=rpois(6,lambda)        # Sample 6 Poisson observations of losses
K=0.5*(prod(1/factorial(x))/exp(6)+prod(2^x/factorial(x))/exp(12))
lambdahat=0.5*prod(1/factorial(x))/(exp(6)*K)+
   prod(2^x/factorial(x))/(exp(12)*K)
LM=c(LM,mean(x))         # Collect sample mean
LBM=c(LBM,0.5*mean(x)+0.75) # Collect Buhlmann premium
LT=c(LT,lambda)          # Collect true lambda
LE=c(LE,lambdahat)       # Collect Bayes estimate
}
mse=sum((LE-LT)^2)/m     # Compute MSE of Bayes estimate
msemean=sum((LM-LT)^2)/m # Compute MSE of sample mean
msebm=sum((LBM-LT)^2)/m  # Compute MSE of Buhlmann premium
mse                      # Output MSE of Bayes estimate
msemean                  # Output MSE of sample mean
msebm                    # Output MSE of Buhlmann premium
```

8.6 Summary and Discussions

The prediction of future random losses can be usefully formulated under the Bayesian framework. Suppose the random loss variable X has a mean $E(X | \Theta) = \mu_X(\Theta)$, and a random sample of $X = \{X_1, X_2, \ldots, X_n\}$ is available. The Bayesian premium is equal to $E[\mu_X(\Theta) | x]$, which is also equal to $E[X_{n+1} | x]$. The former is the Bayesian estimate of the expected loss, and the latter is the Bayesian predictor of future loss. The Bayesian estimate (prediction) is the posterior mean of the expected loss (posterior mean of the future loss), and it has the minimum mean squared error among all estimators of the expected loss.

The Bühlmann credibility estimate is the minimum mean squared error estimate in the class of estimators that are linear in X. When the likelihood belongs to the linear exponential family and the prior distribution is the natural conjugate, the Bühlmann credibility estimate is equal to the Bayesian estimate. However, in other situations the performance of the Bühlmann credibility estimate is generally inferior to the Bayesian estimate.

While the Bayesian estimate has optimal properties, its computation is generally complicated. In practical applications, the posterior mean of the expected loss may not be analytically available and has to be computed numerically.

Exercises

Exercise 8.1 Let $X \sim \mathcal{BN}(m, \theta)$ and $X = \{X_1, \ldots, X_n\}$ be a random sample of X. Assume Θ follows a beta distribution with hyperparameters α and β.

(a) Calculate the posterior mean of $\mu_X(\Theta) = E(X | \Theta)$.
(b) What is the conditional pf of X_{n+1} given the sample data x?

Exercise 8.2 Let $X \sim \mathcal{BN}(m, \theta)$ and $\Theta \sim \mathcal{B}(\alpha, \beta)$. Given the functions $A(\theta)$ and $B(\theta)$ for the $\mathcal{BN}(m, \theta)$ distribution in Table 8.2, identify the functions $a(\alpha, \beta)$ and $b(\alpha, \beta)$ as defined in equation (8.25) so that the $\mathcal{B}(\alpha, \beta)$ distribution is a natural conjugate of $\mathcal{BN}(m, \theta)$. Hence, derive the hyperparameters of the posterior distribution of Θ using equations (8.27) and (8.28).

Exercise 8.3 In Example 8.10, the mean squared error of the expected loss is analytically derived for the sample mean and the Bühlmann credibility estimate, and numerically estimated for the Bayesian estimate. Derive the mean squared errors of the sample mean and the Bühlmann premium as predictors for future loss X_{n+1}. Suggest a simulation procedure for the estimation of the mean squared error of the Bayesian predictor for future loss.

Exercise 8.4 Given $\Theta = \theta$, $X \sim \mathcal{N}\mathcal{B}(r, \theta)$. If the prior distribution of Θ is $\mathcal{B}(\alpha, \beta)$, determine the unconditional pf of X.

Exercise 8.5 Show that the negative binomial distribution $\mathcal{N}\mathcal{B}(r, \theta)$ belongs to the linear exponential family, where r is known and θ is the unknown parameter. Identify the functions $A(\theta)$, $B(\theta)$ and $C(x)$ in equation (8.24).

Exercise 8.6 Given N, X is distributed as $\mathcal{B}\mathcal{N}(N, \theta)$. Derive the unconditional distribution of X assuming N is distributed as (a) $\mathcal{P}\mathcal{N}(\lambda)$, and (b) $\mathcal{B}\mathcal{N}(m, \beta)$, where m is known.

Questions Adapted from SOA Exams

Exercise 8.7 The pf of the annual number of claims N of a particular insurance policy is: $f_N(0) = 2\theta$, $f_N(1) = \theta$ and $f_N(2) = 1 - 3\theta$. Over different policies the pf of Θ is: $f_\Theta(0.1) = 0.8$ and $f_\Theta(0.3) = 0.2$. If there is one claim in Year 1, calculate the Bayesian estimate of the expected number of claims in Year 2.

Exercise 8.8 In a portfolio of insurance policies, the number of claims for each policyholder in each year, denoted by N, may be 0, 1 or 2, with the following pf: $f_N(0) = 0.1$, $f_N(1) = 0.9 - \theta$ and $f_N(2) = \theta$. The prior pdf of Θ is

$$f_\Theta(\theta) = \frac{\theta^2}{0.039}, \qquad 0.2 < \theta < 0.5.$$

A randomly selected policyholder has 2 claims in Year 1 and 2 claims in Year 2. Determine the Bayesian estimate of the expected number of claims in Year 3 of this policyholder.

Exercise 8.9 The number of claims N of each policy is distributed as $\mathcal{B}\mathcal{N}(8, \theta)$, and the prior distribution of Θ is $\mathcal{B}(\alpha, 9)$. A randomly selected policyholder is found to have made 2 claims in Year 1 and k claims in Year 2. The Bayesian credibility estimate of the expected number of claims in Year 2 based on the experience of Year 1 is 2.54545, and the Bayesian credibility estimate of the expected number of claims in Year 3 based on the experience of Years 1 and 2 is 3.73333. Determine k.

Exercise 8.10 Claim severity is distributed as $\mathcal{E}(1/\theta)$. The prior distribution of Θ is inverse gamma with pdf

$$f_\Theta(\theta) = \frac{c^2}{\theta^3} \exp\left(-\frac{c}{\theta}\right), \qquad 0 < \theta < \infty, \, 0 < c.$$

Given an observed loss is x, calculate the mean of the posterior distribution of Θ.

Exercise 8.11 Consider two random variables D and G, where

$$\Pr(D = d \,|\, G = g) = g^{1-d}(1 - g)^d, \qquad d = 0, 1,$$

and

$$\Pr\left(G = \frac{1}{5}\right) = \frac{3}{5} \quad \text{and} \quad \Pr\left(G = \frac{1}{3}\right) = \frac{2}{5}.$$

Calculate

$$\Pr\left(G = \frac{1}{3} \mid D = 0\right).$$

Exercise 8.12 A portfolio has 100 independently and identically distributed risks. The number of claims of each risk follows a $\mathcal{PN}(\lambda)$ distribution. The prior pdf of Λ is $\mathcal{G}(4, 0.02)$. In Year 1, the following loss experience is observed:

Number of claims	Number of risks
0	90
1	7
2	2
3	1
Total	100

Determine the Bayesian expected number of claims of the portfolio in Year 2.

Exercise 8.13 Claim severity X is distributed as $\mathcal{E}(1/\theta)$. It is known that 80% of the policies have $\theta = 8$ and the other 20% have $\theta = 2$. A randomly selected policy has 1 claim of size 5. Calculate the Bayesian expected size of the next claim of this policy.

Exercise 8.14 The claim frequency N in a period is distributed as $\mathcal{PN}(\lambda)$, where the prior distribution of Λ is $\mathcal{E}(1)$. If a policyholder makes no claim in a period, determine the posterior pdf of Λ for this policyholder.

Exercise 8.15 Annual claim frequencies follow a Poisson distribution with mean λ. The prior distribution of Λ has pdf

$$f_\Lambda(\lambda) = 0.4\left(\frac{1}{6}e^{-\frac{\lambda}{6}}\right) + 0.6\left(\frac{1}{12}e^{-\frac{\lambda}{12}},\right), \qquad \lambda > 0.$$

Ten claims are observed for an insured in Year 1. Determine the Bayesian expected number of claims for the insured in Year 2.

Exercise 8.16 The annual number of claims for a policyholder follows a Poisson distribution with mean λ. The prior distribution of Λ is $\mathcal{G}(5, 0.5)$. A randomly selected insured has 5 claims in Year 1 and 3 claims in Year 2. Determine the posterior mean of Λ.

Exercise 8.17 The annual number of claims of a given policy is distributed as $\mathcal{GM}(\theta)$. One third of the policies have $\theta = 1/3$ and the remaining two-thirds have $\theta = 1/6$. A randomly selected policy had two claims in Year 1. Calculate the Bayesian expected number of claims for the selected policy in Year 2.

Exercise 8.18 An insurance company sells three types of policies with the following characteristics:

Type of policy	Proportion of total policies	Distribution of annual claim frequency
A	5%	$\mathcal{PN}(0.25)$
B	20%	$\mathcal{PN}(0.50)$
C	75%	$\mathcal{PN}(1.00)$

A randomly selected policy is observed to have one claim in each of Years 1 through 4. Determine the Bayesian estimate of the expected number of claims of this policyholder in Year 5.

Exercise 8.19 The annual number of claims for a policyholder is distributed as $\mathcal{BN}(2, \theta)$. The prior distribution of Θ has pdf $f_\Theta(\theta) = 4\theta^3$ for $0 < \theta < 1$. This policyholder had one claim in each of Years 1 and 2. Determine the Bayesian estimate of the expected number of claims in Year 3.

Exercise 8.20 Claim sizes follow the $\mathcal{P}(1, \gamma)$ distribution. Half of the policies have $\gamma = 1$, while the other half have $\gamma = 3$. For a randomly selected policy, the claim in Year 1 was 5. Determine the posterior probability that the claim amount of the policy in Year 2 will exceed 8.

Exercise 8.21 The probability that an insured will have at least one loss during any year is θ. The prior distribution of Θ is $\mathcal{U}(0, 0.5)$. An insured had at least one loss every year in the last 8 years. Determine the posterior probability that the insured will have at least one loss in Year 9.

Exercise 8.22 The probability that an insured will have exactly one claim is θ. The prior distribution of Θ has pdf

$$f_\Theta(\theta) = \frac{3\sqrt{\theta}}{2}, \qquad 0 < \theta < 1.$$

A randomly selected insured is found to have exactly one claim. Determine the posterior probability of $\theta > 0.6$.

Exercise 8.23 For a group of insureds, the claim size is distributed as $\mathcal{U}(0, \theta)$, where $\theta > 0$. The prior distribution of Θ has pdf

$$f_\Theta(\theta) = \frac{500}{\theta^2}, \qquad \theta > 500.$$

If two independent claims of amounts 400 and 600 are observed, calculate the probability that the next claim will exceed 550.

Exercise 8.24 The annual number of claims of each policyholder is distributed as $\mathcal{PN}(\lambda)$. The prior distribution of Λ is $\mathcal{G}(2, 1)$. If a randomly selected policyholder had at least one claim last year, determine the posterior probability that this policyholder will have at least one claim this year.

9

Empirical Implementation of Credibility

We have discussed the limited-fluctuation credibility method, the Bühlmann and Bühlmann–Straub credibility methods, as well as the Bayesian method for future loss prediction. The implementation of these methods requires the knowledge or assumptions of some unknown parameters of the model. For the limited-fluctuation credibility method, Poisson distribution is usually assumed for claim frequency. In addition, we need to know the coefficient of variation of claim severity if predictions of claim severity or aggregate loss/pure premium are required. For the Bühlmann and Bühlmann–Straub methods, the key quantities required are the expected value of the process variance, μ_{PV}, and the variance of the hypothetical means, σ^2_{HM}. These quantities depend on the assumptions of the prior distribution of the risk parameters and the conditional distribution of the random loss variable. For the Bayesian method, the predicted loss can be obtained relatively easily if the prior distribution is conjugate to the likelihood. Yet the posterior mean, which is the Bayesian predictor of the future loss, depends on the hyperparameters of the posterior distribution. Thus, for the empirical implementation of the Bayesian method, the hyperparameters have to be estimated.

In this chapter, we discuss the estimation of the required parameters for the implementation of the credibility estimates. We introduce the empirical Bayes method, which may be nonparametric, semiparametric or parametric, depending on the assumptions concerning the prior distribution and the likelihood. Our main focus is on the Bühlmann and Bühlmann–Straub credibility models, the nonparametric implementation of which is relatively straightforward.

Learning Objectives

1 Empirical Bayes method
2 Nonparametric estimation

3 Semiparametric estimation
4 Parametric estimation

9.1 Empirical Bayes Method

Implementation of the credibility estimates requires the knowledge of some unknown parameters in the model. For the limited-fluctuation method, depending on the loss variable of interest, the mean and/or the variance of the loss variable are required. For example, to determine whether full credibility is attained for the prediction of claim frequency, we need to know λ_N, which can be estimated by the sample mean of the claim frequency.[1] For predicting claim severity and aggregate loss/pure premium, the coefficient of variation of the loss variable, C_X, is also required, which may be estimated by

$$\hat{C}_X = \frac{s_X}{\bar{X}}, \tag{9.1}$$

where s_X and $\bar{X}$ are the sample standard deviation and sample mean of X, respectively.

In the Bühlmann and Bühlmann–Straub framework, the key quantities of interest are the expected value of the process variance, μ_{PV}, and the variance of the hypothetical means, σ^2_{HM}. These quantities can be derived from the Bayesian framework and depend on both the prior distribution and the likelihood. In a strictly Bayesian approach, the prior distribution is given and inference is drawn based on the given prior. For practical applications when researchers are not in a position to state the prior, empirical methods may be applied to estimate the hyperparameters. This is called the **empirical Bayes method**. Depending on the assumptions about the prior distribution and the likelihood, empirical Bayes estimation may adopt one of the following approaches:[2]

1 **Nonparametric approach:** In this approach, no assumptions are made about the particular forms of the prior density of the risk parameters $f_\Theta(\theta)$ and the conditional density of the loss variable $f_{X \mid \Theta}(x \mid \theta)$. The method is very general and applies to a wide range of models.

2 **Semiparametric approach:** In some practical applications, prior experience may suggest a particular distribution for the loss variable X, while the specification of the prior distribution remains elusive. In such cases,

---

[1] Refer to the assumptions for full credibility and its derivation in the limited-fluctuation approach in Section 6.2.1. Recall that λ_N is the mean of the claim frequency, which is assumed to be Poisson.

[2] Further discussions of parametric versus nonparametric estimation can be found in Chapter 10.

parametric assumptions concerning $f_{X \mid \Theta}(x \mid \theta)$ may be made, while the prior distribution of the risk parameters $f_\Theta(\theta)$ remains unspecified.

3 **Parametric approach:** When the researcher makes specific assumptions about $f_{X \mid \Theta}(x \mid \theta)$ and $f_\Theta(\theta)$, the estimation of the parameters in the model may be carried out using the maximum likelihood estimation (MLE) method. The properties of these estimators follow the classical results of MLE, as discussed in Appendix A.19 and Chapter 12. While in some cases the MLE can be derived analytically, in many situations they have to be computed numerically.

9.2 Nonparametric Estimation

To implement the limited-fluctuation credibility prediction for claim severity and aggregate loss/pure premium, an estimate of the coefficient of variation C_X is required. $\hat{C}_X$ as defined in equation (9.1) is an example of a nonparametric estimator. Note that under the assumption of a random sample, s_X and $\bar{X}$ are consistent estimators for the population standard deviation and the population mean, respectively, irrespective of the actual distribution of the random loss variable X. Thus, $\hat{C}_X$ is a consistent estimator for C_X, although it is generally not unbiased.[3]

For the implementation of the Bühlmann and Bühlmann–Straub credibility models, the key quantities required are the expected value of the process variance, μ_{PV}, and the variance of the hypothetical means, σ^2_{HM}, which together determine the Bühlmann credibility parameter k. We present below unbiased estimates of these quantities. To the extent that the unbiasedness holds under the mild assumption that the loss observations are statistically independent, and that no specific assumption is made about the likelihood of the loss random variables and the prior distribution of the risk parameters, the estimates are nonparametric.

In Section 7.4 we set up the Bühlmann–Straub credibility model with a sample of loss observations from a risk group. We shall extend this setup to consider multiple risk groups, each with multiple samples of loss observations over possibly different periods. The results in this setup will then be specialized to derive results for the situations discussed in Chapter 7. We now formally state the assumptions of the extended setup as follows:

1 Let X_{ij} denote the loss per unit of exposure and m_{ij} denote the amount of exposure. The index i denotes the ith risk group, for $i = 1, \ldots, r$, with $r > 1$. Given i, the index j denotes the jth loss observation in the ith group, for $j = 1, \ldots, n_i$, where $n_i > 1$ for $i = 1, \ldots, r$. The number of loss observations

---

[3] Properties of estimators will be discussed in Chapter 10.

n_i in each risk group may differ. We may think of j as indexing an individual within the risk group or a period of the risk group. Thus, for the ith risk group we have loss observations of n_i individuals or periods.

2 X_{ij} are assumed to be independently distributed. The risk parameter of the ith group is denoted by θ_i, which is a realization of the random variable Θ_i. We assume Θ_i to be independently and identically distributed as Θ.

3 The following assumptions are made for the hypothetical means and the process variance

$$E(X_{ij} \mid \Theta = \theta_i) = \mu_X(\theta_i), \qquad \text{for } i = 1, \dots, r; \ j = 1, \dots, n_i, \qquad (9.2)$$

and

$$\text{Var}(X_{ij} \mid \theta_i) = \frac{\sigma_X^2(\theta_i)}{m_{ij}}, \qquad \text{for } i = 1, \dots, r; \ j = 1, \dots, n_i. \qquad (9.3)$$

We define the overall mean of the loss variable as

$$\mu_X = E[\mu_X(\Theta_i)] = E[\mu_X(\Theta)], \qquad (9.4)$$

the mean of the process variance as

$$\mu_{\text{PV}} = E[\sigma_X^2(\Theta_i)] = E[\sigma_X^2(\Theta)], \qquad (9.5)$$

and the variance of the hypothetical means as

$$\sigma_{\text{HM}}^2 = \text{Var}[\mu_X(\Theta_i)] = \text{Var}[\mu_X(\Theta)]. \qquad (9.6)$$

For future reference, we also define the following quantities

$$m_i = \sum_{j=1}^{n_i} m_{ij}, \qquad \text{for } i = 1, \dots, r, \qquad (9.7)$$

which is the total exposure for the ith risk group; and

$$m = \sum_{i=1}^{r} m_i, \qquad (9.8)$$

which is the total exposure over all risk groups. Also, we define

$$\bar{X}_i = \frac{1}{m_i} \sum_{j=1}^{n_i} m_{ij} X_{ij}, \qquad \text{for } i = 1, \dots, r, \qquad (9.9)$$

as the exposure-weighted mean of the ith risk group; and

$$\bar{X} = \frac{1}{m} \sum_{i=1}^{r} m_i \bar{X}_i \qquad (9.10)$$

as the overall weighted mean.

The Bühlmann–Straub credibility predictor of the loss in the next period or a random individual of the ith risk group is

$$Z_i \bar{X}_i + (1 - Z_i)\mu_X, \tag{9.11}$$

where

$$Z_i = \frac{m_i}{m_i + k}, \tag{9.12}$$

with

$$k = \frac{\mu_{PV}}{\sigma^2_{HM}}. \tag{9.13}$$

To implement the credibility prediction, we need to estimate μ_X, μ_{PV} and σ^2_{HM}. It is natural to estimate μ_X by $\bar{X}$. To show that $\bar{X}$ is an unbiased estimator of μ_X, we first note that $E(X_{ij}) = E[E(X_{ij} \mid \Theta_i)] = E[\mu_X(\Theta_i)] = \mu_X$, so that

$$
\begin{aligned}
E(\bar{X}_i) &= \frac{1}{m_i} \sum_{j=1}^{n_i} m_{ij} E(X_{ij}) \\
&= \frac{1}{m_i} \sum_{j=1}^{n_i} m_{ij} \mu_X \\
&= \mu_X, \qquad \text{for } i = 1, \ldots, r. \tag{9.14}
\end{aligned}
$$

Thus, we have

$$
\begin{aligned}
E(\bar{X}) &= \frac{1}{m} \sum_{i=1}^{r} m_i E(\bar{X}_i) \\
&= \frac{1}{m} \sum_{i=1}^{r} m_i \mu_X \\
&= \mu_X, \tag{9.15}
\end{aligned}
$$

so that $\bar{X}$ is an unbiased estimator of μ_X.

We now present an unbiased estimator of μ_{PV} in the following theorem.

Theorem 9.1 *The following quantity is an unbiased estimator of μ_{PV}*

$$\hat{\mu}_{PV} = \frac{\sum_{i=1}^{r} \sum_{j=1}^{n_i} m_{ij}(X_{ij} - \bar{X}_i)^2}{\sum_{i=1}^{r}(n_i - 1)}. \tag{9.16}$$

Proof We rearrange the inner summation term in the numerator of equation (9.16) to obtain

$$\sum_{j=1}^{n_i} m_{ij}(X_{ij} - \bar{X}_i)^2 = \sum_{j=1}^{n_i} m_{ij} \left\{ [X_{ij} - \mu_X(\theta_i)] - [\bar{X}_i - \mu_X(\theta_i)] \right\}^2$$

$$= \sum_{j=1}^{n_i} m_{ij}[X_{ij} - \mu_X(\theta_i)]^2 + \sum_{j=1}^{n_i} m_{ij}[\bar{X}_i - \mu_X(\theta_i)]^2$$

$$- 2 \sum_{j=1}^{n_i} m_{ij}[X_{ij} - \mu_X(\theta_i)][\bar{X}_i - \mu_X(\theta_i)]. \qquad (9.17)$$

Simplifying the last two terms on the right-hand side of the above equation, we have

$$\sum_{j=1}^{n_i} m_{ij}[\bar{X}_i - \mu_X(\theta_i)]^2 - 2 \sum_{j=1}^{n_i} m_{ij}[X_{ij} - \mu_X(\theta_i)][\bar{X}_i - \mu_X(\theta_i)]$$

$$= m_i[\bar{X}_i - \mu_X(\theta_i)]^2 - 2[\bar{X}_i - \mu_X(\theta_i)] \sum_{j=1}^{n_i} m_{ij}[X_{ij} - \mu_X(\theta_i)]$$

$$= m_i[\bar{X}_i - \mu_X(\theta_i)]^2 - 2m_i[\bar{X}_i - \mu_X(\theta_i)]^2$$

$$= -m_i[\bar{X}_i - \mu_X(\theta_i)]^2. \qquad (9.18)$$

Combining equations (9.17) and (9.18), we obtain

$$\sum_{j=1}^{n_i} m_{ij}(X_{ij} - \bar{X}_i)^2 = \left[\sum_{j=1}^{n_i} m_{ij}[X_{ij} - \mu_X(\theta_i)]^2 \right] - m_i[\bar{X}_i - \mu_X(\theta_i)]^2. \qquad (9.19)$$

We now take expectations of the two terms on the right-hand side of the above. First, we have

$$\mathrm{E}\left[\sum_{j=1}^{n_i} m_{ij}[X_{ij} - \mu_X(\Theta_i)]^2 \right] = \mathrm{E}\left[\mathrm{E}\left(\sum_{j=1}^{n_i} m_{ij}[X_{ij} - \mu_X(\Theta_i)]^2 \mid \Theta_i \right) \right]$$

$$= \mathrm{E}\left[\sum_{j=1}^{n_i} m_{ij} \mathrm{Var}(X_{ij} \mid \Theta_i) \right]$$

$$= \mathrm{E}\left[\sum_{j=1}^{n_i} m_{ij} \left[\frac{\sigma_X^2(\Theta_i)}{m_{ij}} \right] \right]$$

$$= \sum_{j=1}^{n_i} \mathrm{E}[\sigma_X^2(\Theta_i)]$$

$$= n_i \, \mu_{\mathrm{PV}}, \qquad (9.20)$$

and, noting that $\mathrm{E}(\bar{X}_i \mid \Theta_i) = \mu_X(\Theta_i)$, we have

$$\mathrm{E}\left\{ m_i[\bar{X}_i - \mu_X(\Theta_i)]^2 \right\} = m_i \, \mathrm{E}\left[\mathrm{E}\left\{ [\bar{X}_i - \mu_X(\Theta_i)]^2 \mid \Theta_i \right\} \right]$$

$$= m_i \, \mathrm{E}\left[\mathrm{Var}(\bar{X}_i \mid \Theta_i) \right]$$

$$= m_i \, \mathrm{E}\left[\mathrm{Var}\left(\frac{1}{m_i} \sum_{j=1}^{n_i} m_{ij} X_{ij} \mid \Theta_i \right) \right]$$

$$= m_i \, \mathrm{E} \left[\frac{1}{m_i^2} \sum_{j=1}^{n_i} m_{ij}^2 \, \mathrm{Var}(X_{ij} \mid \Theta_i) \right]$$

$$= m_i \, \mathrm{E} \left[\frac{1}{m_i^2} \sum_{j=1}^{n_i} m_{ij}^2 \left(\frac{\sigma_X^2(\Theta_i)}{m_{ij}} \right) \right]$$

$$= \frac{1}{m_i} \sum_{j=1}^{n_i} m_{ij} \, \mathrm{E}[\sigma_X^2(\Theta_i)]$$

$$= \mathrm{E} \left[\sigma_X^2(\Theta_i) \right]$$

$$= \mu_{\mathrm{PV}}. \tag{9.21}$$

Combining equations (9.19), (9.20) and (9.21), we conclude that

$$\mathrm{E} \left[\sum_{j=1}^{n_i} m_{ij}(X_{ij} - \bar{X}_i)^2 \right] = n_i \mu_{\mathrm{PV}} - \mu_{\mathrm{PV}} = (n_i - 1) \mu_{\mathrm{PV}}. \tag{9.22}$$

Thus, taking expectation of equation (9.16), we have

$$\begin{aligned} \mathrm{E} \left(\hat{\mu}_{\mathrm{PV}} \right) &= \frac{\sum_{i=1}^{r} \mathrm{E} \left[\sum_{j=1}^{n_i} m_{ij}(X_{ij} - \bar{X}_i)^2 \right]}{\sum_{i=1}^{r} (n_i - 1)} \\ &= \frac{\sum_{i=1}^{r} (n_i - 1) \mu_{\mathrm{PV}}}{\sum_{i=1}^{r} (n_i - 1)} \\ &= \mu_{\mathrm{PV}}, \end{aligned} \tag{9.23}$$

so that $\hat{\mu}_{\mathrm{PV}}$ is an unbiased estimator of μ_{PV}. $\square$

Note that equation (9.22) shows that

$$\hat{\sigma}_i^2 = \frac{1}{(n_i - 1)} \left[\sum_{j=1}^{n_i} m_{ij}(X_{ij} - \bar{X}_i)^2 \right] \tag{9.24}$$

is also an unbiased estimator of μ_{PV}, for $i = 1, \ldots, r$. These estimators, however, make use of data in the ith risk group only, and are thus not as efficient as $\hat{\mu}_{\mathrm{PV}}$. In contrast, $\hat{\mu}_{\mathrm{PV}}$ is a weighted average of $\hat{\sigma}_i^2$, as it can be written as

$$\hat{\mu}_{\mathrm{PV}} = \sum_{i=1}^{r} w_i \, \hat{\sigma}_i^2, \tag{9.25}$$

where

$$w_i = \frac{n_i - 1}{\sum_{i=1}^{r} (n_i - 1)}, \tag{9.26}$$

so that the weights are proportional to the degrees of freedom of the risk groups.

We now turn to the estimation of σ_{HM}^2 and present an unbiased estimator of σ_{HM}^2 in the following theorem.

Theorem 9.2 *The following quantity is an unbiased estimator of σ^2_{HM}*

$$\hat{\sigma}^2_{HM} = \frac{\left[\sum_{i=1}^{r} m_i(\bar{X}_i - \bar{X})^2\right] - (r-1)\hat{\mu}_{PV}}{m - \frac{1}{m}\sum_{i=1}^{r} m_i^2}, \tag{9.27}$$

where $\hat{\mu}_{PV}$ is defined in equation (9.16).

Proof We begin our proof by expanding the term $\sum_{i=1}^{r} m_i(\bar{X}_i - \bar{X})^2$ in the numerator of equation (9.27) as follows

$$\begin{aligned}
\sum_{i=1}^{r} m_i(\bar{X}_i - \bar{X})^2 &= \sum_{i=1}^{r} m_i \left[(\bar{X}_i - \mu_X) - (\bar{X} - \mu_X)\right]^2 \\
&= \sum_{i=1}^{r} m_i(\bar{X}_i - \mu_X)^2 + \sum_{i=1}^{r} m_i(\bar{X} - \mu_X)^2 - 2\sum_{i=1}^{r} m_i(\bar{X}_i - \mu_X)(\bar{X} - \mu_X) \\
&= \left[\sum_{i=1}^{r} m_i(\bar{X}_i - \mu_X)^2\right] + m(\bar{X} - \mu_X)^2 - 2(\bar{X} - \mu_X)\sum_{i=1}^{r} m_i(\bar{X}_i - \mu_X) \\
&= \left[\sum_{i=1}^{r} m_i(\bar{X}_i - \mu_X)^2\right] + m(\bar{X} - \mu_X)^2 - 2m(\bar{X} - \mu_X)^2 \\
&= \left[\sum_{i=1}^{r} m_i(\bar{X}_i - \mu_X)^2\right] - m(\bar{X} - \mu_X)^2. \tag{9.28}
\end{aligned}$$

We then take expectations on both sides of equation (9.28) to obtain

$$\begin{aligned}
E\left[\sum_{i=1}^{r} m_i(\bar{X}_i - \bar{X})^2\right] &= \left[\sum_{i=1}^{r} m_i\, E\left[(\bar{X}_i - \mu_X)^2\right]\right] - m\, E\left[(\bar{X} - \mu_X)^2\right] \\
&= \left[\sum_{i=1}^{r} m_i \operatorname{Var}(\bar{X}_i)\right] - m\operatorname{Var}(\bar{X}). \tag{9.29}
\end{aligned}$$

Applying the result in equation (A.115) to $\operatorname{Var}(\bar{X}_i)$, we have

$$\operatorname{Var}(\bar{X}_i) = \operatorname{Var}\left[E(\bar{X}_i \mid \Theta_i)\right] + E\left[\operatorname{Var}(\bar{X}_i \mid \Theta_i)\right]. \tag{9.30}$$

From equation (9.21) we conclude

$$\operatorname{Var}(\bar{X}_i \mid \Theta_i) = \frac{\sigma_X^2(\Theta_i)}{m_i}. \tag{9.31}$$

Also, as $E(\bar{X}_i \mid \Theta_i) = \mu_X(\Theta_i)$, equation (9.30) becomes

$$\operatorname{Var}(\bar{X}_i) = \operatorname{Var}\left[\mu_X(\Theta_i)\right] + \frac{E\left[\sigma_X^2(\Theta_i)\right]}{m_i} = \sigma^2_{HM} + \frac{\mu_{PV}}{m_i}. \tag{9.32}$$

Next, for $\operatorname{Var}(\bar{X})$ in equation (9.29), we have

$$\operatorname{Var}(\bar{X}) = \operatorname{Var}\left(\frac{1}{m}\sum_{i=1}^{r} m_i\bar{X}_i\right)$$

$$= \frac{1}{m^2} \sum_{i=1}^{r} m_i^2 \text{Var}(\bar{X}_i)$$

$$= \frac{1}{m^2} \sum_{i=1}^{r} m_i^2 \left(\sigma_{\text{HM}}^2 + \frac{\mu_{\text{PV}}}{m_i} \right)$$

$$= \left[\sum_{i=1}^{r} \frac{m_i^2}{m^2} \right] \sigma_{\text{HM}}^2 + \frac{\mu_{\text{PV}}}{m}. \tag{9.33}$$

Substituting equations (9.32) and (9.33) into (9.29), we obtain

$$\text{E} \left[\sum_{i=1}^{r} m_i (\bar{X}_i - \bar{X})^2 \right] = \left[\sum_{i=1}^{r} m_i \left(\sigma_{\text{HM}}^2 + \frac{\mu_{\text{PV}}}{m_i} \right) \right] - \left[\left(\sum_{i=1}^{r} \frac{m_i^2}{m} \right) \sigma_{\text{HM}}^2 + \mu_{\text{PV}} \right]$$

$$= \left[m - \frac{1}{m} \sum_{i=1}^{r} m_i^2 \right] \sigma_{\text{HM}}^2 + (r - 1)\mu_{\text{PV}}. \tag{9.34}$$

Thus, taking expectation of $\hat{\sigma}_{\text{HM}}^2$, we can see that

$$\text{E} \left(\hat{\sigma}_{\text{HM}}^2 \right) = \frac{\text{E} \left[\sum_{i=1}^{r} m_i (\bar{X}_i - \bar{X})^2 \right] - (r - 1)\text{E}(\hat{\mu}_{\text{PV}})}{m - \frac{1}{m} \sum_{i=1}^{r} m_i^2}$$

$$= \frac{\left[m - \frac{1}{m} \sum_{i=1}^{r} m_i^2 \right] \sigma_{\text{HM}}^2 + (r - 1)\mu_{\text{PV}} - (r - 1)\mu_{\text{PV}}}{m - \frac{1}{m} \sum_{i=1}^{r} m_i^2}$$

$$= \sigma_{\text{HM}}^2. \tag{9.35}$$

$\square$

From equation (9.16), we can see that an unbiased estimate of μ_{PV} can be obtained with a single risk group, i.e., $r = 1$. However, as can be seen from equation (9.27), $\hat{\sigma}_{\text{HM}}^2$ cannot be computed unless $r > 1$. This is due to the fact that σ_{HM}^2 measures the variations in the hypothetical means and requires at least two risk groups for a well-defined estimate.

As the Bühlmann model is a special case of the Bühlmann–Straub model, the results in Theorems 9.1 and 9.2 can be used to derive unbiased estimators of μ_{PV} and σ_{HM}^2 for the Bühlmann model. This is summarized in the following corollary.

Corollary 9.1 *In the Bühlmann model with r risk groups, denote the loss observations by X_{ij}, for $i = 1, \ldots, r$, with $r > 1$, and $j = 1, \ldots, n_i$. The exposures of X_{ij} are the same, so that without loss of generality we let $m_{ij} \equiv 1$. The following quantity is an unbiased estimator of μ_{PV}*

$$\tilde{\mu}_{PV} = \frac{\sum_{i=1}^{r} \sum_{j=1}^{n_i} (X_{ij} - \bar{X}_i)^2}{\sum_{i=1}^{r} (n_i - 1)}, \tag{9.36}$$

and the following quantity is an unbiased estimator of σ_{HM}^2

$$\tilde{\sigma}_{HM}^2 = \frac{\left[\sum_{i=1}^{r} n_i(\bar{X}_i - \bar{X})^2\right] - (r-1)\tilde{\mu}_{PV}}{n - \frac{1}{n}\sum_{i=1}^{r} n_i^2}, \tag{9.37}$$

where $n = \sum_{i=1}^{r} n_i$. In particular, if all risk groups have the same sample size, so that $n_i = n^*$ for $i = 1, \ldots, r$, then we have

$$\tilde{\mu}_{PV} = \frac{1}{r(n^* - 1)}\left[\sum_{i=1}^{r}\sum_{j=1}^{n^*}(X_{ij} - \bar{X}_i)^2\right]$$

$$= \frac{1}{r}\left[\sum_{i=1}^{r} s_i^2\right], \tag{9.38}$$

where s_i^2 is the sample variance of the losses of the ith group, and

$$\tilde{\sigma}_{HM}^2 = \frac{1}{r-1}\left[\sum_{i=1}^{r}(\bar{X}_i - \bar{X})^2\right] - \frac{\tilde{\mu}_{PV}}{n^*}$$

$$= S^2 - \frac{\tilde{\mu}_{PV}}{n^*}, \tag{9.39}$$

where S^2 is the between-group sample variance.

Proof The proof is a straightforward application of Theorems 9.1 and 9.2, and is left as an exercise. $\qquad\square$

With estimated values of the model parameters, the Bühlmann–Straub credibility predictor of the *i*th risk group can be calculated as

$$\hat{Z}_i\bar{X}_i + (1 - \hat{Z}_i)\bar{X}, \tag{9.40}$$

where

$$\hat{Z}_i = \frac{m_i}{m_i + \hat{k}}, \tag{9.41}$$

with

$$\hat{k} = \frac{\hat{\mu}_{PV}}{\hat{\sigma}_{HM}^2}. \tag{9.42}$$

For the Bühlmann credibility predictor, equations (9.41) and (9.42) are replaced by

$$\tilde{Z}_i = \frac{n_i}{n_i + \tilde{k}} \tag{9.43}$$

and

$$\tilde{k} = \frac{\tilde{\mu}_{PV}}{\tilde{\sigma}_{HM}^2}. \tag{9.44}$$

While $\hat{\mu}_{PV}$ and $\hat{\sigma}^2_{HM}$ are unbiased estimators of μ_{PV} and σ^2_{HM}, respectively, $\hat{k}$ is not unbiased for k, due to the fact that k is a nonlinear function of μ_{PV} and σ^2_{HM}. Likewise, $\tilde{k}$ is not unbiased for k.

Note that $\hat{\sigma}^2_{HM}$ and $\tilde{\sigma}^2_{HM}$ may be negative in empirical applications. In such circumstances, they may be set to zero, which implies that $\hat{k}$ and $\tilde{k}$ will be infinite, and that $\hat{Z}_i$ and $\tilde{Z}_i$ will be zero for all risk groups. Indeed, if the hypothetical means have no variation, the risk groups are homogeneous and there should be no differential weighting. In sum, the predicted loss is the overall average.

From equation (9.10), the total loss experienced is $m\bar{X} = \sum_{i=1}^r m_i \bar{X}_i$. Now if future losses are predicted according to equation (9.40), the total loss predicted will in general be different from the total loss experienced. If it is desired to equate the total loss predicted to the total loss experienced, some readjustment is needed. This may be done by using an alternative estimate of the average loss, denoted by $\hat{\mu}_X$, in place of $\bar{X}$ in equation (9.40). Now the total loss predicted becomes

$$\sum_{i=1}^r m_i[\hat{Z}_i\bar{X}_i + (1 - \hat{Z}_i)\hat{\mu}_X] = \sum_{i=1}^r m_i \left\{ [1 - (1 - \hat{Z}_i)]\bar{X}_i + (1 - \hat{Z}_i)\hat{\mu}_X \right\}. \quad (9.45)$$

As $m_i(1 - \hat{Z}_i) = \hat{Z}_i\hat{k}$, the above equation can be written as

$$\text{Total loss predicted} = \sum_{i=1}^r m_i \left\{ [1 - (1 - \hat{Z}_i)]\bar{X}_i + (1 - \hat{Z}_i)\hat{\mu}_X \right\}$$

$$= \sum_{i=1}^r m_i\bar{X}_i + \sum_{i=1}^r m_i(1 - \hat{Z}_i)(\hat{\mu}_X - \bar{X}_i)$$

$$= \text{Total loss experienced} + \hat{k}\sum_{i=1}^r \hat{Z}_i(\hat{\mu}_X - \bar{X}_i). \quad (9.46)$$

Thus, to balance the total loss predicted and the total loss experienced, we must have $\hat{k}\sum_{i=1}^r \hat{Z}_i (\hat{\mu}_X - \bar{X}_i) = 0$, which implies

$$\hat{\mu}_X = \frac{\sum_{i=1}^r \hat{Z}_i\bar{X}_i}{\sum_{i=1}^r \hat{Z}_i}, \quad (9.47)$$

and the loss predicted for the ith group is $\hat{Z}_i\bar{X}_i + (1 - \hat{Z}_i)\hat{\mu}_X$.

Example 9.1 An analyst has data of the claim frequencies of workers compensations of three insured companies. Table 9.1 gives the data of company A in the last three years and companies B and C in the past four years. The numbers of workers (in hundreds) and the numbers of claims each year per hundred workers are given.

Calculate the Bühlmann–Straub credibility predictions of the numbers of claim per hundred workers for the three companies next year, without and with corrections for balancing the total loss with the predicted loss.

Table 9.1. *Data for Example 9.1*

Company		Years			
		1	2	3	4
A	Claims per hundred workers	–	1.2	0.9	1.8
	Workers (in hundreds)	–	10	11	12
B	Claims per hundred workers	0.6	0.8	1.2	1.0
	Workers (in hundreds)	5	5	6	6
C	Claims per hundred workers	0.7	0.9	1.3	1.1
	Workers (in hundreds)	8	8	9	10

Solution 9.1 The total exposures of each company are

$$m_A = 10 + 11 + 12 = 33,$$
$$m_B = 5 + 5 + 6 + 6 = 22,$$

and

$$m_C = 8 + 8 + 9 + 10 = 35,$$

which give the total exposures of all companies as $m = 33 + 22 + 35 = 90$. The exposure-weighted means of the claim frequency of the companies are

$$\bar{X}_A = \frac{(10)(1.2) + (11)(0.9) + (12)(1.8)}{33} = 1.3182,$$
$$\bar{X}_B = \frac{(5)(0.6) + (5)(0.8) + (6)(1.2) + (6)(1.0)}{22} = 0.9182,$$

and

$$\bar{X}_C = \frac{(8)(0.7) + (8)(0.9) + (9)(1.3) + (10)(1.1)}{35} = 1.0143.$$

The numerator of $\hat{\mu}_{\text{PV}}$ in equation (9.16) is

$$(10)(1.2 - 1.3182)^2 + (11)(0.9 - 1.3182)^2 + (12)(1.8 - 1.3182)^2$$
$$+ (5)(0.6 - 0.9182)^2 + (5)(0.8 - 0.9182)^2 + (6)(1.2 - 0.9182)^2$$
$$+ (6)(1.0 - 0.9182)^2 + (8)(0.7 - 1.0143)^2 + (8)(0.9 - 1.0143)^2$$
$$+ (9)(1.3 - 1.0143)^2 + (10)(1.1 - 1.0143)^2 = 7.6448.$$

Hence, we have

$$\hat{\mu}_{\text{PV}} = \frac{7.6448}{2 + 3 + 3} = 0.9556.$$

The overall mean is

$$\bar{X} = \frac{(1.3182)(33) + (0.9182)(22) + (1.0143)(35)}{90} = 1.1022.$$

The first term in the numerator of $\hat{\sigma}^2_{HM}$ in equation (9.27) is

$$(33)(1.3182 - 1.1022)^2 + (22)(0.9182 - 1.1022)^2$$
$$+ (35)(1.0143 - 1.1022)^2 = 2.5549,$$

and the denominator is

$$90 - \frac{1}{90}[(33)^2 + (22)^2 + (35)^2] = 58.9111,$$

so that

$$\hat{\sigma}^2_{HM} = \frac{2.5549 - (2)(0.9556)}{58.9111} = \frac{0.6437}{58.9111} = 0.0109.$$

Thus, the Bühlmann–Straub credibility parameter estimate is

$$\hat{k} = \frac{\hat{\mu}_{PV}}{\hat{\sigma}^2_{HM}} = \frac{0.9556}{0.0109} = 87.6697,$$

and the Bühlmann–Straub credibility factor estimates of the companies are

$$\hat{Z}_A = \frac{33}{33 + 87.6697} = 0.2735,$$

$$\hat{Z}_B = \frac{22}{22 + 87.6697} = 0.2006,$$

and

$$\hat{Z}_C = \frac{35}{35 + 87.6697} = 0.2853.$$

We then compute the Bühlmann–Straub credibility predictors of the claim frequencies per hundred workers for company A as

$$(0.2735)(1.3182) + (1 - 0.2735)(1.1022) = 1.1613,$$

for company B as

$$(0.2006)(0.9182) + (1 - 0.2006)(1.1022) = 1.0653,$$

and for company C as

$$(0.2853)(1.0143) + (1 - 0.2853)(1.1022) = 1.0771.$$

Note that the total claim frequency predicted based on the historical exposure is

$$(33)(1.1613) + (22)(1.0653) + (35)(1.0771) = 99.4580,$$

Table 9.2. *Data for Example 9.2*

Company	Number of employees	Mean claim amount per employee	Standard deviation of claim amount
A	350	467.20	116.48
B	673	328.45	137.80
C	979	390.23	86.50

which is not equal to the total recorded claim frequency of $(90)(1.1022) = 99.20$. To balance the two figures, we use equation (9.47) to obtain

$$\hat{\mu}_X = \frac{(0.2735)(1.3182) + (0.2006)(0.9182) + (0.2853)(1.0143)}{0.2735 + 0.2006 + 0.2853} = 1.0984.$$

Using this as the credibility complement, we obtain the updated predictors as

$$\text{A}: \ (0.2735)(1.3182) + (1 - 0.2735)(1.0984) = 1.1585,$$
$$\text{B}: \ (0.2006)(0.9182) + (1 - 0.2006)(1.0984) = 1.0623,$$
$$\text{C}: \ (0.2853)(1.0143) + (1 - 0.2853)(1.0984) = 1.0744.$$

It can be checked that the total claim frequency predicted based on the historical exposure is

$$(33)(1.1585) + (22)(1.0623) + (35)(1.0744) = 99.20,$$

which balances with the total claim frequency recorded. ☐

Example 9.2 An insurer sold health policies to three companies. The claim experience of these companies in the last period is summarized in Table 9.2. Suppose company A has 380 employees in the new period, calculate the Bühlmann credibility predictor of its aggregate claim amount.

Solution 9.2 Assuming the claim amounts of the employees within each company are independently and identically distributed, we employ the Bühlmann model. From equation (9.36), we have

$$\tilde{\mu}_{\text{PV}} = \frac{(349)(116.48)^2 + (672)(137.80)^2 + (978)(86.50)^2}{349 + 672 + 978}$$
$$= \frac{24,813,230.04}{1,999}$$
$$= 12,412.84.$$

The overall mean of the claim amounts is

$$\bar{X} = \frac{(350)(467.20) + (673)(328.45) + (979)(390.23)}{350 + 673 + 979}$$

Table 9.3. *Data for Example 9.3*

Company	Mean annual aggregate loss over 3 years	Standard deviation of annual aggregate loss
A	235.35	48.42
B	354.52	76.34

$$= \frac{766,602.02}{2,002}$$

$$= 382.92.$$

We compute the denominator of equation (9.37) to obtain

$$2,002 - \frac{1}{2,002}\left[(350)^2 + (673)^2 + (979)^2\right] = 1,235.83.$$

Thus, from equation (9.37), we have

$$\tilde{\sigma}_{HM}^2 = [(350)(467.20 - 382.92)^2 + (673)(328.45 - 382.92)^2$$
$$+ (979)(390.23 - 382.92)^2 - (2)(12,412.84)]/1,235.83$$
$$= 3,649.66,$$

and the Bühlmann credibility parameter estimate is

$$\hat{k} = \frac{12,412.84}{3,649.66} = 3.4011.$$

For company A, its Bühlmann credibility factor is

$$\hat{Z}_A = \frac{350}{350 + 3.4011} = 0.99,$$

so that the Bühlmann credibility predictor for the claim amount of the current period is

$$(380)\left[(0.99)(467.20) + (1 - 0.99)(382.92)\right] = 177,215.36. \qquad \square$$

Example 9.3 An insurer insures two rental car companies with similar sizes and operations. The aggregate-loss (in thousand dollars) experience in the last three years is summarized in Table 9.3. Assume the companies have stable business and operations in this period, calculate the predicted aggregate loss of company B next year.

Solution 9.3 In this problem, the numbers of observations of each risk group are $n^* = 3$. We calculate $\tilde{\mu}_{PV}$ using equation (9.38) to obtain

$$\tilde{\mu}_{PV} = \frac{(48.42)^2 + (76.34)^2}{2} = 4,086.1460.$$

As the overall mean is

$$\bar{X} = \frac{235.35 + 354.52}{2} = 294.94,$$

using equation (9.39) we obtain $\tilde{\sigma}_{HM}^2$ as

$$\tilde{\sigma}_{HM}^2 = (235.35 - 294.94)^2 + (354.52 - 294.94)^2 - \frac{4,086.1460}{3}$$

$$= 5,738.6960.$$

Thus, the Bühlmann credibility parameter estimate is

$$\tilde{k} = \frac{4,086.1460}{5,738.6960} = 0.7120,$$

so that the estimate of the Bühlmann credibility factor of company B is

$$\tilde{Z}_B = \frac{3}{3 + 0.7120} = 0.8082.$$

Therefore, the Bühlmann credibility prediction of the aggregate loss of company B next year is

$$(0.8082)(354.52) + (1 - 0.8082)(294.94) = 343.09. \qquad \square$$

9.3 Semiparametric Estimation

The unbiasedness of $\hat{\mu}_{PV}$ and $\hat{\sigma}_{HM}^2$ holds under very mild conditions that the loss random variables X_{ij} are statistically independent of each other and are identically distributed within each risk group (under the same risk parameters). Other than this, no particular assumptions are necessary for the prior distribution of the risk parameters and the conditional distribution of the loss variables. In some applications, however, researchers may have information about the possible conditional distribution $f_{X_{ij} \mid \Theta_i}(x \mid \theta_i)$ of the loss variables. For example, claim frequency per exposure may be assumed to be Poisson distributed. In contrast, the prior distribution of the risk parameters, which are not observable, are usually best assumed to be unknown. Under such circumstances, estimates of the parameters of the Bühlmann–Straub model can be estimated using the semiparametric method.

Suppose X_{ij} are the claim frequencies per exposure and $X_{ij} \sim \mathcal{P}(\lambda_i)$, for $i = 1, \ldots, r$ and $j = 1, \ldots, n_i$. As $\sigma_X^2(\lambda_i) = \lambda_i$, we have

$$\mu_{PV} = E[\sigma_X^2(\Lambda_i)] = E(\Lambda_i) = E[E(X \mid \Lambda_i)] = E(X). \qquad (9.48)$$

Thus, μ_{PV} can be estimated using the overall sample mean of X, $\bar{X}$. From (9.27) an alternative estimate of σ_{HM}^2 can then be obtained by substituting $\hat{\mu}_{PV}$ with $\bar{X}$.

Example 9.4 In Example 9.1, if the claim frequencies are assumed to be Poisson distributed, estimate the Bühlmann–Straub credibility parameter k using semiparametric method.

Solution 9.4 We estimate μ_{PV} using $\bar{X} = 1.1022$. Thus, the estimate of σ^2_{HM} is

$$\hat{\sigma}^2_{HM} = \frac{2.5549 - (2)(1.1022)}{58.9111} = 0.005950,$$

so that the semiparametric estimate of the Bühlmann–Straub credibility parameter k is

$$\hat{k} = \frac{1.1022}{0.005950} = 185.24. \qquad \square$$

9.4 Parametric Estimation

If the prior distribution of Θ and the conditional distribution of X_{ij} given Θ_i, for $i = 1, \ldots, r$ and $j = 1, \ldots, n_i$ are of known functional forms, then the hyperparameter of Θ, γ, can be estimated using the maximum likelihood estimation (MLE) method.[4] The quantities μ_{PV} and σ^2_{HM} are functions of γ, and we denote them by $\mu_{PV} = \mu_{PV}(\gamma)$ and $\sigma^2_{HM} = \sigma^2_{HM}(\gamma)$. As k is a function of μ_{PV} and σ^2_{HM}, the MLE of k can be obtained by replacing γ in $\mu_{PV} = \mu_{PV}(\gamma)$ and $\sigma^2_{HM} = \sigma^2_{HM}(\gamma)$ by the MLE of γ, $\hat{\gamma}$. Specifically, the MLE of k is

$$\hat{k} = \frac{\mu_{PV}(\hat{\gamma})}{\sigma^2_{HM}(\hat{\gamma})}. \tag{9.49}$$

We now consider the estimation of γ. For simplicity, we assume $m_{ij} \equiv 1$. The marginal pdf of X_{ij} is given by

$$f_{X_{ij}}(x_{ij} \mid \gamma) = \int_{\theta_i \in \Omega_\Theta} f_{X_{ij} \mid \Theta_i}(x_{ij} \mid \theta_i) f_{\Theta_i}(\theta_i \mid \gamma) \, d\theta_i. \tag{9.50}$$

Given the data X_{ij}, for $i = 1, \ldots, r$ and $j = 1, \ldots, n_i$, the likelihood function $L(\gamma)$ is

$$L(\gamma) = \prod_{i=1}^{r} \prod_{j=1}^{n_i} f_{X_{ij}}(x_{ij} \mid \gamma), \tag{9.51}$$

and the log-likelihood function is

$$\log[L(\gamma)] = \sum_{i=1}^{r} \sum_{j=1}^{n_i} \log f_{X_{ij}}(x_{ij} \mid \gamma). \tag{9.52}$$

The MLE of γ, $\hat{\gamma}$, is obtained by maximizing $L(\gamma)$ in equation (9.51) or $\log[L(\gamma)]$ in equation (9.52) with respect to γ.

---

[4] See Appendix A.19 for a review of the maximum likelihood estimation method. The result in equation (9.49) is justified by the invariance principle of the MLE (see Section 12.3).

Example 9.5 The claim frequencies X_{ij} are assumed to be Poisson distributed with parameter λ_i, i.e., $X_{ij} \sim \mathcal{PN}(\lambda_i)$. The prior distribution of Λ_i is gamma with hyperparameters α and β, where α is a known constant. Derive the MLE of β and k.

Solution 9.5 As α is a known constant, the only hyperparameter of the prior is β. The marginal pf of X_{ij} is

$$
\begin{aligned}
f_{X_{ij}}(x_{ij} \mid \beta) &= \int_0^\infty \left[\frac{\lambda_i^{x_{ij}} \exp(-\lambda_i)}{x_{ij}!} \right] \left[\frac{\lambda_i^{\alpha-1} \exp\left(-\frac{\lambda_i}{\beta}\right)}{\Gamma(\alpha)\beta^\alpha} \right] d\lambda_i \\
&= \frac{1}{\Gamma(\alpha)\beta^\alpha x_{ij}!} \int_0^\infty \lambda_i^{x_{ij}+\alpha-1} \exp\left[-\lambda_i \left(\frac{1}{\beta} + 1 \right) \right] d\lambda_i \\
&= \frac{\Gamma(x_{ij}+\alpha)}{\Gamma(\alpha)\beta^\alpha x_{ij}!} \left(\frac{1}{\beta} + 1 \right)^{-(x_{ij}+\alpha)} \\
&= \frac{c_{ij}\beta^{x_{ij}}}{(1+\beta)^{x_{ij}+\alpha}},
\end{aligned}
$$

where c_{ij} does not involve β. Thus, the likelihood function is

$$
L(\beta) = \prod_{i=1}^{r} \prod_{j=1}^{n_i} \frac{c_{ij}\beta^{x_{ij}}}{(1+\beta)^{x_{ij}+\alpha}},
$$

and ignoring the term that does not involve β, the log-likelihood function is

$$
\log[L(\beta)] = (\log \beta) \left(\sum_{i=1}^{r} \sum_{j=1}^{n_i} x_{ij} \right) - [\log(1+\beta)] \left[n\alpha + \sum_{i=1}^{r} \sum_{j=1}^{n_i} x_{ij} \right],
$$

where $n = \sum_{i=1}^{r} n_i$. The derivative of $\log[L(\beta)]$ with respect to β is

$$
\frac{n\bar{x}}{\beta} - \frac{n(\alpha+\bar{x})}{1+\beta},
$$

where

$$
\bar{x} = \frac{1}{n} \left(\sum_{i=1}^{r} \sum_{j=1}^{n_i} x_{ij} \right).
$$

The MLE of β, $\hat{\beta}$, is obtained by solving for β when the first derivative of $\log[L(\beta)]$ is set to zero. Hence, we obtain[5]

$$
\hat{\beta} = \frac{\bar{x}}{\alpha}.
$$

As $X_{ij} \sim \mathcal{PN}(\lambda_i)$ and $\Lambda_i \sim \mathcal{G}(\alpha, \beta)$, $\mu_{\text{PV}} = \text{E}[\sigma_X^2(\Lambda_i)] = \text{E}(\Lambda_i) = \alpha\beta$. Also, $\sigma_{\text{HM}}^2 = \text{Var}[\mu_X(\Lambda_i)] = \text{Var}(\Lambda_i) = \alpha\beta^2$, so that

---

[5] It can be verified that the second derivative of $\log[L(\beta)]$ evaluated at $\hat{\beta}$ is negative, so that $\log[L(\beta)]$ is maximized. Note that α is a known constant in the computation of $\hat{\beta}$.

$$k = \frac{\alpha\beta}{\alpha\beta^2} = \frac{1}{\beta}.$$

Thus, the MLE of k is

$$\hat{k} = \frac{1}{\hat{\beta}} = \frac{\alpha}{\bar{x}}. \qquad \square$$

9.5 Summary and Discussions

While the hyperparameters of the prior distribution are assumed to be known values in the Bayesian model, they are typically unknown in practical applications. The empirical Bayes method adopts the Bayesian approach of analysis, but treats the hyperparameters as quantities to be obtained from the data. In this chapter, we discuss some empirical Bayes approaches for the estimation of the quantities necessary for the implementation of the credibility prediction.

The nonparametric approach makes no assumption about the prior pdf (or pf) of the risk parameters and the conditional pdf (or pf) of the loss variables. For the Bühlmann–Straub and Bühlmann models, these estimates are easy to calculate. The semiparametric approach assumes knowledge of the conditional pdf (or pf) of the loss variable but not the prior distribution of the risk parameters. We illustrate an application of this approach when the loss variable is distributed as Poisson. When assumptions are made for both the prior and conditional distributions, the likelihood function of the hyperparameters can be derived, at least in principle. We can then estimate the hyperparameters using the MLE method, which may require numerical methods.

Exercises

Exercise 9.1 The claim experience of three policyholders in 3 years is given as follows:

Policyholder		Year 1	Year 2	Year 3
1	Total claims	–	2,200	2,700
	Number in group	–	100	110
2	Total claims	2,100	2,000	1,900
	Number in group	90	80	85
3	Total claims	2,400	2,800	3,000
	Number in group	120	130	140

Determine the Bühlmann–Straub credibility premium for each group in Year 4.

Exercise 9.2 An actuary is making credibility estimates for rating factors using the Bühlmann–Straub nonparametric empirical Bayes method. Let X_{it} denote the rating for Group i in Year t, for $i = 1, 2$ and 3, and $t = 1, \ldots, T$, and m_{it} denotes the exposure. Define $m_i = \sum_{t=1}^{T} m_{it}$ and $\bar{X}_i = (\sum_{t=1}^{T} m_{it}X_{it})/m_i$. The following data are available:

Group	m_i	$\bar{X}_i$
1	50	15.02
2	300	13.26
3	150	11.63

The actuary computed the empirical Bayes estimate of the Bühlmann–Straub credibility factor of Group 1 to be 0.6791.

(a) What are the Bühlmann–Straub credibility estimates of the rating factors for the three groups using the overall mean of X_{it} as the manual rating?
(b) If it is desired to set the aggregate estimated credibility rating equal to the aggregate experienced rating, estimate the rating factors of the three groups.

Questions Adapted from SOA Exams

Exercise 9.3 You are given the following data:

	Year 1	Year 2
Total losses	12,000	14,000
Number of policyholders	25	30

If the estimate of the variance of the hypothetical means is 254, determine the credibility factor for Year 3 using the nonparametric empirical Bayes method.

Exercise 9.4 The claim experience of three territories in the region in a year is as follows:

Territory	Number of insureds	Number of claims
A	10	4
B	20	5
C	30	3

The numbers of claims for each insured each year are independently Poisson distributed. Each insured in a territory has the same number of expected claim frequency, and the number of insured is constant over time for each territory. Determine the empirical Bayes estimate of the Bühlmann–Straub credibility factor for Territory A.

Exercise 9.5 You are given the following data:

Group		Year 1	Year 2	Year 3	Total
A	Total claims		10,000	15,000	25,000
	Number in group		50	60	110
	Average		200	250	227.27
B	Total claims	16,000	18,000		34,000
	Number in group	100	90		190
	Average	160	200		178.95
	Total claims				59,000
	Number in group				300
	Average				196.67

If the estimate of the variance of the hypothetical means is 651.03, determine the nonparametric empirical Bayes estimate of the Bühlmann–Straub credibility factor of Group A.

Exercise 9.6 During a two-year period, 100 policies had the following claims experience:

Total claims in Years 1 and 2	Number of policies
0	50
1	30
2	15
3	4
4	1

You are given that the number of claims per year follows a Poisson distribution, and that each policyholder was insured for the entire two-year period. A randomly selected policyholder had one claim over the two-year period. Using the semiparametric empirical Bayes method, estimate the number of claims in Year 3 for the selected policyholder.

Exercise 9.7 The number of claims of each policyholder in a block of auto-insurance policies is Poisson distributed. In Year 1, the following data are observed for 8,000 policyholders:

Number of claims	Number of policyholders
0	5,000
1	2,100
2	750
3	100
4	50
5 or more	0

A randomly selected policyholder had one claim in Year 1. Determine the semiparametric Bayes estimate of the number of claims in Year 2 of this policyholder.

Exercise 9.8 Three policyholders have the following claims experience over three months:

Policyholder	Month 1	Month 2	Month 3	Mean	Variance
A	4	6	5	5	1
B	8	11	8	9	3
C	5	7	6	6	1

Calculate the nonparametric empirical Bayes estimate of the credibility factor for Month 4.

Exercise 9.9 Over a three-year period, the following claims experience was observed for two insureds who own delivery vans:

Insured		Year 1	2	3
A	Number of vehicles	2	2	1
	Number of claims	1	1	0
B	Number of vehicles	–	3	2
	Number of claims	–	2	3

The number of claims of each insured each year follows a Poisson distribution. Determine the semiparametric empirical Bayes estimate of the claim frequency per vehicle for Insured A in Year 4.

Exercise 9.10 Three individual policyholders have the following claim amounts over four years:

Policyholder	Year 1	Year 2	Year 3	Year 4
A	2	3	3	4
B	5	5	4	6
C	5	5	3	3

Using the nonparametric empirical Bayes method, calculate the estimated variance of the hypothetical means.

Exercise 9.11 Two policyholders A and B had the following claim experience in the past four years:

Policyholder	Year 1	Year 2	Year 3	Year 4
A	730	800	650	700
B	655	650	625	750

Determine the Bühlmann credibility premium for Policyholder B using the nonparametric empirical Bayes method.

Exercise 9.12 The number of claims of each driver is Poisson distributed. The experience of 100 drivers in a year is as follows:

Number of claims	Number of drivers
0	54
1	33
2	10
3	2
4	1

Determine the credibility factor of a single driver using the semiparametric empirical Bayes method.

Exercise 9.13 During a five-year period, 100 policies had the following claim experience:

Number of claims in Years 1 through 5	Number of policies
0	46
1	34
2	13
3	5
4	2

The number of claims of each policyholder each year follows a Poisson distribution, and each policyholder was insured for the entire period. A randomly selected policyholder had three claims over the five-year period. Using semiparametric empirical Bayes method, determine the Bühlmann estimate for the number of claims in Year 6 for the same policyholder.

Exercise 9.14 Denoting X_{ij} as the loss of the ith policyholder in Year j, the following data of 4 policyholders in 7 years are known

$$\sum_{i=1}^{4}\sum_{j=1}^{7}(X_{ij} - \bar{X}_i)^2 = 33.60, \qquad \sum_{i=1}^{4}(\bar{X}_i - \bar{X})^2 = 3.30.$$

Using nonparametric empirical Bayes method, calculate the Bühlmann credibility factor for an individual policyholder.

Part IV

Model Construction and Evaluation

Model construction and evaluation are two important aspects of the empirical implementation of loss models. To construct a parametric model of loss distributions, the parameters of the distribution have to be estimated based on observed data. Alternatively, we may consider the estimation of the distribution function or density function without specifying their functional forms, in which case nonparametric methods are used. We discuss the estimation techniques for both failure-time data and loss data. Competing models are selected and evaluated based on model selection criteria, including goodness-of-fit tests.

Computer simulation using random numbers is an important tool in analyzing complex problems for which analytical answers are difficult to obtain. We discuss methods of generating random numbers suitable for various continuous and discrete distributions. We also consider the use of simulation for the estimation of the mean squared error of an estimator and the p-value of a hypothesis test, as well as the generation of asset-price paths.

10

Model Estimation and Types of Data

Given the assumption that a loss random variable has a certain parametric distribution, the empirical analysis of the properties of the loss requires the parameters to be estimated. In this chapter, we review the theory of parametric estimation, including the properties of an estimator and the concepts of point estimation, interval estimation, unbiasedness, consistency and efficiency. Apart from the parametric approach, we may also estimate the distribution functions and the probability (density) functions of the loss random variables directly without assuming a certain parametric form. This approach is called nonparametric estimation. The purpose of this chapter is to provide a brief review of the theory of estimation, with the discussion of specific estimation methods postponed to the next two chapters.

Although the focus of this book is on nonlife actuarial risks, the estimation methods discussed are also applicable to life-contingency models. Specifically, the estimation methods may be used for failure-time data (life risks) as well as loss data (nonlife risks). In many practical applications, only incomplete data observations are available. These observations may be left truncated or right censored. We define the notations to be used in subsequent chapters with respect to left truncation, right censoring and the risk set. Furthermore, in certain setups individual observations may not be available and we may have to work with grouped data. Different estimation methods are required, depending on whether the data are complete or incomplete, and whether they are individual or grouped.

Learning Objectives

1 Parametric versus nonparametric estimation
2 Point estimate and interval estimate
3 Unbiasedness, consistency and efficiency
4 Failure-time data and loss data

5 Complete versus incomplete data, left truncation and right censoring
6 Individual versus grouped data

10.1 Estimation

We review in this section the basic concepts of estimation, distinguishing between parametric and nonparametric estimation. Properties of parametric estimators will be discussed. Methods of estimation, however, will be postponed to the next two chapters.

10.1.1 Parametric and Nonparametric Estimation

Loss distributions may be estimated using the parametric or nonparametric approach. In the parametric approach, the distribution is determined by a finite number of parameters. Let the df and pdf (or pf) of the loss random variable X be $F(x; \theta)$ and $f(x; \theta)$, respectively, where θ is the parameter of the df and pdf (pf). To economize notations we shall suppress the suffix X in the functions. This convention will be adopted subsequently unless there is a need to be more specific. Furthermore, θ may be a scalar or vector, although for convenience of exposition we shall treat it as a scalar. When θ is known, the distribution of X is completely specified and various quantities (such as the mean and variance) may be computed. In practical situations θ is unknown and has to be estimated using observed data. Let $\{X_1, \ldots, X_n\}$ be a random sample of n observations of X. We denote $\hat{\theta}$ as an estimator of θ using the random sample.[1] Thus, $F(x; \hat{\theta})$ and $f(x; \hat{\theta})$ are the parametric estimates of the df and pdf (pf), respectively. Parametric estimation of loss distributions will be covered in Chapter 12.

On the other hand, $F(x)$ and $f(x)$ may be estimated directly for all values of x without assuming specific parametric forms, resulting in nonparametric estimates of these functions. For example, the histogram of the sample data is a nonparametric estimate of $f(\cdot)$. Nonparametric estimation of loss distributions will be covered in Chapter 11. Unlike the parametric approach, the nonparametric approach has the benefit of requiring few assumptions about the loss distribution.

10.1.2 Point and Interval Estimation

As $\hat{\theta}$ assigns a specific value to θ based on the sample, it is called a **point estimator**. In contrast, an **interval estimator** of an unknown parameter is a

---

[1] An estimator may be thought of as a rule of assigning a point value to the unknown parameter value using the sample observations. In exposition we shall use the terms estimator (the rule) and estimate (the assigned value) interchangeably.

random interval constructed from the sample data, which covers the true value of θ with a certain probability. Specifically, let $\hat{\theta}_L$ and $\hat{\theta}_U$ be functions of the sample data $\{X_1, \ldots, X_n\}$, with $\hat{\theta}_L < \hat{\theta}_U$. The interval $(\hat{\theta}_L, \hat{\theta}_U)$ is said to be a $100(1 - \alpha)\%$ **confidence interval** of θ if

$$\Pr(\hat{\theta}_L \leq \theta \leq \hat{\theta}_U) \geq 1 - \alpha. \tag{10.1}$$

For example, let the mean and variance of $\hat{\theta}$ be θ and $\sigma_{\hat{\theta}}^2$, respectively. Suppose $\hat{\theta}$ is normally distributed so that $\hat{\theta} \sim \mathcal{N}(\theta, \sigma_{\hat{\theta}}^2)$, then a $100(1 - \alpha)\%$ confidence interval of θ is

$$(\hat{\theta} - z_{1-\frac{\alpha}{2}}\sigma_{\hat{\theta}}, \ \hat{\theta} + z_{1-\frac{\alpha}{2}}\sigma_{\hat{\theta}}). \tag{10.2}$$

When $\sigma_{\hat{\theta}}$ is unknown, it has to be estimated and an alternative quantile may be needed to replace $z_{1-\frac{\alpha}{2}}$ in equation (10.2).

10.1.3 Properties of Estimators

As there are possibly many different estimators for the same parameter, an intelligent choice among them is important. We naturally desire the estimate to be *close* to the true parameter value *on average*, leading to the unbiasedness criterion as follows.

Definition 10.1 (Unbiasedness) An estimator of θ, $\hat{\theta}$, is said to be unbiased if and only if $E(\hat{\theta}) = \theta$.

The unbiasedness of $\hat{\theta}$ for θ requires the condition $E(\hat{\theta}) = \theta$ to hold for samples of all sizes. In some applications, although $E(\hat{\theta})$ may not be equal to θ in finite samples, it may approach to θ arbitrarily closely in large samples. We say $\hat{\theta}$ is **asymptotically unbiased** for θ if[2]

$$\lim_{n \to \infty} E(\hat{\theta}) = \theta. \tag{10.3}$$

As we may have more than one unbiased estimator, the unbiasedness criterion alone may not be sufficient to provide guidance for choosing a good estimator. If we have two unbiased estimators, the closeness requirement suggests that the one with the smaller variance should be preferred. This leads us to the following definition.

Definition 10.2 (Minimum Variance Unbiased Estimator) Suppose $\hat{\theta}$ and $\tilde{\theta}$ are two unbiased estimators of θ, $\hat{\theta}$ is more efficient than $\tilde{\theta}$ if $\text{Var}(\hat{\theta}) < \text{Var}(\tilde{\theta})$. In particular, if the variance of $\hat{\theta}$ is smaller than the variance of any other unbiased estimator of θ, then $\hat{\theta}$ is the minimum variance unbiased estimator of θ.

---

[2] Note that $E(\hat{\theta})$ generally depends on the sample size n.

While asymptotic unbiasedness requires the *mean* of $\hat{\theta}$ to approach θ arbitrarily closely in large samples, a stronger condition is to require $\hat{\theta}$ itself to approach θ arbitrarily closely in large samples. This leads us to the property of consistency.

Definition 10.3 (Consistency)[3] $\hat{\theta}$ is a consistent estimator of θ if it **converges in probability** to θ, which means that for any $\delta > 0$,

$$\lim_{n \to \infty} \Pr(|\hat{\theta} - \theta| < \delta) = 1. \tag{10.4}$$

Note that unbiasedness is a property that refers to samples of all sizes, large or small. In contrast, consistency is a property that refers to large samples only.

The following theorem may be useful in identifying consistent estimators.

Theorem 10.1 $\hat{\theta}$ *is a consistent estimator of* θ *if it is asymptotically unbiased and Var($\hat{\theta}$)* $\to 0$ *when* $n \to \infty$.

Proof See the proof of a similar result in DeGroot and Schervish (2002, p. 234). □

Biased estimators are not necessarily inferior if their average deviation from the true parameter value is small. Hence, we may use the **mean squared error** as a criterion for selecting estimators. The mean squared error of $\hat{\theta}$ as an estimator of θ, denoted by MSE($\hat{\theta}$), is defined as

$$\text{MSE}(\hat{\theta}) = \text{E}[(\hat{\theta} - \theta)^2]. \tag{10.5}$$

We note that

$$
\begin{aligned}
\text{MSE}(\hat{\theta}) &= \text{E}[(\hat{\theta} - \theta)^2] \\
&= \text{E}[\{(\hat{\theta} - \text{E}(\hat{\theta})) + (\text{E}(\hat{\theta}) - \theta)\}^2] \\
&= \text{E}[\{\hat{\theta} - \text{E}(\hat{\theta})\}^2] + [\text{E}(\hat{\theta}) - \theta]^2 + 2[\text{E}(\hat{\theta}) - \theta]\text{E}[\hat{\theta} - \text{E}(\hat{\theta})] \\
&= \text{Var}(\hat{\theta}) + [\text{bias}(\hat{\theta})]^2,
\end{aligned}
\tag{10.6}
$$

where

$$\text{bias}(\hat{\theta}) = \text{E}(\hat{\theta}) - \theta \tag{10.7}$$

is the bias of $\hat{\theta}$ as an estimator of θ. Thus, MSE($\hat{\theta}$) is the sum of the variance of $\hat{\theta}$ and the squared bias. A small bias in $\hat{\theta}$ may be tolerated, if the variance of $\hat{\theta}$ is small so that the overall MSE is low.

---

[3] The consistency concept defined here is also called *weak consistency*, and is the only consistency property considered in this book. For further discussions of convergence in probability, readers may refer to DeGroot and Schervish (2002, p. 233).

Example 10.1 Let $\{X_1, \ldots, X_n\}$ be a random sample of X with mean μ and variance σ^2. Prove that the sample mean $\bar{X}$ is a consistent estimator of μ.

Solution 10.1 First, $\bar{X}$ is unbiased for μ as $E(\bar{X}) = \mu$. Thus, $\bar{X}$ is asymptotically unbiased. Second, the variance of $\bar{X}$ is

$$\mathrm{Var}(\bar{X}) = \frac{\sigma^2}{n},$$

which tends to 0 when n tends to ∞. Hence, by Theorem 10.1, $\bar{X}$ is consistent for μ. □

Example 10.2 Let $\{X_1, \ldots, X_n\}$ be a random sample of X which is distributed as $\mathcal{U}(0, \theta)$. Define $Y = \max\{X_1, \ldots, X_n\}$, which is used as an estimator of θ. Calculate the mean, variance and mean squared error of Y. Is Y a consistent estimator of θ?

Solution 10.2 We first determine the distribution of Y. The df of Y is

$$
\begin{aligned}
F_Y(y) &= \mathrm{Pr}(Y \leq y) \\
&= \mathrm{Pr}(X_1 \leq y, \ldots, X_n \leq y) \\
&= [\mathrm{Pr}(X \leq y)]^n \\
&= \left(\frac{y}{\theta}\right)^n.
\end{aligned}
$$

Thus, the pdf of Y is

$$f_Y(y) = \frac{dF_Y(y)}{dy} = \frac{ny^{n-1}}{\theta^n}.$$

Hence, the first two raw moments of Y are

$$E(Y) = \frac{n}{\theta^n} \int_0^\theta y^n \, dy = \frac{n\theta}{n+1},$$

and

$$E(Y^2) = \frac{n}{\theta^n} \int_0^\theta y^{n+1} \, dy = \frac{n\theta^2}{n+2}.$$

From equation (10.7), the bias of Y is

$$\mathrm{bias}(Y) = E(Y) - \theta = \frac{n\theta}{n+1} - \theta = -\frac{\theta}{n+1},$$

so that Y is downward biased for θ. However, as $\mathrm{bias}(Y)$ tends to 0 when n tends to ∞, Y is asymptotically unbiased for θ. The variance of Y is

$$\mathrm{Var}(Y) = E(Y^2) - [E(Y)]^2$$

$$= \frac{n\theta^2}{n+2} - \left(\frac{n\theta}{n+1}\right)^2$$

$$= \frac{n\theta^2}{(n+2)(n+1)^2},$$

which tends to 0 when n tends to ∞. Thus, by Theorem 10.1, Y is a consistent estimator of θ. Finally, the MSE of Y is

$$\text{MSE}(Y) = \text{Var}(Y) + [\text{bias}(Y)]^2$$

$$= \frac{n\theta^2}{(n+2)(n+1)^2} + \frac{\theta^2}{(n+1)^2}$$

$$= \frac{2\theta^2}{(n+2)(n+1)},$$

which also tends to 0 when n tends to ∞.   □

10.2 Types of Data

The estimation methods to be used for analyzing loss distributions depend crucially on the type of data available. In this section, we discuss different data formats and define the notations and terminologies. While our main interests are in loss distributions, the estimation methods discussed are also applicable to data of life contingency. Indeed the adopted terminologies for the estimation methods in the literature have strong connotations of life-contingent data. Thus, we shall introduce the terminologies and estimation methods using examples of life-contingent as well as loss data.

10.2.1 Duration Data and Loss Data

Suppose we are interested in modeling the age-at-death of the individuals in a population. The key variable of interest is then the time each individual has lived since birth, called the age-at-death variable, which involves length-of-time data or **duration data**. There are similar problems in which duration is the key variable of interest. Examples are: (a) the duration of unemployment of an individual in the labor force, (b) the duration of stay of a patient in a hospital, and (c) the survival time of a patient after a major operation. There may be other cases where estimation methods of duration distributions are applicable. Depending on the specific problem of interest, the methodology may be applied to **failure-time data, age-at-death data, survival-time data** or any duration data in general.

In nonlife actuarial risks a key variable of interest is the claim-severity or loss distribution. Examples of applications are: (a) the distribution of medical-cost claims in a health insurance policy, (b) the distribution of car insurance claims, and (c) the distribution of compensations of work accidents. These cases involve analysis of **loss data**.

Depending on how the data are collected, information about individuals in the data set may or may not be complete. For example, in a post-operation survival-time study, the researcher may have knowledge about the survival of patients up to a certain time point (end of the study) but does not have information beyond that point. Such incompleteness of information has important implications for the estimation methods used. We shall define the data setup and notations prior to discussing the estimation methods.

10.2.2 Complete Individual Data

We begin with the case in which the researcher has complete knowledge about the relevant duration or loss data of the individuals. Let X denote the variable of interest (duration or loss), and $X_1, \ldots, X_n$ denote the values of X for n individuals. We denote the observed sample values by $x_1, \ldots, x_n$. However, there may be duplications of values in the sample, and we assume there are m distinct values arranged in the order $0 < y_1 < \cdots < y_m$, with $m \leq n$. Furthermore, we assume y_j occurs w_j times in the sample, for $j = 1, \ldots, m$. Thus, $\sum_{j=1}^{m} w_j = n$. In the case of age-at-death data, w_j individuals die at age y_j. If all individuals are observed from birth until they die, we have a **complete individual** data set. We define r_j as the **risk set** at *time y_j*, which is the number of individuals in the sample exposed to the possibility of death at time y_j (prior to observing the deaths at y_j).[4] For example, $r_1 = n$, as all individuals in the sample are exposed to the risk of death just prior to time y_1. Similarly, we can see that $r_j = \sum_{i=j}^{m} w_i$, which is the number of individuals who are surviving just prior to time y_j.

The following example illustrates this setup.

Example 10.3 Let $x_1, \ldots, x_{16}$ be a sample of failure times of a machine part. The values of x_i, arranged in increasing order, are as follows:

$$2, 3, 5, 5, 5, 6, 6, 8, 8, 8, 12, 14, 18, 18, 24, 24.$$

Summarize the data in terms of the setup above.

Solution 10.3 There are nine distinct values of failure time in this data set, so that $m = 9$. Table 10.1 summarizes the data in the notations described above. From the table it is obvious that $r_{j+1} = r_j - w_j$ for $j = 1, \ldots, m - 1$. □

To understand the terminology introduced, let us assume that all individuals in the data were born at the same time $t = 0$. Then all 16 of them are exposed to

---

[4] The terminology "risk set" refers to the set of individuals as well as the number of individuals exposed to the risk.

Table 10.1. *Failure-time data in*
Example 10.3

j	*y_j*	*w_j*	*r_j*
1	2	1	16
2	3	1	15
3	5	3	14
4	6	2	11
5	8	3	9
6	12	1	6
7	14	1	5
8	18	2	4
9	24	2	2

the risk of death up to time 2, so that $r_1 = 16$. Upon the death of an individual at time $t = 2$, 15 individuals are exposed to death up to time $t = 3$ when another individual dies, so that $r_2 = 15$. This argument is repeated to complete the sequence of risk sets r_j.

We present another example below based on complete individual data of losses. Although the life-contingent connotation does not apply, the same terminology is used.

Example 10.4 Let $x_1, \ldots, x_{20}$ be a sample of claims of a group medical insurance policy. The values of x_i, arranged in increasing order, are as follows:

15, 16, 16, 16, 20, 21, 24, 24, 24, 28, 28, 34, 35, 36, 36, 36, 40, 40, 48, 50.

There are no deductible and policy limit. Summarize the data in terms of the setup above.

Solution 10.4 There are 12 distinct values of claim costs in this data set, so that $m = 12$. As there are no deductible and policy limit, the observations are ground-up losses with no censoring nor truncation. Thus, we have a complete individual data set. Table 10.2 summarizes the data in the notations described above.

The risk set r_j at y_j may be interpreted as the number of claims in the data set with claim size larger than or equal to y_j, having observed claims of amount up to but not including y_j. Thus, 20 claims have sizes larger than or equal to 15, having observed that no claim of amount less than 15 exists. When 1 claim of amount 15 is known, there are 19 claims remaining in the data set. Thus, prior to knowing the number of claims of amount 16, there are possibly 19 claims of amount greater than or equal to 16. Again when 3 claims of amount 16 are known, there are 16 claims remaining in the sample. As the next higher claim

Table 10.2. *Medical claims data in*
Example 10.4

j	y_j	w_j	r_j
1	15	1	20
2	16	3	19
3	20	1	16
4	21	1	15
5	24	3	14
6	28	2	11
7	34	1	9
8	35	1	8
9	36	3	7
10	40	2	4
11	48	1	2
12	50	1	1

is of amount 20, prior to observing claims of amount 20, there are possibly 16 claims of amount greater than or equal to 20. This argument is repeatedly applied to interpret the meaning of the risk set for other values of y_j. $\square$

10.2.3 Incomplete Individual Data

In certain studies the researcher may not have complete information about each individual observed in the sample. To illustrate this problem, we consider a study on the survival time of patients after a surgical operation. When the study begins it includes data of patients who have recently received an operation. New patients who are operated on during the study are included in the sample as well when they are operated on. All patients are observed until the end of the study, and their survival times are recorded.

If a patient received an operation some time before the study began, the researcher has the information about how long this patient has survived after the operation, and the future survival time is conditional on this information. Other patients who received operations at the same time as this individual but did not live until the study began would not be in the sample. Thus, this individual is observed from a population that has been **left truncated,** i.e., information is not available for patients who do not survive until the beginning of the study. On the other hand, if an individual survives until the end of the study, the researcher knows the survival time of the patient up to that time, but has no information about when the patient dies. Thus, the observation pertaining to this individual is **right censored,** i.e., the researcher has the partial information that this individual's survival time goes beyond the study but does not know its exact value.

Table 10.3. *Survival time after a surgical operation*

Ind i	Time ind i first obs	Time since operation when ind i first obs	Time when ind i ends	Status when ind i ends
1	0	2	7	D
2	0	4	4	D
3	2	0	9	D
4	4	0	10	D
5	5	0	12	S
6	7	0	12	S
7	0	2	12	S
8	0	6	12	S
9	8	0	12	S
10	9	0	11	D

While there may be studies with left censoring or right truncation, we shall not consider such cases.

We now define further notations for analyzing incomplete data. Using survival-time studies for exposition, we use d_i to denote the left-truncation status of individual i in the sample. Specifically, $d_i = 0$ if there is no left truncation (the operation was done during the study period), and $d_i > 0$ if there is left truncation (the operation was done d_i periods before the study began). Let x_i denote the survival time (time until death after operation) of the ith individual. If an individual i survives at the end of the study, x_i is not observed and we denote the survival time up to that time by u_i. Thus, for each individual i, there is a x_i value or u_i value (but not both) associated with it. The example below illustrates the construction of the variables introduced.

Example 10.5 A sample of 10 patients receiving a major operation is available. The data are collected over 12 weeks and are summarized in Table 10.3. Column 2 gives the time when the individual was first observed, with a value of zero indicating that the individual was first observed when the study began. A nonzero value gives the time when the operation was done, which is also the time when the individual was first observed. For cases in which the operation was done prior to the beginning of the study Column 3 gives the duration from the operation to the beginning of the study. Column 4 presents the time when the observation ceased, either due to death of patient (D in Column 5) or end of study (S in Column 5). Determine the d_i, x_i and u_i values of each individual.

Solution 10.5 The data are reconstructed in Table 10.4.
Note that d_i is Column 3 of Table 10.3. x_i is defined when there is a "D" in Column 5 of Table 10.3, while u_i is defined when there is a "S" in the column.

Table 10.4. *Reconstruction of Table 10.3*

i	d_i	x_i	u_i
1	2	9	–
2	4	8	–
3	0	7	–
4	0	6	–
5	0	–	7
6	0	–	5
7	2	–	14
8	6	–	18
9	0	–	4
10	0	2	–

x_i is Column 4 minus Column 2, or Column 4 plus Column 3, depending on when the individual was first observed. u_i is computed in a similar way. □

As in the case of a complete data set, we assume that there are m distinct failure-time numbers x_i in the sample, arranged in increasing order, as $0 < y_1 < \cdots < y_m$, with $m \leq n$. Assume y_j occurs w_j times in the sample, for $j = 1, \ldots, m$. Again, we denote r_j as the **risk set** at y_j, which is the number of individuals in the sample exposed to the possibility of death at time y_j (prior to observing the deaths at y_j). To update the risk set r_j after knowing the number of deaths at time y_{j-1}, we use the following formula

$$r_j = r_{j-1} - w_{j-1} + \text{number of observations with } y_{j-1} \leq d_i < y_j$$
$$- \text{number of observations with } y_{j-1} \leq u_i < y_j, \quad j = 2, \ldots, m. \quad (10.8)$$

Note that upon w_{j-1} deaths at failure-time y_{j-1}, the risk set is reduced to $r_{j-1} - w_{j-1}$. This number is supplemented by the number of individuals with $y_{j-1} \leq d_i < y_j$, who are now exposed to risk at failure-time y_j, but are formerly not in the risk set due to left truncation. Note that if an individual has a d value that ties with y_j, this individual is *not included* in the risk set r_j. Furthermore, the risk set is reduced by the number of individuals with $y_{j-1} \leq u_i < y_j$, i.e., those whose failure times are not observed due to right censoring. If an individual has a u value that ties with y_j, this individual is *not excluded* from the risk set r_j

Equation (10.8) can also be computed equivalently using the following formula

$$r_j = \text{number of observations with } d_i < y_j - (\text{number of observations with } x_i < y_j$$
$$+ \text{number of observations with } u_i < y_j), \quad j = 1, \ldots, m. \quad (10.9)$$

Note that the number of observations with $d_i < y_j$ is the total number of individuals who are potentially facing the risk of death at failure-time y_j. However,

Table 10.5. *Ordered death times and risk sets of*
Example 10.6

j	y_j	w_j	r_j	Eq (10.8)	Eq (10.9)
1	2	1	6	—	$6 - 0 - 0$
2	6	1	6	$6 - 1 + 3 - 2$	$9 - 1 - 2$
3	7	1	6	$6 - 1 + 1 - 0$	$10 - 2 - 2$
4	8	1	4	$6 - 1 + 0 - 1$	$10 - 3 - 3$
5	9	1	3	$4 - 1 + 0 - 0$	$10 - 4 - 3$

individuals with $x_i < y_j$ or $u_i < y_j$ are removed from this risk set as they have either died prior to time y_j (when $x_i < y_j$) or have been censored from the study (when $u_i < y_j$). Indeed, to compute r_j using equation (10.8), we need to calculate r_1 using equation (10.9) to begin the recursion.

Example 10.6 Using the data in Example 10.5, determine the risk set at each failure time in the sample.

Solution 10.6 The results are summarized in Table 10.5. Columns 5 and 6 describe the computation of the risk sets using equations (10.8) and (10.9), respectively. It can be seen that equations (10.8) and (10.9) give the same answers.   □

The methods for computing the risk sets of duration data can also be applied to compute the risk sets of loss data. Left truncation in loss data occurs when there is a deductible in the policy. Likewise, right censoring occurs when there is a policy limit. When the loss data come from insurance policies with the same deductible, say d, and the same maximum covered loss, say u, these values are applied to all observations. The example below illustrates a case where there are several policies in the data with different deductibles and maximum covered losses.

Example 10.7 Table 10.6 summarizes the loss claims of 20 insurance policies, numbered by i, with d_i = deductible, x_i = ground-up loss, and u_i^* = maximum covered loss. For policies with losses larger than u_i^*, only the u_i^* value is recorded. The right-censoring variable is denoted by u_i. Determine the risk set r_j of each distinct loss value y_j.

Solution 10.7 The distinct values of x_i, arranged in order, are

$$6, 8, 9, 10, 12, 13, 14, 15, 18,$$

so that $m = 9$. The results are summarized in Table 10.7. As in Table 10.5 of Example 10.6, Columns 5 and 6 describe the computation of the risk sets using equations (10.8) and (10.9), respectively.

Table 10.6. *Insurance claims data of Example 10.7*

i	d_i	x_i	u_i^*	u_i	i	d_i	x_i	u_i^*	u_i
1	0	12	15	–	11	3	14	15	–
2	0	10	15	–	12	3	–	15	15
3	0	8	12	–	13	3	12	18	–
4	0	–	12	12	14	4	15	18	–
5	0	–	15	15	15	4	–	18	18
6	2	13	15	–	16	4	8	18	–
7	2	10	12	–	17	4	–	15	15
8	2	9	15	–	18	5	–	20	20
9	2	–	18	18	19	5	18	20	–
10	3	6	12	–	20	5	8	20	–

Table 10.7. *Ordered claim losses and risk sets of*
Example 10.7

j	y_j	w_j	r_j	Eq (10.8)	Eq (10.9)
1	6	1	20	—	20 – 0 – 0
2	8	3	19	20 – 1 + 0 – 0	20 – 1 – 0
3	9	1	16	19 – 3 + 0 – 0	20 – 4 – 0
4	10	2	15	16 – 1 + 0 – 0	20 – 5 – 0
5	12	2	13	15 – 2 + 0 – 0	20 – 7 – 0
6	13	1	10	13 – 2 + 0 – 1	20 – 9 – 1
7	14	1	9	10 – 1 + 0 – 0	20 – 10 – 1
8	15	1	8	9 – 1 + 0 – 0	20 – 11 – 1
9	18	1	4	8 – 1 + 0 – 3	20 – 12 – 4

Thus, just like the case of duration data, the risk sets of loss data can be computed using equations (10.8) and (10.9). □

Example 10.8 A sample of insurance policies with a deductible of 4 and maximum covered loss of 20 has the following ground-up loss amounts

$$5, 7, 8, 10, 10, 16, 17, 17, 17, 19, 20, 20^+, 20^+, 20^+, 20^+,$$

where 20^+ denotes right censored loss amount of 20. Determine the risk sets of the distinct loss values.

Solution 10.8 Each of the observations has $d_i = 4$, and there are 4 observations with $u_i = 20$. The 8 distinct loss values y_j, with their associated w_j and r_j values, are given in Table 10.8.

Note that all observations from this sample are from a left truncated population. Hence, analysis of the ground-up loss distribution is not possible and only the conditional distribution (given loss larger than 4) can be analyzed. □

Table 10.8. *Results of Example 10.8*

j	y_j	w_j	r_j
1	5	1	15
2	7	1	14
3	8	1	13
4	10	2	12
5	16	1	10
6	17	3	9
7	19	1	6
8	20	1	5

10.2.4 Grouped Data

Sometimes we work with grouped observations rather than individual observations. This situation is especially common when the number of individual observations is large and there is no significant loss of information in working with grouped data.

Let the values of the failure-time or loss data be divided into k intervals: $(c_0, c_1], (c_1, c_2], \ldots, (c_{k-1}, c_k]$, where $0 \leq c_0 < c_1 < \cdots < c_k$. The observations are classified into the interval groups according to the values of x_i (failure time or loss). We first consider complete data. Let there be n observations of x_i in the sample, with n_j observations of x_i in interval $(c_{j-1}, c_j]$, so that $\sum_{j=1}^{k} n_j = n$. As there is no left truncation, all observations in the sample are in the risk set for the first interval. Thus, the risk set in interval $(c_0, c_1]$ is n. The number of deaths in each interval is then subtracted from the risk set to obtain the risk set for the next interval. This is due to the fact that there is no new addition of risk (no left truncation) and no extra reduction in risk (no right censoring). Thus, the risk set in interval $(c_1, c_2]$ is $n - n_1$. In general, the risk set in interval $(c_{j-1}, c_j]$ is $n - \sum_{i=1}^{j-1} n_i = \sum_{i=j}^{k} n_i$.

When the data are incomplete, with possible left truncation and/or right censoring, approximations may be required to compute the risk sets. For this purpose, we first define the following quantities based on the attributes of individual observations:

$$D_j = \text{number of observations with } c_{j-1} \leq d_i < c_j, \text{ for } j = 1, \ldots, k,$$

$$U_j = \text{number of observations with } c_{j-1} < u_i \leq c_j, \text{ for } j = 1, \ldots, k,$$

$$V_j = \text{number of observations with } c_{j-1} < x_i \leq c_j, \text{ for } j = 1, \ldots, k.$$

Thus, D_j is the number of new additions to the risk set in the interval $(c_{j-1}, c_j]$, U_j is the number of right-censored observations that exit the sample in the interval $(c_{j-1}, c_j]$, and V_j is the number of deaths or loss values in $(c_{j-1}, c_j]$. Note the difference in the intervals for defining D_j versus U_j and V_j. A tie of a d value with c_{j-1} is a new addition of risk to the interval $(c_{j-1}, c_j]$. On the other hand, a tie of a death or a right-censored observation with c_j is a loss in the risk set from the interval $(c_{j-1}, c_j]$. This is due to the fact that D_j determines entry into $(c_{j-1}, c_j]$, while U_j and V_j record exits from it.

We now define R_j as the risk set for the interval $(c_{j-1}, c_j]$, which is the total number of observations in the sample exposed to the risk of failure or loss in $(c_{j-1}, c_j]$. We assume that any entry in an interval contributes to the risk group in the whole interval, while any exit only reduces the risk group in the next interval. Thus, for the first interval $(c_0, c_1]$, we have $R_1 = D_1$. Subsequent updating of the risk set is computed as

$$R_j = R_{j-1} - V_{j-1} + D_j - U_{j-1}, \qquad j = 2, \ldots, k. \tag{10.10}$$

An alternative formula for R_j is

$$R_j = \sum_{i=1}^{j} D_i - \sum_{i=1}^{j-1} (V_i + U_i), \qquad j = 2, \ldots, k. \tag{10.11}$$

Note that equations (10.10) and (10.11) can be compared against equations (10.8) and (10.9), respectively.

In the case of complete data, $D_1 = n$ and $D_j = 0$ for $j = 2, \ldots, k$. Also, $U_j = 0$ and $V_j = n_j$ for $j = 1, \ldots, k$. Thus, $R_1 = D_1 = n$, and from equation (10.10) we have

$$\begin{aligned} R_j &= R_{j-1} - n_{j-1} \\ &= n - (n_1 + \cdots + n_{j-1}) \\ &= n_j + \cdots + n_k, \end{aligned} \tag{10.12}$$

using recursive substitution. This result has been obtained directly from the properties of complete data.

Example 10.9 For the data in Table 10.6, the observations are grouped into the intervals: $(0, 4], (4, 8], (8, 12], (12, 16]$ and $(16, 20]$. Determine the risk set in each interval.

Solution 10.9 We tabulate the results in Table 10.9. D_j and U_j are obtained from the d and u values in Table 10.6, respectively. Likewise, V_j are obtained by accumulating the w values in Table 10.7. Note that the sum of D_j equals the total number of observations; the sum of U_j equals the number of right-censored observations (i.e., 7) and the sum of V_j equals the number of uncensored loss observations (i.e., 13). The risk sets R_j are calculated using equation (10.10). □

Table 10.9. *Results of Example 10.9*

Group j	D_j	U_j	V_j	R_j
$(0, 4]$	13	0	0	13
$(4, 8]$	7	0	4	20
$(8, 12]$	0	1	5	16
$(12, 16]$	0	3	3	10
$(16, 20]$	0	3	1	4

10.3 Summary and Discussions

We have reviewed the theories of model estimation and briefly surveyed the use of the parametric and nonparametric estimation approaches. As the estimation methods used are applicable to both duration and loss data, we use examples from both literature. While the terminologies follow the interpretation of age-at-death data, they are also used for loss data. The purpose of this chapter is to define the notations used for complete and incomplete data, as preparation for the discussion of various estimation methods in the next two chapters. In particular, we explain the concept of risk set, and show how this can be computed using individual and grouped data. For each observation we have to keep track of a set of values representing left truncation, right censoring and age at death. The computation of the risk sets requires special care when the observations are incomplete, due to left truncation and/or right censoring. In grouped data some assumptions regarding entry and exit of risks are required. We have discussed one simple approach, although other methods are available.

Exercises

Exercise 10.1 Let $x = (x_1, \ldots, x_n)$ be a random sample of n observations of X, which has mean μ and variance σ^2. Prove that the sample mean $\bar{x}$ and the sample variance s^2 of x are unbiased estimators of μ and σ^2, respectively.

Exercise 10.2 Let $\hat{\theta}_1$ be an estimator of θ, which is known to lie in the interval (a, b). Define an estimator of θ, $\hat{\theta}_2$, by $\hat{\theta}_2 = \hat{\theta}_1$ if $\hat{\theta}_1 \in (a, b)$, $\hat{\theta}_2 = a$ if $\hat{\theta}_1 \leq a$ and $\hat{\theta}_2 = b$ if $\hat{\theta}_1 \geq b$. Prove that $\text{MSE}(\hat{\theta}_2) \leq \text{MSE}(\hat{\theta}_1)$. If $\hat{\theta}_1$ is an unbiased estimator of θ, also show that $\text{Var}(\hat{\theta}_2) \leq \text{Var}(\hat{\theta}_1)$.

Exercise 10.3 Let $x = (x_1, \ldots, x_n)$ be a random sample of n observations of a continuous distribution X with pdf $f_X(\cdot)$ and df $F_X(\cdot)$. Denote $x_{(r)}$ as the rth order statistic, such that $x_{(1)} \leq x_{(2)} \leq \cdots \leq x_{(n)}$. Show that the joint pdf of $X_{(r)}$ and $X_{(s)}$, $r < s$, is

$$\frac{n!}{(r-1)!(s-r-1)!(n-s)!} \left[F_X(x_{(r)})\right]^{r-1} \left[F_X(x_{(s)}) - F_X(x_{(r)})\right]^{s-r-1}$$

$$\times \left[1 - F_X(x_{(s)})\right]^{n-s} f_X(x_{(r)}) f_X(x_{(s)}).$$

If $X \sim \mathcal{U}(0, \theta)$, show that the joint pdf of $X_{(n-1)}$ and $X_{(n)}$ is

$$\frac{n(n-1)x_{(n-1)}^{n-2}}{\theta^n}.$$

For $X \sim \mathcal{U}(0, \theta)$, compute $E(X_{(n-1)})$ and $Var(X_{(n-1)})$. What is the MSE of $X_{(n-1)}$ as an estimator of θ? Compare this against the MSE of $X_{(n)}$. What is the covariance of $X_{(n-1)}$ and $X_{(n)}$?

Exercise 10.4 Let $x = (x_1, \ldots, x_n)$ be a random sample of n observations of a continuous distribution X, with pdf $f_X(x) = \exp[-(x - \delta)]$ for $x > \delta$ and 0 otherwise.

(a) Is the sample mean $\bar{X}$ an unbiased estimator of δ? Is it a consistent estimator of δ?

(b) Is the first order statistic $X_{(1)}$ an unbiased estimator of δ? Is it a consistent estimator of δ?

Exercise 10.5 If $X \sim \mathcal{BN}(n, \theta)$, show that the sample proportion $p = X/n$ is an unbiased estimator of θ. Is $np(1 - p)$ an unbiased estimator of the variance of X?

Exercise 10.6 Suppose the moments of X exist up to order k, and $x = (x_1, \ldots, x_n)$ is a random sample of X. Show that $\hat{\mu}'_r = (\sum_{i=1}^{n} x^r)/n$ is an unbiased estimate of $E(X^r)$ for $r = 1, \ldots, k$. Can you find an unbiased estimate of $[E(X)]^2$?

Exercise 10.7 Let $x = (x_1, \ldots, x_n)$ be a random sample of n observations of $\mathcal{N}(\mu, \sigma^2)$. Construct a $100(1 - \alpha)\%$ confidence interval of σ^2.

Exercise 10.8 Let $x = (x_1, \ldots, x_n)$ be a random sample of n observations of $\mathcal{E}(\lambda)$. Construct a $100(1 - \alpha)\%$ confidence interval of λ.

Exercise 10.9 Applicants for a job were given a task to perform and the time they took to finish the task was recorded. The table below summarizes the time applicant i started the task (B_i) and the time it was finished (E_i).

i	1	2	3	4	5	6	7	8	9	10	11	12	13	14	15	16	17	18
B_i	2	4	4	5	6	7	8	8	8	9	10	11	11	12	15	18	18	20
E_i	7	6	9	12	14	17	14	13	20	21	21	23	20	19	18	24	25	24

Summarize the data, giving the durations of the task, the distinct observed durations and their frequencies, and the risk set at each observed duration.

Exercise 10.10 In a graduate employment survey the starting monthly salary of each respondent, to the nearest hundred dollars, was recorded. The following data are collected:

$$23, 23, 25, 27, 27, 27, 28, 30, 30, 31, 33, 38, 42, 45, 45, 45.$$

What is the risk set at each observed salary?

Exercise 10.11 The Labor Bureau conducted a survey on unemployment in a small town. The data below give the time B_i the unemployed person i reported out of job ($B_i = -k$ if the person was first unemployed k weeks before the survey started) and the time E_i the unemployed person found a job. The survey spanned a period of 20 weeks, and people who remained unemployed at the end of the survey are recorded as U.

i	B_i	E_i/U
1	−4	12
2	−2	9
3	1	6
4	3	16
5	4	12
6	4	18
7	4	19
8	5	U
9	6	19
10	6	U

Compute the risk set at each observed unemployment duration.

Exercise 10.12 Insurance policies have deductibles d and ground-up losses x. Twenty losses are summarized below.

i	d_i	x_i	i	d_i	x_i
1	0	8	11	4	3
2	0	6	12	4	5
3	0	6	13	6	7
4	2	3	14	6	5
5	2	9	15	6	8
6	2	7	16	6	10
7	2	9	17	6	7
8	2	5	18	6	4
9	4	6	19	6	8
10	4	8	20	6	9

Compute the risk set of each observed ground-up loss amount.

Exercise 10.13 Ground-up losses of 25 insurance policies with a deductible of 5 and maximum covered loss of 18 are summarized as follows:

2, 4, 4, 5, 6, 6, 6, 8, 8, 12, 13, 13, 14, 15, 15, 16, 16, 17,

17, 18, 18, 19, 20, 23, 28.

Determine the risk sets of the reported distinct ground-up loss values.

Exercise 10.14 Insurance policies have deductibles d, maximum covered losses 15 and ground-up losses x. Twenty losses are recorded below.

i	d_i	x_i	i	d_i	x_i
1	0	12	11	4	13
2	0	16	12	4	18
3	0	4	13	4	7
4	0	12	14	4	12
5	0	15	15	4	18
6	2	14	16	5	10
7	2	13	17	5	9
8	2	17	18	5	8
9	2	9	19	5	18
10	2	8	20	5	13

(a) Compute the risk set of each observed ground-up loss amount.
(b) If the loss observations are grouped into the intervals: $(0, 5]$, $(5, 10]$ and $(10, 15]$, determine the risk set in each interval.

11

Nonparametric Model Estimation

The main focus of this chapter is the estimation of the distribution function and probability (density) function of duration and loss variables. The methods used depend on whether the data are for individual or grouped observations, and whether the observations are complete or incomplete.

For complete individual observations, the relative frequency distribution of the sample observations defines a discrete distribution called the empirical distribution. Moments and df of the true distribution can be estimated using the empirical distribution. Smoothing refinements can be applied to the empirical df to improve its performance. We also discuss kernel-based estimation methods for the estimation of the df and pdf.

When the sample observations are incomplete, with left truncation and/or right censoring, the Kaplan–Meier (product-limit) estimator and the Nelson–Aalen estimator can be used to estimate the survival function. These estimators compute the conditional survival probabilities using observations arranged in increasing order. They make use of the data setup discussed in the last chapter, in particular, the risk set at each observed data point. We also discuss the estimation of their variance, the Greenwood formula and interval estimation.

For grouped data, smoothing techniques are used to estimate the moments, the quantiles and the df. The Kaplan–Meier and Nelson–Aalen estimators can also be applied to grouped incomplete data.

Learning Objectives

1 Empirical distribution
2 Moments and df of the empirical distribution
3 Kernel estimates of df and pdf
4 Kaplan–Meier (product-limit) estimator and Nelson–Aalen estimator

5 Greenwood formula

6 Estimation based on grouped observations

11.1 Estimation with Complete Individual Data

We first consider the case where we have complete individual observations. We discuss methods of estimating the df, the quantiles and moments of the duration and loss variables, as well as censored moments when these variables are subject to censoring.

11.1.1 Empirical Distribution

We continue to use the notations introduced in the last chapter. Thus, we have a sample of n observations of failure times or losses X, denoted by $x_1, \ldots, x_n$. The distinct values of the observations are arranged in increasing order and are denoted by $0 < y_1 < \cdots < y_m$, where $m \leq n$. The value of y_j is repeated w_j times, so that $\sum_{j=1}^{m} w_j = n$. We also denote g_j as the partial sum of the number of observations not more than y_j, i.e., $g_j = \sum_{h=1}^{j} w_h$.

The **empirical distribution** of the data is defined as the discrete distribution that can take values $y_1, \ldots, y_m$ with probabilities $w_1/n, \ldots, w_m/n$, respectively. Alternatively, it is a discrete distribution for which the values $x_1, \ldots, x_n$ (with possible repetitions) occur with equal probabilities. Denoting $\hat{f}(\cdot)$ and $\hat{F}(\cdot)$ as the pf and df of the empirical distribution, respectively, these functions are given by

$$\hat{f}(y) = \begin{cases} \dfrac{w_j}{n}, & \text{if } y = y_j \text{ for some } j, \\ 0, & \text{otherwise,} \end{cases} \tag{11.1}$$

and

$$\hat{F}(y) = \begin{cases} 0, & \text{for } y < y_1, \\ \dfrac{g_j}{n}, & \text{for } y_j \leq y < y_{j+1}, j = 1, \ldots, m-1, \\ 1, & \text{for } y_m \leq y. \end{cases} \tag{11.2}$$

Thus, the **mean of the empirical distribution** is

$$\sum_{j=1}^{m} \frac{w_j}{n} y_j = \frac{1}{n} \sum_{i=1}^{n} x_i, \tag{11.3}$$

which is the sample mean of $x_1, \ldots, x_n$, i.e., $\bar{x}$. The **variance of the empirical distribution** is

$$\sum_{j=1}^{m} \frac{w_j}{n} (y_j - \bar{x})^2 = \frac{1}{n} \sum_{i=1}^{n} (x_i - \bar{x})^2, \tag{11.4}$$

which is not equal to the sample variance of $x_1, \ldots, x_n$, and is biased for the variance of X.

Estimates of the moments of X can be computed from their sample analogs. In particular, censored moments can be estimated from the censored sample. For example, for a policy with policy limit u, the censored kth moment $E\left[(X \wedge u)^k\right]$ can be estimated by

$$\sum_{j=1}^{r} \frac{w_j}{n} y_j^k + \frac{n - g_r}{n} u^k, \qquad \text{where } y_r \le u < y_{r+1} \text{ for some } r. \qquad (11.5)$$

$\hat{F}(y)$, defined in equation (11.2), is also called the **empirical distribution function** of X. Likewise, the **empirical survival function** of X is $\hat{S}(y) = 1 - \hat{F}(y)$, which is an estimate of $\Pr(X > y)$.

To compute an estimate of the df for a value of y not in the set $y_1, \ldots, y_m$, we may *smooth* the empirical df to obtain $\tilde{F}(y)$ as follows

$$\tilde{F}(y) = \frac{y - y_j}{y_{j+1} - y_j} \hat{F}(y_{j+1}) + \frac{y_{j+1} - y}{y_{j+1} - y_j} \hat{F}(y_j), \qquad (11.6)$$

where $y_j \le y < y_{j+1}$ for some $j = 1, \ldots, m - 1$. Thus, $\tilde{F}(y)$ is the linear interpolation of $\hat{F}(y_{j+1})$ and $\hat{F}(y_j)$, called the **smoothed empirical distribution function**. At values of $y = y_j$, $\tilde{F}(y) = \hat{F}(y)$.

To estimate the quantiles of the distribution, we also use interpolation. Recall that the quantile x_δ is defined as $F^{-1}(\delta)$. We use y_j as an estimate of the $(g_j/(n+1))$-quantile (or the $(100g_j/(n+1))$th percentile) of X.[1] The δ-quantile of X, denoted by $\hat{x}_\delta$, may be computed as

$$\hat{x}_\delta = \left[\frac{(n+1)\delta - g_j}{w_{j+1}}\right] y_{j+1} + \left[\frac{g_{j+1} - (n+1)\delta}{w_{j+1}}\right] y_j, \qquad (11.7)$$

where

$$\frac{g_j}{n+1} \le \delta < \frac{g_{j+1}}{n+1}, \qquad \text{for some } j. \qquad (11.8)$$

Thus, $\hat{x}_\delta$ is a smoothed estimate of the sample quantiles, and is obtained by linearly interpolating y_j and y_{j+1}. It can be verified that if $\delta = g_j/(n+1)$, $\hat{x}_\delta = y_j$. Furthermore, when there are no ties in the observations, $w_j = 1$ and $g_j = j$ for $j = 1, \ldots, n$. Equation (11.7) then reduces to

$$\hat{x}_\delta = [(n+1)\delta - j] y_{j+1} + [j + 1 - (n+1)\delta] y_j, \qquad (11.9)$$

---

[1] Hence, the largest observation in the sample, y_m, is the $(100n/(n+1))$th percentile, and *not* the 100th percentile. Recall from Example 10.2 that if X is distributed as $\mathcal{U}(0, \theta)$, the mean of the largest sample observation is $n\theta/(n+1)$. Likewise, if y_1 has no tie, it is an estimate of the $(100/(n+1))$th percentile. Note that this is not the only way to define the sample quantile. We may alternatively use y_j as an estimate of the $((g_j - 0.5)/n)$-quantile. See Hyndman and and Fan (1996) for more details. Unless otherwise stated, we shall use equations (11.7) through (11.10) to compute the quantile $\hat{x}_\delta$.

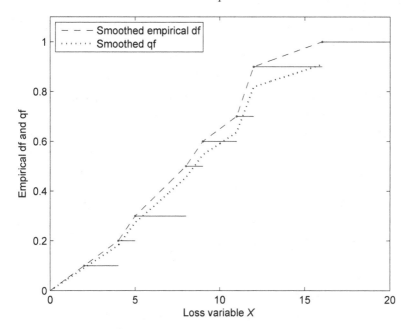

Figure 11.1 Empirical df and qf of Example 11.1

where

$$\frac{j}{n+1} \leq \delta < \frac{j+1}{n+1}, \qquad \text{for some } j. \tag{11.10}$$

Example 11.1 A sample of losses has the following 10 observations

$$2, 4, 5, 8, 8, 9, 11, 12, 12, 16.$$

Plot the empirical distribution function, the smoothed empirical distribution function and the smoothed quantile function. Determine the estimates $\tilde{F}(7.2)$ and $\hat{x}_{0.75}$. Also, estimate the censored variance $\text{Var}[(X \wedge 11.5)]$.

Solution 11.1 The plots of various functions are given in Figure 11.1. The empirical distribution function is a step function represented by the solid lines. The dashed line represents the smoothed empirical df, and the dotted line gives the (inverse) of the quantile function.
For $\tilde{F}(7.2)$, we first note that $\hat{F}(5) = 0.3$ and $\hat{F}(8) = 0.5$. Thus, using equation (11.6) we have

$$\begin{aligned}
\tilde{F}(7.2) &= \left[\frac{7.2 - 5}{8 - 5}\right] \hat{F}(8) + \left[\frac{8 - 7.2}{8 - 5}\right] \hat{F}(5) \\
&= \left[\frac{2.2}{3}\right] (0.5) + \left[\frac{0.8}{3}\right] (0.3) \\
&= 0.4467.
\end{aligned}$$

For $\hat{x}_{0.75}$, we first note that $g_6 = 7$ and $g_7 = 9$ (note that $y_6 = 11$ and $y_7 = 12$). With $n = 10$, we have

$$\frac{7}{11} \le 0.75 < \frac{9}{11},$$

so that j defined in equation (11.8) is 6. Hence, using equation (11.7), we compute the smoothed quantile as

$$\hat{x}_{0.75} = \left[\frac{(11)(0.75) - 7}{2} \right] (12) + \left[\frac{9 - (11)(0.75)}{2} \right] (11) = 11.625.$$

We estimate the first moment of the censored loss $E\left[(X \wedge 11.5)\right]$ by

$$(0.1)(2) + (0.1)(4) + (0.1)(5) + (0.2)(8) + (0.1)(9)$$
$$+ (0.1)(11) + (0.3)(11.5) = 8.15,$$

and the second raw moment of the censored loss $E\left[(X \wedge 11.5)^2\right]$ by

$$(0.1)(2)^2 + (0.1)(4)^2 + (0.1)(5)^2 + (0.2)(8)^2 + (0.1)(9)^2$$
$$+ (0.1)(11)^2 + (0.3)(11.5)^2 = 77.175.$$

Hence, the estimated variance of the censored loss is

$$77.175 - (8.15)^2 = 10.7525. \qquad \qquad \square$$

Note that $\hat{F}(y)$ can also be written as

$$\hat{F}(y) = \frac{Y}{n}, \qquad (11.11)$$

where Y is the number of observations less than or equal to y, so that $Y \sim \mathcal{BN}(n, F(y))$. Using results in binomial distribution, we conclude that

$$E[\hat{F}(y)] = \frac{E(Y)}{n} = \frac{nF(y)}{n} = F(y), \qquad (11.12)$$

and

$$\text{Var}[\hat{F}(y)] = \frac{F(y)[1 - F(y)]}{n}. \qquad (11.13)$$

Thus, $\hat{F}(y)$ is an unbiased estimator of $F(y)$ and its variance tends to 0 as n tends to infinity, implying $\hat{F}(y)$ is a consistent estimator of $F(y)$. As $F(y)$ is unknown, we may estimate $\text{Var}[\hat{F}(y)]$ by replacing $F(y)$ in equation (11.13) by $\hat{F}(y)$. Then in large samples an approximate $100(1 - \alpha)\%$ confidence interval estimate of $F(y)$ may be computed as

$$\hat{F}(y) \pm z_{1 - \frac{\alpha}{2}} \sqrt{\frac{\hat{F}(y)[1 - \hat{F}(y)]}{n}}. \qquad (11.14)$$

A drawback of (11.14) in the estimation of the confidence interval of $F(y)$ is that it may fall outside the interval $(0, 1)$. We will discuss a remedy of this problem later.

11.1.2 Kernel Estimation of Probability Density Function

The empirical pf summarizes the data as a discrete distribution. However, if the variable of interest (loss or failure time) is continuous, it is desirable to estimate a pdf. This can be done using the **kernel density estimation method**.

Consider the observation x_i in the sample. The empirical pf assigns a probability mass of $1/n$ to the point x_i. Given that X is continuous, we may wish to *distribute* the probability mass to a neighborhood of x_i rather than assigning it completely to point x_i. Let us assume that we wish to distribute the mass *evenly* in the interval $[x_i - b, x_i + b]$ for a given value of $b > 0$, called the **bandwidth**. To do this, we define a function $f_i(x)$ as follows[2]

$$f_i(x) = \begin{cases} \dfrac{0.5}{b}, & \text{for } x_i - b \leq x \leq x_i + b, \\ 0, & \text{otherwise.} \end{cases} \tag{11.15}$$

This function is rectangular in shape, with a base of length $2b$ and height of $0.5/b$, so that its area is 1. It may be interpreted as the pdf contributed by the observation x_i. Note that $f_i(x)$ is also the pdf of a $\mathcal{U}(x_i - b, x_i + b)$ variable. Thus, only values of x in the interval $[x_i - b, x_i + b]$ receive contributions from x_i. As each x_i contributes a probability mass of $1/n$, the pdf of X may be estimated as

$$\tilde{f}(x) = \frac{1}{n} \sum_{i=1}^{n} f_i(x). \tag{11.16}$$

We now rewrite $f_i(x)$ in equation (11.15) as

$$f_i(x) = \begin{cases} \dfrac{0.5}{b}, & \text{for } -1 \leq \dfrac{x - x_i}{b} \leq 1, \\ 0, & \text{otherwise,} \end{cases} \tag{11.17}$$

and define

$$K_R(\psi) = \begin{cases} 0.5, & \text{for } -1 \leq \psi \leq 1, \\ 0, & \text{otherwise.} \end{cases} \tag{11.18}$$

Then it can be seen that

$$f_i(x) = \frac{1}{b} K_R(\psi_i), \tag{11.19}$$

where

$$\psi_i = \frac{x - x_i}{b}. \tag{11.20}$$

Note that $K_R(\psi)$ as defined in (11.18) does not depend on the data. However, $K_R(\psi_i)$ with ψ_i defined in equation (11.20) is a function of x (x is the argument

---

[2] Note that the suffix i in $f_i(x)$ highlights that the function depends on x_i. Also, $2b$ is sometimes called the **window width**.

of $K_R(\psi_i)$, and x_i and b are the *parameters*). Using equation (11.19), we rewrite equation (11.16) as

$$\tilde{f}(x) = \frac{1}{nb} \sum_{i=1}^{n} K_R(\psi_i). \tag{11.21}$$

$K_R(\psi)$ as defined in equation (11.18) is called the **rectangular (or box, uniform) kernel function.** $\tilde{f}(x)$ defined in equation (11.21) is the estimate of the pdf of X using the rectangular kernel.

It can be seen that $K_R(\psi)$ satisfies the following properties

$$K_R(\psi) \geq 0, \quad \text{for} - \infty < \psi < \infty, \tag{11.22}$$

and

$$\int_{-\infty}^{\infty} K_R(\psi)\, d\psi = 1. \tag{11.23}$$

Hence, $K_R(\psi)$ is itself the pdf of a random variable taking values over the real line. Indeed any function $K(\psi)$ satisfying equations (11.22) and (11.23) may be called a **kernel function**. Furthermore, the expression in equation (11.21), with $K(\psi)$ replacing $K_R(\psi)$ and ψ_i defined in equation (11.20), is called the **kernel estimate** of the pdf. Apart from the rectangular kernel, two other commonly used kernels are the **triangular kernel**, denoted by $K_T(\psi)$, and the **Gaussian kernel**, denoted by $K_G(\psi)$. The triangular kernel is defined as

$$K_T(\psi) = \begin{cases} 1 - |\psi|, & \text{for} - 1 \leq \psi \leq 1, \\ 0, & \text{otherwise}, \end{cases} \tag{11.24}$$

and the Gaussian kernel is given by

$$K_G(\psi) = \frac{1}{\sqrt{2\pi}} \exp\left(-\frac{\psi^2}{2}\right), \quad \text{for} - \infty < \psi < \infty, \tag{11.25}$$

which is just the standard normal density function.

Figure 11.2 presents the plots of the rectangular, triangular and Gaussian kernels. For the rectangular and triangular kernels, the width of the neighborhood to which the mass of each observation x_i is distributed is $2b$. In contrast, for the Gaussian kernel, the neighborhood is infinite. Regardless of the kernel used, the larger the value of b, the smoother the estimated pdf is. While the rectangular kernel distributes the mass uniformly in the neighborhood, the triangular and Gaussian kernels diminish gradually toward the two ends of the neighborhood. We also note that all three kernel functions are even, such that $K(-\psi) = K(\psi)$. Hence, these kernels are symmetric.

Example 11.2 A sample of losses has the following 10 observations:

$$5, 6, 6, 7, 8, 8, 10, 12, 13, 15.$$

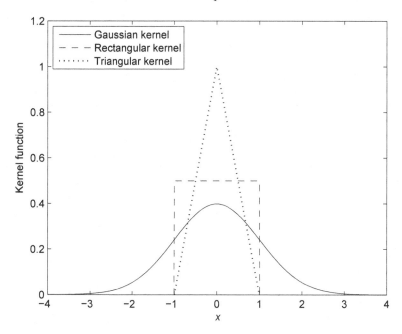

Figure 11.2 Some commonly used kernel functions

Determine the kernel estimate of the pdf of the losses using the rectangular kernel for $x = 8.5$ and 11.5 with a bandwidth of 3.

Solution 11.2 For $x = 8.5$ with $b = 3$, there are six observations within the interval $[5.5, 11.5]$. From equation (11.21) we have

$$\tilde{f}(8.5) = \frac{1}{(10)(3)} \, (6)(0.5) = \frac{1}{10}.$$

Similarly, there are three observations in the interval $[8.5, 14.5]$, so that

$$\tilde{f}(11.5) = \frac{1}{(10)(3)} \, (3)(0.5) = \frac{1}{20}. \qquad \square$$

Example 11.3 A sample of losses has the following 40 observations:

15, 16, 16, 17, 19, 19, 19, 23, 24, 27, 28, 28, 28, 28, 31, 34, 34, 34, 36, 36

37, 40, 41, 41, 43, 46, 46, 46, 47, 47, 49, 50, 50, 53, 54, 54, 59, 61, 63, 64.

Estimate the pdf of the loss distribution using the rectangular kernel and Gaussian kernel, with bandwidth of 3 and 8.

Solution 11.3 The rectangular kernel estimates are plotted in Figure 11.3, and the Gaussian kernel estimates are plotted in Figure 11.4. It can be seen that the

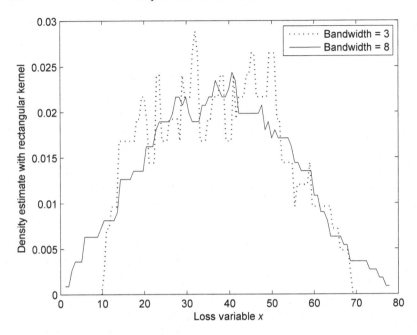

Figure 11.3 Estimated pdf of Example 11.3 using rectangular kernel

Gaussian kernel estimates are smoother than the rectangular kernel estimates. Also, the kernels with bandwidth of 8 provides smoother pdf than kernels with bandwidth of 3. For the Gaussian kernel with bandwidth of 8, the estimated pdf extends to values of negative losses. This is undesirable and is due to the fact that the Gaussian kernel has infinite support and the bandwidth is wide. □

The estimated kernel df, denoted by $\tilde{F}(x)$, can be computed by integrating the estimated kernel pdf. From equation (11.21), we have

$$\tilde{F}(x) = \int_0^x \tilde{f}(x)\,dx$$

$$= \frac{1}{nb} \sum_{i=1}^n \int_0^x K\left(\frac{x - x_i}{b}\right) dx$$

$$= \frac{1}{n} \sum_{i=1}^n \int_{-x_i/b}^{(x-x_i)/b} K(\psi)\,d\psi, \qquad (11.26)$$

where $K(\psi)$ is any well-defined kernel function.

11.2 Estimation with Incomplete Individual Data

We now consider samples with incomplete data, i.e., observations with left truncation or right censoring. Our focus is on the nonparametric estimation of the

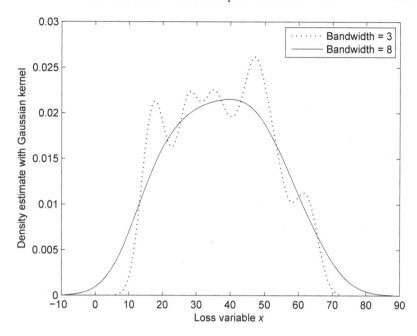

Figure 11.4 Estimated pdf of Example 11.3 using Gaussian kernel

survival function $S(x)$. Suppose the data consist of n observations with m distinct values $0 < y_1 < \cdots < y_m$, with corresponding risk sets $r_1, \ldots, r_m$, and counts of repetition $w_1, \ldots, w_m$ (numbers of times $y_1, \ldots, y_m$ are in the sample). We let $y_0 \equiv 0$, so that $S(y_0) = S(0) = 1$. We shall provide heuristic derivations of the Kaplan–Meier (product-limit) estimator and the Nelson–Aalen estimator of the sf.[3]

11.2.1 Kaplan–Meier (Product-Limit) Estimator

We consider the estimation of $S(y_j) = \Pr(X > y_j)$, for $j = 1, \ldots, m$. Using the rule of conditional probability, we have

$$S(y_j) = \Pr(X > y_1) \Pr(X > y_2 \mid X > y_1) \cdots \Pr(X > y_j \mid X > y_{j-1})$$

$$= \Pr(X > y_1) \prod_{h=2}^{j} \Pr(X > y_h \mid X > y_{h-1}). \tag{11.27}$$

As the risk set for y_1 is r_1 and w_1 observations are found to have value y_1, $\Pr(X > y_1)$ can be estimated by

---

[3] Rigorous derivations of these estimators are beyond the scope of this book. Interested readers may refer to London (1988) and the references therein.

$$\widehat{\Pr}(X > y_1) = 1 - \frac{w_1}{r_1}. \tag{11.28}$$

Likewise, the risk set for y_h is r_h, and w_h individuals are observed to have value y_h. Thus, $\Pr(X > y_h \mid X > y_{h-1})$ can be estimated by

$$\widehat{\Pr}(X > y_h \mid X > y_{h-1}) = 1 - \frac{w_h}{r_h}, \qquad \text{for } h = 2, \dots, m. \tag{11.29}$$

Hence, we may estimate $S(y_j)$ by

$$\hat{S}(y_j) = \widehat{\Pr}(X > y_1) \prod_{h=2}^{j} \widehat{\Pr}(X > y_h \mid X > y_{h-1})$$

$$= \prod_{h=1}^{j} \left(1 - \frac{w_h}{r_h} \right). \tag{11.30}$$

For values of y with $y_j \le y < y_{j+1}$, we have $\hat{S}(y) = \hat{S}(y_j)$, as no observation is found in the sample in the interval $(y_j, y]$.

We now summarize the above arguments and define the Kaplan–Meier estimator, denoted by $\hat{S}_K(y)$, as follows

$$\hat{S}_K(y) = \begin{cases} 1, & \text{for } 0 < y < y_1, \\ \prod_{h=1}^{j} \left(1 - \dfrac{w_h}{r_h} \right), & \text{for } y_j \le y < y_{j+1}, j = 1, \dots, m-1, \\ \prod_{h=1}^{m} \left(1 - \dfrac{w_h}{r_h} \right), & \text{for } y_m \le y. \end{cases} \tag{11.31}$$

Note that if $w_m = r_m$, then $\hat{S}_K(y) = 0$ for $y_m \le y$. However, if $w_m < r_m$ (i.e., the largest observation is a censored observation and not a failure time), then $\hat{S}_K(y_m) > 0$. There are several ways to compute $\hat{S}_K(y)$ for $y > y_m$. First, we may adopt the definition in equation (11.31). This method, however, is inconsistent with the property of the sf that $S(y) \to 0$ as $y \to \infty$. Second, we may let $\hat{S}_K(y) = 0$ for $y > y_m$. Third, we may allow $\hat{S}_K(y)$ to decay geometrically to 0 by defining

$$\hat{S}_K(y) = \hat{S}_K(y_m)^{\frac{y}{y_m}}, \qquad \text{for } y > y_m. \tag{11.32}$$

Example 11.4 Refer to the loss claims in Example 10.7. Determine the Kaplan–Meier estimate of the sf.

Solution 11.4 Using the data compiled in Table 10.7, we present the calculation of the Kaplan–Meier estimates in Table 11.1. For $y > 18$, the sf may be alternatively computed as 0 or $(0.2888)^{\frac{y}{18}}$. □

Example 11.5 Refer to the loss claims in Example 10.8. Determine the Kaplan–Meier estimate of the sf.

Table 11.1. *Kaplan–Meier estimates of*
Example 11.4

Interval containing y	$\hat{S}_K(y)$
$(0, 6)$	1
$[6, 8)$	$1 - \dfrac{1}{20} = 0.95$
$[8, 9)$	$0.95 \left[1 - \dfrac{3}{19} \right] = 0.8$
$[9, 10)$	$0.8 \left[1 - \dfrac{1}{16} \right] = 0.75$
$[10, 12)$	$0.75 \left[1 - \dfrac{2}{15} \right] = 0.65$
$[12, 13)$	$0.65 \left[1 - \dfrac{2}{13} \right] = 0.55$
$[13, 14)$	$0.55 \left[1 - \dfrac{1}{10} \right] = 0.495$
$[14, 15)$	$0.495 \left[1 - \dfrac{1}{9} \right] = 0.44$
$[15, 18)$	$0.44 \left[1 - \dfrac{1}{8} \right] = 0.385$
$[18, \infty)$	$0.385 \left[1 - \dfrac{1}{4} \right] = 0.2888$

Solution 11.5 As all policies are with a deductible of 4, we can only estimate the conditional sf $S(y \,|\, y > 4)$. Also, as there is a maximum covered loss of 20 for all policies, we can only estimate the conditional sf up to $S(20 \,|\, y > 4)$. Using the data compiled in Table 10.8, the Kaplan–Meier estimates are summarized in Table 11.2. $\qquad\square$

For complete data, $d_i = 0$ for $i = 1, \ldots, n$, and there is no u_i value. Thus, $r_1 = n$ and $r_j = r_{j-1} - w_{j-1}$, for $j = 2, \ldots, m$ (see equation (10.8)). Therefore, when the Kaplan–Meier estimate is applied to complete data, we have, for $j = 1, \ldots, m - 1$,

$$\hat{S}_K(y_j) = \prod_{h=1}^{j} \left(1 - \frac{w_h}{r_h} \right) = \prod_{h=1}^{j} \frac{r_{h+1}}{r_h} = \frac{r_{j+1}}{r_1}. \tag{11.33}$$

Table 11.2. *Kaplan–Meier*
estimates of Example 11.5

Interval containing y	$\hat{S}_K(y \mid y > 4)$
(4, 5)	1
[5, 7)	0.9333
[7, 8)	0.8667
[8, 10)	0.8000
[10, 16)	0.6667
[16, 17)	0.6000
[17, 19)	0.4000
[19, 20)	0.3333
20	0.2667

As $r_{j+1} = r_1 - \sum_{h=1}^{j} w_h = r_1 - g_j$, we conclude from equation (11.2) that

$$\hat{S}_K(y_j) = \frac{r_1 - g_j}{r_1} = 1 - \frac{g_j}{n} = 1 - \hat{F}(y_j). \tag{11.34}$$

Furthermore, $\hat{S}_K(y_m) = 0 = 1 - \hat{F}(y_m)$. Thus, the Kaplan–Meier estimate gives the same result as the empirical df when all observations are complete.

We now consider the mean and the variance of the Kaplan–Meier estimator. Our derivation is heuristic and is based on the assumption that the risk sets r_j and the values of the observed loss or failure-time y_j are known. Specifically, we denote $\mathcal{C}$ as the information set $\{y_1, \ldots, y_m, r_1, \ldots, r_m\}$. We also denote W_j as the random variable representing w_j, for $j = 1, \ldots, m$. Now given $\mathcal{C}$, the probability of observing a loss or failure time of value y_j is

$$\Pr(X \le y_j \mid y > y_{j-1}) = \frac{S(y_{j-1}) - S(y_j)}{S(y_{j-1})} = 1 - S_j, \qquad \text{for } j = 1, \ldots, m,$$
$$\tag{11.35}$$

where S_j is defined as

$$S_j = \frac{S(y_j)}{S(y_{j-1})}. \tag{11.36}$$

Hence, given $\mathcal{C}$, $W_1, \ldots, W_m$ are distributed as binomial random variables. Specifically,

$$W_j \mid \mathcal{C} \sim \mathcal{BN}(r_j, 1 - S_j), \qquad \text{for } j = 1, \ldots, m, \tag{11.37}$$

and

$$r_j - W_j \mid \mathcal{C} \sim \mathcal{BN}(r_j, S_j), \qquad \text{for } j = 1, \ldots, m. \tag{11.38}$$

Thus, we have the following results

$$E\left[\frac{r_j - W_j}{r_j} \,|\, \mathcal{C}\right] = S_j \tag{11.39}$$

and

$$E\left[\left(\frac{r_j - W_j}{r_j}\right)^2 \,|\, \mathcal{C}\right] = \frac{S_j(1 - S_j)}{r_j} + S_j^2$$

$$= S_j^2\left[\frac{1 - S_j}{S_j r_j} + 1\right]. \tag{11.40}$$

From equation (11.31), assuming the independence of $W_1, \ldots, W_m$ given $\mathcal{C}$, the mean of the Kaplan–Meier estimator is

$$E\left[\hat{S}_K(y_j) \,|\, \mathcal{C}\right] = E\left[\prod_{h=1}^{j}\left(1 - \frac{W_h}{r_h}\right) \,|\, \mathcal{C}\right]$$

$$= \prod_{h=1}^{j} E\left[\left(1 - \frac{W_h}{r_h}\right) \,|\, \mathcal{C}\right]$$

$$= \prod_{h=1}^{j} S_h$$

$$= \prod_{h=1}^{j} \frac{S(y_h)}{S(y_{h-1})}$$

$$= S(y_j), \tag{11.41}$$

so that $\hat{S}_K(y_j)$ is unbiased for $S(y_j)$. The variance of $\hat{S}_K(y_j)$ is

$$\mathrm{Var}\left[\hat{S}_K(y_j) \,|\, \mathcal{C}\right] = E\left[\left\{\prod_{h=1}^{j}\left(1 - \frac{W_h}{r_h}\right)\right\}^2 \,|\, \mathcal{C}\right] - \left\{E\left[\prod_{h=1}^{j}\left(1 - \frac{W_h}{r_h}\right) \,|\, \mathcal{C}\right]\right\}^2$$

$$= \prod_{h=1}^{j} E\left[\left(1 - \frac{W_h}{r_h}\right)^2 \,|\, \mathcal{C}\right] - \left\{\prod_{h=1}^{j} E\left[\left(1 - \frac{W_h}{r_h}\right) \,|\, \mathcal{C}\right]\right\}^2$$

$$= \prod_{h=1}^{j} S_h^2\left[\frac{1 - S_h}{S_h r_h} + 1\right] - \left[\prod_{h=1}^{j} S_h\right]^2$$

$$= \left[\prod_{h=1}^{j} S_h\right]^2 \left\{\prod_{h=1}^{j}\left[\frac{1 - S_h}{S_h r_h} + 1\right] - 1\right\}$$

$$= [S(y_j)]^2 \left\{\prod_{h=1}^{j}\left[\frac{1 - S_h}{S_h r_h} + 1\right] - 1\right\}. \tag{11.42}$$

Now using the approximation

$$\prod_{h=1}^{j} \left[\frac{1 - S_h}{S_h r_h} + 1 \right] \simeq 1 + \sum_{h=1}^{j} \frac{1 - S_h}{S_h r_h}, \tag{11.43}$$

equation (11.42) can be written as

$$\mathrm{Var}\left[\hat{S}_K(y_j) \mid \mathcal{C}\right] \simeq [S(y_j)]^2 \left(\sum_{h=1}^{j} \frac{1 - S_h}{S_h r_h} \right). \tag{11.44}$$

Estimating $S(y_j)$ by $\hat{S}_K(y_j)$ and S_h by $(r_h - w_h)/r_h$, the variance estimate of the Kaplan–Meier estimator can be computed as

$$\widehat{\mathrm{Var}}\left[\hat{S}_K(y_j) \mid \mathcal{C}\right] \simeq [\hat{S}_K(y_j)]^2 \left(\sum_{h=1}^{j} \frac{w_h}{r_h(r_h - w_h)} \right), \tag{11.45}$$

which is called the **Greenwood approximation** for the variance of the Kaplan–Meier estimator.

In the special case where all observations are complete, the Greenwood approximation becomes

$$\begin{aligned}
\widehat{\mathrm{Var}}\left[\hat{S}_K(y_j) \mid \mathcal{C}\right] &= \left[\frac{n - g_j}{n} \right]^2 \left[\sum_{h=1}^{j} \left(\frac{1}{r_h - w_h} - \frac{1}{r_h} \right) \right] \\
&= \left[\frac{n - g_j}{n} \right]^2 \left[\frac{1}{r_j - w_j} - \frac{1}{r_1} \right] \\
&= \left[\frac{n - g_j}{n} \right]^2 \left[\frac{g_j}{n(n - g_j)} \right] \\
&= \frac{g_j(n - g_j)}{n^3} \\
&= \frac{\hat{F}(y_j)\left[1 - \hat{F}(y_j)\right]}{n},
\end{aligned} \tag{11.46}$$

which is the usual estimate of the variance of the empirical df (see equation (11.13).

Example 11.6 Refer to the loss claims in Examples 10.7 and 11.4. Determine the approximate variance of $\hat{S}_K(10.5)$ and the 95% confidence interval of $S_K(10.5)$.

Solution 11.6 From Table 11.1, we can see that Kaplan–Meier estimate of $S_K(10.5)$ is 0.65. The Greenwood approximate for the variance of $\hat{S}_K(10.5)$ is

$$(0.65)^2 \left[\frac{1}{(20)(19)} + \frac{3}{(19)(16)} + \frac{1}{(16)(15)} + \frac{2}{(15)(13)} \right] = 0.0114.$$

Thus, the estimate of the standard deviation of $\hat{S}_K(10.5)$ is $\sqrt{0.0114} = 0.1067$, and, assuming the normality of $\hat{S}_K(10.5)$, the 95% confidence interval of $S_K(10.5)$ is

$$0.65 \pm (1.96)(0.1067) = (0.4410, 0.8590). \qquad \square$$

The above example uses the normal approximation for the distribution of $\hat{S}_K(y_j)$ to compute the confidence interval of $S(y_j)$. This is sometimes called the **linear confidence interval**. A disadvantage of this estimate is that the computed confidence interval may fall outside the range $(0, 1)$. This drawback can be remedied by considering a transformation of the survival function. We first define the transformation $\zeta(\cdot)$ by

$$\zeta(x) = \log\left[-\log(x)\right], \tag{11.47}$$

and let

$$\hat{\zeta} = \zeta(\hat{S}(y)) = \log[-\log(\hat{S}(y))], \tag{11.48}$$

where $\hat{S}(y)$ is an estimate of the sf $S(y)$ for a given y. Using the delta method (see Appendix A.19), the variance of $\hat{\zeta}$ can be approximated by

$$\widehat{\text{Var}}(\hat{\zeta}) = [\zeta'(\hat{S}(y))]^2 \, \widehat{\text{Var}}[\hat{S}(y)], \tag{11.49}$$

where $\zeta'(\hat{S}(y))$ is the first derivative of $\zeta(\cdot)$ evaluated at $\hat{S}(y)$. Now

$$\frac{d\zeta(x)}{dx} = \left[\frac{1}{-\log x}\right]\left[-\frac{1}{x}\right] = \frac{1}{x \log x}, \tag{11.50}$$

so that we can estimate $\text{Var}(\hat{\zeta})$ by

$$\widehat{\text{Var}}(\hat{\zeta}) = \frac{\widehat{\text{Var}}[\hat{S}(y)]}{[\hat{S}(y) \log \hat{S}(y)]^2} \equiv \hat{V}(y). \tag{11.51}$$

A $100(1 - \alpha)\%$ confidence interval of $\zeta(S(y))$ can be computed as

$$\zeta(\hat{S}(y)) \pm z_{1-\frac{\alpha}{2}} \sqrt{\hat{V}(y)}. \tag{11.52}$$

Taking the inverse transform of Equation (11.47), we have

$$S(y) = \exp\left\{-\exp[\zeta(S(y))]\right\}. \tag{11.53}$$

Thus, a $100(1 - \alpha)\%$ confidence interval of $S(y)$ can be computed by taking the inverse transform of equation (11.52) to obtain[4]

---

[4] As $\zeta(\cdot)$ is a monotonic *decreasing* function, the upper and lower limits of $\zeta(S(y))$ in equation (11.52) are reversed to obtain the limits in equation (11.54).

$$\left(\exp \left[-\exp \left\{ \zeta(\hat{S}(y)) + z_{1-\frac{\alpha}{2}} \sqrt{\hat{V}(y)} \right\} \right] , \right.$$
$$\left. \exp \left[-\exp \left\{ \zeta(\hat{S}(y)) - z_{1-\frac{\alpha}{2}} \sqrt{\hat{V}(y)} \right\} \right] \right) , \qquad (11.54)$$

which reduces to

$$\left(\hat{S}(y)^U, \hat{S}(y)^{\frac{1}{U}} \right) , \qquad (11.55)$$

where

$$U = \exp \left[z_{1-\frac{\alpha}{2}} \sqrt{\hat{V}(y)} \right] . \qquad (11.56)$$

This is known as the **logarithmic transformation method**.

Example 11.7 Refer to the loss claims in Examples 10.8 and 11.5. Determine the approximate variance of $\hat{S}_K(7)$ and the 95% confidence interval of $S(7)$.

Solution 11.7 From Table 11.2, we have $\hat{S}_K(7) = 0.8667$. The Greenwood approximate variance of $\hat{S}_K(7)$ is

$$(0.8667)^2 \left[\frac{1}{(15)(14)} + \frac{1}{(14)(13)} \right] = 0.0077.$$

Using normal approximation to the distribution of $\hat{S}_K(7)$, the 95% confidence interval of $S(7)$ is

$$0.8667 \pm 1.96\sqrt{0.0077} = (0.6947, 1.0387).$$

Thus, the upper limit exceeds 1, which is undesirable. To apply the logarithmic transformation method, we compute $\hat{V}(7)$ in equation (11.51) to obtain

$$\hat{V}(7) = \frac{0.0077}{[0.8667 \log(0.8667)]^2} = 0.5011,$$

so that U in equation (11.56) is

$$\exp \left[(1.96)\sqrt{0.5011} \right] = 4.0048.$$

From (11.55), the 95% confidence interval of $S(7)$ is

$$\{ (0.8667)^{4.0048}, (0.8667)^{\frac{1}{4.0048}} \} = (0.5639, 0.9649),$$

which is within the range $(0, 1)$.

We finally remark that as all policies in this example have a deductible of 4. The sf of interest is conditional on the loss exceeding 4. $\qquad \square$

11.2.2 Nelson–Aalen Estimator

Denoting the cumulative hazard function defined in equation (2.8) by $H(y)$, so that

$$H(y) = \int_0^y h(y)\, dy, \tag{11.57}$$

where $h(y)$ is the hazard function, we have

$$S(y) = \exp\left[-H(y)\right]. \tag{11.58}$$

Thus,

$$H(y) = -\log\left[S(y)\right]. \tag{11.59}$$

If we use $\hat{S}_K(y)$ to estimate $S(y)$ for $y_j \le y < y_{j+1}$, an estimate of the cumulative hazard function can be computed as

$$\begin{aligned}
\hat{H}(y) &= -\log\left[\hat{S}_K(y)\right] \\
&= -\log\left[\prod_{h=1}^{j}\left(1 - \frac{w_h}{r_h}\right)\right] \\
&= -\sum_{h=1}^{j}\log\left(1 - \frac{w_h}{r_h}\right).
\end{aligned} \tag{11.60}$$

Using the approximation

$$-\log\left(1 - \frac{w_h}{r_h}\right) \simeq \frac{w_h}{r_h}, \tag{11.61}$$

we obtain $\hat{H}(y)$ as

$$\hat{H}(y) = \sum_{h=1}^{j}\frac{w_h}{r_h}, \tag{11.62}$$

which is the **Nelson–Aalen estimate of the cumulative hazard function**. We complete its formula as follows

$$\hat{H}(y) = \begin{cases}
0, & \text{for } 0 < y < y_1, \\
\sum_{h=1}^{j}\frac{w_h}{r_h}, & \text{for } y_j \le y < y_{j+1},\, j = 1,\ldots,m-1, \\
\sum_{h=1}^{m}\frac{w_h}{r_h}, & \text{for } y_m \le y.
\end{cases} \tag{11.63}$$

We now construct an alternative estimator of $S(y)$ using equation (11.58). This is called the **Nelson–Aalen estimator of the survival function**, denoted by $\hat{S}_N(y)$. The formula of $\hat{S}_N(y)$ is

$$\hat{S}_N(y) = \begin{cases} 1, & \text{for } 0 < y < y_1, \\ \exp\left(-\sum_{h=1}^{j} \dfrac{w_h}{r_h}\right), & \text{for } y_j \le y < y_{j+1}, j = 1, \ldots, m-1, \\ \exp\left(-\sum_{h=1}^{m} \dfrac{w_h}{r_h}\right), & \text{for } y_m \le y. \end{cases}$$

$$(11.64)$$

For $y > y_m$, we may also compute $\hat{S}_N(y)$ as 0 or $[\hat{S}_N(y_m)]^{\frac{y}{y_m}}$.

The Nelson–Aalen estimator is easy to compute. In the case of complete data, with one observation at each point y_j, we have $w_h = 1$ and $r_h = n - h + 1$ for $h = 1, \ldots, n$, so that

$$\hat{S}_N(y_j) = \exp\left(-\sum_{h=1}^{j} \frac{1}{n - h + 1}\right).$$

$$(11.65)$$

Example 11.8 Refer to the loss claims in Examples 11.6 and 11.7. Compute the Nelson–Aalen estimates of the sf.

Solution 11.8 For the data in Example 11.6, the Nelson–Aalen estimate of $S(10.5)$ is

$$\hat{S}_N(10.5) = \exp\left(-\frac{1}{20} - \frac{3}{19} - \frac{1}{16} - \frac{2}{15}\right) = \exp(-0.4037) = 0.6678.$$

This may be compared against $\hat{S}_K(10.5) = 0.65$ from Example 11.5. Likewise, the Nelson–Aalen estimate of $S(7)$ in Example 11.7 is

$$\hat{S}_N(7) = \exp\left(-\frac{1}{15} - \frac{1}{14}\right) = \exp(-0.1381) = 0.8710,$$

which may be compared against $\hat{S}_K(7) = 0.8667$.   □

To derive an approximate formula for the variance of $\hat{H}(y)$, we assume the conditional distribution of W_h given the information set $\mathcal{C}$ to be Poisson. Thus, we estimate $\text{Var}(W_h)$ by w_h. An estimate of $\text{Var}[\hat{H}(y_j)]$ can then be computed as

$$\widehat{\text{Var}}[\hat{H}(y_j)] = \widehat{\text{Var}}\left(\sum_{h=1}^{j} \frac{W_h}{r_h}\right) = \sum_{h=1}^{j} \frac{\widehat{\text{Var}}(W_h)}{r_h^2} = \sum_{h=1}^{j} \frac{w_h}{r_h^2}.$$

$$(11.66)$$

Hence, a $100(1 - \alpha)\%$ confidence interval of $H(y_j)$, assuming normal approximation, is given by

$$\hat{H}(y_j) \pm z_{1-\frac{\alpha}{2}} \sqrt{\widehat{\text{Var}}[\hat{H}(y_j)]}.$$

$$(11.67)$$

To ensure the lower limit of the confidence interval of $H(y_j)$ to be positive,[5] we consider the transformation

$$\zeta(x) = \log x, \tag{11.68}$$

and define

$$\hat{\zeta} = \zeta(\hat{H}(y_j)) = \log[\hat{H}(y_j)]. \tag{11.69}$$

Thus, using the delta method, an approximate variance of $\hat{\zeta}$ is

$$\widehat{\mathrm{Var}}(\hat{\zeta}) = \frac{\widehat{\mathrm{Var}}[\hat{H}(y_j)]}{[\hat{H}(y_j)]^2}, \tag{11.70}$$

and a $100(1-\alpha)\%$ approximate confidence interval of $\zeta(H(y_j))$ can be obtained as

$$\zeta(\hat{H}(y_j)) \pm z_{1-\frac{\alpha}{2}} \frac{\sqrt{\widehat{\mathrm{Var}}[\hat{H}(y_j)]}}{\hat{H}(y_j)}. \tag{11.71}$$

Taking the inverse transformation of $\zeta(\cdot)$, a $100(1-\alpha)\%$ approximate confidence interval of $H(y_j)$ is

$$\left(\hat{H}(y_j) \left(\frac{1}{U} \right), \hat{H}(y_j) U \right), \tag{11.72}$$

where

$$U = \exp \left[z_{1-\frac{\alpha}{2}} \frac{\sqrt{\widehat{\mathrm{Var}}[\hat{H}(y_j)]}}{\hat{H}(y_j)} \right]. \tag{11.73}$$

Example 11.9 Refer to Examples 11.6 and 11.7. Compute the 95% confidence intervals of the Nelson–Aalen estimates of the cumulative hazard function.

Solution 11.9 For the data in Example 11.6, the Nelson–Aalen estimate of $H(10.5)$ is 0.4037 (see Example 11.8). From equation (11.67), the estimated variance of $\hat{H}(10.5)$ is

$$\frac{1}{(20)^2} + \frac{3}{(19)^2} + \frac{1}{(16)^2} + \frac{2}{(15)^2} = 0.0236.$$

Thus, the 95% linear confidence interval of $H(10.5)$ is

$$0.4037 \pm 1.96\sqrt{0.0236} = (0.1026, 0.7049).$$

---

[5] Note that the cumulative hazard function takes values in the range $(0, \infty)$.

Using the logarithmic transformation, U in equation (11.73) is

$$\exp\left[(1.96)\,\frac{\sqrt{0.0236}}{0.4037}\right] = 2.1084,$$

and the 95% confidence interval of $H(10.5)$ using the logarithmic transformation method is

$$\left\{\frac{0.4037}{2.1084},\,(0.4037)(2.1084)\right\} = (0.1915,\,0.8512).$$

For Example 11.7, the estimated variance of $\hat{H}(7)$ is

$$\frac{1}{(15)^2} + \frac{1}{(14)^2} = 0.0095.$$

The 95% linear confidence interval of $H(7)$ is

$$0.1381 \pm 1.96\sqrt{0.0095} = (-0.0534,\,0.3296).$$

Thus, the lower limit falls below zero. Using the logarithmic transformation method, we have $U = 4.0015$, so that the 95% confidence interval of $H(7)$ is $(0.0345, 0.5526).$ □

11.3 Estimation with Grouped Data

We now consider data that are grouped into intervals. Following the notations developed in Section 10.2.3, we assume that the values of the failure-time or loss data x_i are grouped into k intervals: $(c_0, c_1], (c_1, c_2], \ldots, (c_{k-1}, c_k]$, where $0 \le c_0 < c_1 < \cdots < c_k$. We first consider the case where the data are complete, with no truncation or censoring. Let there be n observations of x in the sample, with n_j observations in the interval $(c_{j-1}, c_j]$, so that $\sum_{j=1}^{k} n_j = n$. Assuming the observations within each interval are uniformly distributed, the empirical pdf of the failure-time or loss variable X can be written as

$$\hat{f}(x) = \sum_{j=1}^{k} p_j f_j(x), \tag{11.74}$$

where

$$p_j = \frac{n_j}{n} \tag{11.75}$$

and

$$f_j(x) = \begin{cases} \dfrac{1}{c_j - c_{j-1}}, & \text{for } c_{j-1} < x \le c_j, \\ 0, & \text{otherwise.} \end{cases} \tag{11.76}$$

Thus, $\hat{f}(x)$ is the pdf of a mixture distribution. To compute the moments of X we note that

$$\int_0^\infty f_j(x)x^r \, dx = \frac{1}{c_j - c_{j-1}} \int_{c_{j-1}}^{c_j} x^r \, dx = \frac{c_j^{r+1} - c_{j-1}^{r+1}}{(r+1)(c_j - c_{j-1})}. \qquad (11.77)$$

Hence, the mean of the empirical pdf is

$$E(X) = \sum_{j=1}^k p_j \left[\frac{c_j^2 - c_{j-1}^2}{2(c_j - c_{j-1})} \right] = \sum_{j=1}^k \frac{n_j}{n} \left[\frac{c_j + c_{j-1}}{2} \right], \qquad (11.78)$$

and its rth raw moment is

$$E(X^r) = \sum_{j=1}^k \frac{n_j}{n} \left[\frac{c_j^{r+1} - c_{j-1}^{r+1}}{(r+1)(c_j - c_{j-1})} \right]. \qquad (11.79)$$

The censored moments are more complex. Suppose it is desired to compute $E[(X \wedge u)^r]$. First, we consider the case where $u = c_h$ for some $h = 1, \ldots, k-1$, i.e., u is the end point of an interval. Then the rth raw moment is

$$E\left[(X \wedge c_h)^r\right] = \sum_{j=1}^h \frac{n_j}{n} \left[\frac{c_j^{r+1} - c_{j-1}^{r+1}}{(r+1)(c_j - c_{j-1})} \right] + c_h^r \sum_{j=h+1}^k \frac{n_j}{n}. \qquad (11.80)$$

However, if $c_{h-1} < u < c_h$, for some $h = 1, \ldots, k$, then we have

$$E\left[(X \wedge u)^r\right] = \sum_{j=1}^{h-1} \frac{n_j}{n} \left[\frac{c_j^{r+1} - c_{j-1}^{r+1}}{(r+1)(c_j - c_{j-1})} \right] + u^r \sum_{j=h+1}^k \frac{n_j}{n}$$

$$+ \frac{n_h}{n(c_h - c_{h-1})} \left[\frac{u^{r+1} - c_{h-1}^{r+1}}{r+1} + u^r(c_h - u) \right]. \qquad (11.81)$$

The last term in the above equation arises from the assumption that $(c_h - u)/(c_h - c_{h-1})$ of the observations in the interval (c_{h-1}, c_h) are larger than or equal to u.

The empirical df at the upper end of each interval is easy to compute. Specifically, we have

$$\hat{F}(c_j) = \frac{1}{n} \sum_{h=1}^j n_h, \quad \text{for } j = 1, \ldots, k. \qquad (11.82)$$

For other values of x, we use the interpolation formula given in equation (11.6), i.e.,

$$\hat{F}(x) = \frac{x - c_j}{c_{j+1} - c_j} \hat{F}(c_{j+1}) + \frac{c_{j+1} - x}{c_{j+1} - c_j} \hat{F}(c_j), \qquad (11.83)$$

where $c_j \le x < c_{j+1}$, for some $j = 0, 1, \ldots, k-1$, with $\hat{F}(c_0) = 0$. $\hat{F}(x)$ is also called the **ogive**. The quantiles of X can then be determined by taking the inverse of the smoothed empirical df $\hat{F}(x)$.

Table 11.3. *Results of Example 11.10*

Interval	c_j	V_j	R_j	$\hat{S}_K(c_j)$	$\hat{F}_K(c_j)$
$(0, 4]$	4	0	13	1	0
$(4, 8]$	8	4	20	$1\left(\dfrac{16}{20}\right) = 0.8$	0.2
$(8, 12]$	12	5	16	$0.8\left(\dfrac{11}{16}\right) = 0.55$	0.45
$(12, 16]$	16	3	10	$0.55\left(\dfrac{7}{10}\right) = 0.385$	0.615
$(16, 20]$	20	1	4	$0.385\left(\dfrac{3}{4}\right) = 0.2888$	0.7113

When the observations are incomplete, we may use the Kaplan–Meier and Nelson–Aalen methods to estimate the sf. Using equations (10.10) or (10.11), we calculate the risk sets R_j and the number of failures or losses V_j in the interval $(c_{j-1}, c_j]$. These numbers are taken as the risk sets and observed failures or losses at points c_j. $\hat{S}_K(c_j)$ and $\hat{S}_N(c_j)$ may then be computed using equations (11.31) and (11.65), respectively, with R_h replacing r_h and V_h replacing w_h. Finally, we use, interpolation method, as in equation 11.84, to estimate other values of the sf $S(x)$ for x not at the end points c_j. The df is then estimated as $\hat{F}(x) = 1 - \hat{S}(x)$.

Example 11.10 Refer to Example 10.9. Compute the Kaplan–Meier estimates of the sf and df.

Solution 11.10 The computations are presented in Table 11.3. The last two columns summarize the estimated sf and df, respectively, at points c_j. The interpolated estimate of the df is plotted in Figure 11.5. For $x > 20$, the geometric decay method is used to compute the estimated sf (see equation (11.32)) and then the estimated df.   □

11.4 R Laboratory

R Codes 11.1 provides the codes to plot the kernel density estimates in Example 11.3. The function density is used to compute the kernel density estimates. We plot the rectangular kernel estimates (see Figure 11.3) and the Gaussian kernel estimates (see Figure 11.4), with two choices of bandwidths.

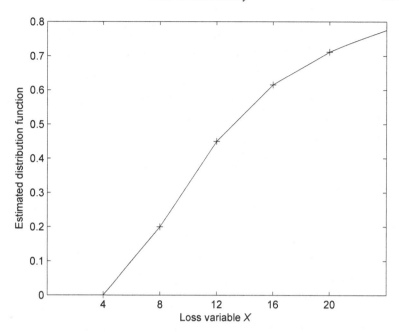

Figure 11.5 Estimated df of Example 11.10 for grouped incomplete data

```
##########################################################
# R Codes 11.1
#
# Example 11.3: Kernel density plots
##########################################################

X=c(15,16,16,17,19,19,19,23,24,27,28,28,28,28,31,34,34,
    34,36,36,37,40,41,41,43,46,46,46,47,47,49,50,50,53,
    54,54,59,61,63,64)
plot(density(X,bw=3,kernel="rectangular"),lty=3,
  xlim=c(0,80), main="Rectangular kernel density
  estimate", xlab="Loss variable x", ylab="Kernel
  density estimate", cex.main=0.7,cex.lab=0.7,
  cex.axis=0.7)
lines(density(X,bw=8,kernel="rectangular"))
legend("topleft",c("Bandwidth = 3","Bandwidth = 8"),
  lty=c(3,1),cex=0.6)
```

```
plot(density(X,bw=3,kernel="gaussian"),lty=3,
  xlim=c(-10,90), main="Gaussian density estimate",
  cex.main=0.7,xlab="Loss variable x",
  ylab="Kernel density estimate",
  cex.lab=0.7,cex.axis=0.7)
lines(density(X,bw=8,kernel="gaussian"))
legend("topleft",c("Bandwidth = 3","Bandwidth = 8"),
  lty=c(3,1),cex=0.6)
```

R Codes 11.2 provides the codes to compute the Kaplan–Meier and Nelson–Aalen estimates of the survival functions and their confidence intervals. The data in Table 10.7 are used. The function cut is used to determine the bin of the x value. Both linear confidence intervals and logarithmic transformed confidence intervals are computed. The results may be compared with those in Examples 11.4, 11.6, 11.8 and 11.9.

```
#####################################################################
# R Codes 11.2
#
# Examples 11.4, 11.6, 11.8 and 11.9:
# Kaplan-Meier and Nelson-Aalen estimation
#####################################################################

y=c(6,8,9,10,12,13,14,15,18)    # y, w and r as in Table 10.7
w=c(1,3,1,2,2,1,1,1,1)
r=c(20,19,16,15,13,10,9,8,4)
breaks=c(0,y,1000)              # 1000 as infinity

s=cumprod(1-w/r)                # KM est, Example 11.4, Table 11.1
x=10.5                          # Select x value
n=cut(x,breaks,right=F,labels=F) # Determine the bin
km=s[n-1]                       # KM est at x
g=km^2*cumsum(w/(r*(r-w)))[n-1] # Greenwood approx var, Eq(11.45)

LL=km-1.96*sqrt(g)
UL=km+1.96*sqrt(g)              # Example 11.6, linear CI of S(10.5)
cat("95% linear confidence interval of S(10.5):",LL,"to ",UL)

v=g/(km*log(km))^2             # Approx var of log-trans, Eq(11.51)
u=exp(1.96*sqrt(v))            # U, Eq(11.56)
LL=km^u
UL=km^(1/u)                    # Log CI of S(10.5)
cat("95% logarithmic confidence interval of S(10.5):",LL,"to ",UL)
```

```
h=cumsum(w/r)                     # NA est of H, Eq(11.63)
s=exp(-h)                         # NA est of S, Eq(11.64)
na=s[n-1]                         # NA est of S(10.5), Example 11.8
hx=h[n-1]                         # NA est of H(10.5), Example 11.9
vna=cumsum(w/r^2)[n-1]            # Var est of H-hat, Eq(11.66)

LL=hx-1.96*sqrt(vna)
UL=hx+1.96*sqrt(vna)              # Example 11.9, linear CI of H(10.5)
cat("95% linear confidence interval of H(10.5):",LL,"to ",UL)

u=exp(1.96*sqrt(vna)/hx)          # U in Eq(11.73)
LL=hx/u
UL=hx*u                           # Example 11.9, log CI of H(10.5)
cat("95% logarithmic confidence interval of H(10.5):",LL,"to",UL)
```

11.5 Summary and Discussions

We have discussed methods of estimating the df and sf of failure-time and loss data, as well as their moments. Cases of complete versus incomplete observations (with left truncation and right censoring), and individual versus grouped data are discussed. The focus is on nonparametric methods in which no parametric functional forms of the distributions are assumed. For incomplete data, the Kaplan–Meier and Nelson–Aalen estimates are two convenient methods to estimate the sf, both for individual as well as grouped data. We have discussed methods of estimating the variance of the estimated sf and df. The confidence intervals of the sf and df based on the linear confidence interval method may give rise to undesirable results with estimated values lying outside the theoretical range. This shortcoming may be remedied using suitable logarithmic transformations.

Exercises

Exercise 11.1 A sample from a distribution X has the following 16 observations:

$$6, 8, 8, 11, 13, 14, 14, 20, 21, 26, 27, 27, 27, 30, 32, 33.$$

(a) Determine the smoothed empirical distribution functions $\tilde{F}(15)$ and $\tilde{F}(27)$.
(b) Determine the smoothed quantiles $\hat{x}_{0.25}$ and $\hat{x}_{0.75}$, and hence the interquartile range $\hat{x}_{0.75} - \hat{x}_{0.25}$.
(c) Compute the mean, the variance and the skewness (see equation (A.28)) of the empirical distribution.
(d) Compute $\text{Var}[(X \wedge 27)]$ and $\text{Var}[(X \wedge 31.5)]$ of the empirical distribution.
(e) If $\tilde{X} = X \,|\, X > 10$, estimate $\Pr(\tilde{X} \leq 25)$ and $\text{E}[(\tilde{X} \wedge 20.5)]$.

Exercise 11.2 A sample of ground-up losses X has the following observations:

$$80, 85, 99, 120, 125, 155, 160, 166, 176, 198.$$

(a) If the policies have a deductible of 90, estimate the expected loss and variance of loss in a loss event, as well as the expected loss and variance of loss in a payment event. Use the sample variance as the variance estimate.
(b) Estimate the probability of X not exceeding 160, and estimate the variance of this estimated probability.

Exercise 11.3 A researcher has collected data on the paired variables (X, Y). However, they have lost the pairing of the data and only managed to keep the unpaired observations, with the values of x being: 2, 7, 4, 6, 8, 7, and the values of y being: 3, 2, 7, 6, 5, 2. What are the maximum and minimum possible sample correlation coefficients of X and Y (see equation (A.50)) based on the empirical data.

Exercise 11.4 A sample of losses X has the following observations:

$$4, 6, 6, 9, 10, 14, 18, 20, 22, 25.$$

(a) Determine the median $\hat{x}_{0.5}$.
(b) If $Y = X \mid X > 5$, determine the median $\hat{y}_{0.5}$.

Exercise 11.5 A sample of losses has the following observations:

$$5, 8, 8, 12, 14, 17, 21, 22, 26, 28.$$

(a) Compute the kernel density estimates $\tilde{f}(10)$ and $\tilde{f}(15)$ using the rectangular kernel with bandwidth of 4 and 6.
(b) Compute the kernel density estimates $\tilde{f}(10)$ and $\tilde{f}(15)$ using the triangular kernel with bandwidth of 4 and 6.

Exercise 11.6 The following grouped data of losses X are given:

$(c_{j-1}, c_j]$	n_j
$(0, 10]$	22
$(10, 20]$	29
$(20, 30]$	38
$(30, 40]$	21
$(40, 50]$	16
$(50, 60]$	8

(a) Compute the mean and the standard deviation of the empirical distribution of X.
(b) Determine $E[(X \wedge 40)]$ and $E[(X \wedge 45)]$ of the empirical distribution of X.
(c) Determine $Var[(X \wedge 40)]$ and $Var[(X \wedge 45)]$ of the empirical distribution of X.
(d) If there is a deductible of 20, compute the expected loss in a loss event using the empirical distribution.
(e) Compute the empirical distribution functions $\hat{F}(40)$ and $\hat{F}(48)$.
(f) What is the 30th percentile of the empirical distribution?

Exercise 11.7 You are given the following grouped loss data:

$(c_{j-1}, c_j]$	n_j
$(0, 100]$	18
$(100, 200]$	29
$(200, 300]$	32
$(300, 400]$	21
$(400, 500]$	12

(a) If the policies have a deductible of 200 and a maximum covered loss of 400, determine the mean and the standard deviation of the loss in a loss event.
(b) If the policies have a maximum covered loss of 280 and no deductible, compute the mean and the standard deviation of the loss in a loss event.

Exercise 11.8 The following grouped data of losses X are given:

$(c_{j-1}, c_j]$	n_j	Total losses	Total squared losses
$(0, 20]$	15	164	2,208
$(20, 40]$	24	628	23,683
$(40, 60]$	26	1,284	68,320
$(60, 80]$	14	1,042	81,230
$(80, 100]$	6	620	52,863

(a) Compute the mean and the standard deviation of the empirical loss distribution.
(b) If there is a maximum loss limit of 60, determine the mean and the standard deviation of the loss in a loss event.

Exercise 11.9 Refer to the duration data in Exercise 10.9.

(a) Estimate the probability of the duration exceeding 8 using the Kaplan–Meier method. Compute the 95% linear confidence interval of this probability.

(b) Estimate the probability of the duration exceeding 3 and less than 6 using the Kaplan–Meier method. What is the estimated variance of this probability?

(c) Estimate the probability of the duration exceeding 8, given that it exceeds 4, using the Kaplan–Meier method. What is the estimated variance of this probability?

(d) Estimate the cumulative hazard function at 10.5, $H(10.5)$, using the Nelson–Aalen method. Compute the 95% linear confidence interval of $H(10.5)$.

Exercise 11.10 Refer to the graduate employment survey data in Exercise 10.10, and denote X as the starting monthly salary in hundred dollars.

(a) Estimate $\Pr(25 \leq X \leq 28)$ using the Kaplan–Meier estimator.

(b) Estimate $\Pr(X > 30 \mid X > 27)$ using the Nelson–Aalen estimator.

Exercise 11.11 Refer to the unemployment survey data in Exercise 10.11.

(a) Estimate the mean unemployment duration using the Kaplan–Meier estimator.

(b) Compute the cumulative hazard function at unemployment duration 12 using the Kaplan–Meier estimator and the Nelson–Aalen estimator.

Exercise 11.12 Refer to the loss data in Exercise 10.12.

(a) Estimate the probability of loss exceeding 9.5, $S(9.5)$, using the Kaplan–Meier estimator. Compute an approximate variance of this estimate.

(b) Compute the 95% linear confidence interval of $S(9.5)$, and compare this against the confidence interval using the logarithmic transformation method.

(c) Estimate the cumulative hazard function at 5, $H(5)$, using the Nelson–Aalen estimator. Compute an approximate variance of this estimate.

(d) Compute the 95% linear confidence interval of $H(5)$, and compare this against the confidence interval using the logarithmic transformation method.

Exercise 11.13 Refer to the loss data in Exercise 10.13. Estimate the mean of the loss payment in a payment event using the Kaplan–Meier and Nelson–Aalen methods. Assume geometrical decay for the survival function beyond the maximum loss observation.

Exercise 11.14 Refer to the loss data in Exercise 10.14.

(a) Compute the 90% logarithmic transformed confidence interval of the probability of loss less than 11 using the Kaplan–Meier method.
(b) Compute the 95% logarithmic transformed confidence interval of the cumulative hazard function at 8 using the Nelson–Aalen method.

Exercise 11.15 Refer to the grouped loss data for the loss variable X in Exercise 10.14 (b).

(a) Estimate $\Pr(X \leq 10)$.
(b) Estimate $\Pr(X \leq 8)$.
(c) Estimate $\Pr(X > 12 \mid X > 4)$.

Questions Adapted from SOA Exams

Exercise 11.16 The 95% linear confidence interval of the cumulative hazard function $H(x_0)$ is (1.54, 2.36). Compute the 95% logarithmic transformed confidence interval of $H(x_0)$.

Exercise 11.17 In a sample of 40 insurance policy losses without deductible, there are five losses of amount 4, four losses of amount 8 and three losses of amount 12. In addition, there are two censored losses of amount 9 and one censored loss of amount 10. Compute the 90% logarithmic transformed confidence interval of the cumulative hazard function at 12, $H(12)$.

Exercise 11.18 In a mortality study with right-censored data, the cumulative hazard function $H(t)$ is estimated using the Nelson–Aalen estimator. It is known that no death occurs between times t_i and t_{i+1}, that the 95% linear confidence interval of $H(t_i)$ is (0.07125, 0.22875), and that the 95% linear confidence interval of $H(t_{i+1})$ is (0.15607, 0.38635). What is the number of deaths at time t_{i+1}?

Exercise 11.19 Fifteen cancer patients were observed from the time of diagnosis until death or 36 months from diagnosis, whichever comes first. Time (in months) since diagnosis, T, and number of deaths, n, are recorded as follows:

T	15	20	24	30	34	36
n	2	3	2	d	2	1

The Nelson–Aalen estimate of the cumulative hazard function at time 35, $\hat{H}(35)$, is 1.5641. Compute the Nelson–Aalen estimate of the variance of $\hat{H}(35)$.

Exercise 11.20 You are given the following information about losses grouped by interval:

$(c_{j-1}, c_j]$	Number of losses V_j	Risk set R_j
$(0, 20]$	13	90
$(20, 40]$	27	88
$(40, 60]$	38	55
$(60, 100]$	21	36
$(100, 200]$	15	18

Estimate the probability of loss larger than 50 using the Nelson–Aalen method.

Exercise 11.21 The times to death in a study of five lives from the onset of a disease to death are: 2, 3, 3, 3 and 7. Using a triangular kernel with bandwidth 2, estimate the density function at 2.5.

Exercise 11.22 In a study of claim-payment times, the data were not truncated or censored, and at most one claim was paid at any one time. The Nelson–Aalen estimate of the cumulative hazard function $H(t)$ immediately following the second paid claim was 23/132. Determine the Nelson–Aalen estimate of $H(t)$ immediately after the fourth paid claim.

Exercise 11.23 Suppose the 95% log-transformed confidence interval of $S(t_0)$ using the product-limit estimator is (0.695, 0.843). Determine $\hat{S}_K(t_0)$.

Exercise 11.24 The claim payments of a sample of 10 policies are ($^+$ indicates a right-censored payment): 2, 3, 3, 5, 5$^+$, 6, 7, 7$^+$, 9 and 10$^+$. Using the product-limit estimator, calculate the probability that the loss of a policy exceeds 8.

Exercise 11.25 You are given the following data for a mortality study:

	Country A		Country B	
t_i	w_i	r_i	w_i	r_i
1	20	200	15	100
2	54	180	20	85
3	14	126	20	65
4	22	112	10	45

Let $\hat{S}_1(t)$ be the product-limit estimate of $S(t)$ based on the data for all countries and $\hat{S}_2(t)$ be the product-limit estimate of $S(t)$ based on the data for Country B. Determine $|\hat{S}_1(4) - \hat{S}_2(4)|$.

Exercise 11.26 In a sample of 200 accident claims, t denotes the time (in months) a claim is submitted after the accident. There are no right-censored observations. $\hat{S}(t)$ is the Kaplan–Meier estimator and

$$c^2(t) = \frac{\widehat{\text{Var}}[\hat{S}(t)]}{[\hat{S}(t)]^2},$$

where $\widehat{\text{Var}}[\hat{S}(t)]$ is computed using Greenwood's approximation. If $\hat{S}(8) = 0.22$, $\hat{S}(9) = 0.16$, $c^2(9) = 0.02625$ and $c^2(10) = 0.04045$, determine the number of claims that were submitted 10 months after an accident.

Exercise 11.27 Eight people joined an exercise program on the same day. They stayed in the program until they reached their weight loss goal or switched to a diet program. Their experience is shown below:

	Time at which ...	
Member	Reach weight loss goal	Switch to diet program
1		4
2		8
3	8	
4	12	
5		12
6	12	
7	22	
8	36	

Let t be the time to reach the weight loss goal, and $H(t)$ be the cumulative hazard function at t. Using the Nelson–Aalen estimator, compute the upper limit of the symmetric 90% linear confidence interval of $H(12)$.

Exercise 11.28 All members of a mortality study are observed from birth. Some leave the study by means other than death. You are given the following: $w_4 = 3$, $\hat{S}_K(y_3) = 0.65$, $\hat{S}_K(y_4) = 0.50$ and $\hat{S}_K(y_5) = 0.25$. Furthermore, between times y_4 and y_5, six observations are censored. Assuming no observations are censored at the times of death, determine w_5.

Exercise 11.29 You are given the following data:

150, 150, 150, 362, 366, 452, 500, 500, 601, 693, 750, 750.

Let $\hat{H}_1(700)$ be the Nelson–Aalen estimate of the cumulative hazard function computed under the assumption that all observations are uncensored, and $\hat{H}_2(700)$ be the Nelson–Aalen estimate of the cumulative hazard function computed under the assumption that all occurrences of the values 150, 500 and

750 are right censored, while the remaining values are uncensored. Determine $|\hat{H}_1(700) - \hat{H}_2(700)|$.

Exercise 11.30 You are given the following ages at time of death for 10 individuals:

$$25, 30, 35, 35, 37, 39, 45, 47, 49, 55.$$

Using a uniform kernel with bandwidth 10, determine the kernel density estimate of the probability of survival to age 40.

Exercise 11.31 For a mortality study with right-censored data, you are given the following:

t_i	w_i	r_i
3	1	50
5	3	49
6	5	k
10	7	21

If the Nelson–Aalen estimate of the survival function at time 10 is 0.575, determine k.

12

Parametric Model Estimation

Some models assume that the failure-time or loss variables follow a certain family of distributions, specified up to a number of unknown parameters. To compute quantities such as average loss or VaR, the parameters of the distributions have to be estimated. This chapter discusses various methods of estimating the parameters of a failure-time or loss distribution.

Matching moments and percentiles to the data are two simple methods of parametric estimation. These methods, however, are subject to the decisions of the set of moments or percentiles to be used. The most important estimation method in the classical statistics literature is perhaps the maximum likelihood estimation method. It is applicable to a wide class of problems: variables that are discrete or continuous, and data observations that are complete or incomplete. On the other hand, the Bayesian approach provides an alternative perspective to parametric estimation, and has been made easier to adopt due to the advances in computational techniques.

Parametric models can be extended to allow the distributions to vary with some attributes of the objects, such as the years of driving experience of the insured in predicting vehicle accident claims. This gives rise to the use of models with covariates. A very important model in the parametric estimation of models with covariates is Cox's proportional hazards model.

We also include in this chapter a brief introduction to the use of copula in modeling the joint distributions of several variables. This approach is flexible in maintaining the assumptions about the marginal distributions while analyzing the joint distribution through the copula function.

Learning Objectives

1 Methods of moments and percentile matching
2 Maximum likelihood estimation

3 Bayesian estimation
4 Cox's proportional hazards model
5 Modeling joint distributions using copula

12.1 Methods of Moments and Percentile Matching

Let $f(\cdot; \theta)$ be the pdf or pf of a failure-time or loss variable X, where $\theta = (\theta_1, \ldots, \theta_k)'$ is a k-element parameter vector. We denote μ'_r as the rth raw moment of X. In general, μ'_r are functions of the parameter θ, and we assume the functional dependence of μ'_r on θ is known so that we can write the raw moments as $\mu'_r(\theta)$. Given a random sample $x = (x_1, \ldots, x_n)$ of X, the sample analogs of $\mu'_r(\theta)$ (i.e., the sample moments) are straightforward to compute. We denote these by $\hat{\mu}'_r$, so that

$$\hat{\mu}'_r = \frac{1}{n} \sum_{i=1}^n x_i^r. \tag{12.1}$$

12.1.1 Method of Moments

The **method-of-moments** estimate $\hat{\theta}$ is the solution of θ in the equations

$$\mu'_r(\theta) = \hat{\mu}'_r, \qquad \text{for } r = 1, \ldots, k. \tag{12.2}$$

Thus, we have a set of k equations involving k unknowns $\theta_1, \ldots, \theta_k$. We assume that a solution to the equations in (12.2) exists. However, there may be multiple solutions to the equations, in which case the method-of-moments estimate is not unique.

Example 12.1 Let X be the claim-frequency random variable. Determine the method-of-moments estimates of the parameter of the distribution of X, if X is distributed as (a) $\mathcal{PN}(\lambda)$, (b) $\mathcal{GM}(\theta)$, and (c) $\mathcal{BN}(m, \theta)$, where m is a known constant.

Solution 12.1 All the distributions in this example are discrete with a single parameter in the pf. Hence, $k = 1$ and we need to match only the population mean $E(X)$ to the sample mean $\bar{x}$. For (a), $E(X) = \lambda$. Hence, $\hat{\lambda} = \bar{x}$. For (b), we have

$$E(X) = \frac{1 - \theta}{\theta} = \bar{x},$$

so that

$$\hat{\theta} = \frac{1}{1 + \bar{x}}.$$

For (c), we equate $E(X) = m\theta$ to $\bar{x}$ and obtain

$$\hat{\theta} = \frac{\bar{x}}{m},$$

which is the sample proportion. □

Example 12.2 Let X be the claim-severity random variable. Determine the method-of-moments estimates of the parameters of the distribution of X, if X is distributed as (a) $\mathcal{G}(\alpha, \beta)$, (b) $\mathcal{P}(\alpha, \gamma)$, and (c) $\mathcal{U}(a, b)$.

Solution 12.2 All the distributions in this example are continuous with two parameters in the pdf. Thus, $k = 2$, and we need to match the first two population moments μ'_1 and μ'_2 to the sample moments $\hat{\mu}'_1$ and $\hat{\mu}'_2$. For (a), we have

$$\mu'_1 = \alpha\beta = \hat{\mu}'_1 \quad \text{and} \quad \mu'_2 = \alpha\beta^2 + \alpha^2\beta^2 = \hat{\mu}'_2,$$

from which we obtain

$$\beta\mu'_1 + \mu'^2_1 = \mu'_2.$$

Hence, the method-of-moments estimates are[1]

$$\hat{\beta} = \frac{\hat{\mu}'_2 - \hat{\mu}'^2_1}{\hat{\mu}'_1}$$

and

$$\hat{\alpha} = \frac{\hat{\mu}'_1}{\hat{\beta}} = \frac{\hat{\mu}'^2_1}{\hat{\mu}'_2 - \hat{\mu}'^2_1}.$$

For (b), the population moments are

$$\mu'_1 = \frac{\gamma}{\alpha - 1} \quad \text{and} \quad \mu'_2 = \frac{2\gamma^2}{(\alpha - 1)(\alpha - 2)},$$

from which we obtain

$$\mu'_2 = \frac{2\mu'^2_1(\alpha - 1)}{\alpha - 2}.$$

Hence,

$$\hat{\alpha} = \frac{2(\hat{\mu}'_2 - \hat{\mu}'^2_1)}{\hat{\mu}'_2 - 2\hat{\mu}'^2_1}$$

and

$$\hat{\gamma} = (\hat{\alpha} - 1)\hat{\mu}'_1.$$

---

[1] Due to the Cauchy–Schwarz inequality, which states that for any $\{x_1, \ldots, x_n\}$ and $\{y_1, \ldots, y_n\}$, $\left(\sum_{i=1}^n x_i y_i\right)^2 \le \left(\sum_{i=1}^n x_i^2\right)\left(\sum_{i=1}^n y_i^2\right)$, we conclude that $\left(\sum_{i=1}^n x_i\right)^2 \le n\left(\sum_{i=1}^n x_i^2\right)$ so that $\hat{\mu}'_2 - \hat{\mu}'^2_1 \ge 0$, with equality only when all x_i are equal. Thus, $\hat{\alpha}$ and $\hat{\beta}$ are positive.

Note that if $\hat{\mu}'_2 - 2\hat{\mu}'^2_1 < 0$, then $\hat{\alpha} < 0$ and the model $\mathcal{P}(\hat{\alpha}, \hat{\gamma})$ is not well defined.[2]

For (c), the population moments are

$$\mu'_1 = \frac{a+b}{2} \qquad \text{and} \qquad \mu'_2 = \frac{(b-a)^2}{12} + \mu'^2_1.$$

Solving for a and b, and evaluating the solutions at $\hat{\mu}'_1$ and $\hat{\mu}'_2$, we obtain

$$\hat{a} = \hat{\mu}'_1 - \sqrt{3(\hat{\mu}'_2 - \hat{\mu}'^2_1)} \qquad \text{and} \qquad \hat{b} = \hat{\mu}'_1 + \sqrt{3(\hat{\mu}'_2 - \hat{\mu}'^2_1)}.$$

However, if $\min \{x_1, \ldots, x_n\} < \hat{a}$, or $\max \{x_1, \ldots, x_n\} > \hat{b}$, the model $\mathcal{U}(\hat{a}, \hat{b})$ is incompatible with the claim-severity data. $\qquad\qquad\qquad\square$

Although the method of moments is generally easy to apply, the results may not be always satisfactory. As can be seen from Example 12.2, the estimates may be incompatible with the model assumption. However, as the sample moments are consistent estimates of the population moments, provided the parameters of the distribution can be solved uniquely from the population moments, the method-of-moments estimates are *consistent* for the model parameters. Of course, incompatibility may still exist when the sample size is small.

We have assumed that the matching of moments is based on the raw moments. An alternative is to consider central moments. For example, for a two-parameter distribution, we may match the sample mean to the population mean, and the sample variance to the population variance. This approach would result in different estimates from matching the raw moments, due to the degrees-of-freedom correction in the computation of the sample variance. In large samples, however, the difference is immaterial.

The method of moments can also be applied to censored or truncated distributions, as illustrated in the following examples.

Example 12.3 A random sample of 15 ground-up losses, X, with a policy limit of 15 has the following observations:

$$2, 3, 4, 5, 8, 8, 9, 10, 11, 11, 12, 12, 15, 15, 15.$$

If X is distributed as $\mathcal{U}(0, b)$, determine the method-of-moments estimate of b.

Solution 12.3 To estimate b we match the sample mean of the loss payments to the mean of the censored uniform distribution. The mean of the sample of 15 observations is 9.3333. As

---

[2] Existence of variance for the Pareto distribution requires α to be larger than 2. Hence, an estimate of $\hat{\alpha} \leq 2$ suggests a misfit of the model, if the variance is assumed to exist.

$$E\left[(X \wedge u)\right] = \int_0^u \left[1 - F(x)\right] dx = \int_0^u \frac{b - x}{b} \, dx = u - \frac{u^2}{2b},$$

and $u = 15$, we have

$$15 - \frac{(15)^2}{2\hat{b}} = 9.3333,$$

so that $\hat{b} = 19.8528$. □

Example 12.4 A random sample of 10 insurance claims with a deductible of 5 has the following ground-up losses:

$$12, \ 13, \ 14, \ 16, \ 17, \ 19, \ 23, \ 27, \ 74, \ 97.$$

If the ground-up loss is distributed as $\mathcal{P}(\alpha, \gamma)$, determine the method-of-moments estimates of α and γ.

Solution 12.4 From Example 3.7, we know that if the ground-up loss is distributed as $\mathcal{P}(\alpha, \gamma)$ and there is a deductible of d, then the distribution of the modified losses in a payment event is $\mathcal{P}(\alpha, \gamma + d)$. Hence, if μ_1' and μ_2' are the first two raw moments of the modified loss payments, from Example 12.2 the method-of-moments estimates of α and γ are

$$\hat{\alpha} = \frac{2(\hat{\mu}_2' - \hat{\mu}_1'^2)}{\hat{\mu}_2' - 2\hat{\mu}_1'^2}$$

and

$$\hat{\gamma} = (\hat{\alpha} - 1)\hat{\mu}_1' - d.$$

Now the modified claim amounts are

$$7, \ 8, \ 9, \ 11, \ 12, \ 14, \ 18, \ 22, \ 69, \ 92,$$

so that $\hat{\mu}_1' = 26.2$ and $\hat{\mu}_2' = 1,468.8$. Hence,

$$\hat{\alpha} = \frac{2[1,468.8 - (26.2)(26.2)]}{1,468.8 - 2(26.2)(26.2)} = 16.3128,$$

and

$$\hat{\gamma} = (16.3128 - 1)(26.2) - 5 = 396.1943.$$

We end this example by commenting that the Pareto distribution cannot be adopted if $\hat{\mu}_2' - 2\hat{\mu}_1'^2 < 0$. Indeed, the estimation of the parameters of the Pareto distribution using the method of moments is generally numerically unstable. □

The classical method of moments can be made more flexible. First, instead of using the raw moments, we may consider a p-element vector-valued function $h(w; \theta)$, where w includes the loss variable of interest (such as the claim amount) as well as some covariates (such as some attributes of the insured), and θ is a k-element vector of parameters. The function $h(w; \theta)$ is defined in such a way that $E[h(w; \theta_0)] = 0$ at the true parameter value θ_0, and $h(w; \theta)$ is called the **orthogonality condition**. For example, when the method of moments is applied to match the first two raw moments, $h(w; \theta)$ is defined as

$$h(w; \theta) = \left[\begin{array}{c} X - \mu_1'(\theta) \\ X^2 - \mu_2'(\theta) \end{array} \right]. \tag{12.3}$$

Having defined $h(w; \theta)$ we estimate its expected value using the sample data, and denote this by $\hat{h}(\theta)$. Thus, the sample estimate of $E[h(w; \theta)]$ with $h(w; \theta)$ given in equation (12.3) is

$$\hat{h}(\theta) = \left[\begin{array}{c} \hat{\mu}_1' - \mu_1'(\theta) \\ \hat{\mu}_2' - \mu_2'(\theta) \end{array} \right]. \tag{12.4}$$

The classical method-of-moments estimation solves for $\hat{\theta}$ such that the sample estimate of $\hat{h}(\theta)$ evaluated at $\hat{\theta}$ is zero. This solution, however, may not exist in general, especially when $p > k$ (we have more orthogonality conditions than the number of parameters). Hence, we modify the objective to finding the value $\hat{\theta}$ such that the sum of squares of the components of $\hat{h}(\hat{\theta})$, i.e., $\hat{h}(\hat{\theta})' \hat{h}(\hat{\theta})$, is minimized. Alternatively, we may consider minimizing a weighted sum of squares $\hat{h}(\hat{\theta})' \Omega \hat{h}(\hat{\theta})$, where Ω is a suitably defined weighting matrix dependent on the data. These extensions have been commonly used in the econometrics literature, in which the method is given the name **generalized method of moments**. In the statistics literature, this approach has been developed as the **estimation-function method**.

12.1.2 Method of Percentile Matching

It is well known that for some statistical distributions with thick tails (such as the **Cauchy** distribution and some members of the **stable distribution family**), moments of *any* order do not exist. For such distributions, the method of moments breaks down. On the other hand, as quantiles or percentiles of a distribution always exist, we may estimate the model parameters by matching the population percentiles (as functions of the parameters) to the sample percentiles. This approach is called **the method of percentile** or **quantile matching**.

Consider k quantities $0 < \delta_1, \ldots, \delta_k < 1$, and let $\delta_i = F(x_{\delta_i}; \theta)$ so that $x_{\delta_i} = F^{-1}(\delta_i; \theta)$, where θ is a k-element vector of the parameters of the df. Thus, x_{δ_i} is the δ_i-quantile of the loss variable X, which we write as $x_{\delta_i}(\theta)$, emphasizing its dependence on θ. Let $\hat{x}_{\delta_i}$ be the δ_i-quantile computed from the sample, as given in equations (11.7) and (11.9). The quantile-matching method solves for the value of $\hat{\theta}$, so that

$$x_{\delta_i}(\hat{\theta}) = \hat{x}_{\delta_i}, \qquad \text{for } i = 1, \ldots, k. \tag{12.5}$$

Again we assume that a solution of $\hat{\theta}$ exists for the above equations, and it is called the **percentile-** or **quantile-matching estimate**.

Example 12.5 Let X be distributed as $\mathcal{W}(\alpha, \lambda)$. Determine the quantile-matching estimates of α and λ.

Solution 12.5 Let $0 < \delta_1, \delta_2 < 1$. From equation (2.36), we have

$$\delta_i = 1 - \exp\left[- \left(\frac{x_{\delta_i}}{\lambda} \right)^\alpha \right], \qquad i = 1, 2,$$

so that

$$-\left(\frac{x_{\delta_i}}{\lambda} \right)^\alpha = \log(1 - \delta_i), \qquad i = 1, 2.$$

We take the ratio of the case of $i = 1$ to $i = 2$ to obtain

$$\left(\frac{x_{\delta_1}}{x_{\delta_2}} \right)^\alpha = \frac{\log(1 - \delta_1)}{\log(1 - \delta_2)},$$

which implies

$$\hat{\alpha} = \frac{\log \left[\dfrac{\log(1 - \delta_1)}{\log(1 - \delta_2)} \right]}{\log \left(\dfrac{\hat{x}_{\delta_1}}{\hat{x}_{\delta_2}} \right)},$$

where $\hat{x}_{\delta_1}$ and $\hat{x}_{\delta_2}$ are sample quantiles. Given $\hat{\alpha}$, we further solve for $\hat{\lambda}$ to obtain

$$\hat{\lambda} = \frac{\hat{x}_{\delta_1}}{[-\log(1 - \delta_1)]^{\frac{1}{\hat{\alpha}}}} = \frac{\hat{x}_{\delta_2}}{[-\log(1 - \delta_2)]^{\frac{1}{\hat{\alpha}}}}.$$

Thus, analytical solutions of $\hat{\alpha}$ and $\hat{\lambda}$ are obtainable.   □

Example 12.6 Let X be distributed as $\mathcal{P}(\alpha, \gamma)$. Determine the quantile-matching estimates of α and γ.

Solution 12.6 Let $0 < \delta_1, \delta_2 < 1$. From equation (2.38), we have

$$\delta_i = 1 - \left(\frac{\gamma}{x_{\delta_i} + \gamma} \right)^\alpha, \qquad i = 1, 2,$$

so that

$$\alpha \log \left(\frac{\gamma}{x_{\delta_i} + \gamma} \right) = \log(1 - \delta_i), \qquad i = 1, 2.$$

We take the ratio of the case of $i = 1$ to $i = 2$ to eliminate α. Evaluating the ratio at the sample quantiles, we obtain

$$\frac{\log\left(\dfrac{\gamma}{\hat{x}_{\delta_1} + \gamma}\right)}{\log\left(\dfrac{\gamma}{\hat{x}_{\delta_2} + \gamma}\right)} = \frac{\log(1 - \delta_1)}{\log(1 - \delta_2)}.$$

This equation involves only the unknown parameter γ. However, it cannot be solved analytically, and the solution $\hat{\gamma}$ has to be computed numerically. Given $\hat{\gamma}$, we can calculate $\hat{\alpha}$ as

$$\hat{\alpha} = \frac{\log(1 - \delta_1)}{\log\left(\dfrac{\hat{\gamma}}{\hat{x}_{\delta_1} + \hat{\gamma}}\right)} = \frac{\log(1 - \delta_2)}{\log\left(\dfrac{\hat{\gamma}}{\hat{x}_{\delta_2} + \hat{\gamma}}\right)}. \qquad \square$$

The above examples show that the quantile-matching method may be straightforward for some models, but numerically involving for others. One question that remains to be answered is the choice of the quantile set δ_i. Given the same data, the use of different quantiles may result in very different estimates of the parameter θ. Nonetheless, for models with analytically difficult pdf and nonexistence of moments, the quantile-matching method may be useful.[3]

12.2 Bayesian Estimation Method

The Bayesian approach to parametric model estimation has been introduced in Section 8.1, in which the emphasis has been on the estimation of the expected value of the claim amount or claim frequency. For the purpose of estimating the unknown parameter θ in a model, the Bayesian approach views θ as the realization of a random variable Θ. The Bayesian estimator of Θ is a decision rule of assigning a value to Θ based on the observed data. The consequence of making a wrong decision about Θ is reflected in a loss function. Given a loss function, the decision rule is chosen to give as small an expected loss as possible. In particular, if the squared-error loss (or quadratic loss) function is adopted, the Bayesian estimator (the decision rule) is the mean of the posterior distribution (given the data) of Θ.

To compute the Bayesian estimate of Θ, we need to obtain the posterior pdf of Θ, denoted by $f_{\Theta \mid X}(\theta \mid x)$. In general, the computation of $f_{\Theta \mid X}(\theta \mid x)$ is quite complex, as it requires the knowledge of the marginal pdf of the data X. We have surveyed in Chapter 8 some conjugate distributions that make the computation of the posterior mean of Θ particularly easy. If the prior pdf is conjugate to the likelihood, the posterior pdf belongs to the same family as the prior.

---

[3] See Adler *et al.* (1998) for the use of quantile-based methods in estimating the stable distributions.

This facilitates the computation of the posterior mean tremendously. Otherwise, numerical computational algorithms have to be adopted to determine the posterior mean. The required computational techniques have been advancing favorably to make the Bayesian approach more viable and easier to adopt.

Example 12.7 Let X be the loss random variable. Consider the following assumptions about the distribution of X and the prior distribution
(a) $X \sim \mathcal{PN}(\lambda)$ and $\Lambda \sim \mathcal{G}(\alpha, \beta)$,
(b) $X \sim \mathcal{GM}(\theta)$ and $\Theta \sim \mathcal{B}(\alpha, \beta)$,
(c) $X \sim \mathcal{E}(\lambda)$ and $\Lambda \sim \mathcal{G}(\alpha, \beta)$.
In each case you have a random sample of n observations $x_1, \ldots, x_n$ of X. Determine the Bayesian estimate of λ in (a) and (c), and θ in (b).

Solution 12.7 For (a) we know from Section 8.2.1 that the posterior distribution of Λ is $\mathcal{G}(\alpha^*, \beta^*)$, where α^* and β^* are given in equations (8.19) and (8.20), respectively. The Bayesian estimate of λ is the posterior mean of Λ, i.e.,

$$\alpha^* \beta^* = \frac{\beta(\alpha + n\bar{x})}{n\beta + 1}.$$

Note that this result is the same as the posterior mean of X_{n+1} as derived in Example 8.7. This is due to the fact that the mean of X_{n+1} is Λ.

For (b) we know from Section 8.2.2 that the posterior distribution of Θ is $\mathcal{B}(\alpha^*, \beta^*)$ where α^* and β^* are given in equations (8.21) and (8.22), respectively. The Bayesian estimate of θ is the posterior mean of Θ, which, from equation (A.103), is

$$\frac{\alpha^*}{\alpha^* + \beta^*} = \frac{\alpha + n}{\alpha + \beta + n + n\bar{x}}.$$

Note that this problem is different from the one in Example 8.8. In the latter example, the interest was in the posterior mean of X_{n+1}, which is equal to the posterior mean of $(1 - \Theta)/\Theta$. In the current problem, our interest is in the posterior mean of Θ.

For (c) we know from Section 8.2.3 that the posterior distribution of Λ is $\mathcal{G}(\alpha^*, \beta^*)$, where α^* and β^* are given in equations (8.23) and (8.24), respectively. The Bayesian estimate of λ is the posterior mean of Λ, i.e.,

$$\alpha^* \beta^* = \frac{\beta(\alpha + n)}{1 + n\beta\bar{x}}.$$

Again, this problem is different from that in Example 8.9, in which we were interested in the posterior mean of X_{n+1}, which is equal to the posterior mean of $1/\Lambda$. □

12.3 Maximum Likelihood Estimation Method

Suppose we have a random sample of n observations of X, denoted by $x = (x_1, \ldots, x_n)$. Given the pdf or pf of $X, f(\cdot; \theta)$, we define the **likelihood function** of the sample as the product of $f(x_i; \theta)$, denoted by $L(\theta; x)$. Thus, we have

$$L(\theta; x) = \prod_{i=1}^{n} f(x_i; \theta), \qquad (12.6)$$

which is taken as a function of θ given x. As the observations are independent, $L(\theta; x)$ is the joint probability or joint density of the observations. We further define the **log-likelihood function** as the logarithm of $L(\theta; x)$, i.e.,

$$\log L(\theta; x) = \sum_{i=1}^{n} \log f(x_i; \theta). \qquad (12.7)$$

The value of θ, denoted by $\hat{\theta}$, that maximizes the likelihood function is called the **maximum likelihood estimator (MLE)** of θ. As the logarithm is a monotonic nondecreasing function, $\hat{\theta}$ also maximizes the log-likelihood function. Indeed, maximization of the log-likelihood function is often easier than maximization of the likelihood function, as the former is the *sum* of n terms involving θ while the latter is a product.

In this section, we discuss the asymptotic properties of the MLE and its applications. We first consider the case where X are independently and identically distributed. This is the case where we have complete individual loss observations. We then extend the discussion to the case where X are not identically distributed, such as for grouped or incomplete data. The properties of the MLE are well established in the statistics literature, and their validity depends on some technical conditions, referred to as **regularity conditions**. We will not elaborate the regularity conditions for the properties of the MLE to hold. Instead, we will only state the standard asymptotic properties of the MLE and discuss its the applications to problems concerning actuarial data.[4]

Appendix A.18 discusses some properties of the likelihood function. We shall summarize some of these results here, with the details deferred to the Appendix. We first consider the case where θ is a scalar. The **Fisher information in a single observation**, denoted by $I(\theta)$, is defined as

$$I(\theta) = \mathrm{E}\left[\left(\frac{\partial \log f(X; \theta)}{\partial \theta}\right)^2\right], \qquad (12.8)$$

---

[4] Readers may refer to Hogg and Craig (1995, Chapter 8), for the proof of the case of random samples. For more advanced results, see Amemiya (1985). An important regularity condition for the asymptotic properties of the MLE to hold is that the support of the distribution does not depend on the unknown parameter. For example, the assumption $X \sim \mathcal{U}(0, \theta)$ violates this condition, as X cannot take any value exceeding θ.

which is also equal to

$$E \left[-\frac{\partial^2 \log f(X; \theta)}{\partial \theta^2} \right]. \tag{12.9}$$

In addition, the **Fisher information in a random sample** X, denoted by $I_n(\theta)$, is defined as

$$I_n(\theta) = E \left[\left(\frac{\partial \log L(\theta; X)}{\partial \theta} \right)^2 \right], \tag{12.10}$$

which is n times the Fisher information in a single observation, i.e.,

$$I_n(\theta) = nI(\theta). \tag{12.11}$$

Also, $I_n(\theta)$ can be computed as

$$I_n(\theta) = E \left[-\frac{\partial^2 \log L(\theta; X)}{\partial \theta^2} \right]. \tag{12.12}$$

For any unbiased estimator $\tilde{\theta}$ of θ, the **Cramér–Rao inequality** states that

$$\text{Var}(\tilde{\theta}) \geq \frac{1}{I_n(\theta)} = \frac{1}{nI(\theta)}, \tag{12.13}$$

and an unbiased estimator is said to be **efficient** if it attains the **Cramér–Rao lower bound**.

The MLE $\hat{\theta}$ is formally defined as

$$\hat{\theta} = \max_{\theta} \{L(\theta; x)\} = \max_{\theta} \{\log L(\theta; x)\}, \tag{12.14}$$

which can be computed by solving the first-order condition

$$\frac{\partial \log L(\theta; x)}{\partial \theta} = \sum_{i=1}^{n} \frac{\partial \log f(x_i; \theta)}{\partial \theta} = 0. \tag{12.15}$$

We now state the asymptotic properties of the MLE for the random-sample case as follows.

Theorem 12.1 *Under certain regularity conditions, the distribution of $\sqrt{n}(\hat{\theta} - \theta)$ converges to the normal distribution with mean 0 and variance $1/I(\theta)$, i.e.,*

$$\sqrt{n}(\hat{\theta} - \theta) \xrightarrow{D} \mathcal{N} \left(0, \frac{1}{I(\theta)} \right), \tag{12.16}$$

where $\xrightarrow{D}$ denotes convergence in distribution.[5]

---

[5] See DeGroot and Schervish (2002, p. 288), for discussions of convergence in distribution.

The above theorem has several important implications. First, $\hat{\theta}$ is asymptotically unbiased and consistent. Second, in large samples $\hat{\theta}$ is approximately normally distributed with mean θ and variance $1/I_n(\theta)$. Third, since the variance of $\hat{\theta}$ converges to the Cramér–Rao lower bound, $\hat{\theta}$ is *asymptotically efficient*.

We now generalize the results to the case where $\theta = (\theta_1, \ldots, \theta_k)'$ is a k-element vector. The **Fisher information matrix** in an observation is now defined as the $k \times k$ matrix

$$I(\theta) = \text{E} \left[\frac{\partial \log f(X; \theta)}{\partial \theta} \frac{\partial \log f(X; \theta)}{\partial \theta'} \right], \qquad (12.17)$$

which is also equal to

$$\text{E} \left[-\frac{\partial^2 \log f(X; \theta)}{\partial \theta \, \partial \theta'} \right]. \qquad (12.18)$$

The Fisher information matrix in a random sample of n observations is $I_n(\theta) = nI(\theta)$. Let $\tilde{\theta}$ be any unbiased estimator of θ. We denote the variance matrix of $\tilde{\theta}$ by $\text{Var}(\tilde{\theta})$. Hence, the ith diagonal element of $\text{Var}(\tilde{\theta})$ is $\text{Var}(\tilde{\theta}_i)$, and its (i,j)th element is $\text{Cov}(\tilde{\theta}_i, \tilde{\theta}_j)$. Denoting $I_n^{-1}(\theta)$ as the inverse of $I_n(\theta)$, the multivariate version of the Cramér-Rao inequality states that

$$\text{Var}(\tilde{\theta}) - I_n^{-1}(\theta) \qquad (12.19)$$

is a nonnegative definite matrix. As a property of nonnegative definite matrices, the diagonal elements of $\text{Var}(\tilde{\theta}) - I_n^{-1}(\theta)$ are nonnegative, i.e., the lower bound of $\text{Var}(\tilde{\theta}_i)$ is the ith diagonal element of $I_n^{-1}(\theta)$. An unbiased estimator is said to be efficient if it attains the Cramér–Rao lower bound $I_n^{-1}(\theta)$.

To compute the MLE $\hat{\theta}$, we solve the first-order condition in equation (12.15). The multivariate version of Theorem 12.1 is stated as follows.

Theorem 12.2 *Under certain regularity conditions, the distribution of $\sqrt{n}(\hat{\theta} - \theta)$ converges to the **multivariate normal distribution** with mean vector 0 and variance matrix $I^{-1}(\theta)$, i.e.,*[6]

$$\sqrt{n}(\hat{\theta} - \theta) \xrightarrow{D} \mathcal{N}\left(0, I^{-1}(\theta)\right). \qquad (12.20)$$

Again, this theorem says that the MLE is asymptotically unbiased, consistent, asymptotically normal and efficient. Thus, its properties are very desirable, which explains its popularity.

---

[6] We use $\mathcal{N}$ to denote a multivariate normal distribution as well as a univariate normal. See Appendix A.19 for some properties of the multivariate normal distribution. Also, 0 denotes a vector of zeros.

The MLE has the convenient property that it satisfies the **invariance principle**. Suppose $g(\cdot)$ is a one-to-one function and $\hat{\theta}$ is the MLE of θ, then the invariance principle states that $g(\hat{\theta})$ is the MLE of $g(\theta)$.[7]

12.3.1 Complete Individual Data

Complete individual observations form a random sample, for which the likelihood and log-likelihood functions are given in equations (12.6) and (12.7), respectively. Maximization through equation (12.15) then applies.

Example 12.8 Determine the MLE of the following models with a random sample of n observations: (a) $\mathcal{PN}(\lambda)$, (b) $\mathcal{GM}(\theta)$, (c) $\mathcal{E}(\lambda)$ and (d) $\mathcal{U}(0, \theta)$.

Solution 12.8 Note that (a) and (b) are discrete models, while (c) and (d) are continuous. The same method, however, applies. For (a) the log-likelihood function is[8]

$$\log L(\lambda; x) = n\bar{x} \log \lambda - n\lambda - \sum_{i=1}^{n} \log(x_i!),$$

and the first-order condition is

$$\frac{\partial \log L(\lambda; x)}{\partial \lambda} = \frac{n\bar{x}}{\lambda} - n = 0.$$

Thus, the MLE of λ is

$$\hat{\lambda} = \bar{x},$$

which is equal to the method-of-moments estimate derived in Example 12.1. For (b) the log-likelihood function is

$$\log L(\theta; x) = n \log \theta + [\log(1 - \theta)] \sum_{i=1}^{n} x_i,$$

and the first-order condition is

$$\frac{\partial \log L(\theta; x)}{\partial \theta} = \frac{n}{\theta} - \frac{n\bar{x}}{1 - \theta} = 0.$$

Solving for the above, we obtain

$$\hat{\theta} = \frac{1}{1 + \bar{x}},$$

which is also the method-of-moments estimate derived in Example 12.1.

---

[7] The invariance principle is not restricted to one-to-one functions. See DeGroot and Schervish (2002, p. 365), for an extension of the result.

[8] Note that the last term of the equation does not involve λ and can be ignored for the purpose of finding the MLE.

For (c) the log-likelihood function is

$$\log L(\lambda; x) = n \log \lambda - n\lambda\bar{x},$$

with the first-order condition being

$$\frac{\partial \log L(\lambda; x)}{\partial \lambda} = \frac{n}{\lambda} - n\bar{x} = 0.$$

Thus, the MLE of λ is

$$\hat{\lambda} = \frac{1}{\bar{x}}.$$

For (d), it is more convenient to consider the likelihood function, which is

$$L(\theta; x) = \left(\frac{1}{\theta}\right)^n,$$

for $0 < x_1, \ldots, x_n \leq \theta$, and 0 otherwise. Thus, the value of θ that maximizes the above expression is $\hat{\theta} = \max\{x_1, \ldots, x_n\}$. Note that in this case the MLE is not solved from equation (12.15).

A remark for the $\mathcal{U}(0, \theta)$ case is of interest. Note that from Theorem 12.1, we conclude that $\text{Var}(\sqrt{n}\hat{\theta})$ converges to a positive constant when n tends to infinity, where $\hat{\theta}$ is the MLE. From Example 10.2, however, we learn that the variance of $\max\{x_1, \ldots, x_n\}$ is

$$\frac{n\theta^2}{(n+2)(n+1)^2},$$

so that $\text{Var}(n \max\{x_1, \ldots, x_n\})$ converges to a positive constant when n tends to infinity. Hence, Theorem 12.1 breaks down. This is due to the violation of the regularity conditions for this model, as discussed in Footnote 4.   □

Example 12.9 Determine the MLE of the following models with a random sample of n observations: (a) $\mathcal{G}(\alpha, \beta)$ and (b) $\mathcal{P}(\alpha, \gamma)$.

Solution 12.9 These models are continuous with two parameters. For (a) the log-likelihood function is

$$\log L(\alpha, \beta; x) = (\alpha - 1)\left[\sum_{i=1}^{n} \log x_i\right] - \frac{n\bar{x}}{\beta} - n \log[\Gamma(\alpha)] - n\alpha \log \beta.$$

This is a complex expression and there is no analytic solution for the maximum. Differentiation of the expression is not straightforward as it involves the gamma function $\Gamma(\alpha)$. On the other hand, if α is known, then there is only one unknown parameter β, and the first-order condition becomes

$$\frac{\partial \log L(\beta; \alpha, x)}{\partial \beta} = \frac{n\bar{x}}{\beta^2} - \frac{n\alpha}{\beta} = 0,$$

so that the MLE of β is

$$\hat{\beta} = \frac{\bar{x}}{\alpha}.$$

For (b), the log-likelihood function is

$$\log L(\alpha, \gamma; x) = n \log \alpha + n\alpha \log \gamma - (\alpha + 1) \sum_{i=1}^{n} \log(x_i + \gamma).$$

The first-order conditions are

$$\frac{\partial \log L(\alpha, \gamma; x)}{\partial \alpha} = \frac{n}{\alpha} + n \log \gamma - \sum_{i=1}^{n} \log(x_i + \gamma) = 0,$$

and

$$\frac{\partial \log L(\alpha, \gamma; x)}{\partial \gamma} = \frac{n\alpha}{\gamma} - (\alpha + 1) \sum_{i=1}^{n} \frac{1}{x_i + \gamma} = 0.$$

Again, an analytic solution is not possible and the MLE have to be solved by numerical methods. If γ is known, then only the first equation above is required, and its solution is

$$\hat{\alpha} = \frac{n}{\sum_{i=1}^{n} \log(x_i + \gamma) - n \log \gamma}.$$

On the other hand, if α is known, we solve for γ from the second first-order condition above. However, analytic solution is still not possible and the problem can only be solved numerically. $\square$

Theorems 12.1 and 12.2 can be used to derive the asymptotic variance of the MLE and hence the confidence interval estimates of the parameters. The example below illustrates this application.

Example 12.10 Determine the asymptotic distribution of the MLE of the following models with a random sample of n observations: (a) $\mathcal{PN}(\lambda)$ and (b) $\mathcal{GM}(\theta)$. Hence, derive $100(1 - \alpha)\%$ confidence interval estimates for the parameters of the models.

Solution 12.10 For (a) the second derivative of the log-likelihood of an observation is

$$\frac{\partial^2 \log f(x; \lambda)}{\partial \lambda^2} = -\frac{x}{\lambda^2}.$$

Thus,

$$I(\lambda) = E\left[-\frac{\partial^2 \log f(X; \lambda)}{\partial \lambda^2}\right] = \frac{1}{\lambda},$$

so that

$$\sqrt{n}(\hat{\lambda} - \lambda) \xrightarrow{D} \mathcal{N}(0, \lambda).$$

As in Example 12.8, $\hat{\lambda} = \bar{x}$, which is also the estimate for the variance. Hence, in large samples $\bar{x}$ is approximately normally distributed with mean λ and variance λ/n (estimated by $\bar{x}/n$). A $100(1 - \alpha)\%$ confidence interval of λ is computed as

$$\bar{x} \pm z_{1-\frac{\alpha}{2}} \sqrt{\frac{\bar{x}}{n}}.$$

Note that we can also estimate the $100(1 - \alpha)\%$ confidence interval of λ by

$$\bar{x} \pm z_{1-\frac{\alpha}{2}} \frac{s}{\sqrt{n}},$$

where s^2 is the sample variance. This estimate, however, will not be as efficient if X is Poisson.

For (b) the second derivative of the log-likelihood of an observation is

$$\frac{\partial^2 \log f(x; \theta)}{\partial \theta^2} = -\frac{1}{\theta^2} - \frac{x}{(1 - \theta)^2}.$$

As $E(X) = (1 - \theta)/\theta$, we have

$$I(\theta) = E\left[-\frac{\partial^2 \log f(X; \theta)}{\partial \theta^2}\right] = \frac{1}{\theta^2} + \frac{1}{\theta(1 - \theta)} = \frac{1}{\theta^2(1 - \theta)}.$$

Thus,

$$\sqrt{n}(\hat{\theta} - \theta) \xrightarrow{D} \mathcal{N}\left(0, \theta^2(1 - \theta)\right),$$

where, from Example 12.8,

$$\hat{\theta} = \frac{1}{1 + \bar{x}}.$$

A $100(1 - \alpha)\%$ confidence interval of θ can be computed as

$$\hat{\theta} \pm z_{1-\frac{\alpha}{2}} \sqrt{\frac{\hat{\theta}^2(1 - \hat{\theta})}{n}}.$$

Note that the asymptotic variance of $\hat{\theta}$ can also be derived using the delta method, together with the result for the variance of the sample mean $\bar{x}$. Readers are invited to show the derivation (see Exercise 12.11). □

12.3.2 Grouped and Incomplete Data

When the sample data are grouped and/or incomplete, the observations are no longer iid. Nonetheless, we can still formulate the likelihood function and compute the MLE. The first step is to write down the likelihood function or log-likelihood function of the sample that is appropriate for the way the observations are sampled.

We first consider the case where we have complete observations that are grouped into k intervals: $(c_0, c_1], (c_1, c_2], \ldots, (c_{k-1}, c_k]$, where $0 \leq c_0 < c_1 < \cdots < c_k = \infty$. Let the number of observations in the interval $(c_{j-1}, c_j]$ be n_j so that $\sum_{j=1}^{k} n_j = n$. Given a parametric df $F(\cdot; \theta)$, the probability of a single observation falling inside the interval $(c_{j-1}, c_j]$ is $F(c_j; \theta) - F(c_{j-1}; \theta)$. Assuming the *individual* observations are iid, the likelihood of having n_j observations in the interval $(c_{j-1}, c_j]$, for $j = 1, \ldots, k$, is

$$L(\theta; n) = \prod_{j=1}^{k} [F(c_j; \theta) - F(c_{j-1}; \theta)]^{n_j}, \qquad (12.21)$$

where $n = (n_1, \ldots, n_k)$. The log-likelihood function of the sample is

$$\log L(\theta; n) = \sum_{j=1}^{k} n_j \log [F(c_j; \theta) - F(c_{j-1}; \theta)]. \qquad (12.22)$$

Now we consider the case where we have individual observations that are right censored. If the ground-up loss is continuous, the claim amount will have a distribution of the mixed type, described by a pf–pdf. Specifically, if there is a policy limit of u, only claims of amounts in the interval $(0, u]$ are observable. Losses of amounts exceeding u are censored, so that the probability of a claim of amount u is $1 - F(u; \theta)$. Thus, if the claim data consist of $x = (x_1, \ldots, x_{n_1})$, where $0 < x_1, \ldots, x_{n_1} < u$, and n_2 claims of amount u, with $n = n_1 + n_2$, then the likelihood function is given by

$$L(\theta; x, n_2) = \left[\prod_{i=1}^{n_1} f(x_i; \theta) \right] [1 - F(u; \theta)]^{n_2}. \qquad (12.23)$$

The log-likelihood function is

$$\log L(\theta; x, n_2) = n_2 \log [1 - F(u; \theta)] + \sum_{i=1}^{n_1} \log f(x_i; \theta). \qquad (12.24)$$

If the insurance policy has a deductible of d, the data of claim payments are sampled from a population with truncation, i.e., only losses with amounts exceeding d are sampled. Thus, the pdf of the ground-up loss *observed* is

$$\frac{f(x; \theta)}{1 - F(d; \theta)}, \qquad \text{for } d < x. \qquad (12.25)$$

If we have a sample of claim data $x = (x_1, \ldots, x_{n_1})$, then the likelihood function is given by

$$L(\theta; x) = \prod_{i=1}^{n} \frac{f(x_i; \theta)}{1 - F(d; \theta)} = \frac{1}{[1 - F(d; \theta)]^n} \prod_{i=1}^{n} f(x_i; \theta), \quad \text{where } d < x_1, \ldots, x_n.$$

(12.26)

Thus, the log-likelihood function is

$$\log L(\theta; x) = -n \log [1 - F(d; \theta)] + \sum_{i=1}^{n} \log f(x_i; \theta).$$

(12.27)

We denote y_i as the modified loss amount, such that $y_i = x_i - d$. Let $y = (y_1, \ldots, y_n)$. Suppose we wish to model the distribution of the payment in a payment event, and denote the pdf of this distribution by $\tilde{f}(\cdot; \theta^*)$, then the likelihood function of y is

$$L(\theta^*; y) = \prod_{i=1}^{n} \tilde{f}(y_i; \theta^*), \qquad \text{for } 0 < y_1, \ldots, y_n.$$

(12.28)

This model is called the **shifted model**. It captures the distribution of the loss in a payment event and may be different from the model of the ground-up loss distribution, i.e., $\tilde{f}(\cdot)$ may differ from $f(\cdot)$.

The above models may be extended and combined in various ways. For example, the data may have policies with different policy limits and/or deductibles. Policies may also have deductibles as well as maximum covered losses, etc. The principles illustrated above should be applied to handle different variations.

As the observations in general may not be iid, Theorems 12.1 and 12.2 may not apply. The asymptotic properties of the MLE beyond the iid assumption are summarized in the theorem below, which applies to a broad class of models.

Theorem 12.3 *Let $\hat{\theta}$ denote the MLE of the k-element parameter θ of the likelihood function $L(\theta; x)$. Under certain regularity conditions, the distribution of $\sqrt{n}(\hat{\theta} - \theta)$ converges to the multivariate normal distribution with mean vector 0 and variance matrix $\mathcal{I}^{-1}(\theta)$, i.e.,*

$$\sqrt{n}(\hat{\theta} - \theta) \overset{D}{\to} \mathcal{N}\left(0, \mathcal{I}^{-1}(\theta)\right),$$

(12.29)

where

$$\mathcal{I}(\theta) = \lim_{n \to \infty} E\left[-\frac{1}{n} \frac{\partial^2 \log L(\theta; x)}{\partial \theta \, \partial \theta'}\right].$$

(12.30)

Note that $\mathcal{I}(\theta)$ requires the evaluation of an expectation and depend on the unknown parameter θ. In practical applications it may be estimated by its sample counterpart. Once $\mathcal{I}(\theta)$ is estimated, confidence intervals of θ may be computed.

Example 12.11 Let the ground-up loss X be distributed as $\mathcal{E}(\lambda)$. Consider the following cases:

(a) Claims are grouped into k intervals: $(0, c_1], (c_1, c_2], \ldots, (c_{k-1}, \infty]$, with no deductible or policy limit. Let $n = (n_1, \ldots, n_k)$ denote the numbers of observations in the intervals.

(b) There is a policy limit of u. n_1 uncensored claims with ground-up losses $x = (x_1, \ldots, x_{n_1})$ are available, and n_2 claims have a censored amount u.

(c) There is a deductible of d, and n claims with ground-up losses $x = (x_1, \ldots, x_n)$ are available.

(d) The policy has a deductible of d and maximum covered loss of u. n_1 uncensored claims with ground-up losses $x = (x_1, \ldots, x_{n_1})$ are available, and n_2 claims have a censored claim amount $u - d$. Denote $n = n_1 + n_2$.

(e) Similar to (d), but there are two blocks of policies with deductibles of d_1 and d_2 for Block 1 and Block 2, respectively. The maximum covered losses are u_1 and u_2 for Block 1 and Block 2, respectively. In Block 1, there are n_{11} uncensored claim observations and n_{12} censored claims of amount $u_1 - d_1$. In Block 2, there are n_{21} uncensored claim observations and n_{22} censored claims of amount $u_2 - d_2$.

Determine the MLE of λ in each case.

Solution 12.11 The df of $\mathcal{E}(\lambda)$ is $F(x; \lambda) = 1 - e^{-\lambda x}$. For (a), using equation (12.21), the likelihood function is (with $c_0 = 0$)

$$L(\lambda; n) = \left[\prod_{j=1}^{k-1} \left(e^{-c_{j-1}\lambda} - e^{-c_j\lambda} \right)^{n_j} \right] \left(e^{-c_{k-1}\lambda} \right)^{n_k},$$

so that the log-likelihood function is

$$\log L(\lambda; n) = -c_{k-1}n_k\lambda + \sum_{j=1}^{k-1} n_j \log \left(e^{-c_{j-1}\lambda} - e^{-c_j\lambda} \right).$$

The MLE is solved by maximizing the above expression with respect to λ, for which numerical method is required.

For (b), the likelihood function is

$$L(\lambda; x) = \left[\prod_{i=1}^{n_1} \lambda e^{-\lambda x_i} \right] e^{-\lambda u n_2},$$

and the log-likelihood function is

$$\log L(\lambda; x) = -\lambda u n_2 - \lambda n_1 \bar{x} + n_1 \log \lambda.$$

The first-order condition is

$$\frac{\partial \log L(\lambda; \boldsymbol{x})}{\partial \lambda} = -un_2 - n_1\bar{x} + \frac{n_1}{\lambda} = 0,$$

which produces the MLE

$$\hat{\lambda} = \frac{n_1}{n_1\bar{x} + n_2 u}.$$

For (c), the likelihood function is

$$L(\lambda; \boldsymbol{x}) = \frac{1}{e^{-\lambda dn}} \left[\prod_{i=1}^{n} \lambda e^{-\lambda x_i} \right],$$

and the log-likelihood function is

$$\log L(\lambda; \boldsymbol{x}) = \lambda dn - \lambda n\bar{x} + n \log \lambda.$$

The first-order condition is

$$\frac{\partial \log L(\lambda; \boldsymbol{x})}{\partial \lambda} = nd - n\bar{x} + \frac{n}{\lambda} = 0,$$

so that the MLE is

$$\hat{\lambda} = \frac{1}{\bar{x} - d}.$$

For (d), the likelihood function is

$$L(\lambda; \boldsymbol{x}) = \frac{1}{e^{-\lambda dn}} \left[\prod_{i=1}^{n_1} \lambda e^{-\lambda x_i} \right] e^{-\lambda un_2},$$

with log-likelihood

$$\log L(\lambda; \boldsymbol{x}) = \lambda dn - \lambda n_1\bar{x} + n_1 \log \lambda - \lambda un_2,$$

and first-order condition

$$\frac{\partial \log L(\lambda; \boldsymbol{x})}{\partial \lambda} = nd - n_1\bar{x} + \frac{n_1}{\lambda} - un_2 = 0.$$

The MLE is

$$\hat{\lambda} = \frac{n_1}{n_1(\bar{x} - d) + n_2(u - d)}.$$

For (e), the log-likelihood is the sum of the two blocks of log-likelihoods given in (d). Solving for the first-order condition, we obtain the MLE as

$$\hat{\lambda} = \frac{n_{11} + n_{21}}{n_{11}(\bar{x}_1 - d_1) + n_{21}(\bar{x}_2 - d_2) + n_{12}(u_1 - d_1) + n_{22}(u_2 - d_2)}$$

$$= \frac{\sum_{i=1}^{2} n_{i1}}{\sum_{i=1}^{2} [n_{i1}(\bar{x}_i - d_i) + n_{i2}(u_i - d_i)]}. \qquad \square$$

Example 12.12 A sample of the ground-up loss X of two blocks of policies has the following observations (d_i = deductible, u_i = maximum covered loss):

Block 1 ($d_1 = 1.4$, $u_1 = \infty$): 0.13, 2.54, 2.16, 4.72, 1.88, 4.03, 1.39, 4.03, 3.23, 1.79,

Block 2 ($d_2 = 0$, $u_2 = 3$): 3.16, 2.64, 2.88, 4.38, 1.81, 2.29, 1.11, 1.78, 0.52, 3.69.

Assuming X is distributed as $\mathcal{W}(\alpha, \lambda)$, compute the MLE of α and λ, and estimate the 95% confidence intervals of these parameters.

Solution 12.12 For Block 1, 2 losses (i.e., 0.13 and 1.39) are below the deductible, and are not observed in practice. There are 8 claims, with ground-up losses denoted by x_{1i}, for $i = 1, \ldots, 8$. The likelihood function of this block of losses is

$$\prod_{i=1}^{8} \frac{f(x_{1i}; \alpha, \lambda)}{1 - F(d_1; \alpha, \lambda)}.$$

Using equations (2.34) and (2.36), the log-likelihood function can be written as

$$(\alpha - 1) \sum_{i=1}^{8} \log x_{1i} + 8 \left[\log \alpha - \alpha \log \lambda\right] - \sum_{i=1}^{8} \left(\frac{x_{1i}}{\lambda}\right)^{\alpha} + 8 \left(\frac{d_1}{\lambda}\right)^{\alpha}.$$

For Block 2, three claims (i.e., 3.16, 4.38 and 3.69) are right censored at $u_2 = 3$. We denote the uncensored losses by x_{2i}, for $i = 1, \ldots, 7$. As there is no deductible, the likelihood function is

$$\left[\prod_{i=1}^{7} f(x_{2i}; \alpha, \lambda)\right] [1 - F(u_2; \alpha, \lambda)]^3.$$

Thus, the log-likelihood function of Block 2 is

$$(\alpha - 1) \sum_{i=1}^{7} \log x_{2i} + 7 \left[\log \alpha - \alpha \log \lambda\right] - \sum_{i=1}^{7} \left(\frac{x_{2i}}{\lambda}\right)^{\alpha} - 3 \left(\frac{u_2}{\lambda}\right)^{\alpha}.$$

The log-likelihood of the whole sample is equal to the sum of the log-likelihoods of the two blocks. Maximizing this numerically with respect to α and λ, we obtain the MLE as (the standard errors of the estimates are in parentheses)[9]

$$\hat{\alpha} = 2.1676 \ (0.5333),$$

$$\hat{\lambda} = 2.9070 \ (0.3715).$$

---

[9] The standard error is the square root of the estimate of the corresponding diagonal element of $\mathcal{I}^{-1}(\theta)$ (see equation (12.30)) divided by $\sqrt{n}$. It is estimated using the sample analog.

Thus, the 95% confidence interval estimates of α and λ are, respectively,

$$2.1676 \pm (1.96)(0.5333) = (1.1223, 3.2129)$$

and

$$2.9070 \pm (1.96)(0.3715) = (2.1783, 3.6352). \qquad \Box$$

Example 12.13 Let the $\mathcal{W}(\alpha, \lambda)$ assumption be adopted for both the ground-up loss distribution and the payment distribution in a payment event (the shifted model) for the data of the policies of Block 1 in Example 12.12. Determine the MLE of these models.

Solution 12.13 For the ground-up loss distribution, the log-likelihood of Block 1 in Example 12.12 applies. Maximizing this function (the log-likelihood of Block 2 is not required), we obtain the following estimates

$$\hat{\alpha} = 2.6040, \qquad \hat{\lambda} = 3.1800.$$

Using equation (2.35), we derive the estimate of the mean of the ground-up loss as 2.8248.

For the shifted model, the log-likelihood function is

$$(\alpha - 1) \sum_{i=1}^{8} \log (x_{1i} - d_1) + 8 \left[\log \alpha - \alpha \log \lambda\right] - \sum_{i=1}^{8} \left[\frac{x_{1i} - d_1}{\lambda}\right]^{\alpha},$$

where $d_1 = 1.4$. The MLE (denoted with tildes) are

$$\tilde{\alpha} = 1.5979, \qquad \tilde{\lambda} = 1.8412,$$

from which we obtain the estimate of the mean of the shifted loss as 1.6509. $\quad \Box$

12.4 Models with Covariates

We have so far assumed that the failure-time or loss distributions are *homogeneous*, in the sense that the same distribution applies to all insured objects, regardless of any attributes of the object that might be relevant. In practice, however, the future lifetime of smokers and non-smokers might differ. The accident rates of teenage drivers and middle-aged drivers might differ, etc. We now discuss some approaches in modeling the failure-time and loss distributions in which some attributes (called the **covariates**) of the objects affect the distributions.

Let $S(x; \theta)$ denote the survival function of interest, called the **baseline survival function**, which applies to the distribution independent of the object's attributes. Now suppose for the ith insured object, there is a vector of k attributes, denoted by $z_i = (z_{i1}, \ldots, z_{ik})'$, which affects the survival function.

We denote the survival function of the ith object by $S(x; \theta, z_i)$. There are several ways in which the differences in the distribution can be formulated. We shall start with the popular **Cox's proportional hazards model.**

12.4.1 Proportional Hazards Model

Given the survival function $S(x; \theta)$, the hazard function $h(x; \theta)$ is defined as

$$h(x; \theta) = -\frac{d \log S(x; \theta)}{dx}, \tag{12.31}$$

from which we have

$$S(x; \theta) = \exp\left(-\int_0^x h(x; \theta)\, dx\right). \tag{12.32}$$

We now allow the hazard function to vary with the individuals and denote it by $h(x; \theta, z_i)$. In contrast, $h(x; \theta)$, which does not vary with i, is called the **baseline hazard function**. A simple model can be constructed by assuming that there exists a function $m(\cdot)$, such that if we denote $m_i = m(z_i)$, then

$$h(x; \theta, z_i) = m_i h(x; \theta). \tag{12.33}$$

This is called the proportional hazards model, which postulates that the hazard function of the ith individual is a multiple of the baseline hazard function, and the multiple depends on the covariate z_i.

An important implication of the proportional hazards model is that the survival function of the ith individual is given by

$$\begin{aligned}
S(x; \theta, z_i) &= \exp\left(-\int_0^x h(x; \theta, z_i)\, dx\right) \\
&= \exp\left(-\int_0^x m_i h(x; \theta)\, dx\right) \\
&= \left[\exp\left(-\int_0^x h(x; \theta)\, dx\right)\right]^{m_i} \\
&= [S(x; \theta)]^{m_i}. \tag{12.34}
\end{aligned}$$

For equation (12.33) to provide a well-defined hazard function, m_i must be positive for all z_i. Thus, the choice of the function $m(\cdot)$ is important. A popular assumption that satisfies this requirement is

$$m_i = \exp(\beta' z_i), \tag{12.35}$$

where $\beta = (\beta_1, \ldots, \beta_k)'$ is a vector of parameters. Based on this assumption, an individual has the baseline hazard function if $z_i = 0$.

The pdf of the ith individual can be written as

$$f(x; \theta, z_i) = -\frac{dS(x; \theta, z_i)}{dx}$$

$$= -\frac{d\,[S(x;\theta)]^{m_i}}{dx}$$

$$= m_i\,[S(x;\theta)]^{m_i-1}\,f(x;\theta), \tag{12.36}$$

where $f(x;\theta) = -dS(x;\theta)/dx$ is the **baseline pdf**. From this equation the likelihood of a sample can be obtained, which depends on the parameters θ and β. Given the functional form of the baseline pdf (or sf), the MLE of θ and β can be computed.

Example 12.14 There are two blocks of policies such that $z_i = 1$ if the insured is from Block 1, and $z_i = 0$ if the insured is from Block 2. We adopt the model in equation (12.35) so that $m_i = e^{\beta}$ if $z_i = 1$, and $m_i = 1$ if $z_i = 0$. Let the baseline loss distribution be $\mathcal{E}(\lambda)$. Suppose there are n_1 losses in Block 1 and n_2 losses in Block 2, with $n = n_1 + n_2$. What is the log-likelihood function of the sample?

Solution 12.14 The baseline distribution applies to losses in Block 2. Note that $m(1) = e^{\beta}$ and $m(0) = 1$. As $S(x;\lambda) = e^{-\lambda x}$ and $f(x;\lambda) = \lambda e^{-\lambda x}$, from equation (12.36), the pdf of losses in Block 1 is

$$f(x;\lambda,1) = e^{\beta}\left(e^{-\lambda x}\right)^{e^{\beta}-1}\left(\lambda e^{-\lambda x}\right) = \lambda e^{\beta - \lambda x e^{\beta}}.$$

The pdf of losses in Block 2 is the pdf of $\mathcal{E}(\lambda)$, i.e.,

$$f(x;\lambda,0) = \lambda e^{-\lambda x}.$$

If the Block 1 losses are denoted by $x_{11},\ldots,x_{1n_1}$ and the Block 2 losses are denoted by $x_{21},\ldots,x_{2n_2}$, the log-likelihood function of the sample is

$$n\log\lambda + n_1\beta - \lambda e^{\beta}\sum_{j=1}^{n_1} x_{1j} - \lambda\sum_{j=1}^{n_2} x_{2j}. \qquad \square$$

The above example shows that the MLE of the full model may be quite complicated even for a simple baseline model such as the exponential. Furthermore, it may be desirable to separate the estimation of the parameters in the proportional hazards function, i.e., β, versus the estimation of the baseline hazard function. For example, a researcher may only be interested in the *relative* effect of smoking (versus non-smoking) on future lifetime. Indeed, the estimation can be done in two stages. The first stage involves estimating β using the **partial likelihood method**, and the second stage involves estimating the baseline hazard function using a nonparametric method, such as the Kaplan–Meier or Nelson–Aalen estimators.

The partial likelihood method can be used to estimate β in the proportional hazards function. We now explain this method using the failure-time data terminology. Recall the notations introduced in Chapter 10 that the observed distinct failure times in the data are arranged in the order $0 < y_1 < \cdots < y_m$, where $m \leq n$. There are w_j failures at time y_j and the risk set at time y_j is r_j. Suppose object i fails at time y_j, the partial likelihood of object i, denoted by $L_i(\beta)$, is defined as the probability of object i failing at time y_j given that some objects fail at time y_j. Thus, we have

$$
\begin{aligned}
L_i(\beta) &= \Pr(\text{object } i \text{ fails at time } y_j \mid \text{some objects fail at time } y_j) \\
&= \frac{\Pr(\text{object } i \text{ fails at time } y_j)}{\Pr(\text{some objects fail at time } y_j)} \\
&= \frac{h(y_j; \theta, z_i)}{\sum_{i' \in r_j} h(y_j; \theta, z_{i'})} \\
&= \frac{m_i \, h(y_j; \theta)}{\sum_{i' \in r_j} m_{i'} \, h(y_j; \theta)} \\
&= \frac{m_i}{\sum_{i' \in r_j} m_{i'}} \\
&= \frac{\exp(\beta' z_i)}{\sum_{i' \in r_j} \exp(\beta' z_{i'})}, \qquad \text{for } i = 1, \ldots, n.
\end{aligned}
\tag{12.37}
$$

The third line in the above equation is due to the definition of a hazard function; the last line is due to the assumption in equation (12.35). Note that $L_i(\beta)$ does not depend on the baseline hazard function. It is also not dependent on the value of y_j.

The partial likelihood of the sample, denoted by $L(\beta)$, is defined as

$$
L(\beta) = \prod_{i=1}^{n} L_i(\beta).
\tag{12.38}
$$

Note that only β appears in the partial likelihood function, which can be maximized to obtain the estimate of β without any assumptions about the baseline hazard function and its estimates.

Example 12.15 A proportional hazards model has two covariates $z = (z_1, z_2)'$, each taking possible values 0 and 1. We denote $z_{(1)} = (0, 0)'$, $z_{(2)} = (1, 0)'$, $z_{(3)} = (0, 1)'$ and $z_{(4)} = (1, 1)'$. The failure times observed are

2 (1), 3 (2), 4 (3), 4 (4), 5 (1), 7 (3), 8 (1), 8 (4), 9 (2), 11 (2), 11 (2), 12 (3),

where the index i of the covariate vector $z_{(i)}$ of the observed failures are given in parentheses.[10] Also, an object with covariate vector $z_{(2)}$ is censored at time 6,

---

[10] For instance, the first failure occurred at time 2 and the covariate vector of the failed object is $z_{(1)} = (0, 0)'$.

Table 12.1. *Computation of the partial likelihood for Example 12.15*

j	y_j	Covariate vector	r_j of covariate $z_{(i)}$ (1)	(2)	(3)	(4)	$L_j(\beta) = \text{num}_j/\text{den}_j$ num_j	den_j
1	2	$z_{(1)}$	3	5	3	3	$m_{(1)}$	$3m_{(1)} + 5m_{(2)} + 3m_{(3)} + 3m_{(4)}$
2	3	$z_{(2)}$	2	5	3	3	$m_{(2)}$	$2m_{(1)} + 5m_{(2)} + 3m_{(3)} + 3m_{(4)}$
3	4	$z_{(3)}, z_{(4)}$	2	4	3	3	$m_{(3)}m_{(4)}$	$\left[2m_{(1)} + 4m_{(2)} + 3m_{(3)} + 3m_{(4)}\right]^2$
4	5	$z_{(1)}$	2	4	2	2	$m_{(1)}$	$2m_{(1)} + 4m_{(2)} + 2m_{(3)} + 2m_{(4)}$
5	7	$z_{(3)}$	1	4	2	2	$m_{(3)}$	$m_{(1)} + 4m_{(2)} + 2m_{(3)} + 2m_{(4)}$
6	8	$z_{(1)}, z_{(4)}$	1	4	1	2	$m_{(1)}m_{(4)}$	$\left[m_{(1)} + 4m_{(2)} + m_{(3)} + 2m_{(4)}\right]^2$
7	9	$z_{(2)}$	0	3	1	1	$m_{(2)}$	$3m_{(2)} + m_{(3)} + m_{(4)}$
8	11	$z_{(2)}, z_{(2)}$	0	2	1	1	$m_{(2)}^2$	$\left[2m_{(2)} + m_{(3)} + m_{(4)}\right]^2$
9	12	$z_{(3)}$	0	0	1	0	$m_{(3)}$	$m_{(3)}$

and another object with covariate vector $z_{(4)}$ is censored at time 8. Compute the partial likelihood estimate of β.

Solution 12.15 As there are two covariates, we let $\beta = (\beta_1, \beta_2)'$. Next we compute the multiples of the baseline hazard function. Thus, $m_{(1)} = \exp(\beta'z_{(1)}) = 1$, $m_{(2)} = \exp(\beta'z_{(2)}) = \exp(\beta_1)$, $m_{(3)} = \exp(\beta'z_{(3)}) = \exp(\beta_2)$ and $m_{(4)} = \exp(\beta'z_{(4)}) = \exp(\beta_1 + \beta_2)$. We tabulate the data and the computation of the partial likelihood in Table 12.1.

If two objects, i and i', have the same failure time y_j, their partial likelihoods have the same denominator (see equation (12.37)). With a slight abuse of notation, we denote $L_j(\beta)$ as the partial likelihood of the object (or the product of the partial likelihoods of the objects) with failure time y_j. Then the partial likelihood of the sample is equal to

$$L(\beta) = \prod_{i=1}^{12} L_i(\beta) = \prod_{j=1}^{9} L_j(\beta) = \prod_{j=1}^{9} \frac{\text{num}_j}{\text{den}_j},$$

where num_j and den_j are given in the last two columns of Table 12.1. Maximizing $L(\beta)$ with respect to β, we obtain $\hat{\beta}_1 = -0.7484$ and $\hat{\beta}_2 = -0.5643$. These results imply $\hat{m}_{(1)} = 1$, $\hat{m}_{(2)} = 0.4731$, $\hat{m}_{(3)} = 0.5688$ and $\hat{m}_{(4)} = 0.2691$. □

Having estimated the parameter β in the proportional hazards model, we can continue to estimate the baseline hazard function nonparametrically using the Nelson–Aalen method. Recall that the cumulative hazard function $H(y; \theta)$, defined by

$$H(y; \theta) = \int_0^y h(y; \theta) \, dy, \tag{12.39}$$

can be estimated by the Nelson–Aalen method using the formula

$$\hat{H}(y; \theta) = \sum_{\ell=1}^{j} \frac{w_\ell}{r_\ell}, \qquad \text{for } y_j \le y < y_{j+1}. \tag{12.40}$$

Now the cumulative hazard function with covariate z_i is given by

$$H(y; \theta, z_i) = \int_0^y h(y; \theta, z_i)\, dy$$

$$= m_i \int_0^y h(y; \theta)\, dy$$

$$= m_i H(y; \theta). \tag{12.41}$$

This suggests that equation (12.40) may be modified as follows

$$\hat{H}(y; \theta) = \sum_{\ell=1}^{j} \frac{w_\ell}{r_\ell^*}, \qquad \text{for } y_j \le y < y_{j+1}, \tag{12.42}$$

where r_ℓ^* is the modified risk set defined by

$$r_\ell^* = \sum_{i' \in r_\ell} m_{i'}. \tag{12.43}$$

Instead of deriving formula (12.42), we now show that the method works for two special cases. First, note that if there are no covariates, all objects have the baseline hazard function so that $m_{i'} = 1$ for all $i' \in r_\ell$. Then $r_\ell^* = r_\ell$, and equation (12.42) gives us the basic Nelson–Aalen formula.[11] On the other hand, if all objects have the same covariate z^* and $m(z^*) = m^*$, then $r_\ell^* = \sum_{i' \in r_\ell} m^* = m^* r_\ell$. Thus, we have

$$\sum_{\ell=1}^{j} \frac{w_\ell}{r_\ell^*} = \sum_{\ell=1}^{j} \frac{w_\ell}{m^* r_\ell} = \frac{1}{m^*} \sum_{\ell=1}^{j} \frac{w_\ell}{r_\ell} = \frac{\hat{H}(y; \theta, z^*)}{m^*} = \hat{H}(y; \theta), \tag{12.44}$$

which is the result in equation (12.42).

Example 12.16 For the data in Example 12.15, compute the Nelson–Aalen estimate of the baseline hazard function and the baseline survival function. Estimate the survival functions $S(3.5; z_{(2)})$ and $S(8.9; z_{(4)})$.

Solution 12.16 The results are summarized in Table 12.2. Note that r_ℓ^* in Column 4 are taken from the last column of Table 12.1 (ignore the square, if any) evaluated at $\hat{\beta}$.

---

[11] Recall that r_ℓ stands for the collection of items in the risk set as well as the number of items in the risk set.

Table 12.2. *Nelson–Aalen estimates for Example 12.16*

ℓ	y_ℓ	w_ℓ	r_ℓ^*	$\dfrac{w_\ell}{r_\ell^*}$	$\hat{H}(y) = \sum_{j=1}^\ell \dfrac{w_j}{r_j^*}$	$\hat{S}(y) = \exp\left[-\hat{H}(y)\right]$
1	2	1	7.8793	0.1269	0.1269	0.8808
2	3	1	6.8793	0.1454	0.2723	0.7616
3	4	2	6.4062	0.3122	0.5845	0.5574
4	5	1	5.5683	0.1796	0.7641	0.4658
5	7	1	4.5683	0.2189	0.9830	0.3742
6	8	2	3.9995	0.5001	1.4830	0.2270
7	9	1	2.2573	0.4430	1.9260	0.1457
8	11	2	1.7842	1.1209	3.0470	0.0475
9	12	1	0.5688	1.7581	4.8051	0.0082

We can now compute the survival functions for given covariates. In particular, we have

$$\hat{S}(3.5; z_{(2)}) = (0.7616)^{0.4731} = 0.8791,$$

and

$$\hat{S}(8.9; z_{(4)}) = (0.2270)^{0.2691} = 0.6710.$$

The values of $\hat{m}_{(2)} = 0.4731$ and $\hat{m}_{(4)} = 0.2691$ are taken from Example 12.15.
□

12.4.2 Generalized Linear Model

While the mean of the loss may or may not be directly a parameter of the pdf, it is often a quantity of paramount importance. If some covariates are expected to affect the loss distribution, it may be natural to assume that they determine the mean of the loss. Thus, a modeling strategy is to assume that the mean of the loss variable X, denoted by μ, is a function of the covariate z. To ensure the mean loss is positive, we may adopt the following model

$$E(X) = \mu = \exp(\beta'z). \tag{12.45}$$

This model is called the **generalized linear model**. The exponential function used in the above equation is called the **link function**, which relates the mean loss to the covariate. The exponential link function is appropriate for modeling loss distributions, as it ensures that the expected loss is positive.

For illustration, if $X \sim \mathcal{PN}(\lambda)$, a generalized linear model may assume that the mean of X, λ, is given by $\lambda = \exp(\beta'z)$, so that the log-likelihood function of a random sample of n observations is (after dropping the irrelevant *constant*)

$$\log L(\beta; x) = \sum_{i=1}^{n} x_i(\beta' z_i) - \sum_{i=1}^{n} \exp(\beta' z_i). \tag{12.46}$$

Example 12.17 If $X \sim \mathcal{G}(\alpha, \beta)$, where the covariate z determines the mean of X, construct a generalized linear model for the distribution of X.

Solution 12.17 We assume $E(X) = \mu = \exp(\delta' z)$.[12] As $E(X) = \alpha\beta$, we write $\beta = \mu/\alpha = \exp(\delta' z)/\alpha$, and reparameterize the pdf of X by α and δ, with z as the covariate. Thus, the pdf of X is

$$f(x; \alpha, \delta, z) = \frac{\alpha^{\alpha}}{\Gamma(\alpha)\mu^{\alpha}} x^{\alpha-1} e^{-\frac{\alpha x}{\mu}} = \frac{\alpha^{\alpha}}{\Gamma(\alpha) \exp(\alpha\delta' z)} x^{\alpha-1} \exp\left(-\alpha x e^{-\delta' z}\right). \square$$

12.4.3 Accelerated Failure-Time Model

In the accelerated failure-time model, the survival function of object i with covariate z_i, $S(x; \theta, z_i)$, is related to the baseline (i.e., $z = 0$) survival function as follows

$$S(x; \theta, z_i) = S(m_i x; \theta, 0), \tag{12.47}$$

where $m_i = m(z_i)$ for an appropriate function $m(\cdot)$. Again, a convenient assumption is $m(z_i) = \exp(\beta' z_i)$. We now denote $X(z_i)$ as the failure-time random variable for an object with covariate z_i. The expected lifetime (at birth) is

$$\begin{aligned}
E[X(z_i)] &= \int_0^{\infty} S(x; \theta, z_i)\, dx \\
&= \int_0^{\infty} S(m_i x; \theta, 0)\, dx \\
&= \frac{1}{m_i} \int_0^{\infty} S(x; \theta, 0)\, dx \\
&= \frac{1}{m_i} E[X(0)]. \tag{12.48}
\end{aligned}$$

The third line in the above equation is due to the change of variable in the integration. Hence, the expected lifetime at birth of an object with covariate z_i is $1/m_i$ times the expected lifetime at birth of a *baseline* object. This result can be further extended. We define the random variable $T(x; z_i)$ as the future lifetime of an object with covariate z_i aged x. Thus,

$$T(x; z_i) = X(z_i) - x \mid X(z_i) > x. \tag{12.49}$$

It can be shown that

$$E[T(x; z_i)] = \frac{1}{m_i} E[T(m_i x; 0)]. \tag{12.50}$$

---

[12] The switch of the notation from β to δ is to avoid confusion.

Thus, the expected future lifetime of an object with covariate z_i aged x is $1/m_i$ times the expected future lifetime of an object with covariate 0 aged $m_i x$. Readers are invited to prove this result (see Exercise 12.24).

Example 12.18 The baseline distribution of the age-at-death random variable X is $\mathcal{E}(\lambda)$. Let z_i be the covariate of object i and assume the accelerated failure-time model with $m_i = \exp(\beta' z_i)$. Derive the log-likelihood function of a sample of n lifes.

Solution 12.18 The baseline survival function is $S(x; \lambda, 0) = \exp(-\lambda x)$, and we have

$$S(x; \lambda, z_i) = S(m_i x; \lambda, 0) = \exp(-\lambda x e^{\beta' z_i}).$$

Thus, the pdf of $X(z_i)$ is

$$f(x; \lambda, z_i) = \lambda e^{\beta' z_i} \exp(-\lambda x e^{\beta' z_i}),$$

and the log-likelihood of the sample is

$$\log L(\lambda, \beta; x) = n \log \lambda + \sum_{i=1}^{n} \beta' z_i - \lambda \sum_{i=1}^{n} x_i e^{\beta' z_i}. \qquad \square$$

12.5 Modeling Joint Distribution Using Copula

In many practical applications, researchers are often required to analyze multiple risks of the same group, similar risks from different groups or different aspects of a risk group. Thus, techniques for modeling multivariate distributions are required. While modeling the joint distribution directly may be an answer, this approach may face some difficulties in practice. First, there may not be an appropriate standard multivariate distribution that is suitable for the problem at hand. Second, the standard multivariate distributions usually have marginals from the same family, and this may put severe constraints on the solution. Third, researchers may have an accepted marginal distribution that suits the data, and they would like to maintain the marginal model while extending the analysis to model the joint distribution.

The use of **copula** provides a flexible approach to modeling multivariate distributions. Indeed, the literature on this area is growing fast, and many applications are seen in finance and actuarial science. In this section, we provide a brief introduction to the technique. For simplicity of exposition, we shall consider only bivariate distributions, and assume that we have continuous distributions for the variables of interest.

Definition 12.1 A bivariate copula $C(u_1, u_2)$ is a mapping from the unit square $[0, 1]^2$ to the unit interval $[0, 1]$. It is increasing in each component and satisfies the following conditions:

1 $C(1, u_2) = u_2$ and $C(u_1, 1) = u_1$, for $0 \leq u_1, u_2 \leq 1$,
2 For any $0 \leq a_1 \leq b_1 \leq 1$ and $0 \leq a_2 \leq b_2 \leq 1$, $C(b_1, b_2) - C(a_1, b_2) - C(b_1, a_2) + C(a_1, a_2) \geq 0$.

A bivariate copula is in fact a joint df on $[0, 1]^2$ with standard uniform marginals, i.e., $C(u_1, u_2) = \Pr(U_1 \leq u_1, U_2 \leq u_2)$, where U_1 and U_2 are uniformly distributed on $[0, 1]$. The first condition above implies that the marginal distribution of each component of the copula is uniform. The second condition is called the **rectangle inequality**. It ensures that $\Pr(a_1 \leq U_1 \leq b_1, a_2 \leq U_2 \leq b_2)$ is nonnegative.

Let $F_{X_1 X_2}(\cdot, \cdot)$ be the joint df of X_1 and X_2, with marginal df $F_{X_1}(\cdot)$ and $F_{X_2}(\cdot)$. The theorem below, called the **Sklar Theorem**, states the representation of the joint df using a copula. It also shows how a joint distribution can be created via a copula.

Theorem 12.4 *Given the joint and marginal df of X_1 and X_2, there exists a unique copula $C(\cdot, \cdot)$, such that*

$$F_{X_1 X_2}(x_1, x_2) = C(F_{X_1}(x_1), F_{X_2}(x_2)). \tag{12.51}$$

Conversely, if $C(\cdot, \cdot)$ is a copula, and $F_{X_1}(x_1)$ and $F_{X_2}(x_2)$ are univariate df of X_1 and X_2, respectively, then $C(F_{X_1}(x_1), F_{X_2}(x_2))$ is a bivariate df with marginal df $F_{X_1}(x_1)$ and $F_{X_2}(x_2)$.

Proof See McNeil *et al.* (2005, p. 187). □

If the inverse functions $F_{X_1}^{-1}(\cdot)$ and $F_{X_2}^{-1}(\cdot)$ exist, the copula satisfying equation (12.51) is given by

$$C(u_1, u_2) = F_{X_1 X_2}(F_{X_1}^{-1}(u_1), F_{X_2}^{-1}(u_2)). \tag{12.52}$$

The second part of Theorem 12.4 enables us to construct a bivariate distribution with given marginals. With a well-defined copula satisfying Definition 12.1, $C(F_{X_1}(x_1), F_{X_2}(x_2))$ establishes a bivariate distribution with the known marginals. This can be described as a *bottom-up* approach in creating a bivariate distribution.

The theorem below, called the **Fréchet bounds** for copulas, establishes the maximum and minimum of a copula.

Theorem 12.5 *The following bounds apply to any bivariate copula*

$$\max\{0, u_1 + u_2 - 1\} \le C(u_1, u_2) \le \min\{u_1, u_2\}. \tag{12.53}$$

Proof See McNeil *et al.* (2005, p. 188).   □

The likelihood function of a bivariate distribution created by a copula can be computed using the following theorem.

Theorem 12.6 *Let X_1 and X_2 be two continuous distributions with pdf $f_{X_1}(\cdot)$ and $f_{X_2}(\cdot)$, respectively. If the joint df of X_1 and X_2 is given by equation (12.51), their joint pdf can be written as*

$$f_{X_1 X_2}(x_1, x_2) = f_{X_1}(x_1) f_{X_2}(x_2) c(F_{X_1}(x_1), F_{X_2}(x_2)), \tag{12.54}$$

where

$$c(u_1, u_2) = \frac{\partial^2 C(u_1, u_2)}{\partial u_1 \, \partial u_2} \tag{12.55}$$

*is called the **copula density**.*

Proof This can be obtained by differentiating equation (12.51).   □

From Theorem 12.6, we can conclude that the log-likelihood of a bivariate random variable with df given by equation (12.51) is

$$\log[f_{X_1 X_2}(x_1, x_2)] = \log[f_{X_1}(x_1)] + \log[f_{X_2}(x_2)] + \log[c(F_{X_1}(x_1), F_{X_2}(x_2))], \tag{12.56}$$

which is the log-likelihood of two *independent* observations of X_1 and X_2, plus a term that measures the dependence.

We now introduce some simple bivariate copulas.[13] **Clayton's copula**, denoted by $C_C(u_1, u_2)$, is defined as

$$C_C(u_1, u_2) = \left(u_1^{-\alpha} + u_2^{-\alpha} - 1\right)^{-\frac{1}{\alpha}}, \qquad \alpha > 0. \tag{12.57}$$

The Clayton copula density is given by

$$c_C(u_1, u_2) = \frac{1 + \alpha}{(u_1 u_2)^{1+\alpha}} \left(u_1^{-\alpha} + u_2^{-\alpha} - 1\right)^{-2 - \frac{1}{\alpha}}. \tag{12.58}$$

Frank's copula, denoted by $C_F(u_1, u_2)$, is defined as

$$C_F(u_1, u_2) = -\frac{1}{\alpha} \log\left[1 + \frac{(e^{-\alpha u_1} - 1)(e^{-\alpha u_2} - 1)}{e^{-\alpha} - 1}\right], \qquad \alpha \ne 0, \tag{12.59}$$

---

[13] For more examples of bivariate copulas, as well as extensions to multivariate copulas, see Denuit *et al.* (2005).

which has the following copula density

$$c_F(u_1, u_2) = \frac{\alpha e^{-\alpha(u_1+u_2)}\left(1 - e^{-\alpha}\right)}{\left[e^{-\alpha(u_1+u_2)} - e^{-\alpha u_1} - e^{-\alpha u_2} + e^{-\alpha}\right]^2}. \tag{12.60}$$

Another popular copula is the **Gaussian copula** defined by

$$C_G(u_1, u_2) = \Psi_\alpha(\Phi^{-1}(u_1), \Phi^{-1}(u_2)), \qquad -1 < \alpha < 1, \tag{12.61}$$

where $\Phi^{-1}(\cdot)$ is the inverse of the standard normal df and $\Psi_\alpha(\cdot, \cdot)$ is the df of a standard bivariate normal variate with correlation coefficient α. The Gaussian copula density is

$$c_G(u_1, u_2) = \frac{1}{\sqrt{1-\alpha^2}} \exp\left[-\frac{\eta_1^2 - 2\alpha\eta_1\eta_2 + \eta_2^2}{2(1-\alpha^2)}\right] \exp\left[\frac{\eta_1^2 + \eta_2^2}{2}\right], \tag{12.62}$$

where $\eta_i = \Phi^{-1}(u_i)$, for $i = 1, 2$.

Example 12.19 Let $X_1 \sim \mathcal{W}(0.5, 2)$ and $X_2 \sim \mathcal{G}(3, 2)$, and assume that Clayton's copula with parameter α fits the bivariate distribution of X_1 and X_2. Determine the probability $p = \Pr(X_1 \leq E(X_1), X_2 \leq E(X_2))$ for $\alpha = 0.001, 1, 2, 3$ and 10.

Solution 12.19 The means of X_1 and X_2 are

$$E(X_1) = 2\Gamma(3) = 4 \qquad \text{and} \qquad E(X_2) = (2)(3) = 6.$$

Let $u_1 = F_{X_1}(4) = 0.7569$ and $u_2 = F_{X_2}(6) = 0.5768$, so that

$$\begin{aligned} p &= \Pr(X_1 \leq 4, X_2 \leq 6) \\ &= C_C(0.7569, 0.5768) \\ &= \left[(0.7569)^{-\alpha} + (0.5768)^{-\alpha} - 1\right]^{-\frac{1}{\alpha}}. \end{aligned}$$

The computed values of p are

α	0.001	1	2	3	10
p	0.4366	0.4867	0.5163	0.5354	0.5734

Note that when X_1 and X_2 are independent, $p = (0.7569)(0.5768) = 0.4366$, which corresponds to the case where α approaches 0. The dependence between X_1 and X_2 increases with α, as can be seen from the numerical results. $\square$

12.6 R Laboratory

R Codes 12.1 provides the codes to compute the MLE of the Weibull distribution for the data in Example 12.2. A function lik is coded to compute the negative log-likelihood function of the data set assuming Weibull distribution. The function optim is used to minimize lik. The standard errors of the MLE are the square roots of the diagonal elements of the inverse of the Hessian matrix.

```
#####################################################################
# R Codes 12.1
#
# MLE of the Weibull distribution for the loss data in Example 12.12
#####################################################################

x1=c(0.13,2.54,2.16,4.72,1.88,4.03,1.39,4.03,3.23,1.79)
x2=c(3.16,2.64,2.88,4.38,1.81,2.29,1.11,1.78,0.52,3.69)
d1=1.4                    # Deductible
u2=3                      # Maximum covered loss

lik=function(b,x1,x2,d1,u2)   # Compute the -ve loglikelihood
{
xx1=x1[x1>d1]
n1=length(xx1)
xx2=x2[x2<u2]
n2=length(xx2)
n3=length(x2)-length(xx2)
a=(b[1]-1)*sum(log(xx1))+n1*(log(b[1])-b[1]*log(b[2]))-
    sum((xx1/b[2])^b[1])+n1*(d1/b[2])^b[1]  # loglikelihood of Block 1
b=(b[1]-1)*sum(log(xx2))+n2*(log(b[1])-b[1]*log(b[2]))-
    sum((xx2/b[2])^b[1])-n3*(u2/b[2])^b[1]  # loglikelihood of Block 2
return(-a-b)              # -ve loglikelihood of the two blocks
}

start = c(2,3)                # Set starting value for optim function
mle=optim(start,lik,x1=x1,x2=x2,d1=d1,u2=u2,hessian=T,
    method="Nelder-Mead")    # Minimize -ve loglikelihood
mlese=sqrt(diag(solve(mle$hessian)))
mle$par                      # Output MLE
mlese                        # Output standard error of MLE
```

R Codes 12.2 provides the codes to estimate the proportional hazard model in Example 12.15. The function plik computes the partial likelihood of the sample as defined in equation (12.38). We then compute the estimates of the hazard multiples with different covariates, which are used to calculate the modified risk sets r_ℓ^* in equation (12.43).

```
####################################################################
# R Codes 12.2
#
# Estimation of the parameters beta in the proportional hazards model
# of Example 12.15
####################################################################

c1=c(3,2,2,2,2,1,1,1,0,0,0,0)
c2=c(5,5,4,4,4,4,4,4,3,2,2,0)
c3=c(3,3,3,3,2,2,1,1,1,1,1,1)
c4=c(3,3,3,3,2,2,2,2,1,1,1,0)
nu=c(1,2,3,4,1,3,1,4,2,2,2,3)  # Index of covariate vector of 12 obs
de=cbind(c1,c2,c3,c4)          # 12 x 4 matrix of risk sets in
                               # Table 12.1
start=c(-0.7,-0.5)             # Set starting values of beta


plik=function(b,de,nu)         # Partial likelihood in Eq(12.38)
{
m=c(1,exp(b[1]),exp(b[2]),exp(b[1]+b[2]))
den=de%*%m
num=m[nu]
return(-prod(num/den))
}


pmle=optim(start,plik,de=de,nu=nu,hessian=F,method="Nelder-Mead")
pmle$par                       # Output estimates of Beta
m=c(1,exp(pmle$par[1]),exp(pmle$par[2]),
  exp(pmle$par[1]+pmle$par[2]))# Estimates of hazard multiples m
unique(de)%*%m                 # Modified risk set, Col 4 of
                               # Table 12.2
```

12.7 Summary and Discussions

We have discussed various methods of estimating the parameters of a failure-time or loss distribution. The maximum likelihood estimation method is by far the most popular, as it is asymptotically normal and efficient for many standard cases. Furthermore, it can be applied to data that are complete or incomplete, provided the likelihood function is appropriately defined. The asymptotic standard errors of the MLE can be computed in most standard estimation packages, from which interval estimates can be obtained. For models with covariates, we have surveyed the use of the proportional hazards model, the generalized linear model and the accelerated failure-time model. The partial likelihood method provides a convenient way to estimate the regression coefficients of the proportional hazards model without estimating the baseline model. Finally, we have introduced the use of copula in modeling multivariate data. This method provides a simple approach to extend the adopted univariate models to fit the multivariate observations.

Exercises

Exercise 12.1 A random sample of n insurance claims with a deductible of d has a ground-up loss distribution following $\mathcal{P}(\alpha, \gamma)$. If the value of α is known, derive the method-of-moments estimate of γ by matching the first-order moment.

Exercise 12.2 The 25th and 75th percentiles of a sample of losses are 6 and 15, respectively. What is $\text{VaR}_{0.99}$ of the loss, assuming the loss distribution is (a) Weibull and (b) lognormal?

Exercise 12.3 The median and the 90th percentile of a sample from a Weibull distribution is 25,000 and 260,000, respectively. Compute the mean and the standard deviation of the distribution.

Exercise 12.4 The following observations are obtained for a sample of losses:

$$20, 23, 30, 31, 39, 43, 50, 55, 67, 72.$$

Estimate the parameters of the distribution using the method of moments if the losses are distributed as (a) $\mathcal{G}(\alpha, \beta)$ and (b) $\mathcal{U}(a, b)$.

Exercise 12.5 A random sample of 10 observations of X from a $\mathcal{L}(\mu, \sigma^2)$ distribution is as follows:

$$45, 49, 55, 56, 63, 71, 78, 79, 82, 86.$$

(a) Estimate μ and σ^2 by matching the moments of X, and hence estimate the probability of X exceeding 80.
(b) Estimate μ and σ^2 by matching the moments of $\log X$, and hence estimate the probability of X exceeding 80.

Exercise 12.6 The following observations are obtained from a right-censored loss distribution with maximum covered loss of 18 (18^+ denotes a right-censored observation):

$$4, 4, 7, 10, 14, 15, 16, 18^+, 18^+, 18^+.$$

Estimate the parameters of the loss distribution using the method of moments if the losses are distributed as (a) $\mathcal{U}(0, b)$, (b) $\mathcal{E}(\lambda)$, and (c) $\mathcal{P}(2, \gamma)$.

Exercise 12.7 Let X be a mixture distribution with 40% chance of $\mathcal{E}(\lambda_1)$ and 60% chance of $\mathcal{E}(\lambda_2)$. If the mean and the variance of X are estimated to be 4 and 22, respectively, estimate λ_1 and λ_2 using the method of moments.

Exercise 12.8 The following observations are obtained from a loss distribution:

$$11, 15, 16, 23, 28, 29, 31, 35, 40, 42, 44, 48, 52, 53, 55, 59, 60, 65, 65, 71.$$

(a) Estimate VaR$_{0.95}$, assuming the loss follows a lognormal distribution, with parameters estimated by matching the 25th and 75th percentiles.
(b) Estimate VaR$_{0.90}$, assuming the loss follows a Weibull distribution, with parameters estimated by matching the 30th and 70th percentiles.

Exercise 12.9 Let X be distributed with pdf $f_X(x)$ given by

$$f_X(x) = \frac{2(\theta - x)}{\theta^2}, \quad \text{for } 0 < x < \theta,$$

and 0 elsewhere. Estimate θ using the method of moments.

Exercise 12.10 Let $\{X_1, \ldots, X_n\}$ and $\{Y_1, \ldots, Y_m\}$ be independent random samples from normal populations with means μ_X and μ_Y, respectively, and common variance σ^2. Determine the maximum likelihood estimators of μ_X, μ_Y and σ^2.

Exercise 12.11 For a loss variable following the $\mathcal{GM}(\theta)$ distribution, the maximum likelihood estimator of θ based on a random sample of n observations is $\hat{\theta} = 1/(1+\bar{x})$. What is the variance of $\bar{x}$? Derive the asymptotic variance of $\hat{\theta}$ using the delta method.

Exercise 12.12 Let $\{X_1, \ldots, X_n\}$ be a random sample from $\mathcal{U}(\theta - 0.5, \theta + 0.5)$. Determine the maximum likelihood estimator of θ and show that it is not unique. If $X_{(i)}$ denotes the ith order statistic of the sample, determine whether the following estimators are maximum likelihood estimators of θ: (a) $(X_{(1)} + X_{(n)})/2$, and (b) $(X_{(1)} + 2X_{(n)})/3$.

Exercise 12.13 The following grouped observations are available for a loss random variable X:

Interval	$(0, 2]$	$(2, 4]$	$(4, 6]$	$(6, 8]$	$(8, \infty)$
No of obs	4	7	10	6	3

Determine the log-likelihood of the sample if X is distributed as (a) $\mathcal{E}(\lambda)$, and (b) $\mathcal{P}(\alpha, \gamma)$.

Exercise 12.14 You are given the following loss observations, where a policy limit of 28 has been imposed:

$$8, 10, 13, 14, 16, 16, 19, 24, 26, 28, 28, 28.$$

(a) If the losses are distributed as $\mathcal{U}(0, b)$, determine the maximum likelihood estimate of b assuming all payments of 28 have losses exceeding the policy limit. How would your result be changed if only two of these payments have losses exceeding the policy limit?

(b) If the losses are distributed as $\mathcal{E}(\lambda)$, determine the maximum likelihood estimate of λ assuming all payments of 28 have losses exceeding the policy limit.

Exercise 12.15 Refer to Example 12.13. Write R codes to verify that the maximum likelihood estimates of the shifted model are $\tilde{\alpha} = 1.5979$ and $\tilde{\lambda} = 1.8412$.

Exercise 12.16 An insurance policy has a deductible of 4 and maximum covered loss of 14. The following five observations of payment are given, including two censored payments: 3, 6, 8, 10 and 10.

(a) If the ground-up losses are distributed as $\mathcal{E}(\lambda)$, compute the maximum likelihood estimate of λ.
(b) If the payment in a payment event is distributed as $\mathcal{E}(\lambda^*)$, compute the maximum likelihood estimate of λ^*.
(c) Compute the maximum likelihood estimates of λ and λ^* if the ground-up loss and the shifted loss distributions are, respectively, $\mathcal{W}(3, \lambda)$ and $\mathcal{W}(3, \lambda^*)$.

Exercise 12.17 The following observations are obtained from the distribution $X \sim \mathcal{E}(\lambda)$: 0.47, 0.49, 0.91, 1.00, 2.47, 5.03 and 16.09. Compute the maximum likelihood estimate of $x_{0.25}$.

Exercise 12.18 A sample of five loss observations are: 158, 168, 171, 210 and 350. The df $F_X(x)$ of the loss variable X is

$$F_X(x) = 1 - \left(\frac{100}{x}\right)^\alpha, \qquad \text{for } x > 100,$$

where $\alpha > 0$. Compute the maximum likelihood estimate of α.

Exercise 12.19 Suppose $\{X_1, \ldots, X_n\}$ is a random sample from the $\mathcal{N}(\mu, \sigma^2)$ distribution.

(a) If σ^2 is known, what is the maximum likelihood estimator of μ? Using Theorem 12.1, derive the asymptotic distribution of the maximum likelihood estimator of μ.
(b) If μ is known, what is the maximum likelihood estimator of σ^2? Using Theorem 12.1, derive the asymptotic distribution of the maximum likelihood estimator of σ^2.
(c) If μ and σ^2 are both unknown, what are the maximum likelihood estimators of μ and σ^2? Using Theorem 12.2, derive the joint asymptotic distribution of the maximum likelihood estimators of μ and σ^2.

Exercise 12.20 Suppose $\{X_1, \ldots, X_n\}$ is a random sample from the $\mathcal{N}(\mu, \sigma^2)$ distribution. Determine the asymptotic variance of $\bar{X}^3$.

Exercise 12.21 Suppose $\{X_1, \ldots, X_n\}$ is a random sample from the $\mathcal{N}(0, \sigma^2)$ distribution. Determine the asymptotic variance of $n/\left(\sum_{i=1}^{n} X_i^2\right)$. [**Hint:** Use result in Exercise 12.19(b).]

Exercise 12.22 Suppose $X \sim \mathcal{E}(\lambda)$ and a random sample of X has the following observations:

$$14, 17, 23, 25, 25, 28, 30, 34, 40, 41, 45, 49.$$

(a) Compute the maximum likelihood estimate of λ.
(b) Estimate the variance of the maximum likelihood estimate of λ.
(c) Compute an approximate 95% confidence interval of λ. Do you think this confidence interval is reliable?
(d) Estimate the standard deviation of the variance estimate in (b).
(e) Estimate $\Pr(X > 25)$ and determine a 90% linear confidence interval of this probability.

Exercise 12.23 Refer to the loss distribution X in Example 12.14. You are given the following losses in Block 1: 3, 5, 8, 12; and the following losses in Block 2: 2, 3, 5, 5, 7. The proportional hazards model is assumed.

(a) Compute the maximum likelihood estimate of β and λ, assuming the baseline distribution is exponential.
(b) Compute the estimate of β using the partial likelihood method, hence estimate the baseline survival function at the observed loss values. Estimate $\Pr(X > 6)$ for a Block 1 risk.

Exercise 12.24 Express the survival functions of $T(x; z_i)$ and $T(x; 0)$ as defined in equation (12.49) in terms of $S(\cdot; \theta, z_i)$. Hence, prove equation (12.50).

Exercise 12.25 Suppose $X \sim \mathcal{PN}(\lambda)$ and a generalized linear model has $\lambda = \exp(\beta z)$ where z is a single index. The following data are given:

x_i	4	6	3	7	5	9	4	10
z_i	1	3	1	2	2	3	1	3

Determine the log-likelihood function of the sample and the maximum likelihood estimate of β.

Exercise 12.26 Refer to Example 12.18. Suppose the covariate is a scalar index z and the following data are given

x_i	10	26	13	17	25	29	34	40	21	12
z_i	2	2	2	2	1	1	1	1	2	2

(a) Determine the log-likelihood function of the sample if the baseline distribution is $\mathcal{E}(\lambda)$, and estimate the parameters of the model.
(b) Determine the log-likelihood function of the sample if the baseline distribution is $\mathcal{P}(3, \gamma)$, and estimate the parameters of the model.

Exercise 12.27 Derive equations (12.58) and (12.60).

Exercise 12.28 Suppose $X_1 \sim \mathcal{E}(\lambda_1)$, $X_2 \sim \mathcal{E}(\lambda_2)$ and Clayton's copula applies to the joint df of X_1 and X_2. You are given the following data:

x_{1i}	2.5	2.6	1.3	2.7	1.4	2.9	4.5	5.3
x_{2i}	3.5	4.2	1.9	4.8	2.6	5.6	6.8	7.8

(a) Compute the maximum likelihood estimates of the model.
(b) Estimate $\Pr(X_1 \leq 3, X_2 \leq 4)$.

Questions Adapted from SOA Exams

Exercise 12.29 There were 100 insurance claims in Year 1, with an average size of 10,000. In Year 2, there were 200 claims, with an average claim size of 12,500. Inflation is found to be 10% per year, and the claim-size distribution follows a $\mathcal{P}(3, \gamma)$ distribution. Estimate γ for Year 3 using the method of moments.

Exercise 12.30 A random sample of 3 losses from the $\mathcal{P}(\alpha, 150)$ distribution has the values: 225, 525 and 950. Compute the maximum likelihood estimate of α.

Exercise 12.31 Suppose $\{X_1, \ldots, X_n\}$ is a random sample from the $\mathcal{L}(\mu, \sigma^2)$ distribution. The maximum likelihood estimates of the parameters are $\hat{\mu} = 4.2150$ and $\hat{\sigma}^2 = 1.1946$. The estimated variance of $\hat{\mu}$ is 0.1195 and that of $\hat{\sigma}^2$ is 0.2853, with estimated covariance between $\hat{\mu}$ and $\hat{\sigma}^2$ being zero. The mean of $\mathcal{L}(\mu, \sigma^2)$ is $\mu_X = \exp(\mu + \sigma^2/2)$. Estimate the variance of the maximum likelihood estimate of μ_X. [**Hint:** See equation (A.200) in the Appendix.]

Exercise 12.32 The pdf of X is

$$f_X(x) = \frac{1}{\sqrt{2\pi\theta}} \exp\left(-\frac{x^2}{2\theta}\right), \qquad -\infty < x < \infty,$$

where $\theta > 0$. If the maximum likelihood estimate of θ based on a sample of 40 observations is $\hat{\theta} = 2$, estimate the mean squared error of $\hat{\theta}$.

Exercise 12.33 The duration of unemployment is assumed to follow the proportional hazards model, where the baseline distribution is exponential and the covariate z is years of education. When $z = 10$, the mean duration of unemployment is 0.2060 years. When $z = 25$, the median duration of unemployment is 0.0411 years. If $z = 5$, what is the probability that the unemployment duration exceeds 1 year?

Exercise 12.34 A proportional hazards model has covariate $z_1 = 1$ for males and $z_1 = 0$ for females, and $z_2 = 1$ for adults and $z_2 = 0$ for children. The maximum likelihood estimates of the coefficients are $\hat{\beta}_1 = 0.25$ and $\hat{\beta}_2 = -0.45$. The covariance matrix of the estimators is

$$\text{Var}(\hat{\beta}_1, \hat{\beta}_2) = \begin{pmatrix} 0.36 & 0.10 \\ 0.10 & 0.20 \end{pmatrix}.$$

Determine a 95% confidence interval of $\beta_1 - \beta_2$.

Exercise 12.35 The ground-up losses of dental claims follow the $\mathcal{E}(\lambda)$ distribution. There is a deductible of 50 and a policy limit of 350. A random sample of claim payments has the following observations: $50, 150, 200, 350^+$ and 350^+, where $^+$ indicates that the original loss exceeds 400. Determine the likelihood function.

Exercise 12.36 A random sample of observations is taken from the shifted exponential distribution with the following pdf:

$$f(x) = \frac{1}{\theta} e^{-\frac{x-\delta}{\theta}}, \quad \delta < x < \infty.$$

The sample mean and median are 300 and 240, respectively. Estimate δ by matching these two sample quantities to the corresponding population quantities.

Exercise 12.37 The distribution of the number of claims per policy during a one-year period for a block of 3,000 insurance policies is

Number of claims per policy	Number of policies
0	1,000
1	1,200
2	600
3	200
≥ 4	0

A Poisson model is fitted to the number of claims per policy using the maximum likelihood estimation method. Determine the lower end point of the large-sample 90% linear confidence interval of the mean of the distribution.

Exercise 12.38 A Cox proportional hazards model was used to study the losses on two groups of policies. A single covariate z was used with $z = 0$ for a policy in Group 1 and $z = 1$ for a policy in Group 2. The following losses were observed:

$$\text{Group 1: 275, 325, 520,}$$
$$\text{Group 2: 215, 250, 300.}$$

The baseline survival function is

$$S(x) = \left(\frac{200}{x}\right)^{\alpha}, \quad x > 200, \ \alpha > 0.$$

Compute the maximum likelihood estimate of the coefficient β of the proportional hazards model.

Exercise 12.39 Losses follow the $\mathcal{W}(\alpha, \lambda)$ distribution, and the following observations are given:

54, 70, 75, 81, 84, 88, 97, 105, 109, 114, 122, 125, 128, 139, 146, 153.

The model is estimated by percentile matching using the 20th and 70th smoothed empirical percentiles. Calculate the estimate of λ.

Exercise 12.40 An insurance company records the following ground-up loss amounts from a policy with a deductible of 100 (losses less than 100 are not reported):

120, 180, 200, 270, 300, 1,000, 2,500.

Assuming the losses follow the $\mathcal{P}(\alpha, 400)$ distribution, use the maximum likelihood estimate of α to estimate the expected loss with no deductible.

Exercise 12.41 Losses are assumed to follow an inverse exponential distribution with df

$$F(x) = e^{-\frac{\theta}{x}}, \quad x > 0.$$

Three losses of amounts 186, 91 and 66 are observed and seven other amounts are known to be less than or equal to 60. Calculate the maximum likelihood estimate of the population mode.

Exercise 12.42 At time 4, there are five working light bulbs. The five bulbs are observed for another duration p. Three light bulbs burn out at times 5, 9 and 13, while the remaining light bulbs are still working at times $4 + p$. If the distribution of failure time is $\mathcal{U}(0, \omega)$ and the maximum likelihood estimate of ω is 29, determine p.

Exercise 12.43 A Cox proportional hazards model was used to compare the fuel efficiency of traditional and hybrid cars. A single covariate z was used with

$z = 0$ for a traditional car and $z = 1$ for a hybrid car. The following observed miles per gallon are given:

Traditional: 22, 25, 28, 33, 39,
Hybrid: 27, 31, 35, 42, 45.

The partial likelihood estimate of the coefficient β of the proportional hazards model is -1. Calculate the estimate of the baseline cumulative hazard function $H(32)$ using an analog of the Nelson–Aalen estimator.

Exercise 12.44 Losses have the following df:

$$F(x) = 1 - \frac{\theta}{x}, \quad \theta < x < \infty.$$

A sample of 20 losses resulted in the following grouped distribution:

Interval	Number of losses
$x \leq 10$	9
$10 < x \leq 25$	6
$x > 25$	5

Calculate the maximum likelihood estimate of θ.

13

Model Evaluation and Selection

After a model has been estimated, we have to evaluate it to ascertain that the assumptions applied are acceptable and supported by the data. This should be done prior to using the model for prediction and pricing. Model evaluation can be done using graphical methods, as well as formal misspecification tests and diagnostic checks.

Nonparametric methods have the advantage of using minimal assumptions and allowing the data to determine the model. However, they are more difficult to analyze theoretically. On the other hand, parametric methods are able to summarize the model in a small number of parameters, albeit with the danger of imposing the wrong structure and oversimplification. Using graphical comparison of the estimated df and pdf, we can often detect if the estimated parametric model has any abnormal deviation from the data.

Formal misspecification tests can be conducted to compare the estimated model (parametric or nonparametric) against a hypothesized model. When the key interest is the comparison of the df, we may use the Kolmogorov–Smirnov test and Anderson–Darling test. The chi-square goodness-of-fit test is an alternative for testing distributional assumptions, by comparing the observed frequencies against the theoretical frequencies. The likelihood ratio test is applicable to testing the validity of restrictions on a model, and can be used to decide if a model can be simplified.

When several estimated models pass most of the diagnostics, the adoption of a particular model may be decided using some information criteria, such as the Akaike information criterion or the Schwarz information criterion.

Learning Objectives

1 Graphical presentation and comparison
2 Misspecification tests and diagnostic checks

3 Kolmogorov–Smirnov test and Anderson–Darling test
4 Likelihood ratio test and chi-square goodness-of-fit test
5 Model selection and information criteria

13.1 Graphical Methods

For complete individual observations, the empirical df in equation (11.2) provides a consistent estimate of the df without imposing any parametric assumption. When parametric models are assumed, the parameters may be estimated by MLE or other methods. However, for the estimates to be consistent for the true values, the pdf assumed has to be correct. One way to assess if the assumption concerning the distribution is correct is to plot the estimated parametric df against the empirical df. If the distributional assumption is incorrect, we would expect the two plotted graphs to differ.

For exposition purpose, we denote $\hat{F}(\cdot)$ as an estimated df using the nonparametric method, such as the empirical df and the Kaplan-Meier estimate, and $F^*(\cdot)$ as a hypothesized df or parametrically estimated df. Thus, $\hat{F}(\cdot)$ is assumed to be an estimate which is entirely data based, and $F^*(\cdot)$ (and the assumption underlying it) is assessed against $\hat{F}(\cdot)$.

Example 13.1 A sample of 20 loss observations is as follows:

$$0.003, 0.012, 0.180, 0.253, 0.394, 0.430, 0.491, 0.743, 1.066, 1.126,$$

$$1.303, 1.508, 1.740, 4.757, 5.376, 5.557, 7.236, 7.465, 8.054, 14.938.$$

Two parametric models are fitted to the data using the MLE, assuming that the underlying distribution is (a) $\mathcal{W}(\alpha, \lambda)$ and (b) $\mathcal{G}(\alpha, \beta)$. The fitted models are $\mathcal{W}(0.6548, 2.3989)$ and $\mathcal{G}(0.5257, 5.9569)$. Compare the empirical df against the df of the two estimated parametric models.

Solution 13.1 The plots of the empirical df and the estimated parametric df are given in Figure 13.1. It can be seen that both estimated parametric models fit the data quite well. Thus, from the df plots it is difficult to ascertain which is the preferred model. □

Another useful graphical device is the *p-p* plot. Suppose the sample observations $x = (x_1, \ldots, x_n)$ are arranged in increasing order $x_{(1)} \leq x_{(2)} \leq \cdots \leq x_{(n)}$, so that $x_{(i)}$ is the ith order statistic. We approximate the probability of having an observation less than or equal to $x_{(i)}$ using the sample data by the sample proportion $p_i = i/(n+1)$.[1] Now the hypothesized or parametrically estimated probability of an observation less than or equal to $x_{(i)}$ is $F^*(x_{(i)})$. A plot of

---

[1] Another definition of sample proportion can be found in Footnote 1 of Chapter 11.

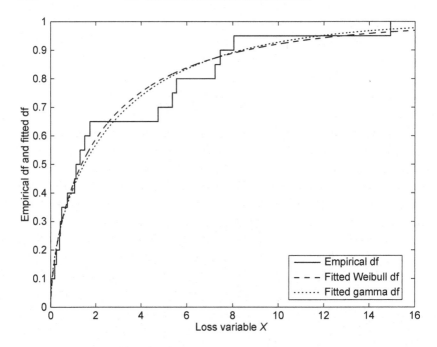

Figure 13.1 Empirical df and estimated parametric df of Example 13.1

$F^*(x_{(i)})$ against p_i is called the *p-p* plot. If $F^*(\cdot)$ fits the data well, the *p-p* plot should approximately follow the 45-degree line.

Example 13.2 For the data and the fitted Weibull model in Example 13.1, assess the model using the *p-p* plot.

Solution 13.2 The *p-p* plot is presented in Figure 13.2. It can be seen that most points lie closely to the 45 degree line, apart from some deviations around $p_i = 0.7$.   □

Another graphical method equivalent to the *p-p* plot is the *q-q* plot. In a *q-q* plot, $F^{*-1}(p_i)$ is plotted against $x_{(i)}$. If $F^*(\cdot)$ fits the data well, the *q-q* plot should approximately follow a straight line.

When the data include incomplete observations that are right censored, the empirical df is an inappropriate estimate of the df. We replace it by the Kaplan-Meier estimate. Parametric estimate of the df can be computed using MLE, with the log-likelihood function suitably defined, as discussed in Section 12.3. The estimated df based on the MLE may then be compared against the Kaplan-Meier estimate.

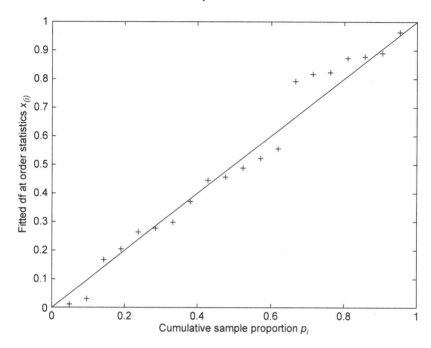

Figure 13.2 *p-p* plot of the estimated Weibull distribution in Example 13.2.

Example 13.3 For the data in Example 13.1, assume that observations larger than 7.4 are censored. Compare the estimated df based on the MLE under the Weibull assumption against the Kaplan-Meier estimate.

Solution 13.3 In the data set three observations are larger than 7.4 and are censored. The plots of the Kaplan-Meier estimate and the estimated df using the MLE of the Weibull model are given in Figure 13.3. For the Kaplan-Meier estimate we also plot the lower and upper bounds of the 95% confidence interval estimates of the df. It can be seen that the estimated parametric df falls inside the band of the estimated Kaplan-Meier estimate. □

For grouped data, the raw sample data may be summarized using a histogram, which may be compared against the pdf of a hypothesized or parametrically fitted model. For estimation using MLE, the log-likelihood given by equation (12.22) should be used. If the method of moments is adopted, the sample moments are those of the empirical distribution, as given by equation (11.80). These moments are then equated to the population moments and the model parameter estimates are computed.

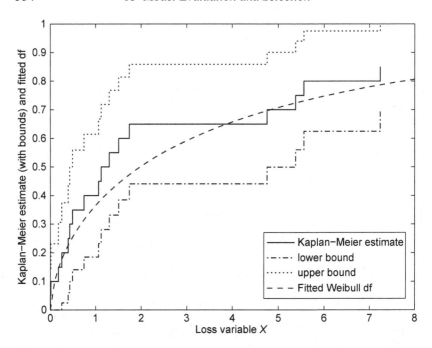

Figure 13.3 Estimated Kaplan-Meier df and estimated Weibull df of Example 13.3

Example 13.4 A sample of grouped observations of losses are summarized as follows, with notations given in Section 11.3:

$(c_{j-1}, c_j]$	(0, 6]	(6, 12]	(12, 18]	(18, 24]	(24, 30]	(30, 50]
n_j	15	45	45	20	15	10

Assuming the losses are distributed as $\mathcal{G}(\alpha, \beta)$, estimate α and β using the MLE and the method of moments.

Solution 13.4 To compute the method-of-moments estimates, we first calculate the sample moments. We have

$$\hat{\mu}_1 = \sum_{j=1}^{6} \frac{n_j}{n} \left[\frac{c_j + c_{j-1}}{2} \right] = 15.6667$$

and

$$\hat{\mu}_2 = \sum_{j=1}^{6} \frac{n_j}{n} \left[\frac{c_j^3 - c_{j-1}^3}{3(c_j - c_{j-1})} \right] = 336.0889.$$

Thus, from Example 12.2, we have

$$\tilde{\beta} = \frac{336.0889 - (15.6667)^2}{15.6667} = 5.7857$$

and

$$\tilde{\alpha} = \frac{15.6667}{5.7857} = 2.7078.$$

The variance of this distribution is 90.6418. On the other hand, using the log-likelihood function of the grouped data as given in equation (12.22), the MLE of α and β are computed as[2]

$$\hat{\alpha} = 3.2141 \quad \text{and} \quad \hat{\beta} = 4.8134.$$

The mean and variance of this distribution are 15.4707 and 74.4669, respectively. Thus, the mean of the two estimated distributions are similar, while the variance of the distribution estimated by the MLE is much lower. $\qquad \square$

13.2 Misspecification Tests and Diagnostic Checks

While graphical methods are able to provide visual aids to assess whether a model fits the data, they do not provide *quantitative measures* about any possible deviations that are not commensurate with the hypothesized model. A formal **significance test** has the advantage of providing a probabilistic assessment of whether a decision concerning the model is likely to be wrong.

A formal significance test may be set up by establishing a **null hypothesis** about the distribution of the losses. This hypothesis is tested against the data using a **test statistic**. Given an assigned **level of significance**, we can determine a **critical region** such that if the test statistic falls inside the critical region, we conclude that the data do not support the null hypothesis. Alternatively, we can compute the probability of obtaining a test statistic more *extreme* than the computed value if the null hypothesis is correct, and call this value the *p*-**value**. The smaller the *p*-value, the more unlikely it is that the null hypothesis is correct. We call statistical significance tests that aim at examining the model's distributional assumptions **misspecification tests**. They are also **diagnostic checks** for the model assumption before we use the model for pricing or other analysis.

In this section, we discuss several misspecification tests for the model assumptions of loss distributions.

---

[2] Note that c_6 is now taken as ∞ for the computation of the log-likelihood.

13.2.1 Kolmogorov–Smirnov Test

We specify a null hypothesis about the df of a continuous loss variable, and denote it by $F^*(\cdot)$. To examine if the data support the null hypothesis, we compare $F^*(\cdot)$ against the empirical df $\hat{F}(\cdot)$ and consider the statistic

$$\max_{x_{(1)} \leq x \leq x_{(n)}} |\hat{F}(x) - F^*(x)|, \tag{13.1}$$

where $x_{(1)}$ and $x_{(n)}$ are the minimum and maximum of the observations, respectively. However, as $\hat{F}(\cdot)$ is a right-continuous increasing step function and $F^*(\cdot)$ is also increasing, we only need to compare the differences at the observed data points, namely, at the order statistics $x_{(1)} \leq x_{(2)} \leq \cdots \leq x_{(n)}$. Furthermore, the maximum may only occur at a jump point $x_{(i)}$ or immediately to the left of it. We now denote the statistic in expression (13.1) by D, which is called the **Kolmogorov–Smirnov statistic** and can be written as[3]

$$D = \max_{i \in \{1,\ldots,n\}} \left\{ \max \left\{ |\hat{F}(x_{(i-1)}) - F^*(x_{(i)})|, |\hat{F}(x_{(i)}) - F^*(x_{(i)})| \right\} \right\}, \tag{13.2}$$

where $\hat{F}(x_{(0)}) \equiv 0$. When we have complete individual observations,

$$\hat{F}(x_{(i)}) = \frac{i}{n}, \tag{13.3}$$

and D can be written as

$$D = \max_{i \in \{1,\ldots,n\}} \left\{ \max \left\{ \left| \frac{i-1}{n} - F^*(x_{(i)}) \right|, \left| \frac{i}{n} - F^*(x_{(i)}) \right| \right\} \right\}. \tag{13.4}$$

If the true df of the data is not $F^*(\cdot)$, we would expect D to be large. Given a level of significance α, the null hypothesis that the data have df $F^*(\cdot)$ is rejected if D is larger than the critical value. When $F^*(\cdot)$ is completely specified (as in the case where there is no unknown parameter in the df) the critical values of D for some selected values of α are given as follows:

Level of significance α	0.10	0.05	0.01
Critical value	$\dfrac{1.22}{\sqrt{n}}$	$\dfrac{1.36}{\sqrt{n}}$	$\dfrac{1.63}{\sqrt{n}}$

Note that the critical values above apply to all df, as long as they are completely specified. Any unknown parameters in the df, however, have to be estimated for the computation of $F^*(x_{(i)})$. Then the critical values above will

---

[3] The Kolmogorov–Smirnov statistic was proposed by Kolmogorov in 1933 and developed by Smirnov in 1939.

not apply. There are, however, some critical values in the literature that are estimated using Monte Carlo methods for different null distributions with unknown parameter values.[4]

When the data are left truncated at point d or right censored at point u, the statistic in (13.1) is modified to

$$\max_{d \leq x \leq u} | \hat{F}(x) - F^*(x) |. \tag{13.5}$$

Equation (13.2) still applies, and the order statistics are within the range (d, u). If some parameters have to be estimated, one of the methods in Chapter 12 can be used. When the observations are not complete, the critical values should be revised downward. The actual value used, however, has to be estimated by Monte Carlo methods.

Example 13.5 Compute the Kolmogorov–Smirnov statistics for the data in Example 13.1, with the estimated Weibull and gamma models as the hypothesized distributions.

Solution 13.5 We denote $F_1^*(x_{(j)})$ as the df of $\mathcal{W}(0.6548, 2.3989)$ evaluated at $x_{(j)}$, and $F_2^*(x_{(j)})$ as the df of $\mathcal{G}(0.5257, 5.9569)$ evaluated at $x_{(j)}$, which are the df of the estimated Weibull and gamma distributions in Example 13.1. We further denote

$$D_{ij} = \max \left\{ \left| \hat{F}(x_{(j-1)}) - F_i^*(x_{(j)}) \right|, \left| \hat{F}(x_{(j)}) - F_i^*(x_{(j)}) \right| \right\},$$

for $i = 1, 2,$ and $j = 1, \ldots, 20$. Note that

$$\hat{F}(x_{(j)}) = \frac{j}{20},$$

as we have complete individual data. See R Codes 13.1 for the computation. The Kolmogorov–Smirnov statistics D for the Weibull and gamma distributions are 0.1410 and 0.1313, respectively, both occurring at $x_{(14)}$. The critical value of D at the level of significance of 10% is

$$\frac{1.22}{\sqrt{20}} = 0.2728,$$

which is larger than the computed D for both models. However, as the hypothesized df are estimated, the critical value has to be adjusted. Monte Carlo methods can be used to estimate the p-value of the tests, which will be discussed in Chapter 15. □

---

[4] See Stephens (1974) for some critical values estimated by Monte Carlo methods.

13.2.2 Anderson–Darling Test

Similar to the Kolmogorov–Smirnov test, the **Anderson–Darling test** can be
used to test for the null hypothesis that the variable of interest has the df $F^*(\cdot)$.[5]
Assuming we have complete and individual observations arranged in the order
$x_{(1)} \leq x_{(2)} \leq \cdots \leq x_{(n)}$, the Anderson–Darling statistic, denoted by A^2, is
defined as

$$A^2 = -\frac{1}{n} \left[\sum_{j=1}^{n} (2j-1) \left\{ \log \left[F^*(x_{(j)}) \right] + \log \left[1 - F^*(x_{(n+1-j)}) \right] \right\} \right] - n.$$

(13.6)

If $F^*(\cdot)$ is fully specified with no unknown parameters, the critical values of
A^2 are 1.933, 2.492 and 3.857 for level of significance $\alpha = 0.10, 0.05$ and 0.01,
respectively. Also, critical values are available for certain distributions with
unknown parameters. Otherwise, they may be estimated using Monte Carlo
methods.

Example 13.6 Compute the Anderson–Darling statistics for the data in Example 13.1, with the estimated Weibull and gamma models as the hypothesized
distributions.

Solution 13.6 The statistics computed using equation (13.6) are 0.3514 and
0.3233, respectively, for the fitted Weibull and gamma distributions. These values are much lower than the critical value of 1.933 at $\alpha = 0.10$. However, as
parameters are estimated for the hypothesized distributions, the true critical
values would be lower. The p-values of the tests can be estimated using Monte
Carlo methods.   □

13.2.3 Chi-Square Goodness-of-Fit Test

The chi-square goodness-of-fit test is applicable to grouped data. Suppose the
sample observations are classified into the intervals $(0, c_1], (c_1, c_2], \ldots, (c_{k-1}, \infty)$,
with n_j observations in $(c_{j-1}, c_j]$ such that $\sum_{j=1}^{k} n_j = n$. The expected number
of observations in $(c_{j-1}, c_j]$ based on $F^*(\cdot)$ is

$$e_j = n \left[F^*(c_j) - F^*(c_{j-1}) \right].$$

(13.7)

To test the null hypothesis that the df $F^*(\cdot)$ fits the data, we define the chi-square
goodness-of-fit statistic X^2 as

$$X^2 = \sum_{j=1}^{k} \frac{(e_j - n_j)^2}{e_j} = \left(\sum_{j=1}^{k} \frac{n_j^2}{e_j} \right) - n.$$

(13.8)

---

[5] This test was introduced by Anderson and Darling in 1952.

Table 13.1. *Results for Example 13.7*

$(c_{j-1}, c_j]$	(0, 6]	(6, 12]	(12, 18]	(18, 24]	(24, 30]	(30, ∞)
n_j	15	45	45	20	15	10
gamma	15.30	45.10	41.35	25.50	12.90	9.85
Weibull	18.40	40.10	40.35	28.00	14.60	8.55

If $F^*(\cdot)$ is fully specified with no unknown parameters, X^2 is approximately distributed as a χ^2_{k-1} (chi-square distribution with $k-1$ degrees of freedom) under the null hypothesis when n is large. For the test to work well, we also require the expected number of observations in each class to be not smaller than 5. If the parameters of $F^*(\cdot)$ are estimated using the **multinomial MLE (MMLE)**, then the asymptotic distribution of X^2 is χ^2_{k-r-1}, where r is the number of parameters estimated. To compute the multinomial MLE, we use the log-likelihood function

$$\log L(\theta; \boldsymbol{n}) = \sum_{j=1}^{k} n_j \log \left[F^*(\theta; c_j) - F^*(\theta; c_{j-1}) \right],$$ (13.9)

where θ is the r-element parameter vector. The log-likelihood $\log L(\theta; \boldsymbol{n})$ is maximized with respect to θ to obtain $\hat{\theta}$.[6] The expected frequency e_j in interval $(c_{j-1}, c_j]$ is then given by

$$e_j = n [F^*(\hat{\theta}; c_j) - F^*(\hat{\theta}; c_{j-1})].$$ (13.10)

Example 13.7 For the data in Example 13.4, compute the chi-square goodness-of-fit statistic assuming the loss distribution is (a) $\mathcal{G}(\alpha, \beta)$ and (b) $\mathcal{W}(\alpha, \lambda)$. In each case, estimate the parameters using the multinomial MLE.

Solution 13.7 The multinomial MLE for the $\mathcal{G}(\alpha, \beta)$ assumption can be found in Example 13.4. We estimate the Weibull case using the multinomial MLE method to obtain the distribution $\mathcal{W}(1.9176, 17.3222)$. For each of the fitted distributions, the expected frequencies are computed and compared alongside the observed frequencies in each interval. The results are given in Table 13.1. Thus, for the gamma distribution, the chi-square statistic is

$$X^2 = \frac{(15)^2}{15.30} + \frac{(45)^2}{45.10} + \frac{(45)^2}{41.35} + \frac{(20)^2}{25.50} + \frac{(15)^2}{12.90} + \frac{(10)^2}{9.85} - 150 = 1.847.$$

---

[6] Note that if the parameters are estimated by MLE using individual observations, X^2 is *not* asymptotically distributed as a χ^2. This was pointed out by Chernoff and Lehmann in 1954. Specifically, X^2 is bounded between the χ^2_{k-1} and χ^2_{k-r-1} distributions. See DeGroot and Schervish (2002, p. 547), for more details.

Similarly, the X^2 statistic for the fitted Weibull distribution is 4.298. The degrees of freedom of the test statistics is $6 - 2 - 1 = 3$ for both fitted distributions, and the critical value of the test statistic at the 5% level of significance is $\chi^2_{3,\,0.95} = 7.815$. Thus, both the gamma and Weibull assumptions cannot be rejected for the loss distribution.   □

13.2.4 Likelihood Ratio Test

The likelihood ratio test compares two hypotheses, one of which is a special case of the other in the sense that the parameters of the model are stated to satisfy some constraints. The unconstrained model is the **alternative hypothesis,** and the model under the parametric constraints is the **null hypothesis.** Thus, the null hypothesis is said to be **nested** within the alternative hypothesis. The constraints imposed on the parameter vector θ can be zero restrictions (i.e., some of the parameters in θ are zero), linear restrictions or nonlinear restrictions. Let $\hat{\theta}_U$ denote the unrestricted MLE under the alternative hypothesis, $\hat{\theta}_R$ denote the restricted MLE under the null hypothesis and r denote the number of restrictions. The unrestricted and restricted maximized likelihoods are denoted by $L(\hat{\theta}_U, x)$ and $L(\hat{\theta}_R, x)$, respectively. The **likelihood ratio statistic**, denoted by ℓ, is defined as

$$\ell = 2 \log \left[\frac{L(\hat{\theta}_U, x)}{L(\hat{\theta}_R, x)} \right] = 2 \left[\log L(\hat{\theta}_U, x) - \log L(\hat{\theta}_R, x) \right]. \qquad (13.11)$$

As $\hat{\theta}_U$ and $\hat{\theta}_R$ are the unrestricted and restricted maxima, $L(\hat{\theta}_U, x) \geq L(\hat{\theta}_R, x)$. If the restrictions under the null are true, we would expect the difference between $L(\hat{\theta}_U, x)$ and $L(\hat{\theta}_R, x)$ to be small. Thus, a large discrepancy between $L(\hat{\theta}_U, x)$ and $L(\hat{\theta}_R, x)$ is an indication that the null hypothesis is incorrect. Hence, we should reject the null hypothesis for large values of ℓ. Furthermore, when the null is true, ℓ converges to a χ^2_r distribution as the sample size n tends to ∞. Thus, the decision rule of the test is to reject the null hypothesis (i.e., conclude the restrictions do not hold) if $\ell > \chi^2_{r,\,1-\alpha}$ at level of significance α, where $\chi^2_{r,\,1-\alpha}$ is the $100(1 - \alpha)$-percentile of the χ^2_r distribution.

Example 13.8 For the data in Example 13.1, estimate the loss distribution assuming it is exponential. Test the exponential assumption against the gamma assumption using the likelihood ratio test.

Solution 13.8 The exponential distribution is a special case of the $\mathcal{G}(\alpha, \beta)$ distribution with $\alpha = 1$. For the alternative hypothesis of a gamma distribution where α is not restricted, the fitted distribution is $\mathcal{G}(0.5257, 5.9569)$ and the log-likelihood is

$$\log L(\hat{\theta}_U, \mathbf{x}) = -39.2017.$$

The MLE of λ for the $\mathcal{E}(\lambda)$ distribution is $1/\bar{x}$ (or the estimate of β in $\mathcal{G}(\alpha, \beta)$ with $\alpha = 1$ is $\bar{x}$). Now $\bar{x} = 3.1315$ and the maximized restricted log-likelihood is

$$\log L(\hat{\theta}_R, \mathbf{x}) = -42.8305.$$

Thus, the likelihood ratio statistic is

$$\ell = 2(42.8305 - 39.2017) = 7.2576.$$

As $\chi^2_{1,0.95} = 3.841 < 7.2576$, the null hypothesis of $\alpha = 1$ is rejected at the 5% level of significance. Thus, the exponential distribution is not supported by the data. $\square$

Example 13.9 For the data in Example 13.1, estimate the loss distribution assuming it is $\mathcal{W}(0.5, \lambda)$. Test this assumption against the unrestricted $\mathcal{W}(\alpha, \lambda)$ alternative using the likelihood ratio test.

Solution 13.9 The unrestricted Weibull model is computed in Example 13.1, for which the fitted model is $\mathcal{W}(0.6548, 2.3989)$. The log-likelihood of this model is -39.5315. Under the restriction of $\alpha = 0.5$, λ is estimated to be 2.0586, and the log-likelihood is -40.5091. Thus, the likelihood ratio statistic is

$$\ell = 2(40.5091 - 39.5315) = 1.9553,$$

which is smaller than $\chi^2_{1,0.95} = 3.841$. Hence, at the 5% level of significance there is no evidence to reject $\alpha = 0.5$ against the alternative hypothesis that the loss distribution is $\mathcal{W}(\alpha, \lambda)$. $\square$

We have discussed four diagnostic checks for modeling. The likelihood ratio test is a general testing approach for restrictions on a model. We may use it to test if the model can be simplified to have a smaller number of unknown parameters. This approach, however, adopts the alternative hypothesis as the maintained model, which is itself not tested. The other three tests, namely, the Kolmogorov–Smirnov test, the Anderson–Darling test and the chi-square goodness-of-fit test, are for testing the fit of a model to the data.

If there are two or more possible models that are non-nested, we may begin by determining if each of these models can be simplified. This follows the **principle of parsimony**, and can be done by testing for parametric restrictions using the likelihood ratio test. The smaller models that are not rejected may then be tested using one of the three misspecification tests. If the final outcome is that only one of the models is not rejected, this model will be adopted. In circumstances when more than one model are not rejected, the decision would not be straightforward. Factors such as model parsimony, prior information and simplicity of theoretical analysis have to be considered. We may also use information criteria for model selection, which helps to identify the model to be adopted.

13.3 Information Criteria for Model Selection

When two non-nested models are compared, the larger model with more parameters has the advantage of being able to fit the in-sample data with a more flexible function and thus possibly a larger log-likelihood. To compare models on more equal terms, **penalized log-likelihood** may be adopted. The **Akaike information criterion**, denoted by AIC, proposes to penalize large models by adding the number of parameters in the model to the negative of its log-likelihood. Thus, AIC is defined as[7]

$$\text{AIC} = -\log L(\hat{\theta};x) + p, \tag{13.12}$$

where $\log L(\hat{\theta};x)$ is the log-likelihood evaluated at the MLE $\hat{\theta}$ and p is the number of estimated parameters in the model. Based on this approach, the model with the smallest AIC is selected.

Although intuitively easy to understand, the AIC has an undesirable property. Consider two models $\mathcal{M}_1$ and $\mathcal{M}_2$, so that $\mathcal{M}_1 \subset \mathcal{M}_2$. That is, $\mathcal{M}_1$ is a smaller model and is nested by $\mathcal{M}_2$. Then, using AIC, the probability of choosing $\mathcal{M}_1$ when it is true converges to a number that is strictly less than 1 when the sample size tends to infinity. In this sense, we say that the Akaike information criterion is *inconsistent*. On the other hand, if the true model belongs to $\mathcal{M}_2 - \mathcal{M}_1$ (i.e., $\mathcal{M}_1$ is not correct, but the true model lies in $\mathcal{M}_2$), then the probability of rejecting $\mathcal{M}_1$ under AIC converges to 1. Hence, the problem of not being able to identify the true model even when we have very large samples occurs when the smaller model is correct.

The above problem of the AIC can be corrected by imposing a different penalty on the log-likelihood. The **Schwarz information criterion**, also called the **Bayesian information criterion**, denoted by BIC, is defined as

$$\text{BIC} = -\log L(\hat{\theta};x) + \frac{p}{2}\log n. \tag{13.13}$$

Thus, compared to the AIC, heavier penalty is placed on larger models when $\log n > 2$, i.e., $n > 8$. Again, the model with the smallest BIC is selected. Unlike the AIC, the BIC is consistent in the sense that the probability it will choose the smaller model when it is true converges to 1 when the sample size tends to

---

[7] Note that exams of the Society of Actuaries define AIC and BIC as the negative of the expressions in equations (13.12) and (13.13), respectively. The model selection rules are thus reversed. Hastie *et al.* (2009) define AIC as two times the expression in equation (13.12) per observation. James *et al.* (2015) provide further discussions on the AIC and BIC, as well as other model selection criteria.

Table 13.2. *Results for Example 13.10*

Model	$\log L(\hat{\theta};x)$	AIC	BIC
$\mathcal{W}(\alpha,\lambda)$	-39.5315	41.5315	42.5272
$\mathcal{W}(0.5,\lambda)$	-40.5091	41.5091	42.0070
$\mathcal{G}(\alpha,\beta)$	-39.2017	41.2017	42.1974
$\mathcal{G}(1,\beta)$	-42.8305	43.8305	45.3284

infinity. Also, as for the case of the AIC, if the true model belongs to $\mathcal{M}_2 - \mathcal{M}_1$, the probability of rejecting $\mathcal{M}_1$ under BIC also converges to 1.

Example 13.10 For the data in Example 13.1, consider the following models: (a) $\mathcal{W}(\alpha,\lambda)$, (b) $\mathcal{W}(0.5,\lambda)$, (c) $\mathcal{G}(\alpha,\beta)$ and (d) $\mathcal{G}(1,\beta)$. Compare these models using AIC and BIC, and comment on your choice of model.

Solution 13.10 The MLE of the four models, as well as their maximized log-likelihood, appear in previous examples. Table 13.2 summarizes the results and the values of the AIC and BIC.

AIC is minimized for the $\mathcal{G}(\alpha,\beta)$ model, giving a value of 41.2017. BIC is minimized for the $\mathcal{W}(0.5,\lambda)$ model, giving a value of 42.0070. Based on the BIC, $\mathcal{W}(0.5,\lambda)$ is the preferred model. □

13.4 R Laboratory

R Codes 13.1 provides the codes to plot the empirical distribution function against the fitted parametric distribution functions of the Weibull and gamma distributions in Example 13.1. The models are fitted by maximum likelihood estimation. The empirical distribution function is computed using the function ecdf. Note that the third argument in pgamma is the parameter rate, which is the reciprocal of the scale parameter β.

```
#####################################################################
# R Codes 13.1
#
# Example 13.1: Empirical df and fitted parametric df (Figure 13.1)
#####################################################################

x=c(0.003,0.012,0.180,0.253,0.394,0.430,0.491,0.743,1.066,1.126,
    1.303,1.508,1.740,4.757,5.376,5.557,7.236,7.465,8.054,14.938)
xx=seq(0,15,0.01)
```

```
plot(ecdf(x),verticals=TRUE,do.p=FALSE,main=
   "Empirical df and fitted parametric df",cex.main=0.8,xlim=c(0,15),
   xlab="Loss variable X",ylab="Empirical and Fitted df",cex.lab=0.8)
lines(xx,pweibull(xx,0.6548,2.3989),lty=3)          # df of Weibull
lines(xx,pgamma(xx,0.5257,1/5.9569),lty=4,col="red")  # df of gamma
legend("bottomright",c("Empirical df","Fitted Weibull df",
   "Fitted gamma df"),lty=c(1,3,4),col=c("black","black","red"),
   cex=0.6)
```

R Codes 13.2 provides the codes to compute the Kolmogorov–Smirnov statistics of the fitted Weibull and gamma distributions in Example 13.5. We use the function pmax to compute the pairwise maximum (see equation (13.4)).

```
################################################################
# R Codes 13.2
#
# Example 13.5: Computation of the Kolmogorov--Smirnov statistic
################################################################

n=length(x)                                # x as in R Codes 13.1
edf=(1:n)/n
edf1=c(0,(1:(n-1))/n)
webdf=pweibull(x,0.6548,2.3989)            # df of fitted Weibull
gamdf=pgamma(x,0.5257,1/5.9569)            # df of fitted gamma
ksweb=max(pmax(abs(edf-webdf),abs(edf1-webdf)))  # KS stat for Weibull
ksgam=max(pmax(abs(edf-gamdf),abs(edf1-gamdf)))  # KS stat for gamma
c(ksweb,ksgam)                             # Output KS statistics
which.max(pmax(abs(edf-webdf),abs(edf1-webdf)))  # Max index for Weibull
which.max(pmax(abs(edf-gamdf),abs(edf1-gamdf)))  # Max index for gamma
```

13.5 Summary and Discussions

We have reviewed some methods for evaluating a fitted model for loss distributions. Graphical tools such as a plot of the estimated df against the empirical df, the *p-p* plot and the *q-q* plot can be used to assess the fit of the model. The key point is to identify if there is any systematic deviation of the parametrically tted model from the sample data.

The likelihood ratio test is applicable to test for parametric restrictions. The purpose is to examine if a bigger and more general model can be reduced to a smaller model in which some parameters take certain specific values. Misspecification tests for the fitness of a hypothesized distribution, whether the parameters are fully specified or subject to estimation, can be performed using the Kolmogorov–Smirnov test, the Anderson–Darling test and the chi-square goodness-of-fit test. When more than one model passes the diagnostic checks, model selection may require additional criteria, such as the principle of parsimony and other considerations. Information selection criteria such as the Akaike and Schwarz information criteria provide quantitative rules for model selection. The Schwarz information criterion has the advantage that it is consistent, while the Akaike information criterion is not.

Exercises

Exercise 13.1 You are given the following loss observations, which are assumed to follow an exponential distribution:

$$2, 5, 6, 9, 14, 18, 23.$$

The model is fitted using the maximum likelihood method.

(a) A p-p plot is constructed, with the sample proportion p_i of the ith order statistic computed as $i/(n + 1)$, where n is the sample size. What are the coordinates of the p-p plot?
(b) Repeat (a) above if p_i is computed as $(i - 0.5)/n$.
(c) Repeat (a) above if the observation "5" is corrected to "6," and the repeated observation is treated as the 2nd- and 3rd-order statistics.
(d) Repeat (b) above if the observation "5" is corrected to "6," and the repeated observation is treated as the 2nd- and 3rd-order statistics.

Exercise 13.2 You are given the following loss observations, which are assumed to come from a $\mathcal{G}(5, 6)$ distribution:

$$12, 15, 18, 21, 23, 28, 32, 38, 45, 58.$$

(a) A q-q plot is constructed, with the sample proportion p_i of the ith order statistic computed as $i/(n + 1)$, where n is the sample size. What are the coordinates of the q-q plot?
(b) Repeat (a) above if the sample proportion is computed as $(i - 0.5)/n$.

Exercise 13.3 Suppose X follows an exponential distribution. A point on the p-p plot of a random sample of X is (0.2, 0.24), and its corresponding coordinates in the q-q plot is $(x, 23.6)$. Determine the value of x.

Exercise 13.4 Suppose X follows a $\mathcal{P}(5, \gamma)$ distribution. A point on the p-p plot of a random sample of X is $(0.246, p)$, and its corresponding coordinates in the q-q plot is (45.88, 54.62). Determine the value of p.

Exercise 13.5 You are given the following observations from a $\mathcal{G}(\alpha, \beta)$ distribution:

$$0.4, 1.8, 2.6, 3.5, 5.4, 6.7, 8.9, 15.5, 18.9, 19.5, 24.6.$$

Estimate the distribution using the method of moments and compute the Kolmogorov–Smirnov statistic of the sample (see R Codes 13.2). What is your conclusion regarding the assumption of the gamma distribution?

Exercise 13.6 Use the data in Exercise 13.5, now assuming the observations are distributed as $\mathcal{W}(\alpha, \lambda)$. Estimate the parameters of the Weibull distribution by matching the 25th and 75th percentiles. Compute the Kolmogorov–Smirnov statistic of the fitted data. What is your conclusion regarding the assumption of the Weibull distribution?

Exercise 13.7 Compute the Anderson–Darling statistic for the $\mathcal{G}(\alpha, \beta)$ distribution fitted to the data in Exercise 13.5. What is your conclusion regarding the assumption of the gamma distribution?

Exercise 13.8 Compute the Anderson–Darling statistic for the fitted $\mathcal{W}(\alpha, \lambda)$ distribution in Exercise 13.6. What is your conclusion regarding the assumption of the Weibull distribution?

Questions Adapted from SOA Exams

Exercise 13.9 A particular line of business has three types of claims. The historical probability and the number of claims for each type in the current year are:

Type	Historical probability	Number of claims in current year
A	0.2744	112
B	0.3512	180
C	0.3744	138

You test the null hypothesis that the probability of each type of claim in the current year is the same as the historical probability. Determine the chi-square goodness-of-fit statistic.

Exercise 13.10 You fit a $\mathcal{P}(\alpha, \gamma)$ distribution to a sample of 200 claim amounts and use the likelihood ratio test to test the hypothesis that $\alpha = 1.5$ and $\gamma = 7.8$. The maximum likelihood estimates are $\hat{\alpha} = 1.4$ and $\hat{\gamma} = 7.6$. The log-likelihood function evaluated at the maximum likelihood estimates is -817.92, and $\sum_{i=1}^{200} \log(x_i + 7.8) = 607.64$. Determine the results of the test.

Exercise 13.11 A sample of claim payments is: 29, 64, 90, 135 and 182. Claim sizes are assumed to follow an exponential distribution, and the mean of the exponential distribution is estimated using the method of moments. Compute the Kolmogorov–Smirnov statistic.

Exercise 13.12 You are given the following observed claim-frequency data collected over a period of 365 days:

Number of claims per day	Observed number of days
0	50
1	122
2	101
3	92
≥ 4	0

The Poisson model is fitted using the maximum likelihood method, and the data are regrouped into four groups: 0, 1, 2 and $\geq$ 3. Determine the results of the chi-square goodness-of-fit test for the Poisson assumption.

Exercise 13.13 A computer program simulated 1,000 $\mathcal{U}(0, 1)$ variates, which were then grouped into 20 groups of equal length. If the sum of the squares of the observed frequencies in each group is 51,850, determine the results of the chi-square goodness-of-fit test for the $\mathcal{U}(0, 1)$ hypothesis.

Exercise 13.14 Twenty claim amounts are randomly selected from the $\mathcal{P}(2, \gamma)$ distribution. The maximum likelihood estimate of γ is 7. If $\sum_{i=1}^{20} \log(x_i + 7) =$ 49.01 and $\sum_{i=1}^{20} \log(x_i + 3.1) = 39.30$, determine the results of the likelihood ratio test for the hypothesis that $\gamma = 3.1$.

Exercise 13.15 A uniform kernel density estimator with bandwidth 50 is used to smooth the following workers compensation loss payments: 82, 126, 161, 294 and 384. If $F^*(x)$ denotes the kernel estimate and $\hat{F}(x)$ denotes the empirical distribution function, determine $|F^*(150) - \hat{F}(150)|$.

Exercise 13.16 The Kolmogorov–Smirnov test is used to assess the fit of the logarithmic loss to a distribution with distribution function $F^*(\cdot)$. There are $n = 200$ observations and the maximum value of $|\hat{F}(x) - F^*(x)|$, where $\hat{F}(\cdot)$ is the empirical distribution function, occurs for x between 4.26 and 4.42. You are given the following:

x	$F^*(x)$	$\hat{F}(x)$
4.26	0.584	0.510
4.30	0.599	0.515
4.35	0.613	0.520
4.36	0.621	0.525
4.39	0.636	0.530
4.42	0.638	0.535

Also, $\hat{F}(4.26^-)$, which is the empirical distribution function immediately to the left of 4.26, is 0.505. Determine the results of the test.

Exercise 13.17 Five models are fitted to a sample of 260 observations with the following results:

Model	Number of parameters	Log-likelihood
1	1	414
2	2	412
3	3	411
4	4	409
5	6	409

Which model will be selected based on the Schwarz Bayesian criterion? Which will be selected based on the Akaike Information criterion?

Exercise 13.18 A random sample of five observations is: 0.2, 0.7, 0.9, 1.1 and 1.3. The Kolmogorov–Smirnov test is used to test the null hypothesis that the probability density function of the population is

$$f(x) = \frac{4}{(1+x)^5}, \quad x > 0.$$

Determine the results of the test.

Exercise 13.19 You test the hypothesis that a given set of data comes from a known distribution with distribution function $F(x)$. The following data were collected (x_i is the upper end point of the interval):

Interval	$F(x_i)$	Number of observations
$x < 2$	0.035	5
$2 \leq x < 5$	0.130	42
$5 \leq x < 7$	0.630	137
$7 \leq x < 8$	0.830	66
$8 \leq x$	1.000	50

Determine the results of the chi-square goodness-of-fit test.

Exercise 13.20 One thousand workers insured under a workers compensation policy were observed for one year. The number of work days missed is given below

Number of days missed	Number of workers
0	818
1	153
2	25
≥ 3	4

The total number of days missed is 230 and a Poisson distribution is fitted, with the parameter estimated by the average number of days missed. Determine the results of the chi-square goodness-of-fit test for the model.

Exercise 13.21 A random sample of losses from a $\mathcal{W}(\alpha, \lambda)$ distribution is: 595, 700, 789, 799 and 1,109. The maximized log-likelihood function is -33.05, and the maximum likelihood estimate of λ assuming $\alpha = 2$ is 816.7. Determine the results of the likelihood ratio test for the hypothesis that $\alpha = 2$.

Exercise 13.22 A sample of claim amounts is: 400, 1,000, 1,600, 3,000, 5,000, 5,400 and 6,200. The data are hypothesized to come from the $\mathcal{E}(1/3,300)$ distribution. Let (s, t) be the coordinates of the p-p plot for claim amount 3,000, and let $D(x)$ be the empirical distribution function at x minus the hypothesized distribution function at x. Compute (s, t) and $D(3,000)$.

Exercise 13.23 You are given the following distribution of 500 claims

Claim size	Number of claims
$[0, 500)$	200
$[500, 1,000)$	110
$[1,000, 2,000)$	x
$[2,000, 5,000)$	y
$[5,000, 10,000)$	$-$
$[10,000, 25,000)$	$-$
$[25,000, \infty)$	$-$

Let $\hat{F}(\cdot)$ be the ogive computed for the sample. If $\hat{F}(1,500) = 0.689$ and $\hat{F}(3,500) = 0.839$, determine y.

Exercise 13.24 Claim size has the following probability density function

$$f(x) = \frac{\theta e^{-\frac{\theta}{x}}}{x^2}, \quad x > 0.$$

A random sample of claims is: 1, 2, 3, 5 and 13. For $\theta = 2$, compute the Kolmogorov–Smirnov statistic.

14

Basic Monte Carlo Methods

Some problems arising from loss modeling may be analytically intractable. Many of these problems, however, can be formulated in a stochastic framework, with a solution that can be estimated empirically. This approach is called Monte Carlo simulation. It involves drawing samples of observations randomly according to the distribution required, in a manner determined by the analytic problem.

To solve the stochastic problem, samples of the specified distribution have to be generated, invariably using computational algorithms. The basic random number generators required in Monte Carlo methods are for generating observations from the uniform distribution. Building upon uniform random number generators, we can generate observations from other distributions by constructing appropriate random number generators, using methods such as inverse transformation and acceptance–rejection. We survey specific random number generators for some commonly used distributions, some of which are substantially more efficient than standard methods. An alternative method of generating numbers resembling a uniformly distributed sample of observations is the quasi-random number generator or the low-discrepancy sequence.

The accuracy of the Monte Carlo estimates depends on the variance of the estimator. To speed up the convergence of the Monte Carlo estimator to the deterministic solution, we consider designs of Monte Carlo sampling schemes and estimation methods that will produce smaller variances. Methods involving the use of antithetic variable, control variable and importance sampling are discussed.

Learning Objectives

1 Generation of uniform random numbers, mixed congruential method
2 Low-discrepancy sequence
3 Inversion transformation and acceptance–rejection methods

4 Generation of specific discrete and continuous random variates
5 Generation of correlated normal random variables
6 Variance reduction techniques
7 Antithetic variable, control variable and importance sampling

14.1 Monte Carlo Simulation

Suppose $f(\cdot)$ is a smooth integrable function over the interval $[0, 1]$, and it is desired to compute the integral

$$\int_0^1 f(x)\, dx. \tag{14.1}$$

Now consider a random variable U distributed uniformly in the interval $[0, 1]$, i.e., $U \sim \mathcal{U}(0, 1)$. Then the integral in (14.1) is equal to $\mathrm{E}[f(U)]$. If the solution of (14.1) is difficult to obtain analytically, we may consider the stochastic solution of it as the mean of $f(U)$. The stochastic solution can be estimated by drawing a random sample of n observations $(u_1, \ldots, u_n)$ from U, and the computed estimate is given by

$$\hat{\mathrm{E}}\,[f(U)] = \frac{1}{n} \sum_{i=1}^n f(u_i). \tag{14.2}$$

By the law of large numbers, $\hat{\mathrm{E}}[f(U)]$ converges to $\mathrm{E}[f(U)]$ when n tends to ∞. Thus, provided the sample size is sufficiently large, the stochastic solution can be made very close to the deterministic solution, at least in probabilistic sense.

There are many deterministic problems that can be formulated in a stochastic framework, such as the solution of differential equations and eigen-value systems. Von Neumann and Ulam coined the use of the term **Monte Carlo method** to describe this technique, which requires the generation of observations as random numbers produced by a computer. This technique can also be extended to study the solution of any simulated stochastic process (not necessarily with a deterministic counterpart), called **statistical simulation**. While some authors require the term simulation to describe a process evolving over time, we would not make this distinction and will treat Monte Carlo method and simulation as synonymous.[1]

Equation (14.2) requires samples of uniform random numbers. Indeed, the generation of uniform random numbers is a main component of a Monte Carlo study. We shall review methods of generating uniform random numbers using congruential algorithms. However, there are problems for which we require

---

[1] See Kennedy and Gentle (1980) and Herzog and Lord (2002) for further discussions of the historical developments of Monte Carlo simulation methods.

random numbers from other distributions. General methods to generate random numbers for an arbitrary distribution using uniform random numbers will be discussed. These include the inverse transformation method and the acceptance–rejection method. As the Monte Carlo method provides an estimated answer to the solution, we shall study its accuracy, which obviously depend on the Monte Carlo sample size. We will also discuss methods to improve the accuracy of the Monte Carlo estimate, or reduce its variance. Techniques such as antithetic variable, control variable and importance sampling will be discussed.

14.2 Uniform Random Number Generators

Independent random variates from the $\mathcal{U}(0, 1)$ distribution can be generated in the computer by dividing random integers in the interval $[0, m)$ by m, where m is a large number. An important method for generating sequences of random integers is the use of the congruential algorithm. We first define the expression

$$y \equiv z \pmod{m}, \tag{14.3}$$

where m is an integer, and y and z are integer-valued expressions, to mean that there exists an integer k, such that

$$z = mk + y. \tag{14.4}$$

This also means that y is the remainder when z is divided by m. The **mixed-congruential method** of generating a sequence of random integers x_i is defined by the equation

$$x_{i+1} \equiv (ax_i + c) \pmod{m}, \qquad \text{for } i = 0, 1, 2, \ldots, \tag{14.5}$$

where a is the **multiplier**, c is the **increment** and m is the **modulus**. The mixed-congruential method requires the restrictions: $m > 0, 0 < a < m$ and $0 \leq c < m$. When $c = 0$, the method is said to be **multiplicative-congruential**.

The integers produced from equation (14.5) are in the interval $[0, m)$. To generate numbers in the interval $[0, 1)$ we divide them by m. To start the sequence of x_i, we need a **seed** x_0. Given the seed x_0, the sequence of numbers x_i is completely determined. However, for appropriately chosen parameters of the congruential algorithm, the sequence will *appear* to be *random*. Indeed, random numbers generated by computer algorithms usually follow deterministic sequences, and are called **pseudo-random numbers**. Such sequences, however, pass stringent tests for randomness and may be regarded as random for practical purposes, i.e.,

$$\frac{x_i}{m} \sim \text{iid } \mathcal{U}(0, 1), \qquad \text{for } i = 1, 2, \ldots. \tag{14.6}$$

Given a seed x_0, when the algorithm produces a value $x_k = x_h$ for certain integers h and k, such that $k > h \geq 0$, the sequence will start to repeat itself. We define the **period of the seed** as the shortest subsequence of numbers, which, by repeating itself, forms the complete sequence generated. Note that given an algorithm, different seeds generally have different periods. The **period of the generator** is the *largest* period among all seeds. Naturally, it is desirable to have pseudo-random number generators with long periods.

Example 14.1 Consider the following mixed-congruential generator

$$x_{i+1} \equiv (3x_i + 1) \pmod{8}.$$

What is the period of (a) $x_0 = 2$ and (b) $x_0 = 4$? What is the period of the generator?

Solution 14.1 For (a), it is easy to show that the sequence of numbers generated is

$$2,\ 7,\ 6,\ 3,\ 2,\ \cdots$$

and this sequence repeats itself. Thus, the period of $x_0 = 2$ is 4. For (b), we have the sequence

$$4,\ 5,\ 0,\ 1,\ 4,\ \cdots$$

Hence, the period of $x_0 = 4$ is again 4. To summarize, for given seed values x_0, the values of x_1 are given as follows:

x_0	0	1	2	3	4	5	6	7
x_1	1	4	7	2	5	0	3	6

All seeds have period 4, and the generated sequences belong to one of the two sequences above. Thus, the period of the generator is 4. □

Congruential algorithms provide efficient methods to generate random sequences. For example, the Super-Duper algorithm has the following formula

$$x_{i+1} \equiv (69{,}069x_i + 1) \pmod{2^{32}}. \tag{14.7}$$

Another simple multiplicative-congruential generator is RANDU, which is defined by the equation[2]

$$x_{i+1} \equiv 65{,}539x_i \pmod{2^{31}}. \tag{14.8}$$

In estimating the integral over the $[0, 1]$ interval, the use of n random points in the interval $[0, 1]$ produces an estimate with a standard error of order $1/\sqrt{n}$.

---

[2] See McLeish (2005) for other congruential generators, as well as other techniques such as shuffling of generators and linear combinations of outputs of generators.

Thus, we describe the error as $O_p(1/\sqrt{n})$, meaning that for large enough n, there is a negligibly small probability of the absolute error exceeding a given bound divided by $\sqrt{n}$. Now instead of using n randomly selected numbers, we may use n *equally spaced* numbers in the interval $[0, 1]$. The use of these equally spaced numbers in equation (14.2) produces a solution for the definite integral by summing the areas of the rectangles approximating the area under the curve $f(\cdot)$. It can be shown that the error of this **numerical integration** is bounded above by a constant times $1/n$, i.e., the error is of order $O(1/n)$.[3] Indeed, if we use the **trapezoidal rule** for the numerical integration, the error is of order $O(1/n^2)$. Hence, the Monte Carlo method is not as efficient as numerical integration for integrals of one dimension.

The scenario, however, changes when we consider multidimensional integrals. For a two-dimensional integral, the error of the Monte Carlo method remains of order $O_p(1/\sqrt{n})$. Using n equally spaced points over the unit square produces distances of order $1/\sqrt{n}$ between the points. Thus, the error in the numerical integration using approximating rectangles is of order $O(1/\sqrt{n})$. In general, when the dimension of the integral is of order d and the trapezoidal rule is used for approximation, the error in numerical integration using evenly spaced points is of order $O(n^{-2/d})$. Hence, for higher dimensional integrals, numerical integration using evenly spaced points becomes unattractive.

Instead of using evenly spaced points over the d-dimensional unit hypercube, we may use **low-discrepancy sequences**. These sequences may be generated using various algorithms, many of which are based on number-theoretic results. They are also called **quasi-random numbers** or **quasi-random sequences**. The numerical integration methods using such sequences are called **quasi–Monte Carlo methods**. Like pseudo-random numbers, the quasi-random sequences are deterministic and so are the error bounds for the numerical integrals using such sequences. The objective of the quasi–Monte Carlo method is to approximate the integral as accurately as possible, and this is done by trying to avoid using repeated choices of sequences. Thus, achieving randomness is not the basic underpinning of this approach. For further details of this method, readers may refer to Boyle *et al.* (1997), Tan ad Boyle (2000) and McLeish (2005).

14.3 General Random Number Generators

In many practical applications, we may be required to generate random numbers from distributions other than $\mathcal{U}(0, 1)$. It turns out that the generation of random numbers following an arbitrary distribution can be done using uniform

---

[3] Note that there is no subscript p for this error, as its bound is deterministic.

random numbers via the inversion transformation. We first define the important **probability integral transform**, which is basically the transformation of a random variable using its distribution function.

Definition 14.1 Let X be a random variable with df $F(\cdot)$. The probability integral transform Y of X is a random variable defined by $Y = F(X)$.

Thus, the probability integral transform is just a df, where the argument is a random variable rather than a fixed number. It turns out that through the probability integral transform we can obtain a random variable that is distributed as $\mathcal{U}(0, 1)$.

Theorem 14.1 *(a) Probability integral transform theorem If X is a random variable with continuous df $F(\cdot)$, then the random variable $Y = F(X)$ is distributed as $\mathcal{U}(0, 1)$. (b) Quantile function theorem Let $F(\cdot)$ be a df, and define $F^{-1}(\cdot)$ as $F^{-1}(y) = \inf\{x : F(x) \geq y\}$, for $0 < y < 1$. If $U \sim \mathcal{U}(0, 1)$, then the df of $X = F^{-1}(U)$ is $F(\cdot)$.*

Proof For Part (a), if $F(\cdot)$ is strictly increasing, the proof is quite straightforward. In this case, for $0 < y < 1$, there exists a unique x such that $F(x) = y$. Furthermore, $Y \leq y$ if and only if $X \leq x$. Thus, if $G(\cdot)$ is the df of Y, then

$$G(y) = \Pr(Y \leq y) = \Pr(X \leq x) = F(x) = y.$$

Hence, $G(y) = y$, which implies $Y \sim \mathcal{U}(0, 1)$. For a general proof requiring $F(\cdot)$ to be continuous only, see Angus (1994).

For Part (b), we note that $X \leq x$ if and only if $U \leq F(x)$. Thus, we conclude

$$\Pr(X \leq x) = \Pr(U \leq F(x)) = F(x).$$

The last equality above is due to the fact that $U \sim \mathcal{U}(0, 1)$. Hence, the df of X is $F(\cdot)$, as required by the theorem. $\qquad\square$

14.3.1 Inversion Method

Part (b) of Theorem 14.1 provides a convenient method to generate a random number with a known df from a uniform random number generator. Provided we can invert the function $F(\cdot)$ to obtain $F^{-1}(\cdot)$, $F^{-1}(U)$ will be a random variable with df $F(\cdot)$. This is called the **inversion method** for generating a random number for an arbitrary distribution.

Example 14.2 Let X have pdf $3x^2$ for $x \in [0, 1]$. Derive an algorithm to generate X. If two random numbers distributed as $\mathcal{U}(0, 1)$ are generated as 0.4521 and 0.8747, what are the values of X generated?

Solution 14.2 We first derive the df of X, which is

$$F(x) = x^3, \qquad \text{for } 0 \leq x \leq 1.$$

Thus, inverting $F(\cdot)$, X may be generated as

$$X = U^{\frac{1}{3}}.$$

For the given values of U generated, the results for X are 0.7675 and 0.9564. □

Example 14.3 Derive algorithms to generate random numbers from the following distributions: (a) $\mathcal{W}(\alpha, \lambda)$ and (b) $\mathcal{P}(\alpha, \gamma)$.

Solution 14.3 For (a), from equation (2.36), the df of $\mathcal{W}(\alpha, \lambda)$ is

$$F(x) = 1 - \exp\left[-\left(\frac{x}{\lambda}\right)^{\alpha}\right].$$

Inverting the df, we generate X using the formula

$$X = \lambda\left[-\log\left(1 - U\right)\right]^{\frac{1}{\alpha}}.$$

As $1 - U$ is also distributed as $\mathcal{U}(0, 1)$, we can use the simplified formula

$$X = \lambda\left[-\log U\right]^{\frac{1}{\alpha}}$$

to generate $\mathcal{W}(\alpha, \lambda)$.

For (b), from equation (2.38), the df of $\mathcal{P}(\alpha, \gamma)$ is

$$F(x) = 1 - \left(\frac{\gamma}{x + \gamma}\right)^{\alpha}.$$

Thus, random numbers from $\mathcal{P}(\alpha, \gamma)$ may be generated using the equation

$$X = \gamma(U^{-\frac{1}{\alpha}} - 1).$$ □

The above examples illustrate the use of the inverse transform of the df to generate continuous random numbers. The inversion method can also be used to generate discrete or mixed-type variables. The example below provides an illustration.

Example 14.4 The ground-up loss X of an insurance policy is distributed as $\mathcal{W}(0.5, 5)$. There is a deductible of $d = 1$ and maximum covered loss of $u = 8$. Derive an algorithm to generate the loss in a loss event variable X_L using a $\mathcal{U}(0, 1)$ variate U. What are the values of X_L generated when $U = 0.8, 0.25$ and 0.5?

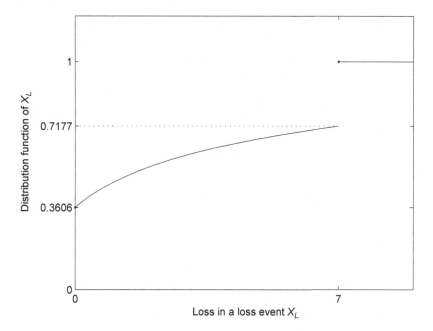

Figure 14.1 Distribution function of X_L in Example 14.4

Solution 14.4 $X_L = 0$ when $X \leq 1$. Thus,

$$F_{X_L}(0) = \Pr(X \leq 1) = \Pr(\mathcal{W}(0.5, 5) \leq 1) = 1 - \exp\left[-\left(\frac{1}{5}\right)^{0.5}\right] = 0.3606.$$

X_L is also right censored at point 7, with

$$\Pr(X_L = 7) = \Pr(X \geq 8) = \exp\left[-\left(\frac{8}{5}\right)^{0.5}\right] = 0.2823.$$

Hence, $\Pr(X_L < 7) = 1 - 0.2823 = 0.7177$, and the df of X_L is

$$F_{X_L}(x) = \begin{cases} 0.3606, & \text{for } x = 0, \\ 1 - \exp\left[-\left(\frac{x+1}{5}\right)^{0.5}\right], & \text{for } 0 < x < 7, \qquad (14.9) \\ 1, & \text{for } x \geq 7. \end{cases}$$

Thus, X_L is a mixed-type random variable, and its df is plotted in Figure 14.1.
    We may invert $F_{X_L}(x)$ as follows to generate a random variate of X_L given a $\mathcal{U}(0, 1)$ variate U

$$X_L = \begin{cases} 0, & \text{for } 0 \leq U < 0.3606, \\ 5\left[-\log\left(1 - U\right)\right]^2 - 1, & \text{for } 0.3606 \leq U < 0.7177, \qquad (14.10) \\ 7, & \text{for } 0.7177 \leq U < 1. \end{cases}$$

When $U = 0.8$, $X_L = 7$. When $U = 0.25$, $X_L = 0$. Finally, when $U = 0.5$, X_L is computed as

$$X_L = 5\left[-\log(1 - 0.5)\right]^2 - 1 = 1.4023.$$

Note that X_L can also be generated by left-truncating and right-censoring a Weibull variate computed using the inversion method. □

While the inversion method is straightforward and easy to understand, there are situations when the df cannot be inverted analytically. When this happens alternative methods may be required to provide an efficient generator of the random numbers.

14.3.2 Acceptance–Rejection Method

The acceptance–rejection method can be used for cases where the df of a random variable has no analytic form or its analytic df cannot be easily inverted (e.g., the normal distribution and the gamma distribution). Let $f(\cdot)$ be the pdf of a random variable X, the df of which cannot be easily inverted, and let Y be another random variable with pdf $q(\cdot)$, for which an easy and efficient generator is available. Assume X and Y have the same support $[a, b]$, and there exists a constant c such that $M(x) \equiv cq(x) \geq f(x)$ for $x \in [a, b]$. We now state the acceptance–rejection procedure for generating random numbers of X, followed by a proof of the validity of the procedure. The steps of the **acceptance–rejection procedure** are as follows:

1 Generate a number x from the distribution with pdf $q(\cdot)$.
2 Generate a number u independently from the $\mathcal{U}(0, 1)$ distribution.
3 If $u \leq f(x)/M(x)$, assign $z = x$, otherwise return to Step 1.

It turns out that the sequence of numbers z obtained from the above procedure have pdf $f(\cdot)$. To prove this statement we consider the df of the random variable Z generated, which is given by

$$
\begin{aligned}
\Pr(Z \leq z) &= \Pr\left(Y \leq z \mid U \leq \frac{f(Y)}{M(Y)}\right) \\
&= \frac{\int_a^z \int_0^{\frac{f(x)}{M(x)}} q(x)\, du\, dx}{\int_a^b \int_0^{\frac{f(x)}{M(x)}} q(x)\, du\, dx} \\
&= \frac{\int_a^z q(x) \left(\int_0^{\frac{f(x)}{M(x)}} du\right) dx}{\int_a^b q(x) \left(\int_0^{\frac{f(x)}{M(x)}} du\right) dx}
\end{aligned}
$$

$$= \frac{\int_a^z q(x)\frac{f(x)}{M(x)}\,dx}{\int_a^b q(x)\frac{f(x)}{M(x)}\,dx}$$

$$= \frac{\int_a^z f(x)\,dx}{\int_a^b f(x)\,dx}$$

$$= \int_a^z f(x)\,dx. \tag{14.11}$$

Note that the second to last equation above is due to the fact that $q(x)/M(x) = 1/c$ for $z \in [a, b]$, and is thus canceled out in the ratio. Finally, differentiating $\Pr(Z \le z)$ with respect to z, we obtain the pdf of Z, which is $f(\cdot)$.

The pdf $q(\cdot)$ is called the **majorizing density**, and the function $M(x) = cq(x)$ is called the **majorizing function**. The principle is to find a majorizing function that *envelopes* the pdf $f(\cdot)$ as closely as possible. For a given majorizing density $q(\cdot)$, c should be chosen to tighten the enveloping of $M(x)$ over $f(x)$, i.e, the optimum c should be

$$c = \inf\{r : rq(x) \ge f(x) \text{ for } x \in [a, b]\}. \tag{14.12}$$

However, even if the optimum c is not used the acceptance–rejection procedure stated above remains valid, albeit there is loss in efficiency.

Example 14.5 Let the pdf of X be

$$f(x) = \frac{2}{\sqrt{2\pi}}\exp\left(-\frac{x^2}{2}\right), \qquad \text{for } x \ge 0.$$

Suppose the majorizing density is selected to be

$$q(x) = e^{-x}, \qquad \text{for } x \ge 0.$$

Discuss the use of the acceptance–rejection procedure for the generation of random numbers of X.

Solution 14.5 X is obtained as the absolute value of the standard normal random variable. Inverse transformation method is intractable for this distribution. Figure 14.2 plots the pdf $f(\cdot)$ and $q(\cdot)$. The two functions cross each other. To create the optimum $cq(\cdot)$, the value of c is $\sqrt{2e/\pi} = 1.3155$.[4] However, any value of $c \ge 1.3155$ may be used to compute the majorizing function and appropriate random numbers will be produced. Figure 14.2 also shows the majorizing function with $c = 1.5$, which is not optimal.

The acceptance–rejection procedure for generating X is summarized as follows:

---

[4] We skip the technical derivation of this result, which can be proved using equation (14.12).

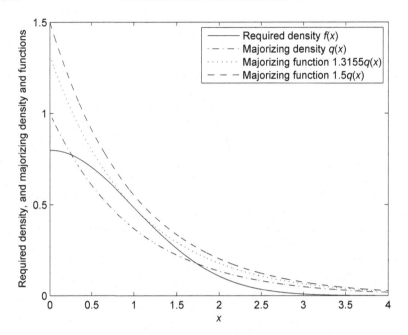

Figure 14.2 Required pdf and majorizing pdf in Example 14.5

Table 14.1. *Illustrative results for Example 14.5*

i	1	2	3	4
u	0.3489	0.9236	0.5619	0.4581
v	0.4891	0.0910	0.5047	0.9057
x	0.7152	2.3969	0.6838	0.0990
$R(x)$	1.8948	0.7438	1.8770	1.3150
Z	0.7152	reject	0.6838	0.0990

1 Generate a number x with pdf e^{-x}. This can be done by computing $x = -\log v$, where v is a random number from $\mathcal{U}(0, 1)$.
2 Generate a number u independently from $\mathcal{U}(0, 1)$.
3 For a selected value of $c \geq 1.3155$, if

$$u \leq \frac{\frac{2}{\sqrt{2\pi}} \exp\left(-\frac{x^2}{2}\right)}{c \exp(-x)} = \frac{2c}{\sqrt{2\pi}} \exp\left(-\frac{x^2}{2} + x\right) \equiv R(x),$$

assign $Z = x$. Otherwise, return to Step 1.
Table 14.1 shows a sample of values of random numbers generated using $c = 1.5$. The last row of values Z are the random numbers having pdf $f(\cdot)$. $\square$

The probability of acceptance in Step 3 of the acceptance–rejection procedure is given by

$$
\begin{aligned}
\Pr\left(U \le \frac{f(X)}{M(X)}\right) &= \int_a^b \int_0^{\frac{f(x)}{M(x)}} q(x)\, du\, dx \\
&= \int_a^b q(x) \left(\int_0^{\frac{f(x)}{M(x)}} du\right) dx \\
&= \int_a^b q(x) \frac{f(x)}{M(x)}\, dx \\
&= \frac{1}{c} \int_a^b f(x)\, dx \\
&= \frac{1}{c}.
\end{aligned}
\tag{14.13}
$$

Thus, we may use $1/c$ as a measure of the efficiency of the procedure.

14.3.3 Generation of Correlated Random Variables

In some Monte Carlo studies, we are required to generate observations that are correlated. For example, in estimating the VaR of a portfolio of assets, we may need to generate returns of the components of the portfolio, which are invariably correlated. In estimating aggregate losses of a block of insurance policies, we may need to generate loss observations that are correlated.

The correlation structure of the random numbers required depends on specific problems. We shall discuss the problem of generating samples of normal random variables that are correlated. This problem is of particular interest, as returns are often assumed to be normal in financial applications (i.e., asset prices are lognormally distributed). Also, the multivariate normal distribution has the nice property that its distribution is completely determined by its mean and variance. We shall discuss the main properties of a multivariate normal distribution, followed by methods of generating correlated multivariate normal variates.

Let $X = (X_1, \ldots, X_k)'$ be a k-element random variable. If X has a multivariate normal distribution, its joint df is completely determined by its mean vector $\mu = (\mu_1, \ldots, \mu_k)'$ and its variance matrix

$$
\Omega =
\begin{bmatrix}
\sigma_1^2 & \sigma_{12} & \cdots & \cdots & \sigma_{1k} \\
\sigma_{12} & \sigma_2^2 & \cdots & \cdots & \sigma_{2k} \\
\vdots & \vdots & \vdots & \vdots & \vdots \\
\vdots & \vdots & \vdots & \vdots & \vdots \\
\sigma_{1k} & \cdots & \cdots & \cdots & \sigma_k^2
\end{bmatrix},
\tag{14.14}
$$

where

$$\mu_i = \mathrm{E}(X_i) \quad \text{and} \quad \sigma_i^2 = \mathrm{Var}(X_i), \qquad \text{for } i = 1, \ldots, k, \tag{14.15}$$

and

$$\sigma_{ij} = \mathrm{Cov}(X_i, X_j), \qquad \text{for } i, j = 1, \ldots, k. \tag{14.16}$$

We will then write

$$X \sim \mathcal{N}(\mu, \Omega). \tag{14.17}$$

If X has a nondegenerate distribution, there exists a lower triangular $k \times k$ matrix C (i.e., the elements in the upper triangle of the matrix are all zero), denoted by

$$C = \begin{bmatrix} c_{11} & 0 & 0 & \cdots & 0 \\ c_{21} & c_{22} & 0 & \cdots & 0 \\ \vdots & \vdots & \vdots & \vdots & \vdots \\ \vdots & \vdots & \vdots & \vdots & \vdots \\ c_{k1} & \cdots & \cdots & \cdots & c_{kk} \end{bmatrix}, \tag{14.18}$$

such that

$$\Omega = CC'. \tag{14.19}$$

The equation above is called the **Choleski decomposition** of Ω. The lower triangular matrix C is obtainable in many statistical packages.

The multivariate normal distribution has some very convenient properties. Let A be a $m \times k$ ($m \le k$) constant matrix and b be a $m \times 1$ constant vector. Then

$$AX + b \sim \mathcal{N}(A\mu + b, A\Omega A'). \tag{14.20}$$

If $Y = (Y_1, \ldots, Y_k)'$ has a multivariate normal distribution with mean vector $\mu = (0, \ldots, 0)' = \mathbf{0}$ and variance matrix $\Omega = \mathbf{I}$ (i.e., the $k \times k$ identity matrix), we write

$$Y \sim \mathcal{N}(\mathbf{0}, \mathbf{I}). \tag{14.21}$$

$Y_1, \ldots, Y_k$ are iid standard normal variates. Furthermore, if we define

$$X = CY + \mu, \tag{14.22}$$

then from equation (14.20) we conclude

$$X \sim \mathcal{N}(C\mathbf{0} + \mu, C\mathbf{I}C') \equiv \mathcal{N}(\mu, \Omega). \tag{14.23}$$

Thus, to generate random numbers of the multivariate normal distribution $X \sim \mathcal{N}(\mu, \Omega)$, we first generate k iid standard normal variates $Y = (Y_1, \ldots, Y_k)'$. Then using equation (14.22), we obtain the required random numbers for X. The generation of standard normal variates will be discussed in Section 14.4.1.

Example 14.6 Let X_1 and X_2 be jointly normally distributed with means μ_1 and μ_2, respectively, variances σ_1^2 and σ_2^2, respectively, and covariance σ_{12}. How would you generate random numbers of X_1 and X_2 given independent random numbers of the standard normal distribution?

Solution 14.6 We first solve for the Choleski decomposition of

$$\Omega = \begin{bmatrix} \sigma_1^2 & \sigma_{12} \\ \sigma_{12} & \sigma_2^2 \end{bmatrix}.$$

It can be easily checked that

$$C = \begin{bmatrix} \sigma_1 & 0 \\ \rho\sigma_2 & \sigma_2\sqrt{1-\rho^2} \end{bmatrix},$$

where ρ is the correlation coefficient, i.e.,

$$\rho = \frac{\sigma_{12}}{\sigma_1\sigma_2}.$$

Hence, if Z_1 and Z_2 are independently distributed $\mathcal{N}(0, 1)$ variates, then we can generate X_1 and X_2 from the equation

$$\begin{bmatrix} X_1 \\ X_2 \end{bmatrix} = \begin{bmatrix} \sigma_1 & 0 \\ \rho\sigma_2 & \sigma_2\sqrt{1-\rho^2} \end{bmatrix} \begin{bmatrix} Z_1 \\ Z_2 \end{bmatrix} + \begin{bmatrix} \mu_1 \\ \mu_2 \end{bmatrix}$$

$$= \begin{bmatrix} \sigma_1 Z_1 + \mu_1 \\ \rho\sigma_2 Z_1 + \sigma_2\sqrt{1-\rho^2}\, Z_2 + \mu_2 \end{bmatrix}.$$

It is easy to verify that $E(X_1) = \mu_1$, $E(X_2) = \mu_2$, $\mathrm{Var}(X_1) = \sigma_1^2$,

$$\mathrm{Var}(X_2) = \rho^2\sigma_2^2 + \sigma_2^2\left(1 - \rho^2\right) = \sigma_2^2,$$

and

$$\mathrm{Cov}(X_1, X_2) = \rho\sigma_1\sigma_2 = \sigma_{12}. \qquad \square$$

14.4 Specific Random Number Generators

Many commonly used distributions cannot be generated by the standard methods reviewed so far, while others can be generated using some specific but more efficient methods. We now discuss the generation of some of these distributions.

14.4.1 Some Continuous Distributions

Normal Distribution

Normal distribution is perhaps one of the most commonly used distributions in statistics. Yet as the df of a normal distribution does not have an analytic expression, the inversion method does not work. A crude method is to invoke the law of large numbers and approximate a normal random variable using the sum of a large number of uniform random numbers. This method, however, is only approximate and is obviously very inefficient in execution.

The **Box–Muller method** generates pairs of standard normal variates from pairs of uniform variates. Let U_1 and U_2 be two independent $\mathcal{U}(0, 1)$ variates. The transformations defined by

$$X_1 = \cos(2\pi U_1)\sqrt{-2 \log U_2},$$
$$X_2 = \sin(2\pi U_1)\sqrt{-2 \log U_2}, \qquad (14.24)$$

produce a pair of independent $\mathcal{N}(0, 1)$ variates X_1 and X_2.

Another algorithm, called the **Marsaglia–Bray method**, uses a mixture distribution together with the acceptance–rejection method. This method, however, requires the generation of more uniform variates. More algorithms for generating normal random variates can be found in Kennedy and Gentle (1980).

Gamma Distribution

The gamma distribution $\mathcal{G}(\alpha, \beta)$ covers several standard distributions as special cases, including the exponential distribution $\mathcal{E}(1/\beta)$ (when $\alpha = 1$), the Erlang distribution (when $\beta = 1$ and α is a positive integer) and the chi-square distribution χ_r^2 (when $\beta = 2$ and $\alpha = r/2$). As the df of a general $\mathcal{G}(\alpha, \beta)$ variable cannot be inverted easily, the inversion method for generating random numbers of $\mathcal{G}(\alpha, \beta)$ does not work.

A gamma random variable with $\beta = 1$ is said to have a standard gamma distribution. As a $\mathcal{G}(\alpha, \beta)$ variate has the same distribution as a $\beta\mathcal{G}(\alpha, 1)$ variate, we only need to consider standard gamma distributions.

From Section 2.2.2, we see that the sum of n independent $\mathcal{E}(1)$ variates is distributed as $\mathcal{G}(n, 1)$. Furthermore, if $U \sim \mathcal{U}(0, 1)$, $-\log U \sim \mathcal{E}(1)$. Hence, if α is an integer (Erlang distribution), $X \sim \mathcal{G}(\alpha, 1)$ can be generated by the equation

$$X = -\sum_{i=1}^{\alpha} \log U_i, \qquad (14.25)$$

where $U_i \sim$ iid $\mathcal{U}(0, 1)$, for $i = 1, \ldots, \alpha$.

If $X_i \sim \mathcal{G}(\alpha_i, 1)$, for $i = 1, 2$, are independently distributed, then $X_1 + X_2 \sim \mathcal{G}(\alpha_1 + \alpha_2, 1)$. Hence, to generate a standard gamma variate $\mathcal{G}(\alpha, 1)$ we may split α into the sum of its largest integer part and a term that is between 0 and 1. Thus, $\mathcal{G}(\alpha, 1)$ is the sum of two gamma variates, one of which has an Erlang distribution and the other has a standard gamma distribution with parameter in the interval $(0, 1)$. We now consider the case of generating a $\mathcal{G}(\alpha, 1)$ variate with $\alpha \in (0, 1)$.

The **Ahrens method** provides an efficient procedure to generate a $\mathcal{G}(\alpha, 1)$ variate with $\alpha \in (0, 1)$ using the acceptance–rejection approach. The required pdf is

$$f(x) = \frac{1}{\Gamma(\alpha)} x^{\alpha-1} e^{-x}, \qquad \text{for } \alpha \in (0, 1), \; x \geq 0. \tag{14.26}$$

The majorizing frequency consists of two segments defined as follows[5]

$$q(x) = \begin{cases} \dfrac{e}{\alpha+e} \, \alpha x^{\alpha-1}, & \text{for } 0 \leq x \leq 1, \\[3mm] \dfrac{\alpha}{\alpha+e} \, e^{1-x}, & \text{for } 1 < x. \end{cases} \tag{14.27}$$

The df of this density, denoted by $Q(\cdot)$, is

$$Q(x) = \begin{cases} \dfrac{e}{\alpha+e} \, x^{\alpha}, & \text{for } 0 \leq x \leq 1, \\[3mm] 1 - \dfrac{\alpha}{\alpha+e} \, e^{1-x}, & \text{for } 1 < x. \end{cases} \tag{14.28}$$

Using the inverse transformation, we can generate a random number X with df $Q(\cdot)$ from a $\mathcal{U}(0, 1)$ variate U as follows

$$X = \begin{cases} \left[\dfrac{(\alpha+e)\,U}{e} \right]^{\frac{1}{\alpha}}, & \text{for } 0 \leq U \leq \dfrac{e}{\alpha+e}, \\[4mm] 1 - \log\left[\dfrac{(1-U)(\alpha+e)}{\alpha} \right], & \text{for } \dfrac{e}{\alpha+e} < U < 1. \end{cases} \tag{14.29}$$

To envelope the pdf $f(\cdot)$ we use the majorizing function $M(x) = cq(x)$, where c is given by

$$c = \frac{\alpha+e}{\Gamma(\alpha)\alpha e}. \tag{14.30}$$

Thus, the majorizing function is

$$M(x) = cq(x) = \begin{cases} \dfrac{1}{\Gamma(\alpha)} x^{\alpha-1}, & \text{for } 0 \leq x \leq 1, \\[3mm] \dfrac{1}{\Gamma(\alpha)} e^{-x}, & \text{for } 1 < x. \end{cases} \tag{14.31}$$

We further note that

$$\frac{f(x)}{M(x)} = \begin{cases} e^{-x}, & \text{for } 0 \leq x \leq 1, \\[2mm] x^{\alpha-1}, & \text{for } 1 < x. \end{cases} \tag{14.32}$$

---

[5] It can be checked that $\int_0^\infty q(x)\, dx = 1$.

Thus, it can be easily checked that $M(x) \geq f(x)$ for $x \geq 0$. We are now ready to state the Ahrens method for the generation of the random variable X with pdf $f(\cdot)$ as follows:

1. Generate a random number u_1 from $\mathcal{U}(0, 1)$. If $u_1 > e/(\alpha + e)$, go to Step 3. Otherwise, continue with Step 2.
2. Set $z = [(\alpha + e) u_1/e]^{\frac{1}{\alpha}}$ and generate independently another random number u_2 from $\mathcal{U}(0, 1)$. If $u_2 > e^{-z}$, go to Step 1, otherwise assign $X = z$.
3. Set $z = 1 - \log [(1 - u_1)(\alpha + e)/\alpha]$ and generate independently another random number u_2 from $\mathcal{U}(0, 1)$. If $u_2 > z^{\alpha-1}$, go to Step 1, otherwise assign $X = z$.

14.4.2 Some Discrete Distributions

We now discuss the generation of two discrete distributions, namely, the binomial and Poisson distributions. Note that while the binomial distribution has a finite support, the support of the Poisson distribution is infinite.

Binomial Distribution

The pf of the binomial distribution $\mathcal{BN}(n, \theta)$ is

$$f(i) = \binom{n}{i} \theta^i (1 - \theta)^{n-i}, \qquad \text{for } i = 0, 1, \dots, n. \qquad (14.33)$$

As the $\mathcal{BN}(n, \theta)$ distribution has a finite support, we can use a simple **table look-up method** to generate the random numbers. We first compute the df of $\mathcal{BN}(n, \theta)$ as

$$F(i) = \sum_{j=0}^{i} \binom{n}{j} \theta^j (1 - \theta)^{n-j}, \qquad \text{for } i = 0, 1, \dots, n. \qquad (14.34)$$

Now a random number X from $\mathcal{BN}(n, \theta)$ may be generated as follows. For a number u generated from $\mathcal{U}(0, 1)$, we set $X = 0$ if $u \leq F(0)$, and set $X = r + 1$ if $F(r) < u \leq F(r + 1)$, for $r = 0, \dots, n - 1$.

Alternatively X can be generated by exploiting the fact that it may be interpreted as the number of successes in n independent trials where the probability of success in each trial is θ. Thus, we generate n random variates U_i, $i = 1, \dots, n$, from $\mathcal{U}(0, 1)$ and compute X as the number of U_i that are less than θ.

Poisson Distribution

As the Poisson distribution has an infinite support, the table look-up method does not work. However, we may make use of the relationship between the exponential distribution and the Poisson distribution to derive an algorithm.

Let $X \sim \mathcal{PN}(\lambda)$ be the number of arrivals of a certain event in a unit time interval. Then the interarrival time Y of the events follows an exponential distribution $\mathcal{E}(\lambda)$, i.e., an exponential distribution with mean waiting time $1/\lambda$. Thus, we can generate Y_i from $\mathcal{E}(\lambda)$ and accumulate them to obtain the *total* waiting time. We then set X to be the largest number of Y_i accumulated such that their total is less than 1, i.e.,

$$X = \min \{n : \sum_{i=1}^{n+1} Y_i > 1\}. \tag{14.35}$$

As Y_i can be generated by $(- \log U_i)/\lambda$, where $U_i \sim \mathcal{U}(0, 1)$, we rewrite the above as

$$
\begin{aligned}
X &= \min \{n : \sum_{i=1}^{n+1} \frac{1}{\lambda}(- \log U_i) > 1\} \\
&= \min \{n : \sum_{i=1}^{n+1} \log U_i < -\lambda\} \\
&= \min \{n : \prod_{i=1}^{n+1} U_i < e^{-\lambda}\}. \tag{14.36}
\end{aligned}
$$

Hence, X can be generated by multiplying uniformly distributed variates. The number of such variates required to generate a single value of X increases with λ.

14.5 Accuracy and Monte Carlo Sample Size

Apart from providing an estimate of the required deterministic solution, Monte Carlo samples can also be used to provide an assessment of the accuracy of the estimate. We may use the Monte Carlo sample to estimate the standard error of the estimated solution and hence obtain a confidence interval for the solution. The standard error may also be used to estimate the required sample size to produce a solution within a required accuracy given a certain probability level.

Example 14.7 The specific damages X covered by a liability insurance policy are distributed as $\mathcal{G}(4, 3)$. The total damages, inclusive of punitive damages, are given by cX, where $c > 1$. The policy has a maximum covered loss of u. Using Monte Carlo methods or otherwise, determine the expected loss of the insured and the probability that the total damages do not exceed u. Discuss the accuracy of your solutions. Consider the case of $c = 1.1$ and $u = 20$.

Solution 14.7 The pdf of X is

$$f(x) = \frac{1}{\Gamma(\alpha)\beta^\alpha} x^{\alpha-1} e^{-\frac{x}{\beta}}, \qquad x \geq 0.$$

We denote the df of $X \sim \mathcal{G}(\alpha, \beta)$ by

$$\gamma_x(\alpha, \beta) = \Pr(X \leq x),$$

and note that

$$\gamma_x(\alpha, \beta) = \gamma_{\frac{x}{\beta}}(\alpha, 1) \equiv \gamma_{\frac{x}{\beta}}(\alpha).$$

The function $\gamma_x(\alpha)$ is also called the (lower) **incomplete gamma function**.

The expected loss is

$$
\begin{aligned}
E\left[(cx) \wedge u\right] &= \int_0^{\frac{u}{c}} cx \, \frac{x^{\alpha-1} e^{-\frac{x}{\beta}}}{\Gamma(\alpha)\beta^\alpha} \, dx + u \int_{\frac{u}{c}}^{\infty} \frac{x^{\alpha-1} e^{-\frac{x}{\beta}}}{\Gamma(\alpha)\beta^\alpha} \, dx \\
&= \frac{c\Gamma(\alpha+1)\beta}{\Gamma(\alpha)} \int_0^{\frac{u}{c}} \frac{x^{(\alpha+1)-1} e^{-\frac{x}{\beta}}}{\Gamma(\alpha+1)\beta^{\alpha+1}} \, dx + u \left[1 - \gamma_{\frac{u}{c\beta}}(\alpha)\right] \\
&= c\alpha\beta\gamma_{\frac{u}{c\beta}}(\alpha+1) + u \left[1 - \gamma_{\frac{u}{c\beta}}(\alpha)\right].
\end{aligned}
$$

Thus, the expected loss can be computed using the incomplete gamma function. Similarly, we can derive the second moment of the loss as

$$
E\left[\left((cx) \wedge u\right)^2\right] = c^2(\alpha+1)\alpha\beta^2 \gamma_{\frac{u}{c\beta}}(\alpha+2) + u^2 \left[1 - \gamma_{\frac{u}{c\beta}}(\alpha)\right],
$$

from which we can compute $\mathrm{Var}[(cx) \wedge u]$.

Now with the given values of $c = 1.1$ and $u = 20$ we obtain

$$E\left[(cx) \wedge u\right] = 12.4608 \qquad \text{and} \qquad \mathrm{Var}\left[(cx) \wedge u\right] = 25.9197.$$

Using a Monte Carlo sample of 10,000 observations, we obtain estimates of the mean and variance of the loss as (these are the sample mean and the sample variance of the simulated losses)

$$\hat{E}\left[(cx) \wedge u\right] = 12.5466 \qquad \text{and} \qquad \widehat{\mathrm{Var}}\left[(cx) \wedge u\right] = 25.7545.$$

The Monte Carlo standard error of $\hat{E}[(cx) \wedge u]$ is

$$\sqrt{\frac{\widehat{\mathrm{Var}}\left[(cx) \wedge u\right]}{10,000}} = \sqrt{\frac{25.7545}{10,000}} = 0.0507.$$

Thus, using normal approximation, the Monte Carlo estimate of the 95% confidence interval of the expected loss is

$$12.5466 \pm (1.96)(0.0507) = (12.4471, \ 12.6461),$$

which covers the true value of 12.4608.

The probability of the total damages not exceeding u is

$$\Pr\left(cX \leq u\right) = \int_0^{\frac{u}{c}} \frac{x^{\alpha-1} e^{-\frac{x}{\beta}}}{\Gamma(\alpha)\beta^\alpha} \, dx = \gamma_{\frac{u}{c\beta}}(\alpha),$$

and we have

$$\gamma_{\frac{20}{(1.1)(3)}}(4) = 0.8541.$$

The Monte Carlo estimate of this probability is the sample proportion of $1.1X \le 20$, which was found to be 0.8543. The 95% confidence interval of the true probability is

$$0.8543 \pm 1.96\sqrt{\frac{(0.8543)(1 - 0.8543)}{10,000}} = (0.8474, 0.8612),$$

which again covers the true probability. □

Example 14.8 Continue with Example 14.7 and modify the total damages to $bX^2 + cX$. Using Monte Carlo methods or otherwise, determine the expected loss of the insured and the probability that the total damages do not exceed u. Discuss the accuracy of your solutions. Consider the case of $b = 0.1$, $c = 1.1$ and $u = 30$.

Solution 14.8 The mean loss is now given by

$$E\left[(bx^2 + cx) \wedge u\right] = \int_0^r (bx^2 + cx)\frac{x^{a-1}e^{-\frac{x}{\beta}}}{\Gamma(\alpha)\beta^\alpha}\,dx + u\int_r^\infty \frac{x^{a-1}e^{-\frac{x}{\beta}}}{\Gamma(\alpha)\beta^\alpha}\,dx,$$

where

$$br^2 + cr = u.$$

We solve for r to obtain

$$r = \frac{\sqrt{c^2 + 4bu} - c}{2b}.$$

Thus, the expected loss is

$$E\left[(bx^2 + cx) \wedge u\right] = b(\alpha + 1)\alpha\beta^2\gamma_{\frac{r}{\beta}}(\alpha + 2) + c\alpha\beta\gamma_{\frac{r}{\beta}}(\alpha + 1) + u\left[1 - \gamma_{\frac{r}{\beta}}(\alpha)\right].$$

We will not derive the variance analytically, but will estimate it using the Monte Carlo method. Using the values $b = 0.1$, $c = 1.1$ and $u = 30$, we obtain

$$E\left[(bx^2 + cx) \wedge u\right] = 21.7192.$$

A Monte Carlo sample of 10,000 observations produced the following estimates

$$\hat{E}\left[(bx^2 + cx) \wedge u\right] = 21.7520 \qquad \text{and} \qquad \sqrt{\frac{\widehat{\text{Var}}\left[(bx^2 + cx) \wedge u\right]}{10,000}} = 0.0867.$$

Thus, a 95% confidence interval estimate of the expected loss is

$$21.7520 \pm (1.96)(0.0867) = (21.5821, 21.9219),$$

which covers the true value.

The probability of the total damages not exceeding u is

$$\Pr(bX^2 + cX \leq u) = \Pr(X \leq r) = \gamma_{\frac{\alpha}{\beta}}(\alpha) = 0.6091.$$

This is estimated by the proportion of Monte Carlo observations of total damages not exceeding 30, and was found to be 0.6076. A 95% confidence interval of the probability of the total damages not exceeding 30 is

$$0.6076 \pm 1.96 \sqrt{\frac{(0.6076)(1 - 0.6076)}{10,000}} = (0.5980, 0.6172),$$

which again covers the true probability.   □

14.6 Variance Reduction Techniques

Consider a deterministic problem with solution equal to $E[f(X)]$, where X is a random variable (not necessarily uniformly distributed) and $f(\cdot)$ is an integrable function over the support of X. The **crude Monte Carlo** estimate of the solution is

$$\hat{E}[f(X)] = \frac{1}{n} \sum_{i=1}^{n} f(x_i), \qquad (14.37)$$

where $(x_1, \ldots, x_n)$ are sample values of X. The accuracy of this stochastic solution depends on the variance of the estimator. We now discuss some methods of sampling and estimation that aim at reducing the variance of the Monte Carlo estimator.

14.6.1 Antithetic Variable

The **antithetic variable method** attempts to reduce the variance of the Monte Carlo estimate through the use of the random numbers generated. To illustrate the idea, consider a Monte Carlo sample of two observations X_1 and X_2. If X_1 and X_2 are iid, The variance of the Monte Carlo estimator is

$$\text{Var}\left(\hat{E}[f(X)]\right) = \frac{\text{Var}[f(X)]}{2}. \qquad (14.38)$$

However, if X_1 and X_2 are identically distributed as X, but *not independent*, then the variance of the Monte Carlo estimator is

$$\text{Var}\left(\hat{E}[f(X)]\right) = \frac{\text{Var}[f(X)] + \text{Cov}(f(X_1), f(X_2))}{2}. \qquad (14.39)$$

Now if $\text{Cov}(f(X_1), f(X_2)) < 0$, the variance of the Monte Carlo estimator is reduced. Random numbers generated in such a way that the functional evaluations at these numbers are negatively correlated are said to be antithetic variables.

If $X_1 \sim \mathcal{U}(0, 1)$, then $X_2 = 1 - X_1 \sim \mathcal{U}(0, 1)$ and is negatively correlated with X_1. It should be noted, however, that for the antithetic variable technique to work well, it is the negative correlation between $f(X_1)$ and $f(X_2)$ that is required. Negative correlation between X_1 and X_2 in itself does not guarantee reduction in the variance of the Monte Carlo estimator.

The above discussion can be generalized to a sample of n observations, in which reduction in the variance may be obtained if the pairwise correlations of $f(X_i)$ are negative. Also, this technique can be extended to the case of a vector random variable.

Example 14.9 Consider the distribution of the loss in a loss event variable X_L in Example 14.4. Estimate $\text{E}(X_L)$ using a crude Monte Carlo method and a Monte Carlo simulation with antithetic variable.

Solution 14.9 To estimate $\text{E}(X_L)$ using the crude Monte Carlo method, we generate a random sample of n variates U_i from $\mathcal{U}(0, 1)$. For each U_i we compute $X_L(U_i)$ using equation (14.10). $\text{E}(X_L)$ is then estimated by

$$\hat{\text{E}}_{\text{CR}}(X_L) = \frac{1}{n} \sum_{i=1}^{n} X_L(U_i).$$

To use the antithetic variable technique, we generate $n/2$ (n being even) $\mathcal{U}(0, 1)$ variates U_i, $i = 1, \ldots, n/2$, and augment this set of numbers by another $n/2$ $\mathcal{U}(0, 1)$ variates by taking $U_{i+\frac{n}{2}} = 1 - U_i$. The sample mean of X_L computed from this set of U_i is the Monte Carlo estimate with antithetic variables, denoted by $\hat{\text{E}}_{\text{AT}}(X_L)$.

We performed a Monte Carlo simulation with $n = 10{,}000$. The sample means and sample variances are

$$\hat{\text{E}}_{\text{CR}}(X_L) = 2.8766, \qquad s_{\text{CR}}^2 = 9.2508,$$

and

$$\hat{\text{E}}_{\text{AT}}(X_L) = 2.8555, \qquad s_{\text{AT}}^{2\cdot} = 9.1719.$$

We can see that the results of the two Monte Carlo estimates of $\text{E}(X_L)$ are very similar. However, there is only a small gain in using antithetic variables in this estimation. If we refer to Figure 14.1, we can see that the probability contents at the two ends of the distribution (at values 0 and 7) are similar. Thus, little negative correlation is induced by taking the complements of the $\mathcal{U}(0, 1)$ variates. □

14.6.2 Control Variable

To estimate $E[f(X)]$ using the control variable, we consider an auxiliary function $g(\cdot)$ and the associated expectation $E[g(X)]$. We select the function $g(\cdot)$ so that it is close to $f(\cdot)$ and yet $E[g(X)]$ is *known*. Now a Monte Carlo estimate of $E[f(X)]$ can be computed as

$$\hat{E}_{CV}[f(X)] = E[g(X)] + \frac{1}{n} \sum_{i=1}^{n} [f(X_i) - g(X_i)]. \qquad (14.40)$$

It is easy to check that $\hat{E}_{CV}[f(X)]$ is an unbiased estimate of $E[f(X)]$. The variance of this estimator is

$$\text{Var}(\hat{E}_{CV}[f(X)]) = \frac{\text{Var}\,[f(X) - g(X)]}{n}, \qquad (14.41)$$

which is smaller than the variance of $\hat{E}_{CR}\,[f(X)]$ if

$$\text{Var}\,[f(X) - g(X)] < \text{Var}\,[f(X)]. \qquad (14.42)$$

Example 14.10 Consider the distribution of the loss in a loss event variable X_L in Example 14.4. Estimate $E(X_L)$ using a Monte Carlo simulation with control variable.

Solution 14.10 To estimate $E(X_L)$ using control variable, we consider a random variable $\tilde{X}_L$ with the following df

$$F_{\tilde{X}_L}(x) = \begin{cases} 0.3606, & \text{for } x = 0, \\ 0.3606 + 0.0510x, & \text{for } 0 < x < 7, \\ 1, & \text{for } x \geq 7, \end{cases}$$

where

$$0.0510 = \frac{0.7177 - 0.3606}{7} = \frac{0.3571}{7}$$

is the slope of the line joining the points $(0, 0.3606)$ and $(7, 0.7177)$. Comparing the above with equation (14.9), we can see that the df of X_L in the interval $[0.3606, 0.7177)$ is now *linearized*. The mean of $\tilde{X}_L$ is

$$E(\tilde{X}_L) = (0.3571)(3.5) + (0.2823)(7) = 3.2260.$$

Given a $\mathcal{U}(0, 1)$ variate U_i, X_L can be generated using equation (14.10), and we denote this by $X_L(U_i)$. Now the inverse transformation of $\tilde{X}_L$ is

$$\tilde{X}_L = \begin{cases} 0, & \text{for } 0 \leq U < 0.3606, \\ (U - 0.3606)/0.0510, & \text{for } 0.3606 \leq U < 0.7177, \\ 7, & \text{for } 0.7177 \leq U < 1. \end{cases}$$

Hence, the Monte Carlo estimate of $E(X_L)$ using the control variable $\tilde{X}_L$ is computed as

$$3.2260 + \frac{1}{n} \sum_{i=1}^{n} \left[X_L(U_i) - \tilde{X}_L(U_i) \right].$$

Note that $X_L(U_i) - \tilde{X}_L(U_i)$ is nonzero only when $U_i \in [0.3606, 0.7177)$, in which case we have

$$X_L(U_i) - \tilde{X}_L(U_i) = 5 \left[-\log (1 - U_i) \right]^2 - 1 - \frac{U_i - 0.3606}{0.0510}.$$

We performed a Monte Carlo simulation with $n = 10{,}000$. The sample mean and sample variance are

$$\hat{E}_{CV}(X_L) = 2.8650, \qquad s_{CV}^2 = 0.3150.$$

Thus, there is a substantial increase in efficiency versus the crude Monte Carlo and Monte Carlo with antithetic variable. $\qquad\qquad\qquad\qquad\qquad\qquad\square$

14.6.3 Importance Sampling

Consider the following integral of a smooth integrable function $f(\cdot)$ over the interval $[a, b]$

$$\int_a^b f(x)\, dx, \tag{14.43}$$

which can be rewritten as

$$\int_a^b \left[(b - a)f(x) \right] \frac{1}{b - a}\, dx. \tag{14.44}$$

Thus, the integral can be estimated by

$$\frac{1}{n} \sum_{i=1}^{n} (b - a)f(X_i), \tag{14.45}$$

where X_i are iid $\mathcal{U}(a, b)$. In general, if $\tilde{X}$ is a random variable with support $[a, b]$ and pdf $q(\cdot)$, the integral in equation (14.43) can be written as

$$\int_a^b f(x)\, dx = \int_a^b \left[\frac{f(x)}{q(x)} \right] q(x)\, dx, \tag{14.46}$$

which can be estimated by

$$\frac{1}{n} \sum_{i=1}^{n} \frac{f(\tilde{X}_i)}{q(\tilde{X}_i)}, \tag{14.47}$$

where $\tilde{X}_i$ are iid as $\tilde{X}$. The estimator in equation (14.47) has a smaller variance than the estimator in equation (14.45) if

$$\text{Var}\left[\frac{f(\tilde{X}_i)}{q(\tilde{X}_i)}\right] < \text{Var}\left[(b-a)f(X_i)\right]. \tag{14.48}$$

The technique of using equation (14.47), with a change of the pdf of the random variable to be generated and the function to be integrated, is called **importance sampling**. From equation (14.48), we can see that the advantage of importance sampling is likely to be large if the variation in the ratio $f(\cdot)/q(\cdot)$ is small over the interval $[a, b]$ (i.e., the two functions are close to each other).

Example 14.11 Consider the distribution of the loss in a loss event variable X_L in Example 14.4. Estimate $E(X_L)$ using a Monte Carlo simulation with importance sampling.

Solution 14.11 Defining $f(U)$ as $X_L(U)$ in equation (14.10), we have

$$
\begin{aligned}
E(X_L) &= \int_0^1 f(x)\, dx \\
&= \int_{0.3606}^{0.7177} \left(5\left[-\log(1-x)\right]^2 - 1\right) dx + \int_{0.7177}^1 7\, dx \\
&= \int_{0.3606}^{0.7177} \left(5\left[-\log(1-x)\right]^2 - 1\right) dx + 1.9761.
\end{aligned}
$$

The integral above is the expected value of

$$(0.7177 - 0.3606)(5[-\log(1-\tilde{U})]^2 - 1),$$

where $\tilde{U} \sim \mathcal{U}(0.3606, 0.7177)$. Thus, we estimate $E(X_L)$ by

$$1.9761 + \frac{0.3571}{n}\sum_{i=1}^n (5[-\log(1-\tilde{U}_i)]^2 - 1),$$

where

$$\tilde{U}_i = 0.3606 + 0.3571U_i,$$

with $U_i \sim$ iid $\mathcal{U}(0, 1)$.

We performed a Monte Carlo simulation with 10,000 observations, and obtained $\hat{E}(X_L) = 2.8654$, with a sample variance of 0.4937. Thus, the importance sampling method produced a big gain in efficiency over the crude Monte Carlo method, although the gain is not as much as that from the control variable method in Example 14.10. □

14.7 R Laboratory

R Codes 14.1 provides the codes to estimate the mean, variance and sample proportion of a censored loss variable using the Monte Carlo method. The ground-up loss is distributed as $\mathcal{G}(4, 3)$. We use the function `pmin` of taking pairwise minimum to compute the censored loss.

```
#####################################################################
# R Codes 14.1
#
# Monte Carlo estimation of the mean, variance and sample proportion
# of the censored loss variables in Examples 14.7 and 14.8
#####################################################################

n=10000                                   # Monte Carlo sample size
b=0.1
c=1.1
u1=20
u2=30
x=rgamma(n,shape=4,scale=3)               # Draw ground-up loss
                                          # sample
xp1=pmin(c*x,u1)                          # Censored loss
                                          # Example 14.7
xp2=pmin(b*x^2+c*x,u2)                     # Censored loss
                                          # Example 14.8
c(mean(xp1),var(xp1),sum(c*x<=u1)/n)       # Results for Example 14.7
c(mean(xp2),var(xp2),sum(b*x^2+c*x<=u2)/n) # Results for Example 14.8
```

14.8 Summary and Discussions

Many deterministic problems can be formulated as a stochastic problem, the solution of which can be estimated using Monte Carlo methods. In a Monte Carlo simulation, random numbers are generated to resemble the sampling of observations. To this effect, efficient algorithms for the generation of uniformly distributed random numbers form a basic component of the method. We have surveyed methods for generating random numbers that are uniformly distributed, from which random numbers following other distributions can be generated using methods such as inversion transformation and acceptance–rejection. For certain commonly used distributions, specific generators are available, which provide efficient algorithms to facilitate the computation. As the solution of the Monte Carlo simulation is a stochastic estimator, its accuracy depends on the variance of the estimator. We discuss methods to improve the efficiency or reduce the variance. Antithetic variable, control variable and importance sampling are some common techniques. The performance of these techniques, however, depends on the actual problems considered and may vary considerably.

Exercises

Exercise 14.1 You are given the following multiplicative-congruential generator

$$x_{i+1} \equiv (16807\, x_i)\ (\bmod\ 2^{31} - 1).$$

Using the modulus function %% in R and the seed $x_1 = 401$, compute the numbers $x_2, \ldots, x_5$ and the corresponding $\mathcal{U}(0, 1)$ variates $u_2, \ldots, u_5$. If the seed is changed to $x_1 = 245987$, determine the new sequence of x_i and u_i.

Exercise 14.2 You are given the following mixed-congruential generator

$$x_{i+1} \equiv (69069\, x_i + 1)\ (\bmod\ 2^{32}).$$

Using the modulus function %% in R and the seed $x_1 = 747$, compute the numbers $x_2, \ldots, x_5$ and the corresponding $\mathcal{U}(0, 1)$ variates $u_2, \ldots, u_5$. If the seed is changed to $x_1 = 380$, determine the new sequence of x_i and u_i.

Exercise 14.3 You are given that $x_1 = 7$, $x_2 = 5$ and

$$x_{i+1} \equiv (5\, x_i + c)\ (\bmod\ 11), \qquad \text{for } i = 0, 1, 2, \ldots.$$

Compute x_{101}.

Exercise 14.4 The RAND function in Excel uses a combination of three multiplicative-congruential generators. The following generators are defined

$$x_{i+1} \equiv (171\, x_i)\ (\bmod\ 30269),$$

$$y_{i+1} \equiv (172\, y_i)\ (\bmod\ 30307),$$

$$z_{i+1} \equiv (170\, z_i)\ (\bmod\ 30323).$$

The $\mathcal{U}(0, 1)$ variates generated by each of the above generators are summed up and the fractional part is taken as the output of the RAND function. This algorithm provides $\mathcal{U}(0, 1)$ variates with a cycle length exceeding 2.78×10^{13}. Using the modulus function %% in R with seeds $x_1 = 320$, $y_1 = 777$ and $z_1 = 380$, compute the next five $\mathcal{U}(0, 1)$ variates.

Exercise 14.5 The inverse Pareto distribution X has the following pdf

$$f(x) = \frac{\alpha \theta x^{\alpha - 1}}{(x + \theta)^{\alpha + 1}},$$

with

$$E(X^{-1}) = \frac{1}{\theta(\alpha - 1)} \quad \text{and} \quad E(X^{-2}) = \frac{2}{\theta^2 (\alpha - 1)(\alpha - 2)}.$$

Suppose $\alpha = \theta = 4$.

(a) How would you generate X variates using the inverse transformation method?

(b) Simulate 50 random variates of X, and estimate $E(X^{-1})$ and $E(X^{-2})$ using the Monte Carlo sample. Compute a 95% confidence interval of $E(X^{-1})$ using your Monte Carlo sample. Does this interval cover the true value?

(c) Use your Monte Carlo sample in (b) to estimate the Monte Carlo sample size required if you wish to estimate $E(X^{-1})$ up to 1% error with a probability of 95%.

Exercise 14.6 The inverse Weibull distribution X has the following pdf

$$f(x) = \frac{\alpha \left(\dfrac{\theta}{x}\right)^{\alpha} e^{-\left(\frac{\theta}{x}\right)^{\alpha}}}{x},$$

with

$$E(X) = \theta\, \Gamma\left(1 - \frac{1}{\alpha}\right) \quad \text{and} \quad E(X^2) = \theta^2\, \Gamma\left(1 - \frac{2}{\alpha}\right).$$

Suppose $\alpha = \theta = 4$.

(a) How would you generate X variates using the inverse transformation method?

(b) Simulate 50 random variates of X, and estimate $E(X)$ and $E(X^2)$ using the Monte Carlo sample. Compute a 95% confidence interval of $E(X)$ using your Monte Carlo sample. Does this interval cover the true value?

(c) Use your Monte Carlo sample in (b) to estimate the Monte Carlo sample size required if you wish to estimate $E(X)$ up to 1% error with a probability of 95%.

Exercise 14.7 Suppose X is distributed with pdf

$$f(x) = 12x^2(1 - x), \quad 0 < x < 1.$$

Using the majorizing density $q(x) = 1$ for $0 < x < 1$, suggest an acceptance–rejection algorithm to generate random variates of X. What is the efficiency measure of your algorithm? Why would you use the acceptance–rejection method rather than the inverse transformation method?

Exercise 14.8 Let $X = U^2$ and $Y = (1 - U)^2$, where $U \sim \mathcal{U}(0, 1)$.

(a) Compute $\mathrm{Var}(X)$, $\mathrm{Var}(Y)$, $\mathrm{Cov}(X, Y)$ and $\mathrm{Var}[(X+Y)/2]$.

(b) Generate 100 random numbers of U and estimate the integral $\int_0^1 u^2\, du$ by simulation. Repeat the computation using the random numbers $1 - U$. Compare the means and the variances the two simulation samples. How would you use the random numbers to improve the precision of your estimates?

Exercise 14.9 Consider the following integral

$$\int_0^1 \frac{e^u - 1}{e - 1} \, du.$$

(a) Estimate the integral using a crude Monte Carlo method with 100 random numbers of $\mathcal{U}(0, 1)$.
(b) Estimate the integral using a Monte Carlo method with antithetic variates. This is done by first generating 50 random numbers $u_i \sim$ iid $\mathcal{U}(0, 1)$ as in (a) above and then use the numbers $1 - u_i$ for a total of 100 random numbers.
(c) Estimate the integral using a Monte Carlo simulation with control variable, with $g(u) = u/(e - 1)$ as the auxiliary function. Use 100 random numbers of $\mathcal{U}(0, 1)$ for your estimation.

Compare the Monte Carlo estimates of the methods above, as well as their standard deviations. Which method provides the best efficiency?

Exercise 14.10 Suppose X_1 and X_2 are jointly distributed as bivariate standard normal variates with correlation of 0.6. Generate 100 observations of (X_1, X_2), and estimate from the sample $\Pr(X_1 \leq 1.2, X_2 \leq 2.1)$. Construct a 95% confidence interval of the probability. If you wish to obtain an estimate with error less than 0.01 with a probability of 95%, what Monte Carlo sample size would you require? [**Hint:** $\Pr(X_1 \leq 1.2, X_2 \leq 2.1) = 0.8783$.]

Exercise 14.11 Suppose $f(\cdot)$ is an integrable function over $[a, b]$ with $0 \leq f(x) \leq c$ for $a \leq x \leq b$. Let

$$\theta = \int_a^b f(x) \, dx.$$

(a) Show that $\theta = (b - a)\mathrm{E}[\, f(X)]$, where $X \sim \mathcal{U}(a, b)$.
(b) Show that $\mathrm{E}[\, f(X)] = c\Pr(Y \leq f(X))$, where $Y \sim \mathcal{U}(0, c)$ and is independent of X.
(c) In a Monte Carlo simulation, n independent pairs of X and Y are drawn and W is the number of cases such that $y \leq f(x)$. Define $\tilde{\theta} = c(b - a)W/n$, which is called the **hit-or-miss estimator** of θ. Show that $\mathrm{E}(\tilde{\theta}) = \theta$ and $\mathrm{Var}(\tilde{\theta}) = \theta[c(b - a) - \theta]/n$.
(d) The crude Monte Carlo estimator $\hat{\theta}$ is defined as $\hat{\theta} = (b - a)\left[\sum_{i=1}^n f(X_i)\right]/n$, where X_i are iid $\mathcal{U}(a, b)$. Show that $\hat{\theta}$ is unbiased for θ and that $\mathrm{Var}(\hat{\theta}) \leq \mathrm{Var}(\tilde{\theta})$.

Exercise 14.12 Let $F(\cdot)$ be the distribution function of $\mathcal{N}(\mu, \sigma^2)$. Show that $F^{-1}(1 - u) = 2\mu - F^{-1}(u)$ for $0 < u < 1$. Suppose X is a variate generated from $\mathcal{N}(\mu, \sigma^2)$. How would you compute an antithetic variate of X?

Questions Adapted from SOA Exams

Exercise 14.13 A mixture variable Y is distributed as $\mathcal{E}(2)$ with probability 0.3 and $\mathcal{U}(-3, 3)$ with probability 0.7. Y is simulated where low values of $\mathcal{U}(0, 1)$ correspond to the exponential distribution. Then the selected component is simulated where low random variates of $\mathcal{U}(0, 1)$ correspond to low values of Y, and Y is computed using the inverse transformation method. The $\mathcal{U}(0, 1)$ variates generated, in order, are 0.25 and 0.69. Determine the value of Y.

Exercise 14.14 N is the number of accidents in a period, and is distributed with pf

$$\Pr(N = n) = 0.9(0.1)^{n-1}, \quad n = 1, 2, \ldots.$$

X_i is the claim amount of the ith accident, and are iid with pdf

$$f(x) = 0.01\, e^{-0.01x}, \quad x > 0.$$

Suppose U and $V_1, V_2, \ldots$ are independent $\mathcal{U}(0, 1)$ variates. U is used to simulate N and V_i are used to simulate the required number of X_i, all using the inverse transformation method, where U and V_i correspond to small values of N and X_i, respectively. The following values are generated: $u = 0.05$, $v_1 = 0.3$, $v_2 = 0.22$, $v_3 = 0.52$ and $v_4 = 0.46$. Determine the total amount of claims simulated for the period.

Exercise 14.15 The return of an asset is zero with probability 0.8 and uniformly distributed on [1000, 5000] with probability 0.2. The inverse transformation method is used to simulate the outcome, where large values of $\mathcal{U}(0, 1)$ generated correspond to large returns. If the first two $\mathcal{U}(0, 1)$ variates generated are 0.75 and 0.85, compute the average of these two outcomes.

Exercise 14.16 The claims of a workers compensation policy follow the $\mathcal{P}(2.8, 36)$ distribution. The df of the frequency of claim N is

n	$\Pr(N \leq n)$
0	0.5556
1	0.8025
2	0.9122
3	0.9610
4	0.9827
5	0.9923
6	1.0000

Each claim is subject to a deductible of 5 and a maximum payment of 30. A $\mathcal{U}(0, 1)$ variate is generated and is used to simulate the number of claims using the inverse transformation method, where small value of $\mathcal{U}(0, 1)$ corresponds to small number of claims. The $\mathcal{U}(0, 1)$ variate generated is 0.981. Then further $\mathcal{U}(0, 1)$ variates are generated to simulate the claim amount, again using the inverse transformation method, where small value of $\mathcal{U}(0, 1)$ corresponds to small amount of claim. The following $\mathcal{U}(0, 1)$ variates are generated: 0.571, 0.932, 0.303, 0.471 and 0.878. Using as many of these numbers as necessary (in the given order), compute the aggregate simulated claim payments.

Exercise 14.17 The df of the number of losses for a policy in a year, N, is

n	$\Pr(N \leq n)$
0	0.125
1	0.312
2	0.500
3	0.656
4	0.773
5	0.855
.	.
.	.

The amount of each loss is distributed as $\mathcal{W}(2, 200)$. There is a deductible of 150 for each claim and an annual maximum out-of-pocket of 500 per policy. The inverse transformation method is used to simulate the number of losses and loss amounts, where small $\mathcal{U}(0, 1)$ variates correspond to small number of loss and amounts. For the number of losses, the $\mathcal{U}(0, 1)$ variate generated is 0.7654. For the loss amounts, the following random numbers are used (in order and as needed): 0.2738, 0.5152, 0.7537, 0.6481 and 0.3153. Determine the aggregate payments by the insurer.

Exercise 14.18 A dental benefit has a deductible of 100 applied to the annual charges. Reimbursement is 80% of the remaining charges subject to an annual maximum reimbursement of 1,000. Suppose the annual dental charges are distributed exponentially with mean 1,000. Charges are simulated using the inverse transformation method, where small values of $\mathcal{U}(0, 1)$ variates correspond to low charges. The following random numbers are generated: 0.30, 0.92, 0.70 and 0.08. Compute the average annual reimbursement.

Exercise 14.19 Total losses are simulated using aggregate loss model and the inverse transformation method, where small values of $\mathcal{U}(0, 1)$ variates correspond to low values of claim frequency and claim size. Suppose claim frequency is distributed as $\mathcal{PN}(4)$ and the $\mathcal{U}(0, 1)$ variate simulated is 0.13;

and claim amount is distributed as $\mathcal{E}(0.001)$ and the $\mathcal{U}(0, 1)$ variates generated are: 0.05, 0.95 and 0.1 (in that order). Determine the simulated total losses.

Exercise 14.20 Losses are distributed as $\mathcal{L}(5.6, 0.75^2)$. The claim payments with deductibles are estimated using simulation, where losses are computed from $\mathcal{U}(0, 1)$ variates using the inverse transformation method, with small $\mathcal{U}(0, 1)$ variates corresponding to small losses. The following $\mathcal{U}(0, 1)$ variates are generated: 0.6217, 0.9941, 0.8686 and 0.0485. Using these random numbers, compute the average payment per loss for a contract with a deductible of 100.

15

Applications of Monte Carlo Methods

In this chapter, we discuss some applications of Monte Carlo methods to the analysis of actuarial and financial data. We first revisit the tests of model misspecification introduced in Chapter 13. For an asymptotic test, Monte Carlo simulation can be used to improve the performance of the test when the sample size is small, in terms of getting more accurate critical values or p-values. When the asymptotic distribution of the test is unknown, as for the case of the Kolmogorov–Smirnov test when the hypothesized distribution has some unknown parameters, Monte Carlo simulation may be the only way to estimate the critical values or p-values.

The Monte Carlo estimation of critical values is generally not viable when the null hypothesis has some nuisance parameters, i.e., parameters that are not specified and not tested under the null. For such problems, the use of bootstrap may be applied to estimate the p-values. Indeed, bootstrap is one of the most powerful and exciting techniques in statistical inference and analysis. We shall discuss the use of bootstrap in model testing, as well as the estimation of the bias and mean squared error of an estimator.

Learning Objectives

1 Monte Carlo estimation of critical values and p-values
2 Bootstrap estimation of p-values
3 Bootstrap estimation of bias and mean squared error.

15.1 Monte Carlo Simulation for Hypothesis Test

In Chapter 13, we discuss some hypothesis tests for model misspecification, including the Kolmogorov–Smirnov test, the Anderson–Darling test and the chi-square goodness-of-fit test. All these tests require large samples to justify the use of an asymptotic distribution for the test statistic under the null. In small samples, the critical values based on the asymptotic distributions may not be accurate. Furthermore, some of these tests require the null distribution to be completely specified, with no unknown parameters. When the parameters are estimated, the distribution of the test statistic is unknown even in large samples.

15.1.1 Kolmogorov–Smirnov Test

We now consider the use of Monte Carlo simulation to estimate the critical values of the Kolmogorov–Smirnov D test when the parameters of the null distribution are unknown. If the null distribution is normal, even if the parameters have to be estimated for the computation of D, the critical values of the D statistic can be estimated using Monte Carlo simulation. This is due to a result in David and Johnson (1948), which states that if the parameters estimated for the null distribution are parameters of *scale* or *location*, and the estimators satisfy certain general conditions, then the joint distribution of the probability-integral transformed observations of the sample will not depend on the *true* parameter values.

The David–Johnson result is important for several reasons. First, the Kolmogorov–Smirnov test is based on the distribution function under the null, which is the probability integral transform (see Definition 14.1) of the sample observations. Second, many commonly used distributions involve parameters of scale and location. For example, for the $\mathcal{N}(\mu, \sigma^2)$ distribution, μ is the location parameter and σ is the scale parameter. The parameter λ in the $\mathcal{E}(\lambda)$ distribution is a location-and-scale parameter. In these cases, the exact distributions of the D statistics under the null do not depend on the true parameter values, as long as the null distribution functions are computed using the MLE, which satisfy the conditions required by the David–Johnson result.

As the null distribution of the D statistic for the normal distribution does not depend on the true parameter values, we may assume *any* convenient values of the parameters without affecting the null distribution. This gives rise to the following Monte Carlo procedure to estimate the critical value of D for a given sample size n:

1 Generate a random sample of n (call this the **estimation sample size**) standard normal variates $x_1, \ldots, x_n$. Calculate the sample mean $\bar{x}$ and sample variance s^2, and use these values to compute the estimated distribution function $F^*(x_i)$, where $F^*(\cdot)$ is the df of $\mathcal{N}(\bar{x}, s^2)$. Then use equation (13.4) to compute D.

Table 15.1. *Results of Example 15.1*

α	n = 20	n = 30
0.10	0.176	0.146
0.05	0.191	0.158
0.01	0.224	0.185

2 Repeat Step 1 *m* times (call this the **Monte Carlo sample size**) to obtain *m* values of D_j, for $j = 1, \ldots, m$.

3 At the level of significance α, the critical value of the Kolmogorov–Smirnov D statistic is computed as the $(1 - \alpha)$-quantile of the sample of *m* values of D, estimated using the method in equations (11.9) and (11.10).

Example 15.1 Estimate the critical values of the Kolmogorov–Smirnov D statistic when the null hypothesis is that the observations are distributed normally, with unspecified mean and variance. Let the estimation sample size *n* be (a) 20 and (b) 30. Assume levels of significance of $\alpha = 0.10, 0.05$ and 0.01.

Solution 15.1 We use the above procedure to estimate the critical values from Monte Carlo samples of size $m = 10,000$. The results are summarized in Table 15.1.

These values are very close to those in Lilliefors (1967), where Monte Carlo samples of 1,000 were used. Compared to the critical values in Section 13.2.1, we can see that when the parameters are estimated the critical values are lower. Thus, if the estimation is not taken into account and the critical values for the completely specified null are used, the true probability of rejection of the correct model is lower than the stated level of significance α. The following critical values are proposed by Lilliefors (1967) for testing normal distributions with unknown mean and variance

Level of significance α	0.10	0.05	0.01
Critical value	$\dfrac{0.805}{\sqrt{n}}$	$\dfrac{0.886}{\sqrt{n}}$	$\dfrac{1.031}{\sqrt{n}}$.

□

If the null hypothesis is that the sample observations are distributed as $\mathcal{E}(\lambda)$, where λ is not specified, to estimate the critical values of the Kolmogorov–Smirnov statistic, the following procedure can be used:

1 Generate a random sample of *n* variates $x_1, \ldots, x_n$ distributed as $\mathcal{E}(1)$. Calculate the sample mean $\bar{x}$ and compute the estimated distribution function $F^*(x_i)$, where $F^*(\cdot)$ is the df of $\mathcal{E}(1/\bar{x})$. Then use equation (13.4) to compute D.

Table 15.2. *Results of Example 15.2*

α	$n = 20$	$n = 30$
0.10	0.214	0.176
0.05	0.236	0.194
0.01	0.279	0.231

2 Repeat Step 1 m times to obtain m values of D_j, for $j = 1, \ldots, m$.
3 At the level of significance α, the critical value of the Kolmogorov–Smirnov D statistic is computed as the $(1 - \alpha)$-quantile of the sample of m values of D, estimated using the method in equations (11.9) and (11.10).

Example 15.2 Estimate the critical values of the Kolmogorov–Smirnov D statistic when the null hypothesis is that the observations are distributed as $\mathcal{E}(\lambda)$, where λ is not specified. The estimation sample size n is (a) 20 and (b) 30. Assume levels of significance of $\alpha = 0.10$, 0.05 and 0.01.

Solution 15.2 We use the above procedure to estimate the critical values from Monte Carlo samples of size $m = 10{,}000$. The results are summarized in Table 15.2.
These values are very close to those in Lilliefors (1969), where Monte Carlo samples of 1,000 were used. Again we can see that when the parameters are estimated, the critical values are lower. The following critical values are proposed by Lilliefors (1969) for testing exponential distributions with unknown mean:

Level of significance α	0.10	0.05	0.01
Critical value	$\dfrac{0.96}{\sqrt{n}}$	$\dfrac{1.06}{\sqrt{n}}$	$\dfrac{1.25}{\sqrt{n}}$.

$\square$

15.1.2 *Chi-square Goodness-of-Fit Test*

As discussed in Section 13.2.3, the asymptotic distribution of the X^2 statistic for the goodness-of-fit test is χ^2_{k-r-1}, where k is the number of groups and r is the number of parameters estimated using the MMLE method. This result holds asymptotically for any null distribution. Yet Monte Carlo simulation can be used to investigate the performance of the test and improve the estimates of the critical values in small samples if required.

Example 15.3 Estimate the critical values of the chi-square goodness-of-fit statistic X^2 using Monte Carlo simulation when the null hypothesis is that the

Table 15.3. *Results of Example 15.3*

	$n = 50$		$n = 100$		$n = 200$		$n = 300$		
α	MLE	MMLE	MLE	MMLE	MLE	MMLE	MLE	MMLE	$\chi^2_{2,1-\alpha}$
0.10	4.71	4.57	4.75	4.61	4.77	4.61	4.76	4.59	4.61
0.05	6.04	5.87	6.13	5.98	6.14	5.99	6.11	5.96	5.99
0.01	9.33	9.21	9.36	9.25	9.40	9.25	9.37	9.20	9.21

observations are distributed as $\mathcal{E}(\lambda)$, where λ is unknown. Compute the X^2 statistics based on the MLE using individual observations as well as the MMLE using grouped data.

Solution 15.3 We group the data into intervals $(c_{i-1}, c_i]$, and use the following four intervals: $(0, 0.4]$, $(0.4, 1]$, $(1, 2]$ and $(2, \infty)$. The MLE of λ using the complete individual data is $1/\bar{x}$. Let $\boldsymbol{n} = \{n_1, \ldots, n_4\}$, where n_i is the number of observations in the ith interval. Using grouped data, the MMLE is solved by maximizing the log-likelihood function

$$\log L(\lambda; \boldsymbol{n}) = \sum_{i=1}^{4} n_i \log \left[\exp(-\lambda c_{i-1}) - \exp(-\lambda c_i)\right]$$

with respect to λ. The X^2 statistic is then computed using equation (13.8). Using a Monte Carlo simulation with 10,000 samples, we obtain the estimated critical values of the X^2 statistic summarized in Table 15.3.

The asymptotic critical values $\chi^2_{2,1-\alpha}$ are shown in the last column. Two points can be observed from the Monte Carlo results. First, the asymptotic results are very reliable even for samples of size 50, if the correct MMLE is used to compute X^2. Second, if MLE is used to compute X^2, the use of $\chi^2_{2,1-\alpha}$ as the critical value will *over-reject* the null hypothesis.   □

15.2 Bootstrap Estimation of p-Value

We have discussed test procedures for which there is a unique distribution of the test statistic under the null hypothesis. This enables us to estimate the critical values or p-values using Monte Carlo simulation. There are situations, however, for which the distribution of the test statistic under the null hypothesis depends on some nuisance parameters not specified under the null. For such problems, tabulation of the critical values is not viable. As an alternative, we may use the **bootstrap method** to estimate the p-value of the test statistic.

Consider a sample of n observations $\boldsymbol{x} = (x_1, \ldots, x_n)$ and a test statistic $T(\boldsymbol{x})$ for testing a null hypothesis H_0. Let the computed value of the test statistic for the sample $\boldsymbol{x}$ be t. Suppose the decision rule of the test is to reject H_0 when t is too large (i.e., on the right-hand extreme tail). Furthermore, assume H_0 contains a nuisance parameter θ, which is not specified. We now consider the estimation the p-value of the test statistic, which is the probability that $T(x)$ is larger than t if the null hypothesis is true, i.e.,

$$p = \Pr(T(X) > t \mid H_0). \tag{15.1}$$

As H_0 contains the nuisance parameter θ, we replace the above problem by

$$p = \Pr(T(X) > t \mid H_0(\hat{\theta})), \tag{15.2}$$

where $\hat{\theta}$ is an estimator of θ. The bootstrap estimate of p can be computed as follows:

1 Let the computed value of $T(x)$ based on the sample x be t, and let the estimated value of θ be $\hat{\theta}$, which may be any appropriate estimator, such as the MLE.
2 Generate a sample of observations from the distributional assumption of $H_0(\hat{\theta})$; call this x^*. Compute the test statistic using data x^* and call this t^*.
3 Repeat Step 2 m times, which is the bootstrap sample size, to obtain m values of the test statistic t_j^*, for $j = 1, \ldots, m$.
4 The estimated p-value of t is computed as

$$\frac{1 + \text{number of } \{t_j^* \geq t\}}{m + 1}. \tag{15.3}$$

The above is a **parametric bootstrap** procedure, in which the samples x^* are generated from a parametric distribution. At level of significance α, the null hypothesis is rejected if the estimated p-value is less than α.

Example 15.4 You are given the following 20 observations of losses:

0.114, 0.147, 0.203, 0.378, 0.410, 0.488, 0.576, 0.868, 0.901, 0.983, 1.049, 1.555, 2.060, 2.274, 4.235, 5.400, 5.513, 5.817, 8.901, 12.699.

(a) Compute the Kolmogorov–Smirnov D statistic, assuming the data are distributed as $\mathcal{P}(\alpha, 5)$. Estimate the p-value of the test statistic using bootstrap.
(b) Repeat (a), assuming the null distribution is $\mathcal{P}(\alpha, 40)$.
(c) Repeat (a), assuming the null distribution is $\mathcal{E}(\lambda)$.

Solution 15.4 For (a), we estimate α using MLE, which, from Example 12.9, is given by

$$\hat{\alpha} = \frac{20}{\sum_{i=1}^{20} \log(x_i + 5) - 20 \log(5)},$$

and we obtain $\hat{\alpha} = 2.7447$. The computed D statistic, with the null distribution being $\mathcal{P}(2.7447, 5)$, is computed using equation (13.4) to obtain 0.1424. To estimate the p-value, we generate 10,000 bootstrap samples of size 20 each from $\mathcal{P}(2.7447, 5)$, estimate α and compute the D statistic for each sample. The generation of the Pareto random numbers is done using the inversion method discussed in Example 14.3. The proportion of the D values larger than 0.1424 calculated using equation (15.3) is 0.5775, which is the estimated p-value. Thus, the $\mathcal{P}(\alpha, 5)$ assumption cannot be rejected at any conventional level of significance.

For (b), the MLE of α is

$$\hat{\alpha} = \frac{20}{\sum_{i=1}^{20} \log(x_i + 40) - 20 \log(40)} = 15.8233.$$

The computed D statistic is 0.2138. We generate 10,000 samples of size 20 each from the $\mathcal{P}(15.8233, 40)$ distribution and compute the D statistic of each sample. The estimated p-value is 0.0996. Thus, at the level of significance of 10%, the null hypothesis $\mathcal{P}(\alpha, 40)$ is rejected, but not at the level of significance of 5%.

For (c), the MLE of λ is

$$\hat{\lambda} = \frac{1}{\bar{x}} = 0.3665,$$

and the computed D value is 0.2307. We generate 10,000 samples of size 20 each from the $\mathcal{E}(0.3665)$ distribution using the inversion method. The estimated p-value of the D statistic is 0.0603. Thus, the assumption of $\mathcal{E}(\lambda)$ is rejected at the 10% level, but not at the 5% level.

To conclude, the Kolmogorov–Smirnov test supports the $\mathcal{P}(\alpha, 5)$ distribution assumption for the loss data, but not the $\mathcal{P}(\alpha, 40)$ and $\mathcal{E}(\lambda)$ distributions.   □

15.3 Bootstrap Estimation of Bias and Mean Squared Error

Bootstrap method can also be used to estimate the bias and mean squared error of the parameter estimates of a distribution. Let us consider the estimation of the parameter θ (or a function of the parameter $g(\theta)$) of a distribution using an estimator $\hat{\theta}$ (or $g(\hat{\theta})$), given a random sample of n observations $x = (x_1, \ldots, x_n)$ of X. In situations where theoretical results about the bias and mean squared error of $\hat{\theta}$ (or $g(\hat{\theta})$) are intractable, we may use the bootstrap method to estimate these quantities.

When no additional assumption about the distribution of X is made, we may use the empirical distribution define by x (see Section 11.1.1) as the assumed distribution. We generate a sample of n observations $x^* = (x_1^*, \ldots, x_n^*)$ by resampling from x with replacement, and compute the estimate $\hat{\theta}^*$ (or $g(\hat{\theta}^*)$) based on x^*. We do this m times to obtain m estimates $\hat{\theta}_j^*$ (or $g(\hat{\theta}_j^*)$), for $j = 1, \ldots, m$. Based on these bootstrap estimates, we can compute the bias and the mean squared error of the estimator $\hat{\theta}$ (or $g(\hat{\theta})$). As x^* are generated from the empirical distribution defined by x, we call this method **nonparametric bootstrap**.

To illustrate the idea, we consider the use of the sample mean and the sample variance as estimates of the population mean μ and population variance σ^2 of X, respectively. Let μ_E and σ_E^2 be the mean and the variance, respectively, of the empirical distribution defined by x. We note that $\mu_E = \bar{x}$ and $\sigma_E^2 = (n-1)s^2/n$, where $\bar{x}$ and s^2 are the sample mean and the sample variance of x, respectively. To use the bootstrap method to estimate the bias and the mean squared error of $\bar{x}$ and s^2, we adopt the following procedure:

1 Generate a random sample of n observations by resampling with replacement from x, call this $x^* = (x_1^*, \ldots, x_n^*)$. Compute the mean $\bar{x}^*$ and variance s^{*2} of x^*.

2 Repeat Step 1 m times to obtain values $\bar{x}_j^*$ and s_j^{*2}, for $j = 1, \ldots, m$.

3 The bias and the mean squared error of $\bar{x}$ are estimated, respectively, by

$$\frac{1}{m} \sum_{j=1}^{m} (\bar{x}_j^* - \mu_E) \quad \text{and} \quad \frac{1}{m} \sum_{j=1}^{m} (\bar{x}_j^* - \mu_E)^2. \tag{15.4}$$

4 The bias and the mean squared error of s^2 are estimated, respectively, by

$$\frac{1}{m} \sum_{j=1}^{m} (s_j^{*2} - \sigma_E^2) \quad \text{and} \quad \frac{1}{m} \sum_{j=1}^{m} (s_j^{*2} - \sigma_E^2)^2. \tag{15.5}$$

It is theoretically known that $\bar{x}$ and s^2 are unbiased for μ and σ^2, respectively. Furthermore, the expected value of $\bar{x}_j^*$ is μ_E and the expected value of s_j^{*2} is σ_E^2, so that the bootstrap estimate of the biases should converge to zero when m is large.

The mean squared error of $\bar{x}$ is

$$\text{MSE}(\bar{x}) = \text{Var}(\bar{x}) = \frac{\sigma^2}{n}, \tag{15.6}$$

which is unknown (as σ^2 is unknown). On the other hand, the bootstrap estimate of the MSE of $\bar{x}$ in equation (15.4) converges in probability to σ_E^2/n, which is known given x. However, when x varies $E(\sigma_E^2/n) = (n-1)\sigma^2/n^2 \neq \text{MSE}(\bar{x})$.

We will not pursue the analytical derivation of $\text{MSE}(s^2)$, which depends on the higher-order moments of X.

Example 15.5 You are given a sample of 20 loss observations of X as in Example 15.4.

(a) Compute the bootstrap estimates of the bias and mean squared error of the sample mean $\bar{x}$.

(b) Compute the bootstrap estimates of the bias and mean squared error of the sample variance s^2.

(c) Compute the bootstrap estimates of the bias and mean squared error of the sample proportion p in estimating $\Pr(X \leq \bar{x})$.

Solution 15.5 From the data, we compute the sample mean (which is also the mean of the empirical distribution μ_E) as 2.7286, the sample variance as 11.5442 and the variance of the empirical distribution σ_E^2 as 10.9670. For (a) and (b), the bootstrap procedure described above is used. Note that the bootstrap estimate of the mean squared error of $\bar{x}$ should converge to

$$\frac{\sigma_E^2}{n} = \frac{10.9670}{20} = 0.5484.$$

For (c), we compute, for the bootstrap sample j, the proportion of observations not exceeding 2.7286, and call this p_j^*. As 14 out of 20 observations in the sample do not exceed 2.7286, the proportion in the empirical distribution is 0.7. The bias and the mean squared error of the sample proportion p are estimated by

$$\frac{1}{m} \sum_{j=1}^{m} (p_j^* - 0.7) \qquad \text{and} \qquad \frac{1}{m} \sum_{j=1}^{m} (p_j^* - 0.7)^2,$$

respectively. Note that p is unbiased for the proportion in the empirical distribution, and

$$\text{Var}(p) = \frac{(0.7)(1 - 0.7)}{20} = 0.0105.$$

Using a bootstrap sample of 10,000 runs, we obtain the results in Table 15.4.

It can be observed that the estimated mean squared error of $\bar{x}$ is very close to its theoretical limit of 0.5484, and so is the estimated mean squared error of p to its theoretical value of 0.0105. Also, the empirical results agree with the theory that the statistics are unbiased. □

We now consider a parametric loss distribution with df $F(\theta)$. The bias and mean squared error of an estimator $\hat{\theta}$ of θ can be estimated using the **parametric bootstrap** method as follows:

Table 15.4. *Results of Example 15.5*

Statistic	Bias	MSE
$\bar{x}$	0.0072	0.5583
s^2	−0.0060	24.2714
p	−0.0017	0.0105

1 Compute the estimate $\hat{\theta}$ using sample data x.
2 Generate a random sample of n observations from the distribution $F(\hat{\theta})$, and estimate θ, called $\hat{\theta}^*$. Repeat this m times to obtain the estimates $\hat{\theta}_j^*$, for $j = 1, \ldots, m$.
3 Estimates of the bias and mean squared error of $\hat{\theta}$ are computed as

$$\frac{1}{m} \sum_{j=1}^{m} (\hat{\theta}_j^* - \hat{\theta}) \qquad \text{and} \qquad \frac{1}{m} \sum_{j=1}^{m} (\hat{\theta}_j^* - \hat{\theta})^2. \qquad (15.7)$$

Note that the bias and mean squared error of $\hat{\theta}$ can also be estimated using the nonparametric bootstrap, in which case the random samples in Step 2 above are generated by resampling with replacement from the data x.

Example 15.6 Refer to the data in Example 15.4. Assume the loss data are distributed as $\mathcal{P}(\alpha, 5)$.

(a) Compute the parametric bootstrap estimates of the bias and mean squared error of the MLE of α.
(b) Compute the nonparametric bootstrap estimates of the bias and mean squared error of the MLE of α.

Solution 15.6 As discussed in Example 15.4, the MLE of α assuming the $\mathcal{P}(\alpha, 5)$ distribution is $\hat{\alpha} = 2.7477$. For parametric bootstrap, we generate the bootstrap samples from the $\mathcal{P}(2.7477, 5)$ distribution and compute the MLE of α in each bootstrap sample. We simulate 10,000 such samples to compute the bias and the mean squared error using equation (15.7). For the nonparametric bootstrap, the procedure is similar, except that the bootstrap samples are generated by resampling with replacement from the original data. The results are summarized in Table 15.5.

We can see that the results of the parametric and nonparametric bootstraps are comparable. We also note that the MLE is upward biased (at the given sample size). □

Table 15.5. *Results of Example 15.6*

Bootstrap method	Bias of $\hat{\alpha}$	MSE of $\hat{\alpha}$
Parametric	0.1417	0.4792
Nonparametric	0.1559	0.5401

15.4 A General Framework of Bootstrap

Bootstrap is a very versatile statistical method with many important applications. In this section, we attempt to provide a framework of the theoretical underpinning of the applications we have discussed. Readers may refer to Davison and Hinkley (1997) for further details of the method.

Let $X = \{X_1, \ldots, X_n\}$ be independently and identically distributed as X with df $F(\cdot)$, which may depend on a parameter θ. Suppose $\xi = \xi(F)$ is a quantity of the distribution (e.g., mean, median, a quantile or a population proportion) and $\hat{\xi} = \hat{\xi}(X)$ is an estimate of ξ based on X. We define

$$\eta(X; F) = \hat{\xi}(X) - \xi(F), \tag{15.8}$$

which is the error in estimating ξ using $\hat{\xi}$. Denoting E_F as the expectation taken using the df F, the bias of $\hat{\xi}$ is

$$E_F[\eta(X; F)] = E_F[\hat{\xi}(X) - \xi(F)] \tag{15.9}$$

and the mean squared error of $\hat{\xi}$ is

$$E_F[\eta(X; F)^2] = E_F[(\hat{\xi}(X) - \xi(F))^2]. \tag{15.10}$$

For another application, let $T(X)$ be a test statistic for a hypothesis H_0 and its value computed based on a specific sample $x = (x_1, \ldots, x_n)$ be $t = T(x)$. We now define

$$\eta(X; F) = T(X) - t. \tag{15.11}$$

If H_0 is rejected when t is too large, the p-value of the test is[1]

$$Pr(T(X) - t > 0 \mid F) = Pr(\eta(X; F) > 0 \mid F). \tag{15.12}$$

In the above cases, we are interested in the expectation or the population proportion of a suitably defined function $\eta(X; F)$. This setup includes the evaluation of bias and mean squared error of an estimator and the p-value of a test, as well as many other applications.

As F is unknown in practice, the quantities in equations (15.9), (15.10) and (15.12) cannot be evaluated. However, we may replace F by a known df F^* and consider instead the quantities

$$E_{F^*}[\eta(X; F^*)] = E_{F^*}[\hat{\xi}(X) - \xi(F^*)], \tag{15.13}$$

$$E_{F^*}[\eta(X; F^*)^2] = E_{F^*}[(\hat{\xi}(X) - \xi(F^*))^2], \tag{15.14}$$

and

$$Pr(T(X) - t > 0 \mid F^*) = Pr(\eta(X; F^*) > 0 \mid F^*). \tag{15.15}$$

---

[1] Tests which are two sided or with critical regions on the left-hand tail can also be defined appropriately.

The above quantities are called the bootstrap approximations. The reliability of these approximations depends on how good F^* is as an approximation to F. If F^* is taken as the empirical distribution defined by x, we have a nonparametric bootstrap. If, however, F^* is taken as $F(\hat{\theta})$ for a suitable estimator $\hat{\theta}$ computed from the sample x, then we have a parametric bootstrap.

As $\hat{\xi}(X)$ and $T(X)$ may be rather complex functions of X, the evaluation of equations (15.13), (15.14) and (15.15) may remain elusive even with known or given F^*. In the case where the sample size n is small and the empirical distribution is used for F^*, we may evaluate these quantities by exhausting all possible samples of X. This approach, however, will not be feasible when n is large or when a parametric df $F(\hat{\theta})$ is used. In such situations, the quantities may be estimated using Monte Carlo methods, and we call the solution the Monte Carlo estimate of the bootstrap approximate, or simply the bootstrap estimate. Specifically, for nonparametric bootstrap, we resample with replacement from x and then compute the sample mean or the sample proportion as required. For parametric bootstrap, however, the samples are generated from the distribution with df $F(\hat{\theta})$.

15.5 R Laboratory

R Codes 15.1 provides the codes to estimate the critical values of the Kolmogorov–Smirnov statistic for a normal distribution with unknown mean and variance. The statistics are based on samples of 20 or 30 observations. The critical values are the quantiles of the bootstrap samples. Some results are reported in Example 15.1.

```
#####################################################################
# R Codes 15.1
#
# Example 15.1: Estimation of critical values of the
# Kolmogorov-Smirnov statistic for normal distribution with
# fitted mean and variance
#####################################################################

nv=c(20,30)                      # Sample size of KS stat
al=c(0.9,0.95,0.99)              # Level of confidence
m=10000                          # Monte Carlo sample size
for (i in 1:length(nv))
{
ksv=NULL                         # Initialize KS stat
n=nv[i]                          # Sample size selected
edf=(1:n)/n
edf1=c(0,(1:(n-1))/n)
for (j in 1:m)
```

```
{
x=rnorm(n)                                  # Draw sample of normal obs
fdf=pnorm(sort(x),mean(x),sd(x))            # Df of fitted normal
ks=max(pmax(abs(edf-fdf),abs(edf1-fdf)))    # KS stat of sample
ksv=c(ksv,ks)                               # Collect computed KS stat
}
cv=as.numeric(quantile(ksv,al))             # Critical values of KS stat
   cat("Sample size =",n,"\n",
       "Critical value at 10%, 5% and 1% confidence level: ",cv,"\n")
}
```

R Codes 15.2 provides the codes to estimate the critical values of the chi-square goodness-of-fit statistic based on the MLE and MMLE in Example 15.3. The function mlik computes the negative of the log-likelihood of the grouped data to be used for minimization using optim for the calculation of the MMLE. Some results are reported in Table 15.3.

```
#######################################################################
# R Codes 15.2
#
# Example 15.3: Estimation of the critical values of the chi-square
# goodness-of-fit statistic based on MLE and MMLE
#######################################################################

set.seed(200)
nv=100                                  # Sample size of chi-square stat
al=c(0.9,0.95,0.99)                     # Critical values
m=10000                                 # Monte Carlo sample size
breaks=c(0,0.4,1,2,100000)              # Define bins
b1=breaks[1:4]                          # Lower bin cutoff
b2=breaks[2:5]                          # Upper bin cutoff
mlik=function(b,nv,b1,b2)
   -sum(nv*log(exp(-b*b1)-exp(-b*b2)))  # -ve loglikelihood of MMLE
MLEV=NULL                               # Initialize sample of MLE
MMLEV=NULL                              # Initialize sample of MMLE
st=1                                    # Start value for MLE
defaultW = getOption("warn")            # Suppress warnings
options(warn = -1)
for (i in 1:m)
{
x=rexp(nv)                              # Generate nv Exp(1) obs
xnv=as.numeric(table(cut(x,breaks)))    # Count numbers in bins
MLE1=1/mean(x)                          # MLE
env1=nv*(exp(-MLE1*b1)-exp(-MLE1*b2))   # Expected frequency for MLE
MLE2=optim(st,mlik,nv=xnv,b1=b1,b2=b2,hessian=F)$par # Compute MMLE
env2=nv*(exp(-MLE2*b1)-exp(-MLE2*b2))   # Expected frequency for MMLE
```

```
C1=sum(xnv^2/env1)-nv          # Chi-square stat for MLE
C2=sum(xnv^2/env2)-nv          # Chi-square stat for MMLE
MLEV=c(MLEV,C1)
MMLEV=c(MMLEV,C2)
}
quantile(MLEV,al)              # Output results for MLE
quantile(MMLEV,al)             # Output results for MMLE
```

R Codes 15.3 provides the codes to estimate the bias and the mean-squared error of the sample mean, sample variance and sample proportion in Example 15.5. The function bootstrap in the package with the same name computes bootstrap sample of a provided function. Functions meanx, varx and px are coded to compute the sample mean, sample variance and sample proportion, respectively, for use in bootstrap.

```
###################################################################
# R Codes 15.3
#
# Example 15.5: Bootstrap estimation of the bias and mean squared
# error of the sample mean, sample variance and sample proportion
###################################################################

x=c(0.114,0.147,0.203,0.378,0.410,0.488,0.576,0.868,0.901,0.983,
    1.049,1.555,2.060,2.274,4.235,5.400,5.513,5.817,8.901,12.699)

library(bootstrap)
nboot=10000                    # Bootstrap sample size
meanx=function(x) mean(x)
varx=function(x) var(x)
px=function(x,c) sum(x<=c)/length(x)

bm=bootstrap(x,nboot,meanx)    # Bootstrap samples of sample mean
bv=bootstrap(x,nboot,varx)     # Bootstrap samples of sample var
bp=bootstrap(x,nboot,px,c=mean(x)) # Bootstrap samples of sample prop
ved=(length(x)-1)*var(x)/length(x) # Population var of empirical dist

mean(bm$thetastar)-mean(x)        # Bias of sample mean
mean((bm$thetastar-mean(x))^2)    # MSE of sample mean
mean(bv$thetastar)-ved            # Bias of sample var
mean((bv$thetastar-ved)^2)        # MSE of sample var
mean(bp$thetastar)-px(x,mean(x))  # Bias of sample proportion
mean((bp$thetastar-px(x,mean(x)))^2) # MSE of sample proportion
```

15.6 Summary and Discussions

We have discussed some applications of Monte Carlo methods for the analysis of actuarial and financial data. Using simulated samples we can estimate the critical values and p-values of the test statistics when their exact values are unknown. These estimates are viable, however, only when there are no nuisance parameters determining the distribution of the test statistic. In cases where nuisance parameters are present, the p-values of the tests can be estimated using bootstrap method. We discuss parametric and nonparametric bootstrap methods. They prove to be very valuable tools for model testing.

Exercises

Exercise 15.1 Let $x = (x_1, \ldots, x_n)$ be a random sample of n observations of X.

(a) How would you estimate the bias and the mean squared error of the sample median as an estimator of the median of X using nonparametric bootstrap?
(b) How would you estimate the bootstrap sample size required if it is desired to estimate the bias of the sample median to within 0.05 with probability of 0.95?
(c) If X is assumed to be exponentially distributed, how would you perform a parametric bootstrap for the above problems?

Exercise 15.2 Let θ denote the interquartile range of X, which is defined as the 75th percentile minus the 25th percentile. You are required to estimate the 95% confidence interval of θ based on the distribution of $\hat{\theta}/\theta$, where $\hat{\theta}$ is the difference between the 75th percentile and the 25th percentile of the sample $x = (x_1, \ldots, x_n)$. How would you estimate the 95% confidence interval of θ using nonparametric bootstrap?

Exercise 15.3 Let (X, Y) be a bivariate random variable with correlation coefficient ρ. You have a random sample of n observations (x_i, y_i), for $i = 1, \ldots, n$ with sample correlation coefficient $\hat{\rho}$.

(a) How would you estimate the bias of $\hat{\rho}$ as an estimator of ρ using nonparametric bootstrap?
(b) If (X, Y) follows a bivariate normal distribution, how would you estimate the bias of $\hat{\rho}$ as an estimator of ρ using parametric bootstrap? [**Hint:** It can be shown that the distribution of $\hat{\rho}$ depends only on ρ, not on the means and standard deviations of X and Y.]

Exercise 15.4 Let $x = (x_1, \ldots, x_n)$ be a random sample of n observations of $X \sim \mathcal{L}(\mu, \sigma^2)$. The coefficient of variation of X is $\theta = [\mathrm{Var}(X)]^{\frac{1}{2}}/\mathrm{E}(X) = (e^{\sigma^2} - 1)^{\frac{1}{2}}$. The maximum likelihood estimate of θ is $\hat{\theta} = (e^{\hat{\sigma}^2} - 1)^{\frac{1}{2}}$, where $\hat{\sigma}^2$ is the maximum likelihood estimate of σ^2. How would you estimate the bias of $\hat{\theta}$ as an estimator of θ using parametric bootstrap?

Questions Adapted from SOA Exams

Exercise 15.5 For an insurance policy covering both fire and wind losses, a sample of fire losses was found to be 3 and 4, and wind losses in the same period were 0 and 3. Fire and wind losses are independent, but do not have identical distributions. Based on the sample, you estimate that adding a policy deductible of 2 per wind claim will eliminate 20% of the insured loss. Determine the bootstrap approximation to the mean squared error of the estimate.

Exercise 15.6 Three observed values of the random variable X are 1, 1 and 4. You estimate the third moment of X using the estimator $\hat{\mu}_3' = \left[\sum_{i=1}^{3} (X_i - \bar{X})^3 \right] / 3$. Determine the bootstrap estimate of the mean squared error of $\hat{\mu}_3'$.

Exercise 15.7 You are given a sample of two values of the distribution X, 5 and 9, and you estimate σ^2, the variance of X, using the estimator $\hat{\sigma}^2 = \left[\sum_{i=1}^{2} (X_i - \bar{X})^2 \right] / 2$. Determine the bootstrap approximation to the mean squared error of $\hat{\sigma}^2$.

Part V

Loss Reserving and Ratemaking

Insurance companies charge premiums for the losses their policies cover. To set adequate and competitive premiums, losses arising from the policies must be reliably predicted based on past data and experience. As insurance claims may take multiple years to settle, actuaries have to account for various factors that may impact future possible losses. We discuss different methods to predict the ultimate aggregate payments of insurance losses, which is the first step in setting the premiums.

Premiums are determined as a markup on the predicted losses to cover expenses and profits. We discuss the loss cost method and loss ratio method for the determination of premiums. Complication may arise when premiums are charged to heterogeneous groups of insured. We discuss methods to revise the differential premium rates for different groups of insured.

16

Loss Reserving

Short-term insurance policies often take multiple years before the final settlement of all losses incurred is completed. This is especially true for liability insurance policies, which may drag on for a long time due to legal proceedings. To set the premiums of insurance policies appropriately so that the premiums are competitive and yet sufficient to cover the losses and expenses with a reasonable profit margin, accurate projection of losses cannot be overemphasized. Loss reserving refers to the techniques to project future payments of insurance losses based on policies in the past.

In this chapter, we discuss three methods of estimating reserves: the expected loss ratio method, the chain-ladder method and the Bornhuetter–Ferguson method. We also consider some variations of these methods, including projecting the aggregate payments using separate projections of claim counts and claim severity.

Learning Objectives

1 Definitions of Calendar Year, Policy Year and Accident Year
2 Earned premiums and reserves
3 Loss ratios and methods of estimating ultimate reserves
4 Methods to develop estimates of claim frequency and severity separately
5 The closure method

16.1 Periods, Premiums and Reserves

As nonlife insurance policies are typically short term, we shall assume these policies to be purchased or renewed annually, unless otherwise stated. While insurance policies can be purchased at any time, actuarial reports are compiled regularly over fixed intervals. Hence, actuaries must be careful in understanding the interaction between the time periods of their reports and the in-force periods of the insurance policies they are reporting. For this matter, it is important to define certain terminologies regarding time periods (years).

First, **Calendar Year (CY)** refers to the period from January 1 to December 31 of a year. The losses paid in a certain CY, however, may be due to a policy issued the year before. Indeed, for certain liability insurance policies there may be a long time lag between a loss occurrence and the final settlement. As we shall see later, it is important to set aside reserves for such policies and estimate their amounts accurately.

Second, **Policy Year (PY)** refers to the year in which the policy is issued. The exposure period of a policy in a certain PY may be over multiple CYs. For example, a policy issued on June 1, 2019, is in force until May 31, 2020. Thus, the exposure period for policies issued in PY 2019 is from January 1, 2019, to December 31, 2020.

Third, **Accident Year (AY)** refers to the year in which a loss (accident) occurs. The policy making the claim may be written in the same CY or in a previous CY. For example, an accident occurring in April 2019 may be for a policy written in January 2019 or December 2018, among other possibilities.

An insurance policy becomes in force upon the payment of a premium. The amount of premium paid is recorded as the **written premium** in a certain period (CY or PY). As the exposure of the policy is for one year, however, the premium is not fully *earned* until the exposure is over. The **earned premium** is the fractional amount of the written premium proportional to the exposure period in the CY or PY when the policy is issued. For example, for a policy with a written premium of 1,000 written on October 1, 2019, the earned premium in 2019 is 250, which is a quarter (the exposure period is a quarter of a year) of the written premium.[1] The **unearned premium** is the difference between the written premium and the earned premium.

Example 16.1 An insurance policy is issued on June 1 of CY1 at an annual premium of 1,200. What is the earned premium of this policy in CY1 if (a) the premium is to be fully paid up front, and (b) the premium is paid by four equal quarterly installments in advance (if there is a claim, the full premium must be paid before the benefits can be disbursed)?

Solution 16.1 The earned premium is the portion of the annual premium covering the relevant in-force period in the CY. It does not depend on the mode

---

[1] In this chapter and the next, all monetary amounts are stated without specifying the currency.

of payment. As the period covered is 7 months, the earned premium in CY1 is

$$1{,}200 \times \frac{7}{12} = 700.$$

□

Example 16.2 An insurance company sells annual workers compensation policies in CY1 with a total amount of 120,000 premiums from May 1 to the end of the year. Assume the policies are sold at a uniform rate throughout this period and calculate the amount of the earned premiums in this period.

Solution 16.2 Let t denote the time (in months) from May 1 of CY1, $0 < t < 8$. For a unit premium received at time t, the earned premium until the end of the year is

$$\frac{8-t}{12}, \qquad \text{for } 0 < t < 8.$$

As policies are sold uniformly throughout the year, t is uniformly distributed in $(0, 8)$ with a density function of $1/8$. Thus, the earned premium from May 1 to the end of CY1 is

$$120{,}000 \int_0^8 \frac{1}{8} \times \frac{8-t}{12} \, dt = \frac{120{,}000}{8 \times 12} \left(\left[8t - \frac{t^2}{2} \right]_0^8 \right) = \frac{120{,}000}{8 \times 12} \times 32 = 40{,}000.$$

□

When an accident is reported, a claim file is opened. The claim amount of each accident will be estimated with the severity of the accident and possible settlement time and inflation taken into account. The aggregate estimated amount of future payments for all opened claim files in addition to the actual payments made is called the **case reserve**. Furthermore, the following reserves must be estimated as well:

1 Provision for future adjustments of known claims.
2 Provision for claim files that are closed but may be reopened.
3 Provision for claims incurred but not reported (**pure IBNR**).
4 Provision for claims reported but not recorded (**RBNR**).

The sum of the four provisions above is called the **gross IBNR reserve** (as opposed to pure IBNR in Item 3) or **bulk reserve**. Note that these four items are unknown and have to be estimated. They are separately itemized so that the actuary can model them using different assumptions.

Good estimates of future losses are important for setting the premium of new policies. Estimates of the total losses should be based on historical data. As some policies have long time lags before the final settlement, accurate loss estimation may require multiple years of data. To this effect, the **table of loss payments** is important for analysis.

Table 16.1. *Table of loss payments*

Year	Incremental loss payments in development year					
	0	1	2	3	4	5
AY1	4,353	1,820	1,542	1,280	980	628
AY2	4,821	1,527	1,728	1,720	1,310	
AY3	5,022	1,872	1,420	1,230		
AY4	5,345	1,920	2,102			
AY5	5,762	2,208				
AY6	6,028					

Table 16.1 is an example of the loss payments of a block of insurance policies over six AYs. The figures in each row trace the incremental payments in subsequent years, called **development years (DY)**. For example, 4,353 (in the first row) is the aggregate of all payments and reserves set aside for future settlement at the end of AY1. This is marked as DY0. Similarly 1,820 is the aggregate of all *additional* payments and reserves set aside for future settlement in the first year after AY1. This row of figures ends at the end of the fifth development year. If the actuary's experience is that policy claims do not take more than five years to settle, reserve development may be assumed to have matured after five years. Note that the incremental figures consist of payments to the insured as well as *changes* in the reserves. If the reserves in the past have been overestimated the updated reserves may be negative and so is the incremental payment. Note that AY6 is the immediate past year and we only have the aggregate payments in development year 0, namely, the end of AY6.

The actuary uses loss data to estimate future losses. In addition to past experience, future losses should also take account of factors such as inflation, technological changes and, changes in consumer behavior as well as changes in regulations. Once future losses are estimated, the loss ratio can be computed. Two notions of loss ratios should be noted: **expected loss ratio** and **permissible loss ratio**. The expected loss ratio is the expected loss amount divided by the premium. Needless to say, this ratio should be less than 1. An expected loss ratio close to 1 suggests that the premium may not be enough to cover the claims. As the losses do not take account of expenses such as administrative costs and sales commissions, care must be taken if such costs are high. On the other hand, the permissible loss ratio is used for pricing. This ratio is usually set a priori to reflect margins for expenses and profit. A low permissible loss ratio will result in a high premium. While the expected loss ratio may be used to estimate future losses and compute loss reserves, the permissible loss ratio is used for setting the premium (also called **ratemaking**).

We now discuss methods of estimating loss reserves. Methods of ratemaking will be discussed in the next chapter.

16.2 Three Methods of Estimating Reserves

In the actuary's books, case reserves are based on filed claims and these figures are known. Sometimes the unknown final payments may be computed as a mark up on the case reserves, resulting in the so-called **case reserves plus** approach. This approach, however, lacks a theoretical basis and is not recommended. In this section, we consider three approaches of estimating the ultimate losses based on available historical data.

16.2.1 Expected Loss Ratio Method

The expected loss ratio method assumes that the risk profiles of the block of policies and the risk environment remain unchanged. The historical loss ratio is used as the future expected loss ratio. The ultimate loss is computed as the earned premium times the expected loss ratio. Reserves to be set aside is the residual of the ultimate losses net the claims paid out. This amount is then adjusted progressively year on year until the final payments are made, with the estimated ultimate payment kept unchanged. Example 16.3 illustrates the use of the expected loss ratio method.

Example 16.3 You are given the data in Table 16.2 for a block of insurance policies. The expected loss ratio is 0.75. Calculate

(a) the total reserve on Dec 31, CY2,
(b) the IBNR reserve on Dec 31, CY2.

Solution 16.3 (a) The expected losses are

$$400,000 \times 0.75 = 300,000.$$

Table 16.2. *Data of Example 16.3*

Date	Action
June 1, CY1	400,000 premiums received
Feb 1, CY2	20,000 losses paid
Sept 1, CY2	10,000 losses paid
Dec 31, CY2	100,000 case reserves paid

Therefore, the total reserve on Dec 31 CY2 is

$$300,000 - 20,000 - 10,000 = 270,000.$$

(b) The IBNR reserve on Dec 31 CY2 is

$$270,000 - 100,000 = 170,000. \qquad \square$$

16.2.2 Chain-Ladder Method

The chain-ladder method uses multiple years of historical loss data to project loss payments for a block of policies. Typically, data of loss payments such as those in Table 16.1 are used. The steps may consist of the following:

1. Construct a table of cumulative loss payments over the development years until all losses are paid.
2. Calculate the **age-by-age development factors** as the ratios of the losses of a development year over the losses of the previous development year.
3. Compute the average age-by-age development factors over multiple AYs. These ratios are called the **link ratios**.
4. Use the link ratios to project future payments of the block until all payments mature.

Example 16.4 uses the data in Table 16.1 to illustrate the use of the chain-ladder method.

Example 16.4 You are given the loss payment data for a block of insurance policies as in Table 16.1. For AY2 through AY6, estimate the reserves in the development years until the payments mature.

Solution 16.4 We first compute the cumulative loss payments up to the last development year. The results are presented in Table 16.3.

We then calculate the development factors as the cumulative payments in DY j over the cumulative payments in DY $j - 1$. For example, for AY1 losses, the ratio of DY1 versus DY0, denoted as "1/0," is

$$\frac{6,173}{4,353} = 1.418.$$

The computed development factors are summarized in Table 16.4.

Next we assume that the loss payment progressions in each AY through their corresponding development years are stable. To summarize their average rates of progression, we calculate the average over different AYs. The number of available development factors varies with the years of development. We compute the average in two ways. First, we compute the arithmetic mean of the

Table 16.3. *Cumulative Loss Payments*

	Cumulative loss payments in development year					
Year	0	1	2	3	4	5
AY1	4,353	6,173	7,715	8,995	9,975	10,603
AY2	4,821	6,348	8,076	9,796	11,106	
AY3	5,022	6,894	8,314	9,544		
AY4	5,345	7,265	9,367			
AY5	5,762	7,970				
AY6	6,028					

Table 16.4. *Loss development factors*

	Loss development factors for development years				
Year	1/0	2/1	3/2	4/3	5/4
AY1	1.418	1.250	1.166	1.109	1.063
AY2	1.317	1.272	1.213	1.134	
AY3	1.373	1.206	1.148		
AY4	1.359	1.289			
AY5	1.383				
Average	1.3700	1.2543	1.1756	1.1213	1.0630
Wt Average	1.3694	1.2546	1.1755	1.1219	1.0630

development factors. For example, for development factor "1/0," we have five ratios, and the arithmetic mean is

$$\frac{1.418 + 1.317 + 1.373 + 1.359 + 1.383}{5} = 1.3700.$$

We compute all the arithmetic means and summarize the results in the second last row of Table 16.4 (simply denoted as "Average"). Another way to compute the average is to weight the ratios with respect to the cumulative payments in the previous development year. We call this the weighted average, denoted by "Wt average" in Table 6.4. For the age-to-age factor "1/0," this is computed as (refer to the cumulative payment figures in Table 16.3)

$$\frac{6,173 + 6,348 + 6,894 + 7,265 + 7,970}{4,353 + 4,821 + 5,022 + 5,345 + 5,762} = 1.3694.$$

The weighted averages of the development factors are summarized in the last row of Table 16.4. With the computed link ratios, we can project the future loss payments for AY2 through AY6 until payments mature. The projections using

Table 16.5. *Projected cumulative payments using*
average link ratios

Year	Development year					
	0	1	2	3	4	5
AY1	4,353	6,173	7,715	8,995	9,975	10,603
AY2	4,821	6,348	8,076	9,796	11,106	**11,805**
AY3	5,022	6,894	8,314	9,544	**10,702**	**11,376**
AY4	5,345	7,265	9,367	**11,012**	**12,348**	**13,126**
AY5	5,762	7,970	**9,997**	**11,753**	**13,179**	**14,008**
AY6	6,028	**8,258**	**10,359**	**12,178**	**13,655**	**14,515**

the average link ratios are summarized in the lower triangle of Table 16.5 (see the boldface figures). For example, the projected cumulative loss payments for AY4 in DYs 3 and 4 are, respectively,

$$9,367 \times 1.1756 = 11,012$$

and

$$11,012 \times 1.1213 = 12,348.$$

The last column of Table 16.5 gives the projected ultimate loss payments for all AYs. The total reserve over all blocks from AY2 through AY6 is the sum of the ultimate losses in the last column (ignoring AY1, which has matured) minus the sum of the cumulative payments to date, namely,

$$(11,805 + \cdots + 14,515) - (11,106 + 9,544 + \cdots + 6,028)$$
$$= 64,830 - 44,015 = 20,815. \qquad \square$$

Modifications to the chain-ladder method as explained are possible. First, the actuary may assign different weights to losses from different AYs in calculating the link ratios. Experience from more recent loss data may be given higher weights. Second, loss payments projected may reflect the rate of inflation as deemed appropriate. Third, the average link ratio computed in the example uses all development factors available in the data. This may be modified by using only the more recent years of losses, such as the latest two or three development factors available.

The chain-ladder method may be used to project the cumulative loss payments or incremental reserves for different DYs. To compute the incremental reserves, we take the differences of the sequential cumulative payments.

16.2.3 Bornhuetter–Ferguson Method

The chain-ladder method of projection depends critically on the cumulative payments up to the latest DY (as represented by the diagonal figures of Table 16.3). If the last cumulative payment is large for some reason (such as the settlement of a big loss toward the end of the year), all subsequent projections will be affected. Usually, if large payments are made in a year, pressure on payments in subsequent year may be mitigated. There is, however, no mechanism in the chain-ladder method to self adjust. Consequently, results projected may not be stable.

The Bornhuetter–Ferguson method is proposed to overcome the above difficulty. Before we outline this method, we define the following notations:

P = Earned premium
r = Expected or permissible loss ratio
R = Cumulative loss payments at the end of DY $j - 1$
R_U = Estimated ultimate losses using the expected loss ratio method
R_C = Estimated ultimate losses using the chain-ladder method
  at the end of DY $j - 1$
m = Ultimate year of loss payments
f_i = Link ratio from DY $i - 1$ to DY i, for $i = 1, \ldots, m$

We assume that all policies are fully settled by the end of DY m. Note that R and R_C refer to the cumulative payments and ultimate projected losses made at the end of DY $j - 1$, respectively. To simplify the notations, however, the index of the DY is suppressed.

Using the above notations, the ultimate losses estimated by the expected loss ratio method is given by

$$R_U = Pr. \tag{16.1}$$

The ultimate loss estimate based on the expected loss ratio method does not depend on the DY. For the chain-ladder method, the projection of the ultimate losses based on the cumulative payments at the end of DY $j - 1$ depends on the chained link ratio f_U (again, index j is suppressed) defined as follows:

$$f_U = \prod_{i=j}^{m} f_i, \tag{16.2}$$

so that

$$R_C = R \prod_{i=j}^{m} f_i = Rf_U. \tag{16.3}$$

Table 16.6. *Earned premiums*

Accident year	AY2	AY3	AY4	AY5	AY6
Earned premium	17,230	17,700	20,000	21,500	23,000

The above equation may be rewritten as

$$R = R_C \times \frac{1}{f_U}. \tag{16.4}$$

As mentioned above, R may be unstable due to fluctuations in payments. We may obtain more stable (estimated) values of cumulative payments by replacing R_C by R_U to obtain

$$\hat{R} = R_U \times \frac{1}{f_U}. \tag{16.5}$$

The Bornhuetter–Ferguson reserve at DY j, denoted by R_B (again the index j is suppressed), is the difference between the ultimate losses estimated by the expected loss ratio method, R_U, and the reestimated cumulative payments $\hat{R}$ at the end of DY j. Thus,

$$R_B = R_U - \hat{R} = R_U - R_U \times \frac{1}{f_U} = R_U \left(1 - \frac{1}{f_U} \right) = Pr \left(1 - \frac{1}{f_U} \right) = Prf, \tag{16.6}$$

where

$$f = 1 - \frac{1}{f_U}. \tag{16.7}$$

Example 16.5 illustrates the use of the Bornhuetter–Ferguson method using the data in Example 16.4.

Example 16.5 In addition to the data in Example 16.4, you are given the information in Table 16.6 regarding the earned premiums of the policies from AY2 to AY6. The expected loss ratio is 0.65 for all policies. Estimate the total required reserves for policies of AY2 to AY6 using the Bornhuetter–Ferguson method.

Solution 16.5 Using the average yearly link ratios computed in Example 16.4 (calculations using the weighted average link ratios can be done similarly), we compute the ultimate link ratios f_U. The results are given in Table 16.7.

We then compute the Bornhuetter–Ferguson reserves R_B and summarize them with the cumulative payments in Table 16.2. These figures are given in boldface in the diagonal cells of Table 16.8.

Table 16.7. *Linked ratios*

	Development year j				
	1	2	3	4	5
f_j	1.370	1.254	1.176	1.121	1.063
f_U	2.408	1.758	1.401	1.192	1.063
f	0.585	0.431	0.286	0.161	0.059

Table 16.8. *Bornhuetter–Ferguson reserves*

	Cumulative loss payments and ultimate reserves development year					
Year	0	1	2	3	4	5
AY1	4,353	6,173	7,715	8,995	9,975	10,603
AY2	4,821	6,348	8,076	9,796	11,106	**663**
AY3	5,022	6,894	8,314	9,544	**1,853**	
AY4	5,345	7,265	9,367	**3,723**		
AY5	5,762	7,970	**6,024**			
AY6	6,028	**8,741**				

For example, for AY2 the Bornhuetter–Ferguson reserve for DY5 is

$$17{,}230(0.65)(0.059) = 663.$$

Similarly, for AY6 the Bornhuetter–Ferguson reserve for DY1 is

$$23{,}000(0.65)(0.585) = 8{,}741.$$

Thus, the total reserve required for the policies from AY2 through AY6 is

$$8{,}741 + 6{,}024 + 3{,}723 + 1{,}853 + 663 = 21{,}004.$$

Note that R_B gives the ultimate reserve required as estimated at DY j. It is not the projected cumulative payments as developed in the chain-ladder method. If we wish to calculate the incremental reserves using the Bornhuetter–Ferguson method, we have to compute R_B over different DYs and then take their differences. The results are summarized in Table 16.9.

For example, for AY4 the incremental reserve for DY4 is

$$20{,}000(0.65)(0.161) - 20{,}000(0.65)(0.059) = 1{,}323.$$

Similarly, for AY5 the incremental reserve for DY3 is

$$21{,}500(0.65)(0.286) - 21{,}500(0.65)(0.161) = 1{,}751. \qquad \square$$

Table 16.9. *Incremental reserves using the*
Bornhuetter–Ferguson method

Year	Incremental loss payments and reserves in development year					
	0	1	2	3	4	5
AY1	4,353	1,820	1,542	1,280	980	628
AY2	4,821	1,527	1,728	1,720	1,310	**663**
AY3	5,022	1,872	1,420	1,230	**1,171**	**681**
AY4	5,345	1,920	2,102	**1,629**	**1,323**	**770**
AY5	5,762	2,208	**2,022**	**1,751**	**1,423**	**828**
AY6	6,028	**2,297**	**2,163**	**1,874**	**1,522**	**885**

Table 16.10. *Cumulative claim counts data*

Year	Cumulative closed number of claims in development year					
	0	1	2	3	4	5
AY1	73	91	93	97	99	101
AY2	73	92	95	99	102	
AY3	71	90	97	101		
AY4	75	93	99			
AY5	78	96				
AY6	80					

16.3 Developing Frequency and Severity Separately

In Chapters 1 and 2, we discuss models for claim frequency and claim severity separately. We then combine the two variables to model aggregate claims in Chapter 3. The projection of aggregate claims using the chain-ladder method may also be done by projecting claim frequency and claim severity separately. These projections are then combined to obtain projections for aggregate claims. It is often found that claim frequency progresses quite regularly and its projections may be more accurate. We now illustrate this approach using the cumulative loss payments data in Table 16.3.

Example 16.6 In addition to the cumulative claim payments data in Table 16.3, you are given the cumulative claim counts data in Table 16.10. Estimate the reserves by projecting the claim counts and claim severity separately.

Table 16.11. *Cumulative average claim sizes*

Year	Cumulative average claim size in development year					
	0	1	2	3	4	5
AY1	59.63	67.84	82.96	92.73	100.76	104.98
AY2	66.04	69.00	85.01	98.95	108.88	
AY3	70.73	76.60	85.71	94.50		
AY4	71.27	78.12	94.62			
AY5	73.87	83.02				
AY6	75.35					

Table 16.12. *Cumulative claim counts projection*

Year	Projected cumulative number of claims in development year					
	0	1	2	3	4	5
AY1	73	91	93	97	99	101
AY2	73	92	95	99	102	**104.06**
AY3	71	90	97	101	**103.58**	**105.67**
AY4	75	93	99	**103.17**	**105.80**	**107.94**
AY5	78	96	**100.72**	**104.96**	**107.64**	**109.81**
AY6	80	**99.89**	**104.80**	**109.22**	**112.00**	**114.27**
	Weighted average link ratio					
	1/0	2/1	3/2	4/3	5/4	
	1.249	1.049	1.042	1.026	1.020	

Solution 16.6 We divide the entries in Table 16.3 by the corresponding entries in Table 16.10 to obtain a table of cumulative average claim amounts in Table 16.11.

Developments of the cumulative claim counts and cumulative average claim sizes are performed separately using the chain-ladder method. Tables 16.12 and 16.13 complete the lower triangles of these projections using the weighted average link ratios.

Finally, we combine Tables 16.12 and 16.13 to obtain the projected aggregate claim payments in Table 16.14. The lower triangle of Table 16.14 is obtained by multiplying the lower triangles of Tables 16.12 and 16.13.   □

The example above applies the chain-ladder method to the cumulative claim counts and cumulative average claim severity separately. Another approach is to model the incremental claim counts and incremental average claim severity

Table 16.13. *Cumulative average claim sizes*
projection

Year	Projected cumulative average claim size in development year					
	0	1	2	3	4	5
AY1	59.63	67.84	82.96	92.73	100.76	104.98
AY2	66.04	69.00	85.01	98.95	108.88	**113.45**
AY3	70.73	76.60	85.71	94.50	**103.35**	**107.68**
AY4	71.27	78.12	94.62	**106.74**	**116.74**	**121.63**
AY5	73.87	83.02	**99.18**	**111.88**	**122.37**	**127.49**
AY6	75.35	**82.64**	**98.72**	**111.37**	**121.80**	**126.91**
Weighted average link ratio						
	1/0	2/1	3/2	4/3	5/4	
	1.097	1.195	1.128	1.094	1.042	

Table 16.14. *Projected cumulative payments using*
separate projections of frequency and severity

Year	Cumulative projected loss payments in development year					
	0	1	2	3	4	5
AY1	4,353	6,173	7,715	8,995	9,975	10,603
AY2	4,821	6,348	8,076	9,796	11,106	**11,805**
AY3	5,022	6,894	8,314	9,544	**10,704**	**11,378**
AY4	5,345	7,265	9,367	**11,012**	**12,351**	**13,128**
AY5	5,762	7,970	**9,989**	**11,744**	**13,171**	**14,001**
AY6	6,028	**8,255**	**10,346**	**12,163**	**13,642**	**14,501**

through the development years. This approach is called the **closure method**. An advantage of this method is that it allows claim severity to reflect the rate of inflation. We illustrate this method using the data above, assuming there is a trending rate of increase of 2% average claim severity per year.

We first construct tables of incremental claim counts and average claim size per claim through the development years, which are summarized in Tables 16.15 and 16.16, respectively. Table 16.15 is derived from Table 16.10, and Table 16.16 is obtained by dividing the entries in Table 16.1 by the entries in Table 16.15.

Next we update the average claim size to the level of the costs in AY6, assuming a trending factor of 2% per year. Thus, we multiply the entries for AY1 in different DYs (first row of Table 16.16) by $(1.02)^5$. This adjustment is performed for other AYs as well. For example, for the entries of AY3, we multiply the average claim size with the factor $(1.02)^3$. The results are given in the upper

Table 16.15. *Incremental claim counts data*

	Incremental closed number of claims in development year					
Year	0	1	2	3	4	5
AY1	73	18	2	4	2	2
AY2	73	19	3	4	3	
AY3	71	19	7	4		
AY4	75	18	6			
AY5	78	18				
AY6	80					

Table 16.16. *Incremental average claim sizes*

	Incremental average claim size in development year					
Year	0	1	2	3	4	5
AY1	59.63	101.11	771.00	320.00	490.00	314.00
AY2	66.04	80.37	576.00	430.00	436.67	
AY3	70.73	98.53	202.86	307.50		
AY4	71.27	106.67	350.33			
AY5	73.87	122.67				
AY6	75.35					

triangle of Table 16.17. We then compute the average of each column to estimate the average claim size at the AY6 cost level. The results are given in the
last row of Table 16.17. For example, the average claim size in DY2 at AY6
cost level is

$$\frac{851.25 + 623.48 + 215.27 + 364.49}{4} = 513.62.$$

We then compute the estimated average claim size in each AY through its
DYs by removing the trended cost. For example, for AY4 in DY3, the average
claim size is

$$\frac{381.69}{(1.02)^2} = 366.87.$$

The lower triangle of Table 16.17 (in boldface) summarizes the estimates of
the average claim size in each AY through to maturity of payments.[2]

---

[2] Note that in Table 16.17, the figures in boldface are at the cost level of the corresponding AY,
while other figures (no boldface) are at the cost level of AY6.

Table 16.17. *Trended incremental average claim sizes*

Year	Trended incremental average claim size in development year					
	0	1	2	3	4	5
AY1	65.84	111.63	851.25	353.31	541.00	346.68
AY2	71.48	86.99	623.48	465.45	472.66	**331.50**
AY3	75.06	104.56	215.27	326.32	**477.60**	**338.13**
AY4	74.15	110.98	364.49	**366.87**	**487.15**	**344.90**
AY5	75.35	125.12	**503.55**	**374.21**	**496.89**	**351.79**
AY6	75.35	**107.86**	**513.62**	**381.69**	**506.83**	**358.83**
	Average incremental severity in development year					
	0	1	2	3	4	5
	72.87	107.86	513.62	381.69	506.83	358.83

Our next step is to work on the progression of the claim closures. Given the total numbers of claims in each AY in the last column of Table 16.12, we calculate the number of claim counts in each DY as a percentage of the remaining ultimate claim counts. The results, given in percentages, are summarized in Table 16.18. For example, for DY0 of AY1, the percentage is

$$\frac{73}{101} = 72.28\%.$$

Further examples are as follows.[3] For DY1 of AY2, the closure percentage is

$$\frac{19}{104.06 - 73} = 61.17\%.$$

For DY2 of AY3, the closure percentage is

$$\frac{7}{105.67 - 90} = 44.67\%.$$

The last row of Table 16.18 summarizes the average claim closure percentage in each DY. These figures are the column averages. They are used as the estimated percentage of claim closures in each DY (for all AYs).

We now complete the lower triangle of Table 16.15, which is given in Table 16.19. Some examples are as follows. For DY3 of AY4, the projected number of claim counts is

$$0.4676(107.94 - 99) = 4.18.$$

---

[3] Refer to Table 16.12 for the claim count development figures.

Table 16.18. *Claim closure percentage*

Year	Claim closure percentage in development year					
	0	1	2	3	4	5
AY1	72.28	64.29	20.00	50.00	50.00	100.00
AY2	70.15	61.17	24.88	44.15	59.29	
AY3	67.19	54.80	44.67	46.14		
AY4	69.48	54.64	40.16			
AY5	71.03	56.59				
AY6	70.00					

Average claim closure percentage in development year					
0	1	2	3	4	5
70.02	58.30	32.43	46.76	54.65	100

Table 16.19. *Projected incremental closed claims*

Year	Projected incremental closed number of claims in development year					
	0	1	2	3	4	5
AY1	73	18	2	4	2	2
AY2	73	19	3	4	3	2.06
AY3	71	19	7	4	2.55	2.12
AY4	75	18	6	4.18	2.60	2.16
AY5	78	18	4.48	4.36	2.72	2.25
AY6	80	19.98	4.63	4.52	2.81	2.32

For DY4 of AY4, we have

$$0.5465(107.94 - 99 - 4.18) = 2.60.$$

We now use the lower triangles of Tables 16.17 and 16.19 to compute the incremental loss payments in each DY for the policies in each AY. The aggregates through the development years give the ultimate reserve. For example, the projected ultimate reserve for AY4 at the end of DY2 is

$$4.18(366.87) + 2.60(487.15) + 2.16(344.90) = 3{,}545.09.$$

In comparison, the estimate based on Table 16.5 is

$$13{,}126 - 9{,}367 = 3{,}759.$$

Similarly, for AY6 the amount of the ultimate reserve at the end of DY0 is

$$19.98(107.86) + \cdots + 2.32(358.83) = 8{,}511.14.$$

In comparison, the estimate based on Table 16.5 is

$$14{,}515 - 6{,}028 = 8{,}487.$$

16.4 Discounting Loss Reserves

Projected future reserves are payments to be made in the future. To reflect the time value of money, we may discount these future reserves at an appropriate rate of interest. We may then add up the discounted reserves to obtain the present value of the future payments for policies the settlements of which have yet to mature. To illustrate this computation, we use the reserves obtained by the Bornhuetter–Ferguson method in Table 16.9.

Example 16.7 Future reserves are obtained by the Bornhuetter–Ferguson method as in Table 16.9. The rate of interest is 4% per annum. Assuming future payments and reserves are paid at the middle of the DY, compute the present value of the total reserves of all unsettled accidents at the end of AY6.

Solution 16.7 We reproduce the reserves computed by the Bornhuetter–Ferguson method in Table 16.20. Note that the payments in the first diagonal entries, namely, 2,297 to 663, will be paid half year from the end of AY6. Similarly, the payments in the second diagonal entries, namely, 2,163 to 681, will be paid one and a half years later. Thus, the total present value of the reserves is

$$\frac{2{,}297 + 2{,}022 + \cdots + 663}{(1.04)^{0.5}} + \frac{2{,}163 + \cdots + 681}{(1.04)^{1.5}}$$
$$+ \frac{1{,}874 + 1{,}423 + 770}{(1.04)^{2.5}} + \frac{1{,}522 + 828}{(1.04)^{3.5}} + \frac{885}{(1.04)^{4.5}} = 19{,}688.29. \qquad \square$$

Table 16.20. *Incremental reserves using the Bornhuetter–Ferguson method*

	\multicolumn{6}{c}{Incremental reserves in development year}					
Year	0	1	2	3	4	5
AY2						663
AY3					1,171	681
AY4				1,629	1,323	770
AY5			2,022	1,751	1,423	828
AY6		2,297	2,163	1,874	1,522	885

16.5 R Laboratory

R Codes 16.1 provides the codes to project the cumulative loss payments until maturity using the chain-ladder method. Example 16.4 is used for illustration, with data drawn from Table 16.1. The codes assume that there are *n* AYs, with losses maturing after $(m - 1)$ DYs. The DYs are thus from 0 to $m - 1$. We also assume that *n* is equal to $m - 1$, so that the numbers of AYs and DYs are the same. Both average link ratio (ALR) and weighted average link ratio (WLR) are computed.

```
#####################################################################
# R Codes 16.1
#
# Projection of cumulative payments using the chain-ladder method as
# illustrated in Example 16.4
#####################################################################

T161.inc=matrix(c(4353,1820,1542,1280,980,628,
        4821,1527,1728,1720,1310,NA,
        5022,1872,1420,1230,NA,NA,
        5345,1920,2102,NA,NA,NA,
        5762,2208,NA,NA,NA,NA,
        6028,NA,NA,NA,NA,NA),
        nrow = 6, byrow = TRUE)   # Incremental losses as in
                                  # Table 16.1
n=nrow(T161.inc)                  # Number of accident years, 1 : n
m=ncol(T161.inc)                  # Number of development years,
                                  # 0 : m-1
T161.cum=matrix(NA,n,m)           # Initialize cumulative losses

for(i in 1:n){T161.cum[i,]=cumsum(T161.inc[i,1:m])} # Compute cum
                                                    # losses
T161.cum                          # Output cumulative losses,
                                  # Table 16.3
ALR=rep(NA,m-1)                   # Initialize average link ratio
WLR=rep(NA,m-1)                   # Initialize wt average link ratio
for(j in 1:(m-1)) {ALR[j]=
  mean(T161.cum[1:(n-j),j+1]/T161.cum[1:(n-j),j])}      # Compute ALR
for(j in 1:(m-1)) {WLR[j]=
  sum(T161.cum[1:(n-j),j+1])/sum(T161.cum[1:(n-j),j])} # Compute WLR

for(i in 2:n)
{T161.cum[i,(m-i+2):m]=T161.cum[i,m-i+1]*cumprod(ALR[(m-i+1):(m-1)])}
T161.cum                          # Output Table 16.5, may use WLR
```

R Codes 16.2 provides the codes to project the reserves using the Bornhuetter–Ferguson method. Example 16.5 is used for illustration, with data drawn from Table 16.1. The lines to input T161.inc in R Codes 16.1 must be run first prior to R Codes 16.2. The results are as in Table 16.9.

```
####################################################################
# R Codes 16.2
#
# Projection of cumulative payments using the BF method as
# illustrated in Example 16.5 (must input T161.inc in R
# Codes 16.1 first)
####################################################################

fu=rev(cumprod(rev(ALR)))                   # fu in Eq(16.2) using ALR
f=1-1/fu                                     # f in Eq(16.7)
fr=c(rev(diff(rev(f))),f[m-1])              # For computing inc BF res
ep=c(17230,17700,20000,21500,23000)         # Earned premiums
elr=0.65                                     # Permissible loss ratio
T161.cum=matrix(NA,n,m)                      # Initialize cumulative
                                             # losses
for(i in 1:n)
{T161.cum[i,]=cumsum(T161.inc[i,1:m])}      # Compute cumulative
                                             # losses
for(i in 2:n)
{T161.cum[i,m-i+2]=ep[i-1]*elr*f[m-i+1]}    # BF res, Eq(16.6),
                                             # Table 16.8
for(i in 2:n)
{T161.inc[i,(m-i+2):m]=ep[i-1]*elr*fr[(m-i+1):(m-1)]}
                                             # Compute inc BF res
                                             # using fr
T161.inc                                     # Output inc BF res,
                                             # Table 16.9
```

16.6 Summary and Discussions

We have discussed methods of estimating future loss payments based on historical data. The methods assume the loss variables, namely, claim counts, claim sizes and aggregate claims, follow some regular patterns in their progression. While these methods assume that the patterns can be extrapolated into the future, the actuary must consider other factors such as regulatory changes and changes in policy terms, which may impact future losses. Nonetheless, it is useful to have a model-based estimate as a benchmark for the actuary and management to deliberate for any necessary modifications.

Exercises

Exercise 16.1 You are given the following information about the sales of the insurance policies of a company:

Year	Written premium
CY1	10,000
CY2	11,000
CY3	12,000
CY4	12,800

For accidents occurring in CY2, 4,000 and 1,500 are paid in DY0 and DY1, respectively. The expected loss ratio is 0.65. Policies are for a one-year period and are sold at a uniform rate throughout the year. Determine the reserves for accidents in CY2 as of the end of DY1 using the expected loss ratio method.

Exercise 16.2 You are given the following loss data of a company:

Accident year	Cumulative loss payments in development year			
	0	1	2	3
AY1	1,000	1,800	2,500	2,850
AY2	1,200	2,000	2,800	
AY3	1,500	2,400		
AY4	1,800			

An actuary projects the reserves using the chain-ladder method with development factors estimated by the volume-weighted average. Assuming all losses are settled within three years, what is the total reserve for accidents in AY2 through AY4?

Exercise 16.3 You are given the following information about the loss payments of an insurance company:

Accident	Cumulative loss payments in development year				
year	0	1	2	3	4
AY1	2,000	3,100	3,800	4,200	4,500
AY2	2,200	3,200	4,000	4,650	
AY3	2,500	3,600	4,500		
AY4	2,600	3,600			
AY5	2,700				

All losses are fully settled within four years. Compute the total IBNR reserve for the accidents in AY2 through AY5 using the chain-ladder method with the age-to-age loss development factors estimated using the arithmetic average.

Exercise 16.4 An actuary has estimated the following link ratios for the chain-ladder method of reserve estimation:

Age-to-age development	Link ratio
1/0	1.8
2/1	1.5
3/2	1.3
4/3	1.2
5/4	1.1

All losses are settled within five years. Cumulative loss payments have been made for recent accidents as follows:

Accident year	Cumulative payments at the end of AY5
AY1	850
AY2	680
AY3	600
AY4	540
AY5	500

Determine the total reserve for all accidents in AY1 to AY5 at the end of AY5.

Exercise 16.5 You are given the following information about the cumulative loss payments of insurance business in the past five years:

Accident year	Cumulative loss payments in development year					Earned premiums
	0	1	2	3	4	
AY1	1,000	1,800	2,500	3,000	3,800	6,400
AY2	1,200	2,100	2,950	3,400		6,500
AY3	1,500	2,600	3,500			6,800
AY4	1,600	2,700				7,000
AY5	1,700					7,500

The following incurred losses have been computed:

Accident year	Cumulative incurred reserves in development year				
	0	1	2	3	4
AY1	1,300	2,200	2,800	3,200	3,800
AY2	1,350	2,300	3,050	3,550	
AY3	1,800	2,900	3,600		
AY4	1,950	3,000			
AY5	2,000				

The expected loss ratio is 0.65. Loss payments mature in four years.

(a) Compute the total case reserve of losses in AY2 through AY5 at the end of AY5.
(b) The chain-ladder method is applied using volume-weighted development factors on the paid loss triangle. Compute the total gross IBNR reserve.
(c) Compute the total gross IBNR reserve using the Bornhuetter–Ferguson method with the link ratios calculated in (b).

Exercise 16.6 You are given the following triangle of cumulative loss payments:

Accident	Cumulative loss payments in development year				
year	0	1	2	3	4
AY1	5,300	6,900	8,200	9,000	9,500
AY2	6,600	8,300	9,800	11,000	
AY3	6,800	9,100	10,200		
AY4	6,950	9,300			
AY5	7,200				

In addition, you also have the following information of the cumulative claims closed:

Accident	Cumulative claims closed in development year				
year	0	1	2	3	4
AY1	120	135	148	154	160
AY2	142	172	186	193	
AY3	144	180	195		
AY4	148	186			
AY5	150				

Losses mature within four years. All link ratios are calculated using arithmetic average.

(a) Project cumulative claim counts and average cumulative claim severity using the chain-ladder method. Using these results, estimate the total ultimate loss payments for accidents in AY2 through AY5.
(b) If the annual trend of claim severity increase is 4%, calculate the incremental loss payments of AY5 for DY1 through DY4 using the closure method.

Exercise 16.7 An actuary projects reserves using the closure method with a severity trending factor of 5% per annum. Percentage of claims closed and average incremental severity trended to CY5 are estimated as follows:

	Development year				
	0	1	2	3	4
Percentage of claims closed	30%	50%	60%	80%	100%
Trended average incremental severity to CY5	200	240	300	340	400

The actuary expects 500 ultimate claim counts for accidents in AY3. If 150 claims are closed in DY0 and also in DY1, compute the projected ultimate amount of loss payments for AY3 at the end of DY1.

Exercise 16.8 You are given the following information about the cumulative loss payments of policies in the past four years:

Accident year	Cumulative loss payments in development year			
	0	1	2	3
AY1	500	900	1,300	1,600
AY2	600	1,100	1,400	
AY3	700	1,300		
AY4	800			

Loss reserves are computed using the chain-ladder method with the link ratios estimated by the volume-weighted averages. Losses mature in four years and reserves are discounted at an effective rate of 4% per annum. Compute the discounted reserves for AY2 through AY4 at the end of AY4.

Questions Adapted from SOA Exams

Exercise 16.9 You are given the following data:

Accident year	Earned premium	Expected loss ratio	Cumulative loss payments through development months			
			12	24	36	48
AY5	19,000	0.90	4,850	9,700	14,100	16,200
AY6	20,000	0.85	5,150	10,300	14,900	
AY7	21,000	0.91	5,400	10,800		
AY8	22,000	0.88	7,200			

There is no development past 48 months. Compute the total indicated loss
reserve using the Bornhuetter–Ferguson method and volume-weighted loss
development factors.

Exercise 16.10 You are given the following information:

Accident	Cumulative paid losses through development months			
year	12	24	36	48
AY5	27,000	49,000	65,000	72,000
AY6	28,000	57,000	71,000	
AY7	33,000	65,000		
AY8	35,000			

Interval	Selected age-to-age paid loss development factors
12–24 months	2.00
24–36 months	1.20
36–48 months	1.15
48–ultimate	1.00

The rate of interest is 5% per annum effective. Calculate the ratio of the
discounted reserves to undiscounted reserves as of December 31, CY8.

Exercise 16.11 You are given the following information:

Accident	Cumulative paid losses in development year						Earned
year	0	1	2	3	4	5	premiums
AY4	1,400	5,200	7,300	8,800	9,800	9,800	18,000
AY5	2,200	6,400	8,800	10,200	11,500		20,000
AY6	2,500	7,500	10,700	12,600			25,000
AY7	2,800	8,700	12,900				26,000
AY8	2,500	7,900					27,000
AY9	2,600						28,000

The expected loss ratio for each accident year is 0.55. Calculate the total loss reserves using the Bornhuetter–Ferguson method and three-year arithmetic average paid loss development factors.

Exercise 16.12 An insurance company was formed to write workers compensation business in CY1. The earned premium in CY1 was 1,000,000. The earned premium growth through CY3 has been constant at 20% per annum at a compounding rate. The expected loss ratio for AY1 is 60%. As of December 31, CY3, the company's reserving actuary believes the expected loss ratio has increased by two percentage points each accident year since the company's inception. Selected incurred loss development factors are as follows:

12 to 24 months	1.500
24 to 36 months	1.336
36 to 48 months	1.126
48 to 60 months	1.057
60 to 72 months	1.050
72 months to ultimate	1.000

Calculate the total IBNR reserve as of December 31, CY3 using the Bornhuetter–Ferguson method.

17

Ratemaking

Ratemaking refers to the determination of the premium rates to cover the potential loss payments incurred under an insurance policy. In addition to the losses, the premium should also cover all the expenses as well as the profit margin. As past losses are used to project future losses, care must be taken to adjust for potential increases in the lost costs. There are two methods to determine the premium rates: the loss cost method and the loss ratio method. Lost cost refers to the losses per unit exposure, whereas lost ratio refers to the fraction of the premium used to cover the losses.

Policy premiums may be charged at different rates, depending on the status and risk features of the covered risk, referred to as different categorizations of risks. The actuary should consider how the overall rates should be revised and how different categories should be charged differently. We study cross categorization represented as territories and classes. The loss cost method and loss ratio method can be applied to revise the overall rate as well as the differential rates for different groups. The two methods will generate the same results if performed correctly.

Learning Objectives

1 Exposure unit, expenses, expected losses and premium
2 Lost cost and loss ratio
3 Trending factor and premium at current rate
4 Policy categorization
5 Policy differentials and overall rate change
6 Credibility weighted rate change

17.1 Exposure, Expenses, Expected Losses and Premiums

Insurance companies charge a premium for the risks they cover. The premiums are quoted per unit of exposure, which is a standardized quantitative measure of possible loss risks. For vehicle insurance, the exposure unit may be a car-year. For workers compensation insurance, it may be the number of workers or a suitable quantification of the size of the group.

The premium charged should be sufficient to cover the expected losses. In addition, it should also cover the expenses involved in selling the policy, as well as a comfortable profit margin. Expenses may be classified into two types: fixed expenses and variable expenses. Fixed expenses include outlays such as rental expenses, utility expenses, salaries and advertising costs, which are incurred irrespective of the number of policies sold. On the other hand, variable expenses include legal costs, regulatory administrative costs and sales commissions, which vary directly with the exposure units.

Expenses may also be associated with losses when they are incurred. These are called **loss adjustment expenses (LAE)**. LAE can be further divided into two categories: **allocated loss adjustment expenses (ALAE)** and **unallocated loss adjustment expenses (ULAE)**. Legal costs are examples of ALAE, while salaries and utility expenses are examples of ULAE.

Profit margin and allowance for contingency should be built in to arrive at the premium. Needless to say, the most important component of the premium is the claimed loss when an accident occurs.

To determine the appropriate premium, we first define the following notations:

P = Premium per unit exposure
V = Profit and variable expenses per unit exposure
F = Fixed expenses per unit exposure
L = Expected or estimated losses per unit exposure

The expected losses L may be estimated by one of the methods discussed in Chapter 16, trended and developed, with LAE included as well.

We assume that profits and variable expenses are determined as a fraction of the premium, so that

$$V = \pi P, \qquad \text{for } 0 < \pi < 1. \tag{17.1}$$

As premium is required to cover the losses, expenses and profits, we have

$$P = L + \pi P + F, \tag{17.2}$$

which implies

$$P = \frac{L + F}{1 - \pi}. \tag{17.3}$$

There are variations to equation (17.3). First, the fixed expenses F may also be determined on a per unit exposure basis and grossed up as a fraction of the premium. In this case, F drops out from the right-hand side of equation (17.2) and the premium is then given by

$$P = \frac{L}{1 - \pi}, \qquad (17.4)$$

where π now includes the "fixed" expenses component as well.

Second, sometimes fixed expenses may not be allowed to be grossed up and may only be incorporated after the gross premium has been determined. In this case, we have

$$P = \frac{L}{1 - \pi} + F. \qquad (17.5)$$

Note that π in equations (17.3) through (17.5) have different interpretations. In all cases, however, $1 - \pi$ is called the **permissible loss ratio**.

The method described above is called the **lost cost method**. It computes the lost costs per unit exposure with a markup for expenses and profits to determine the premium. If we denote P_0 as the current premium and P_1 as the revised premium based on the estimated future losses, the indicated rate change (premium change), denoted by R_P, is given by

$$R_P = \frac{P_1}{P_0} - 1. \qquad (17.6)$$

An alternative method to compute the revised premium, called the **lost ratio method**, compares the loss ratio based on the current premium to the permissible loss ratio. First, we define the **effective loss ratio**, denoted by L_R, as the estimated losses (inclusive of LAE) and fixed expenses per unit exposure as a fraction of the current premium. Thus,

$$L_R = \frac{L + F}{P_0}. \qquad (17.7)$$

The lost ratio method then computes the indicated premium change as

$$\frac{\text{Effective loss ratio}}{\text{Permissible loss ratio}} - 1 = \frac{L_R}{1 - \pi} - 1. \qquad (17.8)$$

From equations (17.3) and (17.7) we have

$$\frac{L_R}{1 - \pi} - 1 = \frac{L + F}{(1 - \pi)P_0} - 1 = \frac{(1 - \pi)P_1}{(1 - \pi)P_0} - 1 = R_P, \qquad (17.9)$$

which shows that the loss cost and loss ratio methods give the same result.

Example 17.1 You are given the following information of an insurance policy:
(i)   Premium rate is 500 per policy,
(ii) Fixed expense is 50 per policy,
(iii) Sales commission is 10% of premium,
(iv) Required profit margin is 8% of premium.

There are no other expenses. If the loss costs are expected to increase by 15% due to inflation, determine the revised premium.

Solution 17.1 We first determine the losses of the existing policy by equation (17.2). Note that $P = 500$, $\pi = 0.10 + 0.08 = 0.18$ and $F = 50$. Hence,

$$500 = L + 0.18(500) + 50,$$

which implies

$$L = 500 - 90 - 50 = 360.$$

The revised premium is then

$$P = \frac{360(1.15) + 50}{1 - 0.18} = 565.85.$$
□

Example 17.2 The current premium rate for an insurance policy is 800. The commission, expenses, profit and losses, as percentages of the premium, are as follows:

(i)	Commission	15%
(ii)	Expenses	15%
(iii)	Profit	8%
(iv)	Losses	62%

Losses and expenses per policy are expected to remain constant for the next period in monetary terms. Determine the premium rate if (a) the commission rate is reduced to 10% of the premium, and (b) the regulator requires the commission to be charged as an expense of 80 per policy.

Solution 17.2 We first compute the monetary amount of losses and expenses per policy, which is

$$(0.15 + 0.62)(800) = 616.$$

This amount will remain unchanged in the next period.
(a) The only variable components are profit and commission, which is $0.10 + 0.08 = 18\%$ of the premium. Hence, the revised premium is

$$P = \frac{616}{1 - 0.18} = 751.22.$$

(b) As commission cannot be grossed up, we first calculate the premium prior to commission, which is

$$\frac{616}{1 - 0.08} = 669.57.$$

Hence, the gross premium is

$$669.57 + 80 = 749.57.$$ □

Example 17.3 An insurance company has losses developed and trended of amount 450,000 on 5,000 exposure units with an existing premium rate of 120. Fixed expenses are 5 per exposure, and the permissible loss ratio is 0.7. Determine the revised premium.

Solution 17.3 We first use the loss ratio method. The effective loss ratio is

$$\frac{450,000}{120(5,000)} = 0.75,$$

and the expense per unit earned premium is

$$\frac{5}{120} = 0.04167.$$

Hence, the indicated rate change is (from equations (17.7) and (17.8))

$$\frac{0.75 + 0.04167}{0.7} - 1 = 0.1310,$$

and the revised premium is $120(1.1310) = 135.71$.

Using the lost cost method, we obtain (from equation (17.3))

$$P = \frac{\dfrac{450,000}{5,000} + 5}{0.7} = \frac{95}{0.7} = 135.71,$$

so that the two approaches give the same answer. □

Note that in the lost cost method, knowledge of the current premium rate is not required. If we know the current premium rate, however, the indicated rate change can be calculated. In contrast, for the lost ratio method we need information of the current premium or total earned premium for the computation of the effective lost ratio. Alternatively, we may express the rate change as a function of the current premium. The computed new rate is the same as that calculated from the lost cost method. For Example 17.3, readers may check that the same answer is obtained for the lost ratio method irrespective of the existing premium rate (i.e., 120) assumed.

17.2 Premium Changes and Earned Premium

Good ratemaking depends on having reliable data on losses and earned premiums. In this section, we focus on the computation of earned premiums over a period of time.

Table 17.1. *Premium changes*

Date	Change
CY1/07/01	+10%
CY3/10/01	+5%

Table 17.2. *Earned premiums*

Year	Earned premiums
CY1	10,000
CY2	11,000
CY3	11,800
CY4	13,200

Actuaries typically use multiple years of data to compute the aggregate losses and earned premiums. As premiums are revised periodically, they change over the sample period of the data set. In addition, when the in-force period of a policy spans multiple years, care must be taken to ensure that the computed earned premiums appropriately reflect changes of the premium over time. A useful approach to aggregate the earned premiums over multiple years is the **parallelogram method**. We illustrate the use of this method in the following examples.

Example 17.4 The premium for a one-year insurance policy had the changes in the past four years as shown in Table 17.1. The earned premiums in each year are given in Table 17.2. Assume the policies are sold at a uniform rate throughout the period. Determine the earned premiums over the four years at the current premium rate (at the end of CY4).

Solution 17.4 Figure 17.1 describes the occasions of rate changes and the progression through time when the premiums are different. Before CY1/07/01, the premium is charged at rate P. Afterwards, the premium increases to $1.1P$ until CY3/10/01, upon which the rate is further increased to $1.1(1.05)P = 1.155P$. The part of the first square above the 45-degree line starting at CY1/07/01 represents earned premiums at the rate P. Thus, the overall earned premium in CY1 is the weighted average of P and $1.1P$ with weights proportional to the area above and below the 45-degree line within the square. Hence, the earned premium in CY1 is

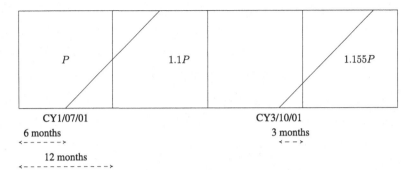

Figure 17.1 Revision of premium for annual policy

$$\left(1 - \frac{6}{12} \times \frac{6}{12} \times \frac{1}{2}\right) P + \frac{6}{12} \times \frac{6}{12} \times \frac{1}{2} \times 1.1P = 1.0125P.$$

Likewise, the earned premium in CY2 is

$$\frac{6}{12} \times \frac{6}{12} \times \frac{1}{2} \times P + \left(1 - \frac{6}{12} \times \frac{6}{12} \times \frac{1}{2}\right) 1.1P = 1.0875P.$$

The earned premium in CY3 is

$$\left(1 - \frac{3}{12} \times \frac{3}{12} \times \frac{1}{2}\right) \times 1.1P + \frac{3}{12} \times \frac{3}{12} \times \frac{1}{2} \times 1.155P = 1.1017P,$$

and the earned premium in CY4 is

$$\frac{9}{12} \times \frac{9}{12} \times \frac{1}{2} \times 1.1P + \left(1 - \frac{9}{12} \times \frac{9}{12} \times \frac{1}{2}\right) \times 1.155P = 1.1395P.$$

As the current premium is $1.155P$, the earned premiums in the four years are

$$10{,}000 \times \frac{1.155}{1.0125} = 11{,}407.41, \qquad \text{for CY1,}$$

$$11{,}000 \times \frac{1.155}{1.0875} = 11{,}682.76, \qquad \text{for CY2,}$$

$$11{,}800 \times \frac{1.155}{1.1017} = 12{,}370.88, \qquad \text{for CY3,}$$

and

$$13{,}200 \times \frac{1.155}{1.1395} = 13{,}379.55, \qquad \text{for CY4.} \qquad \square$$

Example 17.5 The premium for a half-yearly insurance policy had the changes in Table 17.3 in the past four years. The earned premiums in each year are given in Table 17.4. Assume the policies are sold at a uniform rate throughout the period. Determine the earned premiums over the four years at the current premium rate.

Table 17.3. *Premium
changes*

Date	Change
CY1/04/01	+8%
CY2/07/01	+10%
CY3/10/01	+5%

Table 17.4. *Earned
premiums*

Year	Earned premiums
CY1	8,000
CY2	9,000
CY3	10,500
CY4	12,000

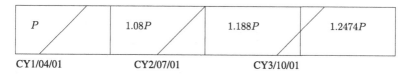

| P | 1.08P | 1.188P | 1.2474P |

CY1/04/01   CY2/07/01   CY3/10/01

Figure 17.2 Revision of premium for half-yearly policy

Solution 17.5 Figure 17.2 describes the occasions of rate changes and the progression of earned premiums. For CY1, the 45-degree line separates the rectangle into two equal parts. Thus, the average premium rate in CY1 is

$$0.5(1.08 + 1.0)P = 1.04P.$$

For CY2, the triangle takes up a quarter of the area so that the average premium rate is

$$[1.08(0.75) + 1.188(0.25)]P = 1.107P.$$

For CY3 and CY4, the average premiums are, respectively,

$$\frac{0.5 \times 0.5 \times 0.5}{2} \times 1.2474P + \left(1 - \frac{0.5 \times 0.5 \times 0.5}{2}\right) \times 1.188P = 1.1917P,$$

and

$$\frac{0.5 \times 0.5 \times 0.5}{2} \times 1.188P + \left(1 - \frac{0.5 \times 0.5 \times 0.5}{2}\right) \times 1.2474P = 1.2437P.$$

Table 17.5. *Exposures*
and losses

Year	Earned exposures	Incurred losses
AY1	560	86,000
AY2	620	102,000
AY3	650	120,000

The earned premiums at current premium rate are

$$8,000 \times \frac{1.2474}{1.04} = 9,595.39, \qquad \text{for CY1,}$$

$$9,000 \times \frac{1.2474}{1.107} = 10,141.46, \qquad \text{for CY2,}$$

$$10,500 \times \frac{1.2474}{1.1917} = 10,990.77, \qquad \text{for CY3,}$$

and

$$12,000 \times \frac{1.2474}{1.2437} = 12,035.70, \qquad \text{for CY4.} \qquad \square$$

17.3 Loss Trending

Loss costs increase with inflation. When historical losses are used to estimate losses for future policies, cost escalation must be taken into account. Actuaries commonly use historical data to estimate the rate of increase in the loss cost. Expected loss costs for a future policy may then be trended using this estimate. The time difference between the occurrence of past losses and future accidents is then used, together with the estimated trending factor, to obtain an estimate of the future losses. The following example illustrates the application of trending.

Example 17.6 The data in Table 17.5 are used for ratemaking. The trending factor is 4% per annum effective. All policies are of one-year terms. The policy premium will be revised on CY4/10/01 and applicable for one year. Future losses are estimated as a weighted average of loss costs in AY1 through AY3, with the weights being 20%, 30% and 50%, respectively. Determine the trended loss cost per unit exposure for the new policy. Assume policy sales and accidents occur uniformly throughout time.

Solution 17.6 The average time of occurrence for accidents in AY1 is AY1/07/01. The new policy will be sold in the period CY4/10/01 through CY5/09/30, with average accident occurrence at CY5/10/01. The average time difference between losses in AY1 and future losses is 4 years and 3 months. Thus, the trended cost per unit exposure using AY1 data is

$$\frac{86,000}{560}(1.04)^{4.25} = 181.43.$$

Combining data from other years with the relevant weights, the estimated trended loss per unit exposure is

$$0.2(181.43) + (0.3)\frac{102,000}{620}(1.04)^{3.25} + (0.5)\frac{120,000}{650}(1.04)^{2.25} = 193.17.$$

$\square$

17.4 Group Differentials and Their Updates

Insurance companies often charge differential rates for their policies, depending on the status and certain characteristics of the insured. In this section we consider a one-way categorization of the insured. For ease of exposition, we call the groups under this categorization *territories*. We shall discuss how to update the premium rates for different territories of policies.

We assume there is a reference territory called the *base group*. This territory typically represents the largest group of policies. Let the premium rate for this group be P_1.[1] Suppose there are m different territories, with premium rates of P_i for $i = 1, \ldots, m$. We denote f_i as the differential so that $P_i = P_1 f_i$ for $i = 1, \ldots, m$ with $f_1 \equiv 1$. When new data are available, the differentials are updated. We consider two approaches for making the changes: loss cost method and loss ratio method.

We first define the following notations:

L_i = Trended and developed aggregate losses (including LAE) of Territory i
E_i = Number of exposure units of Territory i

The loss cost per unit exposure for Territory i, denoted by L_i^C, is

$$L_i^C = \frac{L_i}{E_i}. \tag{17.10}$$

Using the loss cost method, the new or indicated differential for Territory i, denoted by f_i^*, is

$$f_i^* = \frac{L_i^C}{L_1^C}, \qquad i = 1, \ldots, m. \tag{17.11}$$

---

[1] We use the same notation P_1 as in equation (17.6) with different meanings. The difference in definition should be clear in the context.

Table 17.6. *Loss data of three territories*

Territory	Current differential	Earned premiums	Incurred losses
T1	1.0	850,000	600,000
T2	1.2	400,000	280,000
T3	1.5	700,000	560,000

Obviously, $f_1^* = 1$ so that the updated differential for the base group is 1.

For the loss ratio method, we first compute the loss ratio of each territory and denote them by L_i^R. These ratios are the losses per unit of earned premium, so that

$$L_i^R = \frac{L_i}{E_i P_i} = \frac{L_i}{E_i P_1 f_i}, \qquad i = 1, \ldots, m. \tag{17.12}$$

The indicated differentials are then computed as

$$f_i^* = f_i \left(\frac{L_i^R}{L_1^R} \right), \qquad i = 1, \ldots, m. \tag{17.13}$$

It is easy to see that the loss ratio method gives the same answer as the loss cost method. Substituting equation (17.12) into equation (17.13), we obtain

$$f_i^* = f_i \times \frac{L_i}{P_1 E_i f_i} \times \frac{P_1 E_1}{L_1} = \frac{L_i}{E_i} \times \frac{E_1}{L_1} = \frac{L_i^C}{L_1^C}. \tag{17.14}$$

Example 17.7 An insurance policy was sold in three different territories, which are the only categorization. The data in Table 17.6 are used for ratemaking. Determine the indicated differentials using the loss ratio and loss cost methods.

Solution 17.7 T1 is the base group, with $f_1 = 1$. We first compute the loss ratios of the different territories. For T1, we have

$$L_1^R = \frac{600,000}{850,000} = 0.7059.$$

Similarly, for T2 and T3, we have

$$L_2^R = \frac{280,000}{400,000} = 0.7 \quad \text{and} \quad L_3^R = \frac{560,000}{700,000} = 0.8.$$

Hence, the indicated differentials are

$$f_2^* = 1.2 \left(\frac{0.7}{0.7059} \right) = 1.19,$$

and

$$f_3^* = 1.5 \left(\frac{0.8}{0.7059} \right) = 1.70.$$

To use the loss cost method, we first calculate the loss costs per unit exposure, which are

$$L_1^C = \frac{600,000}{850,000/P_1} = 0.7059P_1, \quad \text{for } T1,$$

$$L_2^C = \frac{280,000}{400,000/(1.2P_1)} = 0.84P_1, \quad \text{for } T2$$

and

$$L_3^C = \frac{560,000}{700,000/(1.5P_1)} = 1.2P_1, \quad \text{for } T3.$$

Thus, using the lost cost method, the indicated differentials of T2 and T3 are, respectively,

$$f_2^* = \frac{0.84P_1}{0.7059P_1} = 1.19$$

and

$$f_3^* = \frac{1.2P_1}{0.7059P_1} = 1.70. \qquad \square$$

17.5 Policies with Cross Categorization

We now consider the situation where policy groups are categorized in multiple dimensions. Specifically, we assume that policies are grouped by a two-way cross categorization called "territories" and "classes." We discuss methods of updating the differentials of the territories/classes, and outline methods to revise the overall premium changes as well as new rates for each territory/class.

First, we set up the framework of our model and define our notations. We assume each insurance policy belongs to a certain territory and class, with m territories and n classes. A policy belongs to the (i,j)th group if it is in the ith territory and the jth class. The following notations will be used:

L_{ij} = Aggregate losses (including LAE) of the (i,j)th group
E_{ij} = Exposure units in the (i,j)th group
P_{ij} = Premium rate of the (i,j)th group
f_i = Current differential of the ith territory
f_i^* = Updated differential of the ith territory
g_j = Current differential of the jth class
g_j^* = Updated differential of the jth class

We assume the base group is Territory 1 and Class 1. Thus, the base group premium is P_{11} and $f_1 = g_1 = 1$. We also assume a multiplicative model so that $P_{ij} = P_{11}f_ig_j$. For convenience of notation, we denote $P_{11} \equiv P^*$.

17.5.1 Updating Cross-Categorized Differentials

Without loss of generality we focus on updating the territorial differentials f_i. Again we consider two methods: the loss cost method and the loss ratio method.

The loss cost method involves first of all computing the loss per unit expo-sure. Each territory, however, may have a different distribution of exposure units over different classes. To resolve this issue of nonhomogeneous distribu-tion, we compute instead the loss cost per unit of *adjusted exposure* in the ith territory, which is defined as follows[2]

$$L_i^C = \frac{\sum_{j=1}^n L_{ij}}{\sum_{j=1}^n E_{ij}g_j} = \frac{\text{Losses in Territory } i}{\text{Adjusted exposures of Territory } i}, \tag{17.15}$$

for $i = 1, \ldots, m$. Note that the denominator in the above equation is *not* the actual exposure units, but rather exposure units adjusted for the differen-tials over each class. Using the loss cost method, the indicated differential of Territory i is then computed as

$$f_i^* = \frac{L_i^C}{L_1^C} = \frac{\sum_{j=1}^n L_{ij}}{\sum_{j=1}^n E_{ij}g_j} \times \frac{\sum_{j=1}^n E_{1j}g_j}{\sum_{j=1}^n L_{1j}}, \qquad i = 1, \ldots, m. \tag{17.16}$$

For the loss ratio method, we first calculate the loss ratio for each territory as the loss per unit of earned premium, which is computed as follows:

$$L_i^R = \frac{\sum_{j=1}^n L_{ij}}{\sum_{j=1}^n E_{ij}P_{ij}} = \frac{\sum_{j=1}^n L_{ij}}{P^*f_i \sum_{j=1}^n E_{ij}g_j}, \qquad i = 1, \ldots, m. \tag{17.17}$$

The indicated (revised) differentials are then computed as

$$f_i^* = f_i \left(\frac{L_i^R}{L_1^R} \right). \tag{17.18}$$

We now show that the lost ratio and loss cost methods give the same result. From equation (17.18) we have

$$f_i^* = f_i \left(\frac{L_i^R}{L_1^R} \right)$$

$$= f_i \times \frac{\sum_{j=1}^n L_{ij}}{P^*f_i \sum_{j=1}^n E_{ij}g_j} \times \frac{P^* \sum_{j=1}^n E_{1j}g_j}{\sum_{j=1}^n L_{1j}}$$

---

[2] We use the same notation L_i^C as in equation (17.10). The difference in definition should be clear in the context.

Table 17.7. *Cross categorized data*

	C1		C2	
	Incurred losses	Earned premiums	Incurred losses	Earned premiums
T1	4,000	6,000	5,500	8,000
T2	3,500	5,500	2,300	4,000

$$= \frac{\sum_{j=1}^{n} L_{ij}}{\sum_{j=1}^{n} E_{ij}g_j} \times \frac{\sum_{j=1}^{n} E_{1j}g_j}{\sum_{j=1}^{n} L_{1j}}$$

$$= \frac{L_i^C}{L_1^C}. \tag{17.19}$$

We define the *average premium rate* of Territory i as the earned premium per unit exposure:

$$\text{Average rate of Territory } i = \frac{\sum_{j=1}^{n} E_{ij}P_{ij}}{\sum_{j=1}^{n} E_{ij}}. \tag{17.20}$$

In contrast, we define the *base rate* of Territory i as P^*f_i. Note that the average rate depends on the distribution of the exposure units across different territories, whereas the base rate does not. Furthermore, we have

$$\sum_{j=1}^{n} E_{ij}P_{ij} = P^*f_i \sum_{j=1}^{n} E_{ij}g_j, \tag{17.21}$$

so that

$$\text{Earned premiums} = \text{Base rate} \times \text{adjusted exposures}$$

$$= \text{Average rate} \times \text{exposures.} \tag{17.22}$$

We define the *average class differential* of Territory i as

$$\frac{\sum_{j=1}^{n} E_{ij}g_j}{\sum_{j=1}^{n} E_{ij}} = \frac{\text{Adjusted exposures}}{\text{Exposures}}, \tag{17.23}$$

from which we obtain

$$\text{Base rate} = \text{Average rate} \times \frac{\text{Exposures}}{\text{Adjusted exposure}} = \frac{\text{Average rate}}{\text{Average differential}}. \tag{17.24}$$

Example 17.8 An insurance policy has cross categorization of two territories (T1 and T2) and two classes (C1 and C2). The data in Table 17.7 are available.

Table 17.8. *Loss ratios and loss costs*

	Earned premiums	Incurred losses	Loss ratio	Adjusted exposures	Loss cost
T1	14,000	9,500	0.6786	$14,000/P^*$	$0.6786P^*$
T2	9,500	5,800	0.6105	$10,556/P^*$	$0.5495P^*$
C1	11,500	7,500	0.6522	$11,500/P^*$	$0.6522P^*$
C2	12,000	7,800	0.6500	$10,000/P^*$	$0.7800P^*$

The differentials for C1 and C2 are, respectively, 1 and 1.2, while the differentials for T1 and T2 are, respectively, 1 and 0.9. Determine the indicated differentials of the territories and classes.

Solution 17.8 The loss ratios and loss costs are computed in Table 17.8. The base territory and base class differentials are unchanged at 1. Using the loss ratio method, the indicated differential for T2 is

$$0.9\left(\frac{0.6105}{0.6786}\right) = 0.8097,$$

and that of C2 is

$$1.2\left(\frac{0.6500}{0.6522}\right) = 1.1960.$$

Using the loss cost method, the indicated differential of T2 is

$$\frac{0.5495P^*}{0.6786P^*} = 0.8097,$$

and that of C2 is

$$\frac{0.7800P^*}{0.6522P^*} = 1.1960. \qquad \Box$$

Example 17.9 An insurance policy has cross categorization of territories and classes. The data in Table 17.9 are summarized across three territories, T1 through T3. Compute the indicated differentials of the territories.

Solution 17.9 Using the loss ratio method, we have

$$L_1^R = \frac{68,000}{120,000} = 0.5667,$$

$$L_2^R = \frac{56,000}{80,000} = 0.7000,$$

Table 17.9. *Loss data by territories*

	Current differential	Earned premiums	Incurred losses
T1	1.00	120,000	68,000
T2	1.20	80,000	56,000
T3	1.40	90,000	65,000

and

$$L_3^R = \frac{65,000}{90,000} = 0.7222.$$

Thus, we have

$$f_2^* = 1.2 \left(\frac{0.7000}{0.5667} \right) = 1.4823$$

and

$$f_3^* = 1.4 \left(\frac{0.7222}{0.5667} \right) = 1.7842.$$

For the loss cost method, we use equation (17.21) to obtain the adjusted exposures for T1 through T3, respectively, as

$$\frac{120,000}{P*}, \qquad \frac{80,000}{1.2P*} = \frac{66,667}{P*} \qquad \text{and} \qquad \frac{90,000}{1.4P*} = \frac{64,286}{P*}.$$

From equation (7.15) the loss costs per unit of adjusted exposure for T1 through T3 are, respectively, $0.5667P*$, $0.8400P*$ and $1.0111P*$, from which we obtain

$$f_2^* = \frac{0.8400}{0.5667} = 1.4823$$

and

$$f_3^* = \frac{1.0111}{0.5667} = 1.7842. \qquad \square$$

17.5.2 Overall Rate Change and Balancing Back

We now discuss the methodology of determining the overall rate change as well as the changes in each territory/class using the loss data. Again, this can be done using the loss ratio method or the loss cost method.

For the lost ratio method, we first compute the aggregate losses (trended and developed, inclusive of LAE) and the aggregate earned premiums at current rates. The effective loss ratio, denoted by L_R, is

$$L_R = \frac{\text{Aggregate losses}}{\text{Aggregate earned premiums}} = \frac{\sum_{i=1}^{m} \sum_{j=1}^{n} L_{ij}}{P* \sum_{i=1}^{m} \sum_{j=1}^{n} E_{ij} f_i g_j} \qquad (17.25)$$

and the indicated rate change is

$$R_P = \frac{L_R}{1 - \pi} - 1. \tag{17.26}$$

As in Section 17.1, we may compute the revised base rate as $P^*(1+R_P)$. When we apply this new rate to the indicated differentials with the current exposures, however, the aggregate earned premiums will not in general have the desired rate of increase R_P. A balancing factor is required to achieve the desired increase. We define the old average differential over *all* territories and classes as

$$d = \frac{\sum_{i=1}^{m} \sum_{j=1}^{n} E_{ij} f_i g_j}{\sum_{i=1}^{m} \sum_{j=1}^{n} E_{ij}} \tag{17.27}$$

and the new average differential as

$$d^* = \frac{\sum_{i=1}^{m} \sum_{j=1}^{n} E_{ij} f_i^* g_j^*}{\sum_{i=1}^{m} \sum_{j=1}^{n} E_{ij}}. \tag{17.28}$$

We then compute the balancing factor as

$$\theta = \frac{d}{d^*} \tag{17.29}$$

and the new base rate as

$$P^\dagger = P^*(1 + R_P)\theta, \tag{17.30}$$

with the new rate in the (i,j)th group being

$$P_{ij}^\dagger = P^\dagger f_i^* g_j^*. \tag{17.31}$$

When these new rates are applied to the existing exposures, the aggregate earned premium is

$$\sum_{i=1}^{m} \sum_{j=1}^{n} P_{ij}^\dagger E_{ij} = P^\dagger \sum_{i=1}^{m} \sum_{j=1}^{n} E_{ij} f_i^* g_j^*$$

$$= P^*(1 + R_P)\theta \left[\frac{\sum_{i=1}^{m} \sum_{j=1}^{n} E_{ij} f_i g_j}{\theta} \right]$$

$$= (1 + R_P) \left[\sum_{i=1}^{m} \sum_{j=1}^{n} P^* E_{ij} f_i g_j \right], \tag{17.32}$$

which is the old aggregate earned premium increased at the desired overall rate change of R_P.

To use the lost cost method, we first compute the lost cost per unit exposure, which is

$$\frac{\sum_{i=1}^{m} \sum_{j=1}^{n} L_{ij}}{\sum_{i=1}^{m} \sum_{j=1}^{n} E_{ij}}. \tag{17.33}$$

Table 17.10. *Loss data for AY2*

	C1		C2	
	Earned exposures	Incurred losses	Earned exposures	Incurred losses
T1	500	120,000	620	150,000
T2	450	80,000	300	75,000

As in equation (17.4), we divide the lost cost per unit exposure by the permissible loss ratio to obtain the rate:

$$\frac{\sum_{i=1}^{m}\sum_{j=1}^{n}L_{ij}}{(1-\pi)(\sum_{i=1}^{m}\sum_{j=1}^{n}E_{ij})}. \tag{17.34}$$

We then balance back this rate by dividing it by d^* to obtain the revised new base rate as follows:

$$
\begin{aligned}
\frac{\sum_{i=1}^{m}\sum_{j=1}^{n}L_{ij}}{(1-\pi)(\sum_{i=1}^{m}\sum_{j=1}^{n}E_{ij})d^*} &= \frac{\sum_{i=1}^{m}\sum_{j=1}^{n}L_{ij}}{(1-\pi)(\sum_{i=1}^{m}\sum_{j=1}^{n}E_{ij}f_i^*g_j^*)} \\
&= \frac{\sum_{i=1}^{m}\sum_{j=1}^{n}L_{ij}}{(1-\pi)\sum_{i=1}^{m}\sum_{j=1}^{n}E_{ij}f_ig_j} \times \frac{\sum_{i=1}^{m}\sum_{j=1}^{n}E_{ij}f_ig_j}{\sum_{i=1}^{m}\sum_{j=1}^{n}E_{ij}f_i^*g_j^*} \\
&= P^*\left[\frac{L_R}{1-\pi}\right]\theta \\
&= P^*(1+R_P)\theta \\
&= P^{\dagger}. \tag{17.35}
\end{aligned}
$$

Thus, the loss cost and loss ratio methods give the same result again.

Example 17.10 An insurance policy of one-year term has cross categorization of territories and classes. The data in Table 17.10 are for AY2. Current differentials for T1 and T2 are, respectively, 1 and 1.1, and those for C1 and C2 are, respectively, 1 and 1.2. The permissible loss ratio is 0.65. New rates will be effective on CY4/08/01. The trending factor is 5% per annum effective. Determine the new base rate and rates for each territory/class.

Solution 17.10 We first calculate the base premium rate using the lost cost method. As current rates are centered on CY2/07/01 while future losses for the new rates are centered on CY5/08/01, there is a time difference between the old and new losses of 3.0833 years. We divide the trended and fully developed losses by the exposures to obtain the overall lost cost per unit exposure as

$$\frac{(120,000+150,000+80,000+75,000)(1.05)^{3.0833}}{500+450+620+300} = 246.1680,$$

Table 17.11. *Cross categorized results*

	Adjusted exposures	Loss cost	Indicated differential
T1	1244	217.04	1.0000
T2	810	191.36	0.8817
C1	995	201.01	1.0000
C2	950	236.84	1.1783

so that the new overall premium rate is

$$\frac{246.1680}{0.65} = 406.41.$$

To compute the indicated differential using the lost cost method, we need to calculate the adjusted exposure. For T1, the adjusted exposure is

$$500 + 620(1.2) = 1{,}244,$$

so that the lost cost per unit of adjusted exposure is

$$\frac{270{,}000}{1{,}244} = 217.04.$$

Similar calculations for other territories and classes produce the results in Table 17.11. The new average differential is

$$d^* = \frac{500 + 620(1.1783) + 450(0.8817) + 300(0.8817)(1.1783)}{1{,}870} = 1.0369.$$

After balancing, the new rate for (T1, C1) is

$$\frac{406.41}{1.0369} = 391.96.$$

Other rates are obtained as follows:

$$(\text{T1, C2}): \quad 391.96(1.1783) = 461.84,$$

$$(\text{T2, C1}): \quad 391.96(0.8817) = 345.58$$

and

$$(\text{T2, C2}): \quad 391.96(1.1783)(0.8817) = 407.19. \qquad \square$$

Example 17.11 Loss data are given in Table 17.12. The distribution of the earned exposures in each territory is as shown in Table 17.13.

Table 17.12. *Loss data*

	Current average rate	Loss ratio
T1	150	0.65
T2	120	0.60
T3	110	0.58

Table 17.13. *Earned exposure distribution*

	T1	T2	T3	Current differential
C1	1,500	1,200	900	1.0
C2	800	900	700	1.1
C3	1,000	800	500	0.8

Table 17.14. *Differential by territories*

	Base rate	Current differential	Indicated differential
T1	155.67	1.0000	1.0000
T2	122.96	0.7899	0.7291
T3	111.60	0.7169	0.6397

Overall rate will increase by 4%. Determine the new base rates of the three territories.

Solution 17.11 We first calculate the average differential of each category. For T1, the average differential is (see equation (17.23))

$$\frac{1,500 + 800(1.1) + 1,000(0.8)}{1,500 + 800 + 1,000} = 0.9636.$$

Similarly, the average differentials for T2 and T3 are, respectively, 0.9759 and 0.9857. We then divide the average rate by the average differential to obtain the base rate (see equation (17.24)). Subsequently the current and indicated differentials are obtained in Table 17.14. Next we compute the old average differential and the new average differential. As only the differentials of the territories are updated, to compute the new average differential the old differentials of the classes are used. The old and new average differentials are

Table 17.15. *Loss data*

	Base rate	Earned premiums	Incurred losses	Claim count
T1	105	680,000	400,000	1,200
T2	120	450,000	300,000	820
T3	128	360,000	280,000	600

computed, respectively, as 0.8313 and 0.7912. Hence, the new base rate of T1 is

$$155.67 \times 1.04 \times \frac{0.8313}{0.7912} = 170.10.$$

For T2 and T3, the new base rates are, respectively, $170.10(0.7291) = 124.02$ and $170.10(0.6397) = 108.81$. $\qquad\square$

17.5.3 Credibility Weighting

While the current differential reflects cumulative updating of the differentials through time, the indicated differentials are based on a number of recent years of experience. In line with the experience weighting approach, actuaries need to weight the two sets of differentials for a credibility-weighted value. We denote the credibility weight by Z and compute the credibility-weighted differential as

$$Zf_i^* + (1 - Z)f_i, \qquad i = 1, \ldots, m. \tag{17.36}$$

Full credibility is given to the recent data if $Z = 1$. The credibility factor is close to 1 if the amount of exposures based on which the indicated differential is computed is large. The following example illustrates updating with credibility weighting.

Example 17.12 Loss data are given in Table 17.15. Credibility factor used is

$$Z = \sqrt{\frac{n}{1{,}082}}, \qquad \text{for } n < 1{,}082,$$

and $Z = 1$ for $n \geq 1082$, where n is the number of claim counts. Find the credibility-weighted differentials of the territories.

Solution 17.12 We first apply the loss ratio method. T1 is the base territory, having the largest claim units. T2 and T3 have current differentials of, respectively, $120/105 = 1.143$ and $128/105 = 1.219$. Loss ratios as incurred losses divided by earned premium are then computed, followed by the indicated

Table 17.16. *Differentials by loss ratio method*

	Current differential	Loss ratio	Indicated differential	Z	New differential
T1	1.000	0.5882	1.000	1.0000	1.000
T2	1.143	0.6667	1.295	0.8705	1.275
T3	1.219	0.7778	1.612	0.7447	1.512

Table 17.17. *Differentials by loss cost method*

	Current differential	Adjusted exposures	Loss costs	Indicated differential	New differential
T1	1.000	6,476.19	61.76	1.000	1.000
T2	1.143	3,750.00	80.00	1.295	1.275
T3	1.219	2,812.50	99.56	1.612	1.512

differentials and then the new credibility-weighted differentials. The results are summarized in Table 17.16.

To use the loss cost method, we first calculate the adjusted exposures. The adjusted exposures are the earned premium divided by the base rate (see equation (17.22)). For T1, this is $68,0000/105 = 6476.19$. For T2 and T3, they are, respectively, 3,750.00 and 2,812.50. We then calculate the loss cost per unit of adjusted premium. For T1, this is $40,0000/6,476.19 = 61.76$. For T2 and T3, they are, respectively, 80.00 and 99.56. The indicated differentials as the ratios of the loss costs are computed in Table 17.17. The results are the same as for the loss ratio method. □

17.6 R Laboratory

R Codes 17.1 provides the codes to compute the new premium rates by cross categories as illustrated in Example 17.10.

```
####################################################################
# R Codes 17.1
#
# Computation of new trended premium rates by cross categories as in
# Example 17.10
####################################################################

expos=matrix(c(500,620,450,300),
        nrow = 2, byrow = TRUE)          # Earned exposures
loss=matrix(c(120000,150000,80000,75000),
```

```
            nrow = 2, byrow = TRUE)          # Incurred losses
dc=c(1,1.2)                                  # Existing column diff
dr=c(1,1.1)                                  # Existing row diff
plr=0.65                                     # Permissible loss ratio
aexr=expos%*%dc                              # Adjusted row exposures
aexc=t(expos)%*%dr                           # Adjusted col exposures
lossr=apply(loss,1,sum)                      # Aggregate row losses
lossc=apply(loss,2,sum)                      # Aggregate col losses
lcr=lossr/aexr                               # Loss costs by row
lcc=lossc/aexc                               # Loss costs by col
idr=lcr/lcr[1]                               # Indicated row diff
idc=lcc/lcc[1]                               # Indicated col diff

sexp=as.numeric(sum(expos))                  # Sum of exposures
saexp=as.numeric(t(dr)%*%expos%*%dc)         # Sum of adj exposures
siaexp=as.numeric(t(idr)%*%expos%*%idc)      # Sum of ind adj expos
ds=siaexp/sexp                               # dstar in EQ(17.28)
th=saexp/siaexp                              # theta in Eq(17.29)

tf=1.05^3.0833                               # Trending factor
nbLR=(sum(loss)*tf/(saexp*plr))*th           # LR method new base
                                             # Eq(17.30)
nbLC=(sum(loss)*tf/sexp)/(plr*ds)            # LC method new base
                                             # Eq(17.35)
c(nbLR,nbLC)                                 # Output new base rates
npLR=nbLR*(idr%*%t(idc))                     # Prem by category,
                                             # LR method
npLC=nbLC*(idr%*%t(idc))                     # Prem by category,
                                             # LC method
```

17.7 Summary and Discussions

The loss cost method and loss ratio method are two equivalent approaches to
determine the premium rates. When policies are categorized, the premiums are
charged at differential rates. We discuss methods to revise the differentials.
Experience weighting is applied to balance between current differentials and
estimates based on recent data. Pooled data are used to estimate the overall base
premium, which can be weighted with the revised differential rates to determine
rates for subgroups.

Exercises

Exercise 17.1 You are given the following data about earned premiums and
times of change of rates for a one-year policy in four years:

Year	Earned premiums	Time and rate change
CY1	4,600	07/01: +5%
CY2	5,200	10/01: +8%
CY3	5,800	04/01: +3%
CY4	6,500	10/01: +10%

Calculate the earned premiums for CY1 through CY4 at the rate as of CY4/12/31.

Exercise 17.2 An insurance policy has the following loss costs and expenses per unit exposure:

Losses	1,000 per unit exposure
Variable expenses	10% of gross premium
Commission	8% of gross premium
Profit	12% of gross premium
Fixed expenses	50 per unit exposure

(a) Calculate the gross premium rate.
(b) Losses are expected to increase by 5% and commission is fixed at 100 and is payable on top of the premium. Calculate the revised gross premium rate.

Exercise 17.3 You are given the following data of loss experience in two years:

Year	Earned exposures	Incurred losses
AY1	950	120,000
AY2	1,200	156,000

Experience in AY1 and AY2 are given 30% and 70% weighting, respectively. The losses are trended at an effective rate of 6% per annum. New rates will be implemented on CY4/03/01. The permissible loss ratio is 0.70. Calculate the new gross rate.

Exercise 17.4 You are given the following data of an insurance business in three years:

Year and date of rate change	Rate change	Earned premiums in the year
CY1/11/01	+5%	300,000
CY2/10/01	+8%	450,000
CY3/07/01	+4%	580,000

The contracts are of 6-month terms. Calculate the aggregate earned premiums in the three years at the premium rate of CY3/12/31.

Exercise 17.5 You are given the following data of loss experience:

Territory	Earned exposures	Current differential	Loss ratio
T1	1,500	1.00	0.68
T2	800	0.90	0.75
T3	680	1.15	0.72

The current rate for T2 is 150, and there is an overall rate increase of 6%. Differentials are updated with a credibility factor of (n is the exposure)

$$Z = \sqrt{\frac{n}{1082}}, \qquad \text{for } n \leq 1082,$$

and 1 when $n > 1082$. Determine the new rate for T3.

Exercise 17.6 Data for policies cross categorized by territories (T1 and T2) and classes (C1 and C2) are as follows:

	C1		C2	
	Exposures	Incurred losses	Exposures	Incurred losses
T1	6,800	200,000	3,800	150,000
T2	5,900	280,000	4,200	260,000

T1 and C1 are the base groups. The current differentials of T2 and C2 are respectively, 1.2 and 1.3. The permissible loss ratio is 0.68. Determine the premium rate of the group (T2, C2) using the lost cost method.

Exercise 17.7 Data for exposures of policies cross categorized with three territories (T1, T2 and T3) and three classes (C1, C2 and C3) are as follows:

	C1	C2	C3	Aggregate losses	Average premium
T1	2,000	1,800	800	480,000	120
T2	1,500	1,600	500	380,000	130
T3	1,200	2,000	600	460,000	150
Differential	1.00	1.15	1.40		

Calculate the new base rate for T1, T2 and T3.

Exercise 17.8 You are given the following data for policies over two years:

Year	Earned premiums	Incurred losses
AY2	2,000,000	1,800,000
AY3	3,600,000	3,000,000

New rate will be introduced on CY4/10/01 with a trending factor of 5% per annum effective. Experience data for AY3 and AY2 are given weights of 60% and 40%, respectively. The permissible loss ratio is 0.8. Determine the indicative rate change.

Exercise 17.9 Loss experience of three territories are given below:

Territory	Current differential	Claim count	Earned premiums	Incurred losses
T1	1.00	1,800	50,000	36,000
T2	1.30	900	40,000	28,000
T3	1.40	680	36,000	28,000

Credibility factor is $Z = \sqrt{n/1{,}082}$ for $n \le 1{,}082$ and 1 when $n > 1{,}082$, where n is the claim count. There is an overall rate increase of 6%. Current base rate (for T1) is 120. Determine the new rates for the three territories.

Questions Adapted from SOA Exams

Exercise 17.10 You are given the following earned premiums for three calendar years:

Calendar year	Earned premiums
CY5	7,706
CY6	9,200
CY7	10,250

All policies have a one-year term and policy issues are uniformly distributed throughout each year. The following rate changes have occurred:

Date	Rate change
CY3/07/01	+7%
CY5/11/15	−4%
CY6/10/01	+5%

Rates are currently at the level of CY6/10/01. Calculate the earned premiums for CY6 at the current rate level.

Exercise 17.11 You are given the following data for policies in three territories:

Territory	Earned premiums at current rates	Incurred losses	Claim count	Current differential
T1	520,000	420,000	600	0.60
T2	1,680,000	1,250,000	1,320	1.00
T3	450,000	360,000	390	0.52
Total	2,650,000	2,030,000	2,310	

The full credibility standard is 1082 claims and partial credibility is calculated using the square root rule. Calculate, using the loss ratio method, the indicated territorial differential for T3.

Exercise 17.12 You use the following information to determine the rate change using the loss ratio method:

Accident year	Earned premiums at current rate	Incurred losses	Weight for accident year
AY8	4,252	2,260	40%
AY9	5,765	2,610	60%

The trending factor is 7% per annum effective. Loss development factors are 1.08 for AY8 and 1.18 for AY9. The permissible loss ratio is 0.657. All policies are for one-year terms and are issued uniformly throughout the year with rates effective for one year. Rate change is proposed for CY10/07/01. Calculate the required portfolio-wide rate change.

Exercise 17.13 Policies are written uniformly throughout the year with terms of six months. The following rate changes have occurred:

Date	Rate change
CY1/10/01	+7%
CY2/07/01	+10%
CY3/09/01	−6%

Calculate the factor needed to adjust earned premium of CY2 to the CY3/12/31 level.

Exercise 17.14 You are given the following data for homeowners insurance policies:

Accident year	Loss costs
AY1	1,300
AY2	1,150
AY3	1,550
AY4	1,800

The slope of the straight line fitted to the natural log of the loss costs is 0.1275. Experience periods are 12 months in length. In each year the average accident date is July 1. The current experience period is weighted 80% and the prior experience period is weighted 20% for rate development. New rates take effect CY5/11/01 for one-year policies and will be in effect for one year. Calculate the expected loss cost for these new rates.

Appendix: Review of Statistics

This Appendix provides a review of the statistical tools and literature required for this book. It summarizes background material found in introductory probability textbooks as well as develops required results for use in the main text. Readers who require a quick revision may study this Appendix prior to reading the main text. Otherwise, this Appendix may be used for reference only. For the purpose of being self-contained, some of the results developed in the main text are recapped here.

Students who wish to go deeper in the statistics literature will find the following texts useful: DeGroot and Schervish (2002), Hogg and Craig (1995) and Ross (2006).

A.1 Distribution Function, Probability Density Function, Probability Function and Survival Function

If X is a random variable, the **distribution function (df)** of X evaluated at x, denoted by $F_X(x)$, is defined as

$$F_X(x) = \Pr(X \leq x). \tag{A.1}$$

X is a continuous random variable if its df $F_X(x)$ is continuous. In addition, if $F_X(x)$ is differentiable, the **probability density function (pdf)** of X, denoted by $f_X(x)$, is defined as

$$f_X(x) = \frac{dF_X(x)}{dx}. \tag{A.2}$$

If X is discrete and takes possible countable values x_i for $i = 1, \ldots, n$, where n may be finite or infinite, then the **probability function (pf)** of X is

$$f_X(x_i) = \Pr(X = x_i). \tag{A.3}$$

476

Thus, $f_X(x) = \Pr(X = x_i)$ if $x = x_i$ for some i and zero otherwise. We denote $\Omega_X = \{x_1, x_2, \ldots\}$ as the set of discrete values X can take. For a random variable X, whether continuous or discrete, the set of all possible values X can take (countable if X is discrete and uncountable if X is continuous) is called the **support** of X.

The **survival function (sf)** (also called the **decumulative distribution function** or the **survival distribution function**) of a random variable X, denoted by $S_X(x)$, is

$$S_X(x) = 1 - F_X(x) = \Pr(X > x). \tag{A.4}$$

The df $F_X(x)$ is monotonic nondecreasing, the pdf $f_X(x)$ is nonnegative and the sf $S_X(x)$ is monotonic nonincreasing. Also, we have $F_X(-\infty) = S_X(\infty) = 0$ and $F_X(\infty) = S_X(-\infty) = 1$. If X is positive, then $F_X(0) = 0$ and $S_X(0) = 1$. The following equations express the df in terms of the pdf

$$F_X(x) = \int_{-\infty}^{x} f_X(x) \, dx, \qquad \text{for continuous } X, \tag{A.5}$$

and

$$F_X(x) = \sum_{x_i \leq x} f_X(x_i), \qquad \text{for discrete } X. \tag{A.6}$$

A.2 Random Variables of the Mixed Type and Stieltjes Integral

Some random variables may have a mix of discrete and continuous components. A random variable X is said to be of the **mixed type** if its df $F_X(x)$ is continuous and differentiable in the support apart from at the points belonging to a countable set, say, Ω_X^D. Thus, there exists a function $f_X(x)$ such that[1]

$$F_X(x) = \Pr(X \leq x) = \int_{-\infty}^{x} f_X(x) \, dx + \sum_{x_i \in \Omega_X^D, x_i \leq x} \Pr(X = x_i). \tag{A.7}$$

We use the **differential** $dF_X(x)$ to mean the probability of X in the infinitesimal interval $[x, x + dx)$, i.e.,

$$dF_X(x) = \Pr\{X \in [x, x + dx)\}. \tag{A.8}$$

If $F_X(x)$ has a jump at a point x, i.e., there is a **probability mass** at x, then

$$dF_X(x) = \Pr(X = x). \tag{A.9}$$

On the other hand, if $F_X(x)$ has a derivative $f_X(x)$ at point x, we have

$$dF_X(x) = f_X(x) \, dx. \tag{A.10}$$

---

[1] Note that $f_X(x)$ is the derivative of $F_X(x)$ at the points where $F_X(x)$ is continuous and differentiable, but it is not the pdf of X. In particular, $\int_{-\infty}^{\infty} f_X(x) \, dx \neq 1$.

We use the convenient notation of the **Stieltjes integral** to state that [2]

$$\Pr(a \le X \le b) = \int_a^b dF_X(x), \qquad (A.11)$$

for any interval $[a, b]$ in the support of X. This expression incorporates continuous, discrete and mixed random variables, where the df $F_X(x)$ may be any one of (A.5), (A.6) or (A.7).

A.3 Expected Value

Let $g(x)$ be a function of x, the **expected value** of $g(X)$, denoted by $E[g(X)]$, is defined as the Stieltjes integral

$$E[g(X)] = \int_{-\infty}^{\infty} g(x)\, dF_X(x), \qquad (A.12)$$

which is equal to

$$\int_{-\infty}^{\infty} g(x) f_X(x)\, dx, \qquad \text{if } X \text{ is continuous}, \qquad (A.13)$$

$$\sum_{x_i \in \Omega_X} g(x_i)\, \Pr(X = x_i), \qquad \text{if } X \text{ is discrete} \qquad (A.14)$$

and

$$\int_{-\infty}^{\infty} g(x) f_X(x)\, dx + \sum_{x_i \in \Omega_X^D} g(x_i)\, \Pr(X = x_i), \qquad \text{if } X \text{ is mixed}. \qquad (A.15)$$

Thus, the use of the Stieltjes integral conveniently simplifies the notations. If X is continuous and nonnegative, and $g(\cdot)$ is a nonnegative, monotonic and differentiable function, the following result holds

$$E[g(X)] = \int_0^{\infty} g(x)\, dF_X(x) = g(0) + \int_0^{\infty} g'(x)[1 - F_X(x)]\, dx, \qquad (A.16)$$

where $g'(x)$ is the derivative of $g(x)$ with respect to x. If X is discrete and nonnegative, taking values $0, 1, \ldots$, we have

$$E[g(X)] = g(0) + \sum_{x=0}^{\infty} [1 - F_X(x)]\, \Delta g(x), \qquad (A.17)$$

where $\Delta g(x) = g(x + 1) - g(x)$.

To prove equation (A.16), we note that, using integration by parts, we have

---

[2] For the definition of Stieltjes integral, see Ross (2006, p. 404).

$$\int_0^t g(x)\, dF_X(x) = -\int_0^t g(x)\, d[1 - F_X(x)]$$

$$= -g(t)\,[1 - F_X(t)] + g(0) + \int_0^t g'(x)[1 - F_X(x)]\, dx. \quad (A.18)$$

It is thus sufficient to show that

$$\lim_{t \to \infty} g(t)\,[1 - F_X(t)] = 0. \quad (A.19)$$

The above equation obviously holds if $g(\cdot)$ is nonincreasing. If $g(\cdot)$ is nondecreasing, we have

$$g(t)\,[1 - F_X(t)] = g(t) \int_t^\infty f_X(x)\, dx \le \int_t^\infty g(x) f_X(x)\, dx. \quad (A.20)$$

As $E[g(X)]$ exists, the last expression above tends to 0 as $t \to \infty$, which completes the proof.

A.4 Mean, Variance and Other Moments

The **mean** of X is

$$E(X) = \int_{-\infty}^\infty x\, dF_X(x). \quad (A.21)$$

If X is continuous and nonnegative, we apply equation (A.16) to obtain[3]

$$E(X) = \int_0^\infty [1 - F_X(x)]\, dx = \int_0^\infty S_X(x)\, dx. \quad (A.22)$$

The **variance** of X, denoted by $\mathrm{Var}(X)$, is defined as

$$\mathrm{Var}(X) = E\left\{[X - E(X)]^2\right\} = \int_{-\infty}^\infty [x - E(X)]^2\, dF_X(x). \quad (A.23)$$

The kth **moment about zero**, also called the kth raw moment, of X (for $k \ge 1$), denoted by μ_k', is defined as

$$\mu_k' = E(X^k) = \int_{-\infty}^\infty x^k\, dF_X(x). \quad (A.24)$$

Thus, $\mu_1' = E(X)$. The kth **moment about the mean**, also called the kth **central moment**, of X (for $k > 1$), denoted by μ_k, is defined as

$$\mu_k = E[(X - \mu_1')^k] = \int_{-\infty}^\infty (x - \mu_1')^k\, dF_X(x). \quad (A.25)$$

We have the relationship

$$\mathrm{Var}(X) = E(X^2) - [E(X)]^2, \quad (A.26)$$

---

[3] We need to replace the integral by a summation when X is discrete and nonnegative.

i.e.,

$$\mu_2 = \mu'_2 - (\mu'_1)^2. \tag{A.27}$$

If X is symmetric about the mean μ'_1, the third central moment μ_3 is zero. The standardized measure of **skewness** is defined as

$$\text{skewness} = \frac{\mu_3}{\sigma^3}. \tag{A.28}$$

The standardized measure of the fourth moment is called the **kurtosis**, which is defined as

$$\text{kurtosis} = \frac{\mu_4}{\sigma^4}. \tag{A.29}$$

The kurtosis measures the *thickness* of the tail distribution, with a value of 3 for the normal distribution. The **coefficient of variation** of X is defined as

$$\frac{\sqrt{\text{Var}(X)}}{\text{E}(X)} = \frac{\sqrt{\mu_2}}{\mu'_1}. \tag{A.30}$$

A.5 Conditional Probability and Bayes' Theorem

If A and B are nonnull events in a sample space S, then

$$\Pr(A \mid B) = \frac{\Pr(A \cap B)}{\Pr(B)}, \tag{A.31}$$

which can also be written as

$$\Pr(A \cap B) = \Pr(A \mid B)\Pr(B). \tag{A.32}$$

This is called the **multiplication rule** of probability.

If $B_1, B_2, \ldots, B_n$ are **mutually exclusive and exhaustive events** of S, i.e.,

$$\bigcup_{i=1}^{n} B_i = S \qquad \text{and} \qquad B_i \cap B_j = \emptyset \text{ for } i \neq j, \tag{A.33}$$

then extending the multiplication rule, we have

$$\Pr(A) = \sum_{i=1}^{n} \Pr(A \mid B_i)\Pr(B_i). \tag{A.34}$$

Now applying the multiplication rule to $\Pr(B_i \mid A)$ for any $i \in \{1, 2, \ldots, n\}$, we have

$$\begin{aligned} \Pr(B_i \mid A) &= \frac{\Pr(B_i \cap A)}{\Pr(A)} \\ &= \frac{\Pr(A \mid B_i)\Pr(B_i)}{\sum_{i=1}^{n} \Pr(A \mid B_i)\Pr(B_i)}. \end{aligned} \tag{A.35}$$

This result is called Bayes' Theorem.

A.6 Bivariate Random Variable

The **joint distribution function (joint df)** of the bivariate random variable (X, Y), denoted by $F_{XY}(x, y)$, is defined as

$$F_{XY}(x, y) = \Pr(X \le x, Y \le y). \tag{A.36}$$

If $F_{XY}(x, y)$ is continuous and differentiable with respect to x and y, the **joint probability density function (joint pdf)** of X and Y, denoted by $f_{XY}(x, y)$, is defined as

$$f_{XY}(x, y) = \frac{\partial^2 F_{XY}(x, y)}{\partial x \, \partial y}. \tag{A.37}$$

The pdf of X and Y are, respectively,

$$f_X(x) = \int_{-\infty}^{\infty} f_{XY}(x, y) \, dy, \tag{A.38}$$

$$f_Y(y) = \int_{-\infty}^{\infty} f_{XY}(x, y) \, dx, \tag{A.39}$$

which are called the **marginal pdf**. The **marginal df** of X and Y, denoted by $F_X(x)$ and $F_Y(y)$, can be obtained from the marginal pdf using equation (A.5).

If X and Y are random variables with marginal densities $f_X(x)$ and $f_Y(y)$, respectively, and the joint pdf of X and Y is $f_{XY}(x, y)$, then the **conditional pdf** of X given Y, denoted by $f_{X|Y}(x \mid y)$, is

$$f_{X|Y}(x \mid y) = \frac{f_{XY}(x, y)}{f_Y(y)}. \tag{A.40}$$

The above equation can also be used to compute the joint pdf from the conditional pdf and marginal pdf, i.e.,

$$f_{XY}(x, y) = f_{X|Y}(x \mid y) f_Y(y). \tag{A.41}$$

Let dx and dy be small changes in x and y, respectively. If we multiply $f_{X|Y}(x \mid y)$ by dx we have

$$f_{X|Y}(x \mid y) \, dx = \Pr(x \le X \le x + dx \mid y \le Y \le y + dy). \tag{A.42}$$

Substituting equation (A.39) for $f_Y(y)$ into (A.40), we obtain

$$f_{X|Y}(x \mid y) = \frac{f_{XY}(x, y)}{\int_{-\infty}^{\infty} f_{XY}(x, y) \, dx}. \tag{A.43}$$

X and Y are **independent** if and only if

$$f_{XY}(x, y) = f_X(x) f_Y(y) \tag{A.44}$$

for *all* (x, y) in the support of (X, Y). Using equation (A.40) we can see that equation (A.40) is equivalent to

$$f_{X|Y}(x \mid y) = f_X(x), \qquad \text{for all } x \text{ and } y. \tag{A.45}$$

If X and Y are discrete random variables, the **joint probability function (joint pf)** of X and Y, also denoted by $f_{XY}(x, y)$, is defined as

$$f_{XY}(x, y) = \Pr(X = x, Y = y). \tag{A.46}$$

The **marginal probability function (marginal pf)** of X and Y are analogously defined as equations (A.38) and (A.39).[4]

We now consider the moments of a bivariate distribution. For exposition, we assume X and Y are continuous. The expected value of $g(X, Y)$, denoted by $E[g(X, Y)]$, is defined as

$$E[g(X, Y)] = \int_{-\infty}^{\infty} \int_{-\infty}^{\infty} g(x, y) f_{XY}(x, y) \, dx \, dy, \tag{A.47}$$

if the integral exists. The covariance of X and Y, denoted by $\text{Cov}(X, Y)$, is defined as $E[(X - \mu_X)(Y - \mu_Y)]$, where μ_X and μ_Y are the means of X and Y, respectively. Thus,

$$\text{Cov}(X, Y) = E[(X - \mu_X)(Y - \mu_Y)] = \int_{-\infty}^{\infty} \int_{-\infty}^{\infty} (X - \mu_X)(Y - \mu_Y) f_{XY}(x, y) \, dx \, dy. \tag{A.48}$$

For convenience, we also use the notation σ_{XY} for $\text{Cov}(X, Y)$. From equation (A.48) we can show that

$$\text{Cov}(X, Y) = E(XY) - \mu_X \mu_Y. \tag{A.49}$$

The correlation coefficient of X and Y, denoted by $\rho(X, Y)$, is defined as

$$\rho(X, Y) = \frac{\sigma_{XY}}{\sigma_X \sigma_Y}, \tag{A.50}$$

where σ_X and σ_Y are the **standard deviation** (i.e., the square root of the variance) of X and Y, respectively.

If two random variables X and Y are independent, and $g(x, y) = g_X(x) g_Y(y)$ for some functions $g_X(\cdot)$ and $g_Y(\cdot)$, then

$$E[g(x, y)] = E[g_X(x) g_Y(y)] = E[g_X(x)] E[g_Y(y)], \tag{A.51}$$

where the first two expectations are taken over the joint distribution of X and Y, and the last two expectations are taken over their marginal distributions. For notational simplicity we do not specify the distribution over which the

---

[4] The case when one random variable is discrete and the other is continuous can be defined similarly.

expectation is taken, and let the content of the function of the random variable determine the required expectation.

From equation (A.51), if X and Y are independent, then $E(XY) = E(X)E(Y) = \mu_X\mu_Y$, so that $\sigma_{XY} = 0$ and $\rho(X,Y) = 0$. Thus, independence implies uncorrelatedness. The converse, however, does not stand.

A.7 Mean and variance of sum of random variables

Consider a set of random variables $X_1, X_2, \ldots, X_n$ with means $E(X_i) = \mu_i$ and variances $Var(X_i) = \sigma_i^2$, for $i = 1, 2, \ldots, n$. Let the covariance of X_i and X_j be $Cov(X_i, X_j) = \sigma_{ij}$, the correlation coefficient of X_i and X_j be $\rho(X_i, X_j) = \rho_{ij}$, and $w_1, w_2, \ldots, w_n$ be a set of constants. Then

$$E\left(\sum_{i=1}^{n} w_i X_i\right) = \sum_{i=1}^{n} w_i \mu_i, \tag{A.52}$$

$$Var\left(\sum_{i=1}^{n} w_i X_i\right) = \sum_{i=1}^{n} w_i^2 \sigma_i^2 + \underbrace{\sum_{i=1}^{n} \sum_{j=1}^{n}}_{i \neq j} w_i w_j \sigma_{ij}. \tag{A.53}$$

For $n = 2$, we have

$$\begin{aligned} Var(w_1 X_1 \pm w_2 X_2) &= w_1^2 \sigma_1^2 + w_2^2 \sigma_2^2 \pm 2w_1 w_2 \sigma_{12} \\ &= w_1^2 \sigma_1^2 + w_2^2 \sigma_2^2 \pm 2w_1 w_2 \rho_{12} \sigma_1 \sigma_2. \end{aligned} \tag{A.54}$$

A.8 Moment Generating Function and Probability Generating Function

The **moment generating function (mgf)** of a random variable X, denoted by $M_X(t)$, is a function of t defined by[5]

$$M_X(t) = E(e^{tX}) = \int_{-\infty}^{\infty} e^{tx} \, dF_X(x). \tag{A.55}$$

Given the mgf of a random variable X, the moments of X, if they exist, can be obtained by successively differentiating the mgf with respect to t and evaluating the result at $t = 0$. We observe

$$M_X'(t) = \frac{dM_X(t)}{dt} = \frac{d}{dt}E(e^{tX}) = E\left[\frac{d}{dt}(e^{tX})\right] = E(Xe^{tX}). \tag{A.56}$$

---

[5] If the integral in equation (A.55) does not converge, the mgf does not exist. Some random variables do not have a mgf.

Thus,

$$M_X'(0) = E(X) = \mu_1'. \tag{A.57}$$

Extending the above, we can see that, for any integer r,

$$M_X^r(t) = \frac{d^r M_X(t)}{dt^r} = \frac{d^r}{dt^r} E(e^{tX}) = E\left[\frac{d^r}{dt^r}(e^{tX})\right] = E(X^r e^{tX}), \tag{A.58}$$

so that

$$M_X^r(0) = E(X^r) = \mu_r'. \tag{A.59}$$

If $X_1, X_2, \ldots, X_n$ are independently distributed random variables with mgf $M_1(\cdot), M_2(\cdot), \ldots, M_n(\cdot)$, respectively, and $X = X_1 + \cdots + X_n$, then the mgf of X is

$$M_X(t) = E(e^{tX}) = E(e^{tX_1 + \cdots + tX_n}) = E\left(\prod_{i=1}^{n} e^{tX_i}\right) = \prod_{i=1}^{n} E(e^{tX_i}) = \prod_{i=1}^{n} M_i(t). \tag{A.60}$$

If $X_1, X_2, \ldots, X_n$ are **independently and identically distributed (iid)** with mgf $M(t)$, i.e., $M_i(t) = M(t)$ for $i = 1, 2, \ldots, n$, then we have

$$M_{X_1 + \ldots + X_n}(t) = [M(t)]^n. \tag{A.61}$$

The following are two important properties of a mgf [6]

If the mgf of a random variable X exists for t in an open interval around the point $t = 0$, then all moments of X exist.

If the mgf of two random variables X_1 and X_2 are identical for t in an open interval around the point $t = 0$, then the distributions of X_1 and X_2 are identical. Also, if two distributions are identical, they must have the same mgf.

Another important tool for statistical distributions is the **probability generating function (pgf)**. The pgf of a nonnegative discrete random variable X, denoted by $P_X(t)$, is defined as

$$P_X(t) = E(t^X), \tag{A.62}$$

if the expectation exists. Suppose $\Omega_X = \{0, 1, \ldots\}$, with $\Pr(X = i) = p_i$ for $i = 0, 1, \ldots$, the pgf of X is

$$P_X(t) = \sum_{i=0}^{\infty} t^i p_i. \tag{A.63}$$

---

[6] See DeGroot and Schervish (2002, pp. 205–208), for the details.

The *r*th order derivative of $P_X(t)$ is

$$P_X^r(t) = \frac{d^r}{dt^r}\left(\sum_{i=0}^{\infty} t^i p_i\right) = \sum_{i=r}^{\infty} i(i-1)\cdots(i-r+1)t^{i-r}p_i. \qquad \text{(A.64)}$$

If we evaluate $P_X^r(t)$ at $t = 0$, all terms in the summation vanish except for $i = r$, which is $r!p_r$. Hence, we have

$$P_X^r(0) = r!p_r, \qquad \text{(A.65)}$$

so that given the pgf, we can obtain the pf as

$$p_r = \frac{P_X^r(0)}{r!}, \qquad \text{(A.66)}$$

which explains the terminology pgf.

A.9 Some Discrete Distributions

In this section we present some commonly used discrete distributions, namely, the binomial, Poisson, geometric, negative binomial and hypergeometric distributions.

A.9.1 Binomial Distribution

Let X be the number of successes in a sequence of n independent Bernoulli trials each with probability of success θ. Then X follows a binomial distribution with parameters n and θ, denoted by $\mathcal{BN}(n, \theta)$, with pf

$$f_X(x) = \binom{n}{x}\theta^x(1-\theta)^{n-x}, \qquad \text{for } x = 0, 1, \ldots, n, \qquad \text{(A.67)}$$

where

$$\binom{n}{x} = \frac{n!}{x!(n-x)!}. \qquad \text{(A.68)}$$

The mean and variance of X are

$$\mathrm{E}(X) = n\theta \qquad \text{and} \qquad \mathrm{Var}(X) = n\theta(1-\theta). \qquad \text{(A.69)}$$

The mgf of X is

$$M_X(t) = (\theta e^t + 1 - \theta)^n. \qquad \text{(A.70)}$$

When n is large, X is approximately normally distributed.

A.9.2 Poisson Distribution

A discrete random variable X is said to have a Poisson distribution with parameter λ, denoted by $\mathcal{PN}(\lambda)$, if its pf is

$$f_X(x) = \frac{\lambda^x e^{-\lambda}}{x!}, \qquad \text{for } x = 0, 1, \dots . \tag{A.71}$$

The mean and variance of X are

$$E(X) = \text{Var}(X) = \lambda. \tag{A.72}$$

The mgf of X is

$$M_X(t) = \exp\left[\lambda(e^t - 1)\right]. \tag{A.73}$$

When λ is large, X is approximately normally distributed.

A.9.3 Geometric Distribution

Suppose independent Bernoulli trials, each with probability of success θ, are performed until a success occurs. Let X be the number of failures prior to the first success. Then X has a geometric distribution with parameter θ, denoted by $\mathcal{GM}(\theta)$, and its pf is

$$f_X(x) = \theta(1 - \theta)^x, \qquad \text{for } x = 0, 1, \dots . \tag{A.74}$$

The mean and variance of X are

$$E(X) = \frac{1 - \theta}{\theta} \qquad \text{and} \qquad \text{Var}(X) = \frac{1 - \theta}{\theta^2}. \tag{A.75}$$

The mgf of X is

$$M_X(t) = \frac{\theta}{1 - (1 - \theta)e^t}. \tag{A.76}$$

A.9.4 Negative Binomial Distribution

Suppose independent Bernoulli trials, each with probability of success θ, are performed until r successes occur. Let X be the number of failures prior to the rth success. Then X has a negative binomial distribution with parameters r and θ, denoted by $\mathcal{NB}(r, \theta)$, and its pf is

$$f_X(x) = \binom{x + r - 1}{r - 1} \theta^r (1 - \theta)^x, \qquad \text{for } x = 0, 1, \dots . \tag{A.77}$$

The mean and variance of X are

$$E(X) = \frac{r(1 - \theta)}{\theta} \qquad \text{and} \qquad \text{Var}(X) = \frac{r(1 - \theta)}{\theta^2}. \tag{A.78}$$

These results can be easily obtained by making use of the results in Section A.9.3 and recognizing that X is the sum of r iid geometric random variables with parameter θ. The mgf of X is

$$M_X(t) = \left[\frac{\theta}{1 - (1 - \theta)e^t} \right]^r. \tag{A.79}$$

A.9.5 Hypergeometric Distribution

Consider the probability of getting x blue balls in a random draw of m balls without replacement from an urn consisting of n_1 blue balls and n_2 red balls. The random variable X of the number of blue balls defined by this experiment has the pf

$$f_X(x) = \frac{\binom{n_1}{x} \binom{n_2}{m - x}}{\binom{n_1 + n_2}{m}}, \qquad \text{for } x = 0, 1, \ldots, n_1; \ x \le m; \ m - x \le n_2, \tag{A.80}$$

and is said to have a hypergeometric distribution with parameters m, n_1 and n_2, denoted by $\mathcal{HG}(m, n_1, n_2)$. The mean and variance of X are

$$\mathrm{E}(X) = \frac{mn_1}{n_1 + n_2} \qquad \text{and} \qquad \mathrm{Var}(X) = \frac{mn_1n_2(n_1 + n_2 - m)}{(n_1 + n_2)^2(n_1 + n_2 - 1)}. \tag{A.81}$$

Due to the complexity of the mgf of X, it is not given here.[7]

A.9.6 Summary of Some Discrete Distributions

Table A.1 summarizes the pf, mgf, mean and variance of the discrete distributions discussed in this section.

A.10 Some Continuous Distributions

In this section we present some commonly used continuous distributions, namely, the normal, lognormal, uniform, exponential, gamma, beta, Pareto and Weibull distributions.

---

[7] See Johnson and Kotz (1969, p. 144), for the details.

Table A.1. *Some discrete distributions*

Distribution, parameters, notation and support	pf $f_X(x)$	mgf $M_X(t)$	Mean	Variance
Binomial $\mathcal{BN}(n, \theta)$ $x \in \{0, 1, \ldots, n\}$	$\binom{n}{x}\theta^x(1-\theta)^{n-x}$	$(\theta e^t + 1 - \theta)^n$	$n\theta$	$n\theta(1-\theta)$
Poisson $\mathcal{PN}(\lambda)$ $x \in \{0, 1, \ldots\}$	$\dfrac{\lambda^x e^{-\lambda}}{x!}$	$\exp[\lambda(e^t - 1)]$	λ	λ
Geometric $\mathcal{GM}(\theta)$ $x \in \{0, 1, \ldots\}$	$\theta(1-\theta)^x$	$\dfrac{\theta}{1-(1-\theta)e^t}$	$\dfrac{1-\theta}{\theta}$	$\dfrac{1-\theta}{\theta^2}$
Negative binomial $\mathcal{NB}(r, \theta)$ $x \in \{0, 1, \ldots\}$	$\binom{x+r-1}{r-1}\theta^r(1-\theta)^x$	$\left[\dfrac{\theta}{1-(1-\theta)e^t}\right]^r$	$\dfrac{r(1-\theta)}{\theta}$	$\dfrac{r(1-\theta)}{\theta^2}$
Hypergeometric $\mathcal{HG}(m, n_1, n_2)$ $x \in \{0, 1, \ldots, n_1\},$ $x \le m, m - x \le n_2,$ Denote $n = n_1 + n_2$	$\dfrac{\binom{n_1}{x}\binom{n_2}{m-x}}{\binom{n}{m}}$	Not presented	$\dfrac{mn_1}{n}$	$\dfrac{mn_1n_2(n-m)}{n^2(n-1)}$

A.10.1 Normal Distribution

Let X be a continuous random variable which can take values on the real line. X is said to follow a normal distribution with mean μ and variance σ^2, denoted by $X \sim \mathcal{N}(\mu, \sigma^2)$, if the pdf of X is

$$f_X(x) = \frac{1}{\sqrt{2\pi}\sigma} \exp\left[-\frac{(x-\mu)^2}{2\sigma^2}\right]. \tag{A.82}$$

X is said to be a standard normal random variable if it is normally distributed with mean 0 and variance 1. If $X \sim \mathcal{N}(\mu, \sigma^2)$, then

$$\frac{X-\mu}{\sigma} \sim \mathcal{N}(0, 1). \tag{A.83}$$

The mgf of $X \sim \mathcal{N}(\mu, \sigma^2)$ is

$$M_X(t) = \exp\left(\mu t + \frac{\sigma^2 t^2}{2}\right). \tag{A.84}$$

If X_1 and X_2 are independent random variables with $X_i \sim \mathcal{N}(\mu_i, \sigma_i^2)$ for $i = 1, 2$, and w_1 and w_2 are constants, then $w_1 X_1 + w_2 X_2$ is normally distributed with mean $w_1\mu_1 + w_2\mu_2$ and variance $w_1^2\sigma_1^2 + w_2^2\sigma_2^2$.

Linear combinations of normally distributed random variables (not necessarily independent) are normally distributed.

A.10.2 Lognormal Distribution

Suppose X is a continuous positive random variable. If $\log X$ follows a normal distribution with mean μ and variance σ^2, then X follows a lognormal distribution with parameters μ and σ^2, denoted by $\mathcal{L}(\mu, \sigma^2)$. The mean and variance of X are

$$E(X) = \exp\left(\mu + \frac{\sigma^2}{2}\right), \tag{A.85}$$

$$\mathrm{Var}(X) = \left[\exp\left(2\mu + \sigma^2\right)\right]\left[\exp(\sigma^2) - 1\right]. \tag{A.86}$$

If X_1 and X_2 are independently distributed lognormal random variables with $\log X_i \sim \mathcal{N}(\mu_i, \sigma_i^2)$ for $i = 1, 2$, and w_1 and w_2 are constants, then $Y = X_1^{w_1} X_2^{w_2}$ is lognormally distributed with parameters $w_1\mu_1 + w_2\mu_2$ and $w_1^2\sigma_1^2 + w_2^2\sigma_2^2$. This result holds as

$$\begin{aligned}
\log Y &= \log(X_1^{w_1} X_2^{w_2}) \\
&= w_1 \log X_1 + w_2 \log X_2 \\
&\sim \mathcal{N}(w_1\mu_1 + w_2\mu_2, w_1^2\sigma_1^2 + w_2^2\sigma_2^2).
\end{aligned} \tag{A.87}$$

Products of powers of lognormally distributed random variables (not necessarily independent) are lognormally distributed.

The lognormal distribution has the peculiar property that even though the moments of all finite orders exist, the mgf is infinite for any $t > 0$. The pdf of the lognormal distribution with parameters μ and σ^2 is

$$f_X(x) = \frac{1}{\sqrt{2\pi}\sigma x} \exp\left[-\frac{(\log x - \mu)^2}{2\sigma^2}\right]. \tag{A.88}$$

A.10.3 Uniform Distribution

A continuous random variable X is uniformly distributed in the interval $[a, b]$, denoted by $\mathcal{U}(a, b)$, if its pdf is

$$f_X(x) = \begin{cases} \dfrac{1}{b-a}, & \text{for } x \in [a, b], \\[2mm] 0, & \text{otherwise.} \end{cases} \tag{A.89}$$

The mean and variance of X are

$$E(X) = \frac{a+b}{2} \quad \text{and} \quad \mathrm{Var}(X) = \frac{(b-a)^2}{12}, \tag{A.90}$$

and its mgf is

$$M_X(t) = \frac{e^{bt} - e^{at}}{(b-a)t}.$$ (A.91)

A.10.4 Exponential Distribution

A random variable X has an exponential distribution with parameter λ (> 0), denoted by $\mathcal{E}(\lambda)$, if its pdf is

$$f_X(x) = \lambda e^{-\lambda x}, \qquad \text{for } x \geq 0.$$ (A.92)

The mean and variance of X are

$$E(X) = \frac{1}{\lambda} \qquad \text{and} \qquad \text{Var}(X) = \frac{1}{\lambda^2}.$$ (A.93)

The mgf of X is

$$M_X(t) = \frac{\lambda}{\lambda - t}.$$ (A.94)

A.10.5 Gamma Distribution

The integral

$$\int_0^\infty y^{\alpha-1} e^{-y} \, dy$$ (A.95)

exists for $\alpha > 0$ and is called the gamma function, denoted by $\Gamma(\alpha)$. Using integration by parts, it can be shown that, for $\alpha > 1$,

$$\Gamma(\alpha) = (\alpha - 1) \int_0^\infty y^{\alpha-2} e^{-y} \, dy = (\alpha - 1)\Gamma(\alpha - 1).$$ (A.96)

In addition, if α is an integer, we have

$$\Gamma(\alpha) = (\alpha - 1)!.$$ (A.97)

X is said to have a gamma distribution with parameters α and β ($\alpha > 0$ and $\beta > 0$), denoted by $\mathcal{G}(\alpha, \beta)$, if its pdf is

$$f_X(x) = \frac{1}{\Gamma(\alpha)\beta^\alpha} x^{\alpha-1} e^{-\frac{x}{\beta}}, \qquad \text{for } x \geq 0.$$ (A.98)

The mean and variance of X are

$$E(X) = \alpha\beta \qquad \text{and} \qquad \text{Var}(X) = \alpha\beta^2,$$ (A.99)

and its mgf is

$$M_X(t) = \frac{1}{(1 - \beta t)^\alpha}, \qquad \text{for } t < \frac{1}{\beta}.$$ (A.100)

The special case of $\alpha = r/2$, where r is a positive integer, and $\beta = 2$, is called the chi-square distribution with r degrees of freedom, denoted by χ_r^2.

A.10.6 Beta Distribution

A random variable X is said to have a beta distribution with parameters α and β ($\alpha > 0, \beta > 0$), denoted by $\mathcal{B}(\alpha, \beta)$, if its pdf is given by

$$f_X(x) = \frac{1}{B(\alpha, \beta)} x^{\alpha-1}(1-x)^{\beta-1}, \qquad \text{for } 0 \le x \le 1, \qquad \text{(A.101)}$$

where $B(\alpha, \beta)$ is the beta function defined by

$$B(\alpha, \beta) = \int_0^1 x^{\alpha-1}(1-x)^{\beta-1}\, dx = \frac{\Gamma(\alpha)\Gamma(\beta)}{\Gamma(\alpha+\beta)}. \qquad \text{(A.102)}$$

The mean and variance of the beta distribution are

$$E(X) = \frac{\alpha}{\alpha+\beta} \quad \text{and} \quad \text{Var}(X) = \frac{\alpha\beta}{(\alpha+\beta)^2(\alpha+\beta+1)}, \qquad \text{(A.103)}$$

and its mgf can be expressed as a confluent hypergeometric function. The details will not be provided here.[8]

A.10.7 Pareto Distribution

A random variable X has a Pareto distribution with parameters α and γ ($\alpha > 0, \gamma > 0$), denoted by $\mathcal{P}(\alpha, \gamma)$, if its pdf is

$$f_X(x) = \frac{\alpha\gamma^\alpha}{(x+\gamma)^{\alpha+1}}, \qquad \text{for } x \ge 0. \qquad \text{(A.104)}$$

The df of X is

$$F_X(x) = 1 - \left(\frac{\gamma}{x+\gamma}\right)^\alpha, \qquad \text{for } x \ge 0. \qquad \text{(A.105)}$$

The rth moment of X exists for $r < \alpha$. For $\alpha > 2$, the mean and variance of X are

$$E(X) = \frac{\gamma}{\alpha-1} \quad \text{and} \quad \text{Var}(X) = \frac{\alpha\gamma^2}{(\alpha-1)^2(\alpha-2)}. \qquad \text{(A.106)}$$

The Pareto distribution does not have a mgf.

A.10.8 Weibull Distribution

A random variable X has a 2-parameter Weibull distribution if its pdf is

$$f_X(x) = \left(\frac{\alpha}{\lambda}\right)\left(\frac{x}{\lambda}\right)^{\alpha-1} \exp\left[-\left(\frac{x}{\lambda}\right)^\alpha\right], \qquad \text{for } x \ge 0, \qquad \text{(A.107)}$$

---

[8] See Johnson and Kotz (1970), p. 40, for the details.

where α is the shape parameter and λ is the scale parameter ($\alpha > 0, \lambda > 0$). We denote the distribution by $\mathcal{W}(\alpha, \lambda)$. The mean and variance of X are

$$E(X) = \mu = \lambda\,\Gamma\left(1 + \frac{1}{\alpha}\right) \quad \text{and} \quad \text{Var}(X) = \lambda^2\,\Gamma\left(1 + \frac{2}{\alpha}\right) - \mu^2.$$

$$(A.108)$$

Due to its complexity, the mgf of the Weibull distribution is not presented here.

A.10.9 Summary of Some Continuous Distributions

Table A.2 summarizes the results of the pdf, mgf, mean and variance of the continuous distributions presented in this section.

A.11 Conditional Expectation, Conditional Mean and Conditional Variance

Given two random variables X and Y, and a function $g(x,y)$, the expectation $E[g(X, Y)]$ defined in equation (A.47) can be evaluated by iterative expectations. First, we define the conditional expectation of $g(X, Y)$ given $Y = y$, denoted by $E[g(X, Y)\,|\,y]$, as[9]

$$E[g(X, Y)\,|\,y] = \int_{-\infty}^{\infty} g(x,y)f_{X\,|\,Y}(x\,|\,y)\,dx. \qquad (A.109)$$

Note that $E[g(X, Y)\,|\,y]$ is a function of y (but not x). If we allow y to vary over the support of Y, we treat $E[g(X, Y)\,|\,y]$ as a function of the random variable Y, and denote it by $E[g(X, Y)\,|\,Y]$. Taking the expectation of this function over the random variable Y, we have[10]

$$E\{E[g(X, Y)\,|\,Y]\} = \int_{-\infty}^{\infty} E[g(X, Y)\,|\,y]f_Y(y)\,dy$$

$$= \int_{-\infty}^{\infty}\left[\int_{-\infty}^{\infty} g(x,y)f_{X\,|\,Y}(x\,|\,y)\,dx\right]f_Y(y)\,dy$$

$$= \int_{-\infty}^{\infty}\int_{-\infty}^{\infty} g(x,y)f_{X\,|\,Y}(x\,|\,y)f_Y(y)\,dx\,dy$$

$$= \int_{-\infty}^{\infty}\int_{-\infty}^{\infty} g(x,y)f_{XY}(x,y)\,dx\,dy$$

---

[9] An alternative notation for the conditional expectation is $E_{X\,|\,Y}[g(X, Y)\,|\,y]$, in which the suffix of E explicitly denotes that it is a conditional expectation. We adopt the simpler notation where the suffix is dropped. Also, for simplicity of exposition, we assume X and Y are continuous. The results in this section apply to discrete and mixed random variables as well.

[10] The first expectation on the left-hand side of equation (A.110) is taken over Y and the second expectation is taken over X conditional on $Y = y$.

Table A.2. *Some continuous distributions*

Distribution, parameters, notation and support	pdf $f_X(x)$	mgf $M_X(t)$	Mean	Variance
Normal $\mathcal{N}(\mu, \sigma^2)$ $x \in (-\infty, \infty)$	$\dfrac{\exp\left[-\dfrac{(x-\mu)^2}{2\sigma^2}\right]}{\sqrt{2\pi}\sigma}$	$\exp\left(\mu t + \dfrac{\sigma^2 t^2}{2}\right)$	μ	σ^2
Lognormal $\mathcal{L}(\mu, \sigma^2)$ $x \in (0, \infty)$	$\dfrac{\exp\left[-\dfrac{(\log x - \mu)^2}{2\sigma^2}\right]}{\sqrt{2\pi}\sigma x}$ Does not exist		$e^{\mu + \frac{\sigma^2}{2}}$	$\left(e^{2\mu + \sigma^2}\right)\left(e^{\sigma^2} - 1\right)$
Uniform $\mathcal{U}(a, b)$ $x \in [a, b]$	$\dfrac{1}{b-a}$	$\dfrac{e^{bt} - e^{at}}{(b-a)t}$	$\dfrac{a+b}{2}$	$\dfrac{(b-a)^2}{12}$
Exponential $\mathcal{E}(\lambda)$ $x \in [0, \infty)$	$\lambda e^{-\lambda x}$	$\dfrac{\lambda}{\lambda - t}$	$\dfrac{1}{\lambda}$	$\dfrac{1}{\lambda^2}$
Gamma $\mathcal{G}(\alpha, \beta)$ $x \in [0, \infty)$	$\dfrac{x^{\alpha-1} e^{-\frac{x}{\beta}}}{\Gamma(\alpha)\beta^\alpha}$	$\dfrac{1}{(1-\beta t)^\alpha}$	$\alpha\beta$	$\alpha\beta^2$
Beta $\mathcal{B}(\alpha, \beta)$ $x \in [0, 1]$	$\dfrac{x^{\alpha-1}(1-x)^{\beta-1}}{B(\alpha, \beta)}$	Not presented	$\dfrac{\alpha}{\alpha+\beta}$	$\dfrac{\alpha\beta}{(\alpha+\beta)^2(\alpha+\beta+1)}$
Pareto $\mathcal{P}(\alpha, \gamma)$ $x \in [0, \infty)$	$\dfrac{\alpha\gamma^\alpha}{(x+\gamma)^{\alpha+1}}$	Does not exist	$\dfrac{\gamma}{\alpha - 1}$	$\dfrac{\alpha\gamma^2}{(\alpha-1)^2(\alpha-2)}$
Weibull $\mathcal{W}(\alpha, \lambda)$ $x \in [0, \infty)$	$\left(\dfrac{\alpha}{\lambda}\right)\left(\dfrac{x}{\lambda}\right)^{\alpha-1} e^{-\left(\frac{x}{\lambda}\right)^\alpha}$ Not presented		$\mu = \lambda\,\Gamma\left(1 + \dfrac{1}{\alpha}\right)$	$\lambda^2\,\Gamma\left(1 + \dfrac{2}{\alpha}\right) - \mu^2$

$$= \mathrm{E}[g(X, Y)]. \tag{A.110}$$

Thus, unconditional expectation can be calculated using iterative expectations. This result implies

$$\mathrm{E}[\mathrm{E}(X \mid Y)] = \mathrm{E}(X). \tag{A.111}$$

The conditional variance of X given $Y = y$ is a function of the random variable Y if y is allowed to vary over the support of Y. We denote this conditional variance by $\mathrm{Var}(X \mid Y)$, which is defined as $v(Y)$, where

$$v(y) = \mathrm{Var}(X \mid y) = \mathrm{E}\{[X - \mathrm{E}(X \mid y)]^2 \mid y\} = \mathrm{E}(X^2 \mid y) - [\mathrm{E}(X \mid y)]^2. \tag{A.112}$$

Thus, we have

$$\text{Var}(X \mid Y) = \text{E}(X^2 \mid Y) - [\text{E}(X \mid Y)]^2, \qquad (A.113)$$

which implies

$$\text{E}(X^2 \mid Y) = \text{Var}(X \mid Y) + [\text{E}(X \mid Y)]^2. \qquad (A.114)$$

Now from equations (A.26) and (A.114), we have

$$\begin{aligned}
\text{Var}(X) &= \text{E}(X^2) - [\text{E}(X)]^2 \\
&= \text{E}[\text{E}(X^2 \mid Y)] - [\text{E}(X)]^2 \\
&= \text{E}\{\text{Var}(X \mid Y) + [\text{E}(X \mid Y)]^2\} - [\text{E}(X)]^2 \\
&= \text{E}[\text{Var}(X \mid Y)] + \text{E}\{[\text{E}(X \mid Y)]^2\} - [\text{E}(X)]^2 \\
&= \text{E}[\text{Var}(X \mid Y)] + \text{E}\{[\text{E}(X \mid Y)]^2\} - \{\text{E}[\text{E}(X \mid Y)]\}^2 \\
&= \text{E}[\text{Var}(X \mid Y)] + \text{Var}[\text{E}(X \mid Y)].
\end{aligned} \qquad (A.115)$$

Verbally, the above equation says that the unconditional variance of X is equal to the mean of its conditional (upon Y) variance plus the variance of its conditional (upon Y) mean.

If X and Y are independent, we conclude from equation (A.51) that

$$\text{E}(XY) = \text{E}(X)\text{E}(Y). \qquad (A.116)$$

To compute $\text{Var}(XY)$, we use equation (A.115) and apply conditioning of XY on Y to obtain

$$\begin{aligned}
\text{Var}(XY) &= \text{E}[\text{Var}(XY \mid Y)] + \text{Var}[\text{E}(XY \mid Y)] \\
&= \text{E}[Y^2 \text{Var}(X \mid Y)] + \text{Var}[Y\text{E}(X \mid Y)].
\end{aligned} \qquad (A.117)$$

Since X and Y are independent, $\text{Var}(X \mid Y) = \text{Var}(X)$ and $\text{E}(X \mid Y) = \text{E}(X)$. Thus, we have

$$\begin{aligned}
\text{Var}(XY) &= \text{E}[Y^2 \text{Var}(X)] + \text{Var}[Y\text{E}(X)] \\
&= \text{E}(Y^2)\text{Var}(X) + [\text{E}(X)]^2\text{Var}(Y).
\end{aligned} \qquad (A.118)$$

Note that if we use equation (A.115) and apply conditioning of XY on X, we obtain

$$\text{Var}(XY) = [\text{E}(Y)]^2\text{Var}(X) + \text{E}(X^2)\text{Var}(Y). \qquad (A.119)$$

The equivalence of equations (A.118) and (A.119) can be proved using equation (A.26).

A.12 Compound Distribution

Let N be a discrete random variable that takes nonnegative integer values. We consider a sequence of iid random variables $\{X_1, X_2, \ldots\}$, where $X_i \sim X$ for $i \in \{1, 2, \ldots\}$. Let

$$S = X_1 + \cdots + X_N, \tag{A.120}$$

which is the sum of N iid random variables, each distributed as X, with the number of summation terms N being random.[11] S is said to have a **compound distribution**, with N being the **primary distribution** and X the **secondary distribution**. We denote $E(N) = \mu_N$ and $Var(N) = \sigma_N^2$, and likewise $E(X) = \mu_X$ and $Var(X) = \sigma_X^2$. Using the results on conditional expectations, we have

$$E(S) = E[E(S \mid N)] = E[E(X_1 + \cdots + X_N \mid N)] = E(N\mu_X) = \mu_N\mu_X. \tag{A.121}$$

Also, using equation (A.115), we have

$$\begin{aligned} Var(S) &= E[Var(S \mid N)] + Var[E(S \mid N)] \\ &= E[N\sigma_X^2] + Var(N\mu_X) \\ &= \mu_N\sigma_X^2 + \sigma_N^2\mu_X^2. \end{aligned} \tag{A.122}$$

If N has a Poisson distribution with mean λ, so that $\mu_N = \sigma_N^2 = \lambda$, S is said to have a **compound Poisson distribution**, with

$$Var(S) = \lambda(\sigma_X^2 + \mu_X^2). \tag{A.123}$$

A.13 Convolution

Suppose X_1 and X_2 are independent discrete random variables with common support Ω, and pf $f_{X_1}(\cdot)$ and $f_{X_2}(\cdot)$, respectively, and let $X = X_1 + X_2$. The pf $f_X(\cdot)$ of X is given by

$$f_X(x) = \sum_{x_2, x-x_2 \in \Omega} f_{X_1}(x - x_2)f_{X_2}(x_2) = \sum_{x_1, x-x_1 \in \Omega} f_{X_2}(x - x_1)f_{X_1}(x_1). \tag{A.124}$$

The pf $f_X(x)$ evaluated by either expression in equation (A.124) is called the **convolution** of the pf $f_{X_1}(\cdot)$ and $f_{X_2}(\cdot)$, which may also be written as

$$f_X(x) = (f_{X_2} * f_{X_1})(x) = (f_{X_1} * f_{X_2})(x). \tag{A.125}$$

---

[11] S is defined as 0 if $N = 0$.

Hence, convolutions are *commutative*. If X_1 and X_2 are nonnegative, then equation (A.124) becomes

$$f_X(x) = \sum_{x_2=0}^{x} f_{X_1}(x - x_2) f_{X_2}(x_2) = \sum_{x_1=0}^{x} f_{X_2}(x - x_1) f_{X_1}(x_1), \quad \text{for } x = 0, 1, \ldots.$$

(A.126)

If X_1 and X_2 are continuous, equations (A.124) and (A.126) are replaced, respectively, by

$$f_X(x) = \int_{-\infty}^{\infty} f_{X_1}(x - x_2) f_{X_2}(x_2) \, dx_2 = \int_{-\infty}^{\infty} f_{X_2}(x - x_1) f_{X_1}(x_1) \, dx_1, \quad \text{(A.127)}$$

and

$$f_X(x) = \int_{0}^{x} f_{X_1}(x - x_2) f_{X_2}(x_2) \, dx_2 = \int_{0}^{x} f_{X_2}(x - x_1) f_{X_1}(x_1) \, dx_1. \quad \text{(A.128)}$$

Convolutions may be applied to sums of more than two random variables. Thus, if X_1, X_2 and X_3 are independently distributed, we have

$$f_{X_1+X_2+X_3}(x) = (f_{X_1} * f_{X_2} * f_{X_3})(x). \quad \text{(A.129)}$$

If X_1, X_2 and X_3 are identically distributed with the same pf or pdf $f(\cdot)$, we write equation (A.129) as

$$f_{X_1+X_2+X_3}(x) = (f * f * f)(x) = f^{*3}(x). \quad \text{(A.130)}$$

Thus, for a sum of n iid random variables each with pf or pdf $f(\cdot)$, its pf or pdf is $f^{*n}(\cdot)$.

A.14 Mixture Distribution

Let $X_1, \ldots, X_n$ be random variables with corresponding pf (if X_i are discrete) or pdf (if X_i are continuous) $f_{X_1}(\cdot), \ldots, f_{X_n}(\cdot)$. X_i are assumed to have the common support Ω. A new random variable X may be created with pf or pdf $f_X(\cdot)$ given by

$$f_X(x) = p_1 f_{X_1}(x) + \cdots + p_n f_{X_n}(x), \quad x \in \Omega, \quad \text{(A.131)}$$

where $p_i \geq 0$ for $i = 1, \ldots, n$ and $\sum_{i=1}^{n} p_i = 1$, so that $\{p_i\}$ form a well-defined probability distribution. We call X a **mixture distribution** with a **discrete mixing distribution**.

Now consider a nonnegative random variable (discrete or continuous) with pf or pdf $f(x \mid \theta)$, which depends on the parameter θ. Let $h(\cdot)$ be a function such that $h(\theta) > 0$ for $\theta > 0$, and

$$\int_{0}^{\infty} h(\theta) \, d\theta = 1. \quad \text{(A.132)}$$

A new random variable X may be created with pf or pdf $f_X(x)$ given by

$$f_X(x) = \int_0^\infty f(x \mid \theta) h(\theta) \, d\theta. \tag{A.133}$$

Note that $h(\theta)$ is a well-defined pdf that defines the **continuous mixing distribution**, and X is a mixture distribution with continuous mixing. Furthermore, if we allow $h(\theta)$ to depend on a parameter γ, we may rewrite equation (A.133) as

$$f_X(x \mid \gamma) = \int_0^\infty f(x \mid \theta) h(\theta \mid \gamma) \, d\theta. \tag{A.134}$$

Thus, the mixture distribution depends on the parameter γ, which determines the distribution of θ.

A.15 Bayesian Approach of Statistical Inference

Let $X = \{X_1, X_2, \ldots, X_n\}$ denote a sample of iid random variables each distributed as X, and $x = (x_1, x_2, \ldots, x_n)$ be a realization of the sample. Classical statistical inference assumes that X depends on an unknown *fixed* parameter θ (which may be multidimensional). After X is observed, **statistical inference**, including **estimation** and **hypothesis testing**, concerning the parameter θ is made.

The Bayesian approach of statistical inference assumes that the parameter θ determining the distribution of X is unknown and uncertain. Thus, θ is treated as a random variable, denoted by Θ with support Ω_Θ and pdf $f_\Theta(\theta)$, which is called the **prior distribution** of Θ. Once the data X are observed, the distribution of Θ is revised and the resultant pdf of Θ is called the **posterior distribution** of Θ, with pdf denoted by $f_{\Theta \mid X}(\theta \mid x)$. Denoting $f_{\Theta X}(\theta, x)$ as the joint pdf of Θ and X, and using the result in equation (A.40), we have

$$\begin{aligned} f_{\Theta \mid X}(\theta \mid x) &= \frac{f_{\Theta X}(\theta, x)}{f_X(x)} \\ &= \frac{f_{X \mid \Theta}(x \mid \theta) f_\Theta(\theta)}{\int_{\theta \in \Omega_\Theta} f_{X \mid \Theta}(x \mid \theta) f_\Theta(\theta) \, d\theta}. \end{aligned} \tag{A.135}$$

The conditional pdf of X, $f_{X \mid \Theta}(x \mid \theta)$, is called the **likelihood function**. Multiplying the likelihood with the prior pdf of Θ gives the joint pdf of X and Θ. In classical statistical inference, only the likelihood function matters; the prior pdf does not have a role to play.

Note that the denominator of equation (A.135) is a function of x but not θ. Denoting

$$K(x) = \frac{1}{\int_{\theta \in \Omega_\Theta} f_{X \mid \Theta}(x \mid \theta) f_\Theta(\theta) \, d\theta}, \tag{A.136}$$

we can rewrite the posterior pdf of Θ as

$$f_{\Theta \mid X}(\theta \mid x) = K(x)f_{X \mid \Theta}(x \mid \theta)f_{\Theta}(\theta)$$
$$\propto f_{X \mid \Theta}(x \mid \theta)f_{\Theta}(\theta). \tag{A.137}$$

$K(x)$ is a **constant of proportionality** and is free of θ. It scales the posterior pdf so that it integrates to 1.

The Bayesian approach of estimating θ involves minimizing a **loss function** over the posterior distribution of Θ. The loss function measures the penalty in making a wrong decision with respect to the true value of θ. Thus, if the estimate of θ is $\hat{\theta}$, the loss function is denoted by $L(\theta, \hat{\theta})$. A popular loss function is the **squared-error loss function** defined by

$$L(\theta, \hat{\theta}) = (\theta - \hat{\theta})^2. \tag{A.138}$$

The squared-error loss function is symmetric, as an over-estimation and under-estimation of the same amount incur the same loss. It can be shown that the value of $\hat{\theta}$ that minimizes $(\theta - \hat{\theta})^2$ over the posterior distribution is the **posterior mean**, which is given by

$$\hat{\theta} = E(\Theta \mid x) = \int_{\theta \in \Omega_{\Theta}} \theta f_{\Theta \mid X}(\theta \mid x) \, d\theta. \tag{A.139}$$

This is also called the **Bayes estimate** of θ (with respect to the squared-error loss function).

A.16 Conjugate Distribution

A difficult step in applying the Bayesian approach of statistical inference is the computation of the posterior distribution. As equation (A.135) shows, the posterior pdf is in general difficult to evaluate, as it is the ratio of two terms where the denominator involves an integral. The evaluation of the Bayes estimate is difficult if the posterior cannot be easily computed. It turns out that, however, there are classes of prior pdf which are **conjugate** to some particular likelihood functions, in the sense that the resulting posterior pdf belongs to the same class of pdf as the prior. Thus, for conjugate priors, the observed data X do not change the class of the prior, they only change the *parameters* of the prior.

The formal definition of **conjugate prior distribution** is as follows. Let the prior pdf of Θ be $f_{\Theta}(\theta \mid \gamma)$, where γ is the parameter of the prior pdf, called the **hyperparameter**. The prior pdf $f_{\Theta}(\theta \mid \gamma)$ is conjugate to the likelihood function $f_{X \mid \Theta}(x \mid \theta)$ if the posterior pdf is equal to $f_{\Theta}(\theta \mid \gamma^*)$, which has the same functional form as the prior pdf but, generally, a different hyperparameter. In other words, the prior and posterior distributions belong to the same family of distributions.

We now present some conjugate distributions that are commonly used in Bayesian inference.[12]

A.16.1 The Beta–Bernoulli Conjugate Distribution

Let X be the Bernoulli random variable that takes value 1 with probability θ and 0 with probability $1 - \theta$. Thus, the likelihood of X is

$$f_{X\mid\Theta}(x \mid \theta) = \theta^x(1-\theta)^{1-x}, \qquad \text{for } x = 0, 1. \tag{A.140}$$

Θ is assumed to follow the beta distribution with pdf given in equation (A.101), where the hyperparameters are α and β, i.e.,

$$f_\Theta(\theta; \alpha, \beta) = \frac{\theta^{\alpha-1}(1-\theta)^{\beta-1}}{B(\alpha, \beta)}, \qquad \text{for } \theta \in (0, 1). \tag{A.141}$$

Thus, the joint pdf of Θ and X is

$$f_{\Theta X}(\theta, x) = f_{X\mid\Theta}(x \mid \theta)f_\Theta(\theta; \alpha, \beta) = \frac{\theta^{\alpha+x-1}(1-\theta)^{(\beta-x+1)-1}}{B(\alpha, \beta)}, \tag{A.142}$$

from which we obtain the marginal pdf of X as

$$f_X(x) = \int_0^1 \frac{\theta^{\alpha+x-1}(1-\theta)^{(\beta-x+1)-1}}{B(\alpha, \beta)} \, d\theta$$

$$= \frac{B(\alpha+x, \beta-x+1)}{B(\alpha, \beta)}. \tag{A.143}$$

Substituting equations (A.142) and (A.143) into (A.135), we obtain

$$f_{\Theta\mid X}(\theta \mid x) = \frac{\theta^{\alpha+x-1}(1-\theta)^{(\beta-x+1)-1}}{B(\alpha+x, \beta-x+1)}, \tag{A.144}$$

which is a beta pdf with parameters $\alpha + x$ and $\beta - x + 1$. Hence, the posterior and prior distributions belong to the same family, and the beta distribution is said to be conjugate to the Bernoulli distribution.

Consider now n observations of X denoted by $X = \{X_1, \ldots, X_n\}$. Repeating the derivation above, we obtain

$$f_{X\mid\Theta}(x \mid \theta) = \prod_{i=1}^n \theta^{x_i}(1-\theta)^{1-x_i}$$

$$= \theta^{n\bar{x}}(1-\theta)^{n(1-\bar{x})}, \tag{A.145}$$

and

$$f_{\Theta X}(\theta, x) = f_{X\mid\Theta}(x \mid \theta)f_\Theta(\theta; \alpha, \beta)$$

---

[12] We adopt the convention of "prior-likelihood" to describe the conjugate distribution. Thus, the beta–Bernoulli conjugate distribution has a beta prior and a Bernoulli likelihood.

$$= \left[\theta^{n\bar{x}}(1 - \theta)^{n(1-\bar{x})}\right]\left[\frac{\theta^{\alpha-1}(1 - \theta)^{\beta-1}}{B(\alpha, \beta)}\right]$$

$$= \frac{\theta^{(\alpha+n\bar{x})-1}(1 - \theta)^{(\beta+n-n\bar{x})-1}}{B(\alpha, \beta)}. \tag{A.146}$$

As

$$\int_0^1 f_{\Theta X}(\theta, x)\, d\theta = \int_0^1 \frac{\theta^{(\alpha+n\bar{x})-1}(1 - \theta)^{(\beta+n-n\bar{x})-1}}{B(\alpha, \beta)}\, d\theta$$

$$= \frac{B(\alpha + n\bar{x}, \beta + n - n\bar{x})}{B(\alpha, \beta)}, \tag{A.147}$$

we conclude that

$$f_{\Theta \mid X}(\theta \mid x) = \frac{f_{\Theta X}(\theta, x)}{\int_0^1 f_{\Theta X}(\theta, x)\, d\theta}$$

$$= \frac{\theta^{(\alpha+n\bar{x})-1}(1 - \theta)^{(\beta+n-n\bar{x})-1}}{B(\alpha + n\bar{x}, \beta + n - n\bar{x})}, \tag{A.148}$$

and the posterior distribution of Θ follows a beta distribution with parameters $\alpha + n\bar{x}$ and $\beta + n - n\bar{x}$.

In the above computation we derive the posterior pdf and show that it has the same functional form as the prior pdf, apart from the differences in the parameters. However, following equation (A.137) we could have concluded that

$$f_{\Theta \mid X}(\theta \mid x) \propto f_{X \mid \Theta}(x \mid \theta) f_{\Theta}(\theta)$$

$$\propto \left[\theta^{n\bar{x}}(1 - \theta)^{n(1-\bar{x})}\right]\left[\theta^{\alpha-1}(1 - \theta)^{\beta-1}\right]$$

$$\propto \theta^{(\alpha+n\bar{x})-1}(1 - \theta)^{(\beta+n-n\bar{x})-1}, \tag{A.149}$$

so that the posterior distribution belongs to the same class of distribution as the prior. This is done without having to compute the expression for the constant of proportionality $K(x)$. We shall adopt this simpler approach in subsequent discussions.

A.16.2 The Beta–Binomial Conjugate Distribution

Let $X = \{X_1, X_2, \ldots, X_n\}$ be a sample of binomial random variables with parameters m_i and θ, such that $X_i \sim \mathcal{BN}(m_i, \theta)$ independently. Thus, the likelihood of X is

$$f_{X \mid \Theta}(x \mid \theta) = \prod_{i=1}^{n} \binom{m_i}{x_i} \theta^{x_i}(1 - \theta)^{m_i-x_i}$$

$$= \left[\prod_{i=1}^{n} \binom{m_i}{x_i} \right] \left[\theta^{n\bar{x}} (1 - \theta)^{\sum_{i=1}^{n} (m_i - x_i)} \right]. \tag{A.150}$$

If Θ follows the beta distribution with hyperparameters α and β, and we define $m = \sum_{i=1}^{n} m_i$, the posterior pdf of Θ satisfies

$$\begin{aligned} f_{\Theta \mid X}(\theta \mid x) &\propto f_{X \mid \Theta}(x \mid \theta) f_{\Theta}(\theta; \alpha, \beta) \\ &\propto \left[\theta^{n\bar{x}} (1 - \theta)^{m - n\bar{x}} \right] \left[\theta^{\alpha - 1} (1 - \theta)^{\beta - 1} \right] \\ &\propto \theta^{(\alpha + n\bar{x}) - 1} (1 - \theta)^{(\beta + m - n\bar{x}) - 1}. \end{aligned} \tag{A.151}$$

Comparing this against equation (A.141), we conclude that the posterior distribution of Θ is beta with parameters $\alpha + n\bar{x}$ and $\beta + m - n\bar{x}$. Thus, the beta prior distribution is conjugate to the binomial likelihood.

A.16.3 The Gamma–Poisson Conjugate Distribution

Let $X = \{X_1, X_2, \ldots, X_n\}$ be iid Poisson random variables with parameter λ. The random variable Λ of the parameter λ is assumed to follow a gamma distribution with hyperparameters α and β, i.e., the prior pdf of Λ is

$$f_{\Lambda}(\lambda; \alpha, \beta) = \frac{\lambda^{\alpha - 1} e^{-\frac{\lambda}{\beta}}}{\Gamma(\alpha) \beta^{\alpha}}, \tag{A.152}$$

and the likelihood of X is

$$\begin{aligned} f_{X \mid \Lambda}(x \mid \lambda) &= \prod_{i=1}^{n} \frac{\lambda^{x_i} e^{-\lambda}}{x_i!} \\ &= \frac{\lambda^{n\bar{x}} e^{-n\lambda}}{\prod_{i=1}^{n} x_i!}. \end{aligned} \tag{A.153}$$

Thus, the posterior pdf of Λ satisfies

$$\begin{aligned} f_{\Lambda \mid X}(\lambda \mid x) &\propto f_{X \mid \Lambda}(x \mid \lambda) f_{\Lambda}(\lambda; \alpha, \beta) \\ &\propto \lambda^{\alpha + n\bar{x} - 1} e^{-\lambda \left(n + \frac{1}{\beta} \right)}. \end{aligned} \tag{A.154}$$

Comparing equations (A.154) and (A.152), we conclude that the posterior pdf of Λ is $f_{\Lambda}(\lambda; \alpha^*, \beta^*)$, where

$$\alpha^* = \alpha + n\bar{x} \tag{A.155}$$

and

$$\beta^* = \left[n + \frac{1}{\beta} \right]^{-1} = \frac{\beta}{n\beta + 1}. \tag{A.156}$$

Hence, the gamma prior pdf is conjugate to the Poisson likelihood.

A.16.4 The Beta–Geometric Conjugate Distribution

Let $X = \{X_1, X_2, \ldots, X_n\}$ be iid geometric random variables with parameter θ so that the likelihood of X is

$$f_{X|\Theta}(x \mid \theta) = \prod_{i=1}^{n} \theta(1 - \theta)^{x_i} = \theta^n(1 - \theta)^{n\bar{x}}. \qquad (A.157)$$

If the prior distribution of Θ is beta with hyperparameters α and β, then the posterior pdf of Θ satisfies

$$f_{\Theta|X}(\theta \mid x) \propto f_{X|\Theta}(x \mid \theta) f_\Theta(\theta; \alpha, \beta)$$
$$\propto \theta^{\alpha+n-1}(1 - \theta)^{\beta+n\bar{x}-1}. \qquad (A.158)$$

Thus, comparing equations (A.158) and (A.141), we conclude that the posterior distribution of Θ is beta with parameters

$$\alpha^* = \alpha + n \qquad (A.159)$$

and

$$\beta^* = \beta + n\bar{x}, \qquad (A.160)$$

so that the beta prior is conjugate to the geometric likelihood.

A.16.5 The Gamma–Exponential Conjugate Distribution

Let $X = \{X_1, X_2, \ldots, X_n\}$ be iid exponential random variables with parameter λ so that the likelihood of X is

$$f_{X|\Lambda}(x \mid \lambda) = \prod_{i=1}^{n} \lambda e^{-\lambda x_i} = \lambda^n e^{-\lambda n\bar{x}}. \qquad (A.161)$$

If the prior distribution of Λ is gamma with hyperparameters α and β, then the posterior pdf of Λ satisfies

$$f_{\Lambda|X}(\lambda \mid x) \propto f_{X|\Lambda}(x \mid \lambda) f_\Lambda(\lambda; \alpha, \beta)$$
$$\propto \lambda^{\alpha+n-1} e^{-\lambda\left(\frac{1}{\beta}+n\bar{x}\right)}. \qquad (A.162)$$

Comparing equations (A.162) and (A.152), we conclude that the posterior distribution of Λ is gamma with parameters

$$\alpha^* = \alpha + n \qquad (A.163)$$

and

$$\beta^* = \left[\frac{1}{\beta} + n\bar{x}\right]^{-1} = \frac{\beta}{1 + \beta n\bar{x}}. \qquad (A.164)$$

Thus, the gamma prior is conjugate to the exponential likelihood.

Table A.3. *Some conjugate distributions*

Prior pdf and hyperparameters	Likelihood of X	Hyperparameters of posterior pdf
$\mathcal{B}(\alpha,\beta)$	Bernoulli	$\alpha + n\bar{x}, \ \beta + n - n\bar{x}$
$\mathcal{B}(\alpha,\beta)$	$\mathcal{BN}(m_i,\theta)$	$\alpha + n\bar{x}, \ \beta + \sum_{i=1}^{n}(m_i - x_i)$
$\mathcal{G}(\alpha,\beta)$	$\mathcal{PN}(\lambda)$	$\alpha + n\bar{x}, \ \dfrac{\beta}{n\beta + 1}$
$\mathcal{B}(\alpha,\beta)$	$\mathcal{GM}(\theta)$	$\alpha + n, \ \beta + n\bar{x}$
$\mathcal{G}(\alpha,\beta)$	$\mathcal{E}(\lambda)$	$\alpha + n, \ \dfrac{\beta}{1 + \beta n\bar{x}}$

A.16.6 Summary of Conjugate Distributions

Table A.3 summarizes the conjugate distributions discussed in this section.

A.17 Least Squares Estimation

Consider a regression model with n observations, where the $n \times 1$ vector of the observations of the dependent variable is denoted by $y = (y_1,\ldots,y_n)'$ and the $n \times (k+1)$ matrix of the observations of the regressors is denoted by

$$\mathbf{X} = \begin{bmatrix} 1 & X_{11} & X_{12} & \cdots & \cdots & X_{1k} \\ 1 & X_{21} & X_{22} & \cdots & \cdots & X_{2k} \\ \vdots & \vdots & \vdots & \vdots & \vdots & \vdots \\ \vdots & \vdots & \vdots & \vdots & \vdots & \vdots \\ 1 & X_{n1} & X_{n2} & \cdots & \cdots & X_{nk} \end{bmatrix}. \tag{A.165}$$

Thus, the first column of $\mathbf{X}$ is the vector $\mathbf{1} = (1,\ldots,1)'$, such that the regression has a constant term, and X_{ij} is the ith observation of the jth explanatory variable. We write the regression model in matrix form as

$$y = \mathbf{X}\beta + \epsilon, \tag{A.166}$$

where $\beta = (\beta_0, \beta_1, \ldots, \beta_k)'$ is the vector of regression coefficients and ϵ is the vector of residuals. The regression coefficient β can be estimated using the **least squares method**, which is obtained by minimizing the residual sum of squares (RSS), defined as

$$\begin{aligned} \text{RSS} &= \sum_{i=1}^{n}(y_i - \beta_0 - \beta_1 X_{i1} - \cdots - \beta_k X_{ik})^2 \\ &= (y - \mathbf{X}\beta)'(y - \mathbf{X}\beta) \\ &= y'y + \beta'\mathbf{X}'\mathbf{X}\beta - 2\beta'\mathbf{X}'y, \end{aligned} \tag{A.167}$$

with respect to β. The value of β that minimizes RSS is called the **least squares estimate** of β, denoted by $\hat{\beta}$, and is given by

$$\hat{\beta} = (\mathbf{X'X})^{-1}\mathbf{X'y}. \tag{A.168}$$

$\mathbf{X'X}$ is the $(k+1) \times (k+1)$ **raw sum-of-cross-products** matrix of the regressors, i.e.,

$$\mathbf{X'X} = \begin{bmatrix} n & \sum_{h=1}^{n} X_{h1} & \sum_{h=1}^{n} X_{h2} & \cdots & \cdots & \sum_{h=1}^{n} X_{hk} \\ \sum_{h=1}^{n} X_{h1} & \sum_{h=1}^{n} X_{h1}^2 & \sum_{h=1}^{n} X_{h1}X_{h2} & \cdots & \cdots & \sum_{h=1}^{n} X_{h1}X_{hk} \\ \vdots & \vdots & \vdots & \vdots & \vdots & \vdots \\ \vdots & \vdots & \vdots & \vdots & \vdots & \vdots \\ \sum_{h=1}^{n} X_{hk} & \sum_{h=1}^{n} X_{hk}X_{h1} & \sum_{h=1}^{n} X_{hk}X_{h2} & \cdots & \cdots & \sum_{h=1}^{n} X_{hk}^2 \end{bmatrix}. \tag{A.169}$$

$\mathbf{X'y}$ is the $(k+1) \times 1$ raw sum-of-cross-products vector of the regressor and the dependent variable, i.e.,

$$\mathbf{X'y} = \begin{bmatrix} \sum_{h=1}^{n} y_h \\ \sum_{h=1}^{n} X_{h1}y_h \\ \sum_{h=1}^{n} X_{h2}y_h \\ \vdots \\ \vdots \\ \sum_{h=1}^{n} X_{hk}y_h \end{bmatrix}. \tag{A.170}$$

We now denote the sum-of-cross-products matrix of the **deviation-from-mean** of the k regressors by $\mathbf{M_{X'X}}$, so that the (i,j)th element of the $k \times k$ matrix $\mathbf{M_{X'X}}$ is

$$\sum_{h=1}^{n} (X_{hi} - \bar{X}_i)(X_{hj} - \bar{X}_j), \tag{A.171}$$

where

$$\bar{X}_i = \frac{1}{n} \sum_{h=1}^{n} X_{hi}. \tag{A.172}$$

Likewise, we define the $k \times 1$ vector $\mathbf{M_{X'y}}$ with the ith element given by

$$\sum_{h=1}^{n} (X_{hi} - \bar{X}_i)(y_h - \bar{y}), \tag{A.173}$$

where $\bar{y}$ is the sample mean of y.

Then the least squares estimate of the slope coefficients of the regression model is[13]

$$
\begin{pmatrix} \hat{\beta}_1 \\ \cdot \\ \cdot \\ \cdot \\ \hat{\beta}_k \end{pmatrix} = \mathbf{M}_{X'X}^{-1}\mathbf{M}_{X'y} \tag{A.174}
$$

and the least squares estimate of the constant term is

$$
\hat{\beta}_0 = \bar{y} - \hat{\beta}_1\bar{X}_1 - \cdots - \hat{\beta}_k\bar{X}_k. \tag{A.175}
$$

A.18 Fisher Information and Cramér–Rao Inequality

Let X be a random variable with pdf or pf $f(x; \theta)$, where θ is a parameter. To economize on notations. we drop the suffix X in the pdf or pf. For simplicity of exposition, we assume X is continuous, although the results below also hold for discrete distributions. We assume that the differentiation of a definite integral can be executed inside the integral. This assumption, together with others (such as the existence of derivatives of the pdf), are collectively known as the **regularity conditions**, which, although not elaborated here, will be assumed to hold.

As

$$
\int_{-\infty}^{\infty} f(x; \theta)\, dx = 1, \tag{A.176}
$$

differentiating the equation on both sides, and assuming that we can move the differentiation operation inside the integral, we have

$$
\frac{\partial}{\partial \theta} \int_{-\infty}^{\infty} f(x; \theta)\, dx = \int_{-\infty}^{\infty} \frac{\partial f(x; \theta)}{\partial \theta}\, dx = 0, \tag{A.177}
$$

which can also be written as

$$
\int_{-\infty}^{\infty} \left[\frac{1}{f(x; \theta)} \frac{\partial f(x; \theta)}{\partial \theta} \right] f(x; \theta)\, dx = \int_{-\infty}^{\infty} \left[\frac{\partial \log f(x; \theta)}{\partial \theta} \right] f(x; \theta)\, dx
$$

$$
= \mathrm{E}\left[\frac{\partial \log f(X; \theta)}{\partial \theta} \right]
$$

$$
= 0. \tag{A.178}
$$

If we differentiate the above equation again, we obtain

$$
\int_{-\infty}^{\infty} \left[\left(\frac{\partial^2 \log f(x; \theta)}{\partial \theta^2} \right) f(x; \theta) + \frac{\partial \log f(x; \theta)}{\partial \theta} \frac{\partial f(x; \theta)}{\partial \theta} \right] dx = 0. \tag{A.179}
$$

---

[13] Readers may refer to Johnston and DiNardo (1997, Section 3.1.3) for a proof of this result.

Now the second part of the integral above can be expressed as

$$\int_{-\infty}^{\infty} \frac{\partial \log f(x; \theta)}{\partial \theta} \frac{\partial f(x; \theta)}{\partial \theta} \, dx = \int_{-\infty}^{\infty} \frac{\partial \log f(x; \theta)}{\partial \theta} \left[\frac{\partial \log f(x; \theta)}{\partial \theta} f(x; \theta) \right] dx$$

$$= \int_{-\infty}^{\infty} \left[\frac{\partial \log f(x; \theta)}{\partial \theta} \right]^2 f(x; \theta) \, dx$$

$$= \mathrm{E}\left[\left(\frac{\partial \log f(X; \theta)}{\partial \theta} \right)^2 \right]$$

$$\equiv I(\theta)$$

$$> 0, \qquad (A.180)$$

which is called the **Fisher information** in an observation. From equations (A.179) and (A.180), we conclude that

$$I(\theta) = -\int_{-\infty}^{\infty} \left(\frac{\partial^2 \log f(x; \theta)}{\partial \theta^2} \right) f(x; \theta) \, dx = \mathrm{E}\left[-\frac{\partial^2 \log f(X; \theta)}{\partial \theta^2} \right]. \quad (A.181)$$

Suppose we have a random sample of observations $x = (x_1, \ldots, x_n)$. We define the **likelihood function** of the sample as

$$L(\theta; x) = \prod_{i=1}^{n} f(x_i; \theta), \qquad (A.182)$$

which is taken as a function of θ given x. Then

$$\log L(\theta; x) = \sum_{i=1}^{n} \log f(x_i; \theta). \qquad (A.183)$$

Analogous to equation (A.180), we define the Fisher information in the random sample as

$$I_n(\theta) = \mathrm{E}\left[\left(\frac{\partial \log L(\theta; X)}{\partial \theta} \right)^2 \right], \qquad (A.184)$$

so that from equation (A.183), we have

$$I_n(\theta) = \mathrm{E}\left[\left(\frac{\partial}{\partial \theta} \sum_{i=1}^{n} \log f(X_i; \theta) \right)^2 \right]$$

$$= \mathrm{E}\left[\left(\sum_{i=1}^{n} \frac{\partial \log f(X_i; \theta)}{\partial \theta} \right)^2 \right]. \qquad (A.185)$$

As the observation x_i are pairwise independent, the expectations of the cross product terms above are zero. Thus, we conclude

$$I_n(\theta) = \sum_{i=1}^{n} E\left[\left(\frac{\partial \log f(X_i; \theta)}{\partial \theta} \right)^2 \right] = nI(\theta). \tag{A.186}$$

Let $u(x)$ be a statistic of the sample, such that $E[u(x)] = k(\theta)$, i.e., $u(x)$ is an unbiased estimator of $k(\theta)$. Then we have

$$\text{Var}\,[u(x)] \geq \frac{[k'(\theta)]^2}{I_n(\theta)} = \frac{[k'(\theta)]^2}{nI(\theta)}, \tag{A.187}$$

which is called the **Cramér–Rao** inequality.[14] In the special case $k(\theta) = \theta$, we denote $u(x) = \hat{\theta}$ and conclude

$$\text{Var}(\hat{\theta}) \geq \frac{1}{nI(\theta)}, \tag{A.188}$$

for any unbiased estimator of θ. An unbiased estimator is said to be **efficient** if it attains the **Cramér–Rao** lower bound, i.e., the right-hand side of equation (A.188).

In the case where θ is a k-element vector, the above results can be generalized as follows. First, $\partial \log[f(x; \theta)]/\partial \theta$ is a $k \times 1$ vector. Equation (A.178) applies, with the result being a $k \times 1$ vector. Second, the **Fisher information matrix** in an observation is now defined as the $k \times k$ matrix

$$I(\theta) = E\left[\frac{\partial \log f(X; \theta)}{\partial \theta} \frac{\partial \log f(X; \theta)}{\partial \theta'} \right], \tag{A.189}$$

and the result in equation (A.181) is replaced by

$$E\left[-\frac{\partial^2 \log f(X; \theta)}{\partial \theta \, \partial \theta'} \right], \tag{A.190}$$

so that

$$I(\theta) = E\left[\frac{\partial \log f(X; \theta)}{\partial \theta} \frac{\partial \log f(X; \theta)}{\partial \theta'} \right] = E\left[-\frac{\partial^2 \log f(X; \theta)}{\partial \theta \, \partial \theta'} \right]. \tag{A.191}$$

The Fisher information matrix in a random sample of n observations is $I_n(\theta) = nI(\theta)$. Third, let $\hat{\theta}$ be an unbiased estimator of θ. We denote the variance matrix of $\hat{\theta}$ by $\text{Var}(\hat{\theta})$. Hence, the ith diagonal element of $\text{Var}(\hat{\theta})$ is $\text{Var}(\hat{\theta}_i)$, and its (i,j)th element is $\text{Cov}(\hat{\theta}_i, \hat{\theta}_j)$. Denoting $I_n^{-1}(\theta)$ as the inverse of $I_n(\theta)$, the **Cramér–Rao** inequality states that

$$\text{Var}(\hat{\theta}) - I_n^{-1}(\theta) \tag{A.192}$$

---

[14] See DeGroot and Schervish (2002, p. 439) for a proof of this inequality.

is a nonnegative definite matrix. As a property of nonnegative definite matrices, the diagonal elements of $\text{Var}(\hat{\theta}) - I_n^{-1}(\theta)$ are nonnegative, i.e., the lower bound of $\text{Var}(\hat{\theta}_i)$ is the ith diagonal element of $I_n^{-1}(\theta)$.

If the sample observations are not iid, the Fisher information matrix has to be computed differently. For the general case of a vector parameter θ, the Fisher information matrix in the sample is

$$I_n(\theta) = \text{E}\left[\frac{\partial \log L(\theta; X)}{\partial \theta} \frac{\partial \log L(\theta; X)}{\partial \theta'}\right] = \text{E}\left[-\frac{\partial^2 \log L(\theta; X)}{\partial \theta \, \partial \theta'}\right], \quad \text{(A.193)}$$

where the likelihood function $L(\theta; x)$ has to be established based on specific model assumptions, incorporating possibly the dependence structure and the specific pdf or pf of each observation. For the case of a scalar θ, equation (A.193) can be specialized easily.

A.19 Maximum Likelihood Estimation

We continue to use the notations introduced in Section A.18. Suppose there exists a value that maximizes $L(\theta; x)$ or, equivalently, $\log L(\theta; x)$; this value is called the **maximum likelihood estimate (MLE)** of θ. The maximum likelihood estimator of θ, denoted by $\hat{\theta}$, is formally defined as

$$\hat{\theta} = \max_{\theta} \{L(\theta; x)\} = \max_{\theta} \{\log L(\theta; x)\}. \quad \text{(A.194)}$$

The MLE can be computed by solving the equation

$$\frac{\partial \log L(\theta; x)}{\partial \theta} = \sum_{i=1}^{n} \frac{\partial \log f(x_i; \theta)}{\partial \theta} = 0, \quad \text{(A.195)}$$

called the **first-order condition.** Under some *regularity conditions*, the distribution of $\sqrt{n}(\hat{\theta} - \theta)$ converges to a normal distribution with mean 0 and variance $1/I(\theta)$, i.e., in large samples $\hat{\theta}$ is approximately normally distributed with mean θ and variance $1/I_n(\theta)$. Thus, $\hat{\theta}$ is asymptotically unbiased. Also, as $I_n(\theta) = nI(\theta) \to \infty$ when $n \to \infty$, the variance of $\hat{\theta}$ converges to 0. Hence, by Theorem 10.1, $\hat{\theta}$ is consistent for θ. Furthermore, as the variance of $\hat{\theta}$ converges to the Cramér–Rao lower bound, $\hat{\theta}$ is **asymptotically efficient**.

Suppose $\tau = g(\theta)$ is a one-to-one transformation. Then the likelihood function $L(\theta; x)$ can also be expressed in terms τ, i.e., $L(\tau; x)$, and the MLE of τ, denoted by $\hat{\tau}$, can be computed accordingly. It turns out that $\hat{\tau} = g(\hat{\theta})$, so that the MLE of τ is $g(\cdot)$ evaluated at the MLE of θ.[15]

---

[15] See DeGroot and Schervish (2002, p. 365) for a proof of this result.

Given a function $\tau = g(\theta)$ (not necessarily a one-to-one transformation), using Taylor's expansion, we have[16]

$$\hat{\tau} = g(\hat{\theta}) \simeq g(\theta) + (\hat{\theta} - \theta)g'(\theta). \qquad (A.196)$$

Thus,

$$\sqrt{n}(\hat{\tau} - \tau) \simeq \sqrt{n}(\hat{\theta} - \theta)g'(\theta), \qquad (A.197)$$

so that the asymptotic distribution of $\sqrt{n}(\hat{\tau} - \tau)$ is normal with mean 0 and variance

$$\frac{[g'(\theta)]^2}{I(\theta)}. \qquad (A.198)$$

In general, if the asymptotic variance of $\sqrt{n}(\hat{\theta} - \theta)$ for any consistent estimator $\hat{\theta}$ is $\sigma_{\hat{\theta}}^2$,[17] then the asymptotic variance of $\sqrt{n}(g(\hat{\theta}) - g(\theta))$ is

$$[g'(\theta)]^2 \sigma_{\hat{\theta}}^2. \qquad (A.199)$$

This is known as the **delta method** for the computation of the asymptotic variance of $g(\hat{\theta})$.

The above results can be generalized to the case where θ is a vector of k elements. The MLE solved from equation (A.194) then requires the solution of a system of k equations. Furthermore, the asymptotic distribution of $\sqrt{n}(\hat{\theta} - \theta)$ follows a **multivariate normal distribution** with mean vector 0 and asymptotic variance matrix $I^{-1}(\theta)$. The multivariate normal distribution is a generalization of the univariate normal distribution. It has some important and convenient properties. First, the marginal distribution of each component of a multivariate normal distribution is normal. Second, any linear combination of the elements of a multivariate normal distribution is normally distributed.

Finally, we state the multivariate version of the delta method. If the asymptotic variance of a consistent estimator $\hat{\theta}$ of θ is $\Omega(\theta)$ (a $k \times k$ matrix) and $g(\cdot)$ is a smooth scalar function with a k-element argument, then the asymptotic variance of $\sqrt{n}(g(\hat{\theta}) - g(\theta))$ is

$$\frac{\partial g(\theta)}{\partial \theta'} \Omega(\theta) \frac{\partial g(\theta)}{\partial \theta}. \qquad (A.200)$$

---

[16] $g(\cdot)$ is assumed to be a smooth function satisfying some differentiability conditions.

[17] Here $\hat{\theta}$ is any consistent estimator of θ. It need not be an MLE, and its asymptotic distribution need not be normal.

Answers to Exercises

Chapter 1

1.4 $P_{X^*}(t) = \dfrac{P_X(t) - f_X(0)}{1 - f_X(0)}$

1.5
$$f_X(x) = \binom{6}{x}(0.4)^x(0.6)^{6-x}, \; x = 0, \ldots, 6$$

1.6   (a) $\{0, \ldots, \infty\}$
     (b) $\{0, \ldots, \infty\}$
     (c) $\{0, \ldots, \infty\}$
     (d) $\{0, \ldots, mn\}$

1.7   0.6904

1.8   0.4897

1.9   (a) $E(W) = E(Y)$
     (b) $\mathrm{Var}(W) = \sigma_X^2 \sum_{i=1}^n p_i \geq \sigma_X^2 \sum_{i=1}^n p_i^2 = \mathrm{Var}(Y)$

1.10 (a) $\exp\left[\lambda_1\left(e^{\lambda_2(e^t - 1)} - 1\right)\right]$
     (b) $E(S) = \lambda_1\lambda_2, \quad \mathrm{Var}(S) = \lambda_1\lambda_2(1 + \lambda_2)$
     (c) $f_S(0) = \exp\left[\lambda_1(e^{-\lambda_2} - 1)\right], \quad f_S(1) = f_S(0)\lambda_1\lambda_2 e^{-\lambda_2}$

1.11 (a) $1 - \dfrac{\log[1 - \beta(t-1)]}{\log(1 + \beta)}$
     (b) $[1 - \beta(t-1)]^{-\frac{\lambda}{\log(1+\beta)}}$, i.e., pgf of $\mathcal{NB}(r, \theta)$,

        where $r = \dfrac{\lambda}{\log(1 + \beta)}$ and $\theta = \dfrac{1}{(1 + \beta)}$

1.12 $\Pr(X \geq 4) = 0.1188, \quad E(X) = 1.2256, \quad \mathrm{Var}(X) = 2.7875$

1.13 $\Pr(S = 0) = 0.0067, \quad \Pr(S = 1) = 0.0135, \quad \Pr(S = 2) = 0.0337$

1.14 (a) $\Pr(S = 0) = 0.0907, \quad \Pr(S = 1) = 0.0435, \quad \Pr(S = 2) = 0.0453$
     (b) $\Pr(S = 0) = 0.1353, \quad \Pr(S = 1) = 0.0866, \quad \Pr(S = 2) = 0.0840$

1.15 (a) $\exp\left[\sum_{i=1}^n \lambda_i(t^{x_i} - 1)\right]$
     (b) $\exp\left[-\sum_{i=1}^n \lambda_i\right]$

1.16 $E(S_1) = 8$, $\text{Var}(S_1) = 48$, $E(S_2) = 8$, $\text{Var}(S_2) = 40$

1.17 $P_X(t) = 0.64\,e^{t-1} + 0.32\,e^{2(t-1)} + 0.04\,e^{3(t-1)}$, $E(X) = 1.4$, $\text{Var}(X) = 1.72$

1.18 0.0979

1.19 (a) 0.0111

(b) 0.0422

1.20

x	0	1	2
$\Pr(X_1 = x)$	0.3679	0.3679	0.1839
$\Pr(X_2 = x)$	0.1353	0.2707	0.2707

$\Pr(X_1 + X_2 \le 2) = 0.4232$, note that $X_1 + X_2 \sim \mathcal{PN}(3)$

1.21 primary: $\mathcal{BN}(1, c)$, i.e., Bernoulli with parameter c; secondary: X
X^* is a mixture of a degenerate distribution at 1 and X, with weights $1 - c$
and c, respectively

1.24 $f_S(0) = 0.3012$, $f_S(1) = 0.1807$, $f_S(s) = [0.6 f_S(s - 1) + 1.2 f_S(s - 2)]/s$
for $s \ge 2$

1.25 (a) $P_S(t) = \left[\dfrac{\theta}{1 - (1 - \theta)e^{\lambda(t-1)}} \right]^r$

1.26 $f_X(x) = 0.2 f_X(x - 1)$ with $f_X(0) = 0.8$
$f_X^M(x) = 0.2 f_X^M(x - 1)$ with $f_X^M(0) = 0.4$
mean = 0.75, variance = 0.5625

1.27 $1 - c + c P_S(t)$, where $c = 1/(1 - P_S(0))$ and $P_S(t) = \left[\theta e^{\lambda(t-1)} + 1 - \theta \right]^n$,
assuming primary distribution $\mathcal{BN}(n, \theta)$ and secondary distribution
$\mathcal{PN}(\lambda)$

1.28 $f_S(0) = 0.5128$, $f_S(1) = 0.0393$, $f_S(2) = 0.0619$

1.29 (a) 0.2652

(b) 0.4581

(c) 0.1536

1.30 (a) $M_S(t) = \dfrac{\theta_N}{1 - (1 - \theta_N)(\theta_X e^t + 1 - \theta_X)^n}$,

$P_S(t) = \dfrac{\theta_N}{1 - (1 - \theta_N)(\theta_X t + 1 - \theta_X)^n}$

(b) $M_S(t) = \left[\theta e^{\lambda(e^t - 1)} + 1 - \theta \right]^n$, $P_S(t) = \left[\theta e^{\lambda(t-1)} + 1 - \theta \right]^n$

(c) $M_S(t) = \left[\dfrac{\theta}{1 - (1 - \theta)e^{\lambda(e^t - 1)}} \right]^r$, $P_S(t) = \left[\dfrac{\theta}{1 - (1 - \theta)e^{\lambda(t-1)}} \right]^r$

Chapter 2

2.2 (a) $F_X(x) = e^{-\frac{\theta}{x}}$, $S_X(x) = 1 - e^{-\frac{\theta}{x}}$, $h_X(x) = \dfrac{\theta}{\left(e^{\frac{\theta}{x}} - 1\right)x^2}$, for

$0 < x < \infty$

(b) median = $\dfrac{\theta}{\log(2)}$, mode = $\dfrac{\theta}{2}$

2.3 (a) $S_X(x) = 1 - e^{-\left(\frac{\theta}{x}\right)^\tau}$, $f_X(x) = \frac{\tau}{x}\left(\frac{\theta}{x}\right)^\tau e^{-\left(\frac{\theta}{x}\right)^\tau}$, $h_X(x) = \dfrac{\tau\left(\frac{\theta}{x}\right)^\tau e^{-\left(\frac{\theta}{x}\right)^\tau}}{x\left[1 - e^{-\left(\frac{\theta}{x}\right)^\tau}\right]}$,

for $0 < x < \infty$

(b) median $= \dfrac{\theta}{[\log(2)]^{\frac{1}{\tau}}}$, mode $= \theta\left(\dfrac{\tau}{\tau+1}\right)^{\frac{1}{\tau}}$

2.4 (a) $S_X(x) = 1 - 0.01x$, $F_X(x) = 0.01x$, $f_X(x) = 0.01$, for $x \in [0, 100]$

(b) $E(X) = 50$, $Var(X) = \dfrac{(100)^2}{12}$

(c) median $= 50$, mode $=$ any value in $[0,100]$

(d) 45

2.5 (a) $S_X(x) = 1 - \dfrac{3x^2}{400} + \dfrac{x^3}{4,000}$, $F_X(x) = \dfrac{3x^2}{400} - \dfrac{x^3}{4,000}$,

$h_X(x) = \dfrac{60x - 3x^2}{4,000 - 30x^2 + x^3}$

(b) $E(X) = 10$, $Var(X) = 20$

(c) median $=$ mode $= 10$

(d) 4.667

2.6 2.2705

2.7 mean $= 1.25$, median $= 0.5611$

2.8 e^{-y} for $0 < y < \infty$

2.9 $\dfrac{1}{\pi(1+y^2)}$, for $-\infty < y < \infty$

2.10 (a)

$$F_X(x) = \begin{cases} 0, & x < 0 \\ 0.2, & x = 0 \\ 0.2 + 0.08\left(x - \dfrac{x^2}{40}\right), & 0 < x \le 20 \\ 1, & 20 < x \end{cases}$$

(b) $E(X) = 5.3333$, $Var(X) = 24.8889$

(c) 10

2.11 (a)

$$F_X(x) = \begin{cases} 0, & x < 0 \\ 0.4, & x = 0 \\ 0.4 + 0.6x^4, & 0 < x \le 1 \\ 1, & 1 < x \end{cases}$$

(b) $E(X) = 0.48$, $Var(X) = 0.1696$

(c) 0.9036

2.12 $\dfrac{2}{\sqrt{\alpha}}$

2.13
$$f_X(x) = \begin{cases} 1.7759e^{-2x}, & 0 \le x < 0.8 \\ 2.2199xe^{-2x}, & 0.8 \le x < \infty \end{cases}$$

2.14 (a) $E(X) = \dfrac{\log(5)}{4}$, $\quad \text{Var}(X) = \dfrac{2}{5} - \left[\dfrac{\log(5)}{4}\right]^2$

(b) $\dfrac{1}{4x}\left[e^{-x}\left(1 + \dfrac{1}{x}\right) - e^{-5x}\left(5 + \dfrac{1}{x}\right)\right]$

2.15 $E(X) = 7$, $\quad \text{Var}(X) = 24$

2.16 $x_{0.9} = 4.6697$, $\text{CTE}_{0.9} = 8.2262$

2.17 (a)
$$F_{X_L}(x) = \begin{cases} 0, & x < 0 \\ 1 - e^{-\lambda d}, & x = 0 \\ 1 - e^{-\lambda(x+d)}, & 0 < x < \infty \end{cases}$$

(b)
$$F_{X_P}(x) = \begin{cases} 0, & x < 0 \\ 1 - e^{-\lambda x}, & 0 \le x < \infty \end{cases}$$

(c) $f_{X_P}(x) = \lambda e^{-\lambda x}$, for $x \ge 0$ and 0 otherwise, $E(X_P) = \dfrac{1}{\lambda}$

2.18 (a) 6

(b) 0.8333

(c) 0.1667

2.20 (a) $1 - pe^{-\lambda_1 x} - (1 - p)e^{-\lambda_2 x}$, for $0 < x < \infty$

(b) $\dfrac{pe^{-\lambda_1 d}}{\lambda_1} + \dfrac{(1 - p)e^{-\lambda_2 d}}{\lambda_2}$

2.21 3.4286

2.22 $E(X_P) = 37.5$, $\quad \text{Var}(X_P) = 393.75$

2.23 12.1371

2.24 $E(X_L) = 92.3116$, $\quad \text{Var}(X_L) = 9{,}940.8890$

2.25 without inflation: 54.6716, with inflation: 56.9275

2.29 $\alpha e^{-\alpha y}$ for $0 \le y < \infty$

2.30 6.4745

2.31 3.7119

Chapter 3

3.1 3.0888

3.2 $\theta = 0.2268$, $\quad \beta = 0.0971$

3.3 $\lambda_1 = 1.3333$, $\quad \lambda_2 = 1.5$

3.4 mean = 800, variance = 40,000

3.5 $\left[\dfrac{\theta}{(1 - \beta t)^\alpha} + 1 - \theta\right]^n$

3.6 (a) 0.6561, (b) 0.0820

3.7   (a) 0.0020,   (b) 0.0017

3.8 $\left[\dfrac{1}{3}\left(1 + \dfrac{0.05}{0.05 - t} + \left(\dfrac{0.05}{0.05 - t}\right)^2\right)\right]^5$

3.9   mean = 1.05,   variance = 2.4475

3.10 0.9939

3.11 $\left[0.6(0.5t + 0.3t^2 + 0.2t^3) + 0.4\right]^2$

3.12 (a) & (b): 0.9532

3.13

$$F_{X_1+X_2}(x) = \begin{cases} 0, & x < 0 \\ 0.25, & x = 0 \\ 0.25 + 0.25x + 0.03125x^2, & 0 < x \le 2 \\ 0.5 + 0.25x - 0.03125x^2, & 2 < x \le 4 \\ 1, & 4 < x \end{cases}$$

3.14 0.0313

3.15 15.25

3.16 18

3.17 mean = 19.20, variance = 101.03

3.18 $E(S) = 70$, $\text{Var}(S) = 4{,}433.33$, $E(\tilde{S}) = 44.80$, $\text{Var}(\tilde{S}) = 2{,}909.02$

3.19 compound Poisson distribution with $\lambda = 3$, and $f_X(-2) = 1/3$
      and $f_X(1) = 2/3$

3.20 mean = 30,   variance = 72

3.21 0.7617

3.22 (a) mean = 415,   variance = 19,282.50
      (b) using compound Poisson (other distributions may also be used),
          mean = 415, variance = 20,900

3.23 0.7246

3.24 1.6667

3.25 0.52

3.26 0.2883

3.27 0.0233

Chapter 4

4.6 $\dfrac{\alpha\beta}{1 - \beta\rho}$

4.7 $\text{VaR}_\delta(X) = x_\delta = \lambda\left[-\log(1 - \delta)\right]^{\frac{1}{\alpha}}$

      PH premium $= \lambda\rho^{\frac{1}{\alpha}}\Gamma\left(1 + \dfrac{1}{\alpha}\right)$

4.8   (b) $1 - \dfrac{c}{2}$

      (c) $\text{VaR}_\delta(X) = \begin{cases} \dfrac{\delta}{c}, & \text{for } 0 < \delta < c \\ 1, & \text{for } c \le \delta < 1 \end{cases}$

(d) $\text{CTE}_\delta(X) = \dfrac{1}{1-\delta}\left(\dfrac{c^2-\delta^2}{2c}+1-c\right)$, for $\delta \in (0,c)$

4.9 $\text{VaR}_{0.90}=40$, $\text{VaR}_{0.95}=50$, $\text{VaR}_{0.99}=60$, $\text{CTE}_{0.90}=52$, $\text{CTE}_{0.95}=58$

4.10 (a) $\dfrac{2b\rho}{\rho+1}$, (b) $b\rho$, (c) $\dfrac{b\rho}{2-\rho}$

the PH premium of the Pareto loss distribution is the most sensitive to the risk-aversion parameter

4.11 (a) pure premium $=\dfrac{b}{2}$, expected-value premium $=(1+\theta)\dfrac{b}{2}$

(b) variance premium $=\dfrac{b}{2}+\dfrac{ab^2}{12}$, standard-deviation premium $=\dfrac{b}{2}+\dfrac{ab}{\sqrt{12}}$

(c) $\text{VaR}_\delta = b\delta$, $\text{CTE}_\delta = \dfrac{b(1+\delta)}{2}$

(e) $\text{CVaR}_\delta = \dfrac{b(1-\delta)}{2}$, $\text{TVaR}_\delta = \dfrac{b(1+\delta)}{2}$

4.12 (a) pure premium $=\dfrac{1}{\lambda}$, expected-value premium $=(1+\theta)\dfrac{1}{\lambda}$

(b) variance premium $=\dfrac{1}{\lambda}+\dfrac{\alpha}{\lambda^2}$, standard-deviation premium $=\dfrac{1+\alpha}{\lambda}$

(c) $\text{VaR}_\delta = -\dfrac{\log(1-\delta)}{\lambda}$, $\text{CTE}_\delta = \dfrac{1-\log(1-\delta)}{\lambda}$

(e) $\text{CVaR}_\delta = \dfrac{1}{\lambda}$, $\text{TVaR}_\delta = \dfrac{1-\log(1-\delta)}{\lambda}$

4.13 expected-value premium $=1.2\lambda\alpha\beta$, loading $=\dfrac{0.2}{\beta(1+\alpha)}$

4.14 $\dfrac{\lambda\alpha\beta}{(1-\beta\rho)^{1+\alpha}}$

4.16 (a) $\text{VaR}_{0.95}(P_1) = \text{VaR}_{0.95}(P_2) = 0$

(b)

$P_1 + P_2$	0	100	200
prob	0.9216	0.0768	0.0016

(c) $\text{VaR}_{0.95}(P_1+P_2) = 100 > \text{VaR}_{0.95}(P_1) + \text{VaR}_{0.95}(P_2) = 0$, hence not subadditive

4.17 $\text{VaR}_{0.9}=400$, $\text{CTE}_{0.9}=480$, $\text{CVaR}_{0.9}=80$, $\text{TVaR}_{0.9}=480$

4.20 PH premium of $U = 4^{1-\frac{1}{\rho}}$, PH premium of $V = \dfrac{2\rho}{3-\rho}$

Chapter 5

5.2 3.2299

5.3 0.5312

5.4 0.0237

5.5 adj coeff = 0.4055, max prob = 0.2963
5.6 adj coeff = 0.6755, max prob = 0.2590
5.7 adj coeff = 0.8109, max prob = 0.1975
5.8 0.4
5.9 0.36
5.10 0.199

Chapter 6

6.1 (a) 0.6958
     (b) 2.0781
     (c) 0.0973
     (d) 17.04%
     (e) $\bar{X}$ is approximately normally distributed
6.2 (a) mean = 68,280, variance = 11,655,396
     (b) 0.7699
     (c) $\mu_X = 110.1290$, $\sigma_X = 81.6739$
     (d) 500
6.3 for claim frequency: 983, for claim severity: 456, full credibility attained for claim severity but not claim frequency
6.4 for claim frequency: $2\lambda_F$, for aggregate loss: $\lambda_F(2 + C_X^2)$
6.7 $k = 4.05\%$
     (a) 8,624
     (b) 12,902
6.8 $1.0133\,\lambda_F$
6.9 $2\lambda_F$, $1.4394\,\lambda_F$
6.10 242.9490
6.11 356.8685, 354
6.12 (a) 0.9557
     (b) 1
6.13 1
6.14 24.9038
6.15 16,913
6.16 576.24
6.17 960
6.18 2,468.04

Chapter 7

7.1 $0.4\,c$

7.2 for N: 0.525, for X: 7.25

7.3 $0.1523 + \dfrac{0.725}{c}$

7.4 for N: 6.1348, for X, $c = 20$: 11.7142, for X, $c = 30$: 13.0952

7.6 1.3333

7.7 $\dfrac{x + 1}{\alpha}$

7.8 0.4283

7.9 1.3333

7.10 $\dfrac{\theta - \theta^2}{1.5 - \theta}$

7.11 2.25

7.12 10,622

7.13 16.91

7.14 1.41

7.15 0.9375

7.16 0.8565

7.17 2.40

7.18 0.2222

7.19 0.905

7.20 12

7.21 1,063

7.22 8.3333

7.23 1,138

7.24 2,075

7.25 257.11

Chapter 8

8.1 (a) $\dfrac{m\,(\alpha + n\bar{x})}{\alpha + \beta + mn}$

(b) $\dbinom{m}{x_{n+1}} \dfrac{B(\alpha + n\bar{x} + x_{n+1}, \beta + mn + m - n\bar{x} - x_{n+1})}{B(\alpha + n\bar{x}, \beta + mn - n\bar{x})}$

8.2 $a(\alpha, \beta) = \alpha - 1$, $b(\alpha, \beta) = \dfrac{(\beta - 1) + (\alpha - 1)}{m}$, $\alpha^* = \alpha + n\bar{x}$, $\beta^* = \beta + mn - n\bar{x}$

8.3 for sample mean: 1.75, for Bühlmann premium: 1.6251

8.4 $f_X(x) = \dbinom{x + r - 1}{r - 1} \dfrac{B(\alpha + r, \beta + x)}{B(\alpha, \beta)}$, for $x = 0, 1, \ldots$

8.5 $A(\theta) = \log(1 - \theta)$, $B(\theta) = r \log(\theta)$,
$C(x) = \log[(x + r - 1)!] - \log(x!) - \log[(r - 1)!]$

8.6 (a) $\mathcal{PN}(\theta\lambda)$
(b) $\mathcal{BN}(m, \theta\beta)$

8.7 1.0714

8.8 1.3193

8.9 7

8.10 $\dfrac{x + c}{2}$

8.11 $\dfrac{10}{19}$

8.12 12

8.13 7.2022

8.14 $\mathcal{E}(2)$

8.15 9.8848

8.16 3.25

8.17 3.8293

8.18 0.9420

8.19 $\dfrac{4}{3}$

8.20 0.2126

8.21 0.45

8.22 0.7211

8.23 0.3125

8.24 0.8148

Chapter 9

9.1 Policyholder 1: 23.02, Policyholder 2: 23.20, Group 3: 21.29

9.2 (a) Group 1: 14.355, Group 2: 13.237, Group 3: 11.809
(b) Group 1: 14.428, Group 2: 13.254, Group 3: 11.840

9.3 0.852

9.4 0.323

9.5 0.499

9.6 0.393

9.7 0.575

9.8 0.872

9.9 0.633

9.10 0.778

9.11 687.38

9.12 0.074

9.13 0.221

9.14 0.818

Chapter 10

10.3 $E(X_{(n-1)}) = \dfrac{(n-1)\theta}{n+1}$

$Var(X_{(n-1)}) = \dfrac{2(n-1)\theta^2}{(n+1)^2(n+2)}$

$MSE(X_{(n-1)}) = \dfrac{6\theta^2}{(n+1)(n+2)} > MSE(X_{(n)}) = \dfrac{2\theta^2}{(n+1)(n+2)}$

$Cov(X_{(n-1)}, X_{(n)}) = \dfrac{(n-1)\theta^2}{(n+1)^2(n+2)}$

10.4 (a) $\bar{X}$ is biased and inconsistent

(b) $X_{(1)}$ is biased but consistent

10.5 no, $np(1-p)$ is biased for $Var(X)$

10.6 $\hat{\mu}_2' - s^2$, where s^2 is the sample variance, is unbiased for $[E(X)]^2$

10.7 $\left(\dfrac{(n-1)s^2}{\chi^2_{n-1,1-\frac{\alpha}{2}}}, \dfrac{(n-1)s^2}{\chi^2_{n-1,\frac{\alpha}{2}}} \right)$, where $\chi^2_{r,\alpha}$ is 100α-percentile of the χ^2_r distribution

10.8 $\left(\dfrac{\gamma_{\frac{\alpha}{2}}(n)}{n\bar{x}}, \dfrac{\gamma_{1-\frac{\alpha}{2}}(n)}{n\bar{x}} \right)$, where $\gamma_\alpha(n) = \dfrac{1}{\Gamma(n)} \int_0^\alpha x^{n-1} e^{-x}\, dx$

10.9

y_j	2	3	4	5	6	7	8	9	10	11	12
w_j	1	1	1	3	2	3	1	1	1	1	3
r_j	18	17	16	15	12	10	7	6	5	4	3

10.10

y_j	23	25	27	28	30	31	33	38	42	45
w_j	2	1	3	1	2	1	1	1	1	3
r_j	16	14	13	10	9	7	6	5	4	3

10.11

y_j	w_j	r_j
5	1	10
8	1	9
11	1	8
13	2	7
14	1	5
15	1	3
16	1	1

10.12 Note that the observations of $i = 11$, 14 and 18 are not observable (as $x_i < d_i$) and are removed from the data. Thus, we have (there are no censored data)

y_j	w_j	r_j	Eq (10.8)	Eq (10.9)
3	1	8	—	$8 - 0$
5	2	10	$8 - 1 + 3$	$11 - 1$
6	3	8	$10 - 2 + 0$	$11 - 3$
7	3	11	$8 - 3 + 6$	$17 - 6$
8	4	8	$11 - 3 + 0$	$17 - 9$
9	3	4	$8 - 4 + 0$	$17 - 13$
10	1	1	$4 - 3 + 0$	$17 - 16$

10.13

y_j	w_j	r_j
6	3	21
8	2	18
12	1	16
13	2	15
14	1	13
15	2	12
16	2	10
17	2	8
18	2	6

10.14 (a)

y_j	w_j	r_j	Eq (10.8)	Eq (10.9)
4	1	10	—	$10 - 0 - 0$
7	1	19	$10 - 1 + 10 - 0$	$20 - 1 - 0$
8	2	18	$19 - 1 + 0 - 0$	$20 - 2 - 0$
9	2	16	$18 - 2 + 0 - 0$	$20 - 4 - 0$
10	1	14	$16 - 2 + 0 - 0$	$20 - 6 - 0$
12	3	13	$14 - 1 + 0 - 0$	$20 - 7 - 0$
13	3	10	$13 - 3 + 0 - 0$	$20 - 10 - 0$
14	1	7	$10 - 3 + 0 - 0$	$20 - 13 - 0$
15	1	6	$7 - 1 + 0 - 0$	$20 - 14 - 0$

(b)

Group j	D_j	U_j	V_j	R_j
$(0, 5]$	15	0	1	15
$(5, 10]$	5	0	6	19
$(10, 15]$	0	5	8	13

Chapter 11

11.1 (a) $\tilde{F}(15) = 0.4479$, $\tilde{F}(27) = 0.8125$

(b) $\hat{x}_{0.25} = 11.5$, $\hat{x}_{0.75} = 26.9167$, $\hat{x}_{0.75} - \hat{x}_{0.25} = 15.4167$

(c) mean $= 19.8125$, variance $= 80.1523$, skewness $= -0.0707$

(d) $\text{Var}[(X \wedge 27)] = 62.4336$, $\text{Var}[(X \wedge 31.5)] = 77.0586$

(e) $\widehat{\Pr}(\tilde{X} \le 25) = 0.5231$, $\hat{\text{E}}[(\tilde{X} \wedge 20.5)] = 18.1538$

11.2 (a) loss event: mean $= 47.9$, variance $= 1,469.2111$

payment event: mean $= 59.8750$, variance $= 1,069.5536$

(b) prob $= 0.7$, variance $= 0.21$

11.3 minimum correlation $= -0.9424$, maximum correlation $= 0.8870$

11.4 (a) 12

(b) 14

11.5 (a) for $b = 4$: $\tilde{f}(10) = 0.05$, $\tilde{f}(15) = 0.0375$

for $b = 6$: $\tilde{f}(10) = 0.0417$, $\tilde{f}(15) = 0.0333$

(b) for $b = 4$: $\tilde{f}(10) = 0.0375$, $\tilde{f}(15) = 0.0375$

for $b = 6$: $\tilde{f}(10) = 0.0417$, $\tilde{f}(15) = 0.0333$

11.6 (a) mean $= 25.2985$, standard deviation $= 14.5850$

(b) $\text{E}[(X \wedge 40)] = 23.8060$, $\text{E}[(X \wedge 45)] = 24.5522$

(c) $\text{Var}[(X \wedge 40)] = 148.6972$, $\text{Var}[(X \wedge 45)] = 175.7964$

(d) 8.8433

(e) $\hat{F}(40) = 0.8209$, $\hat{F}(48) = 0.9164$

(f) 16.2754

11.7 (a) mean $= 63.8393$, standard deviation $= 74.4153$

(b) mean $= 200.2321$, standard deviation $= 85.7443$

11.8 (a) mean $= 43.9765$, standard deviation $= 27.4226$

(b) mean $= 38.5412$, standard deviation $= 21.6795$

11.9 (a) prob $= 0.3333$, confidence interval $= (0.1155, 0.5511)$

(b) prob $= 0.2222$, variance $= 0.009602$

(c) prob $= 0.4$, variance $= 0.0160$

(d) $\hat{H}(10.5) = 1.3531$, confidence interval $= (0.5793, 2.1269)$

11.10 (a) 0.3125

(b) 0.7246

11.11 (a) 12.6667

    (b) $\hat{H}_K(12) = 0.3567$, $\hat{H}_N(12) = 0.3361$

11.12 (a) prob = 0.0398, variance = 0.001625

    (b) linear: (−0.0392, 0.1188), lower limit < 0, undesirable

        logarithmic: (0.0026, 0.1752)

    (c) $\hat{H}(5) = 0.325$, variance = 0.0356

    (d) linear: (−0.0449, 0.6949), lower limit < 0, undesirable

        logarithmic: (0.1041, 1.0145)

11.13 Kaplan–Meier: 10.3030, Nelson–Aalen: 11.0322

11.14 (a) (0.2005, 0.5658)

    (b) (0.0948, 0.7335)

11.15 (a) 0.3614

    (b) 0.2435

    (c) 0.5085

11.16 (1.5802, 2.4063)

11.17 (0.2144, 0.5598)

11.18 8

11.19 0.2341

11.20 0.4780

11.21 0.3

11.22 0.3854

11.23 0.7794

11.24 0.36

11.25 0.0667

11.26 10

11.27 1.0641

11.28 2

11.29 0.5833

11.30 0.485

11.31 36

Chapter 12

12.1 $(\alpha - 1)\hat{\mu}_1'$

12.2 (a) 30.1924

    (b) 46.0658

12.3 mean = 97,696.51, standard deviation = 211,005.60

12.4 (a) $\mathcal{G}(6.4470, 6.6698)$

    (b) $\mathcal{U}(13.6674, 72.3326)$

12.5 (a) $\hat{\mu} = 4.1740$, $\hat{\sigma}^2 = 0.0433$, $\widehat{\Pr}(X > 80) = 0.1589$

(b) $\hat{\mu} = 4.1724$, $\hat{\sigma}^2 = 0.0478$, $\widehat{\Pr}(X > 80) = 0.1687$

12.6 (a) $\hat{b} = 28.9286$

(b) $\hat{\lambda} = 0.0443$

(c) $\hat{y} = 39.8571$

12.7 $\hat{\lambda}_1 = 0.1634$, $\hat{\lambda}_2 = 0.3867$

12.8 (a) 97.3093

(b) 75.2438

12.9 $3\bar{x}$

12.10 $\hat{\mu}_X = \bar{x}$, $\hat{\mu}_Y = \bar{y}$, $\hat{\sigma}^2 = \dfrac{\sum_{i=1}^{n}(x_i - \bar{x})^2 + \sum_{i=1}^{m}(y_i - \bar{y})^2}{n + m}$

12.11 $\text{Var}(\bar{x}) = \dfrac{1 - \theta}{n\theta^2}$, $\text{Var}(\hat{\theta}) = \dfrac{\theta^2(1 - \theta)}{n}$

12.12 $X_{(n)} - 0.5 \le \hat{\theta} \le X_{(1)} + 0.5$

(a) yes

(b) no

12.13 (a) $4\log(1 - e^{-2\lambda}) + 7\log(e^{-2\lambda} - e^{-4\lambda}) + 10\log(e^{-4\lambda} - e^{-6\lambda}) + 6\log(e^{-6\lambda} - e^{-8\lambda}) - 24\lambda$

(b) $4\log\left[1 - \left(\dfrac{\gamma}{2+\gamma}\right)^\alpha\right] + 7\log\left[\left(\dfrac{\gamma}{2+\gamma}\right)^\alpha - \left(\dfrac{\gamma}{4+\gamma}\right)^\alpha\right]$

$\qquad + 10\log\left[\left(\dfrac{\gamma}{4+\gamma}\right)^\alpha - \left(\dfrac{\gamma}{6+\gamma}\right)^\alpha\right]$

$\qquad + 6\log\left[\left(\dfrac{\gamma}{6+\gamma}\right)^\alpha - \left(\dfrac{\gamma}{8+\gamma}\right)^\alpha\right] + 3\alpha\log\left(\dfrac{\gamma}{8+\gamma}\right)$

12.14 (a) 37.33 (3 losses exceeding 28), 33.60 (2 losses exceeding 28)

(b) 0.0391

12.16 (a) 0.0811

(b) 0.0811

(c) $\hat{\lambda} = 14.0040$, $\hat{\lambda}^* = 9.7200$

12.17 1.0874

12.18 1.4256

12.19 (a) $\hat{\mu} = \bar{x}$, $\sqrt{n}(\hat{\mu} - \mu) \overset{D}{\to} \mathcal{N}(0, \sigma^2)$

(b) $\hat{\sigma}^2 = \dfrac{\sum_{i=1}^{n}(x_i - \mu)^2}{n}$, $\sqrt{n}(\hat{\sigma}^2 - \sigma^2) \overset{D}{\to} \mathcal{N}(0, 2\sigma^4)$

(c) $\hat{\mu} = \bar{x}$, $\hat{\sigma}^2 = \dfrac{\sum_{i=1}^{n}(x_i - \bar{x})^2}{n}$,

$\sqrt{n}\begin{pmatrix} \hat{\mu} - \mu \\ \hat{\sigma}^2 - \sigma^2 \end{pmatrix} \overset{D}{\to} \mathcal{N}\begin{pmatrix} \sigma^2 & 0 \\ 0 & 2\sigma^4 \end{pmatrix}$

12.20 $\dfrac{9\mu^4\sigma^2}{n}$

12.21 $\dfrac{2^n}{n\sigma^4}$

12.22 (a) 0.0323

(b) 0.00008718

(c) (0.01404, 0.05065), not reliable as sample size is too small

(d) 0.00005034

(e) 0.4455, (0.2417, 0.6493)

12.23 (a) $\hat{\lambda} = 0.2273$, $\hat{\beta} = -0.4643$

(b) $\hat{\beta} = -0.9971$

y	2	3	5	7	8	12
$\hat{S}(y)$	0.8569	0.5947	0.2865	0.1611	0.0416	0.0028

$\hat{S}(6; z_{(1)}) = 0.6305$

12.25 $\log L(\beta; x, z) = -\sum_{i=1}^{n} e^{\beta z_i} + \beta \sum_{i=1}^{n} x_i z_i$, $\hat{\beta} = 0.7511$

12.26 (a) $\log L(\lambda, \beta; x, z) = n \log \lambda + \beta \sum_{i=1}^{10} z_i - \lambda \sum_{i=1}^{10} x_i e^{\beta z_i}$

$\hat{\lambda} = 0.0161$, $\hat{\beta} = 0.6624$

(b) $\log L(\alpha, \gamma; x, z) = n (\log \alpha + \alpha \log \gamma) + \beta \sum_{i=1}^{n} z_i$

$- (\alpha + 1) \sum_{i=1}^{n} \log (x_i e^{\beta z_i} + \gamma)$,

where $\alpha = 3$; $\hat{\gamma} = 188.59$, $\hat{\beta} = 0.6829$

12.28 (a) $\hat{\lambda}_1 = 0.3117$, $\hat{\lambda}_2 = 0.1925$, $\hat{\alpha} = 21.2511$

(b) 0.5352

12.29 26,400

12.30 0.6798

12.31 2,887.55

12.32 0.2

12.33 0.0406

12.34 (−0.476, 1.876)

12.35 $\lambda^3 e^{-1100\lambda}$

12.36 104.4665

12.37 0.9700

12.38 0.9329

12.39 118.3197

12.40 471.3091

12.41 10.1250

12.42 15

12.43 1.0358

12.44 5.5

Chapter 13

13.1 (a) The (x_i, y_i) coordinates are

x_i	y_i
0.125	0.166
0.250	0.365
0.375	0.420
0.500	0.559
0.625	0.720
0.750	0.805
0.875	0.876

(b) the x_i values are: 0.071, 0.214, 0.357, 0.500, 0.643, 0.786, 0.929
  the y_i values are the same as in (a)
(c) the x_i values are the same as in (a)
  the y_i values are: 0.164, 0.416, 0.416, 0.554, 0.715, 0.801, 0.873
(d) the x_i values are the same as in (b)
  the y_i values are the same as in (c)

13.2 (a) & (b): the x_i values are the same for both (a) and (b), but y_i are different

x_i	$y_i(a)$	$y_i(b)$
12	14.16	11.82
15	17.90	16.71
18	20.94	20.21
21	23.77	23.35
23	26.58	26.44
28	29.52	29.68
32	32.77	33.29
38	36.56	37.65
45	41.43	43.60
58	48.95	54.92

13.3 29.0249

13.4 0.2120

13.5 $D = 0.1723 < 0.3678$, the critical value at the 10% level of significance, but this critical value should be adjusted downward due to parametric estimation

13.6 $D = 0.1811 < 0.3678$, the critical value at the 10% level of significance, but this critical value should be adjusted downward due to parametric estimation

13.7 $A^2 = 0.4699 < 1.933$, the critical value at the 10% level of significance, but this critical value should be adjusted downward due to parametric estimation

13.8 $A^2 = 0.3633 < 1.933$, the critical value at the 10% level of significance, but this critical value should be adjusted downward due to parametric estimation

13.9 9.1507

13.10 $X^2 = 7.70$, $\chi^2_{2,\,0.975} = 7.38$ and $\chi^2_{2,\,0.99} = 9.21$; reject null at 2.5% level but not at 1% level

13.11 0.2727

13.12 $X^2 = 7.546$, $\chi^2_{2,\,0.975} = 7.38$ and $\chi^2_{2,\,0.99} = 9.21$; reject null at 2.5% level but not at 1% level

13.13 $X^2 = 37$ and $\chi^2_{19,\,0.99} = 36.191$; reject null at 1% level

13.14 $\ell = 6.901$ and $\chi^2_{1,\,0.99} = 6.635$; reject null at 1% level

13.15 0.025

13.16 $D = 0.111$, reject null at 5% level but not at 1% level

13.17 select Model 1 based on BIC, select Model 4 based on AIC

13.18 $D = 0.6803$, reject null at 5% level but not at 1% level

13.19 $X^2 = 11.022$, $\chi^2_{4,\,0.95} = 9.488$ and $\chi^2_{4,\,0.975} = 11.143$; reject null at 5% level but not at 2.5% level

13.20 $X^2 = 9.36$ and $\chi^2_{2,\,0.99} = 9.21$; reject null at 1% level

13.21 $\ell = 4.464$, $\chi^2_{1,\,0.95} = 3.84$ and $\chi^2_{1,\,0.975} = 5.02$; reject null at 5% level but not at 2.5% level

13.22 $(s, t) = (0.5, 0.5971)$, $D(3000) = -0.0257$

13.23 81

13.24 0.1679

Chapter 14

14.1 for seed 401, x_i are: 6.7396×10^6, 1.6034×10^9, 2.1426×10^9, 1.9729×10^9;
u_i are: 0.0031, 0.7467, 0.9977, 0.9187

for seed 245987, x_i are: 1.9868×10^9, 1.2582×10^9, 1.8552×10^8, 2.0831×10^9;
u_i are: 0.9252, 0.5859, 0.0864, 0.9700

14.2 for seed 747, x_i are: 5.1595×10^7, 3.0557×10^9, 1.7529×10^9, 7.9814×10^8;
u_i are: 0.0120, 0.7115, 0.4081, 0.1858

for seed 380, x_i are: 2.6246×10^7, 3.2404×10^8, 4.2934×10^9, 7.9153×10^8;

u_i are: 0.0061, 0.0754, 0.9996, 0.1843

14.3 7

14.4 0.3479, 0.7634, 0.8436, 0.6110, 0.1399

14.7 Generate u and v independently from $\mathcal{U}(0, 1)$. If $16u/9 > f(v)$, generate another (u, v) again. If $16u/9 \leq f(v)$ output v as value of X. Inverse transformation has no explicit solution.

14.8 (a) $\mathrm{Var}(X) = \mathrm{Var}(Y) = \dfrac{4}{45}$, $\mathrm{Cov}(X, Y) = -\dfrac{7}{90}$, $\mathrm{Var}\left(\dfrac{X+Y}{2}\right) = \dfrac{1}{180}$

14.9 control variable method most efficient, antithetic variate method marginal improvement over crude Monte Carlo method

14.10 $\mathrm{Pr}(X_1 \leq 1.2, X_2 \leq 2.1) = 0.8783$, Monte Carlo sample required = 4,107

14.12 $2\mu - X$

14.13 0.5855

14.14 35.6675

14.15 1,000

14.16 41.8971

14.17 224.44

14.18 522.13

14.19 3,047.02

14.20 614.42

Chapter 15

15.1 (a) Denote the population median by θ and the median of x by $\hat{\theta}$. Draw a sample of n observations from x with replacement, and call this sample x^*, with median denoted by $\hat{\theta}^*$. Perform the sampling m times to obtain m values of $\hat{\theta}_j^*$, for $j = 1, \ldots, m$. The bias of the sample median is estimated by

$$\frac{1}{m}\left[\sum_{j=1}^{m} \hat{\theta}_j^*\right] - \hat{\theta}.$$

The mean squared error of the sample median is estimated by

$$\frac{1}{m}\sum_{j=1}^{m}(\hat{\theta}_j^* - \hat{\theta})^2.$$

(b) Compute the estimate of the variance of $\hat{\theta}^*$ by

$$s^2 = \frac{1}{m-1}\sum_{j=1}^{m}(\hat{\theta}_j^* - \bar{\theta}^*)^2,$$

where $\bar{\theta}^*$ is the sample mean of $\hat{\theta}_j^*$. The required sample size is $(1.96s/0.05)^2$.

(c) The samples x^* are generated from the $\mathcal{E}(1/\bar{x})$ distribution, where $\bar{x}$ is the sample mean of x.

15.2 Draw a sample of n observations from x with replacement, and compute the interquartile range $\hat{\theta}^*$. Perform the sampling m times to obtain m values of $\hat{\theta}_j^*$, for $j = 1,\ldots,m$. Let a and b be the 0.025- and 0.975-quantiles of $\hat{\theta}_j^*/\hat{\theta}$, respectively. The 95% confidence interval of θ is estimated by $(\hat{\theta}/b, \hat{\theta}/a)$.

15.3 (a) Draw a sample of n pairs of observations (x_i^*, y_i^*) from (x_i, y_i) with replacement and compute the sample correlation coefficient $\hat{\rho}^*$. Repeat this m times to obtain $\hat{\rho}_j^*$, for $j = 1,\ldots,m$. The bias of $\hat{\rho}$ is estimated by

$$\frac{1}{m}\left[\sum_{j=1}^{m}\hat{\rho}_j^*\right] - \hat{\rho}.$$

(b) The observations (x_i^*, y_i^*) are simulated from the bivariate standard normal distribution (i.e., $\mu_X = \mu_Y = 0$ and $\sigma_X = \sigma_Y = 1$) with correlation coefficient $\hat{\rho}$. The correlation coefficient $\hat{\rho}^*$ is computed for each sample, and the formula above is used to compute the bias.

15.4 Compute the maximum likelihood estimates $\hat{\mu}$ and $\hat{\sigma}^2$ of μ and σ^2. These are, respectively, the sample mean and $(n-1)/n$ times the sample variance of $\log x_i$, for $i = 1,\ldots,n$. Then simulate n observations x_i^* from $\mathcal{N}(\hat{\mu},\hat{\sigma}^2)$ and compute $(n-1)/n$ times the sample variance, and call this $\hat{\sigma}^{*2}$. Do this m times to obtain $\hat{\sigma}_j^{*2}$ and hence $\hat{\theta}_j^* = (e^{\hat{\sigma}_j^{*2}} - 1)^{\frac{1}{2}}$, for $j = 1,\ldots,m$. The bias of $\hat{\theta}$ is then estimated by taking the sample mean of $\hat{\theta}_j^* - \hat{\theta}$. An alternative procedure is to note that $n\hat{\sigma}^{*2}$ is distributed as a $\hat{\sigma}^2\chi_{n-1}^2$ variable. Thus, each $\hat{\sigma}_i^{*2}$ may be directly simulated as $\hat{\sigma}^2/n$ times a χ_{n-1}^2 variate.

15.5 0.0131

15.6 $\dfrac{44}{9}$

15.7 8

Chapter 16

16.1 1,325
16.2 4,804
16.3 21,817
16.4 3,399
16.5 (a) 850
      (b) 8,937
      (c) 7,320
16.6 (a) 49,103
      (b) DY1: 2,502, DY2: 1,692, DY3: 1,371, DY4: 795
16.7 58,195
16.8 2,697
16.9 23,392
16.10 0.9518
16.11 24,726
16.12 972,040

Chapter 17

17.1 CY1: 5,873.47, CY2: 6,384.97, CY3: 6,653.88, CY4: 7,134.20
17.2 (a) 1,500
      (b) 1,446.15
17.3 218.88
17.4 1,459 thousands
17.5 205.77
17.6 92.42
17.7 T1: 111.10, T2: 112.39, T3: 128.89
17.8 22.48%
17.9 T1: 126.21, T2: 159.91, T3: 187.92
17.10 9,494
17.11 0.5435
17.12 −1.37%
17.13 1.0128
17.14 2,413

References

Adler, R.J., Feldman, R.E., and Taqqu, M.S., 1998, *A Practical Guide to Heavy Tails*, Birkhäuser.

Amemiya, T., 1985, *Advanced Econometrics*, Harvard University Press.

Angus, J.E., 1994, "The probability integral transform and related results," *SIAM Review*, 36, 652–654.

Artzner, P., 1999, "Application of coherent risk measures to capital requirements in insurance," *North American Actuarial Journal*, 3 (2), 11–25.

Artzner, P., Delbaen, F., Eber, J., and Heath, D., 1999, "Coherent measures of risk," *Mathematical Finance*, 9, 203–228.

Bowers, N.L. Jr., Gerber, H.U., Hickman, J.C., Jones, D.A., and Nesbitt, C.J., 1997, *Actuarial Mathematics*, 2nd edition, Society of Actuaries.

Boyle, P., Broadie, M., and Glasserman, P., 1997, "Monte Carlo methods for security pricing," *Journal of Economic Dynamics and Control*, 21, 1267–1321.

David, F.N., and Johnson, N.L., 1948, "The probability integral transformation when parameters are estimated from the sample," *Biometrika*, 35, 182–190.

Davison, A.C., and Hinkley, D.V., 1997, *Bootstrap Methods and Their Application*, Cambridge University Press.

DeGroot, M.H., and Schervish, M.J., 2002, *Probability and Statistics*, 3rd edition, Addison Wesley.

Denuit, M., Dhaene, J., Goovaerts, M., and Kaas, R., 2005, *Actuarial Theory for Dependent Risks: Measures, Orders and Models*, John Wiley.

De Pril, N., 1985, "Recursions for convolutions of arithmetic distributions," *ASTIN Bulletin*, 15, 135–139.

De Pril, N., 1986, "On the exact computation of the aggregate claims distribution in the individual life model," *ASTIN Bulletin*, 16, 109–112.

Dickson, D.C.M., 2005, *Insurance Risk and Ruin*, Cambridge University Press.

Dowd, K., and Blake, D., 2006, "After VaR: the theory, estimation, and insurance applications of quantile-based risk measures," *Journal of Risk and Insurance*, 73, 193–228.

Hardy, M., 2003, *Investment Guarantees*, John Wiley.

Hastie, T., Tibshirani,R., and Friedman, J., 2009, *The Elements of Statistical Learning*, 2nd edition, Springer.

Herzog, T.N., and Lord, G., 2002, *Applications of Monte Carlo Methods to Finance and Insurance*, ACTEX Publications.

Hogg, R.V., and Craig, A.T., 1995, *Introduction to Mathematical Statistics*, 5th edition, Prentice Hall.

Hyndman, R.J., and Fan, Y., 1996, "Sample quantiles in statistical packages," *The American Statistician*, 50, 361–365.

James, G., Witten, D., Hastie, T., and Tibshirani, R., 2015, *An Introduction to Statistical Learning with Applications in R*, Springer.

Jewell, W.S., 1974, "Credible means are exact Bayesian for exponential families," *ASTIN Bulletin*, 7, 237–269.

Johnson, N.L., and Kotz, S., 1969, *Distributions in Statistics: Discrete Distributions*, John Wiley.

Johnson, N.L., and Kotz, S., 1970, *Distributions in Statistics: Continuous Univariate Distributions-I*, John Wiley.

Johnston, J., and DiNardo, J., 1997, *Econometric Methods*, 4th edition, McGraw-Hill.

Jones, B.L., Puri, M.L., and Zitikis, R., 2006, "Testing hypotheses about the equality of several risk measure values with applications in insurance," *Insurance: Mathematics and Economics*, 38, 253–270.

Jones, B.L., and Zitikis, R., 2007, "Risk measures, distortion parameters, and their empirical estimation," *Insurance: Mathematics and Economics*, 41, 279–297.

Kennedy, W.J.Jr., and Gentle, J.E., 1980, *Statistical Computing*, Marcel Dekker.

Klugman, S.A., Panjer, H.H., and Willmot, G.E., 2008, *Loss Models: From Data to Decisions*, 3rd edition, John Wiley.

Lam, J., 2003, *Enterprise Risk Management: From Incentives to Controls*, John Wiley.

Lilliefors, H.W., 1967, "On the Kolmogorov-Smirnov test for normality with mean and variance unknown," *Journal of the American Statistical association*, 62, 399–402.

Lilliefors, H.W., 1969, "On the Kolmogorov-Smirnov test for the exponential distribution with mean unknown," *Journal of the American Statistical association*, 64, 387–389.

London, D., 1988, *Survival Models and Their Estimation*, 2nd edition, ACTEX Publications.

McLeish, D.L., 2005, *Monte Carlo Simulation and Finance*, John Wiley.

McNeil, A.J., Frey, R., and Embrechts, P., 2005, *Quantitative Risk Management: Concepts, Techniques, Tools*, Princeton University Press.

Panjer, H.H., 1981, "Recursive evaluation of a family of compound distributions," *ASTIN Bulletin*, 12, 21–26.

Ross, S., 2006, *A First Course in Probability*, 7th edition, Pearson Prentice Hall.

Stephens, M.A., 1974, "EDF statistics for goodness of fit and some comparison," *Journal of the American Statistical Association*, 69, 730–737.

Tan, K.S., and Boyle, P., 2000, "Applications of randomized low discrepancy sequences to the valuation of complex securities," *Journal of Economic Dynamics and Control*, 24, 1747–1782.

Wang, S.S., 2000, "A class of distortion operators for pricing financial and insurance risks," *The Journal of Risk and Insurance*, 67, 15–36.

Wirch, J., and Hardy, M.R., 1999, "A synthesis of risk measures for capital adequacy," *Insurance: Mathematics and Economics*, 25, 337–347.

Index

Printed in the United States
by Baker & Taylor Publisher Services